ETIQUETTE

The Blue Book of Social Usage

PUBLISHED BY FUNK & WAGNALLS COMPANY, INC.

for

EMILY POST INSTITUTE, INC.

Etiquette: The Blue Book of Social Usage
Children Are People
The Personality of a House
The Emily Post Cook Book

ETIQUETTE

The Blue Book of Social Usage

EMILY POST

FUNK & WAGNALLS COMPANY, INC.

NEW YORK

CONTENTS

4

5

6

7

Children — Special Cards and When To Use Them — Business
Cards — The Vanishing Visit of Empty Form — Fold-over
Cards — The P. P. C. Card — Cards of New or Temporary
Address — Invitation in Place of Returned Visit — "Not at
Home"—No Discourtesy — Paying a Visit to a Lady Who Has
No Maid — Sending Your Card — Visits Which Everyone
Must Pay — Messages Written on Cards — How a First Visit
Is Made — On Opening the Door to a Visitor — Correct Num-
ber of Cards To Leave — When the Visitor Leaves — When
the Lady of the House Is at Home — If a Butler Opens the
Door — The Typical Visitor — How To Enter a Drawing-
Room — How To Sit Gracefully — Postscripts on Visits —
Other Visiting Details — Christmas Cards — Is Husband's or
Wife's Name Written First? — Card for Whole Family —
Cards to Business Acquaintances — A Christmas Card to Some-
one in Mourning — Colored Inks for Gaily Colored Cards —
Birthday and Other Greeting Cards — Answering Visiting-
card Invitation

11

ON THE SUBJECT OF INVITATIONS   91

Wedding Invitations — When—and Why—Two Envelopes?
— Envelopes Should Be Formally Addressed — Envelope and
Invitation in One — Folding and Inserting — Return Addresses
— The Church Invitation — Cards for Reserved Pews — Invitations to Friends in Mourning — The Invitation to the Recep-
tion — Professional Name Added When the Bride Has a Career
— Invitation to a Wedding at the House of a Friend — When
the Bride Has a Stepfather — When the Bride Is an Orphan —
When Her Parents Are Divorced — The Double-Wedding In-
vitation — When Brides Are Not Sisters — When Bridegroom's Family Gives Wedding — The Fewer the Invitations
the Higher Their Value — Invitation to the Reception Only —
An Invitation to a House Wedding Clearly Includes Reception
— Reception at the Club of a Friend — Wedding and Recep-
tion Invitation in One — At Home Cards — Cards of Address
— When the Bride Is a Widow — Concerning a Divorcée's Re-
marriage — A Divorcée's Wedding Ring — When Principals
Are in the Services — Wedding Announcements — The Invi-
tation to a Wedding Anniversary — Answering a Wedding
Invitation — Combination Acceptance and Regret — Other
Formal Invitations — The Invitation to a Ball — Invitation To
Be a Patron — Invitations to a Private Ball — The Ball for a

12

TEAS, COCKTAILS, AND OTHER AFTERNOON PARTIES

13

BALLS AND DANCES

21

ing the Wedding Pictures — Procession to the Church —
Mother Takes Father's Place — At the Church — In Front of
the Ribbons — Seating the Guests — Ushers and Guests Al-
ways Talk — The Bridegroom Waits — The Perfectly Man-
aged Wedding — Here Comes the Bride — The Bridegroom
Advances To Meet the Bride — Her Father Gives Her Away
— The Marriage Ceremony — After the Ceremony — At the
House — The Receiving Line — Ushers at the House — No
Rule about Whether Bride or Bridegroom Is Greeted First —
Receiving Their Guests — The Bride's Table — The Table of
the Bride's Parents — The Bridal Party Eats — The Toast
to the Bride and Groom — Dancing at the Wedding — Into
Traveling Clothes — The Going-away Dress — They're Off!
— Thought for Bridegroom's Parents — Flippancy or Radi-
ance — Wedding Anniversaries — Gifts Not Obligatory —
Further Celebrations Are Not Approved

22

Must One Send a Present? — Presents for Second Marriage —
The Runaway Marriage — Don't Neglect To Send a Re-
ply — What Kind of Gift — Presents from Bridegroom's
Friends — Nearest Relatives May Give Checks — Cards with
Presents — Delayed Presents — What To Wear to a Wedding
— Who Is Intended by "and Family"? — Don't Neglect Your
Child at a Wedding — Arriving at the Church — Aisle Seat
Not Relinquished — Greeting Other Guests — Stranger Fol-
lows Example of Others — From Church to Reception — What
You Do at the Reception — A Sit-down Breakfast — When
You Leave Reception

23

When Both Are Strangers — A Letter of Introduction —Newcomers to a Big City — Making and Keeping Friends — Your
First Visitors — Beware of Immediate Intimacy

24

Selecting a Birth Announcement Card — Newspaper Announcement of Birth — Choosing a Name — Time of Christen-

27

FLAT SILVER AND TABLE-SETTINGS

28

FORMAL DINNERS

32

33

34

35

42

LIST OF PLATES

TO THE READER

Good taste or bad is revealed in everything we are, do, or have. Our speech, manners, dress, and household furnishings—and even our friends —are evidences of the propriety of our taste, and all these are the subject of this book. Rules of etiquette are nothing more than sign-posts by which we are guided to the goal of good taste. These rules are derived from long experience; their basis is always consideration for the feelings, beliefs, and sensibilities of others. The truly considerate person has many qualities—tact, graciousness, charm, hospitality, kindness—that are apparent in every detail of his life. In a word, he has in everything, no matter how insignificant, that indefinable but vitally important element, *good taste.*

In presenting this TENTH EDITION of *Etiquette, The Blue Book of Social Usage,* one is almost compelled to recall the earlier editions and to reflect on the changes that have occurred over the years as they were recorded in each succeeding volume.

Manners of themselves have not changed, of course, but there have been marked changes in our mode of life and in the environment in which we live. What was once considered the tradition of gracious living of the few has in these times of plenty rightly become the heritage of us all. Custom is a mutable thing; yet we readily recognize the permanence of certain social values. Graciousness and courtesy are never old-fashioned, although their expression may change and many conventions of an earlier era have no part in the modern world.

I do think that Americans today are drifting toward, not away from, finer perceptions and good taste. In every period of history the older generation invariably has felt that the younger is speeding swiftly along the road to perdition. We are no different. But I doubt whether the present younger generation is really nearer to that frightful end than any previous one.

To be sure, manners seem to have grown lax, and many of the amenities apparently have vanished. But do these things merely seem so to us today because young men no longer pay party calls and young women are informal? It is difficult to maintain that youth today is so very different from what it has been in other periods of history. I have great confidence that our young people, if they come from homes of charm and graciousness, will in their turn make charming and gracious homes of their own. The unconscious example set by good parents is the greatest influence for good that there is in the world.

A mother should exact precisely the same behavior at home and every day that she would like her children to display in public, and if she expects them to take good manners seriously, she must herself show the same manners to them alone that she shows to "company." Families which exert neither courtesy nor charm when alone can no more deceive other people into believing that either attribute belongs to them than they could hope to hide ugly furniture with gaudy slipcovers. If children see temper uncontrolled, hear malicious gossip, witness arrogant sharp-dealing or lax honor, their own characters can hardly escape perversion.

In the present day of rush and hurry, a few of us allow too little time for home example. To the over-busy or the gaily fashionable, "home" might just as well be a railroad station and "family" passengers who see each other only for a few hurried minutes before taking trains in opposite directions. Any number of busy fathers scarcely know their children at all, and have not stopped to realize that they seldom or never talk to them. And any number of busy mothers spend so much of their increased spare time at meetings or card parties that they never exert themselves to be sympathetic to the problems of their children, or in the slightest degree to influence them. To growl "don't" or "be quiet" is very, very far from being "an influence" on your children's morals, minds, or manners. I cannot emphasize strongly enough the value, particularly in these rush-and-hurry days, of leisurely and relaxed mealtimes, with the whole family together at a dining-room table that is attractively set, and with pleasant conversation in which every member of the family, no matter how young, can participate.

Despite the increasingly frantic pace of our lives, one thing is certain: we have advanced prodigiously in esthetic taste. Never has it been so easy to surround oneself with lovely belongings. One can not go into the shops or pass their windows without being impressed by the ever-increasing availability of beautiful things at prices everyone can afford. In our country we have all the glorious beauty and strength and vitality and courage that belong to youth. At a time when the whole world looks to America for leadership, our country is still youth personified. If we can keep these attributes and add to them perfect taste in living and thinking, we need have no fears about handing down to our children the tradition of gracious living that is the heritage of us all.

IN ANSWER TO A LETTER

ONCE MORE I AM REPRINTING THIS LETTER—AS I HAVE IN former editions—that was sent me at a time when the term *café society* was coined to apply to an unclassifiably mixed group of restaurant and night club habitués in New York. This letter is today as applicable to the subject of this book as it was on the day it was sent me—as is also my answer.

Dear Mrs. Post:

While waiting my turn in a doctor's office, I happened to read in one of America's greatest magazines an amazingly frank article about the publicity-craving of what the author calls café society and evidently believes to be New York's smartest society.

As I finished this story about people whose social position was seemingly proclaimed by being placed by the head waiter at a ringside table, I said to myself, "And so what? Who cares whether the So-and-So's are given a front-row table in a high-priced restaurant, or whether they eat at an automat?"

But to my own surprise I find myself suddenly caring very much, because it is assumed that the rest of us are satisfied to have these same society headliners represent the American social ideal.

This article and hundreds like it depict a world that is pretentious and vulgar. And no one, so far as I know, is saying a word in Society's defense. Or has it no defense? I'd like to know the truth, Mrs. Post; that's why I'm writing to you.

Is it true that these people I have been reading about are the same ones as those whose opinions you so often refer to as authoritative? Or was there (is there) another Best Society, which must have been shamed into seeking greater and greater privacy? And yet this doesn't follow through, because the names figuring conspicuously in several front-page scandals have been those of families whose prestige has always been looked up to as representative of America's Best.

I have been trying to think why I should care. I think it is this: Reformers of sorts may write all they please about the bad taste of Hollywood, but we, the countless "middle-class" people of the nation, look there for entertainment and not for the patterns of highest social and ethical traditions. On the other hand, we not only look to, but are as a nation represented by, those who are assumed to comprise our highest social class.

As you see from the stamping on my letter paper, I live far from New York; and if I, who am so far removed from the super-rich and super-smart of a far-off city, can feel so strongly about this disloyalty to all sense of *noblesse oblige* on the part of those who are thought to be the top, because holding the foremost social citadel of the nation, what must you feel, who all your life have been of the social world of New York?

Perhaps you won't answer me—perhaps you can't. Perhaps the society depicted by these others is what that of all great cities has come to. But if you can, I do wish you would give us who are your readers a reassuring glossary for such terms as "Best Society," "People of Quality," "People of Taste," "The Smart or the Modern or the Fashionable World." Or if you can't, won't you be frank with us who believe you, and who are bringing our children up according to your precepts, and tell us the truth?

Is this society of names advertised and rated by where they walk in the parade and where a head waiter seats them in a restaurant—or by a published list of "ten best-dressed ladies"—also your society? Is the admirable world of Society that I have thought I could read between the lines of what you write real, or do you make it up?

My answer:

No, I do not "make up" the people of whom I write nor the society that I define as "best." But I admit that the reassuring glossary you ask for is almost as difficult to make clear as it would be to separate each color that has gone into the painting of a picture.

In the general picture of this modern day, the smart and the near-smart, the distinguished and the merely conspicuous, the real and the sham, and the unknown general public are all mixed up together. The walls that used to enclose the world that was fashionable are all down. Even the car tracks that divided cities into smart and not-smart sections are torn up.

On the other hand, there are countless private houses whose walls are standing intact and whose shades are pulled down when the indoor lights are lighted. And within the walls of the houses there are enclosures where the owners spend their days and into which intimate friends go at their pleasure. But out in the big concourse, where the reporters gather with their cameras, the crowd is the same public one that goes to the races or to the restaurants, or to the night clubs.

There is nowhere to go to see Best Society on parade, because parading is one thing that Best Society does not intentionally do. And yet it is true (and this is one of the things hardest to make clear) that in the forefront of the public parade are to be found a certain few who are really best. But they are best in spite of, and not because of, the publicity they attract.

When I say that "people of taste do this or think that," I naturally have in mind definite people whose taste is the most nearly perfect among all those whom I know. Or on occasion, perhaps, I go back in memory to the precepts of those whose excellence has remained an ideal.

In other words, when I write of people of quality or fashion or taste, I always select the individual people who ideally serve as models.

Returning to our glossary, Best Society, Best People, or People of Quality can all be defined as people of cultivation, courtesy, taste, and kindness—people, moreover, who are very rarely dissociated from their backgrounds. In thinking of them, you think of their home surroundings, their families, their intimates, their work, their interests. But when you ask for the meaning of smart, fashionable, and modern, the qualities implied may include fastidious taste, alert perceptions, appreciative knowledge of every forward-looking movement of the day; or, on the other hand, it may mean no more than a flair for the trend of the moment—or no less than a love of the limelight.

So you can see how hard it is to try to explain who's who—let alone the much harder what's what. A fact I should like to bring out is that the rating by superficial appearance or the accident of publicity has little to do with an accurate appraisal of intrinsic worth—or worthlessness. Real value is something back of and apart from publicity value. There is all the difference between climbing on the bandwagon in order to be noticed by the public standing on the sidelines, and impulsively jumping on board because one can see better what is at the moment going on.

New York

THE TRUE MEANING
OF ETIQUETTE

·᠊ᢒ[1]ᢎ·᠊

IT WOULD BE CARELESS TO THINK OF ETIQUETTE AS BEING
of importance to none but brides, or diplomats, or perhaps persons lately
elected to political office. There is truly not a single thing that we do,
or say, or choose, or use, or even think, that does not follow—or break—
one of the exactions of taste, tact, ethics, good manners, etiquette—call
it what you will.

Considering manners even in their superficial aspect, no one—unless
he be a hermit—can fail to gain from a proper, courteous, likable approach, or fail to be handicapped by an improper, offensive, resentful one.
Certainly the greatest asset that a man or woman or even a child can
have is charm. And charm cannot exist without the good manners that
come to those who make a continuous practice of kind impulses.

It is hard to say why the word "etiquette" is so inevitably considered
merely a synonym of the word "correct," as though it were no more than
the fixed answer to a sum in arithmetic. In fact, it might be well to pull
the word "correct" out by the roots and substitute "common sense." In
short, I wish that those whose minds are focused on precise obedience to
every precept would instead ask themselves, "What is the purpose of this
rule? Does it help to make life pleasanter? Does it make the social
machinery run more smoothly? Does it add to beauty? Is it essential
to the code of good taste or to ethics?" If it serves any of these purposes,
it is a rule to be cherished; but if it serves no helpful purpose, it is certainly not worth taking very seriously.

On the subject of the thousands of detailed rules essential to all
ceremonial procedures, the importance of knowing the unending details,
such as when to sit and when to stand, what to say and what to do upon
this or that occasion, is most practically illustrated by a church service.
It would be shocking to have people trotting in and out of the pews,
talking out loud, or otherwise upsetting devotional tranquillity. For this
reason we have set rules for all ceremonial functions, so that marriages,

1

christenings, funerals, as well as Sunday services, shall be conducted with ease and smoothness. It is also essential to ease of living that certain mechanical conventions be observed. One of the simplest is that of extending our right hand when shaking hands, but think how confusing it would be if we did not all follow it.

The real point to be made is that rules of etiquette have not been contrived in order to make those who know them seem important and to publicly shame those who happen not to know them. Actually the so-called rules are nothing but the results of long experience handed down for reasons of practicality. This does not mean that the principles of good taste, or of beauty, or of consideration for the rights or feelings of others can ever be discarded. As a matter of fact, good taste is necessarily helpful. It must be the suitable thing, the comfortable thing, the useful thing for the occasion, the place, and the time, or it is not in good taste.

In the same way the code of ethics—which is also known as the code of a gentleman—is an immutable law of etiquette. Too many of us are likely to assume a rich man is of necessity a gentleman. Nothing could be further from the truth, since the quality of a gentleman is necessarily measured only by what he is and what he does—never by what he has. We've all heard the term "nature's nobleman," meaning a man of innately beautiful character who, though never having even heard of the code, follows it instinctively. In other words, the code of ethics is the code of instinctive decency, ethical integrity, self-respect, and loyalty. Decency means not merely propriety of speech and conduct, but honesty and trustworthiness in every obligation. Integrity includes not only honesty but a delicacy of motive and fairness in appraising the motives of others. Self-respect, among many other things, means refusal to accept obligations that one is unwilling to return. This word *unwilling* is of importance, since there is no more contemptible person than one who takes all he can get and gives as little as he can. Loyalty means faithfulness not only to friends, but also to principles.

Etiquette, if it is to be of more than trifling use, must go far beyond the mere mechanical rules of procedure or the equally automatic precepts of conventional behavior. Actually etiquette is most deeply concerned with every phase of ethical impulse or judgment and with every choice or expression of taste, since what one is, is of far greater importance than what one appears to be. A knowledge of etiquette is of course essential to one's decent behavior, just as clothing is essential to one's decent appearance; and precisely as one wears the latter without being self-conscious of having on shoes and perhaps gloves, one who has good manners is equally unself-conscious in the observance of etiquette, the precepts of which must be so thoroughly ingrained that their observance is a matter of instinct rather than of conscious obedience.

"MAY I PRESENT . . ."
—INTRODUCTIONS

·◊[2]◊·

THE MOST CEREMONIOUS INTRODUCTION POSSIBLE IS:

"Mrs. Distinguished, may I present Mr. Traveler?" or

"Mrs. Young, may I present Professor Gray?"

Present is somewhat more formal than the word *introduce,* but introduce is equally proper.

The younger person is introduced to the older, but a gentleman is always presented to a lady, even though he is a gentleman of distinction and the lady be no more than eighteen—especially if she is also a visitor. A young member of the family is introduced to a visitor, "Mr. Eminent, my daughter Cynthia."

No woman is ever presented to a man, except to the President of the United States, a royal personage, or a dignitary of the church.

The correct introduction of either a man or woman is:

TO THE PRESIDENT

"Mr. President, I have the honor to present Mrs. Williams." Or, if officially, "Mrs. Williams of Chicago."

Mrs. Williams bows. If the President offers his hand, Mrs. Williams gives him hers. She does not offer hers should he fail to make this gesture of courtesy—which is of course most unlikely.

TO A REIGNING SOVEREIGN

Much formality of securing placement of one's name on presentation lists is gone through beforehand; at the actual presentation an "accepted" name is repeated from one functionary to another and nothing is said to the king or queen except "Mrs. Williams."

Mrs. Williams curtsies and, if the king offers to shake hands, Mrs. Williams curtsies again as she gives him her hand. If by any chance Mrs. Williams has any objection to curtsying, she must not ask to be presented to the sovereign.

3

TO A CARDINAL

"Your Eminence, may I present Mrs. Williams?"

One who is not a Catholic behaves exactly as to a king, but a Roman Catholic drops on the right knee, places the right hand, palm down, under the cardinal's extended hand and kisses the cardinal's ring.

A woman is always presented to archbishops and monsignors, and it is not incorrect to present her to a priest.

TO DISTINGUISHED PERSONS

A woman is also presented to any member of a reigning family. "Your Royal Highness, or whatever the title, may I present Mrs. Williams?"

But a foreign ambassador is presented. "Your Excellency, may I present you to Mrs. Williams?" Or "Mrs. Williams, may I present His Excellency, the British Ambassador?" An introduction to an archbishop is, "Your Grace, may I present Mrs. Williams?" To those who know him socially, a duke is never "His Grace" nor a lord "His Lordship." A hostess says, "Mrs. Williams, may I present the Duke of Overthere?" or "Lord Blank?" "The Honorable" is merely Mr. Lordson or Mr. Holdoffice. A doctor, a judge, a bishop are addressed and introduced by their titles. Protestant clergymen are usually "Mister" unless they hold the title of Doctor, Dean, or Canon, in which case the surname is added: "Dean Wood," "Doctor Starr," "Canon Cope." A Catholic priest is "Father Kelly." To call him "Mister" is a breach of courtesy.

A senator is always introduced as "Senator Davis," whether he is still in office or not. But the President of the United States, once he is out of office, is merely "Mister" and never "Ex-President."

An ex-governor and an ex-ambassador are both actually "The Honorable." But usually one would in courtesy introduce the latter as "Ex-Ambassador" and the former as "Ex-Governor." On an important occasion one would present "The Honorable John Jones, former Governor of the State of Blank."

GENERAL INTRODUCTIONS

The typical introduction, suitable not only on informal occasions but whenever two individuals are introduced, is the mere pronouncing of two names:

"Mrs. Worldly. Mrs. Norman."

If the two names are said in the same tone of voice, it is not really apparent who is introduced to whom; but by accentuating the more important person's name, it can be made as clear as though the words "May I present" had been used.

The more important name is said with a slightly rising inflection; the secondary as a mere statement of fact. For instance, suppose you say, "There you are!" and then, "It is raining." Use the same inflection exactly and say, "Mrs. Worldly!—Mrs. Younger!"

A man is also introduced, "Mrs. Worldly—Mr. Norman." A mother introducing a man to her daughter would say, "Mr. Eminent—my daughter Mary!" or if she is married "—my daughter Mary Smartlington."

It is discourteous as well as in very bad taste to speak of one's husband as "Mr. Smith" or one's daughter as "Miss Smith." But if one's daughter has a different name, the name can be said with a pause between that makes a parenthesis. "My daughter (pause, and then) Mrs. Smartlington."

The same is true when introducing a step-parent and an acquaintance. In order to avoid confusion if your names are likely to be thought the same, say, "Mrs. Brown—my stepfather," and after a pause add, "Mr. Jones." This is really much more pleasant and approving of him than saying, "Mrs. Brown—my mother's husband."

Although the name of a stranger or of the older or more notable person is properly said first, this is no longer considered of importance —except that a woman's name should be said before that of a man, unless the preposition "to" is used before the lady's name. For instance, if you find yourself saying Mr. Norman's name first, it is quite simple to make this polite by adding, "May I introduce you to Mrs. Maddox?" Or, with greater friendliness, "Mr. Norman, I should like to introduce you to Mrs. Maddox."

Formally, a man introduces another man to his wife. "Mr. Brown, may I present you to my wife?" Or if this seems to you to imply that you are asking Mr. Brown's permission to present him to your wife, you can say, "Mr. Brown, I should like to introduce you to my wife."

A lady introduces her husband to friends and talks about him as "John," and to acquaintances as "my husband." The two names of safety are "my husband" and "my wife," since they are proper no matter to whom you are talking. In business "Mr. Brown" and "Mrs. Brown" are quite correct.

To an old friend a husband would say, "Jim, I want you to meet my wife" (on no account "the wife"!). Then he adds as though in parentheses, "Jim Buyer" or "Mr. Buyer." Or if they are all very young, he probably says, "Mary, this is Bob Ace," since he is really introducing his friend, not to Mrs. Jones, but to Mary.

It might be emphasized that an introduction prefaced by the phrase "This is," when said with an enthusiastic inflection, can express a warmth and charm that other introductions lack. This was once illustrated in London *Punch,* in the drawing of a small boy approaching his mother and holding an abashed small girl by the hand, radiantly exclaiming, "Mummy! THIS is HER!" In the same way a child would introduce a beloved teacher enthusiastically, "Mother, *this* is Miss Brown," or, on the other hand, exclaim, "Miss Brown, *this* is my mother!"—in the sense of "Behold! this is she—my mother."

OTHER FORMS ARE PERMISSIBLE

There are many other forms of introduction which might be called conversational introductions, such as,

"Mrs. Parker, do you know Mrs. Norman?" or

"Mrs. Parker, you know Mrs. Robinson, don't you?"

On no account say, "Do you not?" Best taste always prefers, "Don't you?" Or one may say, "Mrs. Robinson, have you met Mrs. Parker?" or, to attract her attention, "Mary! you have met Mrs. Parker, haven't you?—Mrs. Towne" (Mary's name).

These are all good forms, whether gentlemen are introduced to ladies, ladies to ladies, or gentlemen to gentlemen. In introducing a gentleman to a lady, you may ask Mr. Smith if he has met Mrs. Parker, but you must *not* ask Mrs. Parker if she has met Mr. Smith!

At times a few words of explanation make the introduction of a stranger pleasantly smooth. "Mrs. Worldly! Miss Jenkins—she writes as Grace Gotham." Or, "Mr. Neighbor, I should like you to meet Mr. Tennis—he has just won the tournament at Forest Hills."

This can be very much overdone, as at times it makes it seem that one is trying to impress the world with the importance of one's friends.

INTRODUCING RELATIVES-IN-LAW

A lady introduces her son's wife, formally, to acquaintances, as "My daughter-in-law," or to friends as "Dick's wife." Or, with greater display of affection, "This is my Mary—Dick's wife." But this would be said only to an old friend. To an acquaintance "My daughter-in-law" would depend for its warmth on the tone of voice with which it is spoken. And this, as already noted, is of course an extremely important point in all introductions. By tone alone the same words can convey every shade of feeling from cool indifference to adoration. While the intention of introducing a parent-in-law as simply father and mother is well meant, it may be confusing. It is better to say, "This is my mother-in-law" or, if you prefer, "my husband's mother." When introducing other relatives-in-law, "My husband's sister" and "My brother John's wife" (or "Jim's sister" and "John's wife" to one who knows who they are). These names are more clearly understood than "My sister-in-law."

Although they are not really your relatives-in-law, it is quite proper to speak of the husband of your sister-in-law as "my brother-in-law" and the wife of your brother-in-law as "my sister-in-law."

FORMS TO AVOID

Never say, "Mr. Jones, shake hands with Mr. Smith" or "Mrs. Jones, I want to make you acquainted with Mrs. Smith." And do not say "make you acquainted with," nor in introducing one person to another, call one of them "my friend." You can say "my aunt," or "my sister," or "my cousin"—but to pick out a particular person as "my friend" is bad manners, for it implies that the other person is not.

If you are introducing someone to another who is a very special friend, you may say, "Mrs. Smith, I want you to meet Mrs. Jones." But under no circumstances say, "Mrs. Smith, meet Mrs. Jones." This last phrase lacks friendliness and courtesy.

Do not repeat "Mrs. Jones! Mrs. Smith! Mrs. Smith! Mrs. Jones!" To say each name once is enough, except where it is a foreign one or one that is difficult to pronounce. Then saying this a second time, and slowly, is helpful.

Most people very much dislike being asked their names. To say "What is your name?" is abrupt and unflattering. If you want to know with whom you have been talking, you can almost always find a third person later and ask, "Who was the lady with the gray feather in her hat?" The next time you see her you can say, "How do you do, Mrs. ——?" and call her properly by name.

TITLELESS YOUTH

In no way to be compared with the bad taste of total strangers using first names in introductions, as is so notable on certain radio and television programs, is the younger generation's practice of introducing all friends by first names. This informality is just as suitable to young adults as to teen-agers. Muriel Manners, for example, taking a friend to the country club, greets a group of friends with "Hello, everybody. This is Sally."

If Sarah Stranger is accepted as a member of a certain group, she is at once called Sarah or Sally, or quite likely Sal. To be called Miss Stranger (or Mrs. Stranger if she is in her early twenties) announces that she is not a member of the group. Maybe she does not care to join it—maybe they don't want her—but, whatever the reason, she does not "belong." Obviously, then, introductions among our younger groups are titleless. "Sally Stranger, Lucy and Bob Gilding!" Or "Lucy, this is Sally Stranger," and then to Sally, "That is Bob Gilding, and that is Tom Brown." But even so, a man is always introduced to a girl.

If Muriel were not really a friend of Sarah Stranger, she would introduce her—and her own friends as well—by their titles of Mrs., Miss, or Mr., quite as formally as her mother would. The stranger, by the way, must wait to be called by her first name before calling others by theirs. If you are a younger person, you should never call an older person by his or her first name unless you are asked to. Whether older people choose to have those who are a generation younger call them by their first names is a question for them to decide. The practice of this degree of informality seems today to be increasing.

YOUNG WOMAN TO MAN AT DINNER

When any modern young woman in her twenties finds herself next to an unknown man at a dinner party, she more likely than not merely talks to him without telling him her name. But if he introduces himself to her as "John Blank," she says, "I'm Mary Smith"—unless she has an unwillingness to risk being called "Mary" by a stranger. If so she can say in turn, "I'm one of the Smiths who live on X Street." She would be thought very prissy should she say, "I'm Miss Smith," unless she is well along in her thirties.

It is of course an unbreakable rule that all people who find themselves seated together at table accept the obligation of talking. To sit side by side without speaking is one of the greatest discourtesies a guest can show a hostess.

At a dinner with place-cards, one may show one's card and say, "My name, what's yours?" while looking toward the stranger's card.

AT GENERAL PARTIES

Under all informal circumstances the roof of a friend serves as an introduction, but at a very large party—such as a dance or a formal tea or a wedding reception—it is not customary to speak with those whom you don't know, unless you and another guest find yourselves apart from the others. In such a case you do not introduce yourself, but you perhaps make a casual remark about the beauty of the bride, or a comment upon the weather. Whether to talk or not usually depends upon mutual willingness, except, as already noted, with those sitting on either side of you at lunch or dinner, to whom you must talk, first to one and then to the other, throughout the meal.

WHAT TO SAY WHEN INTRODUCED

Under all possible circumstances the reply to an introduction is "How do you do?" It may be said gladly, casually, coolly, or unthinkingly, as the case may be, and it may be varied in pronunciation or emphasis. "How do you *do?*" "*How* d'you do?" "How d'you *do-oo?*"

It does sound limited, but so is holding one's knife and fork and so is drinking coffee after meals. And one can often say nothing at all—just smile! True, the same smile can become equally monotonous. At all events, when Mr. Bachelor says, "Mrs. Worldly, may I present Mr. Struthers?" Mrs. Worldly says, "How do you do?" Struthers bows, and says nothing. To sweetly echo "Mr. Struthers?" with a rising inflection on "—thers?" is *not* good form. Saccharine chirpings should be classed with crooking little fingers, high handshaking, and other affectations.

People who know better do not say, "Charmed" or "Pleased to meet you." When it is actually true, you can say, "I am *very* glad to meet you." But you may *never* say, "I am pleased to make your acquain-

tance." "Make your acquaintance" is a stilted phrase which has, fortunately, almost died out in recent years. On an occasion when you meet
someone whom you have heard much about and have long wanted to
meet, you may of course say, "Oh, I am so *glad* to meet you"—or possibly—"to meet you at last!" and then go on to say, "John Brown
speaks of you all the time," or whatever may be the reason for wanting
to meet this person.

When a young girl is introduced to another who is the friend of an
intimate friend of her own, she naturally explains, "Mary has so often
talked about you." A girl should say less than this to a boy. She should
not tell him how much Mary has talked about him. A boy, on the other
hand, may properly tell a girl that his roommate is always talking about
how wonderful she is. Often the first remark is the beginning of a conversation. Sidney Struthers is introduced to Muriel Manners. She smiles
and perhaps says, "Tommy tells me you are going to be in New York
all winter." Struthers answers, "Yes, I am an interne at Medical
Center."

The one occasion when something more than "How do you do?" is
necessary is when a friend brings a stranger to your house and tells you,
"I have brought Mrs. Blank, who is visiting us." You reply, "I'm so
glad you did!" Then to the stranger, "I'm delighted to see you, Mrs.
Blank."

SHAKING HANDS

Intimate friends, unless they have not seen each other for a long
time, rarely shake hands when they meet in public or even when they
come in or go out of each other's houses. But the rule that a hostess
must shake hands with every guest whom she has invited to a party is
so ingrained that a well-bred hostess invariably rises and shakes hands
with a guest even though she may have seen her but a few minutes
before.

Gentlemen always shake hands when they are introduced to each
other even if they have to cross a room to do so. Ladies rarely shake
hands when introduced. Boys and girls both follow the example of their
fathers and shake hands when introduced, but not when greeting their
friends—except at a formal party when they shake hands with hostess
or host.

When a gentleman is introduced to a lady, she generally smiles,
bows slightly, and says, "How do you do!" Strictly speaking, it is her
place to offer her hand or not, as she chooses; but if he should extend
his hand, she as a matter of course gives him hers. Nothing could be
more ill-bred than to treat any spontaneous friendliness curtly. In general, it is also the place of a gentleman to whom another is being introduced to offer his hand, and the one being introduced should wait until
he does so before putting out his own.

Those who have been drawn into a conversation do not usually shake hands on parting. But for this there is no fixed rule. One is more likely to shake hands with someone whom one finds sympathetic than with one who is the contrary.

Nearly all rules of etiquette are to a degree elastic, and none more so than those governing the acceptance or rejection of the strangers you meet.

There is a wide distance between rudeness and reserve. You can be courteously polite and at the same time reserved to someone who does not appeal to you, or you can be welcoming and friendly to another whom you like on sight.

WHEN TO RISE

On formal occasions a hostess always stands at the door and the host nearby. Both shake hands with every arrival. On informal occasions they both rise and go forward to greet each guest—a man as well as a woman. The children in the family should rise to receive another child, as well as rise for every grown person who enters the room, and stand until the older person is seated. Grown as well as half-grown members of the family rise to greet guests but do not necessarily shake hands. A woman guest does not stand when introduced to someone at a distance, nor when shaking hands with a friend of her own or with anyone else unless that person be very much older. Should an old lady enter the room in which many other ladies are seated, the others—unless members of the family who live in the house—do not rise, since seven or eight all getting up at once would produce an effect not so much of politeness as of confusion. But every gentleman stands as long as his hostess or any other lady near him does. Nor does he sit if any other gentleman with whom he is talking remains standing. In a restaurant, when a lady bows to him, a gentleman merely makes the gesture of rising slightly from his chair and at the same time bowing. Then he sits down again.

HOW VISITOR TAKES LEAVE

When a visitor is ready to leave, he or she merely stands. To one with whom he has been talking, the visitor says, "Good-by. I hope I shall see you again soon," or "I've enjoyed our talk so much." Naturally a woman is less effusive in what she says to a man than in what she may say to another woman. And yet she may very well exclaim, "I've been completely thrilled!" if he has told her anything that can be truthfully described as thrilling, but not otherwise. Furthermore, any comment in praise of his opinion, or of his achievement, or of an especial work he has done is proper. But any remark flattering to his personal appearance or charm would be in worst possible taste. Whatever pleasant remark one person makes, the other person answers, "Thank you." The one who has told of his adventures perhaps answers, "I think you've been very good to listen to me." Or a woman replies to another who hopes to see her again, "I hope so too," although she is more apt to say simply, "Thank you."

In taking leave of a group of strangers—it makes no difference whether you have been introduced or merely included in their conversation—you bow slightly and smile a "good-by" to any who happen to be looking at you, but you do not attempt to attract the attention of those who are unaware that you are leaving.

ONE PERSON TO A GROUP

On formal occasions, when a great many people are present, one person is not introduced to each and every person there. An arrival may be introduced to one or two people, or he may be left to talk with those nearby without exchanging names.

But at a small lunch, for instance, let us suppose you are the hostess. Your position is not necessarily near, but it is toward the door. Mrs. King is sitting quite close to you, and also Mrs. Lawrence. Miss Robinson and Miss Brown are much farther away. Mrs. Jones enters. You go a few steps forward and shake hands with her, then stand aside, as it were, to see whether Mrs. Jones goes to speak to anyone. If she apparently knows no one, you say, "Mrs. King, Mrs. Jones." Mrs. King, if she is young, rises, shakes hands with Mrs. Jones and then sits down. If Mrs. King is of about the same age as Mrs. Jones, Mrs. King merely extends her hand and does not rise. Having said "Mrs. Jones" once, you do not repeat it immediately, but turning to the other lady sitting near you, you say, "Mrs. Lawrence." You can, if you choose, look across the room and continue, "Miss Robinson, Miss Brown; Mrs. Jones!" The two bow but do not rise.

It is much more practical to repeat the names of those present before that of the new arrival, because the attention of each is attracted by hearing her own name, and she will hear the name of the new arrival, whereas Mrs. Jones is naturally paying attention.

MAKING TOUR OF ROOM A MISTAKE

Typical of many hospitable hostesses who give very large parties is the practice of leading a guest, particularly a stranger, on a tour around the room to make sure that he—or more especially she—shall have been introduced to everyone.

Unfortunately this well-meant procedure is sometimes likely to fail of its friendly intent, because it is more than probable that while she is making this circuit newly arriving guests will claim her attention as hostess, and the stranger will be left standing alone!

In other words the advisable procedure is to seat a stranger with a nearby group, at the same time introducing her to them. But even if the hostess overlooks these introductions, the stranger will not be marooned because well-behaved people *always* talk with those seated near them in the house of a friend. It would be an unforgivable breach of etiquette not to!

At a very big lunch when a newcomer does not at once join one obviously a friend, the hostess places him or her next to one or more earlier arrivals. Although it is courteous to introduce strangers to those who will be seated together at table, it is not really necessary because they quite properly introduce themselves at the table (as described on page 359). In the drawing-room before and after the meal, a guest falls naturally into conversation with those she or he is next to without the giving or asking of names.

WHEN TO INTRODUCE

The question as to when introductions should be made or not made is one of the most elusive points of social knowledge. One occasion that requires introductions is the presentation of everyone to a guest of honor. If one arrives after the receiving line has ended, he must look for this guest and present himself, since it is the height of rudeness to go to an entertainment given in honor of someone and fail to "meet" him. Even when one's memory is too feeble to remember him afterward!

At a dance, when an invitation has been asked for a stranger, the friend who vouched for him should personally present him to the hostess. "Mrs. Worldly, this is Mr. Robinson (or, if he is young, John), whom you said I might bring." The hostess shakes hands and smiles and says, "I am very glad to see you, Mr. Robinson."

A guest in a box at the opera or horse show or county fair introduces to her hostess any gentleman who comes to speak to her, unless other people block the distance between so that an introduction would be forced and awkward.

At a formal dinner—a dinner of ceremony—the host should see that every gentleman either knows or is presented to the lady he is to "take in" to dinner, but, on occasion, at a very large dinner, this is not always practical. A gentleman who does not know Mrs. James Jones, whose name is in his "dinner envelope," is expected to find out who she is and ask to be introduced to her. But if this is difficult, it is entirely correct for him to go up to her, bow slightly, and say, "Mrs. Jones? I'm Henry Smith and I believe that I am to have the pleasure of taking you in to dinner!"

Strangers sitting next to each other at table always introduce themselves. A gentleman says, "I'm Arthur Robinson." Or, showing his place-card, he says, "My name!" Unless he is very "modern," showing his card is especially wise if he is seated next to a young modern who is likely to call him "Arthur" unless she sees "Mr." in writing.

An older lady says, "I'm Mrs. Hunter Jones." A young one says,

"I'm Mary Brown," and perhaps if married adds, "Bob Brown's wife." If her husband is at the dinner she adds, "He is sitting across the table on the right of the lady in the red dress." In any case, as said before, those seated together are obliged to talk: it is an unforgivable breach of manners not to do so. For ways of beginning a conversation, see the suggestions in Chapter 6.

When you are taking a house guest with you to a party and your guest is not known in your neighborhood, it is necessary to remember to introduce him or her to all whom you closely encounter. This does not mean that you should make a grand tour of the room—but merely to remember that unless your guest is unforgettably notable, it is unfair to your hostess to expect her to look after *your* guest, and to have a stranger's name at the tip of her tongue in order to introduce him to her other guests whom he does not know.

At a very large dinner, people are not collectively introduced. After dinner, men in the smoking-room or left at table always talk to their neighbors whether they have been introduced or not, and ladies in the drawing-room do the same.

Quaint writers on etiquette speak of "correct introductions" that carry "obligations of future acquaintance" and "incorrect introductions" that seemingly obligate one to nothing.

Such degrees of introduction are utterly unknown in actual life. According to good manners one person is welcomed by those he comes in contact with because he is well mannered, and doubtless because he is interesting or clever or sympathetic and personally attractive. Another is rejected by those who find him unattractive and boring. Introductions, whether "correct" or "incorrect," can no more add to the charm of the one than they can lessen the unpleasing qualities of the other.

WHEN NOT TO INTRODUCE

It is likely that we all know—or have at least encountered—one of those introduction enthusiasts who can not let one person pass another without insisting that they stop to be introduced.

At a "get-together" club, this is quite all right, but at a large tea or wedding reception, or at any general gathering, repeating never-to-be-remembered names is a mistake, unless there is some special reason for doing so. Such a reason would be the close proximity of a real celebrity and an unrealizing best friend—the latter might be chagrined, should he have missed meeting a person in whom he has an especial interest.

A newly arriving visitor is not introduced to another who is taking leave. Nor is an animated conversation between two persons interrupted —very especially that between a young woman and man—to introduce a third who then joins them without encouragement! It *should* be unnecessary to write this, and the fact that it is being put down must be understood as a definite protest against the all-too-many elderly men and women—both of them—who cannot observe a girl and a man obviously enjoying a conversation without breaking into it.

CONVERSATION WITHOUT INTRODUCTION

On occasions it happens that in talking to one person you want to include another in your conversation without making an introduction. For instance, suppose you are talking in your garden to a seedsman and a friend joins you. You greet your friend, and then include her by saying, "Mr. Smith is suggesting that I dig up these cannas and put in delphiniums." Whether your friend gives an opinion about the change in color of your flower bed or not, she has been made part of your conversation.

HALF-WAY INTRODUCTION OF DOMESTIC EMPLOYEE

Ordinarily the introduction of a maid, or butler, or a chauffeur, or any domestic employee to a guest would be as out of place as introducing the driver of a bus to his passengers. But there are many occasions when, for one reason or another, a half-way introduction is made. For example, Mrs. Kindhart, having offered the use of her car to Celia Lovejoy, says as the chauffeur opens the door at her own house, "Carlson, take Mrs. Lovejoy wherever she wants to go this afternoon, and that will be all for today." Or, again, to a house guest as the maid who is to unpack the visitor's clothes approaches, "Will you give Selma the keys to your bags?" Or to a man, "If you ring four times, Dawson will look after you."

A real introduction is made only when the employee has been long in the family and is held in affectionate esteem. In the South certainly, and very likely elsewhere, a young man would tell his fiancée, "Muriel, this is my Louisa who brought me up!" and to Louisa, "And *you* don't have to be told who *this* is, do you?"

And it is not at all unusual—especially in a small household—for the mistress of the house to introduce—or rather call friendly attention to—one who has been long in her employ, "This is our Hilda" or "Aunt Jane, I'm sure you *remember* Hilda!"

INTRODUCING ONESELF

If there is a good reason for knowing someone, it is quite proper to introduce yourself. For instance, you would say, "Mrs. Worldly, aren't you a friend of my mother's? I am Mrs. John Smith's daughter." Mrs. Worldly says, "Yes, indeed, I am. I am so glad you spoke to me."

But if a strange man says, "Aren't you Muriel Manners?" Muriel says, "Yes," and waits for his explanation; and then if the stranger continues, "I think my sister Millicent—Brown—is a friend of yours," Muriel offers her hand and, smiling, asks, "Are you George or Alec?"

"I'm Alec." Whereupon Muriel probably says, "Well, Alec, I *am* glad to meet you at last."

But unless he is the brother of a friend, or a particular friend of a friend, a man should say, "Are you Miss Manners? I am Arthur Jones. I met you at a dinner at Mrs. Worldly's last winter." Whereupon Muriel would greet him with the usual, "How d'you do, Mr. Jones?"

Obviously, it would be in very bad taste to introduce yourself to Mrs. Worldly if your mother knew her only slightly, or for any man without sufficient reason to introduce himself to Muriel.

NAME BLACK-OUT MADE WORSE BY THE TACTLESS

When you are talking with someone whose name you are struggling to remember, and are joined by a friend who looks inquiringly from you to the nameless person—perhaps even asks you, "Won't you introduce me?"—you are obviously helpless to do anything further than introduce your friend to the stranger by saying to the latter, "Oh, don't you know Mrs. Neighbor?" This can be all right if the stranger is so tactful and understanding as to announce her own name.

But when she says nothing and Mrs. Neighbor makes matters as bad as can be by saying, "You did not tell me your friend's name," and the stranger is so lacking in perceptiveness or kindness as to say nothing, then the situation reaches the depth of embarrassment.

COURTESY TO ONE WHO MAY HAVE FORGOTTEN YOU

When meeting someone who may have forgotten you, you should never say, "You don't remember me, do you?" and then give no further help! Unless the person you speak to greets you by name, you should say at once, "I'm Mrs. Brown or Mary Brown (and then if this does not bring a sign of recognition), we met at the Roberts'."

INTRODUCTION BY LETTER

An introduction by letter is far more binding than any spoken introduction which does not commit you to anything. See Chapter 42.

RECEIVING LINES

If a hostess is giving a very big party for a stranger, the latter receives, standing with her. Arriving people are presented to her, "This is Mrs. Neighbor." She offers her hand. At a smaller, friendly party given for someone who is not a stranger to the majority, she does not receive with the hostess, but sits or stands in a convenient place so that others can go up and talk with her.

Even at large balls and semipublic receptions, the receiving line should be limited to four whenever possible. Although one thinks of a receiving line as being composed entirely of women, there are many occasions when men also are included, and sometimes men receive alone.

"HOW DO YOU DO?"—GREETINGS

··≼[3]≽··

AS EXPLAINED IN THE PRECEDING CHAPTER, THE CORRECT formal greeting is "How do you do?", sometimes abbreviated in friendly fashion to "How d'you do" or even to " 'D'you do." Whether Mrs. Younger is presented to Mrs. Worldly or whether the French ambassador is presented to her, all say the same, or merely bow.

ACKNOWLEDGING INTRODUCTIONS

Following their introduction, one gentleman says to another, "I'm very glad to meet you," or "Delighted to meet you."

Friends greet each other with "Good morning" or "Good evening" or "How are you?" But "Good afternoon" is a business rather than a social greeting. It is sometimes used as a greeting by public speakers, but its more typical use is as a phrase of dismissal. A lady terminates an interview with a stranger who has come to see her on business by bidding him "Good afternoon." On similar occasions she would say, "Good morning" or "Good evening," but not "Good-by" or "Good night" —both of which are said to friends.

"Hello!" This is today as widely accepted among friends as it has always been on the telephone. "Hello, Amanda" or "How 'do, John" are practically interchangeable.

In fact "Hi!" or better "Hie-ya!" gaily said like a telescoped "How are you?" has come into unself-conscious use even by parents who have learned this informal greeting from their children.

Very often in place of the well-worn "How do you do?" or "Hello, Jane!" perhaps more often than not, people skip the words of greeting and say, "I'm so glad to see you!" or "I haven't seen you for ages," or "What have you been doing lately?" The weather, too, fills in with equal faithfulness. "Isn't it a heavenly day!" or "Horrid weather, isn't it?"

THE ANSWER TO "HOW ARE YOU?"

The trait of character which more than any other produces good manners is tact. To one who is a chronic invalid or is in great sorrow

16

or anxiety, a gay-toned greeting "Hello, Mrs. Jones! How *are* you? You look fine!", while kindly meant, is really tactless, since to answer truthfully would make the situation emotional. In such a case she can only reply, "All right, thank you." She may be feeling that everything is all wrong, but to "let go" and tell the truth would open the floodgates disastrously. "All right, thank you" is an impersonal and therefore strong bulwark against further comment or explanation.

As a matter of fact, "All right, thank you" is always the correct and conventional answer to "How are you?" unless there is reason to believe that the person asking really wants to know the state of one's health.

A GENTLEMAN AND HIS HAT IN AN ELEVATOR

A gentleman takes off his hat and holds it in his hand when a lady enters the elevator in an apartment house or hotel—any building which can be classified as a dwelling. He puts it on again in the corridor. A public corridor is like the street, but an elevator in a hotel or apartment house has the character of a room in a house and there a gentleman does not keep his hat on in the presence of ladies.

But in public buildings, such as offices or stores or buildings which contain neither apartments nor assembly rooms, the elevator is considered as public a place as a bus or a trolley car. What is more, the elevators in such business structures are usually so crowded that the only room for a man's hat is on his head!

A GENTLEMAN AND HIS HAT OUT OF DOORS

A situation that requires some dexterity is that of a gentleman who stops on a city street to speak to a lady of his acquaintance, in taking his hat and glove off, and in getting his walking stick and cigarette, should he be encumbered with either, out of the way. This constitutes a maneuver that needs considerable practice to be done without effort, though the process is easy enough to describe. First he transfers cigarette and stick, if necessary, to his left hand; then he removes his hat and transfers it to his left hand, at the same time gripping the fingers of his right glove and pulling it off. He then offers his gloveless right hand to the lady. This explains why men who use walking sticks prefer those with handles that can be crooked over their left arms. If the gentleman and lady walk ahead together, he puts his hat on; but while he is standing in the street talking to her, he must remain hatless, no matter how cold the wind nor how torrid the sun, for so long as she may be pleased to stand and talk to him. Nor may he smoke. In the country he may very well be bare-headed and also be smoking a pipe, but in a city street there is no rudeness greater than for a man to stand talking to a lady with his hat on, cigar, pipe, or cigarette in his mouth.

It should not be necessary to add that, out of doors, every American citizen stands with his hat off at the passing of the flag and when the national anthem is played. If he didn't, some other more loyal citizen might take it off for him. Also every man should stand with his hat off in the presence of a funeral.

A GENTLEMAN LIFTS HIS HAT

Lifting or tipping the hat is a conventional gesture of politeness shown to strangers only, not to be confused with bowing, which is a gesture used to acquaintances and friends. In lifting his hat, a gentleman merely lifts it slightly off his forehead—by the brim of a stiff hat or by the crown of a soft one—and replaces it.

When walking with a friend who bows to a lady who is a stranger to him, a gentleman lifts his hat without either bowing or looking directly at the lady. This is because it is a fixed rule of etiquette that a gentleman must never stare at a lady.

If a lady who is a stranger drops her glove, a gentleman should pick it up, hurry ahead of her, on no account nudge her, offer the glove to her, and say, "I think you dropped this!" The lady replies, "Thank you." The gentleman should then lift his hat and turn away.

If he passes a lady in a narrow space, so that he blocks her way or in any manner obstructs her, he lifts his hat as he passes.

If he gets on a bus and the bus gives a lurch just as he is about to be seated and throws him against another passenger, he exclaims, "I'm sorry!" or "Excuse me." If the passenger is a woman, he lifts his hat as soon as he regains his balance. When a man has to ask someone to let him pass by to enter or leave the bus, he says, "Excuse me!"

If he would be thought a person of good taste he must *not* say, "Pardon *me*!" The word "pardon" is a social pariah except in the complete phrase, "I *beg* your pardon."

We all know that a gentleman does not take a seat ahead of a woman, but if he is sitting and women enter, should they be young, he may in today's habitually crowded buses keep his seat. If a very old woman or a young one carrying a baby enters the bus, a gentleman rises at once, lifts his hat slightly as he indicates the proffered seat, and lifts his hat again when she thanks him.

If the bus is very crowded when he wishes to leave it and a woman is directly in his way, he asks, "May I get through, please?" As she makes room for him to pass, he lifts his hat, if he has a free hand, and says, "Thank you!"

If he is in the company of a lady anywhere in public, he lifts his hat to a man who offers her a seat, or who picks up something she has dropped, or shows her any other civility. He lifts his hat if he asks a woman a question, and always, if, when walking on the street with a lady, she bows to another person.

In other words, a gentleman lifts his hat whenever he says, "Excuse me," "Thank you," or speaks to, or is spoken to by a lady. Needless to say, he always takes his pipe, cigar, or cigarette out of his mouth as he lifts his hat, takes it off, or bows. And a gentleman always lifts his hat to his wife when he encounters her, or joins her, or takes leave of her in public, because, if for no other reason, the public does not know the lady is his wife.

A BOY TAKES OFF HIS HAT

A young boy must learn to take off his hat to a lady or a gentleman. He should also take it off to a girl, or at least lift it. To another boy he either makes a gesture of salute, or waves his hand, or very likely calls out, "Hi, Jimmy!"—unless the boy is with his mother or another lady, in which case he takes off his hat if he knows her.

A GENTLEMAN REMOVES HIS GLOVE

A gentleman *wearing outdoor gloves* never shakes hands with a lady without first removing his right hand glove. But at a ball, or when he is usher at a wedding, he does *not* remove a glove intended to be worn indoors. If in the street he cannot free his left hand to pull his right glove off, he says, "Excuse my glove." But he does not ask that an indoor glove be excused.

A lady *never* takes off her gloves to shake hands—correctly she puts them *on!* An exception would be if she were working in her garden and her gloves were soiled, when she would either remove one or say, showing her hands, "I'm sorry, I can't shake hands."

PERSONALITY OF A HANDSHAKE

A handshake may create a feeling of liking or of irritation between two strangers. Who does not dislike a "boneless" hand extended as though it were a spray of seaweed or a boiled fish? It is equally annoying to have one's hand clutched aloft in grotesque affectation or shaken violently, as though it were being used to clean a spot out of the atmosphere. What woman does not wince at the viselike grasp that cuts her rings into her flesh and temporarily paralyzes every finger?

The proper handshake is made briefly; but there should be a feeling of strength and warmth in the clasp, and one should at the same time look into the countenance of the person whose hand one takes. In giving her hand to a foreigner, a married woman always relaxes her arm and fingers, as it is customary for him to lift her hand to his lips. Except in the movies, the hand of an unmarried girl is *not* kissed. But by a relaxed hand is not meant a wet rag; a hand should have life even though it be passive. A woman should always allow a man who is only an acquaintance to shake her hand; she should never shake his. To a very old friend she gives a much firmer clasp, but he shakes her hand more than she shakes his. Younger women usually shake the hand of the older; otherwise women merely clasp hands, give them a dropping movement rather than a shake, and let go.

GREETINGS FROM YOUNGER TO OLDER

It is the height of rudeness for young people not to go and shake hands with an older lady of their acquaintance when they meet her away from home, especially if she is a hostess to whose house they have often gone. It is not at all necessary for either young women or young men to linger and enter into a conversation, unless the older lady detains them, which she should not do beyond the briefest minute. The one excuse for passing by as quickly as possible is when the older person is a clinging questioner, who won't let any approach of friendliness end without asking for a complete report on the health and occupation of every relative and friend of one who merely wished to bid a polite "Good evening" to one of "the family's" friends.

Older ladies, who detain young people with long stories or questions or who, worse yet, at a dance are always dragging young men up to unprepossessing partners, are studiously avoided and with reason. Otherwise it is inexcusable for any youth to fail in this small exaction of polite behavior. If a young man is talking with someone when an older lady enters the room, he bows formally from where he is, as it would be rude to leave a young girl standing alone while he went up to speak to Mrs. Worldly or Mrs. Toplofty. But a young girl or boy passing near an elderly lady or gentleman can so easily stop a brief moment to say, "How do you do, Mrs. Stevens!" or, "Good evening, Judge Wise!" It is a very trifling thing to do and yet few assets will win greater friendships than this impulse.

When a boy is wearing no hat, he bows to a lady or a gentleman exactly as he would indoors, but he would probably raise his hand and wave to a girl or other boy.

A GENTLEMAN RISES

A gentleman always rises when a lady comes into a room. In public places men do not jump up for every strange woman who happens to approach. But if any woman addresses a remark to him, a gentleman stands as he answers her. In a restaurant, when a lady bows to him, a gentleman merely makes the gesture of rising by getting up halfway from his chair and at the same time bowing. Then he sits down again.

When a lady goes to a gentleman's office on business, he should stand up to receive her, offer her a chair, and should not sit down until after she is seated. When she rises to leave, he must get up instantly and stand for as long as she stands—no matter how long that is—and then go with her as far as the door, which he holds open for her.

THE BOW OF CEREMONY

The standing bow, made by a gentleman when he rises at a dinner to say a few words in response to applause or across a drawing-room at a formal dinner when he bows to a lady or an elderly gentleman, is usually the outcome of the bow taught little boys at dancing school. The instinct of clicking heels together and making a quick bend over from the hips and neck, as though the human body had two hinges, a big one at the hip and a slight one at the neck, and was quite rigid in between, remains in a modified form through life. The man who as a child habitually greeted his mother's guests with a bow, when grown makes a charming bow wholly lacking in self-consciousness. There is no apparent heel-clicking, but a slow-motion camera would show that the motion is there.

THE INFORMAL BOW

The informal bow is merely a modification of the bow of ceremony; it is easy and unstudied, but it should suggest the ease of controlled muscles, not the floppiness of a rag doll.

In bowing on the street, a gentleman should never take his hat off with a flourish, nor should he sweep it down to his knee; nor is it graceful to bow by pulling the hat over the face as though examining the lining. The correct bow when wearing a stiff-brimmed hat is to lift it by holding the brim directly in front, take it off merely high enough to escape the head easily, bring it a few inches forward, the back somewhat up, the front down, and put it on again.

If a man is wearing a soft hat, he takes it by the crown instead of the brim, lifts it slightly off his head, and puts it on again.

A gentleman does not look at a stranger to whom he lifts his hat, but he always looks at a person whom he knows.

The bow to a friend is made with a smile, to a very intimate friend often with a broad grin that fits exactly with the word "Hello"; whereas the formal bow is mentally accompanied by the formal salutation, "How do you do."

THE BOW OF A WOMAN OF CHARM

Nothing is so easy for any woman to acquire as a charming bow. It is such a short and fleeting duty. Not a bit of trouble really; just to incline your head and spontaneously smile as though you thought, "Why, *there* you are! How glad I am to see you!"

Even to a stranger who does her a favor, a woman of charm always smiles as she says, "*Thank* you." As a possession for either woman or man, a ready smile is more valuable in life than a ready wit; the latter may sometimes make enemies, but the former always makes friends.

GREETINGS IN PUBLIC

In Europe a gentleman bows to a lady first; in the United States a lady is supposed to bow first; but today few people observe this formality.

In meeting the same person many times within an hour or so, one does not continue to bow after the second, or at most third, meeting. After that, one either looks away or merely smiles.

Unless one has a good memory for people, it is always better to bow to someone whose face is familiar than to run the greater risk of ignoring an acquaintance. It is often difficult to recognize people whom one has met when they are wearing a different type of dress or hat— sports clothes or evening dress, for instance.

But the habit that causes most unintended rudeness is absent-mindedness. Absorbed in their own thoughts, the unmindful do not hear the voice or see the motions made by someone trying to speak to them. They pass a friend unaware of his proximity. It may be annoying to be passed by an "unseeing" acquaintance, but one should be careful not to confuse absent-minded unseeingness with intentional slight, for it often may be you who have changed in appearance.

THE INTENTIONAL "CUT"

For one person to look directly at another and not acknowledge the other's bow is a breach of civility that only gravest cause can warrant. One must therefore be careful not to confuse poor sight or a forgetful memory with an intentional cut. Anyone whose eyes are not sharp or who is not quick of memory can all too easily fail to recognize good friends as well as newly made acquaintances by whom they were much attracted. This does not excuse the bad memory, but it explains the unintended rudeness.

A "cut" is very different. It is a direct stare of blank denial, and is not only insulting to its victim but embarrassing to every witness. Happily it is practically unknown in polite society.

GREETINGS IN CHURCH

People do not greet each other in church, except at a wedding. At weddings people do speak to friends sitting near them, in a low tone. It would, however, be shocking to enter a church and to hear an undignified and unceremonious babel of voices.

Ordinarily in church, if a friend happens to catch your eye, you may perhaps smile, but never actually bow. If you go to a church not your own and a stranger offers you a seat in his pew, you should, of course, almost soundlessly, say, "Thank you." But you do not greet anyone until you are out in the vestibule or on the church steps, when you naturally speak to your friends as you encounter them.

TAKING LEAVE

Whether you are a man or a woman bidding good-by to a new acquaintance, either man or woman, you shake hands and say, "Good-by. I am very glad (or so glad) to have met you." To one who has been especially interesting or who is somewhat of a personage, you say, "It's been a great pleasure to meet you." The other replies, "Thank you," or "Thank you very much," or "I've enjoyed meeting *you*," or "I'm so glad to have met *you*."

When leaving a party early, you also look for your hostess and say good-by. But you try not to attract more attention than necessary to your going, because this might suggest leaving to others and so start the premature breaking up of the party.

THE USE OF NAMES AND TITLES

··∘[4]∘··

A CENTURY AGO IT WAS NOT UNHEARD OF FOR A WIFE TO
speak always of her husband as "Mr. Jones" and even to call him
"Mr. Jones" herself. The use of first names was restricted to children,
and otherwise they were used only between immediate members of a
family, or by a girl and her fiancé, or by really lifelong friends.

USE OF FIRST NAMES

First names used in public was in such bad form that even young
women and men who had known each other all their lives and habitually
called each other by their first names spoke to each other as "Miss"
or "Mister" when with strangers. And yet, absurd as this prim formality
sounds today, surely there is little to be said for the present-day familiarity in the much too frequent use of first names.

First names should indicate that people know each other well, and
the degree of friendship implied among those beyond college years
should increase in proportion to age. Yet we all know that there are
countless people of middle age and older who seem to think that being
called Sally or Jack by Doris Débutante and Bobby Freshman will take
them back to the same age level.

It may be true that "Sally" or "Jack" does suggest camaraderie; that
"Mrs. Autumn" or "Mr. Sere" does not—and if they individually like
the former, certainly no one else has a right to object—though one
wonders how Mrs. Autumn would feel should she overhear those who,
she has supposed, were accepting her as their own contemporary, say,
"Here comes Old Sal!"

If an older person calls a young man or woman by his or her first
name, he or she is not supposed to call the older person by a first name
simply because of their doing so, unless invited to.

WHAT A CHILD CALLS OLDER PEOPLE

The greater informality which has in many instances encouraged
children to call their parents' friends by their first names can, even

when allowed and approved by the family friends, be quite unfair to the child, if others hearing him criticize this apparent lack of respect as his own bad manners. Children should not call a grown person by his or her first name—unless told to do so by that person.

In many cases, really intimate friends who are devoted to the children—those who do not like the formality of "Mr." and "Mrs." and yet do not want to be called by their first names—suggest nicknames for themselves. Otherwise everyone is of course called "Mr." and "Mrs." There is a reasonable prejudice against a general practice of teaching children to call their parents' friends "Aunt," "Uncle," or "Cousin" when there is not sufficient intimacy and devotion to endorse such a genuinely wished-for relationship.

NAMES FOR PARENTS-IN-LAW

The question of what a bride is to call her parents-in-law is one that has no definite answer, except the old-fashioned, suitable and charming one of "Mother Jones" and "Father Jones," one all too seldom heard today. Among the moderns, choice of names is purely personal. In unusually formal families, for example, one hears "Mr." and "Mrs.," which does to most of us sound very uncaring. Usually—and more naturally—parents-in-law are called by names which mean mother and father, but are not the names which the bride uses for her own parents. Or perhaps they are called "Mr." and "Mrs." until a grandchild's nicknames such as "Mimi" and "Pompy" gradually become theirs. Curiously enough, the less intimate relationships of aunts, uncles, and even grandparents never come into question since, with the exception of his parents, the bride calls all of her husband's relations exactly what he does, and he in turn does the same in speaking of hers. The ban against "Mother" and "Father" is out of consideration for their own. Very few mothers or fathers could be happy to hear their own special names bestowed elsewhere.

REFERRING TO HER HUSBAND

Usually—and correctly—a lady says "my husband" when speaking of him to an acquaintance. But to a friend—or the friend of a friend —she speaks of him as "John." But this does not give anyone else the privilege of calling him John unless particularly asked to do so. In the same way, Mr. Worldly speaks of Edith to intimate friends of course, and also to every woman whom they both know socially, whether they themselves call her Edith or Mrs. Worldly. But to a man not an intimate friend and to a woman who is a stranger, he speaks of her as "my wife." In most business situations if he has occasion to speak of her at all, he would say, "Mrs. Worldly thinks, or says, thus or so. . . ."

When the Duke of Edinburgh, accompanying Queen Elizabeth II, was hailed by a former shipmate in the British Navy, he correctly introduced him to "my wife."

THE WORDS "LADY" AND "GENTLEMAN" ESSENTIAL

It is true that these once beautiful words have become so discredited by their misappropriation that those to whom they most accurately belong have banished their usage for the words *man* and *woman*, even putting man first.

However, an understanding of the true meaning of "lady" and "gentleman" is essential to an understanding of the true meaning of perfect behavior. To say a "man" does thus or so has no meaning other than the mental and physical limitations of every male human being. Furthermore, to say no *man* cheats at cards or strikes a woman in the face, or that no *woman* tries to attract the attention of strange men, would not be true. Each of these statements *is* true of a gentleman and of a lady but not necessarily so of a man or a woman.

As a matter of fact these words, though necessary in a book such as this, are very rarely used in ordinary conversation.

"MISS GRAY," "MISS MARY GRAY," OR "MISS MARY"?

Whether she is half-grown or an elderly spinster, calling an unmarried daughter, sister, or aunt "Miss Mary" is socially correct everywhere, and not alone characteristic of the South. To ask for "Miss Gray" or even "Miss Mary Gray" would imply either that she is living away from home, or that the person asking for her is a stranger probably calling on business. In any case, it definitely would proclaim a stranger to her family.

At the door of a friend's house, at a time when you are not expected and when the maid or butler does not know you, you announce yourself as "Mr. James Polk." If you are expected, you merely say, "Mr. Polk." You would do the same when giving your name to the announcer at a party.

Never under any circumstances should you call yourself "Mr." when announcing yourself to anyone whom you have met socially. To one who evidently does not recognize you, you'd say, "I'm James Polk, a friend of the Joneses," or "Jimmy," if you are very young, and then explain, "We met at Mary Jones's birthday party."

NAME OF SAFETY

The so-called "name of safety" used by every well-bred man, or woman, or child when speaking to a stranger about any member of the family is "my wife," or "my husband," or "my daughter," or "my mother"—or, as necessary, "my sister Alice," "my son George." No matter to whom these merely descriptive names are said, they can't be wrong. On the other hand, should one whom you have met socially speak of her husband as "Mr.," this would be very rude.

When a lady is talking with someone who has presumed to call her husband by his first name and she wishes to register her disapproval of the form of address, she speaks of him as "Mr." as soon as she can bring his name in casually.

WHEN FIRST NAMES ARE IN WORST TASTE

In speaking about other people, one says "Mrs.," "Miss," or "Mr.," as the case may be. It is very bad form to go about saying "Edith Worldly" to those who do not call her Edith, and to speak familiarly of a person whom one perhaps does not even know is done only by the climbers and snobs who speak with familiarity of persons of prominence in order to impress their hearers with their own importance (with usually quite the opposite effect). An exception of course is in speaking of a celebrity whose full name is a trade mark.

ON THE TELEPHONE

On the telephone, a lady says to another whom she knows socially, but who is not on a first-name-calling basis, "Hello, Mrs. Knox? This is Mary Bailey."

Mrs. Knox answers, "Good morning, Mrs. Bailey!"

A gentleman calling a lady of his acquaintance never under any circumstances announces himself as "Mr. Smartling." Instead, if the call is social, he says, "This is George Smartling." But if he were calling on business he would say, "This is Mr. Smartling of Dash & Sons." If he were calling a businessman at his office, he would be likely to say, "This is Smartling of Dash & Sons." For further details about telephone etiquette consult Chapter 37.

JUNIOR EXECUTIVE ANNOUNCES HIMSELF

If you are a junior executive approaching the receptionist in an unfamiliar business office, you announce yourself by whatever name you use on your business card. For example: J. H. Brown or John H. Brown, vice president, or whatever your executive position may be, of Green, Black and Company. If being vice president has no bearing on the reason for your call, it is better taste, because less pretentious, to announce yourself as J. H. Brown from Green, Black and Company.

USE OF TITLE OF DOCTOR

No matter what doctorate of learning a man or woman holds, if his professional service is to the public at large and not limited to the knowledge of a select group, then, according to best present-day usage, he may and even should use the title.

When the title of Doctor is required in order that a person be permitted to follow a profession such as the practice of medicine, surgery, or dentistry, it is used instead of "Mister" at all times.

But when the title is an earned or honorary one, indicating that a man or woman has received a diploma of the highest degree in such faculties as those of divinity, law, philosophy, or literature, it is used only in professional work; in private life he continues to call himself "Mister." This means having his name on visiting-cards and listed in club or social directories as "Mr." or by none at all. His friends and acquaintances will, however, almost certainly call him "Doctor" in courtesy.

MILITARY AND NAVAL TITLES

In contrast to the abbreviation of "Mr." or "Mrs.," which is *never* written in full, it is both correct and courteous to write all military and naval titles in full—especially when addressing a social note. Impersonal communications may, however, quite properly be sent to 2nd Lieut. John Smith or Lieut. Johnson, but neither Cap'n nor Capt. instead of Captain is proper for an Army officer—still less for a Naval one. Col. instead of Colonel and Gen'l instead of General and Adm'l instead of Admiral should never be used. Lieut. Colonel is, however, quite correct; but Maj. General is not.

NAMES LEGALLY CHANGED

Whatever may have been the reason for changing the name by which one has been known, social and business associates should be notified of the change if embarrassing situations are to be avoided. The quickest and simplest way of telling them is to send out formal announcements which read:

Mr. and Mrs. John Original-Name
Announce that by Permission of the Court
They and Their Children
Have Taken the Family Name of
Miller

THE WORDS WE CHOOSE
AND HOW WE USE THEM

·•∋[5]∈•·

THE REASON WHY THE QUALITY OF OUR SPEECH IS SO important is that the measure of our own cultivation is made evident the moment we speak. Nothing so instantly reveals our background— our advantages or disadvantages—as the words we choose and the way we pronounce them. This is because cultivated persons have for generations established by usage an unwritten list of approved and disapproved words and pronunciations. Moreover, since these approvals or prejudices were shared by all persons of social tradition, our speech of today proclaims that we too have inherited the same traditions or that we have not.

SPEECH PROCLAIMS ONE'S POSITION

To compare the world of cultivated society to a fraternity, with the avoidance of certain seemingly unimportant words or speech mannerisms as the sign of recognition, is not a fantastic simile. People of great cultivation invariably use certain expressions and appear instinctively to avoid others; when a stranger uses an avoided one, he proclaims that he does not belong, exactly as a pretended lodge member proclaims himself an outsider by giving the wrong grip or password.

To use English of distinction may seem simple enough; the dictionary is meticulous in its definitions, and grammar determines every word's use. The dictionary reflects cultivated usage; in it words not appropriate for formal speech are labeled archaic, colloquial, popular, slang, or vulgar. The shades of meaning of a word may vary, however, from one locale to another, and there are of course local or regional dialects or accents. Usually, to speak as the cultivated element in one's own home town speaks is sufficient for all social and domestic purposes. Be sure, of course, that you don't follow the speech pat-

29

terns of those to whom affectation is a substitute for true cultivation.

For those who are going to make public speeches, either to the nation at large or to representatives from several areas of the country—perhaps as a candidate for Federal office or as a delegate to a national convention—any markedly local accent or vocabulary may well be a handicap. The reason is that any local accent connotes to the listener a locality-limited mind.

COLLOQUIALISMS AND SLANG

Slang is hardly ever used by truly cultivated people, either in speaking or in writing, unless they are trying to achieve a particular effect. These words have become hackneyed through overuse by the uncultivated; as a result, slang often seems tasteless and trite where vividness and variety of speech were intended. Colloquialisms, on the other hand, are everywhere proper except upon the most formal occasions, such as diplomatic meetings. These words are often heard in informal speech, although they are not in the more formal or literary language.

However, a woman of best society may use slang occasionally and yet leave the impression of her background intact, while an equally attractive and equally well-dressed woman proclaims her lack of background through an overuse of both slang and colloquialisms. Miss Old-lineage may perfectly well say "That's swell" and talk of her "boy friend," but Miss Nobackground instantaneously spoils the effect of her appearance when she calls out, "Say, Murree, that's dandy!"

BE NATURAL

Another aspect of the difficult subject of accepted or excluded words is that, at the illiterate extreme, certain exceptional people can seemingly overcome all handicaps. Persons who say "I come," and "I seen it," and "I done it" prove by their lack of grammar that they have had little education. But they may at the same time have exceptional characters, respected by everyone who knows them, because they are what they seem and nothing else. But the caricature "lady" with the comic-picture "society manner" who says "Pardon me," and talks of "retiring," and "residing," and "desiring," and "performing her ablutions," and "being acquainted with," and "attending" this or that with "her escort," and who curls her little finger while holding her teacup and prates of "cult-your" is not sensitive to the exactions of taste—nor likely to be. The offense of pretentiousness is committed oftener perhaps by women than by men, who are usually more natural and direct. A genuine, sincere, kindly American man or woman can go anywhere and be welcomed by everyone, provided, of course, that he be a man of some natural talent, ability, wit, or grace. One finds him all over the world, **neither** aping the manners of others nor treading on the sensibilities of **those** less fortunate than himself.

Often too we encounter men and women in whose conversation **is** perceptible the influence of much reading of the Bible. Such are seldom if ever stilted, or pompous, or long-worded, but are invariably distinguished for the simplicity and dignity of their English.

In best—meaning most distinguished—society no one arises, or retires, or resides in a residence. One gets up, takes a bath, goes to bed, and lives in a house. In other words, everything that is simple **and direct** is better form than the cumbersome and pretentious.

WORDS AND PHRASES TO AVOID

Never say	*Say instead*
I desire to purchase	I would like to buy
I trust I am not trespassing	I hope I am not in the way (*unless trespassing on private property is actually meant*)
Request (*suitable for third-person invitations or official communications*)	Ask (*the proper word under usual circumstances*)
Will you accord me permission?	Will you let me? *or,* May I?
He expressed a desire to make your acquaintance	He said he would like to **meet you**
Permit me to assist **you**	Let me help you
I presume	I suppose
Tendered him a banquet	Gave a dinner for **him**
Converse	Talk
Partook of liquid refreshment	Had something to drink
A song entitled (*unless used in legal sense*)	A song called
I will ascertain	I will find out
Residence (*except in printing or engraving*)	House
Mansion	Big house
Realtor (*except as a technical term*)	Real estate agent

UNINTENTIONAL VULGARITIES

Make you acquainted with	(*See Introductions, Chapter 2*)
Pardon *me!*	I beg your pardon, *or,* Excuse me! *or,* I'm sorry!
Lovely food	Good food *or* delicious food
Elegant home	Beautiful house *or* place

UNINTENTIONAL VULGARITIES

A stylish dresser	She dresses well, *or,* She wears lovely clothes
Charmed! *or,* Pleased to meet you!	How do you do! *or,* I'm very glad to meet you!
Corsage	*A word cherished by many, but distasteful to the fastidious who prefer the phrase,* flowers to wear
Concur	Agree
Tux	Tuxedo *or* dinner jacket. *The word tuxedo is not so fashionable a word as dinner jacket or coat but its acceptance by millions of Americans—who, outside of a very few super-fashionable communities, might not even know what sort of coat a dinner jacket might be—makes it the more widely understood; it is therefore the better word.*
Galluses	Suspenders, *admissible;* braces, *smartest*
An invite	Invitation

IN BAD TASTE

Formals	Formal clothes
Boy (*when over twenty-one years of age*)	Man
Young lady	Young girl (*proper according to good usage for any unmarried young woman not in business, and not older than the early twenties*)
Gentleman friend	Man friend *or* "a man who is a friend of mine"
Lady friend	Woman friend *or* my best girl
Close friend	A best friend *or* intimate friend; *on occasion,* good friend
Drapes—*this word is an inexcusable vulgarism*	Curtains *are hung at a window;* hangings *as decoration for walls. It is true,* draperies *would be correct for many loopings or*

IN BAD TASTE

	shirrings or pleatings, especially on a woman's dress.
Fellow, chap, character	Man (*or boy, if under twenty-one years of age*)
Photo, mints, auto	*Photo or foto is wrong for* photograph; peppermints; automobile *is one exceptional word that is correctly referred to as* car, *but not* auto
Phone	Telephone; *phone has pushed its way into commercial business but is still a social outcast*
Going steady with	*There is no proper equivalent for the phrase because according to etiquette the situation should not exist; no man is given the exclusive right to be devoted to any girl unless engaged to her.*

TWO WORDS OF THE YOUNG NOW ACCEPTED

Guy	*The socially banned word* guy *has been in best usage by college* "men" *themselves for the last dozen years.* "He's a great guy" *is highest praise. But do not say this unless you are a man, and still young!*
Boy friend *versus* beau	*The* boy friend, *after having long been refused entrance to any of the best houses where the* beau *was warmly welcomed, has now been given a place by the fire in the family living-room, whereas the* beau *is shown into the drawing-room only.*

Many other expressions are provincial, and one who seeks purity of speech should, if possible, avoid them; but as offenses they are small! They include such homey terms as:

Reckon, guess, calculate, *or* figure, *meaning* think.

Folks, *meaning* family.

Visiting with, *meaning* **talking with.**

HOME *versus* HOUSE

In its true meaning, the word "home" is the sentiment, the atmosphere, the spirit, the personality, the hospitality that the room or the apartment of the house in which you dwell expresses. Home is not a synonym for house. To people of taste a house is built of wood or brick or stone. It is shocking to be offered a refrigerator as though it were an attribute of family loyalty. You can love your home, work for your home, and be at home, or have or do whatever you please at home. You can also eat home cooking, do home designing and home sewing, meaning food cooked in your kitchen, designing or sewing done by yourself or done under your roof; but if you are sensitive to the traditions of taste, you never put a piece of furniture in *the* home unless you mean a charitable institution. You would say, "Our home was an old Georgian house," but not "We had a Georgian home."

A FEW WORDS TO AVOID

There are certain words which have been singled out and misused by the indiscriminating until their meaning has been distorted and their value has been destroyed.

Long ago "elegant" was turned from a word denoting the quintessence of refinement and beauty into gaudy trumpery. "*Re*-fined" and "dainty" are both affected. So is "limb" unless you are referring to the branches of a tree. But the pariah of the language is "culture," a word rarely used by those who truly possess it, but so constantly misused by those who understand nothing of its meaning that it is becoming a synonym for vulgarity and imitation. To speak of the proper use of a fingerbowl or the ability to introduce two people without a blunder as being evidence of culture of the highest degree is precisely as though evidence of highest education were claimed for whoever can do sums in addition and read words of one syllable. Culture in its true meaning is widest possible education, *plus* sensitive and discriminating appreciation of excellence. And this is reflected in our speech and more immediately noticed than are any other of our idiosyncrasies.

Whether you should say "girl" or "young woman" when you mean a young person between eighteen and twenty-five years—whether married or not—depends upon whether you are speaking according to the dictionary or according to social traditions. In business one speaks of men and young women always. Socially one speaks of men and girls. This is an arbitrary custom. If, in society, one spoke of men and young women, the scene would immediately shift from ballroom or terrace to office.

If a middle-aged woman is inviting some friends for lunch, she doesn't say, "I'm having the 'girls' over," or "the 'gang' in." She is **inviting some women to lunch.**

FORMAL AND INFORMAL

But the most misused words in the dictionary are "informal" when formality is intended, and "formal" for other occasions which have not an attribute of formality about them! Formal is a synonym for ceremonial. A formal party is always conducted according to rules of ritualistic or established forms of ceremony.

In certain houses—such as Mrs. Worldly's, for instance—formality is inevitable no matter how informal may be her "will you dine informally" intention!

On the other hand, the Kindharts can invite a hundred guests, half of them strangers, and at the same time achieve a party that has nothing formal about it. In short, the ordinary pleasant social intercourse between friends and neighbors should, it is to be hoped, never be characterized as formal.

VERNACULAR OF TODAY

While the word "formal" itself denotes the extreme degree of correctness, its exact opposite is surely illustrated by the following dialogue, which took place between one of yesterday's most distinguished gentlemen and his ought-to-be-equally-distinguished grandson. The two were sitting together at a fashionable beach club, when George called out to a passing friend, "Hey, Jim! D'you know—are we going formal tonight?"

Jim answered, "Yeah—guesso!"

Grandfather looked at George's shorts, sleeveless shirt, and unbuttoned collar. "Tell me," he said, "*What* is meant by 'going formal'?"

The boy shrugged and then half sheepishly replied, "I d'n know! I guess it means we've got to put on ties and the girls'll wear skirts!"

COLORFUL SLANG

The fact that slang is apt and forceful makes its use irresistibly tempting. Coarse or profane slang is beside the mark, but the "movies," "deadly" (meaning dull), "swell" (meaning first-rate), "divine" (meaning pleasant), "hunch," and "O.K." and even such phrases as "and how!" "so what?" "you betcha," and "in a jiff" are words and phrases in such common use—at least by our husbands and sons—that their exclusion would leave our American vernacular rather stilted.

It must be remembered that all slang is so greatly modified by the tone of voice in which it is said that the vocabulary as printed may give an inaccurate impression. Slang, to be acceptable, must be fresh and applicable, or it is as unappetizing as cold mutton gravy. Moreover, it is like underscoring written words, and to be effective must be sparingly used. It is all too easy to fall into the habit of using too much slang.

All colloquial expressions are little foxes that spoil the grapes of perfect diction, but they are very little foxes; the false elegance of stupid pretentiousness, however, is an annihilating blight that destroys root and vine.

PRONUNCIATION

Our pronunciations differ and so to a certain degree do the words we use in each section of our country. A common expression used in Texas might be Greek to a Vermonter. Which means, of course, that if our speech is that of the representative people in our community, we need have no concern as to how those in other sections of the country sound their "r's" or "a's."

Traits of pronunciation which are typical of whole sections of the country, or accents inherited from European parents, and seldom lost entirely, must not be confused with crude pronunciations that have their origin in illiteracy or carelessness. A gentleman of Irish blood may have a brogue as rich as plum cake, or another's accent be a soft Southern drawl, or flat New England, or rolling Western; and to each of these the utterance of the others may sound too flat, too soft, too harsh, too refined, or drawled, or clipped short, but not uncultivated.

To a New York ear, which ought to be fairly unbiased since the New York accent is a composite of all accents, English women chirrup and twitter. But the beautifully modulated, clear-clipped enunciation of a cultivated Englishman, one who can move his jaws and not swallow his words whole, comes as near to perfection in English as the diction of the Comédie Française comes to perfection in French.

The Boston accent is very crisp and in most cases suggestive of best English. On occasion the vowels are flattened—suggestive of London, but not quite.

Then, South, there is much softness, with "I" turned to "ah" and a slight tendency toward a drawl.

The Pennsylvania burr is perhaps the mother of the Western one. The Philadelphians themselves are not at all unaware of it, and nearly all will make fun of themselves by saying glibly: "Owrchie had a mawervelous howrrt" and the "oiyly boiyd choiyped and choiyped." In other words, like those of us from Baltimore who like the sweetness of the "eur," the Philadelphians have no idea of lessening the use of their "r's." They also make fun of their "oi" sound in place of "er."

Chicago calls itself "Chicawgo" and eats "chawklut." "Many Omur-ricuns go on fourun tours and eat awerunges." All of which merely indicates the part of the country we are from.

"Water," pronounced as though it were the watt of electric measure —watter—came, so it is said, from German settlers who pronounced it like "Wasser." "Bot" and "thot" sound ugly to those who pronounce bought and thought with lips shaped like an "O." But it is very possible that bought and thought sound ugly to the others, just as "lowng" and "strowng" sound ugly to the English, who always say "lahng" and "strahng."

Philadelphia's "haow" and "caow" for how and cow, and "mee" for my, are quite as tenaciously preserved as the "water-r" and "thot" of the West.

N'Yawk is supposed to say "yeh" and "Omurica." And "Thuh spoim erl wuz berled" (the sperm oil was boiled). Probably five percent of it does, but as a whole it has no accent, because it is a composite of all pronunciations.

Among the highly cultivated New Yorkers there is perhaps a generally accepted pronunciation which seems chiefly an elimination of the accents of other sections. (No doubt that is what all people think of their own pronunciation.) Or do they not know whether their inflection is right or wrong? Nothing should be simpler to determine. If they pronounce according to a standard dictionary, they are correct; if they don't, they have an "accent" or are ignorant; it is for them to determine which. Such differences as those between saying "wash" or "wawsh," "cahn't" or "can't," "ad*ver*tisement" or "adver*tise*ment" are of small importance. But one who considers himself able to qualify as a person of education should know better than to commit errors such as the following.

These illiterate exaggerated pronunciations are of course *never* given in the dictionary, nor used by highly cultivated people.

Fourun	for	Foreign (*far-ren*)
Otta*m*obile	for	Automo*bile*
Reely	for	Real-ly
Cherce	for	Choice
Fambly	for	Family
Moom pitcher	for	Moving picture
Merrige	for	Marriage
Het and ket	for	Hat and cat
Atha-let-ic	for	Ath-let-ic
Pur runt	for	Parent
Av viator	for	Ay viator
Ar tchi tek	for	Ark ki tect
Jest or jast	for	Just
Fillum	for	Film
Et	for	Ate
Erl	for	Oil (*it's "oi," not "err"*)
Eggsit	for	Exit ("*ex*," *not "eggs" you have for breakfast, "x" as in ax*)

Muh*ree*	for	Ma *rie* ("*a*" *as in fat*)
Luk a mo tuv	for	Lo co mo tive (*first three sylla-bles to rhyme with "go"; "tive" to rhyme with give*)
Strenth	for	Strength (*sound the "g"*)
Sing ging	for	Sing ing (*there is no hard "g" before "ing"*)
Kep	for	Kept (*sound the "t"*)
Ree fined	for	Refined (*accent on "fined"*)
Col-yum	for	Column (*there is no "γ" be-fore "um"*)
The *ay* ter	for	*Thea*-ter
Tempture	for	Temperature
Of-ten	for	Of'en (*the "t" is silent in the modern usage, although orig-inally pronounced*)

The following are pretentious pronunciations:

IN BAD TASTE	IN GOOD TASTE
Cult your	Culchur
Par ris (*with trilled "r" and hissing "s"*)	Paris
At-all	A-tall
Iss-you	Issue (ishue)
Press-i-yus	Precious (preshus)

Incorrect pronunciations most frequently encountered:

Feb u ary	for	Feb ru ary
Toos day	for	T(you)z day
Youman	for	Human
Abzorb	for	Absorb (*the sibilant* s, *not a* z)
Gov er ment	for	Gov ern ment (*second syllable same as in "earn money"*)
Wite	for	White (*say hwite*)

FRENCH WORDS IN ENGLISH

Sprinkling French words throughout English speech does not give elegance to conversation or show great erudition, but on the contrary suggests a limited vocabulary in English. It is true that certain words which have become part of our language are unavoidable and should therefore be said properly. Especially important is it to learn those which have no English equivalents. Many of these are as easy to say as any words in our language, and there is no excuse for their mispronunciation. For instance:

PRONOUNCING FRENCH WORDS

Bouquet is pronounced boo-kay, boo to rhyme with you not go.

Vaudeville is not vaw-da-ville. Say voad—to rhyme with road; leave out "da" and say ville as veal; voad-veal.

Chauffeur is not *show*fer, but show*fur;* accent on the last syllable, which is pronounced fur.

Garage is not gurrodge, but gar-*razhe*—gar as in garret, and zhe like the ge in rouge. Everyone can say rouge—why not gar-razhe?

The bill of fare in every restaurant is not a may-*noo.* The actual French pronunciation has no English equivalent, but the acceptable English is *men* (plural of man)—*you.* This is the *English* word and is not intended to imitate the French.

Corsage—the word corsage definitely describes a carefully arranged bouquet made to be worn by a woman, and when necessary to describe its meaning, the word is proper. According to best taste, however, a fastidious woman merely "wears flowers."

Amateur is easy! But it is *not* "amachure." Say quickly, "I *am at her* house," and you can't help pronouncing amateur perfectly.

One who is engaged is a fiancé, masculine, or fiancée, feminine; both words are pronounced alike. The first syllable is *fee,* same as the fee a doctor charges; the second has no English equivalent, but the nearest is "an" in want. The last syllable is *say*—fee-ahn-*say* as though the final "y" were broken off with an "h" in mid-air. But these syllables are only approximate. Too bad we do not use betrothed—a beautiful word which we all can pronounce—whereas the *an* and *é* are both as bad for us Americans as our "th" is for the French; not one in a thousand of us can say it correctly unless we learned it as very young children.

Première—not prum *eer,* nor prehm *eer,* but pruh *myair.*

Words which perhaps ought to be banned because they cannot be written with the standard sounds of the English alphabet include *bouillon, bon-bon, lingerie,* and *ensemble.* Much better to say clear soup, candy, underthings, and dress with coat to match—in plain English, instead of murdering our own tongue as well as that of the French with "bull yon," "bonn bonn," "long ger ay," and "enn sem-bel." The nearest to "in" in lingerie is like the *an* in sang, long drawn out without pronouncing the g, ger like the g as in rouge, and rie is a *trilled* ree. The nearest to ensemble as "ahn sahm-m-bl"—"en" like a groan of pain.

HOW TO CULTIVATE AN AGREEABLE SPEECH

The often-heard but not too polite expression, "You know she is a lady as soon as she opens her mouth," is not an exaggeration. The first requirement for charm of speech is a pleasing voice. A few singing lessons—even though you have no gift for music and will never sing a note—are of inestimable value in teaching you to place your speaking voice and in teaching you to breathe. A low voice—low in pitch, not in range—is always more pleasing than one forced up against the ceiling and apparently let out through a steam vent in the roof! On the other hand, a voice uttered with so little strength that it threatens to be extinguished or so low as to be heard with effort is even more trying. Making yourself heard is chiefly a matter of enunciation; if you breathe properly and pronounce distinctly, a low voice carries well and delights a sensitive ear. Socially and in a business office, it is annoying to have to ask a "mumbler" to repeat. Few people with loud voices have any idea that their steam-whistle screaming is not only ear-splitting but, in public, extremely bad form, as it attracts the attention of everyone within shouting radius.

As a nation we do not talk so much too fast as too loud. Tens of thousands twang and slur and shout and burr! Many of us drawl and many others of us race tongues and breath at full speed, but, as already said, the speed of our speech does not matter so much. Pitch of voice matters very much, and so do pronunciation and enunciation, both of which are absolutely essential to the comfort of the listener.

There is no better way to cultivate taste in words than by constantly reading books of proved literary standing. But it must not be forgotten that there can be a vast difference between literary standing and popularity, and that many that appear on the "best seller" lists have no literary merit whatsoever.

In recommending the reading of two English authors—Rebecca West and Winston Churchill—as first sources of flawless English, it must not be taken as implying that we ourselves have none of our own. On the contrary, we have so many it would be impossible as well as unfair to concentrate on two.

But it is true that Winston Churchill's war memoirs have a value of "matter" as well as "manner" of writing English that sets a valuable standard. And such writing as that of Rebecca West is of definite advantage to those who are interested in finding an example of English at its *best*.

AVOIDING SELF-CONSCIOUS PRONUNCIATIONS

We should all pay attention to the quality of our speech, but this doesn't mean that we should become self-conscious and affected. It is much better to think about what we want to say than about our manner of saying it! That is, if we have any difficulty in thinking about both.

A "lazee slurrin prununshiashun" is obviously BAD. But an affected "twittah" is just as bad—in some ways worse!

Enunciation is very important. In fact those who are quite deaf can usually hear us better if we speak distinctly than if we shout but run-ur-wor's-t'geth'r!

But do not mistake a clear enunciation for any such absurd affectations as "*Oo*, my deah! So *delight*ed to see youh"—someone *might* talk like that and be a very delightful person! Again, most likely not!

MISUSED BEAUTIFUL WORDS

Precious. Precious, when not referring to a gem, but when used as a term of endearment, is one of the loveliest words in the language. It should for this reason be used only when meaning most beloved, most cherished. A house or a dress is not precious.

In contrast, this word can be used to express irony such as when a completely spoiled child has become a neighborhood menace, the neighbors speak of him with cutting irony as "his mother's 'precious' son."

Gracious. Although the word gracious is one of the most beautiful in our language, it *does* imply an unavoidable flavor of condescension, and it is therefore most suitably applied to an elderly person who is bending down, as it were, from an earlier period of time rather than from an assumed position of superiority. Obviously, it is not suitably said of a very young person who would better be called friendly, lovely, responsive, or charming. "Your gracious invitation" does not mean "your kind invitation."

Party. Party, meaning a social gathering, is in best taste. "Do come and bring your guests or friends," never "you and your party." The word probably crept in because of legal usage. As a synonym for man or person it is a humorous usage.

The Man of Distinction. The man of distinction is a very real loss to the vocabulary of this book because he is now concentrating his attention on a tall glass. A very distinguished man implies definite achievement as well as an impressive personality.

SIMPLE ANGLO-SAXON BEST

In determining the excellence of speech, no general rule is more reliable than to choose the shorter, simpler, and preferably Anglo-Saxon word. As has been mentioned before, those who model their conversation on the Bible, with its beautiful and dignified prose, have the most effective and always correct speech.

There are, however, exceptions to this preference for the shorter word: waistcoat, for example, is a better choice than vest.

The tuxedo, as everyone knows, is the hip-length jacket with dress-suit trousers that is a gentleman's semi-formal evening dress. The word tuxedo, by the way, is known to all of us from the Atlantic Coast to the Pacific, but in Tuxedo where it originated and in cities such as New York, Boston, and Philadelphia, where it first became fashionable, it was and still is called a dinner coat or jacket. In other words whether you call it one name or the other is merely a question of personal choice.

THE CHARMING SPEAKER

No speaker who must search for words to express his thoughts is interesting. Beautiful speech is like a brook that ripples on and on. Irritating speech is like the puffing of a locomotive, each puff broken with "er-er-and-er," the listeners sharing in the search and also sharing in the effort with which each word is pronounced, and never even hearing the thoughts the speaker is trying so desperately to convey.

But the outstanding attribute of the charming speech is brevity. The speech which bores, exhausts, and exasperates is one which goes on and on and *on* with complete disregard of the increasing lethargy of its enforced listeners.

Of course, if you are giving a course of lectures, or have been asked to give a half-hour- or even an hour-long talk, your primary concern will be not brevity but content. In this case, however, you must be sure not to dwell at excessive length on any one point. The long speech which entertains is the one which informs and keeps its listeners interested in the subject.

But, if you have been called upon to "say a few words," remember that the speech which charms is the one which ends to its listener's regret. Even one who is kept speaking by the enthusiasm of the audience will be wise to stop while applause is at its height rather than wait for its perceptible decline.

INCREASING VOCABULARY

There is no better way to cultivate a perfect pronunciation, apart from association with cultivated people, than by getting a small pronouncing dictionary of words in ordinary use, and reading it word by word, marking and studying any that you use frequently and mispronounce. When you know them, read any book aloud to yourself slowly, very carefully pronouncing each word. Look up any words you come across that are not familiar to you, and learn the meaning as well as the correct pronunciation. After you can pronounce the words in the book you have chosen, read it aloud again, this time trying to speak naturally as though you were in conversation with a friend.

A notable lawyer, whose early advantages had not taught him good English, but who won a high reputation for the purity of his speech, improved his vocabulary and pronunciation in this way: For years he wrote words or phrases, a few at a time, on his bathroom mirror with soap! Then he practiced these words by saying them over and over to himself, day after day, while he shaved and dressed. Later on, when these words were thoroughly fixed in his mind, other words were written in their place.

Similar methods have been followed by many men handicapped in youth through lack of education, who have become prominent in public life, and by many women who, likewise handicapped by circumstances, have not only made possible a creditable position for themselves, but have then given their children the inestimable advantage of learning to speak correctly at their mother's knee.

There are available many excellent books containing vocabulary-building instructions, with exercises to help you increase your knowledge of words and test your achievement. The consciousness of these exercises may make you stilted in conversation at first, but by using your new vocabulary constantly this can be overcome with ease.

A postscript of encouragement, however, is that plain speech, which is natural and therefore gives an impression of sincerity, is much more pleasing and friend-making than speech which betrays self-consciousness because not really natural to the speaker.

THE ART OF CONVERSATION

·◦〗 6 〖◦·

IDEAL CONVERSATION IS AN EXCHANGE OF THOUGHT, AND
not, as many of those who worry most about their shortcomings believe,
an eloquent exhibition of wit or oratory. Fortunately for most of us, it
is not necessary to have any very special gift of cleverness to be a person with whom others are delighted to talk. No hostess expects or wants
a guest to carry on a serious conversation during an afternoon visit.

BE CALM! THERE IS NOTHING TO FEAR

If you are one of those who dread meeting strangers because you
are afraid you won't be able to think of anything to say, you might do
well to remember that most of the faults of conversation are committed
not by those who talk little, but by those who talk too much.

A bore is almost always one whose voice is never still. A tactless
person invariably rushes in with what ought never to be said.

On the other hand, those who have great difficulty in carrying on a
conversation are usually those who for reasons known only to themselves are terrified of silence. This terror is very like the terror of sinking
felt by those who are learning to swim. It is not just the first stroke
that overwhelms them, but the thought of all the strokes that must follow.

In the same way it is not making a first remark that is dismaying, but
the endless effort to keep on thinking of further remarks, with the result
that the frightened talker hears not a word said to him because he is so
desperately trying to think of what to say next. So the practical rule for
continuing a conversation is the same as that for swimming: "Don't
panic. Don't splash violently. Just take it calmly."

To change the simile, the old sign at the railroad crossings, "STOP,
LOOK, LISTEN," is excellent advice under many circumstances other than
when waiting to cross the tracks. In conversation, "Stop" means not to
rush recklessly forward; "Look" means pay attention to the expression of
the person with whom you are talking; and "Listen"—meaning exactly

that—is the best advice possible, since the person whom most people love to sit next to is a sympathetic listener who makes others want to talk. It must , of course, be remembered that a sympathetic listener really listens. To hold a fixed expression of sympathy and let your mind wander elsewhere won't do at all.

Ideal conversation is a matter of equal give and take. But unhappily it is too frequently all "take." The voluble talker or chatterer rides his own hobby straight through the hours without giving anyone else, who might also like to say something, a chance to do other than exhaust-edly await the turn that never comes. Once in a while—a very long while—one meets a brilliant person whose talk is a delight; or still more rarely a wit who manipulates every ordinary topic with the agility of a sleight-of-hand performer, to the ever-increasing rapture of his listeners.

But as a rule the man who has been led to believe that he is a brilliant talker has been led to make himself a pest. He is the authority on all subjects! No conversation is possible between others whose ears are within reach of his insistent voice. There is a simple rule by which, if one is voluble, one can at least refrain from being a pest or a bore. And the rule is merely to stop and think.

"THINK BEFORE YOU SPEAK"

Nearly all the faults or mistakes in conversation are caused by not thinking, that is, by lack of consideration. A primary rule for behavior in company, a rule that applies particularly to conversation, is: Try to do and say only that which will be agreeable to others. But alas! There are many people who really should know better, people who would be perfectly capable of intelligent understanding if they did not let their brains remain asleep, if they were not too lazy to be considerate. They go night after night to dinner parties, day after day to other social gather-ings, and absent-mindedly chatter about this or that without ever taking the trouble to think what they are saying and to whom they are saying it! Would a young mother describe a dozen cunning tricks and sayings of the baby to a bachelor who has been helplessly sitting next to her at dinner if she *thought*? A more considerate woman would understand that only a very dear friend would care for more than an *hors d'oeuvre* of the subject.

IF YOU ARE A DOTING MOTHER—DON'T

The older mother is even worse, unless something occurs, often when it is too late, to make her wake up and realize that she not only bores her hearers but prejudices everyone against her children by the unrestraint of her own praise. The daughter who is ceaselessly lauded as the most captivating and beautiful girl in the world seems to the wearied perceptions of enforced listeners uninteresting and plain. In the same way the magnificent son is handicapped by a mother's or a father's pride and love in exact proportion to its displayed intensity.

That great love has seldom perfect wisdom is one of the great tragedies in the drama of life. In the case of the over-loving wife or mother, someone should love *her* enough to make her stop and think that her loving praise is not merely boring her friends but handicapping unfairly those for whom she would gladly lay down her life—and yet few would have the courage to point out this fact to her.

SOME BASIC CONSIDERATIONS FOR CONVERSATIONALISTS

People who talk too easily are apt to talk too much, and at times imprudently. And those who have vivid imaginations are often unreliable in their statements. On the other hand, the "man of silence," who never speaks except when he has something worthwhile to say, tends to wear well among his intimates, but he is not likely to add much to the gaiety of a party. In conversation, as in most things, the popular "middle road" is best. Be neither too silent nor too glib. Know when to listen to others, but know also when it is your turn to carry the conversation.

Try not to repeat yourself, either by telling the same story again and again or by going back over details of your narrative that seemed especially to interest or amuse your hearer. Many things are of interest when briefly told and for the first time; nothing interests when too long dwelt upon or told a second time. The possible exception is something very amusing that you have heard about a neighbor, or more especially her child, which having already told your friend you can then tell another neighbor, and then repeat it later to a third listener in the first person's presence. Avoid this as a habit, however, because an over-dosage of praise is very like ten lumps of sugar in coffee.

Certain subjects, even though you are very sure of the ground upon which you are standing, had best be shunned; such, for example, as the criticism of a religious creed or disagreement with another's political conviction. Also, since few can parry an opponent's thrusts with good temper as well as skill, be careful not to let amiable discussion turn into argument. The tactful person keeps his prejudices to himself, and even when involved in a discussion says, "It seems to me thus and so." One who is well bred never says, "Nothing of the kind!" If he finds another's opinion unreasonable, he tries to find a more pleasant subject.

When someone is talking to you, it is inconsiderate to be repeating, "What did you say?" Those who are deaf are often obliged to ask that a sentence be repeated. Otherwise their irrelevant answers would make them appear half-witted. People who are hard of hearing should use a hearing aid. It makes life more comfortable for them and friends do not have to shout at them. But countless persons, with perfectly good hearing, say, "What?" from force of habit and inattention.

HUMOR IS THE RAREST OF GIFTS

If you know anyone who is gay, beguiling, and amusing, you will, if you are wise, do everything you can to make him prefer your house and your table to any other; for where he is, the successful party is also. What he says is of no moment. It is the twist he gives to it, the intonation, the personality he puts into his quip, or retort, or observation, that delights his hearers, and to his case the ordinary rules do not apply.

Our greatly beloved Will Rogers could tell a group of people that it had rained today and would probably rain tomorrow, and make everyone burst into laughter—or tears if he chose—according to the way it was said. But the forced wit is a bore, and the ordinary rest of us must, if we would be thought sympathetic, intelligent, or agreeable, "go fishing."

FISHING FOR TOPICS

In talking to a stranger whom you have just met and about whom you are in complete ignorance, there is really nothing to do but try one topic after another just as a fisherman searches for the right fly. You "try for nibbles" by asking a few questions, such as "Are you fond of the theatre?" If the answer is, "Yes, very," you can talk theatre. When the subject runs down, you try another, or perhaps you talk of something you have been doing or thinking about—planting a garden, planning a journey, contemplating a job, or similar safe topics. Do not snatch at a period of silence. Let it go for a little while. Conversation is not a race that must be continued at breakneck pace.

MY NAME IS MRS. JOHN JONES

This is sometimes the most practical way to begin a conversation with a stranger seated next to oneself at a dinner party. "That's my husband sitting opposite you. We live in the country and raise prize poultry and dahlias, but we come to town very often in the winter to hear music." The one spoken to is very likely to reply that he lives in the city, knows nothing about music or prize flowers and poultry, but his favorite occupations are golf and fishing. Probably after this you talk fishing and this leads to other things. If these topics fade out, he perhaps asks about poultry and what one must know to take prizes. It's really very simple. Or, another helpful thing, if you are a woman talking to a man, is to ask advice. "We are planning to drive through the South. Do you know about the roads?" Or, "I'm thinking of buying a television set. Which make do you think is best?" In fact, it is safe to ask his opinion on almost anything. Politics, sports, the stock market, the trend of behavior—anything. Or, if you are a man talking to a young woman, ask her what she thinks about life, love, work, amusement, romance, almost any question about the relative values of the things people do or think or try for. If she is an older woman, she will probably talk to *you!*

ADVANCE PREPARATION FOR CONVERSATION

Making an outline of what to say before you go out is sensible only in that it does in some cases inspire self-confidence. This does not mean that you should study a subject and then lecture on it. Heaven forbid! But if you glance through your newspaper, in which every imaginable topic is mentioned, you can't very well go out feeling completely unprepared and stilted. Whatever you do, don't deliberately read up on a topic that you think will give an impression of your cleverness. That is the way bores are made! Be sure to choose topics that truly appeal to you. It doesn't matter so much what the subjects are; your enthusiasm about what you have to say is almost sure to result in a responsive reply from your listener.

And yet, a paradox: If you care too intensely about a subject, it is dangerous to allow yourself to say anything. That is, if you can only lecture about your fixed point of view, then you should never mention it except as a platform speaker. But if, on the other hand, you are able to listen with an open mind, the chances are that you need put no barriers whatever on any subject.

At the present moment Mrs. Oldname and Mrs. Kindhart, really the most devoted of neighbors, are so violently opposed to each other on a certain political question of today that their neighbors have made a rule to which both have amiably agreed: the first person who mentions the forbidden topic must pay a fine.

After all, a conversation between two people is very simple. You find a topic on which you agree—one topic that is pleasant to both. Then you stumble on another about which you don't agree. Careful here! Much better withdraw unless you can argue without bitterness or bigotry. Argument between cool-headed, skilful opponents is a delightful, amusing game, but very, very dangerous for those who may become hot-headed and ill-tempered.

THE TACTLESS BLUNDERER

Thoughts and feelings of seclusion and sacredness are ruthlessly laid bare by such remarks as, "Oh, but your son's lameness is getting much worse!" "I suppose you feel lonely since the death of your daughter?" "Are you really going to be divorced?"

These examples sound unbelievable, yet each of these crude remarks has actually been made on occasion by persons of supposed education who had not a semblance of excuse for their cruelty.

Commonplace examples of tactlessness include the mean-to-be-agreeable elderly man who says to an old acquaintance, "Twenty years ago you were the prettiest girl in Philadelphia." Or, in the pleasantest tone of voice to one whose only son has married, "Why is it, do you suppose, that young wives always dislike their mothers-in-law?"

If you have any ambition to be sought after, you must not talk about the unattractiveness of old age to the elderly, about the joys of dancing and skating to the lame, or about the advantages of ancestry to the self-made. It is also dangerous, as well as needlessly unkind, to ridicule or criticize others, especially for what they can't help. To say, "She looks as though her mother had been scared by a white mouse" may make your listeners laugh at a girl who is very blonde, shy, and pale, but it is a cheap trick and not worth the taking.

A young girl who admired her own facile adjectives said to a casual acquaintance, "How *can* you go about with that squint-eyed girl!" "Because," answered the young man whom she had hoped to impress, "she is my sister."

It is scarcely necessary to say that one whose tactless remarks may ride rough-shod over the feelings of others is not welcomed by many.

THE BORE

It has been said of the bore that he is "one who talks about himself when you want to talk about yourself!" This is superficially true, but a bore might more accurately be described as one who insists on telling you at length something that you don't want to hear about at all. He insists that you hear him out to the bitter end in spite of your plainly shown boredom. He will tell the same story time after time, every tiresome detail is held up and turned about as a morsel of delectability.

On the other hand, to be bored is a bad personal habit, and one only too easy to acquire. As a matter of fact, it is impossible, almost, to meet anyone who has not *something* of interest to tell you if you will but take the trouble to find out what it is. Also you might remember that in every conversation with a dull person, half of the dullness is your own.

There are certain always delightful people who refuse to be bored. Their attitude is that no subject need ever be utterly uninteresting, so long as it is discussed for the first time. Repetition alone is deadly dull. Besides, what is the matter with trying to be agreeable yourself? Not too agreeable. It has been truly said: "Be polite to bores and so shall you have bores always round about you." Furthermore, there is no reason why you should be bored when you can be otherwise. But when you find yourself sitting in the hedgerow with nothing but weeds, there is no reason for shutting your eyes and seeing nothing, instead of finding what beauty you may in the weeds. Cynically, life is too short to waste in drawing blanks; therefore, it is up to you to find as many pictures to put on your blank pages as you possibly can!

SUBJECTS OF CONVERSATION

The safest rule to remember is that conversation must never be on subjects such as details of illnesses, and operations, or household troubles. In fact it is very bad form to talk freely to acquaintances, or worse yet to strangers, about your private concerns.

DANGERS TO BE AVOIDED

In conversation the dangers are very much the same as those to be avoided in writing letters. Talk about things which you think will be agreeable to your hearer. Don't dilate on ills, misfortunes, or other unpleasantnesses. Your audience probably has them too and won't be entertained by yours. Only your nearest and dearest will care how many times you went to the operating room. The one in greatest danger of making enemies is the man or woman of brilliant wit. If sharp, wit tends to produce a feeling of mistrust even while it stimulates. Furthermore, the applause which follows every witty sally becomes in time breath to the nostrils, and perfectly well-intentioned people, who mean to say nothing unkind, in the flash of a second "see a point," and in the next second score it with no more power to resist than a drug addict has to refuse a dose put into his hand!

The mimic is a joy to his present company, but eccentric mannerisms are much easier to imitate than charm of personality, and the subjects of the habitual mimic are all too likely to become enemies.

You need not, however, be dull because you refrain from the rank habit of a critical attitude, which like a weed will spread all over the place if you let it have half a chance. A very good resolve to make and keep, if you would also keep your friends, is never to speak of anyone without, in imagination, having him or her overhear what you say. One often hears the exclamation "I would say it to her face!" At least be very sure that this is true, and not a braggart's phrase, and then— nine times out of ten—think better of it and refrain. Preaching is all very well in a textbook, schoolroom, or pulpit, but it has no place in society. Society is supposed to be a pleasant place; telling people disagreeable things to their faces or talking behind their backs is not a pleasant occupation. To be brutally frank is usually very tactless.

PERSONAL REMARKS

Although personal remarks are likely to be in bad form, it is proper and always pleasant to say something appreciative about something one has done. "Your speech was splendid!" "Such a delicious dinner you gave us," "I've never seen such beautiful flowers," "You always know how to make a room inviting." But it is certainly bad taste to say, "What a lovely nose you have and what an enchanting mouth."

THE OMNISCIENCE OF THE VERY RICH

Why a man, because he has millions, should assume that they confer omniscience in all branches of knowledge is something which may be left to the psychologist or psychiatrist to answer, but most people thrown in contact with millionaires will agree that an attitude of infallibility is typical of a fair majority.

A professor who has devoted his life to a subject modestly makes a statement. "You are all wrong," says the man of millions. "It is this way . . ." Because he can pay for anything he fancies, he considers himself an accredited expert as well as a potential owner. Topics he has a smattering of he simply appropriates; his prejudices are, in his opinion, expert criticism; his taste impeccable; his judgment infallible; and to him the world was created for his sole pleasure. But to the rest of us, who also have to live in it with as much comfort as we can, such persons are certainly elephants at large in the garden. Sometimes we can induce them to pass through gently, but they are just as likely at any moment to pull up our fences, and push the house itself over on our defenseless heads.

There are countless others, of course, often the richest of all, who are authoritative in all they profess, who are human, helpful, and respecters of the garden enclosure of others.

FOR THOSE WHO TALK TOO EASILY

The faults of commission are far more serious than those of omission; regrets are seldom for what you left unsaid.

The chatterer reveals every corner of his shallow mind; one who keeps silent cannot have his depth plumbed.

Don't pretend to know more than you do. To say you have read a book and then give evidence that you have understood nothing of what you have read, proves you a half-wit. No person of real intelligence hesitates to say, "I don't know."

Above all, stop and *think* what you are saying! This is really the most important rule. If you stop, you can't chatter or flounder ceaselessly; and if you *think*, you will find a topic and a manner of presenting your topic so that your neighbor will be interested rather than bored.

Remember also that the sympathetic listener is the delight of delights. The person who seemingly is eager for your news or enthralled with your conversation, who looks at you with a kindling of the face and gives you spontaneous and undivided attention, is the one to whom the "orchid" for the art of conversation would undoubtedly be awarded.

IN PUBLIC PLACES

·◦[7]◦·

CONVENTION RULES THAT A GENTLEMAN, WHETHER WALK-
ing with two ladies or with one, takes the curb side of the pavement;
he should never sandwich himself between two ladies. Taking the curb
side has not been an exaction of courtesy since automobiles removed
the danger of runaway horses, from which the gentleman was once
supposed to protect his fair companion, and today it does seem senseless that he keep circling back of the lady every time they cross a
street, instead of giving her the position of courtesy on his right. In
short, modern rules of behavior approve of his walking on the curb
side of the pavement or on the lady's left as he chooses, but not on any
account on her right and away from the curb at the same time! Keeping the lady on the right is a courtesy strictly observed in Europe.

The reason why a man should neither walk nor sit between two
women is that from one side he can look in the direction of both while
talking with either one, whereas when he is between them then he must
turn away from one when he talks to the other.

DON'T ATTRACT ATTENTION

Not to attract attention to oneself in public is one of the cardinal
principles of etiquette. Shun conspicuous manners and conspicuous
clothes, staring at people, or bumping into them. In public—whether in
the street or in an elevator—one should particularly avoid conversing
in strident tones. Nothing stamps the parvenu more plainly than the
advertisement of his achievements by loud word of mouth. One should
also avoid loudly pronouncing people's names, or making personal remarks that may either attract passing attention or proclaim anyone's
identity. Do not expose your private affairs, feelings, or innermost
thoughts in public. You are knocking down the walls of your house when
you do.

A young man walking with a young woman should be careful to draw
no attention to her or to himself. Too devoted a manner is always conspicuous. He should never grasp her at the elbow and shove her here
and there—unless, of course, to save her from being run over!

GENTLEMEN AND BUNDLES

In Victorian days it was considered necessary for a man to carry anything and everything for the lady he was with, no matter how feminine in appearance or how light in weight the bundle might be. Nowadays, however, the etiquette of toting is determined by practicality. A lady should certainly carry such feminine articles as her purse, gloves, umbrella, and hat box, and she may also carry any lightweight packages. A gentleman must, of course, carry the heavy items—suitcases, golf bags, and even groceries—and he should ask if he can assist her when she has many small packages. Obviously a woman should not allow a man to carry for any distance a heavy or otherwise burdensome package.

Of course, every man should be willing to carry an umbrella that looks like a man's. He should also very willingly carry a woman's field glasses, or her camera, or her polo coat, or indeed anything that might seemingly be his own. But only a very inconsiderate woman would ask him to carry a slender, colored umbrella with a long, delicate handle, or a coat that is conspicuously feminine.

A woman should make sure that any packages she asks a man to carry for her are wrapped neatly and securely. An unthinking young woman who asks an admirer to carry something suggestive of a pillow, done up in crinkled paper and odd lengths of joined string, is likely to find herself wondering why John Newbeau never calls her any more!

A GENTLEMAN OFFERS HIS ARM

To an old lady, or to an invalid, or to any lady on any occasion when she may need his support, a gentleman of course offers his arm, but unless she needs his support she does not take it in the daytime.

In accompanying a lady at night, whether down the steps of a house or when walking a distance, a gentleman should offer his arm, not only because it is a courtesy, but because high-heeled evening shoes can be somewhat difficult to walk in when it is too dark for a woman to see clearly where she is placing her foot.

When he offers his arm, he says, "Will you take my arm?" or perhaps, "You'd better take my arm!" or, "Wouldn't it be easier if you took my arm along here?" Otherwise the only occasions on which a gentleman offers his arm to a lady are in taking her in at a formal dinner, or when he is an usher at a wedding. In walking across a ballroom, except at a public ball in the grand march, it is the present fashion for the younger generation to walk side by side rather than hand on arm. Etiquette does not permit a gentleman to grab a lady by the arm or the elbow, and shove her along. It is only when he is assisting her to get into a car, a taxi, or a bus that it is permitted for him to put his hand under her elbow. When he helps her out, he should alight first and offer her his hand. Over dangerous footing or up a few rickety steps he also goes first and then leans over and offers her his hand, which she takes to steady herself.

Under all ordinary circumstances, indoors or out, the gentleman precedes her only if the way is dangerous or uncertain. The reason for his alighting first from a carriage dates from the era of the horse-drawn vehicle, when the horses might start suddenly, and he stood ready to catch or assist her should she trip. He alights first from a car today because of the habit of getting out of a carriage first. He also precedes her down a very steep or slippery stairway. "Let me go first; the stairs are bad." The idea of protecting her should she slip is quite out of key with the fleet-footed young women of today. Even so, etiquette requires that he make the gesture of stepping into a boat first and being ready to help her. Moreover it is well to remember that charm in a woman still presupposes feminine grace rather than masculine hardihood, which in no way denies the fact that a young woman's helplessness is a thing of the past.

ON COUNTRY BY-PATHS

It is still impossible to imagine a lady walking on a city street and either chewing gum or smoking. Nor does a gentleman walk with a lady on a city street and at the same time smoke. On the other hand, many things which are not done in the city are permissible in the country, where a man's pipe, like his dog, is classically his inseparable companion. That a young woman's cigarette may properly go along with the man, and his pipe, and his dog is now taken for granted in almost every community. It is needless to caution civic-minded people to make sure that all ashes are carefully smothered and matches broken in two, but there are some thoughtless ones who need to be reminded that on a dry, hot summer day, a few weeds may prove to be a tinderbox.

A LADY NOT ON THE LEFT

In former days there was a rule of utmost importance, that a lady was never seated on a gentleman's left, because according to the etiquette of the day a lady "on the left" was *not* a "lady." But today in America all that remains of this rule is that, when equally practical, it is always more polite that a gentleman seat a lady on his right. A few definite rules about sitting on the right include the seating of a guest of honor on the right of the host or hostess or chairman, and the military rule by which the senior officer walks as well as sits on his junior's right. There is also a fixed rule that in her own car a lady always sits on the right-hand side of the rear seat of a car that is driven by a chauffeur. This is the owner's seat, and therefore a woman friend, who of course enters the car first, must remember to take the left-hand seat so that the owner may take her own place, unless she relinquishes it to a guest, such as the wife of the President or the governor, or anyone whom she wishes especially to honor.

THE QUESTION OF PAYING

It is becoming much less customary than it used to be for a gentleman to offer to pay a lady's way, especially if they happen to meet by chance. For example, if a young woman and a man happen to find themselves taking the same train and she stops at the news-stand to buy magazines, the man instinctively starts to pay for them. If she knows him very well and the total is very small, she perhaps lets him pay. But if he is someone she knows slightly or if she has bought several of the higher-priced ones, she answers, "Don't bother; I have it!" and puts the money on the counter. It would be awkward for him to protest, and bad taste to press the point. In this case, too, she buys her ticket and tips the porter for carrying her bag. On the other hand, if she has gone on his invitation to spend the day in the country, or to lunch, or to dinner, or to a theatre, he of course pays for everything.

A courteous gentleman on a train or boat who finds himself sitting next to a lady whom he knows very slightly should not offer to pay for her seat or for anything she may buy from the newsboy. The reason for this rule is that he should on no account put her under obligation to him.

THE ENJOYMENT OF PUBLIC PLACES

Apart from the courtesies which all of us are expected to show to friends and neighbors, there are endless other exactions of ordinary human kindness which we should always show to the public at large, and which we have the right to expect will be shown to us. The following items can not be taken too much to heart by any of us who, no matter how good our intentions, may sometimes forget the rights of or be unaware of the feelings of others.

PICNIC IN PUBLIC

When you picnic anywhere in public, don't forget to choose a place well out of the way of traffic. And do, moreover, make sure not only to tidy up before you leave, so that no trace will be left, but to be careful, while you are eating and opening papers, that you don't carelessly throw them aside where they will blow out on the road. Many of the highways have pleasant wayside parks for picnickers, equipped with rustic tables, safe drinking water, and incinerators. On the property of a private owner the least payment you can make is to be sure that you do nothing that might despoil any of his property.

In the woods, for example, vandal picnickers not only pick flowers, but break off large branches and sometimes even pull out whole bushes (be sure you do not pick any flowers or dig up bushes that are on the conservation list), and drive blithely away leaving cardboard boxes and tin cans scattered behind them. Needless to say, if you picnic in the woods and have lighted a fire, you must make sure that the ashes are out and safely covered over with earth before you leave. Although most picnickers are careful about this, there are many who seem utterly unaware that leaving an untidy mess behind them is a pretty shabby way to repay the owners for your enjoyment of their property.

AT A PUBLIC BEACH

At a public beach the first rule is to avoid crowding—at least as much as you possibly can. Those of us who have children should choose places as near as we can to where the children are going to wade in and out of the water and dig canals and build sand castles. Not only is it dangerous to have little children paddling in the water far away, but it is also natural for a child to fill his pails and run back and forth from his family to the water, kicking sand and spilling water all over those who may be sitting in his path, and, even though they run very steadily, many people are likely to be nervous and fearful of having water poured over them.

It is also important not to let a child thrust its attentions upon strangers. While spontaneous friendliness is one of the most appealing traits a child can have, and most people are inclined to like children, it must nevertheless be remembered that there are those who do not. Therefore, before letting Johnny make himself one of a group of strangers sitting nearby, be sure to notice whether the strangers are showing particular interest in Johnny or if Johnny is alone showing interest in the strangers! And if the latter seems to be the case, call him back immediately!

Do unto others . . . and this means follow the posted rules for the safety and comfort of others—and yourself!

PARKS AND PLAYGROUNDS

Behavior at one of the public parks is practically the same as that at the beach. Again, don't crowd against other groups if you can help it. Don't spread your picnic baskets and personal belongings over two or three tables when your share is one. Although picnicking table manners are less exacting than those at a set table at home, this does not grant to the children the privilege of eating like little savages and offending the sensibilities of your neighbors who see them eat.

On the other hand, the public parks and picnic grounds are excellent training schools in that they teach children to take their turn and be satisfied with their own share of time on the slides, swings, and see-saws, and in any other pleasures offered to all children.

LIFE IN CROWDED CITIES

Even more important than the need for consideration of others on beaches and in parks is that of the dwellers in city flats so closely packed that every sound made by one family can be heard by several others. In fact, sound seems sometimes to be intensified by distance. In the room with the children, their play does not seem overloud; nor does the radio or television set—even one that seems scarcely loud enough to bother anyone not close to it. But to the family living on the floor below, the patter of little feet sounds like a stable full of percherons. The toys they drop seem all of iron! The disc-jockey crashes through each separate convolution of a neighbor's brain. As for young musicians' practicing, there is no manager of an apartment house who is not at his wits' end to solve this chief cause of complaint.

There are certain annoyances to others that can't be helped; babies must sometimes cry, children scream, dogs bark, or someone gets a hacking cough. The best that considerate parents can do is to try to soften such sounds as much as possible by shutting a window temporarily and by trying to train both children and dogs.

An angle that is evidently difficult to comprehend is that in nearly all communal buildings in close-ranged neighborhoods, there are always those few who seemingly show no feelings for others because their own insensitiveness is, as it were, on another wavelength. It is very hard to keep in mind, or even to understand, that there can be sounds which greatly annoy some of us—such as the unceasing sound of a radio or record-player—that do not disturb others at all, whereas some of the things which we don't mind can quite possibly be unbearable to our neighbors.

ENTERTAINING AT A RESTAURANT

⋅⋅∘[8]∘⋅⋅

IN A RESTAURANT OF THE FIRST CLASS A GENTLEMAN leaves his hat and coat in the coatroom or checks them at the entrance of the restaurant. A lady may leave her wrap in the dressing-room, or wear it into the dining-room as she chooses. In this case, after being seated, she merely throws the shoulders of her wrap back of her, over her chair.

In the daytime when lunching at a restaurant, she wears a hat and keeps it on. Despite today's trend toward hatlessness, a hat is always correct with a street dress. At night she wears a hat if in daytime clothes, an evening hat if she chooses with semi-evening or dinner dress, and no hat ever if in formal evening dress.

HOW TO ENTER A RESTAURANT

When you have checked your things and joined your husband or wife or friend, you wait just inside the door of the entrance until the head waiter or hostess comes toward you and shows you to a table.

The waiter pulls out the choice seat first (meaning the seat that he considers choice because it faces into the room or the lake-view or whatever is supposed to be of interest). If you are a lady with a gentleman, you naturally take it, unless for some reason you prefer another. In this case, you stand beside the other chair saying, "I'd rather sit here." A lady who has another lady as her guest offers the choice seat to her.

When there is no waiter at hand to seat them, the gentleman helps his guests. If he is with two ladies, he helps first one and then, at least, makes the gesture of helping the second. He should help a guest before his wife, of course, who by that time has probably seated herself.

The ladies always follow the head waiter and the gentlemen follow them. If a gentleman is giving a dinner for six or more, the ladies stand at the table until told by their host where to sit. Therefore, it causes less confusion if he goes in ahead of his guests. When a husband and wife are hosts, the wife seats the guests, usually going ahead with the most important lady.

58

If they are only four, and none is married, the ladies seat themselves, facing each other. When two married couples dine together, the host and his wife sit opposite each other exactly as they do at a table for six or ten. At a table of eight or other multiples of four, a gentleman sits opposite the host with the hostess on his right or left.

If there is dancing and an older and more important woman is a guest, the host invites her for the first dance; then he dances with the other ladies and finally his wife. A woman should never be left alone at a table.

RESTAURANT WITH BUILT-IN SEATS ALONG THE WALL

In a restaurant that has continuous sofa-seats or banquettes along its walls, two diners are seated side by side against the wall, and the table which is two places wide is pushed in front of them. If four are dining together, the ladies are seated on the sofa, and chairs are placed for the gentlemen facing them across the table.

If the restaurant were very crowded, two diners, who might otherwise be given wall seats, would be seated at a half-width table, at which the lady would be seated against the wall and the gentleman facing her.

IN A RESTAURANT WITH ALCOVES

In a restaurant with alcoves, the ladies go in first and sit against the far wall, facing each other across the table. The gentlemen then sit next to them also facing each other. If a lady and two gentlemen are lunching or dining in an alcove, the lady takes her place first against the wall. If one of the gentlemen is related to her, he sits across from her, and the one not related sits beside her. If this grouping is reversed, the two ladies sit next to the wall, and the man who is the husband of one sits beside the other.

In certain localities husbands and wives are always seated together when out in company. This is a practice contrary to all precepts of etiquette and common sense—for when they go out, if they only talk to each other, they might just as well stay at home.

A GIRL AND A MAN DINING ALONE

The head waiter seats them across a small table for two or across corners at a square table set for four.

On occasion a man, who may want to order a special dish or dishes, gives the order beforehand. Usually, however, the man, the girl, and the waiter hold a three-sided conversation, something like this:

MAN: "What would you like? Fruit cocktail? Oysters? Clams?"

WAITER: "Our shrimps are particularly fine."

MAN to GIRL: "Would you like shrimps?"

GIRL: "Yes, very much," or else, "I'd rather have oysters."

MAN to WAITER: "Please bring one order of shrimps, one of oysters."

MAN to GIRL: "Soup?"

GIRL: "No, I'd like just one dish, chicken—or something like that, and a dessert."

Or when asked what she would like, she says in the beginning what she wants, or she agrees to what he suggests. One point: The girl does not give her order to the waiter but tells the man what she would like and it is he who orders her choice. Unless she knows the man is very well-off, or the restaurant serves *table-d'hôte* meals, the girl ought to show some consideration for her companion's purse. A young woman who says sweetly "yes" to his necessary suggestions—*Hors d'oeuvre?* Soup? Fish? Entrée? Roast? Salad? Dessert? Coffee?—is not very likely to be asked to dine with him soon again—if ever!

If the waiter makes the mistake of serving him first, he asks that the lady be served before him.

GIVING A DINNER OR LUNCH IN A RESTAURANT

When invitations are given beforehand to a lunch or to a dinner in a restaurant, the host or hostess orders the meal in advance, and the guests eat what is put before them exactly as at a dinner in someone's house. When the waiter shows you, as host, the dish he is about to serve, look at it to be sure it is what you ordered and that there is nothing obviously wrong with it. To fuss unnecessarily in a restaurant is in very bad taste, but you do owe it to your guests to see that they are given the best that is available. The waiter will almost surely see that each receives what he or she ordered, that each has butter and that no water glass is empty. But you yourself should have an eye on all such details. When people are invited to dine on the spur of the moment and the host has not made previous preparation, he asks what each would like and then gives the order.

When you as a guest are asked what you would like, it is much better frankly to name a dish or two than to answer, "Oh, anything," which means nothing whatever and leaves the host helplessly staring at that utterly impersonal dictionary of dishes, an *à la carte* menu.

Remember, however, that a considerate guest should not suggest more than either *hors d'oeuvre* or soup and a main course, or else a main course and salad or dessert, followed by demitasse.

At a *table d'hôte*, it is usual for each person in turn to order for himself—and seemingly by a miracle the waiter brings to each exactly what was ordered.

THE DIFFERENCE BETWEEN TABLE D'HÔTE AND À LA CARTE

Table d'hôte means a set price for a complete meal, irrespective of how many courses are ordered. "Club" breakfasts and lunches, "blue plate" dinners, or any meals at fixed prices are *table d'hôte*.

À la carte means that you order from a long list of dishes and you pay for each dish ordered including the bread and butter.

Usually it is very easy to know which is which, because the price follows each item on an *à la carte* menu, whereas no prices are listed on a *table d'hôte* bill of fare. Very often a separate card or a box inset on the *à la carte* menu reads, "Special dinner $3.00" or whatever the price may be, which means that you can order whatever you choose on this special list for three dollars, but that any item taken from the regular bill of fare will be charged for as an extra.

If a guest does not want a cocktail or wine, there is no reason for ordering one. On the other hand, there is no reason why other people should not have what they wish.

Another combination menu becoming very popular is that which has a price following each entrée. This price includes the choice of an *hors d'oeuvre* or a soup; also a salad or a dessert, and choice of coffee, tea, or milk. If any items other than the entrées are followed by a price, this means that there is an additional charge for them.

In an *à la carte* restaurant, the check—meaning a list of what you have ordered with the price of each item and the total of the bill—is brought to you by the waiter who serves you. In restaurants of the first class and in most less expensive ones, it is always turned face down on a plate or a small silver tray. You turn it over and pay the waiter. He then brings your change, and you give him a tip.

TIPPING IN A RESTAURANT

It is impossible to give definite schedules for tipping, because it all depends upon where you go, and upon what you order, and upon the service given you—or that you exact.

That is, if you patronize restaurants of greatest luxury and wear obviously expensive clothes with valuable accessories or if you are critical and difficult to please, greater "compensation" is expected than if your appearance were simpler and your demands less exacting.

It is true that tips have become somewhat higher than they used to be. The ten percent rule of yesterday is today at least fifteen and sometimes even twenty!

In an average restaurant a reasonably accurate rule is still a minimum tip of twenty-five cents for one person or for a bill that totals less than two dollars; forty-five or fifty cents for a bill of three dollars to four dollars.

If you are having a party of ten, twelve, or more, fifteen percent would be quite adequate for the waiters who serve you, and perhaps five dollars to the head waiter if he has taken pains to give you good service. On the other hand, if he does nothing for you further than seating you and handing you a menu, you give him nothing. If the wine steward has served you, he should receive twelve to fifteen percent of the wine bill. The bartender receives ten percent if you have drinks at the bar.

Fifteen percent is the standard tip in any restaurant, twenty in a night club, or if you've been very exacting, or if the service has been excellent. Ten percent is too little anywhere, except perhaps at a lunch counter, and never less than ten cents there.

Patrons who make a practice of tipping waitresses less than waiters are being quite unfair, since the service rendered is the same.

WHEN A WOMAN INVITES A MAN

A situation that caused great embarrassment some years ago but is taken casually today, is that of the woman who wants to invite a man to dine with her. It is best of course to take him to her club if possible—or to a restaurant where she has a charge account and merely signs the check, including the waiter's tip.

If she has no charge account and has to pay the check before her guest, this will be embarrassing. A good plan in this situation is to go to the restaurant beforehand and leave a deposit larger than necessary with the cashier. That will avoid the presentation of a bill and also take care of the waiter's tip. She calls for her change next day, or makes arrangements to have it returned.

In the case of a woman "entertaining" a customer for her company, the probabilities are that the company has accounts in the best restaurants, and she signs the check as the company's representative. If the company has not made arrangements for her to sign the check, she pays cash, and if her guest protests and tries to pay himself, she explains that he is her company's guest, and that the amount of this check is going on her expense account.

RESTAURANT COURTESY

When a lady stopping at a table is introduced to other ladies seated at table, the latter never rise—not even though they be young and the visitor quite old.

Gentlemen at the table do not rise when another gentleman stops on his way by. But when one comes across the room to speak to one of the diners, the latter would then stand to shake hands. The visitor would then ask him please to be seated while he finishes what he has come to say. But if intending to say more than a few words of greeting, he might ask a waiter for a chair or more probably make an appointment with the one he wishes to talk to for a later time.

When a group is dining together and, on entering, sees people whom some know and others do not, the group continues on directly to its table. A public restaurant is scarcely the place for group social introductions beyond those of simplest greeting.

WOMEN WHO PUT ON MAKE-UP AT TABLE

A well-bred woman always avoids making up in public; cosmetics and food do not go together. At the end of a meal, a woman may quickly powder her nose and put on a little lipstick; the best rule is—don't. But to sit and daub at the face in a little mirror for any length of time cannot fail to impress your host or any onlooker with the blemishes this face must have to need such drastic repair!

The one never-to-be-broken rule is: Don't ever use a comb anywhere outside of a dressing room. Don't even slightly rearrange or put your fingers on your hair in any place where food is served. No woman with the faintest trace of fastidious taste could commit this offense.

SHOW CONSIDERATION FOR THE HUSBANDS—PLEASE!

One act of thoughtlessness that causes distress to courteous citizens by others whose intentions are quite as kindly as their impulses are friendly is that of an unobserving woman, who, when entering a crowded restaurant and passing a table at which a friend is dining with her husband, cannot resist stopping for a greeting that lengthens into a dialog of many minutes. The point she overlooks is that during her stay the polite husband is obliged to stand and all too often watch the scarcely tasted food on his plate grow colder and colder.

True, the visitor does from time to time earnestly urge, "Oh, *do* sit down! Oh, *please* don't stand!" Which Mr. Courteous may quite well do, if the restaurant be empty. But in usual circumstances every well-behaved diner at every table would look with contempt upon the ignorance of a man so lacking in courtesy! Lately however the impulse of a husband may quite likely have solved this problem.

Gustav Gourmet, just about to eat a perfect soufflé in a noted restaurant, was forced to stand for a friend of his wife, who stopped at their table. "Oh, *please* sit down! You must not let your soufflé fall!" said she, and having given this permission simply thought him stubborn not to sit. Thereupon he did solve the problem before it was too late by lifting the plate and eating—standing!

Let us hope that long-talking standees will take this anecdote to heart and pass the tables of their friends without pausing.

THE COAT-CHECK TIP

A question often asked by young women is about the fee to the maid in the dressing room—given when she returns the coat check and is helped on with her wrap. This is never less than twenty-five cents— in every restaurant or hotel that is of highest class. The fee to the check-rack boy or girl who takes care of a man's hat and coat in an inexpensive restaurant is ten cents, or in a de luxe restaurant twenty-five.

WHEN WOMEN DINE TOGETHER

When several women are dining out together, the problem of the check is one which can cause concern to and confusion among the waiters, the nearby diners, and the women themselves. Women so seldom are able to separate a check into several parts with grace and speed that the cartoon of feminine heads clustered about the waiter's tab, captioned "Now let's see, Ethel, you had the Tomato Surprise," is familiar to all of us. One way to avoid such a scene is to get separate checks. Or one woman may pay the entire check, and the settling up can be done later. If each one's debt must be figured at the table, at least make sure the best computer in the group gets the chore so that it gets done effortlessly and quietly.

THOSE WHO ARE WELL-BRED SHOW CONSIDERATION TO ALL

To show lack of consideration for those who in any capacity serve us—whether in restaurants, hotels, or stores, or in public places anywhere—is always an evidence of ill-breeding as well as inexcusable selfishness. It is only those who are afraid that someone may encroach upon their exceedingly insecure dignity who show neither courtesy nor consideration except to those whom they think it would be to their advantage to please.

THE OPERA, THE THEATRE, AND OTHER PLACES OF AMUSEMENT

·•⟨ 9 ⟩•·

NOWHERE IS GREATER DIGNITY OF MANNER REQUIRED than in a box at the opera. As people usually dine with their hostess before the opera, they arrive together. The gentlemen assist the ladies to lay aside their wraps; one of the gentlemen, whichever is nearest, draws back the curtain dividing the anteroom from the box, and the ladies enter, followed by the gentlemen, the last of whom closes the curtain again. If there are two ladies besides the hostess, the latter places her more distinguished or older guest in the corner nearest the stage. The seat farthest from the stage is always her own. The older guest takes her seat first, then the hostess takes her place, whereupon the third lady goes forward in the center to the front of the box, and stands until one of the gentlemen places a chair for her between the other two.

This maneuver is necessary because three chairs placed side by side take up the width of the box. The chairs are always arranged by the caretaker in three rows of two, with an aisle between, so that the third lady's chair, brought from the second row, closes the aisle.

One of the duties of the gentlemen is to see that the curtains at the back of the box remain tightly closed, as the light from the anteroom shining into the faces of others in the audience across the house is very disconcerting to them.

A gentleman never sits in the front row of a box, even though he is for a time alone.

Until a few years ago, no gentleman would have thought of being seen in a parterre box unless properly clothed in "white tie and tails," particularly on Monday nights. Today the dinner jacket has almost entirely replaced tails even on Monday! As for the orchestra seats, the dinner jacket is being gradually replaced by the dark business suit.

Women no longer always wear their very best evening dresses in the parterre boxes, and now appear in their simplest, least conspicuous dinner dresses. In the second tier and orchestra many come in cocktail or even day dresses.

GENTLEMEN VISIT THE BOXES

It is the custom for a gentleman who is a guest in one box to pay visits to friends in other boxes during the *entr'actes*. Under ordinary circumstances he must visit none but ladies of his acquaintance and must never enter a box in which he knows only the gentlemen and expect to be introduced to the ladies. A lady's box at the opera is considered as if it were her house, and only those who are welcome visitors in her house should take it upon themselves to go into her box.

It is however quite correct for a gentleman to go into a stranger's box to speak to a lady who is a friend of his, just as he would go to see her if she were staying in a stranger's house. But he should not go into the box of one he does not know, to speak to a lady with whom he is only slightly acquainted, since visits are not paid quite so casually to ladies who are themselves visitors. When a gentleman enters a box, it is obligatory for whoever is sitting behind the lady whom the arriving gentleman has come to see to relinquish his chair. Another point of etiquette is that a gentleman must never leave the ladies of his own box alone. Occasionally it happens that the gentlemen in Mrs. Gilding's box, for instance, have all relinquished their places to visitors and have themselves gone to Mrs. Worldly's, or Mrs. McClellan's, or Mrs. Town's boxes. Mrs. Gilding's guests must, from the vantage point of the Worldly, McClellan, or Town boxes, keep a watchful eye on their hostess and instantly return to her support when they see her visitors about to leave, even though the ladies whom they are visiting be momentarily left to themselves. It is of course the duty of the other gentlemen who came to the opera with Mrs. Worldly, Mrs. McClellan, or Mrs. Town to hurry to them.

A gentleman must never stay in any box that he does not belong in after the lowering of the lights for the curtain. Nor does courtesy either to the musicians or to the audience permit conversation during the performance or during the overture. Box-holders arriving late or leaving before the final curtain do so as quietly as possible and always without talking.

WHAT IS KNOWN AS A "BRILLIANT OPERA NIGHT"

Whether a "brilliant opera night," which one so often heard spoken of before the Second World War, will ever return is something that none can at present answer. In its day, this was generally a night when a leader of fashion, such as Mrs. Gilding or Mrs. Toplofty, was giving a ball, and most of the holders of the parterre boxes were in ball dresses, with an unusual display of jewels. Or a house was particularly "brilliant" if a very great singer were appearing in a new role or a personage of eminence were to be present as especial guest of honor.

BOXES OR ORCHESTRA AT THE THEATRE

At the opera the world of fashion is to be seen in the parterre boxes. At the theatre, however, the choicest seats are those in the center of the orchestra. In fact, most new theatres have no boxes.

A box at the theatre has little to recommend it except that a group can sit together and that one can go out between the acts without crawling across the laps of others. This hardly compensates the three or four of the six box occupants who are able to see only a slice of the stage.

WILL YOU HAVE DINNER AND GO TO A PLAY?

One of the more popular or agreeable ways of entertaining people is to ask them to have dinner and go to a play. Unfortunately, however, theatre tickets in New York, for example, have become so expensive that a party of four is more typical than six—which is the outside number. The old-fashioned one of twenty or over is practically unheard of— except when that of a club.

When a man invites three friends to go to the theatre, he usually takes them to dinner in a restaurant, but hosts living in their own house are likely to have dinner at home.

TICKETS BOUGHT IN ADVANCE

Not only must a host get seats in advance, but he must get good ones. It is little compliment and less pleasure to be invited to spend an evening in theatre seats from which you can neither see nor hear more than half of the performance. It is scarcely necessary to say that one must never ask people to go to a place of public amusement and then stand in line to get seats at the time of the performance.

It is also practical as well as polite to ask, "How near do you like to sit?" and then get seats near to the stage—or to the platform at a concert or a lecture—or somewhat farther back accordingly.

ORDER OF GOING DOWN THE AISLE

If there is no host, the gentleman to whom the hostess has handed the tickets goes down the aisle first and gives the checks to the usher, and the others follow in the order in which they are to sit and which the hostess has directed. It is necessary that each shall know who follows whom.

If it is a party of more than six, the hostess or host gives a seating diagram to each guest at the end of dinner. This shows the number and positions of all of the seats, with each guest's own name plainly starred on her or his seat.

Going down the aisle is not a question of precedence, but a question of seating. The one who is to sit sixth from the aisle, whether a lady or a gentleman, goes first, then the fifth, and so on each in turn.

If a gentleman and lady go to the theatre alone, who goes down the aisle first is determined by where the usher is. If the usher takes the ticket stubs at the head of the aisle, the lady follows the usher. If the usher is not at the head of the aisle, the gentleman with the ticket stubs goes first, until having given them to the usher, he lets the lady precede him the rest of the way. In any event, he stands at the end of their row and lets her take her place first, and then takes the seat on or nearer to the aisle.

Do not, however, judge hastily when this rule is not followed. Arthur Norman, for example, is stone-deaf in his right ear and his wife always sits on his left no matter where that position happens to place her. Others for any similar reasons do the same.

COURTESY AT THE THEATRE

In passing strangers, gentlemen as well as ladies face the stage and always press closely to the backs of the seats they are facing, remembering, however, not to drag anything across the heads of those sitting in the row in front. Some ladies are very careless about their handbags.

If someone is obliged to get up to let you pass, say, "Thank you," or "I'm sorry."

When you are seated and others pass you, you must give them enough room to pass. If you can do this by merely turning your knees sideways, so much the better, especially if the play or movie has started. But if there is so little space that they have to step over your knees, you must of course stand and sit down again—quickly! Remember that during every second you stand, you are cutting off the view of all who are seated behind you.

NO ONE LIKES TO BE CLIMBED OVER

Young people have much to say about the ill manners of certain middle-aged men as well as women, who practically refuse to allow anyone to pass. It is quite true that having to gather up opera glasses, program, and bag, and stand while each person on a long aisle leaves and comes back separately after every act can be far from pleasurable. But if one hasn't sufficient self-control not only to seem but to be amiable about whatever annoyances one encounters, one should at least take enough trouble to avoid the obvious annoyances or else stay at home. As an obvious example, if you do not wish to go out to smoke between the acts why not take pains to get seats away from an aisle instead of on it? In a theatre that has no center aisle, get seats in the mid-center and sit undisturbed. It is true that, where there is a center aisle and seats become less desirable as distance from the aisle increases, it comes to a question of choosing between sitting at the side or being climbed over twice (once out and once in) by everyone in the row, after each act.

HATS OFF

Even if a woman believes her hat to be so small as not to obstruct the view of anyone, she should be amiable about removing it, if asked to do so. Courteous women whose hats are likely to interfere with the view of the one behind them take them off without having to be asked. As a matter of fact, the very sight of an up-rolling brim or a sticking-up bow or feather announces to all who so much as catch a glimpse of it that there sits someone who has no manners.

DRESSING FOR THE THEATRE

The present trend of fashion is toward ordinary day clothes for both men and women—particularly in the smaller communities. However, when sitting "down front" in best seats during an opening night or the opening week of an evening performance of a play or musical comedy, ladies usually wear semi-evening or dinner dresses, and this of course exacts that gentlemen wear tuxedos. Their plans for after the theatre naturally affect their choice of dress, no matter where they are sitting.

THEATRE PESTS

Talking, coughing, rattling programs, jingling bangles—not to speak of those who rattle cellophane when opening candy boxes!—and coming back for each act after the curtain has gone up not only annoy the audience but frequently disturb the actors. Most people are seemingly unaware that sound travels as well one way across the footlights as another. And the comments of those in the first few rows of the audience, and the constant coughing throughout a bronchial disturbance, have actually made it impossible for the company to give a good performance. Very young people love to go to the theatre in droves called theatre parties and absolutely ruin the evening for others who happen to sit in front of them. If Julie and Johnny and Susy and Tommy want to talk and giggle, why not arrange chairs in rows for them in a drawing-room, turn on a radio or the television set as an accompaniment, and let them sit there and chatter!

If those behind you insist on talking, it is always bad manners to turn around and glare. If you are young, they pay no attention; and if you are older—most young people think an angry older person the funniest sight on earth! The small boy throws a snowball at an elderly gentleman for no other reason! The only thing you can do is to say amiably, "I'm sorry, but I can't hear anything while you talk." If they still persist, you can ask an usher to call the manager.

The sentimental should realize that every word said above a whisper is easily heard by those sitting directly in front, and those who discuss family or other private affairs might do well to remember this also.

As a matter of fact, comparatively few people are ever anything but well-behaved. Most people take their seats as quietly and quickly as they possibly can, and are quite as much interested in the play and therefore as attentive and quiet as you are, or they would not have come.

WHEN THE PLAY IS OVER

The gentleman on the aisle, or nearest the aisle, naturally stands in the aisle a moment so that the lady who necessarily follows can walk with him or, if the crowd makes two abreast impossible, precede him. Under nearly all circumstances a lady goes first. An exception to this is where the crowd is really dense; in this case he goes first to make a wedge for her. She follows as closely behind him as possible in order to take advantage of the space he makes for her. In a theatre party of six the first gentleman should let the lady who sat next to him go ahead of him, but usually he does not wait to follow the remaining two.

MAKING UP IN PUBLIC

The well-groomed have no need to do it; others should learn how unattractive it is and avoid doing it. In other days it was always thought that so much as to adjust a hairpin or glance in the glass of a compact was evidence of lack of breeding. For example, when Mrs. Cleveland, in her early twenties, made her first appearance at a state dinner, the British Ambassador, afterwards commenting on the charm of the President's lovely bride, especially noted that "not once during the entire evening did she raise her hands to her dress, her face, or her hair!"

TAKING THEM TO THE THEATRE

No party pleases so many persons so much as being taken to the theatre—whether you are taking a single friend from out of town or engaging all of the orchestra seats in the theatre! A big theatre party has always been a favorite entertainment given for a débutante by very well-to-do parents or grandparents.

The invitations may be written formally or informally. If the party is given by her parents, the débutante very likely writes the invitations herself or even telephones them. But if the party is a formal one and given by a prominent hostess, her general utility invitation usually is filled in, as follows, the phrasing in Roman type being written by hand.

To meet Miss Millicent Gilding
Mrs. Toplofty
requests the pleasure of
Miss Rosalie Gray's
company at   the Thespis Theatre
on   Tuesday the sixth of January
at   8:15
R. s. v. p.

All those who accept the invitation have tickets sent them. Each ticket is accompanied by a visiting-card on which is written:

Please be in the lobby
of the Thespis Theatre at 8:15.

On the evening of the theatre party, Mrs. Toplofty, or whoever the hostess may be, stands in the lobby to receive the guests. As soon as those who are to sit next one another have arrived, they are sent into the theatre. Each pair give their tickets to an usher and sit in the places allotted to them. When all of her guests have arrived, Mrs. Toplofty goes to her own seat.

After the play, cars or taxis drive them to the house of the hostess. Occasionally if the house is large enough, musicians are provided and the young people dance. Usually, however, they have a very simple supper and then go home.

YOU MUST NOT BE LATE!

Nothing is so unfair to others who are keen about whatever it is you are going to see than to make them miss the beginning of a performance through your selfishness in being late.

GOOD MANNERS AT PLACES OF AMUSEMENT

Considerate and polite behavior by each member of an audience is the same everywhere. At outdoor games or at the circus, it is not necessary to stop talking. In fact, a good deal of noise is not out of the way in "rooting" for your favorite team at a match, and silence is not necessary in order to appreciate a circus band's cheerful blare. Of great annoyance to many are the careless smokers.

Another serious annoyance met with at ball games or parades or wherever people occupy seats in the grandstand is that produced by a few in front who get excited and insist on standing up. If those in front stand—those behind naturally have to! Generally people call out, "Down in front!" If they won't stay down, then all those behind have to stay up. Also, open umbrellas entirely blot out the view of those behind!

FINDING SEATS AT THE MOVIES

How one goes down the aisle in a movie—a man and girl, for example—is not a fixed custom. Usually, in a motion picture house where they look for their own seats, they go down the aisle together. Either one, seeing seats that are pleasing, says, "There are two—shall we take those?" The other agrees, or proposes two farther down.

ORDER OF SEATING IN THEATRE

There is no fixed rule about seating four people in a theatre except that a man should sit on the aisle—if they have aisle seats. If two married couples go to the theatre together, they usually do sit so that a man shall not be seated next to his wife. But if Mr. and Mrs. Marshall took Miss Hyer and Mr. Dalton to the theatre, Mr. Marshall would sit on the aisle and then Miss Hyer, then Mr. Dalton, and then Mrs. Marshall. But if Mr. Dalton and Miss Hyer are engaged, the Marshalls would sit together, since the pair who are in love might as well be counted as absent. In other words, sit in whichever order you think most pleasant.

"EXCUSE ME, PLEASE"

This is the typical expression of courtesy when having to disturb anyone, to get to or to leave your seat in a theatre, or any other place.

Should you by any chance have to pass someone a second time—to get something forgotten—you say, "I'm sorry to disturb you," and "Thank you," as they let you pass.

SMOKING BETWEEN THE ACTS

The modern woman usually goes out with a man who wishes to smoke. But if he is with an old-fashioned type of woman who does not smoke, it is quite proper to leave her briefly during one *entr'acte;* or should the play have more than three acts, he might go out for two. Of course, it depends somewhat upon whom he is with. He could leave his wife more often than others, which does not mean he should leave her at each curtain-fall to sit alone until the house is darkened for the curtain's rise.

VISITING-CARDS AND THEIR USES

··⊰[10]⊱··

SOME UNKNOWN MAN IN THE VICTORIAN ERA WAS PROB-
ably the one who first said—"The only mechanical tool ever needed by
a woman is a hairpin." He might have added that with a hairpin, or
today a bobby pin, and a visiting-card she is ready to meet almost any
emergency.

Although the principal use of a visiting-card, at least the one for
which it was originally invented—to be left as an evidence of one person's presence at the house of another—has gradually gone out of favor,
its usefulness seems to keep a nicely adjusted balance. In New York,
for instance, the visiting-card has taken the place of the written note of
invitation to informal parties of every description. Matching envelopes,
larger than the card, should be ordered. Small envelopes may be lost in
the mails. Messages of condolence or congratulation are often written
on visiting-cards.

Whenever you do happen not to have a card of your own with you
to enclose with a present, the shop can usually give you a small white
one to write on and an envelope to match. The only employment of it
which is not as flourishing as formerly is that of being left in quantities
and with frequency at the doors of acquaintances. In these hectic days,
people are simply too busy to make many formal calls. They are still
an expected custom in ultra-conservative groups and in military and
diplomatic circles.

SIZE AND ENGRAVING

The size of visiting-cards varies, necessarily, according to length of
name (a short name on a squarer card than that chosen for a long
name), but a married woman's card is usually from 3 to 3½ inches
wide and from 2¼ to 2½ inches high, although the smaller of these
two dimensions has been for many years in fashion. Very young girls
customarily use a still smaller card. A man's card is narrower in shape

—from 3 to 3¼ inches long, and from 1¼ to 1⅝ inches high. The cards are made of white or cream-white glazed or unglazed bristol board of medium thickness, but those made of thin parchment paper are convenient because a greater quantity may be carried easily.

The engraving much in use is shaded Roman. Script is always good form, and various other letterings, brought out by engravers from time to time, have a temporary vogue, but all overlarge or ornate lettering should be avoided.

All people who live in cities should have the address in the lower right corner, engraved in very small letters. In the country, addresses are less important, as everyone knows where everyone else lives. People who have town and country houses usually have separate cards for each.

In America it is not customary for a married man to have a club address on his card. Unmarried men use the address of a club, especially if they live in transient quarters; but if they do not regularly receive their mail at a club they of course use their home address.

CORRECT NAMES AND TITLES

To be impeccably correct, initials should not be engraved on a visiting-card. A gentleman's card should read "Mr. John Hunter Titherington Smith"; but since names are sometimes awkwardly long, and it is the American custom to cling to each and every one given in baptism, he has his cards engraved "Mr. John H. T. Smith" or "Mr. J. H. Titherington Smith," as suits his fancy. So, although according to established custom he should drop a name or two and be Mr. Hunter Smith or Mr. Titherington Smith, it is very likely that to the end of time the American man, and necessarily his wife, who must use his name as he does, will go on cherishing initials. Her card must of course be the exact duplicate of his, and not read "Mrs. J. Hunter Smith" when his reads "Mr. John H. Smith."

A WIDOW SHOULD KEEP HER HUSBAND'S NAME

In certain localities a curious custom is the discarding by a widow of her husband's Christian name and sometimes her wedding ring as well. Of course if he made her so bitterly unhappy that the thought of him is hateful—and she wishes all to know it!—one can understand her getting rid of everything suggestive of him. But it is impossible to imagine a sorrowing wife's repudiation of a beloved husband's name and ring, the most sacred emblems of her life with him.

A man gives his name to his wife for life—or until she herself through remarriage relinquishes it. A widow, therefore, should always continue to use her husband's Christian names. She is Mrs. John Hunter Titherington Smith (or, Mrs. J. H. Titherington Smith), but never Mrs. Sarah Smith, if she cares at all about good taste.

"MRS. MARY" UNAVOIDABLE IN BUSINESS

In business and in legal matters it is often impossible to avoid addressing a woman by her own Christian name, because she uses it in her signature. But one should never address a personal or social letter "Mrs. Sarah Smith," unless one knows that this is what she prefers to call herself. In best taste a woman who has earned a professional title uses her title or professional name in public, and in private life uses the name of her husband. A spinster who is a practicing physician uses the title of Doctor socially as well as professionally. But if she is, for instance, a Doctor of Philosophy, a woman of taste would not call herself "Doctor" except in a classroom or when introduced as a speaker.

WHEN WIDOW AND SON HAVE SAME NAME

When a widow's son who has the name of his father marries, the widow may have "Sr." added to her name; or if she is the head of the family, she very often omits all Christian names and has her card engraved "Mrs. Smith." (Smith is not a very good name as an example, since no one could very well claim the distinction of being *the* Mrs. Smith. It, however, illustrates the point.) Unless the name is most unusual, this practice may cause confusion with charge accounts and delivery of mail.

This use of Sr. or the omission of the Christian name is necessary if they live at the same address—or in a village where no street address is used. If they live in different cities, both mother and daughter-in-law can be Mrs. John Hunter Smith.

If the widow lives in the same city but at a different address from her son and his wife, she can have her address engraved in small letters at the lower right-hand corner and so identify herself.

For the daughter-in-law to continue to use a card with "Jr." on it when her husband no longer uses "Jr." on his is a mistake made by many people. A wife always bears the name of her husband. To have a man and his mother use cards engraved respectively "Mr. J. H. Smith" and "Mrs. J. H. Smith" and the son's wife a card engraved "Mrs. J. H. Smith, Jr." would announce to anyone upon whom the three cards were left that Mr. and Mrs. Smith and *their* daughter-in-law had called.

It is to avoid this confusion that many "Jr." sons continue to use the "Jr." after their father's death. This is of course incorrect, but when the widow, who is possibly young and the stepmother of the son, does not wish to be known as "Sr." it is the only practical solution.

CARDS OF A YOUNG GIRL

A young girl's cards after she is fourteen, always, and often earlier, have "Miss" before her name, which should be her real and never a nickname: "Miss Sarah Smith," not "Miss Sally Smith."

MEANING OF "JR." AND "2ND"

The fact that a man's name has "Jr." added at the end in no way takes the place of "Mr." His card should be engraved "Mr. John Hunter Smith, Jr.," and his wife's "Mrs. John Hunter Smith, Jr." It is rather the fashion to have the "junior" engraved in full; it is not spelled with a capital J if spelled out.

It is improper for a man to continue adding "Jr." to his name after the death of his father or grandfather. In the same way it is improper to continue calling a boy "John Smith, 3rd," if John Smith, Jr. (or 2nd), has died. "Junior" always means the son—or possibly the grandson—of a man of the same name; "2nd" means the nephew or cousin of a man of the same name. The following diagram will perhaps make this much misunderstood order clear:

Silas Acres

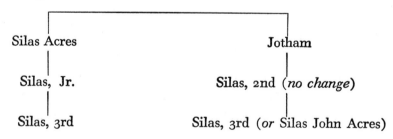

Since there is no way to distinguish between (A) and (B), the latter is usually given a different middle name, and is christened Silas John Acres. Since this changes the name, he has no suffix, and his son could be called Silas John Acres, Jr.

Upon the death of the senior Silas Acres, the names of his family are changed to:

Silas Acres	Jotham
Silas, Jr.	Silas, 2nd (*no change*)
Silas, 3rd	Silas, 3rd (*or* Silas John Acres)

And yet once in a great while and for definite reasons, a son continues to call himself "Jr." after his father has died. For example, when a father has been so celebrated that the son cannot possibly take his father's place, or when the mother is a celebrity who cannot very well be expected to add "Sr." to her name, and sometimes for other reasons, such as professional, when it is practical or very important that the son keep his own identity as junior, he continues to use the suffix. But this is not the usual procedure.

When a mother and daughter are both known professionally, the daughter is "Mary Notable, younger" or "second" because "junior" is a masculine title.

"MR." ON BOY'S CARD

A boy never puts "Mr." on his cards until he leaves school, and many use cards without "Mr." until they have finished college.

TITLES ON CARDS

A doctor, a clergyman, or a military officer in active service, and holders of title-bestowing offices all have their cards engraved with their titles: Doctor Henry Gordon; The Reverend William Goode; Colonel Thomas Doyle; Judge Horace Rush; Senator Widelands. But a person holding high degrees does not add their letters to his name, and his cards are not engraved "Professor" unless he is a teacher of highest rank who holds an established chair in a university.

The double card reads Doctor and Mrs. Henry Gordon, Judge and Mrs. Horace Rush, Professor and Mrs. Scholar, etc. It is always best form to engrave titles in full.

A woman who is divorced takes her maiden name in place of her husband's Christian name. Mrs. Henry Green who was Mabel Smith calls herself Mrs. Smith Green, according to good taste, never Mrs. Mabel Green. If her husband's surname is distasteful, she sometimes takes back her own maiden name—preceded by that of her mother. If her mother was a Miss Brown, her daughter calls herself Mrs. Brown Smith. In business or on the stage she may be known as Miss Mabel Smith but NOT in private life.

DIVORCÉE TAKES NAME OF FIRST HUSBAND

A seemingly accepted custom is that of a widow who remarries, then divorces her second husband and takes back her first husband's name. The propriety of this maneuver depends upon her motive, which is usually that of wanting to have the same name as her children.

The laws of the United States permit anyone to change his or her name without applying to the courts, if he or she is able to give proof that this was done with no intent to defraud.

CARDS OF PERSONAGES

The correct card for a governor is

The Governor of Nevada

on a card that is slightly larger or squarer than an ordinary man's card. Less correct, but not inadmissible, is his ordinary card with Gov-

ernor of Nevada added in small letters under his name. Occasionally an overmodest incumbent objects to the correct form because he thinks it looks too self-important. But he must remember that the card is representative of the highest office of his State and not that of a private citizen.

The card of a mayor may read either

The Mayor of Chicago

or if he prefers

Mr. John Lake
Mayor of Chicago

would also be correct.

A diplomat uses his title and United States of America rather than America or American.

It is unnecessary to continue this list, as each official certainly knows his own name! But it may be as well to add that titles of courtesy have no place either in a signature or on a visiting-card.

The American title of courtesy, The Honorable, unlike this title given to sons of British earls, viscounts and barons, is never correct on a card.

The professional card of a doctor or surgeon is James Smith, M.D. His social card is Dr. or Doctor James Smith, as he prefers. (Dr. is perfectly correct; but Doctor is somewhat better form.)

The visiting-card for a doctor and his wife is engraved Dr. (or preferably Doctor) and Mrs. James Smith. If his wife is also a physician who prefers using her own title, it is best not to use a double card. But if they insist upon this, it must read Dr. James and Dr. Julia Smith. Doctor written in full twice would make many names too long.

If the wife is a practicing physician and her husband is not, their card could be Mr. James and Doctor Julia Smith.

A woman physician who is practicing her profession is Doctor Julia Smith or Julia Smith, M.D.—as she may prefer.

CARDS FOR CHILDREN

That very little children should have visiting-cards is not so "silly" as might at first thought be supposed. To acquire perfect manners, and those graces of deportment that Lord Chesterfield so ardently tried to instil into his son, training cannot begin early enough, since it is through lifelong familiarity with the niceties of behavior that much of the distinction of those to the manner born is acquired. Many mothers think it good training in social personality for children to have their own cards, even though they are used only to send with gifts and upon very rare occasions. They may sound a bit extravagant but are a suggestion for a present from a doting grandmother or aunt.

At the rehearsal of a wedding, the tiny twin flower-girls came carrying their wedding present for the bride between them, to which they had themselves attached their own small visiting-cards. One card was bordered and engraved in pink, and the other bordered and engraved in blue, and the address on each read *"Chez Maman."*

And in going to see a new baby cousin each brought a small 1830 bouquet, and both sent to their aunt their cards, on which, after seeing the baby, one had printed, "He is very little," and the other, "It has a red face." This shows that if modern society believes in beginning social training in the nursery, it does not believe in hampering a child's natural expression.

Children's cards are always smaller than regulation size, and the younger the child, the smaller the card. These cards of their own may also be used for inviting friends to their birthday parties.

SPECIAL CARDS AND WHEN TO USE THEM

The double card, reading "Mr. and Mrs.," is sent with a wedding present, or with flowers to a funeral, or with flowers to a débutante, and is also used in paying formal visits.

A débutante's name may be engraved under that of her mother and such a card would be used most frequently when no coming-out entertainment has been given for the daughter. Her name on her mother's card announces, wherever it is left, that the daughter is grown and eligible for invitations. Although general card-leaving is each year more and more going out of fashion, it is still correct when paying visits to leave the cards of all sons and daughters who are grown and still living with you.

BUSINESS CARDS

Business cards are not to be confused with visiting-cards and they are never used for social purposes. Their principal use is when an employee or an executive of one company makes a business call on another company, or on a client or prospective client. The card of an employee usually has the name and address of the company in the center of the card with the employee's name in the lower left corner and the telephone number in the lower right corner. An executive has his or her name in the center with his or her position in the company in smaller letters under the name. The name and address of the company then is put in the lower left corner, and while the telephone number is often omitted, it is so convenient not to have to look up the number that it is usually put in the lower right corner. Its size is approximately 3½ inches by 2 inches.

THE VANISHING VISIT OF EMPTY FORM

Somewhat more than a generation ago, Mrs. Social Leader, after her annual ball, put all the cards left upon her into a certain box, and

a few weeks later these cards, carefully noted, made up the list of those
to be invited next year, and those whose cards were absent were themselves left out. But about twenty-five years ago the era of informality
set in and has been gaining ground to such extent that, if lists were
kept according to party-call cards, the once-smart hostess would find
herself reduced to the middle-aged oldsters and the climbers, while the
younger world of fashion flocked to whichever night club happened to
be enjoying the greatest popularity at that moment, and cared very
little whether Mrs. Toplofty and Mrs. Social Leader asked them to
their balls or not. And as Society can have distinction and dignity without youth, but not gaiety, hostesses have capitulated and party-calls by
the younger set are no longer exacted or even expected.

But there are circumstances in which even the most indifferent to
social obligations *must* leave cards. For example:

In Washington diplomatic or official circles, if you want to be correct, you leave your cards within three days. But few of us Americans
leading private lives are as punctilious as this.

One must of course return a first visit. Only a serious reason can
excuse rudeness to a stranger that failure to return a first call implies.

Except in Washington, card-leaving has become such a neglected
practice that a neighbor who fails to return a visit should be given the
benefit of the doubt before she is believed intentionally rude. More details for Washington card-leaving will be found in Chapter 51.

FOLD-OVER CARDS

Fold-over cards—known as informals—are convenient when one
wants to write a very brief note but one that requires more space than
is afforded by a visiting-card. Fold-over cards are substitutes for note
paper and must never be left in place of visiting-cards.

THE P. P. C. CARD

This is merely a visiting-card, whether of a lady or a gentleman, on
which the initials P. P. C. (*pour prendre congé*—to take leave) are
written in ink in the lower left corner. This is usually sent by mail to
acquaintances when one is leaving, and means nothing except "I've
gone away—good-by." It is in no sense a message of thanks for especial
kindness, for which a visit should be paid or a note of farewell and
thanks written.

Since there is a tendency at present to translate French words into
English for their more practical use, many are now writing T.s.g.b.!
(To say good-by), which is certainly sensible in this particular instance.

CARDS OF NEW OR TEMPORARY ADDRESS

In a case where change of address is not readily found, a visiting-
card with new address on it is the proper way to notify one's acquain-

tances as well as friends. Most of your friends probably know that you are moving, but it will be helpful if you send them the correct address.

Cards are also sent, with a temporary address written in ink, when one is in a strange city and wishes to notify friends—either men or women—where one is stopping.

INVITATION IN PLACE OF RETURNED VISIT

People who are old friends pay no attention to how often or how seldom one goes to see the other, unless there is an illness, a death, a birth, or a marriage. Nor do they ever consider whose turn it is to invite whom. But first visits should be paid and returned with considerable formality—especially the visit that must be paid after a *first* invitation to lunch or dine or take supper.

If hospitality has been shown you by two or more hostesses together, you are indebted to both or all equally, if you know them equally. But if you have been asked by the only one you know, it is not necessary that you return the hospitality of the other (or others) unless opportunity offers. In any event, when returning the hospitality of these several hostesses, it is never necessary that you invite them together.

"NOT AT HOME"—NO DISCOURTESY

When a servant at a door says "Not at home," this phrase means that the lady of the house is "not at home to visitors." This answer neither signifies nor implies—nor is it intended to imply—that Mrs. Jones is out of the house. This is more polite than "Not receiving," a phrase which actually means the same thing and is used by many people.

To be told, "Mrs. Jones is at home but doesn't want to see you," would certainly be unpleasant. And to "beg to be excused"—except in a case of illness or bereavement—is very chilling. But the message "not at home," given at her door, means merely that she is not sitting in her living room ready to receive visitors. It means *that*, and *nothing* else! Actually she may be resting, or she may be ill, or very busy! She may very well be unpresentable.

If it should happen that, catching a glimpse of you or recognizing your voice, she should call, "Oh, *do* come in. I am at home to *you!*" this certainly is no discourtesy, nor is it "catching her in a lie." It is merely showing great friendliness to you personally, and you should certainly be pleased and not imagine her an untruthful person.

Anyone who talks about this phrase as being a white lie either doesn't understand the meaning of the words, or is going very far afield to look for untruth. To be consistent, these over-literals should also exact that when a guest inadvertently knocks over a teacup and stains a sofa, the hostess, instead of saying, "It is nothing at all! Please don't worry about it," ought for the sake of truth to say, "See what your clumsiness has done! You have ruined my sofa!" And when someone says, "How are you?" instead of answering with conventional politeness, "Very well, thank you," the same truthful one should perhaps take an hour by the clock and mention every symptom of indisposition that she can accurately subscribe to.

While "not at home" is merely a phrase of politeness, to say "I am *out*" after a card has been brought to you is both an untruth and an inexcusable rudeness. Or to have an inquiry answered, "I don't know, but I'll see," and then to have the servant, after taking a card, come back with the message "Mrs. Jones is out" cannot fail to make the visitor feel rebuffed. Once a card has been admitted, the visitor *must* be admitted also, no matter how inconvenient receiving her may be. You may send a message that you are dressing but will be very glad to see her if she can wait ten minutes. The visitor can either wait or say she is pressed for time. But if she does not wait, then it is she who is rather discourteous.

It may be a nuisance to be obliged to remember either to turn an "in" and "out" card in the hall, or to ring a bell and say, "I am going out," and again, "I have come in." But whatever plan or arrangement you choose, no one at your front door should be left in doubt and then repulsed. It is something that does at times occur in the houses of all of us; we run next door or up the street, or we go somewhere just for a moment, never thinking it important to tell whoever answers our door that we have gone. To do this, however, and give a visitor the chance to think we have been at home is bad manners.

PAYING A VISIT TO A LADY WHO HAS NO MAID

Let us say you go to see a stranger who has come to live in your neighborhood, and that when you ring the bell the lady herself opens the door—or let us say you find her sitting on her veranda. In either case you say, "How do you do—I'm Mrs. Jones. I live in the brick house across the street." The new neighbor says, "How do you do. I'm very glad to see you," or "How kind of you to come to see me!" She then invites you into her living-room or asks whether you think it pleasanter on the veranda. In any case you sit and talk. From ten to fifteen minutes is the time allotted for a formal visit. This is not a strict rule, but it is well to keep within this time unless you have much to talk about, and unless your hostess says, "Oh, do stay a little longer" or "Oh, don't go so soon," in which case you stay for a few minutes longer, or say, "I'm sorry! I'd love to but I can't today. Do come and see me soon!" The new neighbor says, "I'll be glad to." You both say, "Goodby," and that's all.

But if the new neighbor, struggling to get her house in order, opens her door to an unexpected visitor, it is obviously human to exclaim frankly, "Oh dear neighbor, I would so very much like to ask you to come in but, as you can *see*, my house and I are in just too much of a turmoil to receive you!" And then probably add, "Won't you *please* come to see me when I get things straightened out?"

SENDING YOUR CARD

Before our cities became so large and traffic became so difficult the rules for leaving cards were important and had to be followed, but today a popular woman would have to spend considerable time on these social amenities. She will probably telephone or mail her card with a brief note written on it.

VISITS WHICH EVERYONE MUST PAY

Paying visits differs from leaving cards in that you must ask to be received. A visit of condolence should be paid at once to a friend when a death occurs in her immediate family, but in this case you ask if Mrs. So-and-so feels like seeing you. And further the would-be visitor asks if there is anything he or she can do. A lady does not call on a man, but writes him a note of sympathy.

When going to inquire for a friend who has been very ill, the question of whether or not you ask to be received depends upon how well you know her. It is always proper as well as thoughtful to take a gift of a book or fruit or flowers, or perhaps something from your kitchen, if you know of something she likes that you or your cook makes and that she is allowed to eat.

When the engagement of a man in your family—or family-in-law— is announced, you must at once go to see his fiancée. Should she be out, you do not ask to see her mother. You do, however, leave a card upon both ladies, and after this you show your future relative whatever hospitality you can.

A visit of congratulation is also paid a new mother and, of course, it is always very pleasing if you can take a present to the baby.

MESSAGES WRITTEN ON CARDS

"With sympathy" or "With deepest sympathy" is written on your visiting-card with flowers sent to a funeral. This same message is written on a card and left at the door of a house of mourning, if you do not know the family well enough to ask to be received.

"To inquire" is often written on a card left at the house of a sick person, but not if you are received.

At the house of a lady whom you know well and whom you are sorry not to find at home, it is friendly to write "Sorry not to see you!" or "So sorry to miss you!"

Bending the corner of a card means merely that the card was left at the door by the visitor and not sent by mail. This has very little sense today when cards are left seldom and mailed, without a message, scarcely ever.

HOW A FIRST VISIT IS MADE

In very large cities (New York, for example) neighbors seldom call on each other. But when strangers move into a neighborhood in a small town or more especially in the country, it is very unfriendly of their neighbors not to call on them. The new residents always must wait for the old residents to call on them—or at least invite only those much younger to come to see them.

Or, if two ladies meet and they are both newcomers, either one may say, "I wish you would come to see me." To which the other replies, "I'd love to."

Everyone invited to a wedding should call upon the bride on her return from the honeymoon. And when a man marries a girl from a distant place, courtesy absolutely demands that his friends and neighbors go to see her as soon as she is at home.

ON OPENING THE DOOR TO A VISITOR

On the hall table in every house, there should be a small silver or other card tray, a pad, and a pencil. The nicest kind of pad is one that, when folded, makes its own envelope, so that a message, when written, need not be left open. There are all varieties and sizes at all stationers.

When the doorbell rings, the servant on duty should look before she opens the door and if she sees that it is a chauffeur or a lady, should have the card tray ready to present on the palm of the left hand. Whoever is on duty at the door or comes to open it should never take the cards in his or her fingers.

CORRECT NUMBER OF CARDS TO LEAVE

When the visitor herself rings the doorbell and the message is "not at home," the butler or maid proffers the card tray on which the visitor lays a card of her own and her daughter's for each lady in the house and a card of her husband's and son's for each lady and gentleman. The number of cards to leave is very simple. You leave your own cards for ladies only, because you do not call upon a gentleman. But your husband's card is left upon every gentleman as well as every lady.

That is all there is to it. But three is the greatest number ever left of any one card. In calling on Mrs. Town, who has three grown daughters and her mother living in the house, and a Mrs. Stranger staying with her whom the visitor was invited to a luncheon to meet, a card on each would mean a packet of six. Instead, the visitor should leave three— one for Mrs. Town, one for all the other ladies of the house, and one for Mrs. Stranger. In asking to be received, her query at the door should be, "Are any of the ladies at home?" Or in merely leaving her cards she should say, "For all of the ladies."

WHEN THE VISITOR LEAVES

The butler or maid must stand with the front door open until a visitor reenters her car, or if she is walking, until she has reached the sidewalk. It is bad manners ever to close the door in a visitor's face, or while she is still going down the front steps.

WHEN THE LADY OF THE HOUSE IS AT HOME

When the door is opened by a waitress or a parlor maid and the lady of the house is in the living-room, the maid leads the way into the living-room.

IF A BUTLER OPENS THE DOOR

The butler reads the card himself, picking it up from the tray; and, going to the door of the drawing-room, he announces: "Mrs. John Jones."

The duration of a formal visit should be in the neighborhood of fifteen minutes. But if other visitors are announced, the first one—on a very formal occasion—may cut her visit shorter. Or if conversation becomes especially interesting, the visit may be prolonged five minutes or so. On *no* account must a visitor stay longer than half an hour.

A hostess always rises when a visitor enters, unless the visitor is a very young woman or man and she is seated behind the tea-table so that rising is difficult. She should always receive a visitor graciously. She says, "How nice of you to come to see me!" Or "I'm very glad to see you. Won't you sit here?"

If the lady of the house is at home but upstairs, the servant at the door leads the visitor into the reception room, saying, "Will you take a seat, please?" and then carries the card to the mistress of the house.

On an exceptional occasion, such as paying a visit of condolence or inquiring for a convalescent, when the question as to whether he will be received is necessarily doubtful, a gentleman does not take off his coat or gloves, but waits in the hall with his hat in his hand. When the servant returning says either, "Will you come this way, please?" or "Mrs. Town is not well enough to see anyone, but Miss Lillian will be down in a moment," the butler then takes the gentleman's hat, helps him off with his coat, and shows the way to the living-room.

THE TYPICAL VISITOR

A gentleman visitor always leaves his hat and coat in the hall and also removes and leaves his gloves—and overshoes, should he be wearing them. A gentleman entering a room in which there are several people who are strangers, shakes hands with his hostess and slightly bows to all the others, whether he knows them personally or not. He, of course, shakes hands with any who are friends, and with all men to whom he is introduced, but with a lady only if she offers him her hand.

HOW TO ENTER A DRAWING-ROOM

To know how to enter a drawing-room is supposed to be a test of social skill. But there should be no more difficulty in entering the drawing-room of Mrs. Worldly than in entering the sitting-room at home. Perhaps the best instruction would be: Take plenty of time; never dash inside and then have to stop when you are halfway into the room to get your bearings.

Before entering a room full of people, it is best to pause on the threshold and see where the hostess is and the most unencumbered approach to her. The way *not* to enter a drawing-room is to dart forward and then stand awkwardly bewildered and looking about in every direction. After greeting the hostess, talk with her for a few moments, and then either join friends of your own or those to whom the hostess introduces you.

HOW TO SIT GRACEFULLY

To sit gracefully one should not perch stiffly on the edge of a straight chair, nor sprawl at length in an easy one. The perfect position is one that is easy, but dignified. In other days, no lady of dignity ever crossed her knees, held her hands on her hips, or twisted herself sideways, or even *leaned back in her chair!* Today all these things are done; and the only etiquette left is on the subject of how not to exaggerate them. No young girl—let alone older lady—should cross her knees when wearing knee-length skirts that are also lacking in fullness; neither should her foot be thrust out so that her toes are at knee level. An arm akimbo is not a graceful attitude, nor is a twisted spine! Everyone, of course, leans against a chair back (except in a box at the opera and in a ballroom). A gentleman who is a guest in a lady's house should not sit on the middle of his backbone with one ankle supported on the other knee, and both as high as his head. If too weak to sit up, he should stay at home.

The proper way for a lady to sit is in the center of her chair, or slightly sideways in the corner of a sofa. She may lean back, of course, and easily, her hands relaxed in her lap, her knees together, or if crossed, her foot must not be thrust forward like a pump-handle, or hooked around the chair leg in vine fashion. On informal occasions she can lean back in an easy chair as far as she chooses. In a ball dress a lady of distinction never really leans backward. One cannot picture a beautiful and high-bred woman, wearing a tiara and other ballroom jewels, *leaning* against anything.

A gentleman may even on very formal occasions lean against the back of his chair, but he must give the appearance of sitting on a chair, not of lying at ease on a sofa. and the sole of at least one of his feet must be flat on the floor.

POSTSCRIPTS ON VISITS

When you are paying a formal visit, the important rules are: Don't outstay other visitors who arrive after you, or one who may have come before you but who is plainly an intimate friend in whose news the hostess seems interested. In such a situation, the rule of safety is to leave after ten minutes.

Do not, however, fidget and talk about leaving. Sit down as though your leaving immediately were not on your mind, but after a very few minutes stand up and say "Good-by" and go.

Never make remarks such as "I'm afraid I have overstayed my welcome" or "I must apologize for hurrying off" or "I'm afraid I have bored you to death talking so much." All such expressions are self-conscious and stupid. If you really think you are staying too long or leaving too soon or talking too much—*don't!*

Above all, don't keep your hostess standing while you make parting remarks for half an hour! Having risen to go, *go!*

OTHER VISITING DETAILS

Visits of condolence are never returned.

A lady never pays a party call on a gentleman. But if the gentleman who has given a dinner has his mother or sister staying with him, and if the mother or sister chaperoned the party, cards should, of course, be left upon her.

Few Americans are so punctilious as to pay their dinner calls within twenty-four hours—if indeed they ever pay them; but it is the height of correctness and good manners to do so.

CHRISTMAS CARDS

The ever-increasing impulse to send out Christmas cards as messages of friendship and good will is plainly not a mere caprice of fashion, but evidence of a country-wide trend toward a broadened and more friendly social relationship.

The present tendency is toward sending personal cards to those whom not many years ago we would have considered rather formal acquaintances.

When ordering Christmas cards the inclusion of Mr. and Mrs. as part of the signature is proper when the names are engraved or printed in imitation of engraving and are put at the head of the message.

For example, "Mr. and Mrs. Christopher Holly send you their best wishes for a Merry Christmas and a Happy New Year." This is certainly better form than "Best Wishes for a Merry Christmas and a Happy New Year, from Mr. and Mrs. Christopher Holly."

Sending cards as bought without any signature and then enclosing a visiting-card is suitable for the extremely impersonal greeting sent to clients or customers or business acquaintances. When sent to friends, it rather suggests evidence of having been ordered too late to have them properly engraved—or perhaps it shows a frugal mind, since if the card is unmarked, it will be just as good as new for the receiver to send on to someone else next year.

An important point to be made is that engraving of names on Christmas cards naturally follows the rules for the engraving of names on visiting-cards. For example, a woman's name should never be engraved without the title of Mrs. or Miss, although a man's card may be left without a title.

IS HUSBAND'S OR WIFE'S NAME WRITTEN FIRST?

When the cards are sent by husband and wife, the one who writes the names courteously writes his or her own name last. But when cards are printed, there is no rule about whether the husband's or the wife's name shall be first. Mary and John seems more polite to Mary, but John and Mary does of course follow the conventional Mr. and Mrs. form. However, when children's names are included, the father's name comes first—always. For example: John and Mary and the Baby is better than Mary and John and the Baby. Sometimes, by the way, a baby's arrival at any time during the year is announced by adding his name on the Christmas cards—John and Mary and their new son Timothy. Cards sent to intimate friends, by a family having several children, might be from The John Smiths—all Five, or from The Smiths —John, Mary, Johnny, Marie, and Tim. There is of course no rule about anything so informal as this.

On the formal cards sent by a widow and her grown son together, or widower and his grown daughter, the name of the parent would be engraved on one line and that of the son or daughter on the line below. Or if written by hand, the parent's name would come first: Aunt Jane and Tim, or Henry Green and Mary Green, or to those who call the parent by the first name, Henry and Mary, each signing his or her name.

Engaged people often send cards together to their intimate friends with their first names either written by hand or printed to match the rest of the printing on an informal card. But their two names together are not suitable when formally engraved.

There is practically no limit to the list of those to whom one may send Christmas cards, beginning with dearest friends and ending with the slightest acquaintances, but they should stop at acquaintances. Tradespeople should not commercialize the spirit of the most beautiful day in the year by sending cards intended to solicit customers. This does not mean that it is improper to send Christmas cards as a purely friendly greeting to customers whom they know personally.

CARD FOR WHOLE FAMILY

When a card is intended for the whole family and one dislikes the ambiguousness of Mr. and Mrs. Brightmeadow and Family, it is best to address the envelope Mr. and Mrs. and then on the card itself and below the wording of the message write in ink "Love to the children too" or "We all in our house send best Christmas wishes to all of you in your house," or whatever message is suitable.

CARDS TO BUSINESS ACQUAINTANCES

When sending cards to a business acquaintance whom one's husband or wife does not know, one properly signs one's name alone; but when the acquaintance is a social one as well or when sending a card to anyone who is really a friend and whom one would very much like one's husband or wife to meet, the name of the latter may be included. Both these customs apply to cases of uncertainty. In the usual case you would do what your own impulse tells you, and send either an impersonal one alone or a friendly one together. And this also applies to people working in business with you, for you, and above you.

A CHRISTMAS CARD TO SOMEONE IN MOURNING

A card to someone who is in deep mourning can be kind if its picture in some way illustrates the birth of Christ or the promise of peace, or if its message be of loving friendly thought. But please do not send a picture of a grave or gravestones—nor on the other hand a gay card shouting "Merry Christmas and Happy New Year." Whether or not those who are themselves in mourning send cards depends entirely upon their own feelings. Naturally they would not send cards to mere acquaintances, but certainly there is no impropriety in wishing their friends happiness, if they can forget their own unhappiness enough to do so. On the other hand, no one could possibly want them to do anything that could add to the strain of what must be to them the hardest of days to endure.

COLORED INKS FOR GAILY COLORED CARDS

Although red and orange and green ink are still rejected for social usage, there is no objection to signing cards in red or other colored ink to match the wording on a gaily informal Christmas card. Also Christmas envelope linings can be as vividly colorful as you please. It is quite all right to paste return address stickers or to write your address on envelopes going to people whose address you are not certain about, or to any you think may not know your own address.

BIRTHDAY AND OTHER GREETING CARDS

Birthday and anniversary cards and all other messages of friendship are charming evidences of good wishes from family and friends. But the engraved or printed card intended as a substitute for a written note of thanks is like a slap in the face to one who went to the trouble and expense of sending a gift.

ANSWERING VISITING-CARD INVITATION

Although it does seem inconsistent to answer a visiting-card invitation, which is scarcely formal, with a note of acceptance or regret written in the third person, nevertheless, this is the accepted convention, probably because its first use was considered as a substitute for the formal, engraved, third-person invitation form which was merely filled in with a few words. At the present time only comparative strangers answer in the third person. Intimate friends invariably reply in kind, "Coming!" "Accept." "Sorry can't come!" And it is reasonable to suppose that the custom will spread further. In fact, even though the third-person reply is conventionally correct, there is no objection whatever to replying to "Fri. Nov. 1, 7:30 o'ck, Buffet supper" on one's own card, "Accept with pleasure Nov. 1" or "So sorry can't accept for Friday."

When leaving your card on one member of a large family, write "For Miss Mary" across the top *over* your name. If she were staying in a hotel or living in an apartment house you would add her surname.

Write on the face, because a message on the back might be overlooked, should the one who receives it read the name and not turn the card over.

ON THE SUBJECT OF INVITATIONS

·∘⟧ 11 ⟦∘·

THE ENGRAVED FORMS OF INVITATIONS AND ANNOUNCE-
ments we use are almost as unchangeably fixed as are the letters of the
alphabet, although many of us can remember a day when thin glossy
paper of large size was in the height of fashion with fairly small lettering made important with somewhat large and shaded flourishings.

Even so, the third-person wording of an invitation and its acceptance
or regret has remained unchanged throughout countless years. It is true
we no longer "present our compliments" and invite our neighbors to
come in "for a dish of tea." On the other hand, the wording of third-
person invitations to a dinner of ceremony or a dance are worded and
engraved exactly as they have always been.

All formal invitations are recognized as such because they are
worded in the third person, and their acceptances and regrets are invariably answered in this same form, and by hand. The words must be
placed on specified lines and centered as evenly as possible. Names of
hosts belong on the first line; "request the pleasure of" on the second;
name of guest on the third; and so on.

Among the many engraved forms adapted to our social, political or
professional life, wedding invitations are of greatest familiarity to us all.

WEDDING INVITATIONS

Invitations to the largest, most elaborate wedding in a great city
consist of an invitation to the church ceremony, enclosing a card of
admission. Intimate friends and relatives receive also an invitation to
the "reception"—which may be a sit-down breakfast or a buffet supper
with preparations for dancing.

Correct invitations to a wedding are always engraved on the first
page of a double sheet of ivory or white note paper, either plain or with
a raised margin called a plate-mark or panel. This is one time, should
the family of the bride have one, when it is proper to have its coat of
arms—or a crest only—embossed without color at top center of the

sheet. Further details for use of heraldry are given in the chapter on "Formal Correspondence." If the family has no authentic coat of arms the invitation bears no device of any kind. The engraving may be in whichever the bride prefers among the several lettering styles offered her by the stationer.

The invitation to the church should always request "the honour"—spelled with a "u"—of your "presence," and never the "pleasure" of your "company." It is the invitation to the reception that requests the "pleasure" of your "company."

WHEN—AND WHY—TWO ENVELOPES?

As a matter of fact, two envelopes are definitely associated with wedding invitations. The inner envelope has no mucilage on the flap, and is addressed to Mr. and Mrs. Brown with neither first name nor address. Then it is put into an outer "mailing envelope" that has mucilage on its flap, addressed side toward the flap. This envelope is then addressed by hand to "Mr. and Mrs. George W. Brown—26 Parkway—Home Town."

In all formal correspondence it is in bad taste to abbreviate the state name, but it is correct to omit it when the invitations are posted for delivery in the same city, or when otherwise unnecessary. New York, for example, need never be written twice.

To those who are only asked to the church, no house invitation is enclosed.

If the wedding is to be in a very small church or chapel and the reception in a very big house, then many will receive invitations to the reception and very few to the ceremony. If it happens that not only the church but also the reception is limited to a very few who are sent hand-written invitations or are given oral invitations, then engraved announcements in place of invitations of any kind are sent to the friends who could not be included as well as to all acquaintances.

The invitations to a large wedding are sent three weeks beforehand; those to a simpler wedding can be mailed as late as ten days before the wedding day.

ENVELOPES SHOULD BE FORMALLY ADDRESSED

Envelopes should *not* be addressed:

Mr. and Mrs. James Greatlake
and Family

The phrase "and Family" has never been approved for invitations by persons of taste because it is considered as too indefinite as to how many of the family are invited. Correctly, Miss Mary Greatlake, or the Misses Greatlake, may be written beneath the names of their parents, but a separate invitation should be sent to "The Messrs." All members of the family not living at the family's home address certainly would have to be sent separate invitations.

The names of children under twelve or thirteen are written on the inner envelopes this way:

Priscilla, Penelope, Harold, and Jim

and enclosed in an outer envelope addressed to "The Misses and Messrs. Greatlake."

On the inside envelopes of the invitations to relatives who are very dear to the bride or to the groom—especially if they are simple people who might not understand that the formality of writing "Mr. and Mrs." is prescribed and not intended to be snobbish, "Aunt Kate and Uncle Tom" or "Grandmother" may be written in the handwriting of the bride or the groom. This, however, is a personal exception and quite apart from etiquette, which is more particularly concerned with the wording of the engraving or with the addressing of the outer envelope.

ENVELOPE AND INVITATION IN ONE

Wedding invitations and announcements are sometimes engraved on a sheet with a gummed flap at the top; when folded, this paper makes its own envelope. This style cannot possibly replace the conventional fine-quality kid-finish paper enclosed in two envelopes—which is in best possible taste. But, if there are no enclosures, it might serve as well as those invitations sent in one envelope—as a paper-saving measure in wartime, for example. But when they are to be had, the two envelopes are always the preferred choice.

FOLDING AND INSERTING

When preparing to send out the invitations, all of the envelopes are addressed first. An envelope-size invitation is inserted in the inner envelope, folded edge down, with the engraved side toward you. An invitation designed to fit a half-size envelope will require a second fold. This second fold should be made with the engraving inside and inserted, folded edge down, into the envelope. With the unsealed flap of this filled inner envelope in the palm of the hand, insert it in the mailing envelope.

NOTE. Engravers may sometimes use tissue sheets to protect the pages from the fresh ink. These tissues should be removed.

RETURN ADDRESSES

Return addresses are not correctly used on invitations and announcements. However, when the address of a far-away friend is in doubt, it is permissible to put your address in the upper left corner of the envelope, so that it may be returned to you if the letter is not delivered.

In the examples of correct wording, spacing, and styles of engraving which follow, it is important to note the omission of punctuation, except after abbreviations and initials and when phrases requiring separation by punctuation occur in the same line.

THE CHURCH INVITATION

The proper form for an invitation to the church ceremony is:

Mr. and Mrs. John Huntington Smith
request the honour of

Miss Pauline Town's

presence at the marriage of their daughter
Mary Katherine
to
Mr. James Smartlington
Tuesday, the first of November
at twelve o'clock
St. John's Church

The invitation may be about 5½ inches wide by 7⅜ inches deep or slightly smaller and folded into its envelope, or about 4⅜ inches by 5¾ inches to go into the envelope without folding; but the fashion in this varies from time to time and other sizes may be used, according to the current fashion.

When the bride's father has a coat of arms, and if it is used, it is always embossed without color on wedding invitations and announcements; but when invitations are sent out in the name of the bride's mother (or of any woman alone), a coat of arms is improper. She can, however, have the device on the shield of her husband's coat of arms impaled with that of her own family on a lozenge.

Apart from the socially correct form of invitation above, some communicants of the Roman Catholic Church use a form in which the phrase "at the marriage of," is replaced by *"at the Marriage in Christ of"*; and where appropriate there is added beneath the name of the groom the lines *"and your participation in the offering of the Nuptial Mass."*

On an actual invitation a device such as this is embossed by the engraver without color and of course does not have the black effect as this printed example.

Plain script is in very best taste for invitations ornamented with a coat of arms or a lozenge.

Mr. and Mrs. Charles Robert Oldname

request the honour of your presence

at the marriage of their daughter

Pauline Marie

to

Mr. John Frederick Hamilton

Saturday, the twenty-ninth of April

at four o'clock

Church of the Heavenly Rest

New York

CARDS FOR RESERVED PEWS

To the family and those intimate friends who are to be seated in specially designated pews, the same admission card which is sent to others may be sent, but with the words "Pew No. —" engraved in the lower left-hand corner, the number of the pew to be written in by hand.

But the more usual and less expensive custom is for the mother of the bride and the mother of the bridegroom each to write on her personal visiting-card the number of the pew reserved for each member of the family and the one which each intimate friend is to occupy.

Pew No. 7

Mrs. John Huntington Smith

600 East Fifty-Seventh Street

A card for a reserved enclosure consisting of a certain number of front pews, although for no special pew, and inscribed "Within the ribbon" may be enclosed with the invitations, or the words may be added in the lower left-hand corner of an appropriate number of the regular admission cards. If admission cards are not necessary, "Within the ribbon" may be written on a visiting-card and included with the invitation.

INVITATIONS TO FRIENDS IN MOURNING

Invitations are sent to persons in mourning even though they undoubtedly will not accept the invitation to the reception and may not go to the wedding itself.

THE INVITATION TO THE RECEPTION

The invitation to the breakfast or reception following the church ceremony is engraved on a card to match the paper of the church invitation and is a little smaller than the size of the latter after it is folded for the envelope.

Mr. and Mrs. John Huntington Smith
request the pleasure of

Miss Pauline Town's

company at breakfast
Tuesday, the first of November
at half after twelve o'clock
43 Park Avenue

R.s.v.p.

The great number of wedding invitations to the church usually sent out excuses to a degree the use of an engraved "your" in place of the full name of each guest written in by hand.

The invitations to the reception, however, should have the name of each guest written in by hand.

Or the following on a small card is enclosed with the invitation to the church:

Reception

immediately following the ceremony

895 Park Avenue

R.S.V.P.

The forms R.s.v.p. and R.S.V.P. are both correct. The former, however, is preferred by the conservative. It is to be noted that in France and in diplomatic circles, the capital letters are the correct form.

PROFESSIONAL NAME ADDED WHEN THE BRIDE HAS A CAREER

When the bride has a career and uses a professional name, and has therefore many professional friends to whom she would like to send invitations, but who are unlikely to know who "Pauline Marie Old-name" could be, the invitations may have her professional name engraved in very small letters and in parentheses under her Christian name:

Pauline Marie
(Pat Bond)

to

Mr. John Frederick Hamilton

This is most practically done by having the name (Pat Bond) added to the plate after the order for regular invitations has been completed. And as many invitations as are to go to her professional friends are then struck off with this addition.

INVITATION TO A WEDDING
AT THE HOUSE OF A FRIEND

In this form the invitations are issued by the parents of the bride, although the wedding takes place at a house other than their own. The names of the parents at the head of the invitation means that *they* are giving the wedding (and assuming all expenses) even though it is taking place at a house not their own.

Mr. and Mrs. Richard Littlehouse

request the honour of

presence at the marriage of their daughter

Betty

to

Mr. Frederic Robinson

Saturday, the fifth of November

at four o'clock

at the residence of Mr. and Mrs. James Sterlington

Tuxedo Park, New York

R.s.v.p.

WHEN THE BRIDE HAS A STEPFATHER

When the bride's own father or mother is not living and she has a step-parent, the invitations are worded:

Mr. and Mrs. John Huntington Smith
request the honour of your presence
at the marriage of her daughter
Mary Alice Towne
etc.

The phrase "their daughter" instead of "her daughter" would be untrue—unless Mr. Smith had adopted her—and cruel to the memory of her father. But in any case, all invitations are sent out by Mr. and Mrs. Smith. It is also important to remember that good taste does not permit "Miss" or "Mrs." as titles to the bride's name except in the three cases that follow.

WHEN THE BRIDE IS AN ORPHAN

If the bride has no relatives and the wedding is given by friends, the wording is:

Mr. and Mrs. John Neighbor
request the honour of your presence
at the marriage of
Miss Elizabeth Orphan
to
Mr. John Henry Bridegroom

If she has brothers, the oldest one customarily sends out her wedding invitations and announcements in his name. Or, if another relative has taken the place of a parent, his or her name is used. The bride, whose several sisters or brothers are younger than she, may prefer to send her invitations in her own name. The following form might be used:

The honour of your presence
is requested
at the marriage of
Miss Elizabeth Orphan
to
etc.

Or she and the bridegroom may announce their own marriage this way:

Miss Elizabeth Orphan
and
Mr. John Henry Bridegroom
announce their marriage
etc.

WHEN HER PARENTS ARE DIVORCED

Properly the invitations and announcements should be sent out by the bride's mother and her present husband's name should be included:

Mr. and Mrs. John Newhusband
request the honour of your presence
at the marriage of her daughter
Mary Oldhusband
etc.

It is possible for Mr. Oldhusband to share in his daughter's wedding. Details are given on page 225.

THE DOUBLE-WEDDING INVITATION

Mr. and Mrs. Henry Smartlington
request the honour of your presence
at the marriage of their daughters

Marian Helen

to

Mr. Judson Jones

and

Amy Caroline

to

Mr. Herbert Scott Adams

Saturday, the tenth of November
at four o'clock
Trinity Church

The elder sister's name is given first.

WHEN BRIDES ARE NOT SISTERS

It is unusual but not unheard of for two brides who have been lifelong friends—or possibly cousins, but with different names—to have a double wedding.

The wording of such invitations must necessarily include the surnames of both parents and brides:

Mr. and Mrs. Henry Smartlington
and
Mr. and Mrs. Arthur Lane
request the honour of your presence
at the marriage of their daughters
Marian Helen Smartlington
to
Mr. Judson Jones
and
Mary Alice Lane
to
Mr. John Gray
etc.

If the surnames of the brides should be omitted, there is, at the moment, danger that strangers may suppose the invitation to be one of those divorced-parent offenses occasionally perpetrated.

WHEN BRIDEGROOM'S FAMILY GIVES WEDDING

In the unusual situation of the young bride coming as a stranger from abroad, or from any distance without her family, it is entirely proper that the groom's family give the wedding and send the invitations in their name. This is the only other case where the title "Miss" is used.

Mr. and Mrs. John Henry Pater
request the honour of your presence
at the marriage of
Miss Marie Mersailles
to
their son
John Henry Pater, junior
etc.

Announcements may also be sent from abroad by her own family.

THE FEWER THE INVITATIONS
THE HIGHER THEIR VALUE

The most *flattering* wedding invitation possible to receive is a note of invitation personally written by the bride:

Dear Mrs. Kindhart
Dick and I are to be married at Christ Church Chantry at noon on Thursday the tenth. We both want you and Mr. Kindhart to

come to the church and afterward to breakfast at my aunt's, Mrs. Salde, at Two Park Avenue.

With much love from us both,

Affectionately,
Helen

The bride would of course write similar notes to the groom's relatives and special friends.

INVITATION TO THE RECEPTION ONLY

On occasion the ceremony is private and a big reception follows. This plan is chosen, for example, where the nearest relative is an invalid who can perhaps go down to the drawing-room with only the immediate families, but could not otherwise be present.

Under these circumstances the invitations to the ceremony are given orally, and general invitations to the reception sent out for a somewhat later hour. The wording for this is:

Mr. and Mrs. John Huntington Smith
request the pleasure of
(name or names written in)   *company*
at the wedding breakfast   (or *reception*)
of their daughter
Millicent Jane
and
Mr. Sidney Strothers
Tuesday, the first of November
at half after twelve o'clock   (or whatever hour)
555 Park Avenue

R.s.v.p.

AN INVITATION TO A HOUSE WEDDING
CLEARLY INCLUDES RECEPTION

The wording of an invitation to a house wedding gives a house address in place of the name of the church, and R.s.v.p. is added. A further invitation to stay on at a house, to which the guest has been already invited, is not necessary.

RECEPTION AT THE CLUB OF A FRIEND

When a wedding reception or any other entertainment is given at a club through the courtesy of a friend of the hostess, the following announcement is always engraved in the lower right corner, "Through the courtesy of Mrs. John Smith Jones." This is put in the right corner because the left corner is reserved for the R.s.v.p.

WEDDING AND RECEPTION INVITATION IN ONE

Occasionally, especially for a country wedding or when the reception is taking place in the assembly room or parish house of the church and everyone is invited to remain, the invitation to the reception or to the breakfast is included in the invitation to the ceremony.

Mrs. Alexander Oldname

requests the honour of

Mr. and Mrs. Worldly's

presence at the marriage of her daughter

Hester

to

Mr. James Town, junior

Tuesday, the twenty-first of October

at three o'clock

Church of the Resurrection

Ridgemont, New York

and afterwards at the reception

Bright Meadows

R.s.v.p.

Or the invitation will read, "At twelve o'clock, Church of the Resurrection, Ridgemont, New York, and afterwards at breakfast at Bright Meadows."

AT HOME CARDS

The bride- and groom-to-be cannot send their future Mr. and Mrs. visiting-card with their address with the wedding invitations. So if they

want their friends to know what their address is to be, an At Home card
is included with the invitation. Today this card is most often as follows:

At Home

after the fifteenth of November

3842 Olympia Drive

Houston 19, Texas

Because At Home with two capitals is usually used for the most
formal invitations, it is better taste to use At home with a small "h."
Twenty-five years ago the card generally used would have read

Will be at home

after October sixteenth

1730 Taylor Street

Del Monte, California

and this would not be incorrect today. The size of the cards is about
4″ by 2¾″.

CARDS OF ADDRESS

If the bride and groom wish to inform their friends of their future
address, the following information is engraved in the lower left corner
of the invitations:

After the first of December
25 Elm Street, Greattown

If announcements are sent out the same form is used or a smaller
card enclosed and the form is the same.

WHEN THE BRIDE IS A WIDOW

Invitations to the marriage of a widow—if she be very young—are sent in the name of her parents exactly as were the invitations for her first wedding, except that her name, instead of being simply Priscilla, is now written as Priscilla Banks Loring, thus:

> *Mr. and Mrs. Maynard Banks*
> *request the honour of your presence*
> *at the marriage of their daughter*
> *Priscilla Banks Loring*
> *to*
> *etc.*

Forms that are not acceptable include a title following a possessive pronoun denoting relationship; equally wrong are "their daughter, Mrs." and "their niece, Miss." One explanation suggested is that, when Mr. and Mrs. Jones announce the marriage of "their daughter, Mary Jones Smith," no one will know that this is her second marriage. It would be difficult indeed to see how it could be plainer. On the other hand, without the Jones in her name she might of course be the daughter of Mrs. Jones, who might first have been a Mrs. Smith, but that this is not the case is shown by "their daughter" instead of "her daughter" in the wording of the invitation. And after all, invitations to second weddings are supposed to be sent to people who surely will have known the Joneses or the bride really well. If they do not recognize any of the names, it would scarcely have been necessary to send announcements or invitations.

Announcements for a young widow's marriage are the same as for a first wedding.

> *Mr. and Mrs. Maynard Banks*
> *announce the marriage of their daughter*
> *Priscilla Banks Loring*
> *etc.*

But the announcement of the marriage of a widow of maturer years reads:

> *Mrs. Mary Hoyt*
> *and*
> *Mr. Worthington Adams*
> *announce their marriage*
> *on Monday, the second of November*
> *One thousand nine hundred and fifty-five*
> *at Saratoga Springs*
> *New York*

In this instance, the objection to a "Mrs." followed by a woman's Christian name is removed since it is Mary, and not Mrs. John, who is being given in marriage. The other instance is that of a professional woman who, having been married, is improperly addressed as "Miss" and who, therefore, will use "Mrs. Mary."

CONCERNING A DIVORCÉE'S REMARRIAGE

Sending out engraved invitations to, or announcements of, the remarriage of a divorcée is never in best taste—nor should a widow choose to have an elaborate second wedding.

On the other hand, the fact that the groom has been divorced does not interfere with the announcement of his new bride's marriage.

A DIVORCÉE'S WEDDING RING

A widow always keeps and wears her wedding ring until she dies or marries again, but to a divorcée her wedding ring can only be a very unhappy symbol, and it is very unlikely that she should wish to keep it. Many have thrown their unlucky rings into the ocean to get rid of them, but it would seem less wasteful to sell them, and then give the money received to the church or her favorite charity or cause. If the divorcée objects to being without a ring and wants to show that she has been married, she can get a new one and wear it on her left hand, or on her right hand, if she wants to show that she might consider a second marriage.

WHEN PRINCIPALS ARE IN THE SERVICES

On the wedding invitations, the name of a bridegroom whose rank is below Commander in the Navy or Captain in the Army is given this way:

John Strong,
2nd Lieutenant, United States Army
or
Ensign, United States Navy

One change (probably permanent) is that Mr. before the name of a bridegroom of lower than senior rank whose rating is indicated on a line below is fast going out of favor. It is still correct, much as Esquire is; but it is used by the few, rather than by the many.

The name of a non-commissioned or an enlisted man in the Armed Forces is engraved John Strong, and Signal Corps, U.S.N.R., or Coast Artillery, U.S.A., or whatever designation is his, in smaller type directly beneath the name on the wedding invitations. Or, if the bride chooses to include Pvt. 1st Class, U.S.A., or Apprentice Seaman, U.S.N.R., social usage is now permitting this.

The name of the bride who is in the Armed Forces is engraved:

marriage of their daughter
Alice Mary
Lieutenant, Women's Army Corps
or
Ensign, WAVES, United States Naval Reserve
or
Lieutenant, Nurse Corps, United States Naval Reserve

When the bride's father is also in the Armed Forces and absent on duty, his name appears as follows:

Major (overseas) and Mrs. John Jones
request the honour of your presence, etc.

If the father is in the Armed Forces and has rank below that of Captain in the Army or Commander in the Navy, the first line of the invitations and announcements is engraved

Mr. and Mrs. John Henry Jones

This form may also be used when the bride's mother is in the Armed Forces.

WEDDING ANNOUNCEMENTS

If no general invitations have been issued to the church, an announcement engraved on note paper like that of the invitation to the ceremony is sent to the entire visiting list of both the bride's and the groom's families. They should be sent as soon after the wedding as possible.

Mr. and Mrs. John Fairplay

have the honour of

announcing the marriage of their daughter

Madeleine Anne

to

Mr. George Followes Highseas

Ensign United States Navy

Tuesday, the twenty-seventh of March

One thousand nine hundred and forty-five

Washington, D. C.

Three forms of phrasing are equally correct: "have the honour to announce," or "have the honour of announcing," or merely the one word "announce." At present, "have the honour of announcing" is in fashion. Also in fashion is "Tuesday, April 24, 1955" in place of "Tuesday, the twenty-fourth of April" on one line and "One thousand nine hundred and fifty-five" on a second line.

Announcements go out in the name of the nearest kin—whether actually present or absent. An invalid mother's name is included in the "Mr. and Mrs." of the invitation. A father's name is included although actually he is abroad.

Announcements are never sent to those who have been invited to the wedding.

An announcement means that, for some reason or other, you were not (or *could not be*) invited. Or that the wedding was very small and no invitations were issued. An announcement requires no gift or acknowledgment except that of your own interest and impulse.

THE INVITATION TO A WEDDING ANNIVERSARY

If the bride and groom are themselves giving the party, the invitations are engraved on a card or sheet of note paper stamped with the year of the marriage and that of the celebration:

1930—1955
Mr. and Mrs. John Longlife
request the pleasure of
(name written in)
company at dinner in honour of
their silver anniversary
etc.

R.s.v.p.

Or, much less formal and more in keeping with the wooden or tin wedding is the sending of an ordinary Mr. and Mrs. visiting-card, on which is written:

1945—1955
(*engraved names on card*)
May 1
9 P.M.
R.s.v.p.

Sometimes the invitations are sent by their children, in which case they may be written informally:

Sally, Mary, and John Brown
hope you will come in
on Friday evening, March 1st
at 9 o'clock
to help celebrate
their parents' Silver Wedding Anniversary

Or they are perhaps more formally engraved:

*In honour of the
Fiftieth Wedding Anniversary of
Mr. and Mrs. John Longlife
their sons and daughters
request the pleasure of*
(name written in)
*company on Tuesday evening, the first of June
at nine o'clock
in the Ballroom of the Towne Club*
R.s.v.p.
John Longlife, Jr.
Towne Club

Invitations to a very simple anniversary tea or evening party are more usually written by hand or are telephoned.

ANSWERING A WEDDING INVITATION

An invitation only to the church requires no answer whatever (except where the wedding is so small that the invitation is a personally written note). An invitation to the reception or breakfast is answered on the first page of a sheet of note paper; and although it is written by hand, the spacing of the words must be followed as though they were engraved. This is the form of acceptance:

Mr. and Mrs. Robert Gilding, Jr.
accept with pleasure
Mr. and Mrs. Smith's
kind invitation for
Tuesday, the first of June

The regret reads:

> Mr. and Mrs. Richard Brown
> regret that they are unable to accept
> Mr. and Mrs. Smith's
> kind invitation for
> Tuesday, the first of June

The inclusion of a definite time is necessary only when accepting an invitation to a lunch or dinner, or when it is important that there has been no misunderstanding about the exact time.

The letter of acceptance or regret omits the first names of Mr. and Mrs. Smith, but the envelope of course reads exactly as on the engraved invitation.

COMBINATION ACCEPTANCE AND REGRET

It is entirely proper for a wife or husband to take it for granted that either one alone will be welcome at a general wedding reception, and to send an acceptance worded as follows:

> Mrs. John Brown
> accepts with pleasure
> Mr. and Mrs. Smith's
> kind invitation for
> Saturday, the tenth of June
> but regrets that
> Mr. Brown
> will be absent at that time

This same wording sent by a husband would merely transpose Mr. and Mrs.

OTHER FORMAL INVITATIONS

All other formal invitations are engraved or written by hand (never printed), on white, suède-finish cards, either plain or plate-marked like those for wedding receptions.

Formal third-person invitations are sometimes written on paper headed by a very small monogram, but never are engraved on paper headed by an address. If the family has a coat of arms this, or the crest, may be embossed without color on all engraved invitations as well as wedding announcements.

The size of the card of invitation varies with personal preference. The most graceful proportion is three units in height to four in width, or four high by three wide.

The lettering is a matter of personal choice, but the plainer the design, the safer. Punctuation is used only where words requiring separation occur on the same line, and in certain abbreviations, such as R.s.v.p. Capital letters for the R.S.V.P., which went out of fashion a few years ago, are at the present moment coming back into favor. The time should never be given as "nine-thirty" but as "half past nine o'clock" or the more conservative form "half after nine o'clock."

THE INVITATION TO A BALL

The word ball is rarely used except in an invitation to a public one, or at least a semi-public one, such as may be given by a committee for a charity or by a club or association of some sort. For example:

The Entertainment Committee of the Greenwood Club
requests the pleasure of your company
at a Ball
to be held at the club house
on the evening of Thursday, the seventh of November
at ten o'clock
for the benefit of
The Neighborhood Hospital
Tickets five dollars

INVITATION TO BE A PATRON

If fifty or more names are to be included in the list of those invited to become patrons, the correct wording is as follows:

The Committee of the Midwinter Ball
has the honour to invite
(name written by hand)
to be a Patron of the Ball
for the benefit of
The Children's Hospital
at the Hotel Grand
Friday evening, the thirtieth of October
at nine o'clock

Usually a card with return envelope is enclosed with the invitation for the convenience of the patron's answer. The most elaborate of these is worded:

I accept the Committee's invitation to be a Patron of the Scholarship Ball, at the Hotel Grand, Friday Evening, October thirtieth. Please reserve for me:

.................Boxes; First Tier (seating eight persons. Supper served in the box) .... $

.................Single Tickets (including Table Reservations on the ballroom terrace, Supper, and All Events of the Evening) .... each $

.................Single Tickets (including Buffet Supper and All Events of the Evening).. each $

Each patron is requested to be responsible for at least four tickets at $............ or $............ each.

As tables will be allotted in the order in which acceptances are received, early reservations are advisable.

Name ....
(Please write name as you wish it to appear on the Patrons' List)

Address ....

Checks, made payable to the Scholarship Committee, should be mailed to Room 540, Blank Building, Blanktown.

INVITATIONS TO A PRIVATE BALL

Invitations to a private ball, no matter whether the ball is to be given in a private house or the hostess has engaged an entire floor of the largest hotel in the world, announce merely that Mr. and Mrs. Somebody will be "At Home"—both words written with capital letters —and the word "Dancing" is added, almost as though it were an afterthought, in the lower left or right corner. *This is the most punctilious and formal invitation that it is possible to send.* It is engraved in script usually, on a card of white bristol board about $5\frac{1}{2}$ inches wide and $3\frac{3}{4}$ inches high. Like the wedding invitation, it has an embossed crest without color, or *nothing*.

The precise form is:

Mr. and Mrs. Davis Jefferson

At Home

Monday, the third of January

at ten o'clock

Town and Country Club

Kindly send reply to
Three Vernon Square

Dancing

but it may of course be engraved in whatever style of lettering the family prefers.

THE BALL FOR A DÉBUTANTE DAUGHTER

Very occasionally an invitation is worded:

Mr. and Mrs. Davis Jefferson
Miss Alice Jefferson
At Home

if the daughter is a débutante and the ball is for her; but it is not strictly correct to have any names except those of the host and his wife above the words "At Home."

Another proper form of invitation when the ball is to be given for a débutante is as follows:

Mr. and Mrs. de Puyster

request the pleasure of

Miss Rosalie Grey's

company at a dance in honour of their daughter

Miss Alice de Puyster

Monday the tenth of January

at ten o'clock

One East Fiftieth Street

R.s.v.p.

The explanation of why the wording "their daughter Miss" is permitted in the invitation to a ball and is forbidden in an invitation to a wedding is that the wedding is a church sacrament. The marriage, a sacrament, of "their daughter Miss" (or "Mrs.") is shocking. But all the young men are invited to meet and to dance with Miss Alice de Puyster. Or, if this explanation is not satisfactory, we must fall back on the fact that social convention has always said "Yes" to one and "No" to the other. The invitation to the ball may also read:

Mr. and Mrs. James Town

Miss Pauline Town

request the pleasure of

Mr. and Mrs. Greatlake's

company on Monday, the third of January

at ten o'clock

One East Fiftieth Street

Dancing

R.s.v.p.

The form most often used by fashionable hostesses is:

Mr. and Mrs. Gilding

request the pleasure of

company at a small dance

Monday, the first of January

at ten o'clock

900 Fifth Avenue

R.s.v.p.

Even though the ball is given for a débutante daughter, her name does not necessarily appear, and it is called a "small dance" whether it is really small or big.

If the dance or dinner, or whatever the entertainment is to be, is given at one address and the hostess lives at another, both addresses are always given.

Mr. and Mrs. Sidney Oldname

request the pleasure of

Miss Pauline Town's

company at a dance

Monday evening, January the third

at ten o'clock

The Fitz-Cherry

Kindly send response to
Brookmeadows,
Long Island

If the dance is given for a young friend who is not a relative, Mr. and Mrs. Oldname's invitations read:

request the pleasure of

company at a dance in honour of

Miss Rosalie Grey

ASKING FOR AN INVITATION

One may never ask for an invitation for oneself anywhere! Nor ordinarily does one ask to bring a house guest to a meal, unless one knows it is a buffet at which one or two unexpected persons could make no difference.

When regretting, it is quite proper to explain that you are expecting to have three week-end guests. Ordinarily the hostess-to-be says, "I'm sorry!" Or if it happens that she may be having a big buffet lunch, or a tea or cocktail party she may say, "*Do* bring them. We will be delighted to have them!"

An invitation for any general entertainment may be asked for a stranger—especially for a house guest—still more especially for a man.

Example:

Dear Mrs. Worldly,
  My nephew, David Park, is staying with us. May I send him to your dance on Friday?
                                            Very sincerely yours,
                                            Caroline Robinson Town

If the nephew had been a niece instead, Mrs. Town would have added, "If it will be inconvenient for you to include her, please do not hesitate to say so." This would give Mrs. Worldly a chance to answer, if necessary, that her list of dancing men was rather short, and that she would be glad to have Mrs. Town send a man as well as Miss Stranger.

But most properly—and probably—Mrs. Worldly sends a telephoned answer, "Mrs. Worldly will be delighted to see Mr. Park (or Miss Stranger) on the tenth."

A young girl may of course ask her hostess if she may bring a man to her dance; and in fact several dancing men would almost certainly be welcomed!

INVITATIONS TO SIMPLE DANCE SENT BY
SEVERAL MEMBERS OF A FAMILY

This form is intended for several junior members of a family to
send out themselves. It may quite properly be written:

> Mary, Sara, and Jack Brown
> hope you will come to their dance
> on Friday evening, December 23rd
> at 9 o'clock
> Do say yes!

THE CARD OF GENERAL INVITATION

Invitations to important entertainments are nearly always specially engraved, so that nothing is written except the name of the person
invited. But for the hospitable hostess, a card which is engraved in
blank, so that it may serve for dinner, luncheon, dance, lecture, musicale, or whatever she may care to give, is indispensable.

Mr. and Mrs. Stevens

request the pleasure of

company at

on

at   o'clock

Two Knob Hill

INVITATIONS TO RECEPTIONS AND TEAS

Invitations to receptions and teas differ from invitations to balls
in that the cards on which they are engraved are usually somewhat
smaller. The words "At Home" with capital letters are changed to "will
be at home" with small letters or "at Home" with a small "a." At present
the wording "at Home" is in fashion. The time is not set at a certain
hour, but extends over a definite period indicated by a beginning and a
terminating hour. Also, except for very unusual occasions, a man's name
does not appear. The name of the débutante for whom the tea is given
is put under that of her mother, and sometimes under that of her sister
or the bride of her brother.

Mrs. James Town
Mrs. James Town, junior
Miss Pauline Town
will be at home
Tuesday, the eighth of December
from five until seven o'clock
850 Fifth Avenue

Because afternoon teas are supposedly given by women, Mr. Town's name is omitted from this invitation, and Mrs. Town brings her daughter out at a tea alone. Mr. Town shares her responsibility if the party is given in the evening, and he, of course, assumes the responsibility of host in the afternoon as well. Just why his name is omitted has no answer further than "It's always been that way."

Mr. Town's name would probably appear with that of his wife if he were an artist and the reception were given in his studio to view his pictures; or if a reception were given to meet a distinguished guest, such as a bishop or a governor, in which case "In honour of the Right Reverend William Ritual" or "To meet His Excellency the Governor of California" would be engraved at the top of the invitation.

Suitable wording for an evening reception:

Mr. and Mrs. James Town
at Home
Tuesday, the eighth of December
from nine until eleven o'clock

This use of the little *a* and capital *H* as in the example above is a new form borrowed from England. It is pleasing, because it emphasizes the hospitable thought of Home and denotes neither the ceremoniousness of At Home nor the impersonal inclusion of one's whole visiting list at an afternoon tea which "will be at home" announces.

THE FORMAL INVITATION WHICH IS WRITTEN

When the formal invitation to dinner or luncheon is written instead of engraved, note paper stamped with house address or personal device is used. The wording and spacing must follow the engraved models exactly.

Mr. and Mrs. John Kindhart

request the pleasure of

Mr. and Mrs. Robert Gilding Jr.'s

company at dinner

on Tuesday, the sixth of December,

at eight o'clock.

If the device stamped on the paper does not contain the address, it is correct to write this below the hour. It is never proper for a telephone number to appear on a formal invitation.

An invitation should *not* be written like this:

Mr. & Mrs. J. Kindhart request the pleasure of Mr. & Mrs. James Town's company at dinner on Tuesday

etc.

This incorrect invitation has three faults:

(1) Letters in the third person must follow the prescribed form, and this does not. (2) The writing is crowded against the margins of the note paper. (3) The full name "John" should be used instead of the initial "J."

RECALLING AN INVITATION

If for illness or other reason invitations have to be recalled, the following forms are correct. They are always printed instead of engraved, there being no time for engraving.

> *Owing to the sudden illness of their daughter*
> *Mr. and Mrs. John Huntington Smith*
> *are obliged to recall their invitations*
> *for Tuesday, the tenth of June*

When an engagement is broken off after the wedding invitations have been issued:

Mr. and Mrs. Benjamin Nottingham
announce that the marriage of their daughter
Mary Katharine
to
Mr. Jerrold Atherton
will not take place

THE FORMAL ACCEPTANCE OR REGRET

Answers to informal invitations are telephoned more often than not.

The formal acceptance of an invitation, whether it be to a dance, a wedding breakfast, or a ball, is identical in general form.

Mr. and Mrs. Donald Lovejoy
accept with pleasure
Mr. and Mrs. Worldly's
kind invitation for dinner
on Monday, the tenth of December
at eight o'clock

The formula for regret:

Mr. Clubwin Doe
regrets that he is unable to accept
Mr. and Mrs. Worldly's
kind invitation for dinner
on Monday, the tenth of December

or

Mr. and Mrs. Timothy Kerry
regret that they are unable to accept
Mr. and Mrs. Smith's
kind invitation for the tenth of December

"Monday, December the tenth" is sometimes used, but the wording above is best form.

In accepting an invitation, the day and hour must be repeated so that, in case of mistake, it may be rectified and prevent one from arriving on a day and hour when one is not expected. But in declining an invitation, it is not necessary to repeat the hour.

It is best to avoid giving last-minute invitations, but if you are faced with a gap at your dinner table due to the sudden illness of a guest, ask only a very good friend to help you out, never an acquaintance.

MORE THAN ONE HOSTESS

If the names of two or more hostesses appear on an invitation, the envelope is addressed to the one at whose house the party is to take place; or, if it is to be at a club or hotel, to all the names exactly as in the invitation. The acceptance usually reads:

> Mrs. Donald Lovejoy
> accepts with pleasure
> the kind invitation of
> Mrs. White and
> Mrs. Black and
> Mrs. Grey
> for Tuesday, the tenth of November
> at half after one o'clock

If, however, only one of the hostesses is known to you, it would be quite permissible to accept "your kind invitation for Tuesday the tenth . . ." and, leaving out all names, address the envelope to which- ever hostess happens to be your friend. You may write the date in numerals: Tuesday, November 10th.

If there is a vast difference in the ages of the hostesses, the name of the older or oldest appears first, but in any case when you answer you must repeat the same order of names that appeared on the invitation.

INVITATION SENT BY AN ORGANIZATION

An example of this type of invitation:

> *The Alpha Chapter*
> *of*
> *Beta Chi Delta*
> *requests the pleasure of your company*
> *on Monday, the twenty-third of February*
> *at four o'clock*
> *at the Beta Chi Delta House*
> *2 Campus Row*

This is answered:

> Miss Mary Jones
> accepts with pleasure
> the kind invitation of
> The Alpha Chapter
> of
> Beta Chi Delta
> for Monday afternoon, February 23rd

VISITING-CARD INVITATIONS

With the exception of invitations to house parties, dinners, and luncheons, the writing of notes is past. For an informal dance, musicale, picnic, for a tea to meet a guest, or for bridge, a lady uses her ordinary visiting-card. The following examples are absolutely correct in every detail—including the abbreviations.

> To meet
> Miss Millicent Gilding
>
> Mrs. John Kindhart
>
> Tues. Jan. 7.
> Dancing at 10. o'ck.
>
>   350 Park Avenue

> Wed. Jan. 8.
> Bridge at 4. o'ck.
>
> Mrs. John Kindhart
>
> R.s.v.p.   350 Park Avenue

A reply to this may be no more than:

> Accepts with pleasure!
> Wednesday at 4.
>
> Mrs. Robert Gilding, junior
>
>   1000 Fifth Avenue

or

Sincere regrets
Wed. Jan. 8

TELEGRAPHED INVITATIONS

That telegrams are rapidly taking the place of telephoned as well as written invitations sent out by hosts and hostesses of highest fashion is not surprising. In the first place nothing is simpler than handing a list of names with a form note to a telegraph operator and letting the telegraph company do the rest. It is difficult to estimate how long it would take to telephone. It would probably take much longer to call each of the fifty numbers (including busy signals and messages left for those not at home, and enforced conversation with those who, answering themselves, talk for half an hour). But the greatest advantage of telegraphing is that, when giving a spur-of-the-moment party, everyone not only answers but answers at once. These may be formal or informal invitations in wording, and the reply follows the form of the invitation.

THE BACHELOR'S INVITATIONS

The bachelor's invitations are the same as those sent out by a hostess. There is absolutely no difference. He himself telephones or else his butler or maid telephones, "Will Mr. and Mrs. Norman dine with Mr. Bachelor on Wednesday?" Or he writes a note or uses the engraved dinner card. In giving a party of any size, it is correct for him to write on his visiting-card.

> Saturday, April 7.
> at 4. o'ck.
>
> Mr. Anthony Dauber
>
> To hear Tonini play.   Park Studio

This card of an artist is somewhat larger than a man's ordinary visiting-card. But it would be proper for any host alone to send for any informal party he cares to give—except a sit-at-table dinner. It would be quite all right for a buffet supper or luncheon.

DO NOT SEND TINY ENVELOPES THROUGH THE MAIL

Because the Post Office definitely requests that no very small envelopes be sent through the mail, envelopes of a practical size for mailing should be ordered for visiting-cards or other small-sized cards.

(Small envelopes have to be hand-stamped, are easy to lose, and slow up the mounting work of a busy post office.) These larger envelopes, being thinner but of the color and texture of the cards, do not look unmatched, especially since nearly all of us know they actually are matched!

INFORMAL INVITATIONS AND THEIR ANSWERS

Informal invitations are those which are written in the second person, and, though called informal because they have greater latitude than the utterly prescribed pattern of the third-person invitation and reply, they too follow a fairly definite formula. The *colon* is not used after the form of address in a social note. Either no punctuation or a comma, as you prefer.

The informal dinner and luncheon invitation is not spaced according to set words on each line, but is written merely in two paragraphs.

Dear Mrs. Steele
    Will you and Mr. Steele dine with us on Thursday, the seventh of January, at eight o'clock?
    Hoping so much to see you then, I am
                            Very sincerely
                               Caroline Robinson Town

or to a young woman newly engaged to a man unknown to the writer of this invitation:

Dear Phyllis
    Will you and your fiancé lunch with us this coming Saturday, at one o'clock?
    Looking forward to meeting him,
                               Affectionately
                               Caroline

THE INFORMAL NOTE OF ACCEPTANCE OR REGRET

Dear Mrs. Town
    It will give us much pleasure to dine with you on Thursday the seventh at eight o'clock.
    Thanking you for your kind thought of us,
                               Sincerely yours
                               Constance Style

Wednesday

Or:

Dear Mrs. Town

We are so sorry that we cannot accept your kind invitation for Saturday because of another engagement.

With many thanks for thinking of us, and hope to see you soon.

Sincerely

Ethel Norman

To more intimate friends (although usually telephoned):

Dear Caroline

Will you and John dine with us next Monday (the eighth) at seven o'clock promptly, and go afterward to the new opera?

Affectionately

Emily

Acceptance:

Dear Emily

John says "Yes!" and I am simply thrilled at the thought of hearing the new opera and—with you.

With love.

Caroline

Regret:

Dear Emily

John WON'T!

You were sweet to ask us, but he doesn't like opera, and he has been so ill I have to spoil him for a little while.

Much love, and I know you will understand.

Affectionately

Caroline

Informal:

Dear Maisie

Will you and Jack (and the baby and nurse, of course) come out Friday the 28th and stay for ten days? Morning and evening trains take only forty minutes, and it won't hurt Jack to commute for the week-days between the two Sundays! I am sure the country will do you and the baby good, or at least it will do me good to have you here.

With much love.

Affectionately

Susan

To intimate friends:

Dearest Trudy

WHEN will you come? And of course I mean all of you! Don't write me such nonsense as that it is too much to descend upon us five strong! I should be delighted if you were ten! I mean it.

As you know, the house is plain but perfectly comfortable, and you certainly know that seeing the children (and hearing them) about the place is just what Tom and I like best!

So we are back at the beginning.

When? and for how long? The very longest long you can make it! All of July and August, too! Please!

Your devoted
Paula

Dear Bob

How about spending the Fourth with us? From Friday the second to Thursday the eighth—surely you can stay away from the office till Monday the twelfth? Can't you?

Sally

Dearest Sally

Am I never to see you again? Won't you come out for a week in June? Any one you will. Do! I'll come in and get you the day and hour you say.

Devotedly
Lucy

Answer:

Dearest Lucy

Yes, with joy! Will be ready and waiting June 8 at three. It will be heavenly to see you!

Devotedly
Sally

BRIEF NOTES AT PRESENT IN FASHION

One may write a note on the front page of a small sheet of note paper, quite as typically as on the inside of a folded card.

Dear Alice
Will you lunch on Monday at 1:30 here?
Affect'ly
Grace

Answer:

> Dear Grace
> Love to! 1:30 Monday!
> Devotedly
> Alice

TYPICAL NOTES OF YOUNGER GENERATION

Cora darling
> Giving big lunch 1:30 Jan. 26. You've *got* to come.
> Kit

Answer:

> All right darling! I've written it down.
> Cora

THE FORMAL INVITATION BY TELEPHONE

Informal invitations are usually given by telephone, and it is also proper to telephone formal invitations. Such calls, if placed and received by members of the household staff, should follow a prescribed form:

"Is this LEnox 2-0100? Will you please ask Mr. and Mrs. Smith if they will dine with Mrs. Grantham Jones next Tuesday, the tenth, at eight o'clock? Mrs. Jones's telephone number is REgent 4-0011."

The answer:

"Mr. and Mrs. Huntington Smith regret very much that they will be unable to dine with Mrs. Jones on Tuesday, the tenth, as they are engaged for that evening."

Or:

"Please tell Mrs. Jones that Mr. and Mrs. Smith are very sorry they will be unable to dine with her next Tuesday, and thank her for asking them."

Or:

"Please tell Mrs. Jones that Mr. and Mrs. Smith will dine with her on Tuesday, the tenth, at eight o'clock, with pleasure."

The formula is the same, whether the invitation is to dine or lunch, or play bridge or tennis or golf, or motor, or go on a picnic.

"Will Mrs. Smith play bridge with Mrs. Grantham Jones this afternoon at the Country Club, at four o'clock?"

"Hold the wire, please. . . . Mrs. Smith will play bridge with pleasure at four o'clock."

REMINDER CARDS AND NOTES

When invitations have been telephoned, cards reminding guests of their acceptance are in good usage and very sensible. Those who entertain a great deal have cards engraved with blank spaces to fill in with the word lunching, dining, playing bridge, or whatever.

To remind you
that you are
with Mrs. John Smith
on   at   o'clock

Otherwise you write on your visiting-card: "To remind you—Wednesday 10th, 7:30."

To expected house guests, one perhaps writes a note.

Dear Helen
    Just to remind you that you and Dick are coming here on the sixth.

                                      Love
                                      Muriel

INVITATION TO COMMENCEMENT

Each school, college, and university follows its own established customs for Commencement Week. (See Chapter 15, "Popularity and Hospitality at College.") Of the varying forms of invitation to Commencement Exercises sent, the following is the most usual:

The President and Faculty
of Hotchkiss College
request the pleasure of your company
at the Commencement Exercises
on Wednesday morning
the twentieth of June
at eleven o'clock
in the Sterling Gymnasium

Each graduate encloses his or her own card.

THE FORMAL AFTERNOON TEA-TABLE

Chocolate, either hot or iced, often takes the place of the punch bowl.
The tea service is omitted for a wedding collation and the wedding cake added.

THE EVERYDAY AFTERNOON TEA-TABLE
A charming custom for informal entertaining of friends and family.

TEAS, COCKTAILS, AND OTHER AFTERNOON PARTIES

⟨ 12 ⟩

AFTERNOON PARTIES RANGE FROM THE VERY DIGNIFIED reception, through the more or less formal tea dance or tea, to the quite casual cocktail party. The reception has today become primarily a state affair, a public or semi-public gathering in honor of a prominent personage or an important event. Receptions most frequently take place on the diplomatic or civic levels, and arrangements are usually handled by specially designated committees.

The major difference between a reception and a tea is one of atmosphere, like the difference in furnishing twin houses. A reception always takes itself seriously. A tea, no matter how formal it pretends to be, is friendly and inviting. We do not go to be impressed or instructed, but to enjoy seeing our friends and be seen by them.

TEA DANCES

The afternoon tea dance can take the place of yesterday's débutante ball. It may equally well be given to introduce a new daughter-in-law. If it is to be so important as to be a substitute for a ball, the invitations are engraved on a white card and worded:

Mrs. Grantham Jones

Miss Muriel Jones

At Home

on Tuesday, the third of December

from four until seven o'clock

The Fitz-Cherry

Dancing

Today, such invitations, especially those to introduce the bride of a son, are usually written on a visiting-card of the hostess with "To meet Mrs. Robert E. Cavanaugh, Jr." across the top.

To meet Mrs. Grantham Jones, Jr.

Mrs. Grantham Jones

Tuesday, Dec 3,
from 4 until 7 O'clock.
Tea and dancing

It was customary, in times past, to invite the hostess' complete general visiting list, but today a general visiting list usually is smaller and so the invitations are limited to the special friends of the hostess and all the young people it is possible to think of. Also nowadays, houses large enough for dancing are comparatively few, and growing fewer. A coming-out tea is usually given at a club-house or in the small ballroom of a hotel. Remember, however, it is a mistake to choose too large a room, for too much space for too few people gives an effect of emptiness which is always indirectly suggestive of failure; also one must not forget that an undecorated public room needs more people to make it look "trimmed." Although a "crush" may be unpleasant, it does always give the effect of "success." Nothing is more dismal than a half-empty room with bored-looking guests.

The arrangements for a tea with dancing are much the same as for a dance. A grouping of branched smilax behind which the musicians sit (unless they sit on stage), perhaps a few trailing green vines here and there, and the débutante's own bouquets banked on tables nearby where she stands to receive form the typical decoration.

Whether in a hotel, club ballroom, or a private drawing-room, the curtains over the windows are drawn, and the lights lighted as though for a dance in the evening. Further details that might be useful are given in Chapter 13, "Balls and Dances," and in Chapter 14, "The Débutante."

AFTERNOON TEA MENU IS LIMITED

Usually only tea, chocolate, breads, and cakes are served. In some localities coffee is offered instead of the chocolate, and the term "A Coffee" instead of "A Tea" has gained popularity. There may be all sorts of sandwiches, made with rolls and made with bread. There may be layer cake, sliced cake, and all imaginable kinds of little cakes, but nothing more elaborate is necessary. (Hot breads are reserved for the informal varieties of teas.) At the end of the table or on a separate table nearby, there are bowls or pitchers of orangeade or lemonade or punch for the dancers, exactly as at an evening dance.

Guests go to the table and ask whoever is "pouring" for chocolate or tea and help themselves to the sandwiches or cakes, which they eat standing at the table—with cup and saucer held in the left hand.

AFTERNOON TEAS WITHOUT DANCING

Afternoon teas without dancing are given in honor of visiting celebrities, new neighbors, or engaged couples, or a new daughter-in-law, or to "warm" a new house, or for a house guest from another city; or, as is the case most often, for no reason other than that the hostess feels hospitably inclined.

The invitation is a visiting-card of the hostess with "To meet Mrs. Harvey Montgomery" across the top of it and "Jan. 10, Tea at 4 o'clock" in the lower corner, opposite the address.

THE LADIES WHO POUR

At a tea of this description, tea and chocolate may be passed on trays or poured by two intimate friends of the hostess. The ladies who pour are always especially invited beforehand, and are always chosen because they can be counted on for their gracious manners to everyone and under all circumstances. Sometimes after an hour, the first two are relieved by two other intimate friends of the hostess.

It does not matter that a guest going into the dining room does not know the deputy hostesses who are pouring. It is perfectly correct for a stranger to say, "May I have a cup of tea?"

The one pouring should smile and answer, "Certainly! How do you like it? Strong or weak?"

If the visitor says, "Weak," she adds *boiling* water and, watching for the guest's indication, adds sugar, cream (good tea calls for milk, though it seems to be always called cream!) or lemon. Or, preferring chocolate, the guest asks the hostess at the other end of the table for a cup of that. If either hostess is surrounded with people, she smiles as she hands it out, and that is all. But if she is unoccupied and her momentary guest-by-courtesy is alone, she makes a few pleasant remarks. Very likely when asked for chocolate she says, "How nice of you! I have been feeling very neglected. Everyone seems to prefer tea." Whereupon the guest ventures that people are afraid of chocolate because they are counting their calories or because it is often so hot. After an observation or two about the beauty of the table or how delicious the little cakes look, the guest finishes her chocolate.

If the table hostess is still unoccupied, the guest smiles and slightly nods good-by; but if the hostess is talking with someone else, she leaves without farewell.

If another lady coming into the dining-room is a friend of one of the table hostesses, the new visitor draws up a chair, if there is room, and drinks her tea or chocolate at the table. But as soon as she has finished, she should give her place to a later arrival. Except in a public tea-room, a tea-table is seldom set with places. But at a table where deputy hostesses are pouring, and especially at a tea that is informal, a number of chairs are usually available for those who like to take their tea at the table.

Whether or not strangers standing in a queue or at the table in the dining-room at very large and formal entertainments speak to each other, depends upon the friendliness or aloofness, or possibly shyness, of individuals. But at a luncheon, a dinner, or any small party, the roof of a friend serves as an introduction, and strangers who find themselves *seated* together always talk with each other.

THE INFORMAL DAILY TEA-TABLE

The everyday afternoon tea-table is familiar to everyone; there is not the slightest difference in its service, whether in the tiny one-room apartment of the newest bride, or in the drawing-room of Mrs. Worldly of Great Estates. Always the tea-tray stands on a low table in front of the hostess, who pours. For convenience, the tea-table should be of the drop-leaf variety because it can be more easily moved about in a room than a larger solid one.

Its height should be five or six inches above the knees of the hostess, which of course depends upon the height of the chair or sofa that she always sits upon. It is usually about 26 inches high, between 24 to 26 inches wide, and from 27 to 36 inches long, or it may be oval or oblong. A table that has a second deck above the main table is not good because the tea-tray perched on the upper deck is neither graceful nor convenient. A tea-wagon is not in the best taste for *tea!* One of chromium and glass for cold drinks of all sorts which require a quantity of bottles, servers, and glasses is definitely more beautiful as well as most practical because it does not spot or stain.

THE TEA-TABLE

But to return to the table prepared for the correct serving of tea. Except on a table of chromium and glass or with a mirror top, a cloth must always be placed on the table before putting down the tray. It may barely cover the table, or it may hang half a yard over the edges. A yard and a quarter is the average size. A tea cloth may be colored, but the conventional one is of white linen, with little or much needlework or lace, or both, or appliquéd designs.

A tray big enough to hold everything except the plates of food is then placed on the table. The tray may be a massive silver one that requires strong arms for lifting, or it may equally well be of lacquered tôleware. Many of these lacquered trays are exquisite in design and color. Many of the old Chinese or English ones are also priceless. The Mexican bright tin tray is often used. In any case, on it should be the most important item of the tea equipment—a *practical* kettle in which the water should have been boiling before being brought in, with a spirit lamp under it. If carried in by a maid, it is lighted as soon as the tray is set down but *never before,* as a terrible accident can too easily occur. Her uniform or a dainty organdy apron needs only a stray spark to turn her into a flaming torch.

On the tray also is an empty teapot, a caddy of tea, a tea strainer and slop bowl, cream pitcher and sugar bowl, and, on a glass dish, thin slices of lemon.

In a house without any servants the hostess would of course set the tray with everything except the boiling water before her guests arrive, leaving the water kettle on the range in the kitchen. When she is ready for tea, she fills the tea-tray kettle from the kitchen kettle and carries it in.

As already said—especially in a small house—the tea-tray is equally smart if made of modern and not expensive tin, the tea set of china, and the water kettle of glass. There is a fascination in watching water come to a boil through a glass kettle that is entirely lost in the solidity of silver.

Cups and saucers and a stack of little tea plates, all to match, with a napkin about twelve inches square, to match the tea cloth, folded on each of the plates, like the filling of a layer cake, complete the arrangements. Each plate is lifted off with its own napkin. Then on the tea-table, back of the tray, or on the shelves of a separate curate (a stand made of three small shelves one above the other and each big enough to hold a dish or plate or platter), are three varieties of tea foods.

FOOD FOR TEA

The typical variety would be one plate of cake, one of sandwiches, and one of hot bread, but the selection of these items is limited only by the imagination and the skill of the hostess. Many provide no more than crackers or wafers or cookies. Others pile an extra table as well as the curate with toasted crumpets or muffins, or hot buttered oatmeal wafers—cinnamon toast as well as pastry, or cheesecakes and sandwiches of several varieties. All of which is of less importance to the subject of etiquette than the reminder that any such offering as English muffins toasted and buttered and accompanied by a helping of jam must also be accompanied by a small-sized knife and also a fork. The typical implements made for fruit are perfect for this jam-and-muffin require-

ment. The new porcelain-handled ones, decorated with a fruit or vegetable design, are inexpensive and most attractive. They are also very
necessary.

Small tea forks for pastries or "gooey" cakes and small knives to
spread jam and to cut crumpets or English muffins are obviously essential to comfort.

GOOD TEA IS EASILY MADE

Correctly, the hostess herself makes the tea and pours it.

The most important item of the tea service is boiling water, and
plenty of it. The least amount of water not actually bubbling as it is
poured over tea leaves turns the flavor to hay! (A fact that not one hotel
in a thousand takes note of!) Nothing is easier than tea-making; nothing is rarer than the hostess who knows *how!*

To make good tea. First, rinse the pot with a little boiling water to
heat the teapot and pour it into the slop bowl. Then put in a rounded
teaspoonful of tea leaves or one tea-bag for each person or half this
amount if the tea is superquality. Then pour on enough *actually boiling* water to cover the tea leaves about half an inch. It should steep at
least five minutes, or for those who like it very strong, ten, before additional boiling water is poured on. Now pour half tea, half boiling water
for those who like it "weak"; pour it straight for those who like it strong.

The cup of *good* tea should be too strong without the addition of a
little lively boiling water which gives it freshness. The tea is still good
for half an hour if the cup is rinsed and *actually boiling* water is poured
over a half or a third of a cupful of tea. But if the water is not boiling
hard the standing tea will not be fit to drink.

IF TEA MUST STAND

When tea has to stand a long time and for many guests, the ideal
way to make tea is to make it in a big kettle on the kitchen range, very
strong, and let the tea actually boil three to four minutes on the range;
then pour it through a sieve or filter into your hot teapot. The tea will
not become bitter. Moreover, you do not need a strainer! It does not
matter if it gets quite cold. The boiling water poured over no more than
the tablespoonful of tea is hotter than most of us can drink at once.

TEA AT DINING TABLE

Quite a number of hostesses are having tea served at the dining-
room table. Many moderns, for instance, think it simpler and more
comfortable for eight or ten or even for six.

The great majority of hostesses, however, prefer to serve it in the
living-room, with little individual tables placed next to each guest.
These tables are either glass-topped or of stain-resistant enamel or
lacquered wood, and hold plate and cup and saucer, a glass or ashtray,

or any of the other things that must otherwise be balanced on one's knees.

When offering a cup, the hostess asks, "How do you like your tea?" Her guest answers, "Strong, with lemon and one lump," or "Weak, please, no sugar, quite a lot of cream." And it is poured accordingly, tea in cup first, then water, then sugar, then a slice of lemon, or else little or much cream as desired.

If there are likely to be more than five or six people for tea, water must be kept boiling in the kitchen kettle so that it will quickly again come to a boil for replenishing the kettle on the tea-table.

Those sitting near the hostess put out their hands for their cup and saucer. If any ladies are sitting farther off and a gentleman is present, he, of course, rises and takes the tea from the hostess to the guest. He also then passes the curate, afterward putting it back where it belongs and resumes his seat. If no gentleman is present, a lady gets up and takes her own tea which the hostess hands her and carries it to her own little individual table, comes back, takes a plate and napkin, helps herself to what she likes, and goes to her place. If there are no little tables, she either surreptitiously draws near to any shelf-offering piece of furniture, or manages as best she can to balance plate and cup and saucer on her lap.

DRINKS SERVED AT TEA

At an informal or everyday tea a modern hostess often asks a guest who has refused a cup of tea if he or she would like anything else, a whiskey and soda, or cocktail. But it is still not a cocktail party because tea is offered first and is what most of her guests take.

COCKTAIL PARTIES

A cocktail party has become the most popular way for the modern hostess to entertain more guests than she can possibly have to dinner in the limited space of her house or apartment. They may be of any size, from ten or twelve people who can easily be served by the host or hostess alone, to a crowd of as many as can be contained in the available space, with everyone standing almost in imitation of the five o'clock rush hour on the subway.

Let me here make a plea for two or more small parties, rather than trying to invite to a single one all to whom an invitation is due. And by small I mean a party where there will not be more guests than those who can find places to sit. After all even three parties of fifteen will not really cost any more for food and drink than one of forty-five or fifty, and the extra man or waitress needed to serve the larger number can be dispensed with. Further, and what is most important, the guests at the small party will all be comfortable and able to enjoy conversation with each other, which is certainly not the case when they are standing pressed together and where there is no place to put down a glass, or even a burning cigarette for that matter.

If the rooms are large many can be invited, and one or two bartenders engaged for the afternoon, who will stand behind a table and mix and serve drinks for the guests who come to the table. Food is put on another table, and one or more caterer's men see that the platters of food are often replenished, collect used glasses, and constantly empty ashtrays.

DRINKS THAT ARE SERVED

The Martini is still the most popular cocktail, with an Old-Fashioned, or Scotch or Bourbon "on the rocks" gaining in favor. In hot weather Daiquiris, Gin-and-Tonics, or Tom Collinses at least seem to be cooling. The modern trend though is for guests who prefer a longer drink than a cocktail to ask for a Scotch and soda. There must of course always be something non-alcoholic to drink for those who prefer it, such as ginger ale or fruit juice.

INVITATIONS TO COCKTAIL PARTIES

A cocktail party is so informal that invitations to one may be in any form. At the moment the one most often seen is folded like an informal. It often has a picture of a rooster or a cocktail glass on the outside, and inside, "Cocktails at —— o'clock" or "Cocktails from 5 to 7," on such and such a date and the name of the hostess and her address. Otherwise the invitations are often telephoned, written on visiting-cards, or telegraphed.

It is polite and thoughtful to answer cocktail invitations even though they seldom have R.S.V.P. on them.

WHAT TO SERVE WITH COCKTAILS

At a cocktail party you may serve literally every sort of in-fingers-eaten *hors d'oeuvre* or appetizers that you think taste good and look tempting. Olives (either chilled or wrapped in bacon and broiled), or very tiny sausages, broiled; canapés, or thin bread rolled around cheese or bacon, skewered and toasted, or crackers spread with sandwich paste, crabmeat, or lobster in mouthful pieces, or shrimps on little wooden picks with which to dip them in mayonnaise or colorful sauces are favorites.

Before a meal, it is not customary to serve a great variety of canapés. One or two varieties of appetizers on one platter are ample.

Cocktails served before a meal are either made in the pantry and passed on a tray by a servant, or else mixed in the living room and handed around by the host.

SAYING "NO" AT A COCKTAIL PARTY

Why anyone should find it harder to say "No, thank you" to a cocktail than to shellfish or strawberries makes very little sense. If one should answer *"Certainly not!"* in a disapproving tone of voice, it would be extremely rude! But a polite "No, thank you!" is the courteous way of refusing. If pressed further, say seriously, "No—really, I can't!" or as one member of Alcoholics Anonymous says smilingly but firmly, "No can take." In his case, the censure of everyone who knows his situation would rise against anyone so unthinking as to urge him.

HOW TO REFUSE COCKTAILS

If you refuse cocktails or any other alcoholic beverages, it would be very rude to your hosts to let your manner or tone of voice give an impression of disapproval, instead of merely declining for yourself.

If you actually do disapprove and do happen to find yourself out of sympathy with the company you are in, you can leave reasonably soon. It is not only permissible, but best all around for others as well as for yourself to make a polite excuse and leave. There is, however, no excuse for bad manners—ever!

THE DISCOURTESY IS HOST'S NOT GUEST'S

On the other hand the rudeness of a guest who shows disapproval of his host is not any more inexcusable than the thoughtlessness of a host who offers no thirst-quenching fruit juice or tea to a guest who may, for any reason, not wish to take a stimulant. In this particular situation the tomato juice, or whatever it may be, can be kept sealed in its container in the refrigerator rather than prepared only to be wasted. But it should be offered.

In the same way every hostess, unless she is sure of the tastes of her guests, should be prepared to offer caffeine-free coffee as an alternate to regular after-dinner coffee. Or if she herself prefers caffeine-free coffee, she should offer her guests regular coffee as well.

YOUNG PEOPLE AFRAID TO SAY "NO"

The most serious "No, thank you" problem is of course that of young people who are afraid of saying "No" to whatever others suggest, because they fear it may lessen their popularity. Wanting to be popular is natural. It is also natural to go along with the crowd, do what the others are doing, and think what they think. In matters which are not important this is quite the right thing to do. But when a small inner voice says, "Don't do that! It's cheap; it's wrong," then it is time to say "No," and hold to it. As for real popularity—it does not really belong to the sheep, after all.

In school, in college, in politics, or anywhere else, the person who follows a leader into doing things with which his own conscience does not agree is taking the first step, not toward success, but toward being held in contempt even by those whom he follows. A real leader is one who says "No" lightly, and yet this "No" has an immutable finality. Such a person says very little about what he will or won't do. In fact, he rarely forces his opinion upon anyone, but if asked, he gives his answer as truthfully, as uncritically, and as briefly as possible, especially if he thinks his opinion may be in serious disagreement with that of the other persons. Such people are respected and never lose the confidence of their friends.

"NO" SHOULD BE AS FRIENDLY AS "YES"

Of course, the obvious point to be made is that frankness must be adjusted to courtesy by means of the warmth of one's manner. It is quite amazing how frank we can be when our manner is sympathetic, eager, or appreciative. We can say "No" and make it sound almost as pleasant as "Yes." On the other hand, we can say "No" and make it sound cold, critical, and almost as affronting as a blow. We can say, "I'm sorry, no," and make it sound a poignant regret, or as casual and light-hearted as the flitting of a butterfly. Or it can come down upon the sensibilities of others with the weight of a sledge-hammer.

The secret of how this is done is first of all an innate attitude by which, while we refuse, we hold no criticism of those who do not agree with us. At the very moment we set ourselves up with an "I am better than thou" attitude, we become as intolerable to others as we ourselves are intolerant.

THE GARDEN PARTY

The really formal garden party is so far out of key with the ever-increasing simplicity of today, that its briefest outline would seem quite sufficient for all practical purposes.

Its first requirement is a garden with an unusual amount of walk-about space, either lawn or terrace, which is set out with chairs and tables—either under garden umbrellas, or placed in the shade. Further than this, in every other respect it is exactly the same as any outdoor wedding reception if one omits the bride and groom and their attendants.

PARTIES IN THE GARDEN

A party in the garden is as different from a garden party as a simple buffet supper is from a dinner of ceremony. If many people are expected, a large table is set as for an afternoon tea, outdoors—the weather permitting—or else on the veranda or in the dining-room, and the accent is on cold beverages. Tea is iced and has plenty of mint and usually lemon, and perhaps other fruit juices are added. If there is chocolate, it is cold and poured into glasses with whipped cream. Food consists of nothing but breads and cakes. These can be of whatever variety, and as many or few as one may choose. Usually there are thin sandwiches cut either in diamond or heart shapes but not otherwise fancy.

A very pleasant hospitality that is popular with those having lovely gardens is that of being at home in the garden on several successive Saturdays or Sundays, or possibly on several days in the same week. The object is to show the garden when it is at its very best. There is a period in almost every garden when it is just a little more beautiful than it is likely to be at another time, as when the tulips and spring flowers are a riot of color or when the roses are at their peak. These invitations, usually written on visiting-cards, are "At home in the garden" (or other similar phrasing) and then the dates and hours:

> Mon. Wed. and Sat.
> July 20-22-25
> between 5 and 6 o'ck

BALLS AND DANCES

·◦⟨ 13 ⟩◦·

ALTHOUGH GREAT PRIVATE BALLS HAVE BECOME ALMOST
unknown in the past forty years, this book would be incomplete if
descriptions of all balls of splendor were omitted. This therefore is the
way one is given.

HOW TO GIVE A BALL

If the hostess does not put all the arrangements into the hands of
a social specialist, she makes an appointment to see the manager of the
hotel she prefers, or of other suitable assembly rooms, and finds out
which evenings are available. She then telephones—or most likely the
manager telephones for her—and engages the two best orchestras for
the evening when both the orchestras and the ballroom are at her dis-
posal. It is also important to try to select an evening not already taken
by another hostess who would be likely to ask too many of the same
young people she intends to invite.

Of the two, music is of more importance than choice of place. You
cannot give a ball or a dance that is anything but a dull promenade
if you have dull music. At all balls there must be two orchestras, so
that the moment one finishes playing the other begins. At dignified
private balls, dancers do not stand in the middle of the floor and clap
as they do elsewhere because the music does not stop until the ball is
over.

Having secured the music and engaged the ballroom, dressing-rooms,
and lounge or other rooms—where guests can talk and smoke, and very
probably play cards—as well as the main restaurant after it is closed to
the public, the hostess next makes out her list and orders and sends out
her invitations.

INVITATIONS

The fundamental difference between a ball and a dance is that,
while only those of approximately one age are asked to a dance, ball

invitations include all the personal friends of the hostess, no matter what their age.

If the ball is for a débutante, all the débutantes whose mothers are on the general visiting list are asked, as well as all young dancing men in these same families. All the débutante's own friends are of course asked, but older members of their families are not necessarily included, unless they happen to be friends of the hostess.

BORROWING A LIST

A lady who has a débutante daughter, but who has not given any general parties for years—or ever—and whose daughter, having been away at boarding school or abroad, has therefore very few friends of her own, must necessarily, in sending out invitations to a ball, take the list of young girls and men from a friend or a member of her family.

In a small community it is especially cruel to leave out any of the young people whose friends are all invited, and a hostess can, of course, be as generous as she chooses in allowing extra invitations for friends of friends.

ASKING FOR AN INVITATION TO A BALL

It is always permissible to ask a hostess if you may bring a dancing man who is a stranger to her; men who dance are always in demand, and the more the better, but it is rather difficult to ask for an invitation for an extra girl, no matter how pretty she is, unless she is to be looked after by the person asking for the invitation. In that case the hostess is delighted to invite her. Invitations for older people are rarely asked for. Nor are invitations ever asked for persons whom the hostess already knows. This is a definitely established rule of etiquette which assumes that she would have sent them an invitation had she cared to. It is, however, not at all out of the way for an intimate friend to remind her of someone who, in receiving no invitation, has more than likely been overlooked.

DECORATIONS

Ball decorations have on occasions been literally astounding, but as a rule no elaboration is undertaken other than greens in corners and trailing vines wherever most effective.

SUPPER

The sit-down supper is the most elaborate ball supper, but a buffet supper that begins at one and continues until three or later, and to which people go when they feel like it, is in highest fashion. A sit-down supper is always served in the restaurant, which is closed to the public at one o'clock; the entrance is then curtained or shut off from the rest of the hotel. The tables are decorated with flowers and the supper service opened for the ball guests. Guests sit where they please, either "making up a table," or a man and his partner finding a place wherever there are two vacant chairs. At a private ball guests do not pay for anything or tip the waiters because the restaurant is for the time being the private dining room of the host and hostess.

Suppers are no longer as elaborate as they used to be. Years ago no balls were given without champagne at supper.

There is always an enormous glass bowl of punch or orangeade— sometimes two or three bowls, each containing a different iced drink —in a room adjoining the ballroom. And in very cold climates it is the thoughtful custom of some hostesses to have a cup of hot chocolate or bouillon offered each departing guest. This is especially welcome at a holiday dance in the country for those who have a long drive home. And infinitely better than the "one for the road" offered to one who is driving a car!

A DANCE

A dance is merely a ball on a smaller scale. Fewer people are asked to it, and it usually has simpler decorations and refreshments.

But the real difference is that invitations to balls always include older people—as many as, if not more than, younger ones. The invitations to a dance for a débutante, for instance, include none but very young girls and young men; or, if the dance is given by a hostess for herself, it includes only her personal group of intimate friends.

A dance, as well as a ball, may be given in the banquet room or smaller ballroom of a hotel, or in the assembly or ballroom of a club.

Simple dances as well as other informal parties will be found in Chapter 32, "Simple Party-Giving."

A BALL IN A PRIVATE HOUSE

For a ball there is always an awning and a red carpet down the front steps of the house. A chauffeur at the curb opens the car doors. If there is a great crush, there is a detective in the hall to investigate anyone who does not have himself announced to the hostess. In fact, is has become customary in New York and other big cities to have admission cards engraved and sent to all those who have accepted.

All the necessary appurtenances, such as awning, red carpet, coat-hanging racks, ballroom chairs, as well as crockery, glass, napkins, waiters, and food, can be supplied by hotels or caterers. In houses like the Gildings', footmen's liveries to match those of their own footmen are kept in reserve to be worn by the caterer's men. In other words, fifteen of the twenty footmen in Gildings' liveries who wait at big parties are caterer's men and five, or fewer, their own.

Unless a house has a ballroom, which practically none has today, the room selected for dancing must have all the furniture moved out of it; and if there are adjoining rooms and the dancing room is not especially big, it adds considerably to the floor space to put no chairs around it. Those who dance seldom sit around a ballroom, anyway, and the more informal grouping of chairs in the hall or library is a better arrangement than the wainscot row or wallflower exposition grounds. The dance floor, it goes without saying, must be smooth and waxed.

THE HOSTESS MUST BE PROMPT

The hostess must be ready to receive on the stroke of the hour specified in her invitations. If the ballroom opens on a foyer at the head of a stairway, she usually receives at this place. Otherwise she receives in the ballroom near the door of entrance.

Guests arriving are announced, and after shaking hands with the hostess, they pass on to the ballroom. A man who has received an invitation through a friend is usually accompanied by the friend, who presents him. Otherwise, when the butler announces him to the hostess, he says, "Mrs. Norman tells me you said that I might come." And the hostess shakes hands and says, "How do you do. I am very glad you came."

THE PERFECT HOST

The duty of seeing that guests are looked after, that shy youths are presented to partners, that shyer girls are not left on the far wallflower outposts, that the dowagers are taken in to supper, and that elderly gentlemen are provided with good cigars in the smoking room, falls to the perfect host.

Hosts and hostesses should try to see that their guests are having a pleasant time. Guests have a responsibility too. Once they have accepted an invitation, they should be pleasant and act as if they were having a good time, no matter how dull the party might be.

BALLROOM ETIQUETTE

A ballroom is still the one background against which gentlemen and ladies behave with almost exaggerated decorum. Ladies do not sit with crossed knees lolling against their chairs. Properly a lady doesn't lean back at all when she is sitting on one of the little gold chairs that are usually around the edge of the room against the wall. Neither a man nor a woman can smoke in a ballroom without destroying the distinction of the whole assemblage.

But even so, an onlooker who has been brought up to know the balls of a generation ago is too often impressed at any modern ball with the gracelessness of the young people who walk across a ballroom floor. The athletic young woman of today strides across the ballroom floor as though she were on the golf course; the happy-go-lucky one ambles— shoulders stooped, arms swinging, hips and head in advance of chest;

others trot, others shuffle, others make a rush for it. The young girl who can walk across a room with grace is rare.

Older gentlemen still give their arms to older ladies in all promenading at a ball, since the customs of a lifetime are not broken by one short and modern generation. Those of today walk side by side. At public balls, when there is a grand march, the lady always takes her partner's right arm.

DUTY DANCES

Every young man must dance at least once with the hostess, the girl or girls the dance is given for, the hostess of a dinner he went to before the dance, and both girls he sat beside at dinner. He must of course at a dance to which he brought a girl dance the first dance with her. He must also watch during the evening to be sure she is not stuck too long with any one partner, and take her home after the dance.

DISTINCTION VANISHED WITH COTILLION

The glittering display of tinsel satin favors that used to be the featured and gayest decoration of every ballroom is gone; the cotillion leader, his hands full of seat checks, his manners a cross between those of Lord Chesterfield and a traffic policeman, is gone; and much of the distinction that used to be characteristic of the ballroom is gone with the cotillion. There is no question that a cotillion was prettier to look at than a mob scene of dancers crowding each other for every few inches of progress.

The reason why cotillions were conducive to good manners was that people were on exhibition, where now they are unnoticed components of a general crowd. When only a sixth, at most, of those in the room danced while others had nothing to do but watch them, it was only natural that those on exhibition should dance as well as they possibly could, and since their walking across the room and asking others to dance by "offering a favor" was also watched, grace of deportment and correct manners were not likely to deteriorate.

The cotillion usually takes place following the supper at a ball. All the gentlemen and their ladies are seated on small gilt chairs around the sides of the ballroom. The cotillion leader indicates by motioning to fifteen or more couples that they are to dance. After a short interval the music is stopped, and the dancers go to the favor table where each lady is given a favor. On receiving it, she then presents it to one of the gentlemen who is still seated. He, in turn, then temporarily leaves his partner and dances with the lady giving him the favor.

In the same way each gentleman of the first group receives a favor for the lady he will choose from those seated with whom he will then dance.

Those who in this way have not been called out remain seated and watch the dancing until the music stops. Those of the first group then seat themselves and the cotillion leader motions out a second group of fifteen who dance, receive and give favors as before. This is repeated again for each succeeding group until the supply of favors is exhausted.

There are always a small group dancing and a larger number watching, providing the incentive to look one's loveliest and handsomest and to dance one's very best. The girls, of course, vied with each other to secure the greatest number of favors, which were often of considerable value.

USHERS ARE VERY HELPFUL

The hostess who would insure the success of a dance of any size chooses from among the young men whom she knows best a number who are tactful and self-possessed to act as ushers. They are recognized by white or other distinguishing boutonnières as deputy hosts. They must see that wallflowers are not left decorating the seats in the ballroom, and it is also their duty to relieve any young man who has too long been planted beside the same "rosebud."

The ushers have little chance to follow their own inclinations, and unless the honor of being chosen by a prominent hostess has some measure of compensation, the appointment—since it may not be refused—is a doubtful pleasure. An usher has the right to introduce any man to any girl without knowing either one of them personally, and without asking permission. He may also ask a girl (if he has a moment to himself) to dance with him, whether he has ever met her or not, and he can also leave her promptly, because any stag called upon by an usher must dance. The usher in turn must release every stag he calls upon by substituting another, and the second by a third, and so on. In order to make a ball "go," meaning to keep everyone dancing, the ushers have on occasions spent the entire evening in relief work.

At a ball where there are ushers, a girl standing or sitting alone would at once be rescued by one of them, and a rotation of partners presented to her. If she is hopeless—meaning a poor dancer—even the ushers are helpless! The answer is of course that she must either learn to dance or seek her popularity elsewhere.

On the other hand, on an occasion when none of her friends happen to be present and there are no ushers, even the greatest belle of the year can spend an equally distressing evening.

The greatest advantage of ushers is that their presence gives courage to many a young man because assured of rescue to dance with a girl he would otherwise avoid.

DANCE PROGRAMS

The program or dance-card has some undeniable advantages. A girl can give as many dances as she chooses to whomever she chooses; and a man can be sure of having not only many but uninterrupted dances with the one he most wants to be with—provided she is willing. Why the dance-card is unheard of at private balls is probably because the youth of today does not care to take his pleasure on schedule. He likes to dance when the impulse moves him; he also likes to be able to stay or leave when he pleases. In New York there are often two or three dances given on the same evening, and he likes to drift from one to the other just as he likes to drift from one partner to another, or not dance at all if he does not want to. A man who writes himself down for the tenth dance must be eagerly appearing on the stroke of the first bar. And if he does not engage his partners busily at the opening of the evening, he cannot dance at all—he may not want to, but he hates not being able to.

So again we come back to the problem of the average young girl, whose right it is, because of her youth, to be light-heartedly happy—and not to be terrified, wretched, and neglected. The best solution seems to be for her to belong to a group; or the problem may be solved if her hostess has been thoughtful enough to have efficient ushers at her dance.

THE ADVANTAGE OF BEING ONE OF A GROUP

If a number of young girls and young men come together—better yet, if they go everywhere together, always sit in a flock, always go to supper together, always dance with one another—they not only have a good time, but the girls will be popular with drifting odd men also. If a man knows that, having asked a girl to dance, one of her group will inevitably cut in, he is eager to dance with her. He knows that he will not be marooned with her. Or if he can take her to the others when they have danced long enough, he is not only delighted to be with her for a while but to sit with her and the others off and on throughout that and every other evening, because since there are always some of them together he can leave them again the moment he chooses.

A certain group sits in precisely the same place in a ballroom, to the right of the door, or to the left, or in a corner. One might almost say they form a little club; they dance as much as they like, but come back "home" between whiles. They all go to supper together, and whether individuals have partners or not is scarcely noticeable, not even known by themselves.

CUTTING IN

When one of the stags sees a girl whom he wants to dance with dance past, he darts forward, lays his hand on the shoulder of her partner, who relinquishes his place in favor of the newcomer, who then dances with the girl until a third in turn does the same to him.

When cutting in, the following rules must be observed:

1. The partner who was first dancing with a girl must not cut back

on the man who took her from him. He can cut in on a third man if he wants to, especially if he is giving her a rush.

2. He must not continue to cut in on the same man when the latter dances with other partners.

REFUSING TO DANCE

If a girl is sitting in another room, or on the stairs, with a man alone, a second one should not interrupt or ask her to dance. If she is sitting in a group, he can go up and ask her, "Don't you want to dance some of this?" She then either smiles and says, "Not just now—I am very tired," or if she likes him, she may add, "Come and sit with us!"

To refuse to dance with one man and then immediately dance with another is an open affront to the first one—excusable only if he was intoxicated or otherwise actually offensive so that the affront was justifiable. But under ordinary circumstances, if she is dancing, she must dance with everyone who asks her; if she is not dancing, she must not make exceptions.

A girl who is dancing may not refuse to change partners when another cuts in. This is the worst phase of the cutting-in custom; those who particularly want to dance together are often unable to take a dozen steps before being interrupted. Once in a while a girl will shake her head "No" to a stag who darts toward her. But that, under most circumstances, is considered rude. And there are young men who make it a rule never again to ask a girl to dance who has once refused to dance with them.

Another unhappy phase of cutting in is that the man with whom she dances best invariably makes her own dancing conspicuously graceful, and therefore every stag in the room wants to cut in. On the other hand, a man who dances like a jumping-jack, stamping on her toes, is not only a torture to her but makes her seem almost as awkward as he, and no one comes to her rescue. If he doesn't know the polka, the mambo, or the latest dance steps, he should say so. A wise girl therefore stops dancing at once, saying, "Let's sit out the rest of this dance." This, by the way, according to a trend of today, may also be suggested by the man.

ASKING FOR A DANCE

When a man is introduced to a girl, he says, "Would you care to dance?" She either replies, "Certainly" or "Yes, I'd like to very much," or usually she says nothing but gets up, or turns to him, and dances. At the end of the dance, whether it has lasted one minute or sixty, the man says, "Thank you!" or "Thanks ever so much!" On occasion he adds, "That was wonderful!" In this case she says, "Thank you," casually not seriously.

If they have danced only a few steps, ordinarily she says nothing when cut in on, unless she says gaily, "See you again!"

At the end of quite a long dance, when he says, "Thank you," she also says, "Thank *you*."

A girl never asks a man to dance, or to go to supper with her, though she may, if she is one of a flock, say, "Come and sit at our table!" This however would not imply that in sitting at their table he is supposed to sit next to her.

In asking a girl to go to supper, a man says, "May I take you to supper?" He should never say, "Have you a partner?" as she is put in an awkward position. To have to answer, "No, I haven't" is a belittling statement. And for him to add, "Sorry, I was going to take you to him!" makes the situation impossibly awkward. If he has a supper partner, he must go and find her. He says, "I'm so sorry I have to find my supper partner; if I leave you here, can your partner find you?" To this she has to say, "Yes, indeed" or "Just leave me by the door" (or wherever a partner is most likely to ask her). This is somewhere near the stag line but not thrust into it.

A BALL IS NOT A DANCING SCHOOL

Since a girl may not without rudeness refuse to dance with a man who cuts in, a man who does not know how to dance is inexcusably inconsiderate if he cuts in on good dancers. If at home, or elsewhere, a girl volunteers to teach him, that is another matter, but the ballroom is no place to practice.

SUPPER CLUBS AND CABARETS

In London, supper clubs are clubs in reality; but, with very few exceptions, those in America are merely restaurants or night clubs to which the public goes after the theatre. People sit at small tables ranged around a small dancing floor space upon which a gay floor-show performance is given. Before and after the performance there is general dancing.

Those sitting at the same table dance only with each other; there is little if any interchange of cordialities between the groups at different tables.

These clubs come properly under the head of restaurants, for which details of behavior are to be found in Chapter 8.

THE DÉBUTANTE

·‹[14]›·

"PRESENTING A DÉBUTANTE TO SOCIETY," NEVER BEFORE and rarely long past her eighteenth birthday, has a quaint flavor, reminiscent of social customs long past. And yet it is not at all out of order for a present-day mother to give whichever of the following entertainments she may choose for her daughter's "coming out," meaning being presented to society. The most elaborate of these, possible only to parents of means, is a ball. Less elaborate, and far more popular, is a small dance which presents the débutante to her own friends. Third, is a tea dance. (Sending out a mother's visiting-card, with her daughter's name below her own to announce to the world that the daughter is eligible for invitations, is rarely used.) Today's débutante usually comes out at a big dance which, except in a very large city, may well be for all the débutantes of the year or for a smaller group of girls, or it may be even a dance given cooperatively by a group of parents who get together and share the expense of a coming-out party for their daughters.

A DÉBUTANTE BALL

The ball for a débutante is the typical ball! The débutante "receives" standing beside her mother or whoever else may be hostess, and farthest from the entrance, whether that happens to be on the latter's right or left. As they enter, the guests approach the hostess first, who, as she shakes hands with each, turns to the débutante and, repeating the name that has been announced to her, says, "My daughter" or "You remember Cynthia, don't you?" or merely "Cynthia."

Each arriving guest shakes hands with the débutante as well as with the hostess; if there is a queue of people coming at the same time, there is no need of saying anything beyond "How do you do?" and passing on as quickly as possible. If there are no others entering at the moment, each guest makes a few pleasant remarks—for instance, "How beautiful your bouquets are!" A friend of her mother probably says, "Cynthia dear, how lovely you are tonight" or "Your dress is enchanting!" Her boy friend exclaims, "My, you look wonderful tonight!" The girls assure her, "Your dress is simply divine!"

It is still customary in most cities to send a débutante a bouquet at her coming-out party. They may be bouquets really, or baskets, or other decorative flowers, and are sent by relatives, friends of the family, her father's business associates, as well as by younger men who are her friends. These bouquets are always banked as a background for her when she stands to receive. The débutante always holds one of the bouquets while receiving, sometimes the same one, sometimes several in succession so as not to show partiality to any special giver.

FRIENDS OF THE DÉBUTANTE RECEIVE WITH HER

At a ball, where the guests begin coming at eleven o'clock, the débutante stands beside the hostess, usually her mother, and receives until about twelve o'clock—later if guests continue to arrive. Then she is free to join the dancing, and usually dances the first dance with her father.

At all coming-out parties, the débutante invites a few of her best girl friends to receive with her. Being asked to receive means little more than being described afterward in the society columns of the press. Actually they rarely stand in line, and other than adding to the lovely picture, they have no duties beyond that of their own amusement.

AT SUPPER

The débutante goes to supper with a partner whom she herself chooses—meaning that she always makes up her own table which includes her most intimate friends. If she is very popular and does not wish to center her attention on one man, an easy way out is to ask her brother. Her table is usually in the center of the dining-room, and somewhat larger than the other tables surrounding it. Also, a card on it says "reserved." If the supper is a buffet one, the débutante's special group sits together wherever they find space.

The afternoon tea dance to introduce a débutante is described in the chapter on teas, and the very small dance needs little comment, because, except for size and decoration, its pattern is precisely the same. When the dance, whether in the evening or at tea time, is given in a private house most of the furniture is, of course, rearranged.

WHAT SHE WEARS

At a ball, the débutante wears her very prettiest evening dress. Old-fashioned sentiment prefers that it be white and that it ought to suggest something light, airy, gay and, above all, young. For one who prefers to wear colors, a pastel—faint rose, pale blue, or light yellow—

is perfectly suitable. But not scarlet or Yale blue, and on no account black, no matter how sophisticatedly chic she thinks she would look in it.

At an afternoon tea the débutante wears a semi-evening dress. Her mother wears an afternoon dress, not an evening one. Both mother and daughter wear gloves, and neither they, nor the young girls receiving, wear hats. Hats are of course worn at a wedding reception because it follows a religious service.

ADVICE TO A DÉBUTANTE

Let us suppose a worldly godmother is speaking, and that you are a young girl on the evening of your coming-out ball. You are excited! Of course you are! It is your evening! There is music, and there are lights, and there are flowers everywhere, tables heaped with bouquets— all for you! You are young and gay, and you have on the dress that of all those you looked at seemed to you the prettiest. Even your mother and married sister have for the moment become, for all their smartness, merely background; and you alone are the center of the picture. Up the wide staircase to the ballroom come those persons of importance—who mean "the world." They are coming on purpose to see *you!* You can't help feeling that the glittering dresses of the beautiful women, the gleaming white shirt-fronts of the men, as well as the best clothes of all the younger people, were all put on for you.

You shake hands and smile to a number of older ladies and gentlemen. Then suddenly, half-way up the stairs you see Josie and Ann and Alan and Harold. Of course your attention is drawn to them. You are vaguely conscious that the butler is shouting some stupid name you never heard of—that you don't care in the least about. Your mother's voice is saying, "Mrs. Zzzzz——"

Impatiently you give your hand to someone—you haven't the slightest idea who it is. So far as your interest is concerned, you might as well be brushing away annoying flies. Your smiles are directed to Josie and Ann. As they reach the top of the stairs, you dart forward and enter into an excited conversation, deliberately overlooking a lady and gentleman who, without trying further to attract your attention, pass on. Later in the winter, you will perhaps wonder why you alone among your friends were not invited to the cabaret party of the Holmes. The answer is that the lady and gentleman of whom you were so rudely unaware happened to be Mr. and Mrs. Holmes. Probably friends of your mother or business associates of your father. Sooner or later rudeness always exacts a toll. And now you have entirely forgotten that you are a hostess, and furthermore that you have the whole evening, beginning at supper, when you can talk to these friends of yours! You can dance with Alan, and Harold, and Jimmy, all the rest of the evening; you can spend most of your time with them for the rest of your life if you and they choose. But at a party of which you are the hostess, commonest civility demands that you behave courteously to *all* your guests.

It takes scarcely five seconds to listen to the name that is said to you, to look at the one to whom the name belongs, to put out your hand willingly and not as though doing something hateful to you, and with a smile say, "How do you do, Mrs. Holmes?" who then passes on. It takes no longer to be cordial and attentive than to be distrait and casual and rude, yet the impression made in a few seconds of time may easily gain or lose a friend. When no other guests are arriving, you can chatter to your own friends as much as you like; but as you turn to greet another, you must show pleasure, not annoyance, in giving her or him your attention.

A happy attitude to cultivate is to think that strangers are like packages in a grab-bag, and that you can never tell what any of them may prove to be until you know what is inside the outer wrappings!

As friends who have sent you flowers approach, you must thank them; you must also write later an additional note of thanks to older people. But to your relatives or your own intimate friends, your oral thanks, if appreciatively made, are sufficient.

A FEW DON'TS

Don't think that because you have a pretty face, you need neither intelligence nor manners. Don't think that you can be rude to anyone and escape being disliked for it.

Whispering and giggling are always rude. Everything that shows lack of courtesy toward others is rude.

If you would be thought likable, don't nudge, or paw, or finger people. Don't hold hands or walk arm-about-waist in public. Don't allow anyone to paw you. Petting is cheap—and pawing common. Don't hang on anyone for support, unless necessary! Don't lope across a dance floor swinging your arms. Don't talk or laugh loudly enough to attract attention, and on no account force yourself to laugh. Nothing is flatter than laughter that is lacking in mirth. If you laugh only because there is something irresistibly funny, the chances are that your laugh will be irresistible too. In the same way, a smile should be spontaneous, because you *feel* happy, and pleasant. Nothing has less allure than a mechanical grimace or a pinned-on grin, as though you were trying to imitate a toothpaste advertisement.

YESTERDAY'S BELLES

Some years ago the measuring rod of a young girl's social success was the number of her partners in a ballroom. Today, although ballroom popularity is still important and pleasant, it is by no means the

CHILDREN
ARE
PEOPLE

by

EMILY POST

Author of

Etiquette—*The Blue Book of Social Usage*

The Personality of a House

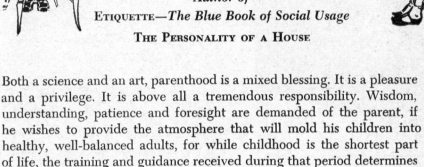

Both a science and an art, parenthood is a mixed blessing. It is a pleasure and a privilege. It is above all a tremendous responsibility. Wisdom, understanding, patience and foresight are demanded of the parent, if he wishes to provide the atmosphere that will mold his children into healthy, well-balanced adults, for while childhood is the shortest part of life, the training and guidance received during that period determines the remainder of life.

Emily Post has written CHILDREN ARE PEOPLE to help parents in their training of children and in the building of a foundation for enduring comradeship. This volume proves her own understanding of youngsters and of the kind of guidance they need to become well-bred, well-balanced adults—happy and successful at meeting life's problems.

In this warm and sympathetic book, Mrs. Post covers children's growth from birth to young adulthood. She gives answers to countless puzzling problems and many practical ideas for handling troublesome situations. With insight and wisdom she tells how to develop the child, and at the same time she shows how the child develops the parent, for as they teach children, parents in turn learn from their offspring. Stories drawn from her own memory and vast experience color every chapter; sentiment and humor enliven every page.

A perennial best seller in a brand new edition, this popular guide has been brought up to date with today's people and events. From the first page to the last, CHILDREN ARE PEOPLE is highly informative, extremely valuable and thoroughly delightful.

Illustrations from the book by George A. Brettell and
Henrietta McCraig Starrett.

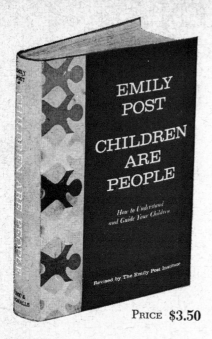

EMILY
POST

CHILDREN
ARE
PEOPLE

*How to Understand
and Guide Your Children*

Revised by The Emily Post Institute

Price **$3.50**

CONTENTS

FUNK & WAGNALLS COMPANY, Inc. • **360 Lexington Ave., New York 1**

beginning and end that it used to be. Even if you aren't as light as a snowflake on your feet, you can still have a good time.

As repeated several times in this book, the day of the belle is past; beaux belong to the past too. Today is the day of woman's equality with man; and if in proving her equality she has come down from a pedestal, her pedestal was perhaps a theatrical property at best and not to be compared for satisfaction with the level ground of the entirely solid position she now occupies.

There was a time when wallflowers went night after night to balls where they either sat beside a chaperon or spent the evening in the dressing room in tears. Today a young girl who finds she is not a ball-room success avoids ballrooms and seeks her success elsewhere. She sizes up the situation exactly as a boy might size up his chances of making the baseball or the football team, or in trying out for the oboe spot in the band. Perhaps she is a good swimmer or a good sport on a rough hiking trip.

TODAY'S SPECIALISTS

The girl of today soon discovers, if she does not know it already, that to be a ballroom success it is necessary first of all to dance really well, and to treat each partner or a man who cuts in on her as if he were Fred Astaire, although he may step on her ankles. A girl may be as beautiful as a young Diana or as fascinating as Circe, but if she is heavy or steps on her first partner's toes, never again will he ask her to dance. And the news spreads in an instant.

The girl of today therefore knows she must learn to dance well, which is difficult, since superb dancers are born, not made; or she must go to balls for supper only, or not go at all. Or perhaps she skates or hunts, or plays a really good game of tennis or golf, each one of which opens a vista leading to popularity and the possibilities for a good time, which was after all the mainspring of old-fashioned ballroom success.

And since the day of femininity that is purely ornamental is a "has been," it is the girl who does things well who finds life full of interests and of friends and of happiness. The old idea that measures a girl's popular success by the number of trousered figures around her has also passed. It is quality, not quantity, that counts; and the girl who surrounds herself with indiscriminately chosen and possibly cheap youth excites, not the envy, but the derision of other people. To the highest type of young girl today it makes very little difference whether, in the inevitable group in which she is perpetually to be found, there are more men than girls or the opposite.

This does not mean that human nature has changed—hardly that! There always are and doubtless always will be any number of women who love to parade a beau just as they love to parade a new dress. But the tendencies of the time do not encourage the tasteless parading attitude. It is not considered a triumph to parade a new beau every day any more than to parade a new dress every day, but rather an evidence of lack of discriminating taste.

THE SECRET OF POPULARITY

The secret of popularity is unconsciousness of self, enthusiastic interest in almost anything that turns up, a genuine interest in people, and inward generosity of thought and impulse outwardly expressed in good manners.

AT COLLEGE

·◦[15]◦·

YOUNG MEN AND GIRLS, DURING THEIR FOUR YEARS IN college, not only are receiving an academic education, but also are taking part in the social life of their school. Etiquette on the campus must cover some rather specialized situations, but there is one basic consideration that *always* applies: Whatever constitutes proper and decent behavior for young men and girls anywhere is correct in any college situation.

PERSONAL POPULARITY

Of course, your decision to attend college is a very serious one, and should be made chiefly because of your wish for further education, or to study for a particular career. As is true of everything, you may expect to gain from your studies in proportion to the time and interest you devote to them. But surely you do not want or expect your years in college to be a "grind," devoted solely to the acquisition of book-learning. To be able to make people like you, to get on easily with those who are thrown into close and continued contact with you, and to make friends is of vital importance to you now, and will be all the rest of your life.

The best way to make yourself liked and to make friends is to like people enough to become interested in what interests them, and to be outgoing and friendly. Don't overlook this rule! The truly interested and outgoing person is very rare. Most of us go through life mentally wrapped in the cotton wool of our own affairs. We go about thinking of what *we* are going to do, what *we* hope or fear is going to happen to *us*, instead of thinking or caring about what happens to those about us.

Sensitive awareness of the reactions of others is a priceless gift. There are far too many of us who never note the effect that our unthinking speech or behavior is quite plainly having upon the feelings of others. If you would be liked by those with whom you come in contact, you should cultivate sensitiveness of perception. This does not mean, of course, that you should become oversensitive. Our sensitiveness must have for its object the understanding of the points of view and feelings of others. To let this sensitiveness center about ourselves is to make us easily offended or hurt. We develop a sense of inferiority when our vision becomes focused inward—it is as if we had put our heads into mirror-lined divers' helmets. If we have this tendency we should remember that most people intend no offense to us, and usually are not thinking about us at all; and those who are have only kind intentions, unless we have made ourselves disagreeable.

PROBLEMS OF THE VERY CLEVER

Although many people think that those who are intelligent are usually unpopular, this is not necessarily the case. But there are special difficulties that the very clever encounter in making friends. The very clever girl, for example, may make an average young man feel inferior, while an equally clever man may resent her rivalry. Her friends, therefore, are likely to be limited to the few who are more clever than she.

The real handicap of a man who is clever is the likelihood of his seeming conceited. It is of course just as unfortunate to *seem* as to *be*. This is often the cause of the unpopularity of the shy, whose self-consciousness may well be misinterpreted as self-satisfaction. If only the shy might be inoculated with a little real conceit! But those of us who do not have the problem of shyness should shun any hint of conceit in our behavior toward others.

DO GOOD LOOKS COUNT?

This question cannot be answered with an unqualified "Yes." Attractive looks are an asset, certainly, but a bright, responsive personality is far more friend-making than great beauty—even for a girl. True, the great beauty may get easily what others have to work for. On the other hand, these others know that what *they* get is more likely to be securely theirs. Men, too, will find that the possession of a charming personality will be of more value than any "matinee idol" appearance. Good grooming, however, is the one aspect of good looks that always counts. You should always make a neat, clean appearance. Campus clothing should be casual and comfortable, suited to the informal activities of the college day. You should never overdress, but neither should you go to the other extreme and wear to class the dungarees which were perfectly appropriate for hanging dance decorations in the gymnasium.

WHEN IT'S YOUR TURN TO TALK

Although slang may be a "lingua franca" among students, it has no place in the lecture room or when addressing members of the faculty.

Don't let the use of slang become so habitual that you can't express yourself in perfect English.

On the campus, be outspoken when the subject is one that really matters to you, but don't overplay the capital "I." Absent-mindedness on the subject of your own abilities is a most valuable habit. You can be sure that your outstanding abilities will be recognized by others, and much more appreciated if they are not pointed out by you!

At bull sessions where every imaginable subject is discussed, you should remember to allow others to express their opinions. Don't force others to listen by shouting. Keep your raised voice for cheering at games. One of the best ways to make friends is to learn to understand the points of view of others. Above all, never take a group discussion too seriously or personally and leave with a chip on your shoulder or with hurt feelings.

IN A CO-EDUCATIONAL COLLEGE

Accept the companionship of girls or men, as the case may be, impersonally, without measuring each member of the opposite sex as if she or he were a prospective wife or husband.

When encountering a man and girl obviously engrossed in conversation, do not join them. Nod briefly if you happen to catch the eye of either, but pass by without changing your pace. If they want a third, they will call to you.

In many activities in which men and girls compete for positions, such as the college newspaper, the girl must realize that she stands solely upon her ability, and not upon her beauty, or her personal charm.

WELCOME THE WELCOMING COMMITTEE

Granted, your first days in college will be harried and hurried, but they'll also be a lot of fun. You'll be learning new things, meeting new people, and adapting to a whole new life. Orientation or Welcome Week is included in the first-of-the-semester activities at many colleges. It is a time devoted exclusively to the freshman, for in this week there are group meetings to explain such matters as study programs, registration routine, the faculty-advisor system, and other facts of campus life. Faculty members are available for the new students to meet and talk with. There is also generally an evening devoted to a presentation of extra-curricular activities, with representatives from each student group describing its program and membership qualifications.

Orientation Week is a busy procession of events, all devoted to helping the new student feel at home in his new environment. If you will welcome the Welcoming Committee with interest and cordiality, you will receive the full benefits from this special time—in addition to acquiring many first-of-the-year friends that will be yours for four years and possibly for life.

DORMITORY LIFE

Consideration is the key to successful dormitory living, whether it be for a roommate, your hall mates, the dormitory personnel, or the maintenance staff. The facilities of the dormitory are yours, but they're also your roommates'. This means sharing the mirror, the shower, the desk, the lounge; it means preserving the life of all dormitory property; it means keeping "your side" in order. It also means being considerate of your roommate's sleeping—and studying—habits, and observing the Quiet Hours which the dormitory imposes.

Obeying the regulations which every dormitory must enforce will not make you a "goody-goody." It is merely showing *thoughtfulness* to those among whom you must live, for dormitory rules are only designed to make the living of many together congenial.

A custom much to be deplored, but not likely to disappear, is that of borrowing among dormitory mates. Avoid borrowing like the plague, but you must of course respond graciously when asked to lend an article of yours, whether you accept or refuse the request. If you *must* borrow, don't do so at the last minute, and always take better care of borrowed property than of your own. Whether you borrow a book or a sweater, its prompt return to the owner as soon as you have finished with it is essential.

The house mother is there to guide you, not to guard you. Treat her with the respect you would show any older person, but also with friendliness. Dropping into her apartment-suite with a few friends for a chat before dinner is a gesture which takes little time, but will be appreciated for its thoughtfulness. Never, of course, allow yourself to impose on her time or otherwise become a nuisance.

Christmas gifts to the house mother and tips to the staff are certainly in order. The manner of presentation depends on campus custom. Usually a box is passed, with a tip being collected for those on the household staff, and the gift from all presented to the house mother; otherwise, a small remembrance can be given individually.

IN CLASS AND AFTER

The professor or lecturer in a college classroom may be more remote than was the teacher in your high-school classroom, but you nevertheless owe him quiet, attention, and your fully alert mental powers.

In college, the responsibility for handing in assignments on time is *yours*, even though you may not be pressured and reminded to do so.

When you recite in class, speak so that you can be heard by the professor as well as your fellow-students. But talk only if you have something to contribute, or if you really don't understand a point. Killing time in the classroom is a trick of many pseudo-scholars, but such vocal antics will fool nobody but the student himself!

The student encounters faculty members not only in the classroom, but also in joint student-faculty committee meetings, departmental teas, extra-curricular activities, and on the campus. Not even the increased informality of today permits treating the most "hail-fellow-well-met" young instructor as "one of the boys." A professor should never be addressed as "Doc" or "Prof." If, however, a graduate assistant himself requests it, it is all right to call him by his first name. But in general faculty members should be treated with the respect due to their position and age.

With a host of extra-curricular activities confronting him, the student must selectively determine which ones interest him the most. He may choose among those that supplement academic interests, such as a history, education, or pharmacy society, or a Cosmopolitan Club which offers opportunities to speak the language of his major, or among those that provide a contrast to them, such as religious organizations, student government, and any kind of athletic club.

You will miss a lot if you don't join in any of these activities during your years in college. On the other hand, if you're inclined to be an "organization man," remember that moderation is always the wisest course. Consider Joe College, for example: he is an officer of the Men's Athletic Association, a member of the Players' Club, the basketball team, and a Greek fraternity, and he writes for the humor magazine. Always busy, Joe has no time for his studies. Even worse, he has made too many acquaintances, and too few friends.

Every club, no matter how informal, functions through some degree of parliamentary procedure. Respect for the rights and opinions of other members and the Chair is essential. *Robert's Rules of Order* may not be followed to the letter, but being able to conduct a meeting is one of the responsibilities of a club officer.

Participating in extra-curricular activities is an excellent way to make new friends. You will encounter fellow-students whose leisure interests are similar to your own, but whom you might not meet during your regular academic hours.

THE GREEK PICTURE

Fraternities and sororities are an integral feature of most campuses throughout the country, but it would be a mistake to believe they are essential to a collegiate social life. Whatever the Greek picture on your campus may be, follow your own individual tastes and needs in deciding whether to affiliate with a fraternity or remain an Independent.

Fraternity-house living ideally is "brotherhood under one roof," but in reality it becomes forty or so distinct individuals who share a bond of social fraternity. This bond of brotherhood is in fact one of the advantages of belonging to a fraternity, and it often forms a basis for post-collegiate social life. Then too, there is the cooperative endeavor of group work, whether it be channeled to raise money for a charity or to build a decorative float for Homecoming.

To the neophyte, Rush Week appears to be a confusing jumble of parties, faces, and favors. Its purpose is to afford both the rushee and the fraternity or sorority an opportunity to get to know each other so that interests and personalities can find a meeting ground in the pledging of new members. Each fraternity usually gives an Open House to initiate Rush Week, followed by a succession of smaller parties until, by the end of the week, the rushee has decided which of several fraternities he is most interested in, and the fraternity has determined which rushee will receive bids. The most important thing to remember about Rush Week behavior is that *naturalness* is the only key (as on all occasions) to self-presentation. If you are yourself, and not someone you think a fraternity expects you to be, then your hosts will like you for what you are—yourself!

Don't "push" or be presumptuous during rushing season. The Interfraternity Council and National Panhellenic have set up regulations which strongly prohibit such things as hot-boxing (cornering a rushee and promising a bid). A rushee has no claim whatsoever on any fraternity, even if his father was once a member, and should in no way let it be known that he anticipates receiving a bid.

THE BIG SOCIAL EVENTS

Every campus has a series of special social events scheduled throughout the academic year, such as Homecoming or Winter Carnival. These occasions are the result of much preparation, and have a pattern established by tradition or by the ingenuity of this year's steering committee.

One school's Homecoming might start on Friday night with a campus variety show. Saturday morning is the parade, with floats representing the efforts of fraternities, sororities, and dormitories. The Homecoming game on Saturday afternoon is probably followed by teas at all the houses for visiting alumni. Saturday night there will certainly be a formal dance to mark the climax of the weekend festivities.

Etiquette for these activities is the same as for any events in which young people participate. Cooperation with the organizing committees is necessary for everyone's enjoyment of the occasion. Consideration of others is particularly important here because of the large group involved, and means arriving on time at the theatre, being unostentatiously "part of the crowd" at the game, and being a good representative of your school, your group, and most important, yourself.

You should remember that the Homecoming Weekend is in honor of the alumni. Members of the class of '27, having their reunion, may seem pretty far removed from your college situation. They may even be "old fogies!" But they are loyal alumni, giving financial and moral support to your school, and they should be given respect and consideration. A little outgoingness from your group would do much to make these returning alumni enjoy their visit to your campus.

FRATERNITY WEEKEND

To the members of a fraternity, one of the most important events of the year is their annual weekend. It may take place in the fall or in the spring, and—if it is a men's college—may bring an influx of girls to the campus. There may be a Friday night informal party at the fraternity house; on Saturday a beach or lake all-day party, complete with a picnic and softball, or perhaps a ski excursion in mid-winter. Saturday night is the fraternity formal dance, held at a country club or hotel ballroom, usually preceded by a sit-down dinner. Sunday the fraternity members and their dates may go to church together, and, after Sunday dinner at the house, the weekend closes.

Though the girl pays for her own transportation to and from the campus, the man should, as soon as she has accepted his written invitation, inform her of the train or bus schedules. If it is impossible for him to meet her, he should arrange for a fraternity brother to be there, or see that a taxi will be available.

The girl may stay in the college's chapter house of her sorority, in the girls' dormitory, or at a local hotel, perhaps sharing a room with another "import." The man should make all the arrangements, and enough in advance to enable his date to have the most comfortable and convenient accommodations available. He, of course, assumes the financial obligations.

He also pays for all her meals, for all transportation after she arrives at the local railroad depot, and for the flowers he gives her the night of the formal dance. He would be well advised to inspect his wardrobe more than one week in advance of the weekend, and make sure his evening clothes, dress shirt, and the other garments he intends to wear are ready for use.

Whether the man's date is from his campus or from out of town, he owes her all the courtesies due a guest. He shouldn't leave her alone while he hobnobs with his fraternity brothers. Though he is in his element, she may not be in hers, and his thoughtful attentiveness to her will enhance the enjoyment of the weekend for all.

WHAT SHALL SHE WEAR?

The first question that Meg probably asks her mother, even as she reads the invitation, is "What can I wear?" And almost always this will be followed by, "Oh Mother, I *must* have . . ." and her list may run on through half a dozen formidable items. The cost of clothes for the occasion may be a real problem, or it may be that Meg can afford to buy everything her heart desires. In either case, practicality would limit both the buying and the packing to the fewest possible items.

It is always a temptation to a girl to take along every attractive thing she owns or can buy, but she should realize that she may have to share with another girl a minimum of closet room and drawer space. The only sensible way for Meg to make a list of necessary clothes is to decide what is suitable for each of the events that will take place, and whenever possible to wear clothes already in her wardrobe.

Meg's clothes list for a typical weekend should be based on the following schedule: For traveling, a simple, dark dress or suit is always neat. For Friday night's informal party or theatrical, Meg should wear a shirtwaist or sheath dress, in silk or fine wool, and carry a small purse. For Saturday, casual sports clothes, suitable to the season and the activity, and low-heeled shoes are appropriate.

Saturday night is the formal dance, for which Meg wears her prettiest evening dress and accessories. Her clothes, by the way, must have the effect of simplicity suitable to her age. The boy who invited Meg wants his friends to see her as he remembers her at home; he does not want a blasé woman who looks thirty-five, instead.

Sunday dinner is to be served at noon, and Meg should wear the suit or dress in which she arrived, since she will leave for home immediately afterward on an afternoon train.

According to this schedule, one traveling dress, one theatre dress, one sport outfit, and one evening dress is all Meg will need. If she travels in a warm, loose coat it can double as an evening wrap. A pretty robe or a pair of slacks might be added for lounging. Be sure to take the proper accessories—jewelry, shoes, purse, gloves—and undergarments for each costume.

If the college is in a warm climate, Meg should naturally take linen or cotton dresses. But for a winter weekend in the north, her clothes should be warm and include heavy gloves and galoshes. Nothing could be less appealing to a young man than a girl in such unsuitable clothes that she can take no part in any outdoor sports. High-heeled evening slippers for walking on snow, and gossamer clothes when the thermometer is zero, will not seem alluring to any boy, but will make him wish he hadn't handicapped himself with such a nuisance.

THE THANK-YOU PRESENT

Except for whatever she may get in the way of clothes, a girl's expenses are limited to those of traveling. It is true that in a number of colleges it is the rather charming custom to contribute toward a thank-you present donated to the house. Usually one who has been at the previous year's house party fixes a box with a money slit in it and each girl puts into it what she can. No one knows how much each puts in. Whatever amount has been collected is then entrusted to the house president to buy some item for the house—if possible this will be marked with the date, and known thereafter as the present from the girls of that year's party.

DON'TS FOR ALL HOUSE PARTY VISITORS

To begin with packing: DON'T put off looking at your bag until the last moment, unless it is new or you know it is in perfect condition. DON'T arrive with a shabby, down-at-heel suitcase with handle half off or lock broken, or packed with straps carelessly hanging out, which to every fastidious man will discount the effect of your otherwise lovely appearance as completely as though you wore unshined shoes. Neat, compact, good-looking luggage will please a man much more than the smartest hat ever bought.

DON'T forget to dress mentally as you pack. Stockings? Now, shoes? Slip? Dress? What goes with it? Belt, clips or flowers or other accessories, bag, etc. No one is less likely to be pleasing than the girl who begins to borrow from the other girls, or sends a boy on repeated trips to the drugstore for the comb, or toothpaste, or whatever else she forgot. And yet: DON'T make your luggage one inch bigger or one ounce heavier than necessary, unless you are driving your own car! Any girl who brings more than one moderate-sized bag will not add to her popularity either with the others who are going in the same car or with her host who meets her at the station, and perhaps has to carry this extra weight up a steep hill to the house where she is to stay. DON'T forget that on holiday occasions in small college towns there may not be taxis or cars for more than about one out of ten. Therefore DON'T count on being that one.

Upon your arrival at the house, DON'T greet the house mother and other chaperons as though they were inanimate objects upon whom you need waste no attention. DON'T show an alive and interested manner toward the boys and indifference toward the girls. When you are shown to the room which you are to share with another girl, DON'T claim the bed you like best by throwing your bag on it. At least make the gesture of asking the other girl if she cares which she takes.

DON'T take up more than exactly your share of the closet space and drawer space. If you have brought too many things for the space that is yours, you must leave some of them packed in your bag, and leave the bag neatly closed.

DON'T monopolize the bathroom; remember that others are waiting. If you have a bathroom to yourself at home, all the more reason for remembering this. DON'T leave your personal belongings around on all the bedroom furniture. DON'T leave powder scattered over everything. Later, when you pack to leave, DON'T leave powder or smears of lipstick, or bobby pins in the bureau drawer. Also open dresser drawers wide to be sure you have not left panties or other very personal items behind. DON'T pretend to have forgotten an especially fetching scrap of nylon and lace, in the belief that it will increase Toby's interest in you. This is a cheap trick and he will recognize it for what it is. DON'T leave rubbish behind you, either. Remember that the men may have to move back into the house before there is time to have their rooms cleaned. DON'T forget, throughout your stay, to respect the wishes of the house mother and other chaperons. Be sure to say good-by to her and to the others, and to thank them for their many kindnesses.

But now, to turn back to the evening of your arrival—at the time, let us say, when you all congregate before dinner and introductions are made. In the fraternity house with no outsiders except each brother's best girl, the introductions would very likely be not only by first names but by nicknames: "Sally, this is Slim," and Babe, and so on. But if outsiders are included, then introductions will be "Miss Jones, Mr. Lake."

DON'T however wait for introductions under the house roof. Friendliness should be your natural inclination. It would be too bad to be thought a snob when you are really only shy. If you are afraid you won't make friends, don't forget that nearly every other girl is feeling exactly the same!

If you don't know anything about the boy seated beside you at dinner, ask your personal host, who should be seated at your left, about him first so as to know what to talk to him about. It is cynical advice, but it is as true today as it was in the day of Aspasia that a man is rarely bored if you talk—but with some intelligence—about him. DON'T, however, get his abilities confused with those of someone else, and DON'T in any case lay flattery on with a trowel!

At the dances, greet the chaperons as though you liked them. The moment of enthusiastic attention that courtesy demands is one of the easiest and most rewarding social investments you can make.

DON'T refuse to dance with anyone who cuts in.

Throughout the days of your visit, DON'T think only of what you like to do; that is, DON'T insist on playing ping-pong if your host would like you to make a fourth at bridge—unless your ping-pong is expert, and your bridge is very bad indeed. In this case tell him you would be delighted to play, only you know how sorry everyone else will be if you do. But in general to do whatever the majority suggest is no more than what is expected of you everywhere—unless what is suggested is something you think is wrong. For instance, there is no obligation to drink anywhere at any time—unless you choose to. (For tact in refusing cocktails, see Chapter 12.)

DON'T be jealous of every attention your best boy friend pays to another girl. The more you show your dislike for this interest, the more jealous he is likely to try to make you. Don't show that you hate to be teased or you'll be a target for even those who never thought of teasing until you showed how badly you take it.

Don't show chagrin or disappointment. The fundamental secret of the popular house guest is to show delight in everything pleasing, and to be blind, deaf, and insensible to annoyance or disappointment. Above all, don't do anything that can seem unappreciative of the efforts made for your pleasure by the man who is your host. It is not playing the part of a fascinating woman of the world to try to impress him with your powers by attracting one of his classmates; on the contrary, it is the maneuver of an extremely stupid as well as vain young woman, whose lack of loyalty to a brother is resented by every member of his fraternity. The real siren is one who makes all other men wish they were in her host's shoes. Never, therefore, should you risk letting one of them think your treatment of a friend of theirs unfair, even though your motive may be free from guile. Certainly you can like his friends, but chiefly because they are his friends, but don't look upon them as prospective scalps you would like to hang from your belt.

Above all, don't forget that the friendship of other girls is the crown of your own success. Popularity with girls may not make you popular with men, but earning their dislike by treating them with contempt and by trying to take their boy friends will end in ostracism of yourself. The really popular girl is popular with girls as well as boys.

In short, don't try to be the house party coquette in an attempt to see how many of the men you can add to your chain of admirers! It is natural that every man wants the girl he asks to this big social event at his fraternity to be liked by all his brothers. But you must not confuse the friendliness shown you under these circumstances with that which might otherwise be given to you for yourself alone. Remember that there is a close bond in the brotherhood that is much stronger than any interest in a strange girl.

GRADUATION

Any definite schedule for Commencement Week cannot be given, since it differs in each of our thousands of colleges. But let us suppose that graduation exercises take place on a Monday. On the Friday preceding, there is probably a senior ball. This is as different in character from all the house-party dances that have preceded it throughout the year as a christening is from a children's party!

Instead of scenes of romance multiplied almost as many times as there are girls or men in college, the commencement picture is of a festivity that includes the whole family. Parents, grandparents, aunts, uncles, and little brothers and sisters arrive in hordes.

Because visiting families stay either at the hotel, or the inn, or in the houses of those who take in guests during this period, a graduate's best girl usually comes with his family. Or perhaps she has already made arrangements to go with her own family (when a brother or relative is also a member of the graduating class), or if neither his nor her family will be there, she may come with an intimate girl friend whose family is going also. She goes to her friend's fraternity house, of course, to dinner, or to afternoon tea, or to whatever entertainment each house gives for its visitors during this week.

Another typical event of Commencement Week is a baseball game on Saturday afternoon. This is either a serious game between the home team and that of a neighboring college, or possibly a burlesque between the present team and picked stars of yesterday. And on Saturday night perhaps a show is put on by the graduates of five, or ten, or fifteen years back. Or possibly on Saturday evening there is a torchlight parade that ends in dancing around a bonfire made of barrels and boxes into which are thrown the books of whatever subject each student disliked most.

The most important event on the week's calendar is the Sunday morning service in chapel, at which the baccalaureate sermon is preached. The sermon is addressed to the students, but the families and friends are expected to be present also. In the afternoon, the president of the college and his wife are most probably at home to students and their families, and the rest of this day is spent much as each fraternity, sorority, or group has arranged.

Graduation also brings the necessity for observing many details of courtesy which should be emphasized. A note of thanks written by hand and on note paper must go to everyone who has sent a present either to a young graduate man or woman. This note need not be long, but it should express appreciation and be written as promptly as possible.

"I can't thank you enough, dear Aunt Agatha, for the check you sent me, which will be a wonderful help toward—" (whatever it is to be used for); or, "Dear Aunt Martha, Thank you for the beautiful flowers you sent me. They could not take your place, but they were a reminder of your loving thought." Or, "Dear Uncle Charles, Your letter was the finest thing possible to receive. And I shall certainly try to do my best in the job you are offering me."

Since invitations to graduation exercises are usually limited to a very small number for each student, it is improper to send announcements that say So-and-So will be graduated on such-and-such a day. To send them out afterward, as all other announcements are sent, would be entirely proper although not often done.

CLOTHES FOR COLLEGE

Although this book is not concerned with the subject of fashion, the following comments are in answer to the high school graduates who each year ask about the clothes that they will need as freshmen in college. Since the majority explain that their budget is small, it may be comforting to realize that among the clothes you now have it is probable that your favorite ones, which for this reason have been time and again seen by everyone at home, will be brand-new to everyone at college.

Moreover, even if you are one of those fortunate few who can buy everything new, it will be much better to wait and see what the other girls will be wearing, so that instead of having chosen clothes that you may quite possibly find all wrong, you will be able to get what you actually need. In most large towns and cities, department stores and specialty shops have College Shops with experienced saleswomen to guide you.

Your campus clothes may be as informal as the rules and customs of your college permit. Remember, however, not to make the mistake of going into town, or wherever life is conventional, without changing into clothes which will be in keeping with those surroundings.

THE CHAPERON
AND HER MODERN COUNTERPARTS

·•>[16]<•·

IT IS HARD FOR THE MODERN GENERATION TO UNDER-
stand the position of the chaperon of yesteryear. We are likely to think
of a chaperon as having been a kind of policewoman professionally
employed to look after the morals, as well as the manners, of a young
girl. Although the chaperon has largely become a lost convention, there
are still a few situations in which a genuine chaperon is required. Today,
however, parental *training* has largely taken the place of the chaperon's
protection.

A RESIDENT CHAPERON FOR THE
YOUNG GIRL WHO LIVES ALONE

No young girl still in, or barely out of, her teens should live alone.
A young girl who has no parents usually is able to find a home with
other relatives. But in the case of a young girl who has no immediate
family but an ample estate, her guardians customarily engage a resident chaperon to look after her and to protect her reputation from Mrs.
Grundy and her ilk, until she marries or becomes old enough to persuade
a doubting world that she is thoroughly able to protect herself. (The
"age of reason" may be considered to begin after graduation from college, or in some cases even high school. An unmarried young woman
who has a career may quite properly take a small apartment with two
or three friends, or live in a women's residence hotel.

A resident chaperon must first of all be a lady, but she need not
be an old lady! She can perfectly well be a reasonably young unmarried woman, or an older woman, either single or widowed. Usually
the chaperon keeps the house, but she is never called a "housekeeper."
Nor is she a secretary, although she probably draws the checks and
audits the bills.

If she is to be of any real use, a chaperon must be a person of wisdom as well as sympathy and tact, for it is of vital importance that
confidence exist between the chaperon and her charge. No young girl

is likely to be influenced by the opinions of one in whom she has not learned to believe. If the girl has any really objectionable companions, for instance, the chaperon's criticism of them must be accurate and their failings serious according to the standards in which the girl herself believes, if it is to be effective.

THE HOUSE MOTHER: A RESIDENT
CHAPERON FOR MANY YOUNG GIRLS

The most usual chaperon today is the house mother, who, as her title implies, is a substitute mother for the girls or young women in her charge. She is to be found in preparatory boarding schools, college dormitories, or metropolitan women's residence hotels.

The house mother should have the qualities mentioned above. She should be neither inquisitive nor interfering, except for seriously considered, valid reasons, since she must serve as an advisor to the young girls. Charm is a necessary quality, because she will be meeting and greeting the parents, girl friends, and beaux of her charges. She'll also be asked to serve at teas, be at the head of reception lines, and preside at luncheons, dinners, and other social occasions.

In addition to these duties, the house mother may be in charge of the kitchen staff and make up or approve the weekly menus. She supervises the houseboys' duties of lawn work, keeping the trunk room in order, and all maintenance work around the house. She also superintends the cleaning staff and any other personnel needed for the efficient running of the house.

Genuine friendliness and kindness are at least as important as being charmingly gracious when a visiting V.I.P. is on hand. A house mother must offer friendship to all the girls under her wing, and not show favoritism to the few to whom she may feel partial.

A GIRL IS HER OWN BEST CHAPERON

From an ethical standpoint, the only chaperon worth having in the present day is a young girl's own efficiency in chaperoning herself. The girl who has been trained to appraise every person and situation she meets needs no one to sit beside her and tell her what to do. She must develop expertness in handling situations herself, since the modern girl is allowed to go without protection. She must be able to gauge the reactions of various types of persons, particularly of men, under varying circumstances. She must learn to judge which man has the instincts of a gentleman, and which is likely, if given the opportunity, to exhibit traits quite different. The girl who, in addition to trained judgment, has the right attributes of proper pride and character needs no chaperon—ever. But if she lacks these qualities, not even Argus could watch over her!

BEWARE OF "MRS. GRUNDY" EVEN TODAY

Apart, however, from the consideration of ethics, which is concerned with what the girl herself thinks or feels, or the motives behind what she says or does, there still remain the appearances to be considered! Many young people today are foolishly inclined to ignore this; they feel they can act independently of public opinion.

It is necessary to act with propriety in the eye of the world for the same reason that one does not shout in the street: if you would keep your affairs private, you should never let yourself become a subject for public discussion. There are too many people like Mrs. Grundy even in this modern day, whose gossip still influences a world which seldom takes the trouble to sift appearance from fact.

To be sure, Mrs. Grundy is a disagreeable old woman who has nothing to do but meddle in affairs which do not concern her. She probably lives in a solid, well-preserved, brownstone house equipped with periscope, telescope, and radar, and situated on a bleak hill so that nothing interferes with her view. Her business in life is to track down and destroy the good name of every woman who comes within range. The pretty young woman living alone is her special quarry. The news of her every going out and coming in, of everyone whom she receives, when they come, how long they stay, and at what hour they go, is checked with a stopwatch and is spread posthaste. However, a young woman who behaves with natural propriety is not likely to excite the gossip of Mrs. Grundy, who is looking for the juciest morsels she can find.

WHEN MAY A YOUNG GIRL ENTERTAIN IN
HER PARENTS' HOME?

In recent years it has become proper not only for a débutante, but also for her little sister of thirteen or so, to invite friends to a party without the necessity of chaperonage other than that of her parents' roof. Parents should, however, arrange to be present at some time during the party. Perhaps they could be home when their daughter's guests arrive, and then leave the young people alone for a few hours, returning to serve the refreshments or bid the guests good-by.

A girl of sixteen could properly invite a boy she knows well to have dinner with her in her parents' home on an evening when they are dining out, with, of course, their consent. The age at which a girl may go out alone with a boy in the evening, and how late she may stay out, will vary according to the responsibility of the girl herself and the custom of the community. Only a parent can make the exact decision. In general, a girl of fourteen may go out with a boy to an early movie, or even to an early dinner in a good restaurant; most of the parties she goes to will however be those at the homes of friends, or dances organized by her school. Her parents should at all times know where and with whom she is.

PARENTS WHO ARE OVERPROTECTIVE

Many parents, unfortunately, become overprotective of their teen-aged children, restricting their activities and friendships unreasonably. Perhaps they are afraid that more lenient guidance would give the impression that they are indifferent to their daughter's well-being. They should realize that overzealous guarding will hamper their child's development of responsibility and judgment, and that unnecessary restriction may separate her from her friends. It is admittedly difficult to achieve the middle road of reasonable supervision, but it is important to the child's social development to receive freedom as well as guidance during these years of adolescence.

SOME PROPRIETIES THAT SHOULD STILL BE OBSERVED

If a young girl's family is not at home she must not, on returning from a party, invite or allow any man to "come in for a while." If he persists, she should answer casually but firmly, "Sorry, another time," and bid him "good night." However, if her parents are home and have been notified, it is perfectly all right to invite her friend in for a sandwich and a half hour of conversation. He should not overstay his welcome, and if he sees the family is tired and the hour late he should leave.

Several years ago, some members of the Junior League started a practice that is quite sensible—merely telephoning home just before leaving a dance. The telephone call gives the mother time to tidy her hair and put on a fresh wrapper before coming to the door. This is not unreasonable from the daughter's point of view. If she has poise, loyalty, and is sure of herself, she can make her practice of telephoning an evidence of respect for her mother, and there will be no more question about her going to the telephone than about going to get her coat! Moreover, if she has these attributes of character, she will agree that the type of man who might resent her mother's presence is not one of the type that she hopes to marry.

An unmarried young girl should not go on overnight auto trips with any young man, even with her fiancé, since convention still decrees that she may not stop in a hotel with a young man unchaperoned. However, a girl of eighteen may perfectly well go on a weekend trip with several couples to a ski resort or a dude ranch. In this case the presence of a few other girls in the party is sufficient protection.

THE CHAPERON AT A SCHOOL DANCE

Chaperons for a school dance may be recruited from among the faculty, the parents of the students, or other townspeople; they may be single persons or married couples. Chaperons are the ringside participants at the dance, responsible for the general discipline and order of those dancing. A school dance should be fun, and the chaperons should never put a damper upon it, but should rather enhance the party by their own enjoyment of it. While a chaperon is not expected to serve as a "bouncer," he or she should be prepared to put down the firm foot of authority when some young person gets too boisterous.

A committee of one or a few may be in charge of securing the chaperons for the gala evening. The committee should select two or three chaperons who will be congenial with one another and with whatever the event is to be. The individual who would be a very suitable chaperon at a Senior Prom might be only a wet blanket at a Winter Carnival. It is thoughtful to invite chaperons at least two weeks in advance so they can obtain baby-sitters or make any other necessary arrangements. If you are asking single persons, it is kind to tell them they may bring escorts. The same committee is responsible for buying flowers for the women, and for writing thank-you notes to each chaperon after the dance.

Chaperons are somewhat at the mercy of the students during a dance. Since it is not their party, nor are their contemporaries present, they can have a dull evening unless the young people, as the party-givers and -goers, help to make it enjoyable for them. Greet them early in the evening and introduce your friends. Chat with them occasionally during the evening. It would be extremely thoughtful if a young man asked a woman who is alone to dance, or if a young couple exchanged partners for a dance with a chaperoning couple.

And, of course, bid the chaperons good night, and thank them for having come to your dance.

WHEN A BACHELOR ENTERTAINS

The bachelor-about-town may occasionally entertain in his apartment, perhaps for a large group at a cocktail party, or for a few friends at dinner. Propriety decrees that four is a better number than two for a small dinner party. A young woman visiting a man's apartment alone is still frowned upon, and talked about, by Mrs. Grundy, and a wise girl avoids a tête-à-tête in a bachelor's apartment. A hard and fast rule, however, cannot be made, since the answer will always be determined by the girl herself. Her character is her chaperon, and will provide the ethical standard in each situation.

A young woman's very acceptance of a man's dinner-for-two invitation shows her confidence that her host is a gentleman who will not ply her with cocktails for nefarious purposes, and his behavior should certainly justify her confidence. It is best if she knows him quite well before accepting such an invitation. Regardless of the relationship, it is hoped that the theatre or another party will follow the dinner for two.

If she is invited for coffee and conversation at the young man's apartment after the theatre, the young woman may suggest having them in her own apartment or, even better, in a restaurant.

A BACHELOR'S HOUSE PARTIES

Young men who either live out of the metropolitan area or who have a country house may give week-end house parties to which both men and women are invited. The host's mother or sister would be the best possible chaperon; any married couple would, of course, be suitable, or the mother of one of the young people could be the chaperon.

The bachelor as host should be sure that sleeping accommodations for his guests are adequate and comfortable. If conditions are somewhat primitive at his country house, he should see to it that the women have precedence in using the bathroom. He should arrange for transportation into town for any guests who may wish to go to church.

The male guests may offer to share some of the expenses of such a weekend, and their host may accept this offer if he chooses. But any bachelor who undertakes to entertain for a weekend must expect to pay all the expenses himself. If, however, his guests are intimate friends, he may ask them to contribute to the expenses when he invites them.

With domestic help becoming more and more a thing of the past, the bachelor may with all ease of conscience ask his female guests to help in preparing some or all of the meals. This is not only allowed, but it can add greatly to the fun of the party.

A good guest at such an informal house party should be sure to help at "clean-up" time, and of course keep his own things in order.

DATING

·◦⟧ 17 ⟦◦·

THE CARTOON DEPICTING A GIRL CONFIDING TO HER friend, "We met in the strangest way—we were formally introduced!" is not too far removed from the realities of today's casual way of life. Young people in high school or college are apt to begin friendships on the school steps, in the student room, or in the classroom. Acquaintances formed in this way are not "pick-ups," a derogatory term referring to a much more public kind of encounter which is *never* correct. A gentleman may not use a lunch counter, bus, or retrieved glove as the basis for an introduction to a young woman; the traditionally correct formal introduction, made by a mutual friend, is still necessary.

THE "BLIND DATE"

The "blind date" is a peculiarly American variation of the formal introduction, which in this case is made indirectly and for the express purpose of arranging a date. Mrs. Towne thinks that Gloria Gorgeous and John Handsome would enjoy each other's company. She first makes sure that John would be interested in calling Gloria; then she asks Gloria if it is all right to give her telephone number to an interested young man. Only after both parties have indicated that they are willing to be so introduced should Mrs. Towne give Gloria's telephone number to John. As one modern young woman explains, "A blind date merely requires an interested, cupidizing third party for a new friendship to blossom!"

HOW TO ASK HER FOR A DATE

A young man may properly ask any girl to whom he's been introduced for a date, at any time. Usually he uses the telephone, but there is no reason why he should not ask her in person when he sees her.

When telephoning, make sure your identity is established immediately and definitely: "This is Jim Brown. We met at Mrs. Worldly's."

174

Then a minute or two of "small talk": "How are you? Hasn't it been a lovely spring day?"—and then state your purpose. Here, too, you must be specific; never say, "What are you doing Saturday night?" and leave her wondering whether you are or are not asking for a definite date. If you say, "I've managed to get two tickets for *Romeo and Juliet* for Saturday night. I hope you can come with me," she will know what and when—as well as what to wear—and she can give you a definite answer. If she says she'd love to go with you on Saturday, you can say, "Good. Shall I call for you at seven-thirty?" or, "How about dinner first?" Decide on the time, say something like, "I'm looking forward to seeing you," and end the conversation.

Some young people do not know how far in advance a date should be made. Many men are too negligent to make their week-end plans before Thursday, and they are likely to discover that the more popular young women have already made their week-end plans well before then. A woman would like to have at least five days ahead for an invitation to an informal evening, two to three weeks ahead for a formal dance or dinner. This is not as unreasonable as it sounds because she may need the time to buy a new dress or arrange an appointment with the hairdresser. In any case she should be given as much time as possible.

WHEN SHE MUST PLEAD
A PREVIOUS ENGAGEMENT

If she is really busy, and really sorry, she should refuse in such a way that the man will be encouraged to try again. This requires diplomacy and charm. Keeping her apology brief, general, and sincere— "I'm so sorry. I've already made other plans"—is better than going into detail about her aunt who has come to town. She can encourage him to call again by suggesting another night ("I'm so sorry I can't make it Friday. Perhaps the following week. . . .") or she can ask for a "raincheck."

Refusing because she does not care enough for the young man's company to want to spend a whole evening with him is also a problem in diplomacy. She should not be rudely blunt; neither should she be coy enough to encourage him to try again. "I'm so sorry, but I've already made plans for Saturday" is sufficient.

The man who is refused may try again, if he thinks the refusal was of the first type. However, if he receives three refusals in a row, he may assume she's not interested, and forget her and her telephone number.

DON'T CANCEL ANY ENGAGEMENT
UNLESS ABSOLUTELY NECESSARY

Illness, business, family ties—there are a variety of legitimate reasons that may cause a date to be broken. The receipt of a more desirable invitation is, however, never sufficient reason for canceling an appointment. Should it be necessary, for a valid reason, for you to break a date, notify the person concerned immediately, explaining as briefly as possible why you cannot keep the appointment and perhaps try at that time to make another.

The practice of willfully not keeping an appointment, known as "standing up," is inexcusable, and is practiced only by a boor. A well-bred person will not plan an appointment with someone he does not care to spend time with; but if he is trapped into making such a date he will feel in honor bound to keep it.

DURING THE DATE

The man must call for his date at her home, and only if he knows her well and if there is good and sufficient reason (such as an early dinner appointment in the city) may he meet her at some other convenient place. It is the man's responsibility to plan and to pay for everything they do that evening—transportation, entertainment, and food. The planning is very important, and the schedule should not be given to the young woman or left to the last minute. The man's dress should, of course, be appropriate for the events he has planned. And he must be on time.

The woman must be ready promptly; there is no truth in the old saw about "keeping him waiting." She should be dressed suitably, assuming the young man has told her what they are going to do; if he has been vague, a simple basic dark dress will be in the best taste. It is always better to be under- than over-dressed. Should she discover that her date is dressed for bowling while she thought they were going to a cocktail party, she should excuse herself for ten minutes—no more!—while she hastily changes into something more casual. The young woman of today has learned that she needs a well-balanced wardrobe for the varied events in her active life, and the wise one keeps her different clothes in good condition, and ready to be put on at a moment's notice (see Chapter 39, "The Clothes of a Lady").

When the young man arrives, the girl should introduce him to her parents or roommates. The man who takes a few minutes to chat with her parents makes a good impression. She should join in the conversation briefly before saying, "Shall we go now?" and then get her hat, coat, handbag, and gloves.

During the evening she participates with enthusiasm in whatever activities have been planned. At the end of the evening it is she who suggests that it is time to go home. No matter how hard he tries to prolong the evening by suggesting a brandy, coffee, or a walk, she should stick to her decision and insist on being taken home.

At her door, he thanks her for the pleasure of her company; she thanks him for an enjoyable evening. He may say, "I'll call you next week," or even make another date then and there. But if he is not interested in seeing her again, he says nothing but "Good night."

MAY A GIRL RUN AFTER A MAN?

Catlike, she may do a little stalking! But run? Not a step. The freedom of today allows her to go to meet him half-way, but the girl who runs, runs after a man who runs faster. How, then, may she do her stalking without seeming to be running?

She may invite him to any sort of party, so long as it is not just a sit-at-home party of two. If she is invited to dinner and asked to bring an escort, or if she herself is giving a party for several couples, she of course asks the man of her choice to be her guest for the evening. She may invite a man she likes but whom she has been unable to see for several weeks because of previous engagements; inviting him will assure the man of her interest, and may be the start of a happy relationship.

She may also indicate to a young man that she wouldn't mind if he telephones, or if she works near his office she can suggest meeting at lunch time. Or she might say, to a young man who works or goes to school in another town and whom she knows at all well, "I'll answer, if you write to me." She may also buy tickets, but not often, for an entertainment, and then telephone him: "I have been given two tickets for the game (or the theatre) for Saturday. Would you like to go with me?"

It isn't so much what she does, as the way she does it. A girl who is apparently impersonal, who is catlike in disguising her intent, may pursue quite actively and with success, while one who bounds in pursuit, like a puppy let loose, has lost the prize at the start. All of which is just common sense.

A QUESTION OF MONEY

Even today, when women associate with men in business, in politics, and in fact in every activity, we nevertheless cling to one convention that many may consider obsolete—no matter what the circumstances, the man pays the check. On those occasions in business when a man is the guest of a woman, she can handle the situation most tactfully and thoughtfully by arranging to pay for the entertainment beforehand (see also page 62).

Any question of money that is not handled with tact and brevity becomes embarrassing to all concerned. Frankness is always the best rule. If a young man of moderate means is asked to join in a game of cards after dinner, it is up to him to say, "I don't play for money" or, "I only play for a tenth of a cent," instead of waiting for the game to end and possibly finding himself seriously in debt. When playing any game for money it is not only correct but very important not to begin until someone has asked "What are we playing for?" (Obviously, when the players habitually play together and always for the same stakes, this is not necessary.) The considerate hostess will make sure that her invitation cannot place a guest in an embarrassing situation.

When several couples are dining together in a restaurant, there are two ways of having the checks presented. The fairer is to have separate checks for each couple, so that each man pays for exactly what he and his own guest have ordered. The other is to divide the total check in equal parts among the men, and this occasionally means that a man and a girl who have ordered coffee and doughnuts must help pay for the extravagance of another couple who ordered caviar and champagne. If one couple chooses to give an especially extravagant order, the man should insist on paying his and his guest's check separately.

Only when agreed upon in advance by all concerned may women as well as men pay their own checks, the true "Dutch treat."

HOW CAN THE MAN OF LOW INCOME
ENTERTAIN THE GIRL OF HIS CHOICE?

The woman of character knows that it is the man himself, and not his manner of entertaining, that matters. But the problem of how a man of small means can entertain his date remains. Though many types of entertainment will be beyond reach of his wallet, a little ingenuity will help him to find inexpensive entertainments—perhaps an open-air concert, a visit to a local museum, or even a walk.

So, to you who hesitate because you do not think that whatever you have in mind is good enough for the nicest girl in the world, the advice is: Ask her, by all means, to whatever you can afford. In fact, the way she responds is a measure of the quality of girl she is, and of her liking for you. The important thing is to be unself-consciously frank yourself, and never pretend that you are richer than you are.

HOW CAN THE WOMAN HELP?

The woman is sometimes able to make things easier in a man's financially strained situation. For instance, if the young man has asked her to the movies, and she knows this is really all he can afford, she may offer to extend the evening by suggesting, "How about having dinner at my apartment first?" In a restaurant she should not order the most expensive item on the menu, unless the man indicates what he expects her to order by saying, "Their sirloin is wonderful. Would you like some?" If his budget is too low for steak he recommends the fried chicken—and perhaps chooses a more modest restaurant the next time. He should never feel obligated to recommend the most expensive item to his date, and have to order the least expensive dish for himself when she accepts his suggestion in the belief that he can afford it. A young woman of sensibility will not enjoy one bite of the tastiest steak under these circumstances.

THE IMPORTANCE OF PUNCTUALITY

Promptness is a responsibility and an obligation, more important than ever before in these busy times when most of us have to keep to a definite schedule in order to do all the things we have to cram into each day. Everyone hates to be kept waiting, and it is very inconsiderate not to keep your engagements promptly, unless you have an unquestionably valid excuse.

When you know you are going to have to be late, it is only reasonable to telephone the other person and tell him that you will be delayed, and for how long.

THREE IS A CROWD

A situation that bothers most people at some time is the inescapable presence of a third person who cannot see two people evidently interested in each other without wedging himself or herself between them. Often the persistent third person is just a natural barnacle and bore who does not realize he (or she) is intruding, but the third person most difficult to tolerate or get rid of is the supposed friend who purposely intrudes, perhaps trying to break up the friendship of the first two.

Let us say that Mary and John encounter Mary's friend Mabel on the campus as they are about to go boating, and Mabel says, "I know you two want to go out in the canoe by yourselves." Or "I know you don't want me tagging along," obviously expecting them to contradict her. Or even worse, "Mary dear, don't worry about leaving me alone. Of course any time you want me I'd love to go, but I wouldn't think of it unless you invite me!" After which, what can Mary do except invite her—or let John think she is being cruel to her lonely friend?

Therefore, if you are Mabel, you should bear in mind that John is Mary's especial friend and not yours. If you have an especial one of your own, you know very well that you wouldn't want to have Mary overhear and join in every word you and he say to each other. Not that you say anything that shouldn't be overheard, but two are company and a third is a whole neighborhood listening on a party wire!

DON'T NEGLECT YOUR GIRL FRIENDS!

Many girls make the mistake of boasting of boredom when compelled to be with girls alone, as though this were an asset. The girl who tells other girls that *she* understands men—implying that the others, poor things, are lacking in sense as well as charm—is not instilling feelings of envy and admiration in the hearts of her hearers, but feelings of resentment against her conceit and of contempt for her stupidity.

The mistake, of course, is in boasting, and not in preferring the companionship of men to girls. Girls who enjoy great popularity are most likely to be those who recognize the necessity of having friendships with girls as well as men. The girl who really has a capacity for friendship with men rarely boasts of it.

"GOING STEADY" AND "PINNING"

The dating habits of young people today include some customs that were unknown a short generation ago. Perhaps to the chagrin of many parents and teachers, "going steady" has become a fact of American teen-age life. Gone is the traditional stag line at the high school dance; today a girl usually dances only with her escort. When a boy and girl date each other consistently, they are considered by their contemporaries to be "going steady." Usually they have an agreement that neither is to date anyone else, and this may even be formalized by an exchange of friendship rings or identification bracelets.

This is for several reasons an unfortunate practice, and it is the wise young person who widens instead of narrowing his circle of friends. Many girls fear not having a date for Saturday night, and some boys are afraid to be told "no" when they call a girl for a date. But these young people are putting limits on the development of their own social personalities when they limit their dating friendships. Only by meeting many other young people of varied backgrounds and interests can a boy or girl broaden his or her own experience and gain enough insight to be capable of making a good choice of a partner when the time comes.

The presentation of a fraternity badge by a college man to his girl, known as "pinning," may be merely another type of "going steady," or it may mean that the couple are "engaged to be engaged," depending on the customs of that particular college. Generally the couple intends marriage but in the somewhat distant future, and this relationship allows them to examine their compatibility without committing themselves formally to an engagement. It is not considered proper for a girl to give a man her sorority pin, or to collect fraternity pins as trophies of her dates. If the "pinned" couple "breaks up," the girl is expected to return the pin to the young man. In many cases, "pinning" does lead to a formal engagement and then to marriage.

After leaving college, of course, unmarried young men and women do not follow these customs, which seem to have significance only among the high school or college community. Although a couple in their late twenties or thirties may be dating each other exclusively, there will usually be no formalizing of their relationship until they decide to become engaged.

ENGAGEMENTS

·❦[18]❦·

THE VERY FIRST THING THEY DO AFTER HE PROPOSES, AND she says "Yes" to him and they perhaps have spent a very short time in realization of their happiness, is the duty of at once seeing her father or whoever is head of her family and ask for his or possibly her consent. If her father refuses, she then is faced with the problem of changing her "Yes" to "No," or else marrying in opposition to her parents. There are, of course, unreasonable parents; but even so, there is no excuse for the most unfilial act of all—deception. The honorable young woman who has made up her mind to marry in spite of her parents' disapproval, announces to them, if she can, that on such and such a day her wedding will take place. If this is impossible, she at least refuses to give her word that she will not marry. The height of dishonor is to give her word while intending to break it.

THE ENGAGEMENT USUALLY APPROVED

In most instances, however, when John goes to see Mary's father, the latter has a perfectly good idea of what he has come to say and has for some time been more than a little perturbed about how he will word his answer to his prospective son-in-law.

It may be that John's finances seem to the father not to be quite up to supporting his daughter, and he may decide to give some sort of allowance to her which will make the life of the young couple less of a struggle. But if her father is not able himself to make up for the shortcomings of John's finances he may have to advise that they wait before marrying or even possibly before approving of the engagement. On the other hand, if everything is satisfactory, he makes no objection to an immediate announcement.

THE ENGAGEMENT RING

It is doubtful whether he who produced a ring from his pocket upon the instant that she said "Yes" ever existed outside of romantic

novels. In real life, it is both correct and wise that HE consult HER taste
—which may quite possibly be gratified, especially since there is a
trend toward a return to the sentiment of our grandmothers for one's
own birthstone instead of the present day's reduction of a possible
diamond solitaire to one of minute size. In any case, the fiancé then goes
alone to the jeweler, explains how much he can afford, and has a selection of rings set aside. He then brings his fiancée into the store and lets
her choose from among them the one she likes best.

It might be a charming one of platinum and diamond design, or if
he is very lucky he may have inherited a diamond which removed from
its old-fashioned setting of gold will be beautiful when transferred to
platinum. Or, as already noted, it may be that there will be a lovely
ring of more important size in her own birthstone.

One quite noticeable effect upon the ideas of today is the widespread
fashion of using costume jewelry, beside which the tiny diamond has
temporarily at least lost out in its appeal. On the other hand, the also
real, though semiprecious, gem stone of size is taking its place. An
effectively big aquamarine is today's first choice as a solitaire diamond's
substitute. An amethyst, or topaz, or transparent tourmaline are all at
present appealing to the girl whose hand is not so conspicuously white
as well as small as to set off the gleam of the littlest of solitaires.

THE BRIDE'S BIRTHSTONE

JANUARY   *Garnet* (Its rather dark glow makes a pleasing engage-
            ment ring). The *zircon*, a white crystal-clear stone, makes a
            very attractive ring and closely resembles a diamond particu-
            larly when square cut and kept brilliantly clean. Because it
            does resemble a diamond, many a bride will, I am afraid, fear
            that people will feel she is trying to fool them into thinking
            it really is a diamond. There is also a beautiful steely-blue
            variety.

FEBRUARY   *Amethyst* (Big one; square cut effective).

MARCH   *Aquamarine*, first; then *bloodstone* or *jasper*. (Aquamarine,
            square cut—a present fashion and a really beautiful substitute
            for a diamond).

APRIL   *Diamond* (The stone of stones but high-priced when of first
            quality).

MAY   *Emerald* (Also very costly if perfect in color and without
            noticeable flaw).

JUNE   *Pearl* (Nothing more becoming to a very beautiful smooth
            white hand).

JULY   *Ruby* (Of very high value when of the desirable pigeon blood
            color).

AUGUST   *Sardonyx, peridot* (a rare and beautiful stone), or *carnelian*.

SEPTEMBER   *Sapphire* (A favorite engagement ring of yesterday).

OCTOBER   *Opal* (The opal is the stone of good fortune for those born in October, but believed to be unlucky for those not born in this especial month).

NOVEMBER   *Topaz.*

DECEMBER   *Turquoise* or *lapis lazuli.*

IF SHE WANTS TO GIVE HIM A RING

Suitability is the point of very first importance to make in every question concerning good taste and this is especially important in choosing a ring for a man.

If he is a diplomat, or in an office, or in any position which is in great measure social, and he does no manual work other than holding a pen or pencil or paint brush, a quite conspicuous ring can be entirely correct especially if becoming to his hand. Anything suggesting lightness instead of solidity would be unsuitable.

In the following list, birthstones are considered as a masculine possibility. The phrase "deeply sunk" means a quite heavy ring of plain gold of varying width and thickness (known as a "Gypsy hoop") that is quite flat across the back but becomes sufficiently broad and heavy toward the center of the front to hold a single stone or not unusually three stones. The single or center one at very largest is a quarter of an inch in diameter or if a diamond appreciably smaller. When a man's ring is set with three stones this means that two small matching stones or more likely diamonds are sunk into the gold on either side of the center one but not touching and never set in prongs. Touching stones held in prongs are as feminine as is any other apparel of a woman.

JANUARY   *Gold seal* ring alone possible; neither garnet nor zircon is suitable. (Gold snake ring, very much in fashion long ago, is rarely seen today. It would, however, be in perfectly good taste.)

FEBRUARY   *Cat's eye* sunk in plain gold makes a beautiful ring for a man.

MARCH   *Bloodstone* typical for seal ring.

APRIL   *Diamond;* only a very small one set deep in plain gold and worn on little finger. An overlarge diamond on the finger of a man is the hallmark of the vulgar.

MAY   *Gold seal* ring. Emerald too light and bright and feminine for a man.

JUNE   *Agate seal* ring.

JULY   *Onyx*—the perfect seal ring.

AUGUST   *Carnelian* makes a most beautiful seal ring set in gold but looks well only on a smooth white hand (it is much the same test as a pearl on a woman's hand).

SEPTEMBER   *Sapphire;* a not very big one cut *en cabochon* set deeply in plain platinum; is in good taste.

OCTOBER   Opal impossible for a man. One of the darkly colored *tourmalines* cut *en cabochon* and sunk in plain gold.

NOVEMBER   *Topaz* makes a seal ring attractive, and looks well set in heavy gold.

DECEMBER   Turquoise impossible. *Lapis lazuli* sunk in gold a possibility, if he has a good-looking hand.

Even if he is one who uses his hands roughly, he can as a matter of fact wear a ring if it gives the impression of unspoilable sturdiness.

The prospective bride must not be upset if he doesn't want one. Some men simply do not like to wear rings.

ENGAGEMENT RING ETIQUETTE

The engagement ring is worn for the first time in public on the day of the announcement. *But the engagement ring is not essential to the validity of the betrothal.* Many confuse the engagement ring with the wedding ring, and believe the former is as indispensable as the latter—which is not the case. The wedding ring is a requirement of the marriage service. The engagement ring is simply evidence that he proposed marriage and that she answered, "Yes!"

Countless wives have never had an engagement ring at all. Many another has received her ring long after marriage, when her husband was able to buy the ring he had all along wanted her to have. Some brides prefer to forego an engagement ring, and put the money it would have cost toward furnishing their future home.

IF SHE GIVES HIM AN ENGAGEMENT PRESENT

It is not obligatory, or even customary, for the girl to give the man an engagement present; but there is no impropriety in her doing so. In fact, if she wants to call it that, she can even give him an engagement ring! The most usual presents include such articles as the following: a set of studs and a matching pair of cuff links, or a watch band or a key chain, or a cigarette case. Probably because the giving of an engagement ring is his particular province, she very rarely gives him a ring or, in fact, any present at all. But there is no impropriety in her giving him a ring if she wants to. If he is to have a wedding ring she buys that, of course!

HIS PARENTS CALL ON HERS

A troublesome custom which follows the acceptance of the engagement is that correctly the parents of the man go to call on the parents of the girl. At least his mother goes at once to see hers. After the en-

gagement is announced, all of the near relatives of the bridegroom-to-be
—sisters, brothers, aunts, and even cousins, if they are close to him—
should go at once and call upon the bride and her family. If they do
not live in the same city, letters of welcome to the girl should be written.
The telephone, of course, can help two families that live at a distance
to know each other. Much awkwardness—at times even unhappiness—
has resulted from not being aware of this convention. If for any reason
the man's family does not call on the parents of the girl, the latter
should be very careful not to permit an oversight to develop into a
situation that may cause great distress. The point to be made is
that this time should be a happy one for the young couple, and that
both sets of parents should act with spontaneity and in a spirit of
friendship.

It is also of great importance that the girl try to understand and to
accept the attitude of her future family (whatever it may be) and that
she must *not* stand inflexibly upon what she unwittingly might consider
to be her own rights. After all, the objective that she should keep in mind is
the happiness of the relationship between herself and her future in-laws.

PERSONAL ANNOUNCEMENT

Usually a few days—perhaps a week—before the formal announcement the girl and man both write to their aunts, uncles, and
cousins, and to their most intimate friends, telling of their engagement,
asking them not to tell anyone until the determined date. This is so
that they will not read of it first in the newspapers. It is expected, however, that these relatives, as soon as they receive the news, call on the
bride. She must, of course, return these visits as soon as possible.

If his people are in the habit of entertaining, they should very soon
ask her with her fiancé to lunch or to dinner, or, after the engagement
is publicly announced, give more general parties in her honor. If, on
the other hand, they are very quiet people, their calling upon her is
sufficient in itself to show their welcome.

In case of a recent death in either immediate family, the engagement should be quietly announced by telling families and intimate
friends.

THE FORMAL ANNOUNCEMENT

The formal or public announcement is made by the parents of the
bride-to-be. This is done intimately either by notes, or at a dinner, or
other gathering, and after that publicly through the newspapers. Engraved announcements are not correct.

The public announcement is made by notifying the society editor of
the daily papers that Mr. and Mrs. John Jones of 100 Park Avenue are
announcing the engagement of their daughter, Mildred, to Mr. George

Brown, son of Mr. and Mrs. Emerson Brown of New Orleans. If the families concerned are prominent, a photograph of the fiancée will be asked for; if it is not, the paper probably does not have space for it.

It is entirely proper to include a photograph of Mildred with the announcement, and if the paper has sufficient space in that day's issue it will be published. But if the column space is crowded, it may then be possible that the announcement will be cut to the fewest lines and perhaps even omitted.

As a matter of fact, the failure of the press notice—while disappointing—is not important, since all the best friends of both families will have received the news personally, by telephone or telegram or written notes from the bride or bridegroom, or from their parents.

When a party is given for the purpose of announcement, the news is told by the girl herself or her mother, as the guests arrive and find the fiancé standing beside them. Or perhaps, if the party is a dinner, it is told by the father, who rises and proposes a toast to the health of his daughter and future son-in-law.

When a girl is an orphan, her engagement is announced by her nearest relative—grandparent, aunt, or older sister. If she has no relative, she gives the announcement to the paper: "The engagement of Miss Mary Smith, daughter of the late Mr. and Mrs. Samuel Smith, is announced, to Mr. ——" etc., without making the announcement in the name of anyone. This form is also sometimes used when her parents live very far away.

When parents are divorced the engagement is announced preferably by her mother—unless she lives with her father and does not see her mother. However, the other parent's name should be mentioned in the notice. Or both names are given to the newspapers impersonally, this way: "The engagement of Miss Mary Robinson, daughter of Mr. Stephen Robinson and Mrs. Smith Robinson (or Mrs. John Jones, if her mother is married again), is announced, to Mr. Henry Brown, son of ——" etc.

The engagement of a spinster of forty or more is properly announced by both her and her fiancé by letting friends and relatives know very shortly before the wedding. A widow announces her second engagement the same way, although both may if they choose give the announcement to the society editors of the papers.

NOVELTY ANNOUNCEMENTS

To those who ask about using a novel way to announce an engagement, convention is not partial to names on balloons, or a sash tying the left arm of the girl to the right arm of the man. Yet there is really no logical objection to whatever may be pleasing to you. Whether you let a cat out of a bag with your names written on a ribbon around its neck, or distribute bouquets and boutonnières tagged with both names, or whether guests receive the glad tidings in telegrams used as place-cards, there is not a rule in the world to hamper your own imagination.

THE TOAST

This is the conventional announcement made by the father of the bride at a dinner: After directing that all glasses at the table be filled, the host rises, lifts his own glass, and says: "I propose we drink to the health of Mary and the young man she has decided to add permanently to our family, James Smartlington."

Or

"A standing toast: To my Mary and to her—Jim!"

Or

"I want you to drink to the happiness of a young pair whose future welfare is close to the hearts of all of us: Mary (holding up his glass and looking at her) and Jim!" (looking at him). Everyone except Mary and Jim rises and drinks a little of whatever the beverage may be. They then congratulate the young couple, and Jim is called upon for a speech!

Generally rather fussed, Jim rises, the color of a black raspberry sherbet, and says something like this: "I—er—we—thank you all very much indeed for all your good wishes," and sits down. Or if he is an earnest rather than a shy youth, perhaps he continues, "I don't have to tell you how lucky *I* am; the thing for me to do is to prove, if I can, that Mary has not made the mistake of her life in choosing me, and I hope that it won't be very long before we see you all at our own table with Mary at the head of it and I, where I belong, at the foot." Or, "I can't make a speech and *you* know it. But I surely am lucky and *I* know it."

IF NO SPEECH IS MADE

The prevailing custom in New York and other big cities is for the party to be given on the afternoon or evening of the day of announcement. In this case, the engagement is never proclaimed to the guests as an assembled audience. The news is "out" and everyone is supposed to have heard it. Those who have not cannot long remain ignorant, as the groom-elect is either receiving with his fiancée, or brought forward by her father and presented to everyone he does not know. Everybody congratulates him and offers the bride-to-be wishes for her happiness.

ENGAGEMENT PRESENTS

It is not unusual for a bride-to-be to receive a few engagement presents sent either by her very intimate friends, her godparents, or by members of her fiancé's family as special messages of welcome to her. But it is not necessary to give engagement as well as wedding presents.

Engagement showers will be found in Chapter 33, "Neighborhood Social
Customs."

ENGAGED COUPLE IN PUBLIC

There is said to be still preserved somewhere in Massachusetts a
whispering reed through the long hollow length of which lovers were
wont to whisper messages of tenderness to each other while separated
by a room's length and the inevitable chaperonage of the fiancée's entire
family.

From those days to the present of unrestricted demonstration from
which one is on occasion made to feel like withdrawing in embarrassment are the two extremes.

Entirely proper of each is their frank approval of whatever the other
may do or say, and their radiant look, and even more proper is their
obvious friendliness toward all people, their air of wishing the whole
world to be beautiful for everybody because it is so beautiful to them.
That is love—as it should be! And its evidence is a very sure signpost
to their future happiness.

ETIQUETTE OF ENGAGED PEOPLE

It is unnecessary to say that an engaged man shows no marked
interest in other women. Often it so happens that engaged people are
together very little because he is away at work, lives in another city,
or for other reasons. Rather than sit home alone, she may, of course,
go out with her friends, but she must avoid going out with any one man
or being seen out with any one man alone. In short, she remains visibly
within the general circle of her group.

SHOULD A LONG ENGAGEMENT BE ANNOUNCED?

Whether to announce an engagement that must be of long duration is not a matter of etiquette but of personal preference. On the
general principle that frankness is always better than secretiveness, the
situation is usually cleared by announcing it.

THE ENGAGED COUPLE AND THE CHAPERON

The question of a chaperon differs with locality. It is perhaps
sufficient to say that if a man is thought worthy to be accepted by a
father as his daughter's future husband, he should be considered worthy
of trust no matter how far any situation they might find themselves in
may be lacking in propriety.

PRESENTS WHICH MAY AND WHICH MAY NOT
BE ACCEPTED

The fiancée of a young man who is "saving in order to marry"
would be lacking in good taste as well as good sense were she to en-

courage or allow him extravagantly to send her many flowers and other charming but wasteful presents. On the other hand, however, if the bridegroom-elect has ample means, she may accept anything he chooses to select, except wearing apparel or anything that can be classified as maintenance.

It is perfectly proper for her to drive his car, and she may select furniture for their house, which he may buy or have built. But, if she would keep her self-respect, she must not live in the house or use its furniture until she is given his name. He may give her all the jewels he can afford; he may give her a fur scarf, but not a fur coat. The scarf is an ornament; the coat is wearing apparel. If she cannot afford to buy a new dress, she may have to be married in the prettiest dress she already has, but her wedding dress and the clothes she wears away on her wedding day must not be supplied by the groom nor, under most circumstances, even by his family.

There are, of course, exceptions. If his mother has long known the girl and loves her dearly, there is no reason why she should not give her everything she chooses. But it would be starting life on a false basis, and putting herself in a category with women of another class, to be lodged and clothed by any man, whether he is soon to be her husband or not.

THE BROKEN ENGAGEMENT

If the engagement should be so unfortunate as to be broken off, the engagement ring and all other gifts of value must be returned to the giver. A notice reading "The engagement of Miss Sara Black and Mr. John Doe has been broken by mutual consent" should be sent to the newspapers which announced the engagement.

BUYING THE WEDDING RING—OR RINGS

Later on, or it may be immediately, it is not only customary but important that the bride go with the groom when he buys the wedding ring. The reason is that since she may not intend to take it off, it stays for life on her finger, and she should be allowed to choose the style she prefers. No ring could be in better taste than the plain band of gold, either yellow or white. A diamond band, no matter how fashionable, is much more suitable as a guard than as a wedding ring. This is because the under side of a diamond band must be cleaned constantly and moreover a lost diamond replaced every so often. But even more, it doesn't look like a traditional wedding ring.

THE BRIDEGROOM'S RING

If the bridegroom wishes to have a ring, the bride buys a plain gold band to match hers but a little wider—or it may be any type of ring he prefers and she is able to buy—at the same time. A man's ring is most fashionably worn on the fourth finger although the third is equally correct. Formerly men's wedding rings were worn only on the right hand, but the left hand is equally correct.

MARKING THE ENGAGEMENT AND WEDDING RINGS

The wedding ring may be engraved with whatever sentiment the bridegroom chooses. On the broad rings of many years ago it was not unusual to have a quotation of twenty-five letters or more, as well as the initials A.Y.X. and L.M.N., September 2, 1900. On the rings of today, however, A.B.Z. and L.M.M., Sept. 2, 1956, is invariably chosen.

The mounting of the modern engagement ring is usually so narrow that "A. to L. — 4, 16, '56" is the most that space can be found for— and at that a magnifying glass is needed to read the letters.

The bridegroom's ring is also marked with initials or a sentiment, as the bride chooses.

PLANNING FOR
THEIR FUTURE HOME

⋅⊰[19]⊱⋅

A TROUSSEAU, ACCORDING TO THE DERIVATION OF THE word, was "a little trusse or bundle" that the bride carried with her to the house of her husband. In modern times the "little bundle" sometimes requires the services of a van to transport.

THE HOUSEHOLD TROUSSEAU

At present the extravagant trousseau of yesterday's daughters of the very wealthy are dwindling to items of actual requirement. Household linen enough to run an enormous house—and for a lifetime—is a thing of the past. Few modern linen closets would hold them. The well-appointed house of today's bride will be adequately equipped with the following items:

BED LINEN (Amounts are for each bed, and these quantities would also take care of an occasional guest.)
   8 sheets (a good grade of cotton percale)
   6 pillow cases (12 for double bed)
   2 blanket covers (washable silk or fine cotton)
   2 quilted mattress pads
   1 lightweight wool blanket
   1 electric blanket (dual control for double bed)
   1 heavyweight wool or wool blend blanket (double or single depending on climate)
   1 down-filled comforter (if climate requires)
   1 cotton-filled comforter or cotton blanket (for summer)
   1 comforter for winter (preferably eiderdown)
   2 bedspreads

BATH LINEN (Quantities per person)
   6 large bath towels
   6 small towels to match

4 washcloths to match

6 linen face towels

6 or 8 smaller linen towels (for guests' use)

1 or 2 shower curtains for each bathroom (nylon or plastic)

2 bath mats for each bathroom

KITCHEN

6 linen glass towels

6 sturdy dish and china towels

6 dishcloths

If you are having a maid to sleep in, then you will have to buy extra bed and bath linen for her. Small bath towels and washcloths are needed for a maid who comes in by the day. Terry cloth towels are very practical because they show only soil. Huck towels rumple the moment they are used.

TABLE LINEN

1 damask tablecloth, white or pastel color, 3½ yards long (if you ever plan to give a dinner for as many as twelve seated at one table—or a cloth 2½ to 3 yards to fit a smaller table)

12 napkins to match, 24″ x 24″

In any case, remember a damask cloth is very useful for a buffet setting because, with a felt pad under it, every inch of space is available —which is not the case with the bare table spaces if mats are used. A handkerchief linen cloth inset with lace is also practical with the addition of a heat-protecting mat under any exceptionally hot platter or dish.

Small place-mats of linen or lace with runner to match are most practical. A dozen mats with one runner can be used permanently as your one and only tablecloth. Merely rinse and press mats when anything is spilled on them or put them into the wash, and take fresh ones from your reserve.

Whether or not you will join the appreciators of tablecloths of plastic is a question worth considering, since they fill a very real need in today's economy of living. In fact, a practically invisible one, when laid over a regular tablecloth, makes possible the daily use of your tablecloths of finest damask or needlework and lace, an example of perpetuity. These are particularly useful if young children eat at the family table. Paper napkins complement the plastics and are so attractively made today that they solve quite practically one household problem. However, where a linen, damask, or other fabric cloth is used on the table the napkins should, of course, match in character. But the new paper products have a welcome use at informal meals when they are of adequate size, fine smooth texture and firm body, quite preferably white—still they *are* informal and should be used in company with other casual table appointments.

A DELIGHTFUL SETTING FOR MODERN HOSPITALITY

Friendliness rather than formality is expressed in every detail.

A DINNER SERVICE OF SIMPLICITY AND PLEASING CHARM

Decorative plastic tablecloths, useful for so many purposes, are surprisingly helpful so that one or two are almost a must for today's house —unless your house is to be run on a fastidiously formal and very extravagant scale.

Although damask tablecloths are still the conventional requirement for a formal dinner, they are so exacting in their requirements of laundering as to be practical in none but extravagantly run houses in which facilities are provided to put a freshly laundered cloth as well as napkins on the table every time it is set.

If your dining-room is likely to be very small, possibly an alcove adjoining your living-room which will not permit seating as many people as you will on occasion want to have at a dinner or lunch party, then it might be practical to get three sturdy, and they must be sturdy, bridge tables, with matching damask tablecloths and napkins. They will be more pleasing in appearance if they are matching and of a color that is becoming to your room. Odd tablecloths grouped together are not pleasing, and give the impression of a haphazard household.

If you like an afternoon tea-table set with a cloth, then have two of these perhaps merely embroidered or perhaps with fillet lace insertions—as well as embroidered—each with a dozen little 12″ tea napkins.

MARKING LINEN

It is, of course, very decorative for the linen to be embroidered with monogram or initials. An initial designed with additional embellishment to give the appearance of a monogram is more effective than two initials—and usually the cost is less!

Long tablecloths are marked on either side of center, midway between table center and edge of table. Small yard-and-a-half square tablecloths are marked at one corner midway between table center and corner or side edge. Square monograms look well set in line with the table edge; irregular ones look best at corner.

Afternoon tea cloths have monograms if there is any linen area where a monogram can be embroidered. Otherwise monograms or initials are put on the napkins only.

Very large damask napkins are marked in center; others are marked in one corner—cross-cornered usually, but sometimes straight. To decide about the place for marking the napkins, always fold the napkin exactly as it is to be folded for use, and then make a light pencil outline in the center of the folded napkin.

Sheets are always marked with base of letters toward hem—when on the bed, the monogram is right-side up and can be read by a person standing at foot of bed—and it is put at half the depth at which the sheet is turned back. Typical modern pillow cases are marked half-way between edge of case and beginning of the pillow. On square French pillow cases the monogram is put cross-cornered with top of initials to corner.

Towels are of course marked so that, when they are folded and hung on the rack, the marking is centered.

Monograms should be in proportion to the size of the linen. If **it is** too small, it will look skimpy; if too large, it is too conspicuous.

WHAT INITIALS TO CHOOSE

Years ago, according to etiquette, when Muriel Brown Jones married Henry Ross, not a piece of linen or silver in their house was marked otherwise than "M.B.J." But as this long proved a confusing and senseless custom, it is now recognized as more practical to mark everything with the bride's future initials: "M.J.R."

When she has three initials, the smartest marking on silver—or other metal or leather articles—is the triangle of block letters—last name initial at the top:

R

M J

According to present-day taste, all overlong and fancy letters should be avoided. If a single initial is to be used, Old English is always excellent.

TABLE CHINA AND GLASS

Today the stores are filled with such entrancing sets of pottery, plasticware, and china in every variety imaginable, thick, thin, plain, or decorated, that the problem is not to find sufficiently attractive table decorations in china, but to decide from among the many to choose from. There is however one item of important advice. Keep in mind the subject of replacements. And remember that any pattern not easily replaced means that breakage will leave you helplessly handicapped. It is always wise to ask if a pattern is in open stock. Beyond this, details of importance to consider are: Soap-bubble thin glass, or glass that is very finely chased or cut, is naturally most becoming to porcelains, whereas the heavier glassware is best suited to pottery.

To what extent china (whether porcelain, or pottery, or plastic) is to take the place of silver hollow-ware must be decided by each bride. China is of course so easily cared for compared with the polishing of silver hollow-ware that it may be preferred for breakfast and tea service. Its disadvantage is that it is all too easily broken or marred. The suggestion however is offered that the supposedly essential silver tea service is no longer the central feature of the bride's silver equipment that it once was.

But let us consider a few general principles that apply to a table set with china: Its one exaction is that it be in harmony; meaning that it have some matching detail—such as texture or at least a repeated note of color. In other words, service plates of one variety, bread and butter plates of another variety, centerpiece of another, dishes for sweets **or** foods of another, candlesticks of still another, would look like an odd-lot table selected at random unless these pieces were closely allied.

Whether you choose decorated china or that which is plain, is a matter of your own choice. All white china of the same color and texture need not match in pattern or shape, but it would be unpleasing for example to use translucent milk glass with opaque white earthenware. China of any other plain color would necessarily depend upon the color of the cloth or table upon which it is to be set.

Whether to buy a complete set of matching china for breakfast, and another for dinner and supper (or lunch), or whether to have a breakfast service, and odd dinner plates in eights or dozens, perhaps in a different pattern for each course, is to be decided; there are advantages and disadvantages of both. First, the advantage of buying an assembled set of china that contains complete service for breakfast, lunch, and dinner for 4, 6, 8, or 12 place-settings is that you pay half the amount or even less than you would pay for the same number of pieces bought separately. The second advantage is that everything being of the same pattern, you need never consider whether dishes and platters, bread and butter plates, and service plates match for each course.

The disadvantages are that in most of the made-up sets (particularly the very large ones) there are too many items of one sort and too few of others.

For example, few households need a dozen egg cups and cereal saucers; they do not balance well with a dozen medium-sized plates which must be used for almost every course at every meal.

In fact an account of personal experience might be used to illustrate this situation:

It goes back to a day when I myself became responsible for the upkeep of four houses which were rented furnished. At a sale I bought four identical sets of china. The best I can say for the pattern is that it was "not bad"; its quality, fair, and each set included about 150 pieces! The closing-out price was absurdly small. I put a sufficient amount of one set in each house and stored the left-over items in my attic to serve as a replacement supply. (I thought I was very clever.) But in the end, all four sets had the same broken pieces, the pattern had not been open stock (one reason for its being on sale), and I was left with four dozen side dishes which had never been used by anyone, four dozen egg cups, a collection of dish covers, sauce boats, and dozens of saucers with scarcely a cup that had a handle on it. Or a plate that wasn't chipped! There was nothing to do with any of it, therefore, except to fill a barrel and send it to the give-away heap for anyone who might care for an odd dish cover or a few egg cups or cupless saucers.

Strictly speaking, there is no such thing as a "glass trousseau"; the really correct "trousseau" is of linen—for her house and herself both (to the last is added other wearing apparel).

Silver is *not* trousseau but a very principal gift—which does, however, consist of a definite list of items. Glass may very well come into this category. A "glass trousseau"—if we *coin* this phrase—would include from six to twelve of:

> Water tumblers (or goblets)
> Iced-tea glasses (useful for any tall drink)
> Fingerbowls, with
> Matching glass dessert plates
> Medium-sized "wine" glasses (for claret, white wine, or ordinary fruit juice)

Of course what may be added to these depends on the habits and customs of the bride and groom, such as cocktail glasses, fruit juice glasses, sherbet glasses, etc. Liqueur glasses, for example, are useful for nothing else.

MAKE YOUR LIST FIRST

Before buying your china, therefore, it is most important to make certain that you are buying from a long-established, open-stock pattern which will make replacements fairly certain. Varieties of especial safety are the Canton blue-and-white and the Dresden white china with flowers, or almost any variety of white edged with gold. These are all easily enough matched—even if not precisely, then nearly enough—as to make extra plates or cups and saucers easily found. It is very important to make a list of what you are going to need for the tables you will probably set, beginning with breakfast, and ending with the highest number you are likely to invite to luncheons or suppers or dinners.

Be firm with yourself in preparing your list so that you will not be "carried away" by the always tempting but unnecessary items. If your new house is going to be small, you probably won't have shelf space for them.

PREPARATIONS FOR A WEDDING

·◦ɪ 20 ɪ◦·

THIS CHAPTER BEGINS WITH A COMPLETE DESCRIPTION OF the most elaborate wedding possible. Not because more than a minority among us will be able—or want to—carry out every detail, but because it is the complete pattern. In other words, it is important to explain all possible details of perfection so that you can follow as many as you find practical and pleasing to you!

It is beautiful, impressive, and the bride's day-of-days. But remember, the groom has a place in it too and his wishes should be consulted. If the wedding is to be a large formal one, expert help should be arranged for well in advance to avoid last-minute confusion. Otherwise father may be irritated, mother jittery, the bride in tears, and the groom cross.

THE WEDDING EXPENSES

In explanation of the following directions: Each detailed expense begins with the wedding of greatest elaborateness and highest cost and then whenever possible a second direction follows in italics to explain a correct alternate at lesser expense.

The first fact to remember is that all the expenses of a wedding belong to the bride's parents. The cost of a wedding varies as much as the cost of anything else that one has or does. A big fashionable wedding can total several thousand dollars, and even a simple one entails considerable outlay if it is to be of considerable size. This cost can, however, be modified by those who are capable of doing many things themselves instead of employing professional service at every point.

THE BRIDE'S PARENTS PROVIDE

1. Engraved invitations to ceremony, with enclosures to the reception. On occasion, announcements instead of, or supplementary to, invitations. *While true engraving is most beautiful and a required expense for a wedding of superperfection and extreme formality, there is at*

least one new method of simulating engraving which is very pleasing and entirely suitable when cost must be counted. In justice to the skill of the engravers it is perhaps fair to explain that copperplate engraving is like an ornament of diamonds compared with smart costume jewelry; those who can afford it naturally prefer diamonds, but the other is much in fashion as a pleasing substitute for the many who must count cost.

2. The service of a professional secretary who compiles a single guest list from the various ones provided her; addresses the envelopes, both inner and outer; encloses the proper number of cards; seals, stamps, and mails all the invitations or announcements. *This item of cost may be omitted if the work is done by members or friends of the family.*

3. The trousseau of the bride, which may consist not only of everything to wear in great variety and lavish detail, but household linen of finest quality. *Or it may consist of the wedding dress, the going-away dress, and one or two others, with pretty, simple underthings and other accessories.*

4. Floral decorations of church and place of reception. Bouquets for the bride and bridesmaids, corsage bouquets for both mothers, and a boutonnière for the father of the bride. *This expense can be eliminated by using garden or field flowers or carrying prayer books.* In many American communities it is customary for the groom to provide the bouquet carried by the bride. In others it is the custom for the bride to send boutonnières to the ushers, and for the groom to order the bouquets of the bridesmaids. In New York's smartest world, the bride's as well as the bridesmaids' bouquets are looked upon as part of the decorative arrangements, all of which are provided by the bride's parents. Though the groom does not give the bride her bouquet, he does send her flowers to wear away and supplies the ushers' as well as the best man's and his own boutonnières.

5. Choir, soloists, and organist at church. *Choir and soloists unnecessary.* And a fee to the sexton.

6. Orchestra at reception. This may mean fifty pieces with two leaders; or it may mean a piano, violin, and drum; or a violin, harp, and guitar—*or a phonograph.*

7. Automobiles for the bridal party from the house to the church and to the reception and for the bride and groom to drive away in, unless they are going on their journey in a car of their own.

8. The refreshments, which may be the most elaborate sit-down luncheon *or the simplest afternoon tea.*

9. Boxes of wedding cake, also the big one (the former necessary at every wedding of importance; the latter alone indispensable). *Latter can be made of white cake.*

10. Champagne, if served, is one of the biggest items of expense; *a fruit punch, on the other hand, is of moderate cost.*

11. The bride's presents to her bridesmaids. They may be jewels of value or *trinkets of trifling cost.* Also hotel accommodations for bride's attendants if necessary.

12. A wedding present to the bride—*not counting her trousseau which is merely part of the wedding.*

13. The bride gives a wedding present or a wedding ring, or both, to the groom, *if she especially wants to. Not necessary, but becoming customary.*

14. Photographs taken of the bridal party. *Not generally given to attendants;* if a bridesmaid or usher wishes to have a wedding photograph she or he may properly order a print from the photographer.

15. Awnings for church and house correct at all very large and formal weddings—especially in the city. *Required in country in very bad weather only.*

THE BRIDEGROOM'S EXPENSES

1. The engagement ring—as handsome as he can afford.

2. A wedding present to the bride—jewels if he is able, always something for her personal adornment.

3. His bachelor dinner if he gives one.

4. The bride's bouquet, where local custom requires it.

5. The marriage license.

6. A personal gift to his best man and to each of his ushers. Their hotel expenses, if necessary, unless they are invited to stay with neighbors.

7. To each of the above he gives their wedding ties and boutonnières, also gloves, if they are to be worn. He buys his own boutonnière.

8. The wedding ring.

9. The clergyman's fee.

10. From the moment the bride and groom start off on their wedding trip, all the expenditure becomes his.

BREACH OF ETIQUETTE FOR BRIDEGROOM
TO GIVE WEDDING

No matter whether a wedding is to be large or tiny, there is a supposedly fixed rule that the reception must be either at the house of the bride's parents, or grandparents, or other relatives, or else in assembly rooms rented by her family. Etiquette has always decreed that the groom's family may give entertainments of whatever description they choose for the young couple after they are married; but the wedding breakfast as well as the trousseau of the bride, however simple these may need to be, must be furnished by her own side of the house!

There might be circumstances, however, where it would be caviling not to break this rule. If, for instance, the bride were without family, she might perfectly well be married in the church or the rectory, and go afterward to the house of the bridegroom's parents for breakfast or for the reception. After all, there are few rules that permit no exceptions under extenuating circumstances. But in the average case—where the girl is known slightly or perhaps not at all by the family of the bridegroom—she would put herself in a false position and bring criticism upon her own family's inability to assume the wedding obligations which properly belong to them.

WHEN, WHERE, AND HOW BIG SHALL THE WEDDING BE?

Before deciding the date of the wedding the bride, or more probably her mother, must find out definitely on which day the clergyman who is to perform the ceremony will be available, and also make sure the church is bespoken for no other service. If it is to be an important wedding she must also confirm the time available for the church with that which is possible for the caterer, or the hotel, or the club.

The next step is to decide the time of day that will be best for the ceremony. Religion, climate, local custom, and transportation schedules may be important factors, as well as the bride and groom's own plans for their wedding trip. Also, due consideration should be given to the probable convenience of a majority of the relatives and friends who will want to come.

Having settled upon a day and hour, she next decides on the number of guests that can be provided for; this is determined by the type of reception intended, as explained above, as well as by the size of the bride's house or the place that her family can afford for the reception.

Remember, too, that if the reception comes at a customary meal hour, a substantial wedding breakfast or collation must be provided. In this case, expense may restrict the number of guests invited to the reception.

Only a very small church or chapel however would limit the number of guests invited to the ceremony.

THE INVITATIONS

The bride-elect and her mother then go to the stationer and decide details, such as size and texture of paper and style of engraving, for the invitations. The order is given about two months or as far as possible in advance for the engraving of all the necessary plates, and for a moderate number of invitations or announcements, which may be increased later when the lists are completed and the definite number known.

For all details of wedding forms, see Chapter 11.

BOTH MOTHERS MAKE WEDDING LISTS

The bride's mother then consults with the groom, or more likely with his mother, about how the house list is to be divided between them.

If the families have long been friends, and it is decided that one hundred may be included at the breakfast, this would probably suggest that some seventy names would be the same, and this would mean then that each would be able to add fifteen of their own to the seventy who are already on their shared list. But if they have never known each other well and their friends are unknown to each other, each would have to limit her list to fifty.

On the other hand, if the groom's people live in another place and this may mean that not more than twenty will be able to come, the bride's mother will be able to invite as many as will result in eighty acceptances. Both mothers may risk being a little overliberal because there are always a few who, having accepted, are then prevented for one reason or another from coming.

It is always safe to invite an overlarge number of friends who live at a distance. Very few outside of the immediate family and most intimate friends are likely to take a long trip—except in thought and expressed by means of telephone or telegraph.

Of course it is true that the number of guests of each of the two mothers is not always evenly divided. It does, in fact, often happen that all of the members of one family are insatiable accumulators of friends, while the other is incurably aloof. In this case the wedding list would in all fairness be divided eighty to the first and twenty to the other. The sum one hundred is used of course merely for convenience. The actual total may more than probably be multiplied several times.

CHURCH INVITATIONS UNLIMITED

Invitations to a big church wedding are always sent to the entire visiting list, and often to business acquaintances of both families, no matter how large the combined number may be or whether they will by any chance be present or not. Even people in deep mourning are included, as well as those who live thousands of miles away, for the invitations not merely proffer hospitality but are messengers carrying the news of the marriage.

After a house wedding or a private ceremony, where invitations had to be limited to relatives and personal friends of the young couple, general announcements are sent out to the entire visiting list.

When, as often happens, one family is several times the size of the other family, and has also a list of intimate friends that is twice the length of that of the other, a certain number of pews within the ribbons that will be unoccupied by the smaller family are made available for members of the larger family.

These are of course allotted according to personal agreement by the two mothers. Usually the extra seats are not "within the ribbons," but in the case of an overlarge family as well as really intimate friends, the smaller family might relinquish one or two fairly close pews to the larger one.

MAKING LIST FOR LARGE WEDDING

In the cities where a Social Register or other Visiting Book is published, people find it easiest to read it through, marking "XX" in front of the names of family members and intimate friends who *must* be asked to the house, and a check, √, in front of those to be asked to the church only, or to have announcements sent them. If the reception list is unavoidably limited, certain names are marked with a single "X," meaning that these are to have house invitations if possible. Names which do not appear in the printed list are added, of course, as they are thought of. In country places and smaller cities, or where a published list is not available or sufficient, use the telephone book.

A word of warning: To leave out old friends because you think them unimportant and to include comparative strangers because they seem to be of great importance, not only shows a want of loyalty and proper feeling, but invites the contempt of those very ones whom such snobbery seeks to impress.

Four lists, therefore, are combined in sending out wedding invitations; the bride and the groom make one each of their own friends, to which is added the visiting list of the bride's family, made out by her mother or other near relative, and the visiting list of the groom's family, made out by his mother or a relative. When the lists have been completed, the bride's mother counts the combined number of double XX's, and if she finds that the guests can include, let us say fifty more, she tells the bridegroom's mother that she can change twenty-five single X names into double ones. On the other hand, should the total number of double XX's be too many, distress in having to cut the list is the result.

At a typical wedding, friends are asked to the reception as well as to the church, and acquaintances to the church only. If the wedding is to be in the house or is otherwise very small, so that none but families and intimate friends are invited, announcements are sent to all uninvited acquaintances.

When lists are very long, the compiling is usually done by a professional secretary, who also addresses the envelopes, encloses the proper number of cards, and seals, stamps, and posts the invitations. The address of a professional secretary can always be furnished by the stationer. Where lists do not run to great length, the envelopes are addressed and the invitations sent out by the bride herself and some of her friends who volunteer to help her.

HOW MANY BRIDESMAIDS OR OTHER ATTENDANTS?

This question is answered by: How many friends has she whom she has "always promised" to have with her on that day? Has she a large circle of intimates or only one or two? Her sister is always maid (or matron) of honor. If she has no sister of suitable age, she chooses her most intimate friend.

In addition to a maid or matron of honor, a bride may have a veritable procession; eight or ten bridesmaids, junior bridesmaids, flower girls, pages, and a ring bearer.

At an average New York wedding there are four or six bridesmaids. Sometimes or in rare cases where a bride's best friends have all married before her, all the "maids" may be "matrons." Married friends of the bride who serve as her bridesmaids are called "bridesmaids" and not "bridesmatrons." Although it is not very suitable to have young married women as bridesmaids and then have an unmarried girl as maid of honor, this rule is usually broken in the case of a bride's unmarried sister.

Although a bride need have no attendants, it is best that she have at least one. The picture of her father holding her bouquet and stooping to adjust her train would be difficult to witness with gravity.

As ushers and bridesmaids are chosen from only most intimate friends of the bride and groom, it is scarcely necessary to suggest how to word the asking! Usually they are told at the time of announcing the engagement that they are expected to serve; or they are told whenever one happens to meet them. If school or college friends who live at a distance are among the number, letters are necessary. Such as:

"Mary and I are to be married on the tenth of November, and, of course, you are to be an usher." Usually he adds, "My dinner is to be on the seventh at eight o'clock at ——," naming the club or restaurant.

It is unheard of that a man refuse the honor unless a bridegroom, for snobbish reasons, asks someone who is not really a friend at all. Of course, the groom is careful not to ask someone who he knows will have problems of time and distance that will be difficult to overcome.

It is entirely correct for a married man to act as usher, or for a married woman to be matron of honor, when neither the wife of the first nor the husband of the second is asked to take part. In fact—though there is no rule against it—it is most rare, if ever, that a man and wife both serve at the same wedding. The one not officiating is of course invited to the wedding, but not necessarily invited to sit at the bridal table.

THE COST OF BEING BRIDESMAID

With the exception of the flowers they carry, which are presented by the bride, every article worn by the bridesmaids, flower girls, or pages, although chosen by the bride, must be paid for by the wearers.

It is perhaps an irrefutable condemnation of the modern wedding display that many a young girl has had to refuse the joy of being in the wedding party because a complete bridesmaid's outfit costs a sum that neither she nor her parents are able to meet. And as it is seldom that the bride herself is in a position to give six or eight complete costumes, much as she may want all her most particular friends with her on her day of days, it is often difficult for her to offer to pay for the outfit of but one of her bridesmaids.

Unless her bridesmaids have unusually deep purses, the bride who has a conscience tries to choose clothes that will not be too expensive. Yesterday the tender-hearted bride who, for the sake of their purses, sent her bridesmaids to an inexpensive dressmaker to have their clothes made, and to a little hat-place around the corner, was likely to have a rather dowdy little flock fluttering down the aisle in front of her. Today, however, department stores as well as specialty shops are prepared to submit enchanting ready-to-wear models that can be ordered in different colors, or even materials, and at almost whatever the budget decided upon may be.

The other expenses are shared this way: All attendants of the bride and bridegroom pay for their own transportation from wherever they are to wherever the wedding is to take place. "Conveyance of the bridesmaids" means merely to and from the church and the bride's house, etc. The girls are always the guests of the bride and the men the guests of the bridegroom, from the moment they arrive in the bride's town until they leave.

SUITABILITY OF THE BRIDE'S DRESS

At her first wedding a bride suitably wears a dress of white and a bridal veil whether she be sixteen or forty! Naturally a veil of tulle would be too youthful for the bride of forty, just as a veil of yellowed lace would be unsuitable at sixteen.

The traditional bridal material is satin for all seasons of the year. Its weight would be affected by the season—a very heavy satin for the winter and a lighter weight for the summer.

In addition to satin, other materials suitable for autumn and midwinter weddings, are faille, velvet, and moiré antique. In the spring, lace and taffeta. In midsummer, chiffon, organdy, mousseline-de-soie.

Her slippers are of white satin or moiré. But whatever she chooses she should be sure that they are comfortable because she not only has to walk up the aisle in them, but she has to stand at the reception.

A very young bride in a veritable cloud of tulle is at her loveliest. Lace of course adds dignity and is most becoming to a mature bride when definitely cream in color rather than unrelieved white.

It is very important that a bride in her thirties or over choose a veil and dress both of a becomingly creamed white, particularly if the dress be of satin.

There is really a very marked difference in the becomingness to the skin of an almost imperceptible accent of blue or pink or ivory.

For a bride beyond her twenties, the right one of these off-white tints is as flattering as the wrong one is cruel.

THE BRIDE'S VEIL

The face veil is rather old-fashioned, and is appropriate only for a very young bride of a demure type. The tradition is that a maiden is too shy to face a congregation unveiled, and reveals her face only when she is a married woman.

If she chooses to wear a veil over her face up the aisle and during the ceremony, the front veil is always a short, separate piece about a yard square, gathered on an invisible band, and pinned with a hairpin at either side, after the long veil is arranged. It is taken off by the maid of honor when she gives the bride's bouquet back to the bride at the conclusion of the ceremony.

At present the veil is usually mounted by a milliner on a foundation, so that it need merely be put on. But every girl has her individual idea of what she wishes her wedding veil to be, and may choose rather to put it together herself, or have it done by some particular friend whose taste and skill she especially admires.

The length of the train of the bride's dress depends somewhat upon the size of the church. In a large church the train can be very long; in a small chapel, short. A moderately short train extends one yard on the ground. The length of the train also depends to some extent on the height of the bride. The dress should be on the conservative side of fashion.

If short, loose gloves happen to be in fashion, she merely pulls the glove off at the altar, but if she wears elbow-length or longer evening gloves, usually the under seam of the wedding finger of the glove is ripped for about two inches, and the bride need only pull the tip off to have the ring put on. Or, if the wedding is a small one, she wears no gloves at all.

If a bride chooses to be married in a traveling dress, she has no bridesmaids, though she often has a maid or matron of honor. A traveling dress is either tailor-made, if she is going directly to a boat or train, or a morning or an afternoon dress, such as she would wear away after a big wedding.

JEWELRY SUITABLE FOR BRIDE

If the gift of the bridegroom is jewelry the bride always wears it even though it may be composed of colored stones. Otherwise she wears colorless jewelry such as a pearl necklace or possibly a pin of pearls or diamonds.

MAKE-UP

As a warning against the too blatant use of cosmetics, it may not be out of place to quote the comments made by a man of great distinction who, having seen nothing of the society of very young people for many years, had to go to the wedding of a niece. It was one of the biggest weddings of the spring season in New York. The flowers were wonderful; the bridesmaids were many and beautiful. Afterward, the family talked long about the wedding, but the distinguished uncle said nothing. Finally, he was asked pointblank, "Don't you think the wedding was too lovely? Weren't the bridesmaids beautiful?"

"No," said the uncle, "I did not think it was lovely at all. Every one of the bridesmaids was so powdered and painted and mascaraed that there was not a sweet or fresh face among them. I can see a procession just like them any evening at a musical comedy! One expects unrestrained make-up in a theatre, but in the house of God it is shocking!"

THE BRIDESMAIDS' COSTUMES

The costumes of the bridesmaids—slippers, stockings, dresses, bouquets, gloves, and hats—are selected by the bride, without considering or even consulting them as to their taste or preferences. This rule is important to note. On occasion a bride will try to consult them and get all to agree, but long experience has proved that six girls almost certainly quarrel over six opposed ideas. Bridesmaids, therefore, customarily wear and pay for what the bride chooses. That is the rule. The only consolation is that, if they are ugly, she gets full blame. If they are lovely, she gets the credit. The bridesmaids are always dressed exactly alike as to texture of materials and model of making, but sometimes their dresses differ in color. The two who follow the ushers might wear pale green, the next two peach, and the next two violet, and the maid of honor yellowish cream; and all carry the same kind of flowers.

The dress of the maid or matron of honor, by the way, never precisely matches that of the bridesmaids, though it is usually similar but reversed in color. For example: If the bridesmaids wear peach dresses trimmed with blue and blue-trimmed peach hats and have bouquets of delphinium, the maid of honor wears the same dress in blue, with peach trimming, has a blue hat trimmed with peach, and carries talisman roses.

Sometimes the bridesmaids wear the same color, but in graduated value. The first two would wear American Beauty rose, the next two a lighter tint, and the next two a still lighter color, while the maid of honor would be in palest flesh pink. Although a bride seldom cares to run the risk of having the white of her attendants detract from the effect of the single whiteness of her dress, an all-white wedding could be entrancing, especially in a garden with a background of dense, dramatic green, like the high-hedged Italian ones.

The other important item is the selection of a material for the bridesmaids' dresses that will complement the material of the dress of the bride. Perhaps the bride's dress might be of fine white lace (stiffly starched) and the bridesmaids' of taffeta; or if in the South, she might wear taffeta and put them in organdy or organzine trimmed with taffeta. Or they might all wear the same soft lustrous satin and let the bride's veil and train alone make the difference.

WHAT THE BRIDESMAIDS CARRY

The bridesmaids almost always carry flowers—bouquets sometimes, or baskets, but usually sheaves which they hold on their outside arms. Those walking on the right side hold them on the right arm with the stems pointing downward to the left; and those on the left hold their flowers on the left arm, with stems toward the right. Bouquets or baskets are, however, held in front.

Sometimes bridesmaids carry muffs in winter, or in summer fans or parasols, more often flower-filled baskets or hats made into baskets by tying their wide brims together with ribbons. Flowers matching those in the basket might be worn in the hair, in which case the bridesmaids need not buy either hats or hair ornaments.

BRIDESMAID IN MOURNING

A bridesmaid who is in mourning may wear colors on this one day, as bridesmaids' dresses are looked upon as uniforms, not individual costumes.

JUNIOR BRIDESMAIDS

Young girl attendants, aged from about seven to fourteen, who are too big to be flower girls and too young to be regular bridesmaids, are junior bridesmaids. Their clothes are modified copies of those worn by the bridesmaids.

FLOWER GIRLS AND PAGES

Flower girls and pages are dressed in quaint old-fashioned dresses and suits of white silk or satin of whatever period the bride fancies as being especially picturesque. Or perhaps they are dressed in their ordinary white clothes, with wreaths and bouquets for the girls and white boutonnières for the boys.

RING BEARERS

As it happens, these are unknown in the smart world of New York, but they are very popular in many other American localities. And if the bride would like to have her little brother or nephew perform this office, he is, of course, dressed in white, carries the ring on a small firm white cushion, and walks ahead of her.

The ring is either lightly sewed to the cushion or fastened by having an ordinary pearl-headed flower pin thrust into the center of **the** cushion and the ring encircling this. The best man should be shown beforehand whether he is to pull or lift it off.

TRAIN BEARERS

Train bearers, as the name implies, hold the bride's train. They, too, must be very little boys and dressed in white. The train trailing smoothly by itself is really more assuring than a train in the hands of very little children whose manner of bearing it is apt to be uncertain, to say the least.

Both boys and girls wear slippers with a strap and white socks. If they are dressed in white, their slippers are of course white; but if they wear color, their slippers are colored, either to match their clothes or of a contrasting color—more often the latter. As everyone knows, children's strap slippers come in several colors; otherwise white ones are easily dyed. Kid is in better taste than satin.

At important weddings little girls often wear picture bonnets. At simpler weddings they wear narrow wreaths on their heads. These should be carefully measured for size and must be neat in outline. Small artificial flowers are far better for this purpose than real flowers, which are likely to be ragged as well as too heavy.

JUNIOR USHERS

For a boy who is too big to be a ring bearer and too young to be an usher, a very useful position (especially if there are two) is that of running the ribbons in front of the pews. When there are two, one takes the right aisle, the other one the left, and then they stand in front holding the ribbon.

When there is only one boy, he can quite well run the ribbon up the left aisle and stand in front of the first pew until the bride's father takes his place. Then he can put the ribbon in front and stand in front of it.

THE HEAD USHER

In certain localities courtesy designates the usher who is selected to take the bride's mother up the aisle as the head or first usher.

Very occasionally, too, a nervous groom appoints an especially reliable friend head usher so as to be sure that all details will be carried out, including the prompt and proper appearance at the church of the other ushers. The ushers divide the arrangements among themselves. The groom decides who goes on which aisle. One volunteers or is asked to look out for the bride's coming and to notify the groom. Another is detailed to take the two mothers up the aisle. But very often this arrangement is arbitrarily decided by height. If one mother is very tall and the other very short, each goes up with a different usher.

BEST MAN AND USHERS

No matter how small the wedding, the bridegroom always has a best man. It is not an unbreakable rule, but it hints of a family quarrel if the brother of the bridegroom is not best man, or the sister of the bride is not maid of honor, unless, of course, brother or sister is many years senior or junior. When the bridegroom has no brother, his next selection is his most intimate friend; or, if deciding upon this best one is difficult, he perhaps chooses the brother of the bride.

"Groomsmen" is supposedly an obsolete term; it is still used in some parts of the country, but the word generally used today is ushers. The number of ushers is in proportion to the size of the church and the number of guests invited. At a house wedding, ushers are often merely honorary, and the bridegroom may have many or none, as he chooses.

BRIDE'S USHER AND GROOM'S BRIDESMAID

Unless attendants are limited to her sister and his brother, a brother of the bride, or if she has no brother, then her favorite cousin is always asked by the groom to be usher out of compliment to her. The bride returns the compliment by asking the sister of the groom who is nearest her own age to be bridesmaid, or if he has no sister, she asks a cousin. If she is to have a number of bridesmaids—especially if the groom has no sister—she very often shows her courtesy by asking the groom to name a particular friend of his. The bride in asking the groom's bridesmaid does not say, "Will you be one of my bridesmaids because Jim wants me to ask you?" If the bridesmaid is not a particular friend of the bride, she knows perfectly that it is on Jim's account that she has been asked. It is the same with the bride's usher. If the groom is choosing six to eight or ten ushers, he often includes one who is an especial friend of the bride, and asks him exactly as he asks the others.

When the homes of the bride and bridegroom are a great distance apart, so that none but the bridegroom's immediate family can make the journey to the wedding, it is not unusual—if he has no brother—that he choose his father or even stepfather as his best man. The ushers are chosen from among the friends of the bride. It is not unusual that his father serve as best man—at any time.

THE BRIDEGROOM'S WEDDING CLOTHES

(1) MOST FORMAL WEDDING, DAYTIME

 Cutaway coat
 Waistcoat to match (or white, if the bridegroom prefers)
 Gray-striped trousers or black with white pin stripes
 Stiff white shirt
 Wing collar

Black and white tie or gray tie, either four-in-hand or bow; or gray or white ascot, if preferred

Plain black shoes and socks. Shoes should be freshly polished and have new soles and heels. Some bridegrooms blacken the soles of their shoes with waterproof shoe dye so that when they kneel at the altar, their shoes look dark and neat.

White boutonnière

White buckskin gloves preferred, but when gray is chosen, they should be as light as possible

Spats, seldom worn today, but when worn, must match the color of gloves

Silk hat

Equally smart, but slightly less formal: Black sack coat; other details the same as for cutaway except hat: black Homburg, derby, or, in summer, Panama

Malacca stick, if any (any stick is rare today)

(2) Most Formal Wedding, Evening

Full dress (tail coat, stiff white shirt, wing collar, white lawn tie, white waistcoat)

White evening gloves

White boutonnière

Patent leather pumps or oxford ties

Black socks

Hat and stick same as (1); opera hat, if preferred, but *not* an ebony cane

(3) Less Formal Wedding, Daytime

Dark blue suit

White shirt

Wing or starched turn-down collar

Blue and white tie, bow or four-in-hand

Black socks and calfskin oxford shoes

White boutonnière

No gloves

Gray or black Homburg hat

(4) Less Formal Evening Wedding

Dinner coat (Tuxedo)

White waistcoat smartest in New York, but not generally customary elsewhere

Black silk tie

White boutonnière

No gloves

Patent leather oxford shoes

Opera hat smartest; otherwise, black Homburg or a derby; in summer, a straw or Panama

(5) SUMMER DAYTIME WEDDING IN COUNTRY

> Either dark blue or gray flannel coat and waistcoat (or if coat double-breasted, no waistcoat)
>
> White or gray flannel or white linen trousers
>
> With blue coat, blue and white tie; with gray coat, black and white tie or plain gray
>
> White buckskin shoes and white wool or lisle socks, or plain dark blue or gray socks (matching coat)
>
> Stiff straw hat or Panama
>
> No gloves

(6) INFORMAL DAYTIME WEDDING IN TORRID WEATHER

> All white Palm Beach or linen suit
>
> Plain dark blue or black tie, bow or four-in-hand
>
> White socks
>
> White buckskin shoes
>
> White handkerchief

(7) EVENING WEDDING IN A TROPICAL CLIMATE

> White dinner coat, double-breasted so as to avoid waistcoat
>
> Black tie, and other details same as (4)

See Chapter 40, "The Clothes of a Gentleman," for more information about the correct accessories for evening and daytime formal wear.

WHAT THE BEST MAN AND USHERS WEAR

At the most correct and formal daytime wedding, the best man wears precisely what the bridegroom wears. The groom and best man often wear ties that are different from those worn by the ushers, and occasionally white waistcoats. Otherwise the two principal men are dressed like the ushers.

To make sure that his ushers will be alike in so far as it is imperative, a fastidious bridegroom sends each one typewritten instructions covering every detail of the equipment required. For example:

> Wedding rehearsal on Tuesday at St. Bartholomew's Church at 5 P.M. Wedding on Wednesday at 4 P.M.   Date.
>
> Please wear for the wedding:
>
> Black calfskin low shoes
>
> Plain black socks
>
> Gray striped trousers—the darkest you have
>
> Morning coat (cutaway) and single-breasted black waistcoat
>
> White dress shirt; cuffs to show three-quarters of an inch below coat sleeves
>
> Stand-up wing collar
>
> Tie and gloves are enclosed. (*Groom had already found out size of gloves and also size of collars, since bow ties had been selected.*)

Boutonnière will be at the church
Be at the church yourself at a quarter before five o'clock Tuesday
and at three o'clock sharp Wednesday

ALIKE? YES. DUPLICATES? NO.

It is of greatest importance that in dress each usher be almost a counterpart of his fellows, if the picture is to be perfect. Everyone knows what a ragged-edged appearance is produced by a company of recruits whose uniforms are from odd lots. The clothes of the bride's father need not match those of the ushers, but they must look well with theirs.

That one word "almost" in the above paragraph is important to mention: The clothes of the men of the bridal party including bridegroom and best man and ushers should NOT match too precisely.

Their ties, boutonnières, and gloves are exactly alike of course, because they are gifts from the bridegroom, and not bought individually. But otherwise, there should be differences in stripes of trousers, shape of waistcoats, and slight but quite apparent differences in materials and measures of coats, to avoid giving the impression of being members of a chorus. This possible resemblance to a musical comedy chorus is also a sound reason why it is in bad taste to permit the bridesmaids to walk with the ushers.

WHAT OTHER CLOTHES FOR THE BRIDE'S TROUSSEAU?

It is impossible for anyone but the bride herself to answer the question of what clothes she will need and of what variety. It all depends: Is she to be in a big city for the winter season, or at a resort for the summer? Is she going to travel, or live quietly? It is impractical to get more outer clothes than she has immediate use for; fashions change too radically.

On the subject of underthings, one can dip into any of the women's magazines devoted to fashion and understand at first sight that the furnishings which may be put upon the person of one young female would require a catalog as long and varied as that of a seedsman. An extravagant trousseau contains every article illustrated—and more besides—and by the dozens! But it must not for a moment be supposed that every bridal trousseau requires an outlay possible only to parents who are very rich and also very indulgent.

BRIDEGROOM'S TROUSSEAU FOR THE HONEYMOON

The clothes the bridegroom will need for his wedding trip depend naturally upon where they are going, and how. If they are going by train or bus with numerous stopping places, the smallest and fewest items to carry is the obvious objective. Airlines charge for excess baggage, and sometimes refuse to carry it even for an extra charge. But if they are going in their own car where there is plenty of room for suit-cases, they can easily take everything they think they might have use for.

If going to any place where he and his bride will want to dress for dinner, he must of course add the type of evening clothes he is likely to need, whether this be no more than a dark business suit with white shirt, or a dinner coat, or even possibly white tie and tails.

If they are going to a large city, he will need two business suits—not necessarily new, but good as new—and two pairs of shoes to wear alternately. He should choose suits which look well with the same overcoat or topcoat—which let us hope is either blue or dark gray, if it is also to be worn with evening clothes.

If they are going on a journey by plane, train, or boat and stopping perhaps at a coast or country resort, then he should take clothes for whatever sports they are likely to follow.

So much for the groom as he appears in public. And now to answer the question, "How important are the groom's clothes to the bride?" Every bride will certainly notice when her husband, in her opinion, looks particularly well. The husband may not be able to afford a large and fashionable wardrobe, but he should be careful to buy clothes of a neat, becoming, and conservative style. It is far better to have a few suits that are good in both quality and taste, than to have a multitude of poorly-made, ill-fitting suits of garish pattern and cheap fabric.

The neatness and cleanliness of her husband's personal belongings is likely to be of particular importance to a bride. He should pay particular attention to their neat appearance so that when they are laid out on the bureau or on the bathroom shelf, there are no brushes with bristles looking chewed off or matted down, nor any dingy shaving things, nor half-empty toothpaste tubes that are twisted and smeared.

A dressing-gown of simplest variety that is fresh and washable is to be preferred to one of silk brocade that is bedraggled. Let his slippers and underwear be new, and his pajamas attractive in color. Actually, none of these items need be new if they *look* nice and fresh. A young man should care for his personal belongings not only to make an impression on his bride, but also so they will not age before their time and need frequent replacing.

CLOTHES OF THE BRIDE'S MOTHER

At any hour between 8 A.M and 6 P.M., the mother of the bride wears a daytime dress, preferably light in color or bright—never black unless relieved with color. Her dress varies in degree of elaborateness according to the other wedding preparations. For example, at a formal wedding (bridal dress, bridesmaids, large reception) her dress follows an equally formal pattern, even to a long skirt. She always should wear hat and gloves and usually wears flowers, although these last are not a requirement.

In the evening, dinner dresses are in best taste. If a dress is cut low, something must be worn over the shoulders in church. Flowers or other hair ornaments or perhaps veiling or a chiffon scarf would fill the requirements for head covering in church when it is not in current fashion to wear evening hats.

As a rule, the mother of the bride leaves her wrap in the vestibule with those of the bridesmaids. If she knows that the church is likely to be draughty and has an attractive fur piece, she might carry or wear this. Otherwise, someone will have to put a light wrap in the pew for her just before she herself comes up the aisle. In other words, the bride's mother should not wear or carry anything that might spoil the effect of her dress.

CLOTHES OF THE BRIDE'S FATHER

There is no hard and fast rule governing the clothes of the bride's father. In other words he may wear whatever is becoming to him, or he may wear whatever the bridegroom is going to wear.

Ordinarily a young father wears a cutaway like that of the bridegroom and his ushers. If they, however, wear black sack coats with their striped trousers and her father is both young and slim-waisted, he may very properly wear the same. But it would not be quite suitable for him to wear the less formal as well as more youthful sack coat, when the younger men are wearing cutaways.

BRIDEGROOM'S MOTHER AND FATHER

Since the two mothers stand together to receive at the reception, the bridegroom's mother should if possible choose a dress similar in type to that chosen by the bride's mother. Obviously, one should not wear a tailored street dress if the other is wearing a long formal semi-evening dress.

The bridegroom's father naturally wears the same type of clothes as those worn by the bride's father. In other words, cutaway in the daytime, tail coat in the evening. He has, however, no part in the ceremony and therefore what he wears is not so important.

THE CLOTHES OF THE GRANDFATHERS

For the grandfathers of the bride or groom (or both) cutaways with four-in-hand ties or possibly frock coats with ascot cravats would be suitable. Whether to choose the latter or a cutaway would depend upon personal becomingness.

OTHER MEMBERS OF THE FAMILIES

The sisters and brothers and grandparents wear clothes similar in type to those worn by the mothers and fathers. Children always wear their best party clothes.

ON WEARING BLACK

Nearest relatives should not choose black unless they wear nothing else ever, and, in this case, its somberness should be relieved with some trimming of color. This even applies to one who is wearing mourning; the color in this case would have to be violet.

THE MOST ELABORATE WEDDING POSSIBLE

Whether in the city or the country, the church is decorated with masses of flowers in some such elaborateness as standards, or sprays tied to the pew ends, as well as the floral embellishment of the chancel. The service is perhaps conducted by a bishop or another distinguished clergyman, with an assistant clergyman, and accompanied by a full choral service, possibly with the addition of a celebrated church soloist. The clothes of the bride and her maids are chosen with seeming disregard of cost.

Later, at the reception, there is not only a floral background against which the bridal couple receives, but every room has been adorned with greens and flowers. An orchestra—actually two, so that the playing may be without intermission—is hidden behind smilax or other greenery in the hall or wherever most convenient. A huge canopied platform is built on the lawn or added to the veranda or built out over the yard of a city house. It is packed with small tables, each seating four or six or possibly eight, as may be preferred or, more likely, as space suggests.

DETAILS OF A SIT-DOWN BREAKFAST

The general sit-down breakfast is the most elaborate wedding reception possible and except in great houses—such as a few of those in Newport—is always supplied by a caterer, who brings all the food, tables, chairs, napery, china, and glass, as well as the necessary waiters. The butler and footmen of the house may assist or oversee, or be detailed to other duties.

In many large houses, a canopied platform is built next to the veranda, on the lawn, or over the yard. The platform is filled with little tables. In the center is the large one reserved for the bridal party. At a large breakfast a second table is reserved for the parents of the bride and groom and a few especially invited friends.

Place-cards at the bride's table and at the parents' table are of white bristol board embossed in silver to match the monograms on the wedding-cake boxes. Or plain white cards may have a strap cut—like a double buttonhole—and small white flowers thrust under the strap.

Place-cards are not put on any of the small tables. All the guests, except the few placed at the two reserved tables, sit with whom they like. Sometimes they do so by prearrangement, but usually they sit where they happen to find friends—and room!

Small menu cards printed in silver are usually put on all the tables. Sometimes these cards have the crest of the bride's father embossed at the top, but usually the initials of the bride and groom are stamped in silver to match the wedding-cake boxes.

Example:

Lobster Newburg
Suprême of Chicken
Peas
Aspic of Foie Gras
Celery Salad
Ices
Coffee

There may be bouillon instead of lobster Newburg, or there may be soft-shelled crabs or oyster pâté, or another sea food. The main dish may also be broiled chicken—half of a squab or chicken for each guest—sweetbreads and mushrooms, or chicken pâté.

Any variety of aspic with celery salad may be served.

Individual ices are accompanied by little cakes of assorted variety.

At a wedding breakfast of this extreme elaborateness, the only correct beverage has always been champagne. A substitute is at best "a poor thing." Orange juice and ginger ale, or white grape juice and ginger ale, with sugar and mint leaves, are two attempts at a satisfying non-alcoholic cup.

THE TYPICALLY "PERFECT" WEDDING

What one might call the typically perfect wedding is merely a modification of the one outlined above. The chancel of the church is decorated—but less lavishly—except perhaps in summer, when garden flowers are to be had in profusion. Sometimes there are flowers at the ends of the ten to twenty reserved pews, or possibly only at the ends of the two pews that mark the beginning of the ribboned section.

There is occasionally a choral service and a distinguished officiating clergyman. Except for the background against which the bride and groom receive, there is very little floral decoration at the reception.

A number of small tables in the downstairs rooms of the house may seat fifty or perhaps a hundred guests. Typically however (whether simple or lavish) the collation is set out on the dining table and the guests eat standing. The bridal table is necessarily placed in another room, or in summer possibly on the porch or in the garden. If the bride has no attendants, she chooses a few of her best friends as well as the ushers to sit at the table with them.

THE STAND-UP BREAKFAST OR SUPPER

For the stand-up breakfast, or for the more typical collation in the afternoon or evening, a single long table is set in the dining-room. It is covered with a plain white damask cloth. In the center is a centerpiece of white flowers. On it are piles of plates (preferably white, or white and gold), stacks of napkins, and rows of spoons and forks at intervals.

Usually the bridal table is set elsewhere. If not, the wedding cake is the feature of the buffet, put at the center of one side of this table with a centerpiece of white flowers behind it or two floral pieces flanking it. At an elaborate high-noon breakfast there is usually a big urn at one end filled with bouillon, and one filled with chocolate at the other. In four evenly spaced places are two cold dishes, such as chicken and celery salad, or ham mousse with chopped hearts of lettuce. The hot dishes may be creamed crab meat, chicken à la king, or chicken croquettes. Whatever the choice is, there are two or three cold dishes and at least two hot dishes. Of first importance is to select food that can be easily eaten with a fork while the plate is held in the other hand. There should also be finger rolls and sandwiches substantial yet small enough to eat easily. Tiny sandwiches are very appetizing.

There are dishes filled with fancy cakes, chosen for looks as much as taste. Usually there are also peppermints, caramels, and chocolates. Ice cream is the typical dessert.

After-dinner coffee is put on a side table, as is champagne or its substitute, punch.

THE HOUSE WEDDING

A house wedding involves slightly less expenditure but has the disadvantage of limiting the number of guests. The ceremony is exactly the same as that in a church, except that the procession advances through an aisle of white satin ribbons from the stairs down which the bridal party descends, to the improvised altar. Chairs for the immediate families have usually been placed within a marked-off enclosure, but sometimes space is merely kept free for them to stand in.

Directly in front of the place reserved for the clergyman, there is a cushioned bench for the bride and groom to kneel on during the prayers of the ceremony. Often this bench is backed by an altar rail. In this case the bench is usually six or eight inches high, and between three and four feet long; at the back of it an upright on either end supports a crosspiece or altar rail. It can be made in the roughest fashion by any carpenter, or amateur, as it is entirely hidden under leaves and flowers. On the kneeling surface of the bench are placed cushions rather than flowers, because the latter stain. All caterers have the necessary standards to which ribbons are tied, like the wires to telegraph poles. The top of each standard is usually decorated with a spray of white flowers.

At a house wedding the bride's mother stands at the door of the room in which the ceremony is to be and receives people as they arrive. But the groom's mother merely takes her place near the altar with the rest of the immediate family. The ushers are purely ornamental, unless the house is so large that pews have been installed and the guests are seated as in a church. Otherwise the guests stand wherever they can find places behind the aisle ribbons. Just before the bride's entrance, her mother goes forward and stands in the reserved part of the room. In an apartment the procession starts in the foyer or bedroom hall. Otherwise the ushers go up to the top of the stairway. The wedding march begins and the ushers come down two and two, followed by the bridesmaids, exactly as in a church, the bride coming last on her father's arm. The clergyman and the groom and best man have, if possible, reached the altar by another door. If the room has only one door, they go up the aisle a few moments before the bridal procession starts.

A HOUSE WEDDING AT LEAST EXPENSE

When there are no garden flowers to be had, a suitable background can be made by drawing heavy curtains or hanging curtains of damask or velvet or any plain fabric from the picture molding across any flat wall space. Against this the colorful clothes of the maid of honor or bridesmaids and, above all, the bride's white dress and veil are entirely effective.

For music, nothing could be more beautiful than the phonograph records of organ and choir music purposely made for weddings.

Even at the smallest wedding possible, the clergyman would enter, followed by the bridegroom; the bride would then enter with her father, or alone, and the wedding service would be read.

The collation might consist of nothing but ginger ale or fruit juice, wedding cake, and a few varieties of sandwiches. The refreshments may be placed on a small table covered with a tea-cloth.

HOUSE WEDDING DIFFERS FROM CHURCH WEDDING

The chief difference between a church and house wedding is that the bride and groom do not take a single step together. The groom meets her at the point where the service is read. After the ceremony, there is no recessional. The clergyman withdraws, an usher removes the prayer bench, and the bride and groom merely turn where they stand, and receive the congratulations of their guests, unless, of course, the house is so big that they receive in another room.

When there is no recessional, the groom always kisses the bride before they turn to receive their guests. At a church wedding the groom does not kiss her at the altar unless the officiating clergyman is the bride's father or other very near relative, who instead of shaking hands with her would naturally kiss her. In this case, of course, the groom kisses her first. It is against all tradition for anyone to kiss the bride before her husband does.

There are seldom many bridal attendants at a house wedding—two to four ushers, and one to four bridesmaids—unless the house is an immense one.

At the smallest wedding possible, where only the immediate families are present, they very often all sit together at one lunch or dinner table. (See diagram below.)

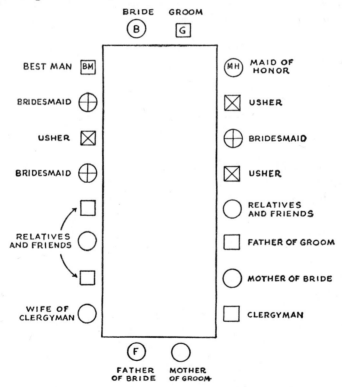

In the country, a house wedding may be performed in the garden, with the wedding procession under the trees and tables out on the lawn —a perfect plan for California or other rainless-season states, but often difficult to arrange along the Atlantic seaboard where rain is all too likely to spoil everything.

At a very simple stand-up breakfast the details would be the same, except that in place of the elaborate cold dishes there would be one hot dish and one salad. If chicken salad is served, there should be a hot dish of eggs or creamed fish. Moreover, if the hot dish is chicken croquettes or chicken à la king, there is a salad of mixed vegetables. The bouillon and ice cream are served as above-stated for the big wedding.

Usually, but not always, there is a bride's table, decorated exactly as that described for a sit-down breakfast, and placed perhaps in the library; but there is no special table for the bride's mother and her guests—or for anyone else.

MODERN SIMPLIFICATION OF WEDDING COLLATION

In New York eating between meals is distinctly going out of fashion, and even the bridal table is more often eliminated than not. The table is set exactly as for afternoon tea, to which is added the wedding cake, of course, and an arrangement of white flowers. Tea is at one end and chocolate at the other. Champagne or fruit punch, and a few dishes of thin sandwiches and little cakes are added, and that is all.

THE EVENING WEDDING

All through the South and generally throughout the West smartest weddings are celebrated at nine o'clock in the evening. There is a reason for the evening wedding in the South. The heat of the day has passed and the coolness of the evening, which lends itself better to festivities and to dancing, which has always been a wedding-supper feature, prevails.

The details are precisely the same as those for the morning or afternoon. In fashionable Southern circles the bride and bridesmaids wear dresses that are perhaps more elaborate and more "evening" in type, and the bridegroom, as well as all men present, wear full evening clothes and the women dress as though going to a ball. For the church ceremony, the women should wear light scarfs of some sort around their shoulders and over their hair, in compliance with the regulations forbidding the uncovering of women's heads and shoulders in consecrated places of worship.

In simpler communities the guests wear exactly what they would wear to evening service in church—a good dress and hat by the women, and dark daytime suits of clothes by the men.

THE EARLY MORNING WEDDING

Among Roman Catholics, an eight o'clock morning wedding is not unusual, and its details are precisely the same as for later hours. But for others, who are perhaps boarding an early morning train or ship, and who would especially like the informality to which such an hour lends itself, a wedding may be carried out as follows:

The bride could wear any simple dress. She would wear a veil, of course, but of tulle instead of lace, either falling to the hem of her dress or of finger length. She would carry a bouquet of moderate size, and no gloves, unless she carries a prayer book instead of a bouquet.

Her attendants might wear the simplest sort of morning dresses and hats; the groom and his best man, business suits or flannels. And the breakfast menu, really breakfast, might be fruit, coffee and hot biscuits.

In fact, a small, early morning wedding—where everyone is dressed in morning clothes, and where the breakfast suggests the first meal of the day—can be perfectly enchanting.

ORTHODOX AND REFORM JEWISH WEDDINGS

The Orthodox wedding ceremony differs somewhat from the Reform Jewish ceremony. In the Orthodox ceremony, the bride is veiled and is escorted under a cloth canopy supported by four poles, usually held by hand, by the father and mother. The groom is escorted by his parents. Hats are worn by all men attending the ceremony. Within recent years, the canopy, called "chupah," has been made stationary, that is, the posts rest upon a platform. Sometimes the canopy is made of flowers instead of cloth—the underlying idea being that there must be a covering over the heads of the couple to be married.

The service is read in Hebrew. The groom places a ring upon the finger of the bride, repeating the following formula: "Thou art consecrated unto me with this ring, according to the law of Moses and Israel." The officiating minister then makes the benediction over the wine, giving the groom and bride the goblet, from which they drink. A document is read in Aramaic, giving in detail the pledge of fidelity and protection on the part of the groom toward the bride, and also indicating the bride's contribution toward the new household. At the conclusion of the ceremony, a glass is broken, symbolizing the fact that one must never overlook, even at the height of happiness, the possibility of misfortune.

In the Reform service, the vernacular is used in addition to Hebrew, and the canopy may be dispensed with. The young couple may decide to include many traditional elements in their wedding ceremony; they should consult with their rabbi about this a few weeks beforehand. The groom is usually ushered in by his best man, and the bride is escorted on the arm of her father. The matron of honor, the bridesmaids, and the ushers function in the regular way. The groom repeats either the Hebrew formula or its English equivalent. The bride and groom also drink wine out of the same cup, symbolizing the cup of joy. Usually the clergyman delivers a brief address upon the significance of marriage.

ROMAN CATHOLIC BETROTHALS AND WEDDINGS

The engagement, or Rite of Betrothal, in which a couple is solemnly betrothed to marry at some future time, is becoming increasingly popular, although it is not a requirement. It is a private ceremony and requires no special dress or invitation. As the ceremony usually takes place in a church parish house or rectory, suitable arrangements as to time and place are to be made with the officiating priest.

The wedding of the Roman Catholic Church is customarily centered around the Nuptial Mass celebrated between eight A.M. and noon. In as much as the Nuptial Mass follows the schedule of masses in most parishes, it is often necessary for the engaged couple to make arrangements at the rectory several months in advance. The banns, an announcement of intention to marry, are usually proclaimed from the pulpit three times or are published in the church calendar prior to the wedding. The couple should therefore complete church arrangements before making reception plans. It is also recommended, though not obligatory, that the Catholic members of the bridal party receive Holy Communion at the Nuptial Mass, at which guests receiving the invitation to do so may partake.

Whether the bride and groom and best man and maid of honor, or the whole bridal party are permitted within the altar rail is determined by individual church practice. Since some churches have strict rules about the social accompaniments of the wedding, it is incumbent on the couple to ascertain the restrictions in advance and to be guided by them.

Although afternoon weddings usually take place between four and five o'clock, they may be held any time from one to six. A Catholic wedding may take place any time during the year; but during the closed seasons of Lent and Advent the Nuptial Blessing is not given, unless, under extraordinary circumstances, permission is granted by the bishop.

A BIG CHURCH MADE SMALL

If the wedding is to be in a large church instead of a chapel and only a comparatively few pews are to be occupied, the effect of emptiness may be overcome entirely by making a hedge of branches or potted shrubbery across the pews that form the boundary. The altar, chancel, and necessary pews would be lighted brilliantly and the pews behind the screen of greens left dark, thus making the church seem as small as need be.

If there is no side door, a narrow opening would have to be left in the aisle to admit the guests, but the bridal party would enter from the vestry instead of going up the long aisle. Or at less expense, if there are choir stalls, they may be used as pews and the church so lighted as to include only the chancel. This arrangement gives to the smallest possible wedding all the solemn beauty of church surroundings, including the music of the organ.

RECEIVING IN CHURCH, A FRIENDLY CUSTOM

When the marriage takes place in a church and there is to be no reception afterward, the bride and groom often follow the friendly and charming custom of waiting after the recessional in the vestibule of the church, with the bridal party and their parents, in order to receive the good wishes of the congregation as it leaves.

THE DOUBLE WEDDING

At a double wedding, the two bridegrooms follow the clergyman and stand side by side, each with his best man behind him; the groom of the older sister nearer the aisle. The ushers—one half, friends of the first, and the others, friends of the second bridegroom—go up the aisle together. Then come the bridesmaids of the older sister followed by her maid of honor, who walks alone. The older sister follows, leaning on her father's arm. Then come the bridesmaids of the younger sister, her maid of honor, and last, the younger bride on the arm of a brother, uncle, or nearest male relative.

The first couple ascends the chancel steps and takes their place at the left side of the altar rail, leaving room at the right side for the younger bride and her bridegroom. The father stands just below his older daughter. The brother takes his place in the first pew.

The ceremony is a double one, read to both couples, with the particular responses made twice. The father gives both brides away—first, his older daughter, and then his younger. Then he takes the place which must be saved for him beside his wife in the first pew.

At the end of the ceremony, the older sister and her husband turn and go down the aisle first. The younger couple follows. The bridesmaids of the older are followed by those of the younger; the ushers follow last.

WHEN BRIDES "ATTEND" EACH OTHER

It is not usual, but it is quite possible, for each bride at a double wedding to serve as maid of honor for her sister. Each in turn holds the other's bouquet during her betrothal ceremony.

But the wise bridegroom, if he dispenses with a best man and uses the services of his brother groom, keeps his own bride's ring in his own waistcoat pocket.

SEATING PARENTS AT A DOUBLE WEDDING

One difficulty of a double wedding is the seating of the parents of the two bridegrooms, who must either share the first pew or draw lots for the occupation of first or second. These questions they must decide for themselves.

Occasionally the brides are cousins, in which case the front pew on the bride's side must be shared by both mothers, the older sister—or sister-in-law—being given the aisle seat.

THE SECOND MARRIAGE

The fact that a bridegroom has been married previously has no bearing on the wedding preparations which may be made by his maiden bride.

WIDOW

The marriage of a widow differs from that of a maid in that she cannot wear a bridal veil, orange blossoms, or a myrtle wreath, which are emblems of virginity; nor does she have bridesmaids, though she may have a maid or matron of honor.

If she has not done so long before, she should either remove, or else transfer, her first wedding and engagement rings to the third finger of her right hand as soon as she becomes engaged. When her second engagement ring is given her she of course discards the first engagement ring, and if her second marriage is to take place soon she removes her wedding ring as well. By and by it may be that she will again wear her first engagement ring on her right hand. This, however, depends upon the feelings of her second husband. If she knows that he objects, her future happiness may quite possibly depend upon its permanent discard.

Usually a widow writes personal notes of invitation to a very quiet wedding, but this is no reason why she cannot have a lovely wedding. Sometimes—especially if she is young and her family and the groom's are very large—it becomes necessary to send out engraved forms. (See Chapter 11.)

Although she usually chooses a dress and hat of color, she may, if she wishes, wear all white; but of course not a bridal veil nor orange blossoms.

A wedding in very best taste for a widow is held in a small church or chapel, a few flowers or some branched greens in the chancel the only decoration. There would be two ushers or quite possibly none. There are no ribboned-off seats, as only very intimate friends are invited. Usually the bride wears an afternoon street dress and hat, which may be of color or may equally well be white. There may be a family dinner afterward, or the simplest afternoon tea. In any case the breakfast, tea, or dinner is, if possible, at the bride's own house, and the bridal pair may stay where they are and have their guests take leave of them, and then drive away afterward.

DIVORCÉE

Whether or not a divorcée may be married in her church depends upon the circumstances of her divorce on which would depend the approval of her clergyman. Usually the marriage takes place in her own house, performed either by a clergyman or a justice of the peace. A small reception follows.

A BRIDE'S BOUQUET

A BRIDE'S BOUQUET

    This design is used when the bride carries a Bible or prayer book.

She of course may not wear a typical white bridal dress and veil, nor orange blossoms. In fact, if she prefers to wear white, it should be a simple street-length gown worn with a hat. Otherwise she chooses any style of dress she prefers.

Engraved invitations are not in good taste; handwritten notes or possibly messages on visiting-cards are best.

WHEN DIVORCED PARENTS REMAIN FRIENDLY

Because it is obviously happier for the children when friendliness rather than hatred exists between their divorced parents, yesterday's ban against the bad taste of any approach of one to the other is gradually being lifted. According to modern precept, if friendly relationship has been possible, not only Mary's parents but also both of her step-parents are present not only at the church but even possibly at the house. The one unbreakable ban remaining is the sending of a joint wedding invitation by the divorced parents—together!

WHEN THEY ARE NOT FRIENDLY

In the entire subject of etiquette, there is perhaps no situation which brings such unavoidable distress as the wedding of a daughter whose parents are divorced, with both families bitterly estranged. This is especially unhappy for the bride who loves her father and all of his family quite as much as—sometimes even more than—she loves her mother and her family. Yet according to the exactions of chivalry, the wedding of their daughter must be given by her mother.

It is true that she does drive with her father to the church, walks with him up the aisle, and even has him share (very briefly) in the marriage ceremony. But he does not have so much as a glimpse of her after the ceremony, since he does not go to the reception given by his ex-wife and, quite possibly, her present husband.

It is also probable that no member of his family—neither the grandparents nor the aunts or uncles of his daughter—has so much as a glimpse of their granddaughter or their niece on her wedding day, since it is quite possible that those who care most are the very ones who do not go even to the church.

HOW DIVORCED FATHER SHARES THE WEDDING

Happily, however, an entirely proper and practical solution was devised by a father and his daughter a short time ago. In fact, it is said that several others have already followed suit.

In this case the parents' divorce had been so bitter as to result in the estrangement of both families. The bride knew very well that few of her nearest relatives on her father's side would be at the church. She knew also that after giving her away her father would leave the church as promptly as possible and that neither he nor any of his immediate family, nor of his most especial friends—many of them hers too—would be at the reception.

Speaking of this at about the time "the day" was definitely set, the bride and her father hit upon a solution so simple the wonder is that it was never adopted years ago.

The new plan was this: On the day the invitations to the wedding were posted by her mother and stepfather, the following invitations to a small second gathering were sent out by her father:

> *Mr. John Pater*
> *requests the pleasure of your company*
> *at the wedding supper of his daughter*
> *Mary*
> *and her bridegroom*
> *James Martin*
> *Saturday, the tenth of April*
> *at half after six o'clock*
> *oo Beacon Street*

One change in the mother's invitations (insisted on by Mary) was the unusual hour five o'clock. Another deviation from the established wedding procedure was this detail: instead of leaving the reception at her mother's in their traveling clothes, the bride remained in her bridal dress and veil and carried her bouquet; the bridegroom was in his cutaway. In these clothes they left the house, accompanied by her bridesmaids and his ushers (also of course in their wedding clothes), and all drove to the home of her father.

After they had greeted his family and special friends (and not a few neutral ones who had come from her mother's house), a buffet supper was served. At the end of this, the bride and groom changed into traveling clothes, which had been sent to her father's house earlier that day, and departed under the customary shower of rice.

For the children who care equally for their parents, a family divorce brings unavoidable unhappiness; and to the bride whose love for her father and his family is quite as great as her love for her mother and her family, the just-given plan is a very important contribution to thoughtful kindness which is always the test of perfect behavior!

IF WEDDING IS GIVEN BY BRIDE'S FATHER

In the few instances where the wedding is given by the bride's father and stepmother while her own mother is also living, this is evidence that the daughter has made her home with her father instead of her mother.

The second wife does not go to the church and the bride's mother does not go to the house. The bride's own mother sits in the front pew with members of her family, but not her second husband. The bride's father gives her away and then takes his place in one of the farther-back pews behind his ex-wife.

SEATING DIVORCED PARENTS OF THE BRIDEGROOM

Even if they have remained on friendly terms it would be in very bad taste to seat any divorced parents together.

His mother and whomever she would like to have with her should be given the first pew on the bridegroom's side of the church, and the father and others of his family seated in the third pew behind. At a large reception their presence need not be conspicuous nor make anyone uncomfortable.

DEFINITE ARRANGEMENTS SHOULD BE MADE
FOR FLOWERS

If any amount of decoration is to be ordered for the church and the reception, the bride and her mother should go as soon as possible to see their florist, and ask him for an estimate for the decoration of the church and house, and for the bridesmaid's bouquets. Whether they or the bridegroom are to order the bride's own bouquet depends upon the custom of the community, as said before.

In certain cities, yesterday's custom of considering the bride's bouquet (on occasion even those of the bridesmaids) the responsibility of the bridegroom still prevails. Where this custom is followed, the corsage bouquet is often inserted in the center of the larger bouquet and removed when the time for throwing the bouquet to the bridesmaids comes, if this tradition is followed, or later when the bride dresses for going away. Of course the flowers appear as if they were one bouquet. But in the majority of cities it is the modern fashion for the bride's parents to order the bride's bouquet as well as those of the bridesmaids when they order the decoration of the church and house.

The bridegroom sends the bride a "corsage bouquet" to wear when she leaves the house with him. In certain communities it is customary for him to send flowers for the mothers and grandmothers to wear at the wedding. He always buys the boutonnières for his ushers, his best man, and himself—but not for the bride's father, who, unless he is a widower, receives his boutonnière from his own "bride," the bride's mother.

Apart from the bouquets of bride and bridesmaids which they carry, and the boutonnières of the bride's father, bridegroom, best man, and ushers, no other flowers are necessary. As a matter of fact, the decorations at all weddings in all seasons consist in greatest degree—and most often wholly—of smilax and plants of green. It is in fact true that a confusion of flowers detracts from the dresses and bouquets of the bride and the bridesmaids.

IF PICTURES ARE TO BE TAKEN

A professional photographer should be engaged as far ahead of time as possible, especially if the wedding is to be in April, June, or November.

On this subject, pictures of the decorations of church, house, or tables always are taken before the ceremony, as are a few "portraits" of the bride, alone or with her bridesmaids, shortly before they leave for the church, or at home go downstairs, or possibly when they have the final fitting of their dresses. Additional pictures are almost always taken of the whole bridal group just before the bride and groom change into traveling clothes. Candid-camera pictures of the wedding and the reception—beginning with one of the bride leaving the house for the church and ending with the departure of the happy pair for their honeymoon—are becoming increasingly popular. If the actual ceremony is to be photographed, the permission of the clergyman must be secured.

MUSIC

The question as to the kind of music that may be played in the church is in the province of the choirmaster or the organist. However, at a majority of weddings, the march from Wagner's *Lohengrin* has come to be almost as essential to the beauty of the wedding procession as the bride and her bridesmaids. The recessional is usually that of Mendelssohn. If the bride and groom have their hearts set on music which they are advised is considered too worldly to be played in their church, they can of course have many of these selections played at the reception.

On occasion a notable singer—or even possibly an organist—who is a member of the bride's or bridegroom's family, or perhaps merely an especial friend, may quite properly be included in the musical selection. But it would be very discourteous to invite an outsider without consulting, and receiving the consent of, the church organist.

WEDDING CAKE

Wedding cake is an essential of every wedding reception. Black fruit cake is traditional, and most expensive. Also used are light fruit cake and pound cake. When an extra smaller cake intended only for the bridal party has favors in it it is usually lady cake or pound cake. In this case there is a much larger official wedding cake on the big dining table. And it is this cake that the bride and groom together cut as a preparatory-to-feasting ceremony.

At the most elaborate breakfast where the guests are seated at small tables and served by waiters, the only wedding cake is the small one on the bridal table reserved for the bride and groom and their attendants. At this table the bride, assisted by the groom, cuts the first slice which they then share. The family butler or the caterer's head man then cuts sufficient slices for those seated at the table and passes the cake, or it is served with ice-cream.

Sometimes there are two sets of favors hidden in the cake between the two sections marked as in the illustration with three orange-blossom buds or by match ends wrapped in silver foil or other easily seen markers to distinguish the sections to be cut. The bridesmaids' favors are always on the bride's side, and the ushers' on the side of the groom.

Various articles have either been wrapped in waxed paper and baked in the cake, or each, wrapped in silver foil, has been pushed between the two marked sections through the bottom of the cake at short intervals. The bridesmaids find a ten-cent piece for riches, a little gold ring for "first to be married," a thimble or little parrot or cat for "old maid," a wishbone for the "luckiest." On the ushers' side, a button or dog is for "old bachelor," and a miniature pair of dice is a symbol of a lucky chance in life.

Good advice on cutting a black fruit cake is to make a straight perpendicular thrust with the point of the knife and follow this with a sequence of similar thrusts. Any attempt to bring the knife blade down as though it were a lever will meet with crumbling resistance on the part of the cake. It is also best to cut fairly thick slices and cut these again into cubes. Very few cutters can cut large fruit cakes thin.

Many think the best way to cut it is in straight horizontal lines all the way across the cake. Then cut each of these vertically after laying them on a cutting board. To cut a big cake into V-shaped pieces is likely to result in a few icing-covered chunks and a heap of crumbs in the center.

But if you have a baker or caterer cut it, his accustomed way will very definitely be the best way. After all, that which is fitted into the boxes is always smooth-edged and even as can be. They are rectangles, not wedges!

A new fashion at wedding receptions is to have the matches that are on the tables or that are passed to guests with the cigarettes be white match books, ornamented with the combined initials of the bride and groom, to match the individual white wedding cake boxes.

The wedding cake for all of those seated at other tables has been put into individual white boxes tied with white satin ribbon and ornamented with the combined initials of the bride and groom. These boxes are stacked on a table close beside the front door. Each departing guest is expected to take one. On occasion when another member of a family has been expected but prevented from coming, a second box may be taken home to him or her. Otherwise, it is very bad manners to take more than one's own box.

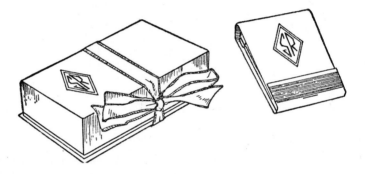

At a smaller wedding, a cake—usually of several tiers and large enough to serve everyone—is provided. The bridal couple cuts the first slice from the projecting bottom tier. After this, a waiter cuts slices until the bottom tier has been cut away. The cake then is removed from the table, and the tiers are separated and cut into slices. The baker has supported each tier on a heavy cardboard disk. When possible, the small top layer surmounted by figurines is set aside for the bride and groom to keep. At any rate, a large piece should be saved for them.

LISTING THE WEDDING PRESENTS

But now to return to the invitations, which are mailed about three weeks before the wedding—unless it is to be a very small one, in which case the invitations are sent out about two weeks before.

If the presents, which begin to arrive as soon as the cards are out, are likely to be many, each one should be entered at once in the gift book. There are many kinds published for the purpose, but any ruled blank book about eight to ten inches square will answer the purpose. The usual model spreads across the double page as follows:

Present Received	Article	Sent by	Sender's Address	Where Bought	Thanks Written
May 20	Silver Dish	Mr. and Mrs. White	1 Park Place	Criterion's	May 20
May 21	12 Plates	Mr. and Mrs. Hardy	2 South Street	Crystal's	May 21

All gifts as they arrive should be numbered with a paste-on sticker, and a corresponding number listed in the gift book. There might be many silver dishes and also dozens of plates—meaning that a sticker goes on one of each design or pattern.

THE BRIDE'S THANKS

In return for the many presents showered upon a happy bride, there is a corresponding task which may not be evaded.

On a sheet of note paper—not a folded visiting-card—and in her own handwriting, she must send a separate letter for each present she receives—and, if humanly possible, she writes each letter of thanks on the day the present arrives. If she does not, they soon get ahead of her and her whole honeymoon is taken up with note-writing. For wording of bride's notes, see Chapter 42.

Notes of thanks can be very short, but they should be written with as little delay as possible. When a present is sent by a married couple, the bride writes to the wife and thanks both, "Thank you for the lovely present you and Mr. Jones sent me." Or she may begin her letter, "Dear Mr. and Mrs. Jones, Thank you *both*," etc.

NEVER SEND AN ENGRAVED CARD OF THANKS

It would not be possible to overemphasize the inexcusable rudeness of the bride who sends a printed or even an engraved card of thanks for wedding presents sent her. Whoever devised this flagrant affront to the traditions of common decency was, obviously, more concerned with making sales to stationers than with acquiring knowledge of the precepts of polite behavior.

A young woman who had many friends but, as it happened, little knowledge of social usage, was led to send out engraved cards announcing

> *Miss Nono Betta*
> *Hereby Acknowledges*
> *Your Kind Gift*
> *And Sends You Her Appreciative Thanks*

It is scarcely necessary to add that appreciative thanks are not expressed in this way. In the case of the young woman in question, her presents stopped like a turned-off faucet as soon as the news of her rudeness spread.

In no way to be confused with the engraved cards of thanks sent out by a social service bureau, in place of the bride's personal letters of

thanks, are the rather especial advance acknowledgments of gifts from
dear friends made by the bride's family on unusual occasions. Such, for
example, as the hurried marriage of a bridegroom who must leave
quickly on foreign service. In this case it is probable that the bride's
mother or sisters will have to send brief notes explaining, "Mary had
gone when your lovely present came. She will, of course, write you as
soon as she receives it." If it is not practical to forward it, her mother
should write a description from which Mary sends her "thanks for the
lovely tray" or whatever her mother described.

Ordinarily, a printed acknowledgment to be followed later by a note
of thanks seems a waste of effort; a minute or two more would complete
a note of thanks to enclose in each stamped and addressed envelope instead of addressing and stamping every acknowledgment twice. Also
it seems pretentious because it implies that so many presents were expected that special preparations were made in advance to take care of
the avalanche. Moreover, this engraved notice, which attracts formal
attention to the promised letter, exacts that the letter be longer and
better than an unheralded note in which a few brief sentences could
say all that is necessary.

WHEN THE PRESENTS ARE SHOWN

There is absolutely no impropriety in showing the presents at the
wedding reception. The only reason for not showing them is lack of
space in a small house or, of course, an apartment. If there is an extra
sitting-room, such as a library, they are shown there. Otherwise a bedroom from which all the furniture has been removed is suitable. Tables
covered with plain white damask tablecloths are put like counters around
the sides of the room. In recent years the display of the presents has often
been omitted.

ARRANGING THE PRESENTS

Not so much in an effort to parade her possessions as to do justice
to the kindness of the many people who have sent them, a bride should
show her appreciation of their gifts by placing each one in the position
of greatest advantage. Naturally, all people's tastes are not equally
pleasing to the taste of the bride—nor are all pocketbooks equally filled.
Very valuable presents are better put in close contrast with others of
like quality—or others entirely different in character. Colors should be
carefully grouped. Two presents, both lovely in themselves, can be made
completely destructive of each other if the colors are allowed to clash.

Usually china is put on one table, silver on another, glass on another,
laces and linens on another. But pieces that jar when appearing together
must be placed as far apart as possible and perhaps even moved to other
surroundings. A badly designed piece of silverware should not be left
among beautiful examples, but be put among china ornaments, or other

articles that do not reveal its lack of fineness by too direct comparison. For the same reason imitation lace should not be put next to real, nor stoneware next to Chinese porcelain. To group duplicates is another unfortunate arrangement. Eighteen pairs of pepper pots or fourteen sauce boats in a row might as well be labeled: "Look at this stupidity! What can she do with all of us?" They are sure to make the givers feel at least a little chagrined at their choice.

DISPLAYING CHECKS

Ordinarily, it would be in very bad taste to display gifts of money. But because it would not be fair to a generous check-giving relative or very intimate friend of the family to have it supposed that he or she sent no gift at all, it is quite proper to display checks with amounts concealed. This is done by laying them out on a flat surface one above the other so that the signatures alone are disclosed. The amount of the one at the top is covered with a strip of opaque paper and then a sheet of glass laid over them all. The glass should be sufficiently large to lay other presents around the margin to keep a curious someone from lifting it.

WHETHER CARDS ARE LEFT ON

There is no definite rule as to whether or not the cards that are sent with the gifts are removed. There is no impropriety in leaving them on, which certainly saves members of the family from repeating many times who sent this and who sent that! This would be especially difficult for a bride whose father is a State governor, or a mayor, or a much-loved clergyman, or notable person in the business community, and who therefore receives an unusual number of presents.

DISPLAYING THE TROUSSEAU

Household linen, especially if very beautiful, is often displayed with the wedding presents, but in cities such as New York, Washington, or Boston, it has never been considered good taste to make a formal display of the bride's personal trousseau. She may, of course, show intimate friends some of her things, but her trousseau is never spread out on exhibition. Objection to her doing so may, however, be removed if it is the custom of the place in which she lives.

EXCHANGING WEDDING PRESENTS

Some people think it discourteous if a bride changes the present chosen for her. But it has been a time-honored custom to permit a bride to exchange all duplicate presents, and no friends should allow their feelings to be hurt, unless they have chosen the present with a particular sentiment. A bride never changes the presents chosen for her by her own family or by the bridegroom's family, unless especially told that she may do so. But to keep twenty-two saltcellars and sixteen silver card trays when she has no pepper pots or coffee spoons or vegetable dishes would be putting sentiment above sense.

THE BRIDESMAIDS' LUNCHEON

In many American communities brides ask their bridesmaids to a farewell luncheon, just as in other communities the bride is given a shower. (See Chapter 33.)

There is no especial difference between a bridesmaids' luncheon and any other lunch party, except that the table is elaborately decorated, usually in pink, with bridesmaids' roses or the bride's chosen colors for the wedding. There is a bride's cake—lady cake with pink icing—and there are favors in the cake and candies wrapped in pink papers on which are written sentimental verses or "fortunes," and altogether it is a "lovely party."

In any event, the typical scene during the days before a wedding is one of packages arriving, and bridesmaids and other intimate friends running in and out of the house at all hours of the day, looking at new presents as they come, perhaps helping the bride to write the descriptions in the gift book or to arrange them in the room where they are to be displayed.

The bride usually goes to oversee the last fittings of the bridesmaids' dresses in order to be sure that they are as she wants them. This final trying-on should be arranged for several days at least before the wedding, so there may be sufficient time to make any alterations that are found necessary. Often the bride tries on her wedding dress at the same time, so that she may see the effect of the whole wedding picture as it will be; or should she prefer, she tries on her dress at another hour alone.

GIFTS FOR THE BRIDE'S ATTENDANTS

Usually her bridesmaids lunch with her, without any "party preparations," or come in for tea, the day before the wedding, and on that day the bride gives each of them her present, which is always something to wear. The typical bridesmaid's present is a bracelet, earrings, a pin, a clip, or other trinket, and this, according to the means of the bride, may have great or scarcely any intrinsic value. The gift to her maid or matron of honor may well match those given the bridesmaids or be quite different. If it is something that can be engraved such as a small silver tray, the date and the initials of the bride and groom commemorate the occasion.

BRIDESMAIDS' AND USHERS' DINNER

If a wedding is held in the country, or if most of the bridesmaids or ushers come from a distance and are therefore staying at the bride's house or with her friendly neighbors, there is naturally a dinner, in order to provide for the visitors. But where the wedding is in the city—especially when all the members of the bridal party live there also—the custom of giving a bridesmaids' and ushers' dinner has gone out of fashion. If the bridal party is asked to dine at the house of the bride on the evening before the wedding, it is usually for the purpose of seeing that they go to the church for rehearsal, which is of all things the most important. More often the rehearsal is in the afternoon, after which they all go to the bride's house for tea, allowing her parents to have her to themselves on her last evening home, and giving her a chance to go early to bed so as to look her prettiest on the morrow.

THE BACHELOR DINNER

Popularly supposed to be a frightful orgy, the bachelor dinner was in truth, more often than not, a sheep in wolf's clothing. As a matter of fact, an orgy was never looked upon with favor by any but silly and misguided youths, whose idea of a howling good time was to make a howling noise, chiefly by singing at the top of their voices and breaking glasses. A boisterous picture, but scarcely a vicious one! Especially as a lot of the cheapest glassware was always there for the purpose.

The breaking habit originated with drinking the bride's health and breaking the stem of the wine glass, so that it "might never serve a less honorable purpose." And this same time-honored custom is followed to this day. Toward the end of the dinner the bridegroom rises, and holding a filled champagne glass aloft says, "To the bride!" Every man rises, drinks the toast standing, and then breaks the delicate stem of the glass. The impulse to break more glass is natural to youth, and probably still occurs and it is not hard to understand. The same impulse is seen at every county fair where enthusiastic youths delight in shooting or throwing balls at clay pipes and ducks and crockery.

Aside from toasting the bride and its glass-smashing result, the bridegroom's farewell dinner is exactly like any other "man's dinner."

GIFTS FOR THE USHERS

The bridegroom's gifts to his ushers are usually put at their places at the bachelor dinner. Cufflinks are the most popular gift. Silver or gold pencils, belt buckles, key rings, cigarette cases, billfolds, or other small and personal articles are suitable. The present to the best man is approximately the same as, or slightly handsomer than, the gifts to the ushers.

THE BRIDEGROOM'S PRESENT TO THE BRIDE

He is a very exceptional and enviable man who is financially able to take his fiancée to the jeweler and let her choose what she fancies. Customarily and better the bridegroom goes shopping alone and buys the handsomest ornament he can afford. If he has great wealth, a diamond pendant, brooch, or bracelet, or if he hasn't, the simplest bangle or charm. But whether his gift is of great or little value, it must be something for her personal adornment.

THE BRIDE'S PRESENT TO THE BRIDEGROOM

The bride need not give a present to the groom, but she usually does if she can. Her favorite gift is something permanent and for his personal use—ranging from cufflinks to a watch or ring.

REHEARSAL IS IMPORTANT

The bride always directs her wedding rehearsal, but never herself takes part in it, as that is supposed to be bad luck. Someone else, anyone who happens to be present, is appointed as a stand-in.

Most of us are familiar with the wedding service, and its form seems simple enough. But, unless one has by experience learned to take care of details, the effect is hitchy and disjointed. It is not that awkward happenings are serious offenses; but any detail that destroys the smoothness of the general impression is disastrous to dignity, which is the qualification necessary above all in every ceremonial observance.

HOW THE PROCESSION IS DRILLED

At an elaborate Protestant wedding with choral service, the choir enters in advance of the hour set for the ceremony, and does not form any part of the wedding procession. But at an important Catholic wedding—in St. Patrick's Cathedral in New York, for instance—the choristers wearing lace-trimmed surplices over cassocks lead the wedding procession, singing as they go. The ushers immediately follow them.

In any event, whether the wedding be Catholic or Protestant, the most elaborate possible or small and simple, the organist must always be at the rehearsal, as one of the most important details is marking the time of the wedding march. Witnesses of most weddings can scarcely imagine that a wedding march is a march at all; more often than not, the heads of ushers and bridesmaids bob up and down like something boiling in a pot. A perfectly drilled wedding procession, like a military one, should move forward in perfect step, rising and falling in a block or unit. To secure perfection of detail, the bars of the processional may be counted so that the music comes to an end at precisely the moment the bride and groom stand side by side at the chancel steps. This is not at all difficult; it merely takes time and attention.

A wedding rehearsal should proceed as follows:

First of all, it is necessary to determine the exact speed at which the march is to be played. The ushers are asked to try it out. They line up at the door, walk forward two and two. The audience, consisting of the bride and a few or many members of the families, decides whether the pace looks well. It must not be fast enough to seem brisk, nor slow enough to be funereal. At one wedding the ushers were told to count two beats as one and the pace was so slow that they all waddled in trying to keep their balance. On the other hand it is unsuitable to trot briskly up the aisle of a church.

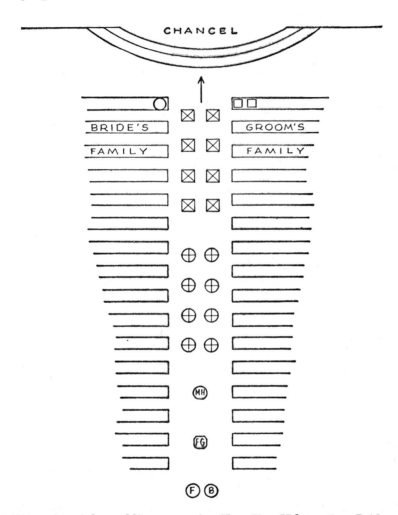

Formation of the wedding procession. Key: ☒ — Ushers; ⊕ — Bridesmaids; MH — Maid of honor; FG — Flower girl; F — Father; B — Bride.

The audience having decided the speed, and the organist having noted the tempo, the entire procession, including the bridesmaids and the stand-in for the bride on her father's arm, goes out into the vestibule and makes its entry. Remember, the father is an important factor in the ceremony and must take part in the rehearsal.

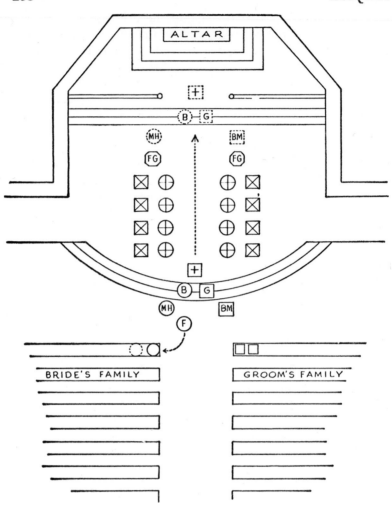

Group at the altar. Key: + — Minister; B — Bride; G — Groom; MH — Maid of honor; BM — Best man; FG — Flower girl; ⊠ — Ushers; ⊕ — Bridesmaids; F — Father of the bride.

The procession is arranged according to height, the two shorter ushers leading—unless others of nearly the same height are found to be more accurate pacemakers. The bridesmaids come directly after the ushers, two and two, also according to height, and again the shorter in the lead. After the bridesmaids, the maid or matron of honor walks alone; flower girls come next, if there are any; and last of all, the understudy bride leaning on the arm of the father, with pages, if she has any, holding up her train. Each pair in the procession follows the two directly in front by four paces or beats of time. In the vestibule, everyone in the procession must pay attention to the feet directly in front; the pace-

makers can follow the army sergeant's example and say very softly,
"Left, left!" At the end the bride counts eight beats before she and the
father put the left foot forward. The whole trick is starting; after that
they just walk naturally to the beat of the music, but keeping the ones
in front as nearly as possible at the same distance.

At the foot of the chancel, the ushers divide. In a small church, the
first two go up the chancel steps and stand at the top, one on the right,
the other on the left. The second two go a step or two below the first.
If there are more, they stand below again. Chalk marks can be made on
the chancel floor if necessary, but it ought not to be difficult, except for
very little children who are flower girls or pages, to learn their positions.

In a big church they go up farther, some of them lining the steps
or all of them in front of the choir stalls. The bridesmaids also divide,
half on either side, and always stand in front of the ushers. The maid
of honor's place is on the left at the foot of the steps, exactly opposite
the best man. Flower girls and pages are put above or below the bridesmaids, wherever it is thought "the picture" is best.

The grouping of the ushers and bridesmaids in the chancel or lining
the steps also depends upon their number and the size of the church. In
any event, the bridesmaids stand in front of the ushers, half of them on
the right and half on the left. They never stand all on the bride's side,
and the ushers on the groom's.

CHURCH WITH TWO MAIN AISLES

In a church with two main aisles, the guests are seated according
to aisles and not according to the church as a whole. All of the seats on
the right aisle belong to the bride's family and guests. The left aisle
belongs to the bridegroom.

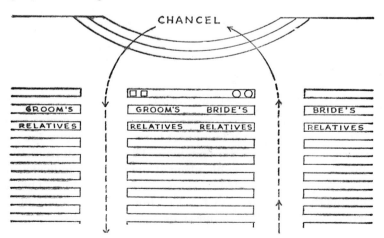

Church with two main aisles. Key: ○○ — Bride's parents; □□ —
Groom's parents.

The bride's mother is seated in the front pew at the left (as always) of the bride's aisle—exactly as she would be in a center-aisle church. On the other side of the church the bridegroom's mother occupies the front pew on the right of the groom's aisle (also as always).

For the processional, the bride's (right) aisle is chosen because people naturally turn to the right rather than to the left. After the ceremony, the bride and groom come down the groom's (left) aisle. These directions make it quite clear why the aisles are necessarily chosen so as to place the immediate families in center pews. The left pew must be entered from the aisle at the right. If the bride's mother were to choose the left aisle, this would seat her in a side pew instead of a center one.

Using one aisle in church with two main aisles. Key: OO — Bride's parents; □□ — Groom's parents.

However, if the church is very large and the wedding small, so that only the right aisle is used, then the bride's family sits on the left of this aisle and the groom's family on the right, while the marriage takes place at the head of this aisle.

ENTRANCE OF THE BRIDEGROOM

The clergyman who is to perform the marriage comes into the chancel from the vestry. At a few paces behind him follows the groom, who in turn is followed by the best man. The groom stops at the foot of the chancel steps and takes his place at the right, as indicated in the diagram on page 238, and his best man stands behind him. The ushers and bridesmaids always pass in front of him and take their places as noted above. When the bride approaches, the groom takes only a step to meet her.

A more effective greeting of the bride is possible—but only if the door of the vestry opens into the chancel, so that on following the clergyman, the groom finds himself at the top instead of the foot of the chancel steps. He goes forward to the right-hand side (his left), his best man behind him, and waits where he is until the bride approaches. He then goes down the steps to meet her—which has a more gallant effect than to stand at the head of the aisle and wait for her to join him.

At the rehearsal the real bride watches carefully how the substitute bride takes her left hand from the real father's arm, shifts her bouquet from her right hand to her left, and gives her right hand to the real bridegroom. In the performance proper the groom takes her right hand in his own right hand and draws it through his left arm, at the same time turning toward the chancel. If the service is undivided and all of it is to be at the altar, this is necessary, as the bride always goes up to the altar leaning on the arm of the groom. If, however, the marriage ceremony is to be read at the foot of the chancel, which is done at many weddings, he may merely take her hand in his left one and stand as they are.

THE ORGANIST'S CUE

The organist stops at the moment the bride and groom have assumed their places. That is the cue to the organist as to the number of bars necessary for the processional. After the procession has practiced "marching" two or three times, everything ought to be perfect. The organist, having counted the necessary bars of music, can readily give the leading ushers their music cue—so that they can start on the measure that will allow the procession and the organ to finish together. The organist can, and usually does, stop short, but there is a better finish if the bride's giving her hand to the groom and taking the last step that brings her in front of the chancel are timed so as to fall precisely on the last bars of the processional.

NO WORDS REHEARSED

No words of the service are ever rehearsed, although all the places to be taken by the several participants in the marriage ceremony are rehearsed.

The substitute for the bride takes the bridegroom's left arm and goes slowly up the steps to the altar. The best man follows behind and to the right of the groom, and the maid of honor, or first bridesmaid, leaves her companions and moves forward at the left of the bride. The substitute for the bride, in pantomime, gives her bouquet to the maid of honor; the best man, in the same way, hands the ring to the groom, this merely to see that they are at a convenient distance for the services they are to perform. The recessional is played, and the procession goes out in reversed order—bride and groom first, she on his right arm, then bridesmaids, then ushers, again all taking pains to fall into step with the leaders.

WHEN THE BRIDE DOES NOT WEAR BRIDAL DRESS

For some time an increasing number of brides have protested against the impractical amount of money spent on a white satin bridal dress which can be worn only once. Many prefer a party dress in a becoming color that can be worn times without number. This same handicap of buying impractical clothes is also of serious concern to her bridesmaids. A lovely effect might easily be created by a bride in a pale and fragile picture dress, with her bridesmaids also in pretty party dresses.

A SIMPLE, LOVELY, AND PERFECT WEDDING

Therefore, starting with a practical dress, becoming as to color and practical for future utility, let us consider the details that are essential to a perfect wedding and see how many can be eliminated.

Perfection is always the result of matching details. Bridesmaids' dresses must match, so too must the clothes of the ushers.

A wedding processional must be something more than one young woman in a street dress followed by another young woman also in street dress, walking with a man in a business suit! In simplest outline the pattern of a church wedding is this:

AT THE CHURCH

Arriving guests are seated by the ushers, who should not be too solemn of mien. Neither, on the other hand, should they be less than dignified. Each usher offers his arm to each lady he escorts. Usually he and she exchange a few brief low-voiced comments about the weather or the church decorations, or in praise of the bride and groom.

Finally the bride arrives! As the first notes of the processional are sounded, the bridegroom, followed by his best man, takes his place at the foot of the chancel steps. The processional is headed by the ushers, followed by the bridesmaids, and then the bride on her father's right arm.

If there is a flower girl, she should not scatter petals, but should carry a basket of beautifully arranged flowers. An apparently empty basket filled with "petals," usually confetti, is not decorative. Moreover confetti gets into and onto everything and is most annoying. Walking up the aisle pulling flowers to pieces is vandalism—no less!

One detail of the processional is important: Everyone must of course keep time with the march as played, but the tempo chosen by the organist should be that of a natural walk—not too draggingly slow. As a matter of fact, this same admonition might be given at the rehearsal of every wedding; although when the bride has a very long train, a somewhat slower pace adds dignity.

SIMPLEST RECEPTION REQUIREMENTS

If there is to be no reception, the bride and groom can go out into the vestibule of the church to receive the congratulations of their friends. For the reception, midafternoon is the best time, because only lightest refreshments are necessary. If it were in the morning, followed by a high-noon breakfast, that would mean substantial food; and in the evening one rather expects an elaborate wedding—evening clothes. An afternoon reception can, however, be very simple. All that is required is a fruit punch in which to drink the bride's and groom's health and the wedding cake. More than this would include either tea or coffee and thin sandwiches.

The decoration of the table at the reception, and the wedding cake, should of course be white.

THE "WHY" OF CERTAIN FIXED RULES

According to a correctly conducted wedding the ushers always head the processional alone, followed by the bridesmaids in a separate group, also alone.

Should the bridesmaids walk with the ushers the impression would be of multiple brides and grooms, or the grand march at a ball, or most likely of all, chorus men and girls on a musical comedy stage.

The reason the bride's father gives her his right arm is that a gentleman's right arm is the arm of courtesy. To place a lady on his left (unless unavoidable) is a definite discourtesy and on occasion an actual indignity. She does, it is true, take her place at the bridegroom's left during the ceremony, during which she is somewhat toward the right of the clergyman. When she comes down the aisle, she then walks on the right of her husband—and always stands on his right at the reception.

A MARRIAGE AT THE PARSONAGE

Marriages are often performed in the clergyman's study or in another room at the parsonage or parish house. Although the words marriage and wedding are the same in meaning, the latter to most people connotes the picturesque ceremonial of long-established custom.

On such an occasion the clergyman should be notified ahead of time regarding the hour set. The bride and bridegroom go together, and are met at the parsonage by the members of their families and the two or three friends invited. When all are assembled, the bridegroom tells the clergyman they are ready. The clergyman takes his place. The bride and bridegroom stand before him and the service is read. Afterward those present congratulate them, and that is all. Of course they may all go to the house of the bride or of a witness, or to a restaurant, and have lunch, or tea, or dinner, together. At such a marriage the bride rarely wears a white wedding dress and veil, but it is entirely proper for her to do so if she chooses—especially if they are going to the home of a friend for a wedding dinner afterward. If the marriage is performed by a magistrate, however, a wedding dress is entirely out of keeping.

THE CLERGYMAN'S FEE

The fee of the clergyman may range anywhere from ten dollars to one or two hundred dollars, according to the means of the groom and the importance of the wedding. Whatever the amount, it is enclosed in an envelope and taken in charge by the best man, who hands it to the clergyman in his vestry room immediately after the ceremony.

When the clergyman comes from a distance either because he is a relative, or schoolmaster, or a friend of the bridegroom's family, his traveling and hotel accommodations are, of course, paid by the groom or his family.

THE WEDDING DAY

⊰[21]⊱

ON THE DAY OF THE WEDDING, THE BUSIEST PERSON IS
the best man! Quite literally, he finds himself thrust into a position that
is a combination of trained nurse, valet, general manager of the entire
wedding procedure as well as the bridegroom's best friend, whose understanding is unfailing.

Bright and early in the morning (if it's to be a daytime wedding),
he hurries to the house of the bridegroom, generally before the latter
is up. Very likely they breakfast together. In any event, he takes charge
of the groom precisely as might a guardian. He takes note of his patient's general condition; if he is normal and fit, so much the better. If
he is up in the air with nerves, the best man must bring him to earth
and calm him down as best he can.

BEST MAN'S DUTIES

His first duty is to see that everything necessary for the journey is
packed, and that the groom does not absent-mindedly put the furnishings of his room in his luggage and leave all his clothing behind in the
closet. If the groom is to wear formal clothes, those which he is to wear
away are put in the right bag to be taken to wherever the reception is
taking place where he, as well as the bride, must change from wedding
clothes into traveling ones. The best man becomes expressman if the
first stage of the wedding journey is to be to a hotel in town. He puts
all the groom's luggage into his own car or a taxi, drives to the bride's
house, carries the bag with the groom's traveling suit in it to the room
set aside for his use—perhaps the dressing room of the bride's father or
the bedroom of her brother. He then collects—according to prearrangement—the luggage of the bride and drives with that of both bride and
groom to the hotel where accommodations have already been engaged,
sees that their bags are placed in their room and that everything is as
it should be. If he is well-to-do in addition to being thoughtful, he may
himself have flowers put about as a decorative welcome. He also registers

for the newly-weds, secures the hotel key, returns to the house of the groom, gives him the key, and assures him that everything at the hotel is in readiness. This maneuver allows the young couple, when they arrive, to go quietly to their own room without attracting the notice of anyone, as would be the case if they arrived with baggage on which supposed-to-be-humorous friends have tied white ribbons, and were con-spicuously led by a bellboy whose manner unmistakably proclaimed, "Bride and Groom!"

Or, if they are traveling by boat or train, the best man takes the baggage to the station, checks the large pieces, and fees a porter to see that the hand luggage is put in the proper stateroom or car seats. If they are going by car, he takes the luggage out to the garage and personally stows it in their car.

BEST MAN AS VALET

His next duty is that of valet. He must see that the groom is dressed and ready early, and be ready with a styptic pencil if he cuts himself shaving. He may need to find his cuff links or even to point out the "missing" clothes that are lying in full view. He must also be sure to ask for the wedding ring and the clergyman's fee, and put them in his own pocket. A very careful best man carries an extra ring in case of one's being lost during the ceremony. (This can be returned to the jeweler if not needed.)

BEST MAN AS COMPANION-IN-ORDINARY

With the bride's and groom's luggage properly stowed, the ring and fee in his pocket, the groom's traveling clothes at the bride's house, the groom in complete wedding attire, and himself also ready, the best man has nothing further to do but be gentleman-in-waiting to the bride-groom until it is time to escort him to the church, where he becomes chief of staff.

HEAD USHER

At a big wedding, it is well to pick the usher who has had the most experience to be head usher. He then assigns, according to their height, the order in which the ushers are to walk in the processional and where each is to stand during the ceremony.

He also tells each usher to which lady of the families he is to hurry back up the aisle, after the recessional, and escort to the vestibule.

AT THE HOUSE OF THE BRIDE

Meanwhile, if the wedding is to be at noon, dawn will not have much more than broken before the house—at least below stairs—becomes bustling.

Even if the wedding is to be at four o'clock, it will still be early in the morning when the business of the day begins. But let us suppose it is to be at noon. If the family is one used to assembling at an early breakfast table, it is probable that the bride herself will come down for this last meal alone with her family. They will, however, not be allowed to linger long at the table. The caterer will be clamoring for possession of the dining-room; the florist will by that time have dumped heaps of wire and greens into the middle of the living-room, if not beside the table where the family is still communing with its eggs. The doorbell has long ago begun to ring. At first there are telegrams and special delivery letters; then come the last-moment wedding presents, notes, messages, and over all the insistent and ceaseless ringing of the telephone.

Next, excited voices in the hall announce members of the family who come from a distance. They all want to kiss the bride, they all want rooms to dress in, they all want to talk. Also comes the hairdresser to do the bride's or her mother's, or aunt's or grandmother's hair; add, too, anyone else who may have been thought necessary to give final beautifying touches to the feminine members of the household. The dozen and one articles from the caterer are meanwhile being carried in at the service door: made dishes and raw materials from which others are to be made; folding chairs, small tables, chinaware, glassware, napery, knives, forks, and spoons. It has become a struggle to get in or out of the kitchen or through the doorway.

The bride's mother consults the florist for the third and last time as to whether the bridal couple would not better receive in the library, because of the picture window which lends itself easily to the decoration of a background, and because the room is, if anything, larger than the drawing-room. And for the third time, the florist agrees about the advantage of the window, but points out that the library has only one narrow door and that the drawing-room is much better, because it has two wide ones, and the guests going into the room will not be blocked in the doorway by those coming out.

The best man turns up and wants the bride's luggage, which of course "is not quite ready."

The head usher comes to ask whether the Joneses who are to be seated in the fourth pew are the tall dark ones or the blond ones; and whether he would not better put some of the Titheringtons, who belong in the eighth pew, also in the seventh, as there are nine Titheringtons, and the Parkers in the seventh pew are only four.

A bridesmaid-elect hurries up the steps, runs into the best man carrying out the luggage. Much conversation and giggling and guessing where the luggage is going. Best man very important, also very noble, and silent. Bridesmaid shrugs her shoulders, dashes up to the bride's room and dashes down again.

More presents arrive. The furniture movers have come and are carting unimagined quantities of chairs, tables, sofas, and whatnots up the stairs to the attic and down the stairs to the cellar. It is all very like an anthill. Some are steadily going forward with the business in hand, but others, who have become quite bewildered, seem to be scurrying aimlessly this way and that, picking something up only to put it down again, and getting in the way.

THE LIVING-ROOM

Here, where the bride and groom are to receive, and from which most of the furniture has been removed, one cannot tell yet what the decoration is to be—but a flowering background of some sort, before which they will stand, is gradually taking shape.

THE DINING-ROOM

The dining-room, too, blossoms with plants and flowers. Perhaps its space, and that of a canopy which has been put up in the garden or city back yard adjoining, is filled with little tables, or perhaps a single row of camp chairs stands flat against the walls. In the center of the room the dining table, pulled out to its fullest extent, is being decked with trimmings and utensils which will be needed later when the spaces left at intervals for various dishes shall be occupied. Preparation of these dishes is meanwhile going on in the kitchen.

THE KITCHEN

The caterer's chefs in white cooks' caps and aprons are in possession of the situation, and their assistants run here and there, bringing ingredients as they are told. Or perhaps the caterer brings everything already prepared, in which case the waiters are busy unpacking the big tin containers and arranging whatever method is used for keeping hot food hot until it is to be served. Huge tubs of cracked ice, in which the ice-cream containers are buried, are standing in the shade in the areaway or out in the back yard.

LAST PREPARATIONS

Back again in the living-room, the florist and his assistants are still tying and tacking and arranging and adjusting branches and garlands and sheaves and bunches, and the floor is a litter of twigs and strings and broken branches. The photographer is asking that the central decoration be finished so he can group his pictures; the florist tells him to go jump in the lake!

The house is as cold as open windows or air conditioning can make it, to keep the flowers fresh, and to avoid stuffiness. The doorbell continues ringing, and the parlor maid finds herself a contestant in a marathon, until someone decides that card envelopes and telegrams shall be left in the front hall.

A first bridesmaid arrives. She at least is on time. All decoration activity stops while she is looked at and admired. Panic seizes someone! Confusion reigns! The time is too short, nothing will be ready! Someone else, realizing the bridesmaid is far too early, says so, and that there is no end of time.

Upstairs everyone is still dressing. The father of the bride—one would suppose him to be the bridegroom himself—is trying on most of his shirts, and the floor is strewn with discarded ones! The mother of the bride is hurrying into her wedding array so that she will be ready for any emergency, as well as ready to superintend the finishing touches to her daughter's dress and veil.

IN THE BRIDE'S ROOM

As the hour approaches, everyone seemingly is in her room; her mother, her grandmother, three aunts, two cousins, three bridesmaids, four small children, two friends, her maid, the dressmaker, and an assistant. Every little while the parlor maid brings a message or a package. Her father comes in and goes out at regular intervals, in sheer nervousness. The rest of the bridesmaids gradually appear and distract the attention of the audience so that the bride has moments of being allowed to dress undisturbed. At last even her veil is adjusted and all present gasp their approval: "How sweet!" "Dearest, you are too lovely!" and, "Darling, how wonderful you look!"

Her father reappears. "If you are going to have the pictures taken, you had better all hurry!"

"Oh, Mary," shouts someone, "what have you on that is

> Something old, something new,
> Something borrowed, something blue,
> And a lucky sixpence in your shoe?"

"Let me see," says the bride. " 'Old,' I have old lace; 'new,' I have lots of new! 'Borrowed,' and 'blue'?" A chorus of voices: "Wear my ring," "Wear my pin," "Wear mine! It's blue!" and someone's pin, which has a blue stone in it, is fastened under the trimming of her dress and serves both needs. If the lucky sixpence—a dime will do—is produced, she must at least pay in discomfort for her "luck."

TAKING THE WEDDING PICTURES

Having pictures taken before the ceremony is a dull custom, because it is tiring to sit for one's photograph at best. And to attempt posing at the moment when the procession ought to be starting is as trying to the nerves as it is exhausting, but to wait until afterward is either to delay the reception or to risk spoiling the pictures with costumes that are no longer fresh.

At a country wedding, and this risk is taken, it is easy to take the pictures out on the lawn at the end of the reception and just before the bride goes to dress; this time is always chosen when the bridegroom and his ushers are to be included in the wedding picture. Sometimes in a town house they are taken in an upstairs room at that same hour. But usually the bride is dressed and her bridesmaids arrive at her house fully half an hour before the time necessary to leave for the church; and pictures of the group, as well as several of the bride alone, are taken with special lights against the background where she will stand and receive.

PROCESSION TO THE CHURCH

Whether the pictures are taken before the wedding or after, the bridesmaids always meet at the house of the bride, where they also receive their bouquets. When it is time to go to the church, there are several cars drawn up at the house. The bride's mother drives away in the first, usually alone, or she may, if she chooses, take one or two bridesmaids in her car; but she must reserve room for her husband, who will return from church with her.

The maid of honor, bridesmaids, and flower girls follow in as many cars as may be necessary.

Last of all comes the bride's car, which always has a wedding appearance. The chauffeur wears a small bunch of white flowers on his coat, and white gloves, and has all the tires painted white. The bride drives to the church accompanied only by her father. Her car arrives last of the procession, and stands without moving, in front of the awning, until she and her husband—in place of her father—return from the ceremony and drive back to the house for the breakfast or reception.

MOTHER TAKES FATHER'S PLACE

If it should happen that the bride has neither father nor any very near male relative or guardian, she may walk up the aisle alone. At the point in the ceremony where the clergyman asks, "Who giveth this woman to be married?" her mother stays where she is standing in her proper place at the end of the first pew on the left and bows her head very distinctly to indicate "I do." There is no rule against her going forward as the bride's father would have done, but this would be unusual.

AT THE CHURCH

Meanwhile, about an hour before the time for the ceremony, the ushers arrive at the church and the sexton turns his guardianship over to them. They leave their hats in the vestry or in the coat room. Their boutonnières, sent by the groom, should be waiting in the vestibule. These should be in charge of a boy from the florist, who has nothing else on his mind but to see that they are there, that they are fresh, and that the ushers get them and put them on. Each man puts one in his buttonhole, and also puts on his gloves. The head usher decides, if the groom has not already told them, to which ushers are assigned the center and to which the side aisles. Those of the ushers who are the most likely to recognize the various friends and members of each family should be detailed to the center aisle. A brother of the bride, for instance, is always chosen for this aisle because he should be best able to recognize and look out for the family's best friends. A second usher should be either a brother of the groom or a near relative who is able to recognize the family and intimate friends of the groom. The parents of the bride always sit in the first pew on the left, facing the chancel; the groom's parents in the first pew on the right. If the church has two aisles, her parents sit on the left of right aisle, and his on the right of left aisle.

IN FRONT OF THE RIBBONS

The first six to twenty pews on either side of the center aisle (depending upon the size of the families) are marked off with ribbons into a reserved enclosure. This is done by fastening a lead sinker or stone, or anything to weigh each end of a length of white satin ribbon, from three to four inches wide and just long enough to reach across the aisle and drop over the ends of the pews and rest on the pew seats, and thus make a barrier across the aisle at this point. The families sit in front of the ribbons, as do the very few most intimate friends. The seats in front of the ribbons are all reserved—not only on ushers' lists, but also by cards sent to individual guests. As a guest belonging in front of the ribbons is escorted up the aisle, the usher lifts one end of the ribbon from its anchorage, drops it to the floor, and leads the guest to the proper seat. Coming down the aisle again, he picks up the ribbon and drops it over the end of the pew.

A few pews may be taken from one family to give to the other when the one family is very small and the other large. Let us say the bride needs eleven pews and the groom three. Since a ribbon cannot very well be run from the back of the third pew on his side to the back of the eleventh on hers, seven pews are ribboned off on each side, and all beyond the first three on his side are filled as though they were hers. This often occurs when the bridegroom is from a distant part of the country and few members of his family and almost none of his friends can be present.

SEATING THE GUESTS

It is the duty of the ushers to show all guests to their places. An usher offers his right arm to each lady as she arrives, whether he knows her personally or not. If the vestibule is very crowded and several ladies are together, he sometimes gives his arm to the oldest and asks the others to follow. But this is not done unless the crowd is great and the time short, otherwise he asks them to wait until he can come back or another usher is available.

The usher does not offer his arm to a man unless he is quite old and it is obvious that he may need assistance. If he is accompanied by a younger man he is asked to follow so that he can seat them together.

If the usher thinks a guest belongs in front of the ribbons, though she fails to present her card, he always asks, "Have you a pew number?" If she has, he then shows her to her place. If she has none, he asks whether she prefers to sit on the bride's side or the groom's, and gives her the best seat vacant in the unreserved part of the church.

At one time, lists of all the guests were given to the ushers, with pew numbers following, for almost the whole church. From every point of view, the typewritten list was bad. First, it wasted time. As everyone arrived at the same moment and every lady was supposed to be taken personally up the aisle "on the arm" of an usher, the time consumed while each usher looked up each name on several gradually rumpling or tearing sheets of paper may be easily imagined. Besides this, one who is at all intimate with either family cannot help feeling in some degree slighted when, on giving his name, he sees the usher look for it in vain.

The present way is simple. Members of the two families and a few most interested friends—such as the mothers of the bridesmaids—have numbered pew-cards. These are quite possibly limited to no more than the three or four front pews on either side of the aisle. All of the other guests are seated according to the general rule of first come first served.

USHERS AND GUESTS ALWAYS TALK

Ushers are not supposed to escort guests in total silence, even when they are strangers. A few casual remarks are made—perhaps about the weather or the decorations—in a low voice, but not whispered or solemn.

The deportment of the ushers should be natural, but dignified and quiet in consideration of the fact that they are in church. They must not trot up and down the aisles in a bustling manner; yet they must be fairly swift and efficient, as the vestibule is packed with guests (most of whom arrive at the same time) and all have to be seated as expeditiously as possible.

The guests without reserved cards should arrive early in order to find good places. Members of the families and the few guests who have places in front of the ribbon come later.

THE BRIDEGROOM WAITS

Meanwhile, about fifteen minutes before the wedding hour, the groom and his best man—both in cutaway coats, top hats, boutonnières, and white buckskin (not glazed kid) gloves—walk or drive to the church and enter the side door which leads to the vestry. They sit there, or in the clergyman's study, until the sexton or an usher comes to say that the bride has arrived. They then wait for and follow the clergyman and take their places.

THE PERFECTLY MANAGED WEDDING

At a perfectly managed wedding, the bride arrives exactly one minute after the hour in order to give the last comer time to find a place. A maid or other volunteer is waiting in the vestibule to help the bride and bridesmaids off with their wraps and to hold them until they are needed after the ceremony. The groom's mother and father also are waiting in the vestibule. As the bride's mother drives up, an usher hurries off to tell the groom of her arrival. Any brothers or sisters of the bride or groom who are not to take part in the wedding procession and have arrived in their mother's car are now taken by ushers to their places in the front pews. The moment the entire wedding party is in the church, the doors between the vestibule and the church are closed. No one is seated after this, except the parents of the young couple.

The proper procedure should be carried out with military exactness and is as follows:

The groom's mother goes up the aisle on the arm of the head usher and takes her place in the first pew on the right; the groom's father follows alone and takes his place beside her. The same usher returns to the vestibule and immediately escorts the bride's mother. He should then have time to return to the vestibule and take his place in the procession—his position depending upon his height. The beginning of the wedding march should sound just as the usher returns to the foot of the aisle.

To repeat: *No person should be seated after the entrance of the mother of the bride.* Nor must anyone be admitted to the side aisles while the mother of the bride is being ushered down the center one. Her entrance should not be detracted from by late arrivals scuttling into their seats behind her. Guests who arrive late must stand in the vestibule or go into the gallery.

The sound of the music is also the cue for the clergyman to enter the chancel, followed by the groom and the best man. The two latter wear gloves but have left their hats and overcoats in the vestry room.

The groom stands on the right-hand side at the head of the aisle; but if the vestry opens into the chancel, he sometimes stands at the top of the first few steps. He removes his right glove and holds it in his left hand. The best man remains always directly back and to the right of the groom, and does not remove his gloves.

HERE COMES THE BRIDE

As already described, the processional advances. First come the ushers two by two, four paces apart; then the bridesmaids—if any—at the same distance exactly; then the maid of honor alone; then the flower girls—if any; then the ring bearer—if any; then, at a *double distance* (eight paces), the bride on her father's *right* arm.

THE BRIDEGROOM ADVANCES TO MEET THE BRIDE

As the bride approaches, the groom waits at the foot of the steps, unless he comes down the steps to meet her. The bride relinquishes her father's arm, changes her bouquet from her right to her left arm, and gives her right hand to the groom. The groom, taking her hand in his right, puts it through his left arm—just her finger tips should rest near the bend of his elbow—and turns to face the chancel as he does so. It does not matter whether she keeps his arm, or whether they stand hand in hand, or merely side by side at the foot of the chancel in front of the clergyman.

HER FATHER GIVES HER AWAY

Her father has remained where she left him, on her left and a step or two behind her. The clergyman stands a step or two above them and reads the betrothal. When he says, "Who giveth this woman to be married?" the father goes forward, still on her left, half-way between her and the clergyman, but not in front of either. The bride turns slightly toward her father and gives him her right hand. (She does not remove her glove.) The father puts her hand in that of the clergyman, signifying by his reply, "I do." He then takes his place next to his wife at the end of the first pew on the left.

The clergyman, holding the bride's hand in his own right, takes the bridegroom's hand in his left and very deliberately places the bride's hand in that of the bridegroom.

THE MARRIAGE CEREMONY

A soloist or the choir then sings while the clergyman slowly ascends to the altar before which the marriage is performed. The bride and groom follow slowly, the fingers of her right hand on his left arm.

The maid of honor, or else the first bridesmaid, moves out of line and follows on the left-hand side until she stands immediately below the bride. The best man takes the same position exactly on the right behind the groom. At the termination of the anthem, the bride hands her bouquet to the maid of honor—or her prayer book to the clergyman. If the bride wishes her own prayer book to be used for her marriage she carries it instead of a bouquet. And the bride and groom plight their troth.

When it is time for the ring, the best man produces it from his pocket.

The wedding ring must not be put above the engagement ring. On her wedding day a bride either leaves her engagement ring at home when she goes to church or she wears it on her right hand. Afterward she wears it above her wedding ring.

When the bridegroom is also to have a ring, the maid of honor hands it to the bride at the moment that the best man gives her ring to the groom, and the bride puts it on his finger immediately after she has received her ring from him. The ceremony then proceeds.

AFTER THE CEREMONY

At the conclusion of the ceremony, the minister congratulates the new couple. The organ begins the recessional. The bride takes her bouquet from her maid of honor—who lifts the bride's veil, if she has worn one over her face. She then turns toward her husband—her bouquet in her right hand—and puts her left hand through his right arm, and they descend the steps.

The maid of honor, handing her own bouquet to a second bridesmaid, follows a short distance after the bride, at the same time stooping and straightening out the long train and veil. The bride and groom go on down the aisle. The best man disappears into the vestry room. At a perfectly conducted wedding he does not walk down the aisle with the maid of honor. The maid of honor recovers her bouquet and walks alone. If a bridesmaid performs the office of maid of honor, she takes her place among her companion bridesmaids, who go next; and the ushers go last.

The best man has meanwhile dashed out of the side entrance and around to the front to give the groom his hat and coat.

Sometimes the sexton takes charge of the groom's hat and coat and hands them to him at the church door as he goes out. But in either case the best man always hurries around to see the bride and groom into their car, which has been standing at the entrance to the awning since she and her father alighted from it.

All the other conveyances are drawn up in the reverse order from that in which they arrived. The bride's car leaves first; next come those of the bridesmaids; next that of the bride's mother and father; next that of the groom's mother and father. Then follow the nearest members of both families, and finally all the other guests in an order determined only by their being able to find their conveyances.

The best man goes back to the vestry, where he gives the fee to the clergyman, collects his own hat and coat, and goes to the bride's house or wherever the reception is to be held.

To return to the ceremony for a moment: As soon as the recessional is over, the ushers hurry back and escort to the door all the ladies who were in the first pews, according to the order of precedence; the bride's mother first, then the groom's mother, then the other occupants of the first pew on either side, then the second and third pews, until all members of the immediate families have left the church. Meanwhile it is a breach of etiquette for other guests to leave their places. At occasional weddings, just before the bride's arrival, the ushers run ribbons down the whole length of the center aisle, fencing the congregation in. As soon as the occupants of the first pews have left, the ribbons are removed and all the other guests go out by themselves. The ushers are by that time hurrying to the bride's house to make themselves useful at the reception.

AT THE HOUSE

An awning makes a covered way from the edge of the curb to the front door. At the lower end the chauffeur, or one of the caterer's men, stands to open the automobile doors and gives return checks to the chauffeurs and their employers. Inside the house an orchestra is playing in the hall or library, and everything is in perfect order. The bride and groom have taken their places in front of the elaborate setting of flowering plants that has been arranged for them.

THE RECEIVING LINE

The only actual receiving line is that of the bride and groom and the bride's attendants. The ushers and best man have no place in the receiving line.

The bride's mother greets the guests at the door of entrance to the room. It is true that often the bridegroom's mother and possibly his father comprise a receiving line of three. Or possibly the bride's father makes a fourth. Very often the two fathers walk about together, leaving the two mothers to receive alone.

The bridegroom's mother almost always receives with the bride's mother if she is from another town. But if she is as well known to the

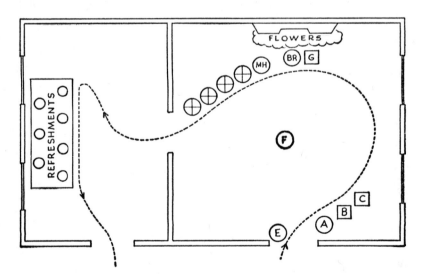

Progress of guests. Key: E — Announcer; A — Mother of bride; B — Mother of groom; C — Father of groom; F — Father of bride; G — Groom; Br — Bride; MH — Maid of honor; ⊕ — Bridesmaids.

FLORAL DECORATION OF CHANCEL AND AISLE

Where there are two aisles, decoration at the pew ends is duplicated for the bride's aisle and for the groom's aisle.

THE BRIDE'S TABLE

A charmingly set and decorated table. The guests' tables are set like it, without the elaborate floral decoration.

guests as the bride's mother, she is likely to receive in another part of
the room where her own friends can talk with her at greater length.
The bride's mother of course decides upon whatever arrangements she
thinks will be most pleasant for all concerned.

In any case the bride's mother always stands near the door of entrance to the principal room. Facing her and just inside this door is her
own butler, or an announcer furnished by the caterer. He asks each
guest his or her name and then repeats it aloud. The guests shake hands
with the hostess, and, making some polite remark about the "beautiful
wedding" or "lovely bride," continue in line to the bridal pair. If there
is no one announcing, guests unknown to the hostess announce their
own names.

All the guests should shake hands with the groom's mother whether
they know her or not, and say a few words of greeting if she is a
stranger, or otherwise say something pleasant about the wedding, the
bride, or the groom. The bride's father sometimes stands beside his wife,
but he usually circulates among his guests just as he would at a ball
or any other party where he is host.

The groom's father is a guest and it is not the obligation of strangers
to speak to him, unless he stands beside his wife and receives. But it is
certainly courteous, especially if he is a stranger, to introduce oneself
and tell him how well one likes his son or his new daughter-in-law—
or, best of all, both.

USHERS AT THE HOUSE

At a small wedding the duty of ushers is personally to take guests
up to the bride and groom as soon as they have greeted the bride's
mother and anyone receiving with her. But at a big reception where
the guests outnumber ushers fifty or a hundred to one, being personally
conducted is an honor accorded only to the old, the celebrated, or the
usher's own best friends. All the other guests stand in line by themselves
and await their turn.

NO RULE ABOUT WHETHER BRIDE OR BRIDEGROOM
IS GREETED FIRST

The bride always stands on the bridegroom's right. The direction
of the queue depends upon the plan of the room. If, in the room shown
on page 256, the door to the dining-room were at the right, the mothers
would stand at left and the queue would naturally swing away from
that door and approach the line from the opposite direction, and guests
would greet the bride first, instead of the bridegroom.

Usually the bride and groom receive against the wall opposite the
door of entrance; but this is not a fixed rule, and they choose whichever
side of the room will make the most convenient background. This is
usually made of leaves and flowers, but may equally well be the closed

curtains of a window or other draperies hung from the picture molding.

The bride stands on the bridegroom's right, the maid of honor at the right of the bride. Usually all the bridesmaids stand on the right of the maid of honor, but sometimes (depending on the space) half stand at the right of the maid of honor and the other half on the left of the bridegroom.

RECEIVING THEIR GUESTS

To a relative or friend of the bride, but a stranger to the groom, the bride always introduces her husband, saying "Jim, this is Aunt Kate!" or "Mrs. Neighbor, *this* is Jim!" or, formally, "Mrs. Faraway, may I present my husband?"

The groom, on the approach of an old friend of his, says, "Mary, this is Cousin Carrie" or "Mrs. Denver, Mary" or "Hello, Steve. Mary, this is Steve Michigan." If Steve is an older man or old-fashioned, he says, "How do you do, Mrs. Smartlington!" And Mary says, "How do you do. Jim often speaks of you!" If he is young or modern, he says, "I'm glad to meet you, Mary." And she replies, "I'm glad to see *you*, Steve."

The bride with a good memory thanks each arriving person for the gift sent her: "Thank you so much for the lovely candlesticks" or "The platter is just what we wanted." The person who is thanked says, "I am so glad you like it," or "I hoped you might find it useful," or "I didn't have it marked, so that in case you have a duplicate, you can change it." But these verbal thanks do not lessen her obligation to write an additional thank-you note. If she has received a large number of presents and if she doesn't trust her memory, she had better not run the risk of thanking Mr. and Mrs. Worthington for a glass ashtray when they sent a piece of sterling silver.

These fragments of conversation are given merely to indicate the sort of things people usually say. There is, however, one real rule: Do not launch into a conversation about yourself, how you feel or look, or what happened to you, or what you wore when you were married! Your subject should be confined to the young couple themselves, their wedding, their future.

Above all, be brief in order not to keep those behind waiting longer than necessary. If you have anything particular to tell them, you can return later when there is no longer a line. But even then any long conversation is out of place.

To all expressions of best wishes and congratulations, the bride and groom need only answer "Thank you." (See Chapter 22 for what to say to the bride and groom.)

Usually it is easier to have the refreshments ready for guests as soon as they have passed down the receiving line—particularly if the reception is a large one. Some are sure to want to leave early or to have other engagements.

THE BRIDE'S TABLE

The feature of the wedding breakfast always is the bride's table. Placed sometimes in the dining-room, sometimes on the veranda, or in a room apart, this table is always decorated with white garlands, or sprays, or other white flowers, and in front of the bride, as its chief ornament, is the wedding cake—always elaborately iced, and often surmounted by little figures depicting the bride and groom.

The bride and groom always sit next to each other, she at his right, the maid or matron of honor at his left. The best man is at the right of the bride. Around the rest of the table are bridesmaids and ushers alternately. Sometimes one or two others—intimate friends who were not included in the wedding party—are asked to the table. When there are no bridesmaids, the table is always made up of such intimate friends.

THE TABLE OF THE BRIDE'S PARENTS

The table of the bride's parents differs from other tables in nothing except its larger size and the place-cards for those who have been invited to sit there. The groom's mother always sits on the right of the bride's father, and opposite them the groom's father is on the right of the mother of the bride. The other places at the table are occupied by especially intimate friends of the bride's parents or distinguished guests, who may or may not include the clergyman who performed the ceremony. If a bishop or dean performed the ceremony, he is always included at this table and is placed at the left of the hostess, and his wife, if present, sits at the bride's father's left.

When the wedding guests are to be served standing up, the only sit-down table is of course the one for the bridal party.

THE BRIDAL PARTY EATS

When the queue of arriving guests has dwindled and melted away, the bride and groom decide that it is time they go to breakfast. Arm in arm they lead the way to their own table, followed by the ushers and bridesmaids.

The decoration of the table, the service, and the food are exactly the same whether the other guests are seated or standing. At dessert the bride cuts the cake. (See "Wedding Cake," page 228.)

THE TOAST TO THE BRIDE AND GROOM

At a sit-down bridal table champagne is poured as soon as the first course has been served. The glass of the bride is filled first, then that of the bridegroom, and then on around the table, starting with the maid of honor at the groom's left and ending with the best man seated at the right of the bride. Then someone—it may be anyone (although it is really the duty of the best man)—proposes a toast to the bride and bridegroom. All (except the bride and groom) rise, raise their glasses, and drink the toast. Then the groom rises and replies with thanks for them both, and that is all. But there is no reason why other toasts may not be drunk should anyone care to propose them; for instance, the groom might wish to propose a toast to the bride's mother. Although at a large reception these are necessarily confined to individual groups. People also make speeches, if they feel like it, but these are not at all necessary and should on no account be more than a few seconds long.

DANCING AT THE WEDDING

On leaving their table the bridal party begin the dancing—or possibly join the dancing which by now has started in the living-room or wherever the wedding group received. The bride and groom dance at first together. Her father-in-law usually asks for the second dance and then her father. The groom follows the same pattern, and dances with his mother-in-law. Then each with bridesmaids or ushers, or other guests. The bride's father asks the groom's mother for the first dance and his father asks the bride's mother. Sometimes the bride and groom continue dancing so long that those who had intended staying for the "going away" grow weary and leave—which is often exactly what the young couple wants! And unless they have to catch a train, they usually stay until the "crowd thins" before going to dress for their journey. At last the bride signals to her bridesmaids and leaves the room. They all gather at the foot of the stairs. About half-way to the upper landing as she goes up, she throws her bouquet, and they all try to catch it. The one who succeeds is supposed to be the next married. If she has no bridesmaids, she collects a group of other girls and throws her bouquet to them.

Sometimes if a very close relative is too ill to attend the wedding, the bouquet is sent to her.

INTO TRAVELING CLOTHES

When the reception has been at her parents' house, the bride goes up to the room that has always been hers, followed by her mother, sisters, and bridesmaids, who stay with her while she changes into her traveling clothes. As soon as the bride has gone upstairs, the groom goes to the room reserved for him and changes into the traveling clothes which the best man has already taken there for him.

THE GOING-AWAY DRESS

A bride necessarily chooses her going-away dress according to the journey she is to make. The bride and groom of good taste try to avoid being conspicuous in clothes that look too new.

But to return to the wedding. The groom, having changed his clothes, waits upstairs until the bride appears in her going-away clothes. All the ushers shake hands with them both. His immediate family, as well as hers, has gradually collected. Any that are missing are sent for. The bride's mother gives her a last kiss; her bridesmaids hurry downstairs to have plenty of rice ready and to tell everyone below as they descend, "Here they come!" A passage from the stairway and out the front door, all the way to their automobile, is left free between two rows of eager guests, their hands full of rice.

THEY'RE OFF!

Down the stairs, out through the hall, into the car, slam the door, and they are off!

The wedding guests stand out on the street or roadway looking after them for as long as a vestige can be seen—and then gradually disperse.

THOUGHT FOR BRIDEGROOM'S PARENTS

At the end of the wedding and as soon as she is in her traveling dress a thoughtful bride will send a bridesmaid or someone out into the hall and ask her husband's parents to come and say good-by to her.

It is very easy for a bride to forget this act of thoughtfulness and for a groom to overlook the fact that he cannot stop to bid his parents good-by on his way out of the house, and many a mother and father, seeing their son and new daughter rush past without even a glance from either of them, have returned home with a let-down feeling and with an ache in their hearts. One naturally exclaims, "But how stupid of them! Why didn't they go upstairs?" But often the groom's parents are strangers; may never have met their new daughter until only a few days before the wedding, and if by temperament they are shy or retiring people, they hesitate to go upstairs in an unknown house until they are invited to do so. So they wait, feeling sure that in good time they will be sent for. Meanwhile the bride forgets; and it does not occur to the groom that, unless he makes an effort while upstairs, there will be no opportunity in the dash down to the car to recognize them any more than anyone else.

FLIPPANCY OR RADIANCE

A completely beautiful wedding is not merely a combination of wonderful flowers, beautiful clothes, smoothness of detail, and delicious food. These, no matter how pleasing, are external attributes. The spirit, or soul of it, must have something besides; and that something is seen in the behavior and in the expression of the bride and groom.

The most beautiful wedding ever imagined could be turned from sacrament to circus by the indecorous behavior of the groom and the flippancy of the bride. She must not reach up and wigwag signals while she is receiving, any more than she must wave to people as she goes up and then down the aisle of the church. She must not cling to her husband as though unable to stand, or lean against him or the wall, or any person or thing. She must not swing her arms as though they were dangling ropes. She must not switch herself this way and that, and she must not shout; and above all she must not, while wearing her bridal veil, smoke a cigarette. No matter how young or natural and thoughtless she may be, she *must*, during the ceremony and the short time that she stands beside her husband at the reception, act with dignity.

The happiness of both the bride and groom must dominate a perfect wedding. An unhappy looking bride, an uncomfortable looking groom, turns the greatest wedding splendor into sham. Without love it is a sacrament profaned, and the sight of a tragic-faced bride strikes chill to the heart.

The radiance of a truly happy bride is so enhancing that even a plain girl is made beautiful. A happy bridegroom quite plainly may have the quality of radiance, but it is different—more directly glad. They both look as though there were sunlight behind their eyes, as though their mouths irresistibly turned to smiles in visible proof of perfect happiness which endears them to all beholders and gives beauty to even the simplest little wedding.

WEDDING ANNIVERSARIES

The eight anniversaries known to us all are:

> 1 year, Paper
> 5 years, Wood
> 10 years, Tin
> 15 years, Crystal
> 20 years, China
> 25 years, Silver
> 50 years, Gold
> 60 years, Diamond

Because the first wedding anniversary is of great importance and the selection of paper gifts is comparatively limited, the trend toward making plastics also an accepted first year gift is too appealing to disallow.

Until comparatively modern times, the eight anniversaries were all that were acknowledged. About fifty years ago, anniversaries were added until there was one for each year up to fifteen, and one for every five years after that.

1 year, Paper or plastics. 2 years, Calico or cotton. Calico is the more amusing word and suggests, perhaps, a more amusing party. 3 years, Leather. 4 years, Silk. 5 years, Wood. 6 years, Iron. 7 years, Copper or woolen. 8 years, Electric appliances (which shows that innovation has supplemented tradition). 9 years, Pottery.

10 years, to the Tin of this year is now added aluminum. 11 years, Steel. 12 years, Linen. 13 years, Lace. 14 years, Ivory.

15 years, Crystal, as it has ever been, and of course it includes everything made of glass. After this there are four giftless anniversaries and then:

20 years, China. 25 years, the Silver Wedding Anniversary, which has surely been celebrated more often than all the others put together. 30 years, Pearls. 35 years, Coral and jade. 40 years, Ruby. 45 years, Sapphire. 50 years, the Golden Wedding Anniversary. 60 years, Diamond.

Suitable parties to celebrate any of the earliest wedding anniversaries are a housewarming or perhaps a stork shower, a calico fancy-dress party, a barn dance, a treasure hunt, or any informal party that appeals to the imagination. For that matter, it can also be a surprise party arranged for the bride and groom by their friends. The first years suggest much more informal gatherings than the Silver Wedding, for example, which is perhaps celebrated by a big dinner at little tables, or a dance to which everyone who was a guest at the wedding is invited. The most important anniversary, the Golden Wedding (50 years), is usually celebrated by a somewhat formal afternoon or evening meal at home, or by a family dinner either in the evening or at midday after which additional relatives, friends, and neighbors come in to offer their congratulations.

GIFTS NOT OBLIGATORY

No one must feel that a present is obligatory, especially when the anniversary year is one which suggests an item of value. Sometimes the invitation carries a line, "Please omit gifts." Intimate friends, however, usually take or send something if possible. Flowers are of course always an appropriate remembrance of such an occasion or any anniversary.

FURTHER CELEBRATIONS ARE NOT APPROVED

Approval by society in general is definitely withheld from an attempt not only to multiply the wedding anniversary celebrations, but to increase excessively the values of the gifts.

The first emphatic protest is against the proposed celebration of three silver weddings—the first one on the fifth anniversary, second on the sixteenth, and the third on the traditional completion of the twenty-fifth year.

Fantastic is the only word for the proposal that the ten-years-married bride and bridegroom shall receive diamond jewelry in place of the tinware that has hitherto been customary.

But the suggestion that they *celebrate* their *golden wedding* at the completion of fourteen years together, certainly seems to indicate a callous opinion that because of the increasing number of divorces a couple staying together fourteen years is as rare today as it used to be to find one ready to celebrate their fiftieth anniversary.

That any couple who chooses to do so may celebrate each and every anniversary they please, is one thing, but to set up any such standards of value as these items suggest would be preposterous. (For anniversary invitations, see Chapter 11.)

THE WEDDING GUEST

·›[22]‹·

THE MERE FACT OF RECEIVING AN ANNOUNCEMENT, OR even an engraved invitation to the church, obligates you to much or nothing according to your personal situation or impulse.

In other words an announcement informing you that a marriage has taken place between Mary Anthony and John Ballard will probably require no attention whatever further than changing the name of the bride in your address book.

MUST ONE SEND A PRESENT?

If you are an intimate friend of the bride or groom or of their families and you are not invited to the wedding reception, you would not be expected to send a present, unless, of course, there was no reception. Obviously the more personal the invitation the greater the obligation to send a gift. An invitation by written note definitely indicates that you are considered an especially dear friend and you will therefore probably want to send a present. And you must always send a present to one who is marrying into your immediate family.

While it is not an obligation, most people who accept an invitation to a wedding reception do feel like sending a present.

PRESENTS FOR SECOND MARRIAGE

An occasional few special friends and perhaps close relatives send presents for a second marriage, but there is no obligation—nor should there be any expectation—of your doing so unless they were both strangers to you at the time of their earlier marriages.

THE RUNAWAY MARRIAGE

To elope, according to the dictionary, is to run away from home with a lover or paramour, but to most of us an elopement means that a young couple have run off and gotten married, probably without the consent of the young girl's parents. I am sure, however, that many elopements have had their quiet blessing, with the supposedly runaway couple and the bride's parents wishing to avoid the bother and expense of a big wedding. Whether they had approved before the wedding or had decided after it to make the best of what has happened, the bride's parents send out the announcement in their name.

Should the parents be unalterably opposed to the wedding and wish the world to know that they are withholding their blessing, they do not send out the announcements. The married pair then will send them out themselves.

One receiving an announcement either in the name of the parents or without their names is in no way obligated, nor even expected to send a present. If, of course, anyone out of love or affection for either the bride or the groom wishes to give them something, this will be an especially appreciated gesture.

DON'T NEGLECT TO SEND A REPLY

It is most inconsiderate as well as impolite not to send a reply to a wedding invitation which includes R.s.v.p.

Remember that the family will have had to make, or order, definite preparation for every guest who does not send word to the contrary. Failure to reply causes extra trouble and expense.

WHAT KIND OF GIFT

Typical wedding presents include almost anything ornamental as well as useful for the furnishing of a house or the setting of a dining table, from a piece of silver to a glass ashtray, a picture frame to a clock, a paper cutter to a lamp, a cigarette box to an occasional table or chair. Naturally, the less you know about the future living plans of the bride and groom, the more necessary it is to choose a gift that can be used by anyone living anywhere.

Many gifts are beautified by marking; a certain few require it. Objects of plain silver or of untooled leather are enhanced by engraved or tooled initials. Linen, unless heavily embroidered or lace-inserted, seems rather impersonal without an embroidered monogram or initials.

The most important thing is that your gift be lovely and useful. To fulfil these two requirements, it need not be expensive. No bride or groom would want you to spend more than you can afford. One type of gift to avoid is the dust-catching ornament.

PRESENTS FROM BRIDEGROOM'S FRIENDS

You seldom send a present to the bridegroom. Even if you are an old friend of his and have never met the bride, your present is sent to her—unless you send two presents, one in courtesy to her and one in affection to him. Rather often friends of the bridegroom do pick out things suitable for him, such as a cigar box or decanter or rather mascu-

line-looking desk sets, etc., which are sent to her but are obviously
intended for his use.

NEAREST RELATIVES MAY GIVE CHECKS

Nearest relatives may properly give their gifts in the form of
money. Since checks given as wedding presents are usually of important
size and frequently intended for a definite purpose, they are not necessarily drawn to the bride. Often they are drawn to them jointly; on
occasion they are drawn to him. The check to be cashed after the wedding is drawn to John and Mary Smith. Godparents also sometimes send
checks so that the bride can make her own choice—perhaps a coffee
table or an occasional chair or whatever she wants. (For display of
checks with the other wedding presents, see Index.)

It has long been considered by custom that gifts to the bridal pair
are in fact the property of the bride, if that unpleasant term must be
used for such things as gifts sent to her at the time of her wedding.
Under certain circumstances, however, there have been court rulings
(usually in cases of separation or divorce) that have awarded certain
property rights to the husband; these cases have largely revolved around
instances of considerable monetary value and where the intent of the
giver could to some extent be determined.

CARDS WITH PRESENTS

A visiting-card is practically always enclosed with a wedding present; sometimes it is left blank but usually you write "Best wishes" or
"All best wishes for your happiness." If you have no visiting-card at
hand, write the same message on a blank card and sign it. If you are
very little older than she, you sign it "John and Mary Friendly." If you
are a friend of her or John's parents, you would write "With best wishes
from ———" and place it so that "Mr. and Mrs. Your Name" engraved
on your card forms the signature. And be sure your address is included
—unless you are certain that the bride knows it.

DELAYED PRESENTS

If, because of illness or absence, a present is not sent until after
the wedding, a note should accompany it, giving the reason for the
delay. Delayed presents are sent to Mr. and Mrs. Newlywed at their
own new address.

WHAT TO WEAR TO A WEDDING

Always, the choice of clothes depends upon the size and time of
the wedding as well as the customary practices of the community.
Wedding guests are wearing simpler clothes than they used to do.
Women wear street length day dresses before noon. At noon and up to

six o'clock, skirts may be longer. Hats are a requirement and gloves are correct.

At very big daytime weddings, correct clothes for men used to be gray striped trousers with a cutaway coat or the less formal black sack suit. (For further details, see Chapter 20.) However, today very few men wear anything more formal than plain business suits, either dark blue or dark gray. During hot weather, especially at simple seashore and country weddings, white suits or white or light gray flannel trousers with plain flannel coats are suitable. The sport coat of today is as out of place for a guest as it would be for a groom!

In certain cities, especially in the South where evening weddings are customary, tail coats are still exacted. In those of less formality the tuxedo coat is the only one ever worn in the evening. In simpler communities, men wear plain navy-blue suits on all dress occasions in the evening as well as during the day.

As a general rule, at a formal evening wedding the women wear low-neck-and-no-sleeves evening dresses, with flowers or feathers or hair ornaments, or perhaps a lace scarf over their hair and shoulders, in church. At a very simple wedding in the evening or during the day, they wear afternoon dresses, sometimes with small becoming hats or else a flower.

When not going to the reception, whatever clothes are worn habitually to church are correct.

Children always wear their best party clothes.

WHO IS INTENDED BY "AND FAMILY"?

An invitation reading "and Family" does include each and every member of the family living under the same roof—this means every child from walking and talking age (at about two) up to great-grandparents. Married daughters or sons who live in their own houses are not included because, if invited, they are sent separate invitations.

DON'T NEGLECT YOUR CHILD AT A WEDDING

Guests in general should *not* take their children unless they have received invitations. And even then not unless they themselves will look after them. Well-behaved children are very sweet at a wedding but, when out of hand, they can be most annoying to everyone and detract from the solemnity of the occasion.

ARRIVING AT THE CHURCH

Hold your card of admission ready to give to the man who will ask for it at the door. When you enter the church, go as far as the foot of the center aisle; if you get there early there will be plenty of seats. Wait until one of the ushers comes up to you. If you are a member of either family or a very intimate friend of the bride or the groom, you will tell him your name. If it is a wedding at which those to sit in the pews in front of the ribbons have been sent cards with a pew number he will ask you for your card. At a wedding without pew cards he would look on his "in front of the ribbons" list in order to seat you. If you say nothing, he will ask you whether you are a friend of the bride or of the groom, in order to seat you on her or his side of the aisle. In any case, a lady puts her hand on the inside of his proffered arm, and he escorts her to a seat; a gentleman alone walks beside the usher or if he comes with a lady he follows the usher and the lady, unless there is room for the three of them to walk abreast.

AISLE SEAT NOT RELINQUISHED

If you have arrived early enough to be given an aisle seat, there is one rule of etiquette which is a seeming contradiction to politeness, and therefore important to know: It is entirely proper that you keep your aisle seat, no matter who or how many enter the pew later. Now and then an inconsiderate late-comer, seeing someone much younger or a stranger sitting on the aisle, unfairly demands, "Move up, please." Nine out of ten well-bred people do so, instinctively, and find themselves pushed along to a sixth seat in. To stand up where you are and to make room for the late-comers to pass you and take their places farther in is all that is required by etiquette, even though the one on the aisle be a young man and the newcomer an elderly woman. In other words, pew seats at a wedding are held exactly as reserved seats are held in a theatre.

The guests without reserved cards should arrive first in order to find good places should they wish them. Members of the families and the few guests who have places in front of the ribbon can, and usually do, come later.

GREETING OTHER GUESTS

At a wedding it is also proper to smile and bow slightly to people you know—even to talk briefly in a very low voice to a friend sitting next to you; but when you find yourself among strangers, you just sit quietly until the processional starts.

STRANGER FOLLOWS EXAMPLE OF OTHERS

In most of the Protestant churches, the congregation then rises and stands throughout the service. In any case, if you are in a church of a religion other than your own, you merely observe those in front of you; stand if they stand, kneel if they kneel, and sit if they sit.

When the service is over and the recessional has passed by, those in the pews farther back must wait in their places until the immediate families in the front pews have left. If you wait until those around you start to leave, you will be sure of not making any mistake.

FROM CHURCH TO RECEPTION

When invited to the reception you are expected to go directly from the church to wherever the reception is to be held. But do give the bridal party a little while to arrange for wedding pictures and form the receiving line. If you are a lone stranger, it will be better to walk or drive around for fifteen minutes or so, to let the house get crowded, so that your aloneness will be less noticeable. Except at out-of-town weddings for which the guests arrive by special train, no provision is ever made for taking any of the guests from the church to the house. You go in your own car, or you call a taxi, or, if the distance is short, you walk.

WHAT YOU DO AT THE RECEPTION

Whether in a house or hotel, you will be met at the entrance by someone who tells you, "Ladies' dressing-room to the right" (or wherever it is). You leave your wrap, if you choose to, but you do not take off your hat or your gloves. And then you go to the door of the room in which the reception is held. You will see people going in and hear a man announcing their names. As you approach, he asks you, "What name, please?" and you give your name with title. If he says nothing, you say to *him*, "Miss Pauline Panic" or "Mrs. John Jones." He then repeats in a clear rather than loud voice, though it may sound loud to you, "Miss Pauline Panic." Then you go through the door. The bride's mother will be standing close beside you. She offers you her hand, smiles, and if you are unknown to her, she says, "How do you do." If she knows you, she says whatever is suitable. In the first place, you also say, "How do you do"; in the second, you reply to what she says to you. If she says, "I'm very glad to see you," you answer, "Thank you" or "It was very kind of you to invite me," and add something pleasant about the bride, the day, or the wedding in general. If the groom's mother is standing next to her, you must shake hands with her too, whether you are introduced to her or not. Even if you know both of the mothers very well, there would really be no time to say more than perhaps something such as "What a lovely day Mary and John have for the wedding!" or "How beautiful Mary looks!" You then join the queue of guests who are waiting to greet the bride and groom. You congratulate the groom, but you wish the bride happiness, because it is a breach of good manners to congratulate a bride on having secured a husband.

If you are in doubt about being known to either of them, you give your name, shake hands with the bride, and add, "I wish you every happiness!" Then you shake hands with the groom and say, "Congratulations, and all good wishes." If the bride does not introduce you because she is being greeted by someone following you, and the groom seems to be trying to remember your name, you tell him who you are. Otherwise, you don't.

In the excitement of the day, the bride and groom may easily forget the names even of their best friends, and they are quite likely not to remember Aunt Mary, who last visited ten years ago. It is thoughtful for a guest to mention her name even though she thinks she is known to the couple. Never choose this moment to play "Guess who I am," as some unbelievably inconsiderate people do.

If a young woman has been invited to bring a friend who is unknown to the bride and groom, she should introduce her friend to them both.

You greet any of the bridesmaids who are friends of yours. Otherwise you walk on—or smile perhaps if you happen to be looking directly at one of them who also looks at you. But there is no chance to stop and really talk to anyone unless you arrived early, or else so late that no one is waiting behind you.

After greeting the bride and groom, you look around for friends of your own. If you see no one whom you know well enough to join, the best thing to do is to make your way slowly and nonchalantly to wherever refreshments are being served.

You take your time to look at the table and then either ask one of the waiters to serve you, or help yourself to what you want. You can linger and nibble as long as you like, or sit down and watch people; and you may speak to anyone who is alone and looks willing to be spoken to.

A SIT-DOWN BREAKFAST

If you are a stranger at a sit-down breakfast, you cannot very well join a group of people whom you do not know. Therefore, it is best to go into the dining-room as soon as you can, and sit down at an unoccupied table, and let others join you. If you wait until every table has several people sitting at it, you have no alternative but to run the risk of making yourself an unwelcome intruder.

WHEN YOU LEAVE RECEPTION

When you want to leave you just do so. It is not necessary or even polite to attract attention to your going if it is soon after your arrival. You do smile at anyone you happen to be talking with and say something about being sorry you have to leave early—and go.

A NEWCOMER TO THE COMMUNITY

·◦⟨ 23 ⟩◦·

THE BRIDE WHO IS A STRANGER, BUT WHOSE HUSBAND and his family are well known in the community has no problem other than to make herself liked. The best way to do this is to be ready to like others, to be interested in what interests them, and to try to adapt herself to their points of view. This does not mean that she is to be double-faced, but merely that she is not to ride roughshod over their pet prejudices before she has even discovered what they are.

The bride, for example, who comes from Chicago or San Francisco to Bright Meadows and rudely criticizes the smaller town's ways, who insists on comparing Bright Meadows' new six-story office building with fifty-story skyscrapers, is being not merely discourteous but stupid.

WHEN BOTH ARE STRANGERS

Let us say the young Lakes from Chicago are about to move to Strangetown, where John Lake will manage the new branch office his firm has just opened. Business is the usual reason for moving to a new community. John will, of course, meet a few people through business. If the town is small and characteristically friendly, Mary will probably get to know her neighbors quickly. The Lakes will become members of the church and, by participating in a variety of church and community activities, gradually enlarge their acquaintance.

A LETTER OF INTRODUCTION

Before the Lakes left Chicago, they told Mrs. Oldname about John's new location, and Mrs. Oldname offered to send a letter introducing the young couple to a friend of hers in Strangetown.

A letter of introduction is better sent than taken in person by the newcomers. If the Lakes themselves were to take a letter to Mrs. Welcome, this lady would be obliged, whether she felt like it or not, to show them immediate and particular hospitality, or risk affronting both the newcomers and the writer of the letter. A letter of introduction sent by Mrs. Oldname and telling her friend about Mary and John Lake

gives Mrs. Welcome time to consider when and how best she may introduce the young couple to other and congenial young people. It does not
force the Lakes upon the intimate hospitality of Mrs. Welcome as a
letter taken by them to her would do.

NEWCOMERS TO A BIG CITY

Because so many young people have the notion that life in a great
city is glamorous, those who come from a small, neighborly community
into a huge city of titanic size and crushing indifference are likely to
be greatly disappointed and unhappy. The young bride will find herself bereft of a position such as she had at home, or would have had
in almost any other community. This is not because the great city
refuses to accept her; it might put her on a pedestal if it knew of her
existence—and this is the very point! In a city of several million people,
how *can* one young bride be found, no matter how lovely she is! But
in a small town she would not remain for long an unrecognized stranger.
If she walked down Main Street a dozen times, dozens of people would
have seen her twelve times.

If you plan to move to one of our large cities, try not to go into
a neighborhood where you will know no one at all. If you have some
friends or relatives in the city, try to find an apartment within easy
traveling distance of them. Or perhaps a man's business associates in
a new city can recommend a neighborhood with which they are familiar.
But if you know no one at all in the city, you may be more at home in a
suburb where the casual informality will provide new friends easily.

But even if you do take an apartment in, let's say, the heart of New
York, you will, in time, find a circle of friends. Even in the largest city in
the world, people can be friendly. Just give a few of them a chance to get
to know you. You'll meet your next-door neighbors in the laundry room
or the elevator, or in the park one block away. If you have a career,
you as well as your husband will be likely to meet people of similar
interests through business. Become an *active* member of the nearest
church of your denomination; perhaps it has a Young Couples' Club, a
Bible Study class, or some other activities you both can participate in.
The YMCA and similar organizations sponsor a variety of clubs and
classes. And every large city has several universities offering evening
extension courses. Study French literature or interior decorating and
make friends with the others taking the same courses. Above all, be
sure to keep busy; never stay at home moping about the town you came
from. The bigger the city you move to, the more there is for you to do
and discover in it.

MAKING AND KEEPING FRIENDS

The young woman in a new town has a choice between making
herself liked or finding herself with many acquaintances but no friends.

The best ingredients for likableness are a happy expression of countenance, an unaffected manner, and a sympathetic attitude. A young woman with an affected pose and bad or conceited manners will never make friends anywhere. The best rule to follow, as always, is: be your own natural, charming, gracious self.

The newcomer should particularly avoid forcing herself on her neighbors. It is fatal to be pushing or presumptuous. She should remain natural when anyone approaches her, but she should not herself approach anyone more than half-way. A smile to the passing acquaintance, the friendlier the better, is never out of place, but after smiling she should continue on. Never grin weakly and cling. A really well-bred person is as charming as possible to all but effusive to none. Enthusiasm should, of course, be shown to friends, in contrast to the more impersonal courtesy displayed to strangers.

YOUR FIRST VISITORS

Very likely some of your new neighbors will come to call before your home is ready to receive visitors. If they find you at the top of a stepladder or in a paint-spattered smock, you are really in luck. If you think about it, you will realize that this is a far more friendly setting than a formal hostess-visitor scene could be. Before you know it, you will be showing your neighbors the objects you have painted and the curtain material you are going to sew; and before they know it, they are giving you their best advice which perhaps you take or perhaps you don't; and by the time they go they seem like friends, and probably they soon become just that.

BEWARE OF IMMEDIATE INTIMACY

If you wish never to seem to be a snob, beware of rushing into intimacy with every welcoming but not especially congenial neighbor, and then later having to break with your earlier friends when you meet people you really like. After you have been in Strangetown for a while, you will come to know people whose interests are the same as your own. You can avoid suddenly having to neglect those with whom you were too intimate at first, if you are reserved and selective when making friends.

If, however, you *are* a snob, and transfer yourself from the Nextdoor circle to the Highhill circle merely because the Highhills are richer or more important, you will deserve the opinion that others will most certainly have of you.

Between being a snob and being discriminating is the entire distance between being contemptible and admirable—between worst and best.

THE NEW BABY

·◦⟨ 24 ⟩◦·

THE FIRST ANNOUNCEMENT OF THE BIRTH OF A BABY IS usually made to the nearest and dearest friends and relatives as soon as the proud father or delighted grandparents can get to the telephone. Some time before the blessed event actually takes place, the prospective parents usually visit a stationer's and select an announcement card to be sent to the entire list of the friends of both grandparental families when the time comes. After the birth, and as soon as the name is determined, the father notifies the stationer, and in a few days the cards are ready. The new mother can address the envelopes while she is still in the hospital.

SELECTING A BIRTH ANNOUNCEMENT CARD

The nicest type of birth announcement, and one that is happily coming back into general use, consists simply of a very small card with the baby's name and birth date on it, tied with a white or pastel ribbon to the upper margin of the "Mr. and Mrs." card of the parents.

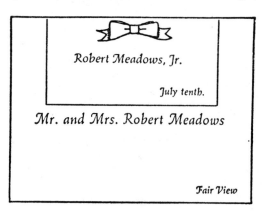

A large variety of commercially designed announcement cards, with space for the baby's name, date of birth, and parents' names to be written in by hand, are also available, and have been very much used in recent years. The least desirable of these include such data as the baby's weight and length, and some coy phrasing or cute design. One such card, which no person of refinement could select, shows a baby's head peering out of a white package carried by a stork, and says: "My mommy and daddy want me to tell you I landed." Good taste rules that the simplest card is the best, *always!*

NEWSPAPER ANNOUNCEMENT OF BIRTH

In the week following the birth, the father may send a release to the local newspapers announcing the event: "Mr. and Mrs. Robert Meadows of 202 Park Avenue, New York City, happily announce the birth of Robert Jr. on July 10, 1959, at Doctors Hospital. They have one daughter, Jane, 4. Mrs. Meadows is the former Miss Mary Gilding." Or, "Mr. and Mrs. Robert Meadows (nee Gilding) of 202 Park Avenue, New York City, happily announce the birth of Jane's brother, Robert Jr., on July 10, 1959, at Doctors Hospital." The same announcement may be sent to the editor of the church newsletter or bulletin.

CHOOSING A NAME

Parents should be careful to avoid giving the baby a name that will be a handicap, because it is too long, or difficult to pronounce clearly, or it forms an unpleasant combination with the last name. Simple Anglo-Saxon or biblical names will go well with most family names. It is nice for a name to have some significance, perhaps through its original meaning, or because it is traditionally carried by some member of the family. A child may also be named for a highly respected national figure or a beloved friend. Many Christian first sons are given the same name as their fathers; when a child is named for a parent he may be given a middle name different from that of the parent, and in adult life he may decide to be known as "R. William Meadows," instead of "Robert Meadows, Jr." Roman Catholic babies, by canon law, are named after a saint. Although they may be called any diminutive, their baptismal certificates must record a saint's name as the baby's first or middle name. Most Jewish babies are traditionally named for a deceased relative, and thus the name of a loved one is perpetuated.

TIME OF CHRISTENING

In other days of stricter observances, a baby was baptized in the Roman or High Episcopal church on the first, or possibly the second, Sunday after its birth. In the Catholic church the baptism still takes place when the baby is very young—usually not over a month old—and always in the church or baptistry (unless its baptism is *in extremis*). In Protestant churches the average age for christening is from two to six months, although in some denominations or under special conditions children may not be christened until they are several years old. In all churches it is customary for the mother to be present if she is able.

ASKING THE GODPARENTS

Before setting the day of the christening, the godparents should be asked and their consent obtained. They may be asked to serve when the baby's arrival is announced to them, and occasionally before; or perhaps when they visit the hospital. In Protestant practice there are usually two godfathers and one godmother for a boy, two godmothers and one godfather for a girl. A Catholic baby usually has one godparent of the same sex as the child, and may have both a godfather and godmother.

It is perfectly correct to send a note if the godparent lives at a distance, or he may be asked by telegraph: "IT'S A BOY. WILL YOU BE GODFATHER?" But in any case do not write anything so formal as, "My husband and I sincerely hope that you will consent to be our son's godmother." It would be the height of presumption to ask anyone so slightly known as this wording implies to fill so intimate a position.

If a godparent whom the parents particularly want is unable to be present at the christening, a proxy quite simply acts for him or her at the ceremony, the consent of the real godparent having first been given; it is considerate for the real godparent to send a note authorizing the proxy to the clergyman.

One must never ask any but a most intimate friend to be a godmother or godfather, since it is a responsibility not lightly to be undertaken and also one difficult to refuse. Godparents are chosen from among friends rather than relatives, since one advantage of godparents is that they add to the child's stock of relatives so that, should the child be left alone in the world, its godparents become its protectors. But when a child is born with plenty of relatives who can be called upon for assistance, godparents are often chosen from among them.

The obligation of being a godparent is essentially a spiritual one; therefore the godparent should be of the same faith as the parents. The godparent must see that the child is given religious training and that he is confirmed at the proper time. Beyond this obligation he is expected to take a special interest in the child, much as a very near relative would do. At the christening he gives the baby as nice a present as he can afford. The typical gift is a silver mug or porringer, inscribed: "*Robert Meadows, Jr. / December 5th, 1955 / From his godfather / John Strong.*" Other typical presents are a silver fork and spoon, a silver comb and brush set, a government bond, or a trust fund to which the donor may add each year until the child is grown.

CHRISTENING INVITATIONS

Usually, christening invitations are given over the telephone, or in a personal note to "Dear Lina and Jeff" or "Mr. and Mrs. Kindhart," and

signed "Mary" or "Mary Meadows." Or a message may be written on
the "Mr. and Mrs." card of the parents, saying simply: *Baby's christening, St. Mary's Church, Jan. 10. 3 o'ck. Caudle at our house afterward.*"
All invitations to a christening should be very friendly and informal.

CLOTHES AT A CHRISTENING

The baby's christening dress is often one that was worn by the baby's
mother, father, or even one of its grand- or great-grandparents. Everything the baby wears on this occasion should be white, although this is
merely a custom and not a church requirement. The traditional christening dress is long and made of sheer, soft material with lace and hand-
embroidery trim, and is worn with delicate, long petticoats. It is not
necessary to go to the expense of buying a traditional christening dress
if there is no family heirloom; any long, plain white dress will do. However, some very pretty christening dresses are now available in the
new miracle fabrics, and they are quite inexpensive.

The guests at a christening wear what they would wear to church.
The mother wears a light-colored dress; she should not wear black on
this occasion.

THE CHRISTENING IN CHURCH

The clergyman, of course, is consulted about the place and hour for
the christening before the godparents are asked. The ceremony may take
place at the close of the regular Sunday service; the guests remain after
the rest of the congregation leaves. Roman Catholic parishes generally
schedule baptisms for a specified time on Sunday afternoons, and the
parents make an appointment at the rectory in advance. If a large party
is planned to follow a Protestant christening, it is best to choose a week-
day and an hour when the church is not being otherwise used. Guests
seat themselves in the pews nearest the font.

As soon as the clergyman appears, the baby's coat and cap are taken
off and the godmother, holding the baby in her arms, stands directly in
front of the clergyman. The other godparents stand beside her, and
relatives and friends nearby.

The godmother who is holding the baby must be sure to pronounce
its name distinctly; in fact it is wise, if the name is long or unusual, to
print it on a slip of paper and give it to the clergyman beforehand, since
whatever name the clergyman pronounces is fixed for life. More than
one baby has been given a name not intended for it. The godmother
states the given name or names only, and not the surname.

As soon as the ceremony is over, the baby and all its relatives and
friends go to the house of the parents or grandparents where a caudle
party—the traditional caudle usually replaced by punch or champagne—
has been arranged.

Baptism is a sacrament of the church, for which no fee is ever required. A donation, however, is usually presented in an envelope to the clergyman after the ceremony, commensurate with the elaborateness of the christening.

A HOUSE CHRISTENING

If permitted by the church to which the baby's parents belong, the house christening is a safer and prettier ceremony—safer, because the baby is not likely to catch cold by being taken out and brought in, and prettier, because the baby's dress has not been crushed by having a coat put over it and taken off and also because a baby brought down from the nursery without any fussing is generally "good," since his routine has not been upset.

The arrangements for a house christening are quite simple, the only necessary decoration being the font. This is always a bowl—usually of silver (often borrowed)—put on a small, high table. A white napkin on the table suggests a restaurant rather than a ritual and is, therefore, an unfortunate choice; most people prefer to cover the table in a dark fabric, such as old brocade or velvet. Flowers are arranged around the bowl in a flat circle, the blossoms outside, the stems toward the center and covered by the base of the bowl.

At the hour set for the ceremony, the clergyman enters the room and takes his place at the font. The guests naturally make way, forming an open aisle. The godmother carries the baby and follows the clergyman; the other godparents walk behind her, and all stand near the font. At the proper moment the clergyman takes the baby, baptizes it, and hands it back to the godmother, who holds it until the ceremony is over.

After performing the ceremony, the clergyman, if he wears vestments, goes to a room that has been set apart for him, changes into his street clothes, and then returns to the living-room as one of the guests.

THE CHRISTENING PARTY

The only difference between an ordinary informal tea and a christening tea is that the latter features christening cake and caudle. The christening cake is generally a white "lady" cake elaborately iced, sometimes with the baby's initials and garlands of pink sugar roses. When a real caudle is served, it is invariably a hot eggnog, drunk out of little punch cups. But today champagne or punch is usually substituted for the caudle. Guests eat the cake as a sign that they partake of the baby's hospitality and are therefore its friend, drink the caudle to its health and prosperity. But by this time the young host or hostess is peacefully asleep in the nursery.

JEWISH CEREMONIES FOR THE NEWBORN

On the eighth day after birth, in the ceremony known as *Brith Milah*, a boy is initiated into the Jewish covenant between man and God.

The circumcision is accompanied by a religious ceremony during which the boy is named. After the ceremony, which today usually takes place in a special room in the hospital, there is a light collation. The guests drink to the baby's future and toast the parents, grandparents, and godparents (there is always a godfather and usually a godmother). Relatives and close friends are invited to the *Brith* by telephone or informal note. They dress as they would for any service in a synagogue, and both men and women customarily wear hats.

Girls are named in the synagogue on the first Sabbath after birth, when the father is called up to the Torah. Sometimes the naming is postponed until the mother is able to be present. In some Reform congregations, boys are also named in the synagogue (in addition to being named at the *Brith*) when both parents are present, and a special blessing is pronounced by the rabbi. The mother may be hostess at the collation following the service. Friends and relatives may be invited to attend the religious service during which the baby will be named.

The ceremony of redemption of the first-born, the *Pidyon Ha-Ben*, which takes place only if the first-born is a boy, is performed when the baby is thirty-one days old. According to ancient custom described in the Bible, the first-born son was dedicated to the service of God. It became customary for a *Kohen* (a descendant of the priestly tribe) to redeem the child from this obligation, entrusting him to the care of his father for bringing up in the Jewish faith. The *Pidyon Ha-Ben*, consisting of a brief ceremony and a celebration, is held in the home, informal notes of invitation having been sent about ten days previously to close friends and relatives.

PRESENTS FOR BABY AND MOTHER

Everyone who receives a birth announcement card should write a note of congratulations to the new parents, or a note may be enclosed in a gift. It is not necessary to send a present, however, even if you receive an announcement. Gifts may be sent for the baby, addressed to the parents at home, or you may bring your present with you when you visit the hospital. It is thoughtful to bring something for the new mother, too—cologne (if she uses it), or handkerchiefs, perhaps.

ANNOUNCEMENT OF ADOPTION

It is a nice gesture to send a card announcing this happy event to your friends and relatives. A card such as this will also bring reassuring comfort to the child later on, should she ever doubt her place in the hearts of those who chose her to be their own: "*Mr. and Mrs. Nuhome / have the happiness to announce / the adoption of / Mary / aged thirteen months.*" Or, if announcements are sent during the legal proceedings, the above is changed to read: "*have the happiness to announce / the arrival / and prospective adoption of . . .*"

FUNERALS

·⊲[25]⊳·

IN A TIME OF BEREAVEMENT, WHEN WE STAND BAFFLED
and alone, etiquette performs its most real service by smoothing the
necessary personal contacts and making sure that the last rites of our
beloved shall be performed with beauty and gravity. Intimate friends
are expected to go to the house of mourning and ask if they can be of
service.

Depending on the faith, friends can be helpful and can be of real
service to the grief-stricken family. The family has to make many de-
cisions in most Protestant and Reform Jewish faiths. Roman Catholic and
Orthodox rituals follow a more rigid rule, but there are still some deci-
sions for the family, or nearest relative, or a close friend to make.

As far as possible the funeral should be in keeping with a man's life.
It would not be appropriate to have a large funeral for a man who was
a scholar or a research scientist who led a quiet life and had a small
circle of friends.

NOTIFY PEOPLE

If members of the immediate family are not already present, the
first act of someone at the bedside of the deceased is to notify them and
one or two intimate friends whose capability as well as sympathy can
be counted on.

If the deceased had suffered a long illness, and the family has become attached to the trained nurse, no one is better fitted than she to
turn her ministrations from the one whom she can no longer help to
those who now have a very real need for her care. She, a friend, or a
member of the family must look after many details.

NEWSPAPER NOTICE

One of the first things to do is to put into the newspapers a notice
of the death and—as soon as it is known—a statement of the time and
place of the funeral. The form can be selected from among those appearing in the daily press. If this notice appears in several papers and

several times, the person who has charge of the funeral expenses must remember to ask for the total amount, for it can be an appreciable item.

Except for those relatives and intimate friends who received telephoned or telegraphed messages asking them to come to the house at once, everyone is expected to consider this newspaper announcement notification enough.

When the notice reads "Funeral private" and neither time nor place is given, very intimate friends are given this information; others understand that they are not expected to be present.

The notification of a private funeral is telephoned or written on the personal card of the relative or friend in charge, "Mr. Brown's funeral will be at Christ Church, Monday at eleven o'clock."

Sometimes the notice reads, "Please omit flowers." This wish should be strictly followed, particularly if the service is being held in a Catholic or very "high" Episcopal church to which flowers are not admitted, and friends may send a donation in the name of the deceased to some charitable organization. (Perhaps the notice lists a particular charity that the deceased was interested in.)

THE FUNERAL DIRECTOR

After consulting members of the family about their wishes in the matter, a friend who knows the family's taste and purse consults the funeral director and discusses carefully the specification of all details, so that everything necessary may be arranged for and unnecessary items omitted. A family which prefers a very elaborate funeral is of course given every aid toward this end. Most people have moderate rather than unlimited means, and it is not unheard of that a small estate is seriously depleted by too lavish funeral expenses. Therefore it is most important that a funeral director of known integrity be chosen, probably recommended by the clergyman, or more likely by the sexton of the church.

Fortunately our ideas about funerals have changed; the day of costly funerals is past. Now the trend is toward simple ones which do not leave the widow in debt. At the time of bereavement she is, of course, emotionally upset and may not know too much about her late husband's finances.

The person in charge delivers clothes in subdued colors, usually such as were worn to church by the deceased, to the funeral director though some still prefer shrouds. Young girls in their teens are buried in white and children in their Sunday school clothes. Men are buried in a cutaway or a dark blue or dark gray suit.

THE CLERGYMAN

Since the deceased or the family are probably church members, their clergyman is notified immediately and asked to officiate at the service.

No fee is ever asked by the clergyman, but those who would like to give something in appreciation of his services may and should do so. The fee may be anything from $10.00 for a very small funeral service to $100.00 for a very elaborate one.

A bill rendered by the sexton includes all necessary charges for the church.

HONORARY PALLBEARERS

The member of the family who is in charge will ask, either when they come to the house or by telephone or telegraph if they are at a distance, six or eight men who are best friends of the deceased to be the pallbearers. When a man has been prominent in public life, he may have twelve or more from among his political or business associates as well as his lifelong friends. Members of the immediate family are never chosen, as their place is with the women of the family. One cannot refuse an invitation to be a pallbearer except because of illness or absence from the city.

The pallbearers meet a few minutes before the time set for the service, in the vestibule of the church.

Honorary pallbearers serve only at church funerals. They do not carry the coffin. This service is performed by the assistants of the funeral director, who are expertly trained.

Although "casket" does more accurately describe the modern box shape and is moreover the word used by many funeral directors, the old-fashioned word "coffin" is usually preferred by the conservative.

EMBLEM OF MOURNING ON THE DOOR

To indicate that there has been a death in the house the funeral director may hang streamers on the front door; white ones for a child, black and white for a young person, or black for an older person. Flowers are, of course, most beautiful and naturally the choice of those who can afford them. Usually they are ordered directly from their own florist or quite possibly the funeral director orders them. White flowers for a young person, purple for one that was older. These are removed by a member of the funeral establishment before the family returns from the services.

A FRIEND OF THE FAMILY IN CHARGE

One who is an intimate friend or member of the family should be near the front door to see the countless people with whom details have to be arranged, to admit to the family anyone they may want to see, and to give news to or take messages from others, and accept telegrams.

As people come to the house to inquire and offer their services, he asks them to attend to whatever there is that has to be done. The first friend who hurries to the house—in answer to the telephone message which announced the death—is asked to break the news to an invalid connection of the family, or he may be sent to the florist to order the flowers for the door, or to the station to meet a child arriving from school.

AN ACCURATE LIST OF FLOWERS

Whoever takes charge of the flowers must carefully collect all the notes and cards. On the outside of each envelope is written a description of the flowers that came with the card. Sometimes this is done by the florist and the cards are delivered to the bereaved family after the funeral. For example:

Large spray Easter lilies tied with white ribbon

Laurel wreath with gardenias

Long sheaf of white roses—broad silver ribbon

Without such notations, the family has no way of knowing anything about the flowers that people have sent. Moreover, these descriptions are necessary when writing notes of thanks.

Some friends send potted plants or arrangements to the house. These cards are removed and noted for later acknowledgments.

ARRANGING THE FLOWERS

If the family is Protestant, an hour before the time set for the service one or two women friends go to the church to help the florist and perhaps an assistant arrange the flowers which have already been placed in the chancel. Their chief duty is to see that flowers sent by relatives are given a prominent position. The differences in names of out-of-town people may confuse the florist. Effective grouping and fastening of the heavy wreaths and sprays is difficult for novices, no matter how perfect their taste may be, and the florist is capable of doing a more effective job.

"SITTING UP" NO LONGER CUSTOMARY

Unless the deceased be a prelate or personage whose lying-in-state is a public ceremony, or unless it is the particular wish of the relatives, the solemn vigil through long nights by the side of the casket is not a requirement of love for the departed.

Everything is done to avoid unnecessary evidence of the change that has taken place. In many instances, the person who has died is left lying in bed or on a sofa in a negligée, if a woman, or dressing gown, if a man, and with flowers placed about the room. In any event, the last attentions are paid in accordance with the wishes of those most nearly concerned.

If people are "sitting up" at the wish of relatives, there are usually two groups who "spell" each other and suitable refreshments such as coffee, sandwiches, and cake are provided. Needless to say, no alcoholic beverages are served.

CONDUCT OF FRIENDS

When you hear of the death of a friend, you should go at once to the house, write "With sympathy" on your card, and leave it at the door. Or you write a letter to the family. In either case you send flowers, addressed either to the funeral of —— (name of the deceased) —— or otherwise to the nearest relative. The latter method is preferable when the relative is a friend. But the former method is followed if the deceased alone was known to you.

On the card accompanying the flowers, and addressed to one of the family, you write "With sympathy," "With deepest sympathy," "With heartfelt sympathy," or "With love and sympathy." If there is a notice in the papers requesting that no flowers be sent, you send none. On the other hand you do send flowers to any bereaved person who is particularly in your thoughts; a few flowers sent from time to time— possibly long afterward—are especially comforting in their assurance of continued sympathy.

If the notice reads "Funeral Private," you do not go unless you have received a message from the family that they wish you to come.

On the other hand, all members of the family find out when the funeral is to take place and go to it without waiting to be notified.

Above all it is heartlessly delinquent not to go to the public funeral of one with whom you have been associated in business or other interests, or to whose house you have been often invited, or where you are an intimate friend of the immediate members of the family.

It is no longer considered necessary to wear black when you go to a friend's funeral unless you sit with the family or have been asked to be one of the honorary pallbearers, but you should choose clothes that are dark and inconspicuous.

Enter the church as quietly as possible, and as there are no ushers at a funeral, seat yourself where you approximately belong. Only a very intimate friend should take a position far up on the center aisle. If you are merely an acquaintance, you should sit toward the rear of the church.

WHEN IT IS REQUESTED THAT NO FLOWERS BE SENT

Catholics often send a "spiritual bouquet" (a Mass said for the deceased). Also, a present-day custom is to make a donation in memory of the deceased, especially if there was an organization in which he or she was personally interested. Flowers may be sent to the house or a funeral home, but are not taken to the cemetery. In some dioceses, flowers are admitted in the Catholic church for the funeral service of a small child. This custom varies and the regulations would have to be checked with the local parish.

One never sends flowers to an Orthodox Jewish funeral, and often the Conservative or Reform church prefers not to have them.

CHURCH FUNERAL

The church funeral is the more trying in that the family has to leave the seclusion of the house and be in the presence of a congregation. On the other hand many find the solemnity of a church service with the added beauty of choir and organ helpfully soothing.

As the time appointed for the funeral draws near, the congregation gradually fills the church. The first few pews on the right side of the center aisle are always left empty for the family and those on the left for the pallbearers.

The trend today is to have the casket closed. Protestants may follow their own wishes. At a Catholic or Jewish service it is obligatory that the casket be closed.

THE PROCESSIONAL

At most funerals of today, the processional is omitted. The coffin, with one or several floral pieces on it—or covered with a pall of needlework belonging to the church or one of flowers—is placed on a stand at the foot of the chancel a half-hour before the service. The family enter from the vestry and take their place in the front pews unobserved.

Should the family prefer that there be a processional, it forms in the vestibule. If there is to be a choral service, the minister and the choir enter the church from the rear, and precede the funeral cortège. Directly after the choir and clergy, come the honorary pallbearers, two by two; then the coffin covered with flowers; and then the family—the chief mourner being first, walking with whoever is most sympathetic to him or her.

Usually each woman leans upon the arm of a man. But two women or two men may walk together, according to the division of the family. If the deceased is one of four sons and there is no daughter, the mother and father walk together immediately after the body of their child, and they are followed by the two elder sons and then the younger, and then the nearest woman relative.

Although the arrangement of the procession is thus fixed, it is of greater importance that those in deepest affliction should each be placed next to the one whose nearness may be of most comfort. A younger child who is calm and soothing would be better next to his mother than an older one who is of more nervous temperament.

At the chancel the choir takes its accustomed place, the clergyman stands at the foot of the chancel steps, the honorary pallbearers take their places in the front pews on the left, and the casket is set upon a stand previously placed there for the purpose. The actual bearers of the casket, who are always professionals furnished by the funeral director, walk quietly to inconspicuous stations on the side aisles. The family occupy the front pews on the right side; the rest of the procession fills vacant places on either side. The service is then read.

THE RECESSIONAL

Upon the conclusion of the service, the procession moves out in the same order as it came in, except that the choir remains in its place. Outside the church, the casket is put into the hearse, the family enter automobiles waiting immediately behind the hearse, and the flowers are put into a covered vehicle. It is very vulgar to fill open landaulets with floral offerings and make a parade through the streets. Or they are taken in a closed car by assistants from the funeral home, following a different route and are placed beside the grave before the hearse and those attending the burial service arrive.

FEW GO TO THE BURIAL

If the burial is in the churchyard or otherwise within walking distance, the congregation naturally follows the family to the graveside. Otherwise, the general congregation no longer expects, nor wishes to go to the interment, which—except at a funeral of public importance— is witnessed only by the immediate family and the most intimate friends. The long line of vehicles that used to stand at the church, ready to be filled with mere acquaintances, is proper only for a public personage.

FUNERAL AT THE HOUSE

Many prefer a house funeral. It is simpler, more private, and obviates the necessity that those in sorrow face people, for the nearest relatives may stay apart in an adjoining room where they can hear the service yet remain in seclusion.

MUSIC

A few decades ago there seldom was music at house funerals because at that time nothing could substitute for the deep, rich tones of the organ. At the present time, however, phonographic recordings of organ and choir music are excellent and readily available, and may be used most helpfully for a beautiful addition to a house funeral.

HOUSE ARRANGEMENT

Arrangements are usually made to hold the service in the drawing-room. The coffin is placed in front of the mantel, or between the windows, but always at a distance from the door. It is usually set on stands brought by the funeral director, who also supplies enough folding chairs to fill the room without crowding.

At a house funeral, the relatives either take their places near the casket or stay apart in seclusion. If the women of the family come into the drawing-room, they wear hats, as in a church.

All other women keep their wraps on. The men wear their overcoats or carry them on their arms and hold their hats in their hands, unless it is summer when no one would be wearing coats.

It is unusual for any but a small group of relatives and intimate friends to go to the cemetery from the house. There the grave will have been lined with boughs and greens—to lessen the impression of bare earth.

THE FUNERAL HOME OR CHAPEL

In recent years, because many people live in hotels and small apartments, the establishments of funeral directors have assumed a new prominence. In the more important ones, there is a chapel, actually a small and often very beautiful non-sectarian church. There are also many retiring rooms and reception rooms where the families may remain undisturbed or receive the condolences of their friends.

A MEMORIAL SERVICE

Under some circumstances, as when the deceased has died in a far country, a memorial service is held instead of a funeral.

Notice of this service is put into the obituary column of the paper, or, in a small town, people are telephoned and each given a short list of his own nearest neighbors whom he is asked to notify.

These services are very brief. In general outline, two verses of a hymn are sung. Then follow short prayers and a very brief address about the work and personality of the one for whom the service is held. The service is closed with a prayer and two verses of another hymn.

Usually, no flowers, except a few for the altar, are sent. On occasion when flowers are sent, they are arranged as bouquets (not sheaves) so that they may be put into the wards of a hospital without having to be taken apart and rearranged.

ACKNOWLEDGMENT OF SYMPATHY

In the case of a very prominent person, where messages of condolence, many of them impersonal, mount into the thousands, the sending of engraved cards to strangers is proper, such as

> *The Governor and Mrs. State*
> *wish gratefully to acknowledge*
> *your kind expression of sympathy*

or

Senator Michigan
wishes to express his appreciation of
..............................'s
sympathy in his recent bereavement

But under no circumstances should such cards be sent to those who have sent flowers or to intimate friends who have written personal letters.

When someone with real sympathy in his heart has taken the trouble to select and send flowers, or has gone to the house and offered what service he might, or has in a spirit of genuine regard written a personal letter, the receipt of words composed by a stationer and dispatched by a professional secretary would be exactly as though his outstretched hand had been pushed aside.

A personal message on a fold-over visiting-card is all anyone asks for. It takes but a moment to write "Thank you for your beautiful flowers," or "Thank you for your kind sympathy" or "Thank you for all your kindness." Nor is it much more of an effort to write: "Thank you, dear Mrs. Smith, for your beautiful flowers and your kind sympathy," or "Your flowers were so beautiful! Thank you for them and for your loving message," or "Thank you for your sweet letter. I know you meant it!" or "I cannot half tell you how much all your loving kindness has meant to me."

Recently a most unfortunate custom has sprung up, that is, the funeral director supplies printed cards, and the recipient merely signs his or her name to it. A poor return, indeed, for a beautiful spray of flowers or even a bouquet of garden flowers.

ANOTHER MAY WRITE FOR ONE IN MOURNING

If the list is very long, or the person who has received the flowers and messages is in reality unable to perform the task of writing, some member of the family or possibly a near friend may write for her or him, "Mother (or whoever it is) asks me to thank you for your beautiful flowers and kind message of sympathy." No one expects more than a short message of acknowledgment, but that message should be *seemingly personal*, and written by hand!

MOURNING

During the past twenty-five years no other changes in etiquette have been so great as those of the conventions of mourning. Until then the regulations for mourning were definitely prescribed according to the precise degree of relationship of the mourner. One's real feelings, whether of grief or comparative indifference, had nothing to do with the outward manifestation one was expected to show as a sign of respect.

A greater and ever greater number of persons today do not believe in going into mourning at all. There are some who believe, as do the races of the East, that great love should be expressed in rejoicing in the rebirth of a beloved spirit instead of selfishly mourning their own earthly loss. It is however certain that the number of these that can attain this spirit is few indeed. Most of us merely do the best we can to continue to keep occupied, to make the necessary adjustments as best we can, and to avoid casting the shadow of our own sadness upon others.

THE CRÊPE VEIL IS NO MORE

It is a very healthy sign that the crêpe veil is no more except at the funeral, and usually it is not worn then—nor does one wear a thick veil of any sort after the funeral. Mourning materials are, however, still definitely prescribed as follows:

MOURNING MATERIALS

Cotton, linen, woolen, and all lusterless silks are suitable for deepest mourning. Uncut velvet is as deep mourning as crêpe, but cut velvet is not mourning at all! Nor is satin or anything shiny. The only lace permissible is a plain or hemstitched net known as "footing."

A very perplexing decree is that clothes entirely of white are deepest mourning, but the addition of a black belt, or hat, or gloves produces second mourning.

Patent leather and open-toe-and-heel-shoes are not mourning. And stockings of beige or any other light shade is the one way a woman all in black announces she is NOT in mourning.

More than a minimum of jewelry with mourning is not in good taste. Habitual jewelry, especially items of utility, such as a watch or a pin that really fastens one's dress, are permissible; and of course one continues to wear one's engagement ring no matter if it be of brightest color. A string of pearls is proper and either pearl or diamond earrings —particularly on older women who have habitually worn them.

Any costume jewelry is tabu.

MOURNING PROPRIETIES GREATLY LIBERALIZED

The liberalizing of mourning conventions is due to the fact that the crêpe veil no longer exists; therefore, the depth of mourning which it represented no longer exists. Those who are wearing mourning do not now go to balls or other conspicuously formal parties, nor take a leading part in purely social activities. On the other hand, anyone who is in public life, in business, or who has a professional career must, of course, continue to fulfil the exactions of his career. The fact that many women have gone into business or are following careers is another cause of the lightening of mourning and the shortening of its duration.

The normal routine of children should not be curtailed—more than ever they need to romp and play.

A WIDOW'S MOURNING

As an example of how things can change in not so many years, a widow formerly never wore any but woolen materials, made as plain as possible, with deep-hemmed, turn-back cuffs and collar of white organdy. On the street she wore a small crêpe bonnet with a widow's cap border of white crêpe organdy and a long veil of crêpe that swathed her from head to within a few inches of the ground—and was worn frequently for life. Today this costume, even for one on the far side of eighty, is unimaginable.

A widow of mature years may still—if she chooses—wear mourning for life. On the other hand, deep mourning for a year, followed by another year of second mourning, is now considered extreme, and more than six months is very rare.

THE YOUNG WIDOW

The young widow, if she wishes to wear mourning, should wear all-black for six months, and then according to fashion of today she usually goes into colors within any intervening second mourning. She should, of course, *never* remain in mourning for her first husband after she has decided she can be consoled by a second.

There is no reason why a woman—or a man—should not, in time, find such consolation. But to welcome the attentions of a new suitor while still in mourning is likely to be thought heartless—especially if the marriage had been a happy one.

MOURNING FOR COUNTRY WEAR

Except for elderly ladies to wear to church, somber black clothes are not appropriate in the country—ever! All gray mixtures with a black band on the left sleeve of the jacket or else clothes in dull materials of white are most suitable. Actual sports clothes may be of any inconspicuous mixture, with black arm band on the left sleeve.

MOURNING WORN BY A MOTHER

A mother who has lost a grown son or daughter wears all-black for six months or a year, depending on her inclination, and after that second mourning for so long as she cares to. All-white or tweeds with arm band should be worn in the country. "Second mourning" means absence of red, blue, green, and yellow.

MOURNING FOR A DAUGHTER OR SISTER

A daughter or sister wears mourning for a long season and second mourning for another season. Counting by season is very practical because of clothes. When going into mourning in the spring or summer, wear deep mourning until winter clothes are appropriate; then change to second mourning, or vice versa.

MOURNING FOR BUSINESS WOMEN

Since mourning is the outward evidence of a personal frame of mind which has no place in the impersonal world of business, mourning which attracts attention is as unsuitable in an office as a black uniform would be on a soldier.

Inconspicuous mourning, on the other hand, is entirely proper. The fact that a woman invariably wears a black dress, or a gray mixture suit, attracts no attention if she has a little white at the throat. Too solid black, including a black-bordered handkerchief, would be out of place in the office.

If a woman arrives at her office a day or so after the death of a close relative in the clothes she ordinarily wears, no one looks askance. She also must consider the effect her wearing mourning would have on any customers she comes into contact with.

MOURNING FOR MEN

It is entirely correct for a man to go into mourning by the simple expedient of putting a black band on his hat and on the left sleeve of his clothes. Also he wears black shoes, gloves, socks, and ties, and white instead of colored linen. In the country a young man continues to wear his ordinary golf clothes and shoes and sweater—no matter how gay, and without any sleeve band. But he must wear a black tie and a white shirt and carry an all-white handkerchief.

The sleeve band is from three and a half to four and a half inches in width and is of dull cloth on overcoats or winter clothing, and of serge on summer clothes. The sleeve band of mourning is sensible for many reasons, the first being that of economy.

Except for the one black suit bought for the funeral and kept for church on Sunday or some other special occasion, only men who are both well-to-do and elderly go into black clothes. The deep black band on the hat is also rarely seen, because a high silk hat is seldom worn in American communities.

There is an objection to even a sleeve band on business clothes: the implied bid for sympathy, which most men want to avoid. Many men, therefore, go to the office with no evidence of mourning other than a black tie and black socks.

LITTLE CHILDREN NEVER WEAR BLACK

For either of their parents little children may, of course, be kept in white—which is the favorite color to choose for them anyway. But on no account should a child be put into black.

BEHAVIOR EXACTED OF CHILDREN

Many people are uncertain about whether children who have lost a parent should participate in their usual school activities and after-school entertainments. The answer is that they of course take part in sports and even a school concert or play. However, they should not go to a purely social party, such as an annual school dance, within two or three months of the death of a parent.

THEY ALSO MOURN WHO DO NOT WEAR BLACK

So many women, as well as men, follow occupations which preclude the wearing of mourning, that each year the number increases of those who show the mourning in their hearts only by the quiet dignity of their lives.

THE WELL-APPOINTED HOUSE

·❧[26]❧·

EVERY HOUSE HAS AN OUTWARD APPEARANCE TO BE MADE
as presentable as possible, and an interior continually to be set in order
and cleaned. For those that dwell within it there are meals to be prepared and served, linen to be laundered and mended, personal clothes
to be brushed and pressed, and perhaps children to be cared for.

Beyond these fundamental necessities, luxuries can be added indefinitely, such as splendor of architecture, of gardening, and of furnishing,
with every refinement of service imaginable. With all this genuine
splendor possible only to the greatest establishments (and they are
becoming fewer and fewer), a little house can no more compete than
a diamond weighing but half a carat can compete with a stone weighing fifty times as much. And this is a good simile, because the perfect
little house may be represented by a corner cut from precisely the same
stone and differing therefrom merely in size, whereas the house in bad
taste and improperly run may be represented by a diamond that is off
color and full of flaws, or merely a piece of glass that can suggest a gem
of value only to those as ignorant as its owner.

A gem of a house may be no size at all, but its lines are honest, and
its painting and furnishing in good taste. As for its upkeep, its path or
sidewalk is beautifully neat, steps scrubbed, brasses polished, and its
bell answered promptly by a trim maid with a low voice and quiet,
courteous manner or by the mistress herself—all contribute as unmistakably to the impression of quality as the luxury of a palace whose bronze
door is opened by the smartest of footmen.

But the mansion of bastard architecture and crude detail, with its
brass indifferently clean, with coarse lace behind the plate glass of its
golden-oak door, and the bell answered at eleven in the morning by a
butler in an ill-fitting dress suit and wearing a mustache, might as well
be placarded, "Here lives a vulgarian who has never had an opportunity
to approach the outermost edges of cultivation." As a matter of fact, the

knowledge of how to make a house distinguished both in appearance and in service is harder to learn than how to present a distinguished appearance oneself and to acquire presentable manners.

The personality of a house is indefinable, but there never lived a lady of great cultivation and charm whose home, whether a mansion or a tiny apartment, did not reflect the charm of its owner. Houses without personality are a series of walled enclosures with furniture standing about in them. Sometimes their lack of charm is baffling; every article is correct and perhaps even beautiful, but one has the feeling that the decorator made chalk marks indicating the exact spot on which each piece of furniture is to stand. Other houses are filled with things of little intrinsic value, often with much that is shabby, and yet they have that inviting atmosphere, that air of unmistakable rightness, which is an unfailing indication of highly cultivated people.

"BECOMING" FURNITURE

Suitability is a test of good taste always—the dress to the occasion, the article to the place, the furniture to the background. And yet to combine many periods in one and commit no anachronism—to put something French, something Spanish, something Italian, and something English into an American house and have the result the perfection of American taste—is a feat that has been accomplished time and again—by those who know *how*!

A woman of great taste follows fashion in house furnishing, just as she follows fashion in dress, in general principles only. She wears what is becoming to her own type and personality, and she puts into her house only such articles as are becoming to it.

That a quaint old-fashioned house should be filled with quaint old-fashioned pieces of furniture, in size proportioned to the size of the rooms, and that rush-bottomed chairs and rag rugs have no place in a marble hall, need not be pointed out. But to an amazing number of persons, proportion seems to mean nothing at all. They will put a huge piece of furniture in a tiny room so that the effect is one of painful indigestion; or they will crowd things all into one corner so that it seems about to capsize into the floor below; or they will spoil a really good room by the addition of senseless and inappropriately cluttering objects, in the belief that because they are valuable they must be beautiful, regardless of suitability. Sometimes a room is marred by "treasures" clung to for reasons of sentiment.

If you happen to collect old glass, it should be kept in one room, one you do not use daily and that can be shown to other people who are interested. But it should not be scattered all over table tops so that your house has the appearance of a museum or antique shop.

THE BLINDNESS OF SENTIMENT

It is almost impossible for any of us to judge accurately about things to which we have been accustomed throughout a lifetime. A chair that was grandmother's, a painting father bought, the silver that has always been on the dining-room table—are all so much a part of ourselves that we are sentiment-blind to their defects and incongruity in new surroundings.

For instance, the portrait of a Colonial officer, among others, had always hung in Mrs. Oldname's dining-room. One day an art critic, whose knowledge was better than his manners, blurted out, "Will you please tell me why you have that dreadful thing in this otherwise perfect room?" Mrs. Oldname, somewhat taken aback, answered rather wonderingly, "Is it dreadful?—Really? I have a feeling of affection for him and his dog!"

The critic was merciless. "If you call a cotton-flannel effigy a dog! And as for the figure, it is equally false and lifeless! It is amazing how anyone with your taste can bear looking at it!" In spite of his rudeness, Mrs. Oldname saw then that what he said was quite true; but not until the fact had been pointed out to her. Gradually she grew to dislike the poor officer so much that he finally became relegated to the attic. In the same way most of us have possessions that have "always been there," or perhaps "treasures" which we love for some association, that are probably as bad as can be, to which habit has blinded us, though we would not have to be told of their hideousness were they seen by us in the house of another. Or perhaps they are not bad in themselves. Perhaps even they are quite beautiful, but unsuitable in the place in which they are and to the objects surrounding them.

It is not to be expected that all people can throw away every esthetically unpleasing possession with which nearly every house of fifty years ago was filled; but those whose pocketbook and sentiment will permit would add greatly to the beauty of their houses by throwing out the bad. Far better have stoneware plates that are good in design than costly porcelain that is bad in decoration. Expensiveness, in other words, is never a criterion of taste.

The only way to determine what is good and what is horrible is to study and try to understand the principles underlying what is good—from books, in museums, in art classes at the universities, and in the magazines devoted to the decorative arts.

Be very careful, though. Do not mistake modern eccentricities for "art." There are, quite literally, frightful things in vogue at times—flamboyant and discordant colors, grotesque deformities, designs that cannot possibly be other than bad, because aside from striking novelty there is nothing good about them.

SERVICE AND SERVANTS

The subject of "appointments," meaning decoration and furnishing of a house, is really outside the province of this book, which is that of neither architecture nor decoration. The "appointments" of this chapter's concern are, therefore, those related to service.

In these days of "do-it-yourself" housekeeping, a large household staff is rare indeed. Most women of today have help with the housecleaning chores once or twice a week. Beyond that, they may hire a combination cook-waitress to assist on a special occasion. Even the one-servant household is a thing of the past to most of us.

Nevertheless, this chapter describes in detail the running of a great establishment. Why? Because a book such as this would be incomplete without the inclusion of every detail concerned with the running of a house, great or small. And, more practically, because this information will be useful to the many women of today who have occasion to hire temporary household help.

But before going into the various details of service, it may be well to speak of the unreasoning indignity cast upon the honorable vocation of a servant.

There is an inexplicable tendency, in this country certainly, for working people in general to look upon domestic service as an unworthy if not altogether degrading vocation. The cause may perhaps be found in the fact that this same scorning public, having for the most part little opportunity to know first-class servants, take it for granted that ignorant "servant girls" and "hired men" are representative of their kind. Therefore, they put upper-class servants in the same category—regardless of whether they are uncouth and illiterate, or persons of refinement who have been not only expertly trained in their own special field, but in most instances have also had the great advantages of many cultivating environments.

And yet so insistently has this obloquy of the word "servant" spread that everyone sensitive to the feelings of others avoids using it exactly as one avoids using the word "cripple" when speaking to one who is slightly lame. Yet are not the best of us "servants" in the church? And the highest among us, "servants" of the people and the state?

To be a slattern in a vulgar household is scarcely an elevated employment, but neither is belonging to the lower ranks of any other calling.

HOW CAN ANY HOUSE
REQUIRE A SCORE OF SERVANTS?

The answer is, it can't, unless the house is of a size that in this, our day, has become virtually obsolete. Even "Golden Hall" and "Great

Estates" often have both had their guest wings and ballrooms shut off and their staffs reduced to half their former size. Neither is kept up as it was—although the formality of the pattern remains the same. In other words, the change is one of reduced numbers rather than of lowered standards. Even though there is a reduction in the number of employees, the general requirements of each department remain the same, whether they be the concern of many, or one alone.

For what one might call complete service (meaning service that is adequate at all times) the minimum number is three; i.e., a cook, a butler or waitress, and a housemaid. The reason why this number is necessary is that the waitress (or butler) and the housemaid are on alternate shifts in staying in and going out, the waitress being on duty to answer bell and telephone and serve tea one afternoon, and the housemaid taking her place the next and also serving dinner (or supper) one evening in the week and every other Sunday. One of these also takes the place of the cook on her evening out. When the schedule has been established, their days off should not be shifted around unless it is really necessary. If it is, try to give them sufficient notice so that they can rearrange their plans for their time off.

It stands to reason that one may expect more nearly perfect service from a "specialist" than from one whose functions are multiple. But when there are two—each one of whom is capable of taking over for the other on her time off—the house can be run perfectly so far as essentials go. And service could be handicapped if, when the waitress goes out, the cook does not substitute for her, and still further if, when the cook goes out, there is no one to prepare the meal.

Whether you have one servant or many, consideration for them—for their feelings as well as their working conditions—is essential.

THE MANAGEMENT OF A GREAT HOUSE

The management of a house of greatest size is divided usually into several distinct departments, each under its separate head. The housekeeper has charge of the appearance of the house and of its contents; the manners and looks of the housemaids and parlor maids, as well as their work in cleaning walls, floors, furniture, pictures, ornaments, and books; taking care of linen is her responsibility.

The butler has charge of the pantry and dining-room. He engages all footmen, apportions their work, and is responsible for their appearance, manners, and efficiency. He is also responsible for silver and wines.

The cook is in charge of the kitchen, under-cook, and kitchen maids.

The nurse, the personal maid, and cook are under the direction of the lady of the house. The butler and the valet as well as the chauffeur and gardener are usually engaged by the gentleman of the house. When garage or garden requires under-men, the head chauffeur usually, and the head gardener always, engages his assistants.

THE HOUSEKEEPER

In a very big house the housekeeper usually lives in the house. Smaller establishments often have a visiting housekeeper who comes for as long as she is needed each morning. The resident housekeeper has her own bedroom, bath, and sitting-room always. Her meals are brought to her by an especial kitchen maid, called in big houses the "hall girl," or occasionally the butler details a footman to that duty.

In an occasional house all the servants, the gardener as well as the cook and butler and nurses, come under the housekeeper's authority; in other words, she superintends the entire household exactly as a very conscientious and skilled lady of the house would do herself if she gave her whole time and attention to it. She is always called Mrs. Hart, never by her given name.

THE BUTLER IN A GREAT HOUSE

The butler is not only the most important servant in every big establishment, but it is by no means unheard of for him to be both steward and housekeeper—meaning by this, however, that although he perhaps supervises the cook's orders or even goes to market, the cook is not otherwise under his supervision, and neither, of course, is the children's nurse, or the lady's maid.

Where there is no housekeeper, and the butler takes her place, he engages not only the menservants but the housemaids, parlor maids, and even on occasion the chef.

But normally in the house of lesser size, the butler has charge of the dining-room and pantry, or possibly the whole parlor floor. In all smaller establishments, the butler is always the valet—and in many great ones he is valet to his employer, even though he details a footman to look after the sons of the family or visitors.

In a small house the butler works a great deal with his hands and not so much with his head. In a great establishment, the butler works very much with his head, and with his hands very little.

At Golden Hall, when guests used to come in dozens at a time, his stewardship—even though there was a housekeeper—was not a job which a man of small ability could fill. He had perhaps twenty men under him at big dinners, ten who belonged under him in the house always; he had the keys to the wine cellar and the combination of the silver safe. He also chose the china and glass and linen as well as the silver to be used each day, and oversaw the setting of the table and the serving of all food.

At all meals he stands behind the chair of the lady of the house so that at the slightest turn of her head he need only take a step to be within reach of her voice. The husband, by the way, is "head of the house," but the wife is "head of *his* table."

At tea time the butler oversees the footman who places the tea-table, puts on the tea cloth, and carries in the tea tray, and also the tray of cocktails, if these are served. Then Hastings himself places the individual tables—small tables or stands with nothing on them, so that each guest may have a convenient place on which to put down a cup and saucer, or glass, tea plate, and ashtray.

THE BUTLER IN A SMALLER HOUSE

In a smaller house the butler also takes charge of the wines and silver, and does very much the same as the butler in the larger house, except that he has less overseeing of others and more work to do himself. Where he is alone, he does all the work—naturally. Where he has either one footman or a parlor maid, he always cleans the silver and answers the front door and telephones, and passes the main courses at the table. The assistant passes the secondary dishes and also washes dishes and cleans the dining-room and pantry. Every other afternoon they take turns in answering the door and serving tea.

The butler is also valet not only for the gentleman of the house but for any gentlemen guests as well.

A description of the useful butler will be found later on in this chapter under the heading "Valet-Butler Alone."

WHAT THE BUTLER WEARS

The butler never wears the livery of a footman. In the early morning he wears an ordinary sack suit, black or very dark blue, with a dark, inconspicuous tie. For luncheon or earlier, if he is on duty at the door, he wears black trousers with gray stripes, a double-breasted, high-cut, black waistcoat, and black swallow-tailed coat without silk on the revers, a white stiff-bosomed shirt with standing collar, and a black four-in-hand tie.

In fashionable houses the butler does not put on his dress suit until six o'clock. The butler's evening dress differs from that of his employer in a few details only; he has no braid on his trousers, and the silk on his lapels (if any) is narrower; but the most distinctive difference is that a butler wears a black waistcoat and a white lawn tie, and a gentleman always wears a white waistcoat with a white tie, or a white waistcoat and a black tie with a dinner coat, but *never* the reverse.

It should be unnecessary to add that none but the unwitting would employ a butler or any other house servant who wears a mustache. And to allow him to open the door collarless and in shirt sleeves is in the worst possible taste.

A butler never wears gloves, nor a flower in his buttonhole. He sometimes wears a very thin watch chain in the daytime, but none at night. He never wears a scarf pin or any jewelry that is for ornament alone. His cufflinks should be as plain as possible, and his shirt studs white enamel ones that look like linen.

The butler's clothes are usually provided by his employer, but in occasional communities he is expected to provide his own.

THE HOUSE FOOTMAN

Several menservants who assist in waiting on the table come under the direction of the butler and are known as footmen. In an old-fashioned house of comfort, but not of conspicuous style, a single assistant to the butler is called "the second man" rather than footman. Except in really palatial houses, footmen would be too much like a gold-plated dinner service bought for use in a cottage. One who never comes into the dining-room is known as a utility man. The duties of both a footman and a utility man include cleaning the dining-room, pantry, lower hall, entrance vestibule, sidewalk, attending to the furnace, carrying wood to any open fireplaces in the house, cleaning the windows, cleaning brasses, cleaning all shoes and boots, carrying everything that is too heavy for the parlor maids or moving furniture for them to clean behind it, valeting all gentlemen who either live in or are guests in the house, setting and, in the case of the footman, waiting on table, attending the front door, telephoning and writing down messages, and cleaning and polishing silver.

In a small house the butler polishes silver, but in a very big house one of the footmen is silver specialist and does nothing else. Nothing? If there is to be a party of important size, he puts on his livery and joins the others who line the hall and bring dishes to the table. But he does not assist in setting the table, in washing dishes, or in cleaning anything whatsoever—except silver. Nor does he wear livery except as noted above.

The butler himself usually answers the telephone; if not, it is answered by the first footman. The first footman is deputy butler and takes his place whenever the butler is off duty.

The footmen also take turns in answering the door. In houses of great ceremony like those of the Worldlys and the Gildings, there are always two footmen at the door when anyone is to be admitted: one to open the door, and the other to conduct a guest into the drawing-room. But if formal company is expected, the butler himself is in the front hall with one or two footmen at the door.

THE FOOTMAN'S LIVERY

People who have big houses usually choose a color for their livery and never change it. Maroon and buff, for instance, are the colors of the Gildings; all their automobiles are maroon with buff lines and cream-colored or maroon linings. The chauffeurs and outside footmen wear maroon liveries. The house footmen wear ordinary footmen's liveries, maroon trousers and long-tailed coats with brass buttons and maroon-and-bug striped waistcoats. A house footman wears this same livery no matter what the hour of the day, except of course when he is actually engaged in doing his work, at which time he wears an apron over his waistcoat and shirt sleeves are rolled up. He does not appear in an apron and without his coat in the front part of the house except in the morning when he is cleaning rooms on the first floor.

The regulation livery always has trousers and coat to match, buttons of either brass or silver, stiff starched collar and shirt, white lawn tie, striped waistcoat, and white cotton gloves. The number of buttons on the tails of the coat is determined by the employer's personal idea of smartness. Usually there are three on each side of the front of a coat in addition to two linked together on each side of the front edge to hold the coat nearly closed over the waistcoat. On the tails of the coat there is a row of four buttons at their top, with two under these four. Below the two is a second row of four buttons with two again below.

When giving a big dinner or other party, Mrs. Gilding adds as many caterer's men as necessary. All are dressed in her livery, a supply of which is always kept on hand, and in order.

The extravagant liveries not uncommonly seen until some forty years ago which included black satin knee breeches and patent leather pumps with silver buckles have, of course, gone the way of powdered wigs and all other overelaborations of yesterday.

As already noted, it is of first importance that a butler be flawlessly neat: Clean-shaven, hair well cut, and fingernails cared for as well as clean. A smart butler may, however, be quite elderly. Graying hair can impart great dignity—particularly in a very formal house.

THE CHAUFFEUR

The position of chauffeur differs from that of the other domestic employees in two respects. The first is that he has no regular days off. Second, he usually finds and pays for his own board and lodging. Sometimes a single man may eat with the servants in the kitchen, but this is not usual. Sometimes, too, there may be a room over the garage or perhaps a whole apartment—especially above a garage that has been converted from a stable—in which he and his family may live. Although he seemingly gets higher wages than any of the other servants, it must be remembered that living expenses have to be deducted from his pay, whereas the wages of other servants are clear.

When traveling, the employer always pays for the chauffeur's room and meals for so long as they are away from home.

His uniforms are furnished him by his employer.

His duties are irregular, sometimes extremely so. In a large family, particularly where there are half-grown or grown daughters, a chauffeur's life can be inhumanly strenuous. He can, for example, be expected to take the younger children to school, come back and take the lady shopping, go back to school for the children, drive various members of the family during the afternoon, come back and take his employers out to dinner, go back later to fetch them, and perhaps take them or a débutante daughter to a supper club or ball. Or, if his employers are home that evening, he may perhaps have to stand on the sidewalk to open the car doors of the arriving guests, and again when they depart.

On the other hand, there are places in which the chauffeur is almost a man of leisure; his employer, perhaps, is an old lady who goes to church on Sunday morning from eleven to half-past twelve, who likes to drive from three to five every afternoon, and who goes out to dinner, or to a concert, or to the theatre perhaps not oftener than once a week. Both of these extremes can be encountered in almost every city. The typical schedule is midway between the two. Perhaps he has long driving days intermixed with short ones. But every considerate employer tells his chauffeur as far in advance as he can when he knows he is not going to want the car, since it is only under these circumstances that the chauffeur may himself make any personal engagements.

When the car is in a private garage and the chauffeur has no helper, he must of course wash it and take care of it himself. In a public garage the washing is done for him and the interior of the car is also brushed out by the garage attendant. A lady's town car is usually locked by the chauffeur and he alone takes care of its interior.

A chauffeur never carries a robe on his arm as a footman does when waiting at the door for his employer. Properly, the lap robe is laid in deep full-length folds on the far side of the seat. As soon as the occupants have taken their places, the chauffeur reaches across and, holding the edge of the fold, draws it toward him across their laps. Upon arriving at a destination, if a doorman or a chauffeur is stationed on the sidewalk, he remains seated; otherwise he leaves his seat and holds open the door for the occupants to alight. In assisting a lady or possibly a gentleman who is elderly, the chauffeur presents his forearm held horizontally with his wrist bent inward so that the person alighting puts her or his hand upon his sleeve as though it were a balustrade.

He touches his hat at the close of any order given him, unless the car is in motion, when he merely nods his acknowledgment.

It is unnecessary to add that a chauffeur may never smoke when seated in his employer's car even though it be unoccupied, nor may he smoke when standing on the sidewalk waiting for his employer.

No employer is expected to show leniency to a chauffeur who has driven while intoxicated.

THE COOK OR CHEF

The cook is always in charge in the kitchen. In a small house, or in an apartment, she is alone and has all the cooking, and the cleaning of the kitchen and larder to do, the basement or kitchen bell to answer, and the servants' table to set and their dishes as well as her kitchen utensils to wash. In a larger house, the kitchen maid does all cleaning of the kitchen and pots and pans, answers the basement bell, sets the servants' table and washes the servants' table dishes. In a still larger house, the second cook cooks for the servants always, and for the children sometimes, and assists the cook by preparing certain plainer portions of the meals, the cook preparing all dinner dishes, sauces, and the more elaborate items on the menu. Sometimes there are two or more kitchen maids who merely divide the greater amount of work between them.

In most houses, the cook does all the marketing. She sees the lady of the house every morning and submits the day's menus for her to approve or change.

SUBMITTING THE MENU

In a house of largest size—at the Gildings', for instance—the chef writes in his "book" every evening the menus for the next day, whether there is to be company or not. None, of course, if the family is to be out for all meals. This book is sent up to Mrs. Gilding with her breakfast tray. It is a loose-leaf blank book of rather large size. The day's menu sheet is on top, but the others are left in their proper sequence underneath, so that by looking at her engagement book to see who dined with her on such a date and then looking at the menu for that same date, she knows—if she cares to—exactly what the dinner was.

If she does not like the chef's choice, she draws a pencil through the items to be left out and writes in something else. If she has any orders or criticisms to make, she writes them on an envelope pad, folds the page, and seals it so that no one but the chef himself can read any criticism she may want to make, and puts the note in the book.

If the menu is to be changed, the chef rewrites it; if not, the page is left as it is, and the book is kept in the kitchen.

The butler always goes down into the kitchen shortly after the book has come down and copies the day's menus on a pad of his own. From this he knows what table utensils will be needed.

The reason for this system is that, in houses where there is a great deal of entertaining, it is much simpler for the butler to be able to go and see for himself than to ask the cook, and forget, and ask again; or for the cook to forget, and then—disturbance—because the butler did not send down the proper silver dishes or have the proper plates ready.

THE COOK'S DRESS

The cook always wears a white dress and usually a high apron with pockets, white stockings, and white shoes. She is expected to furnish her clothes herself, but her aprons and uniforms (and her hair coverings if she wears them) are laundered for her. A certain few fastidious cooks wear small white kerchief-shaped caps when they are preparing food. It is to be hoped that this custom may become universal, since nothing in the world is so revolting as even the thought that a sudden breeze is quite likely to blow a hair into the food.

The most practical of these are triangles of fine white linen, or muslin, or nylon. The center is held tight against the nape of the neck, and the two side corners tied over the center corners above the forehead. Nothing could be simpler to make, to tie on, or to launder, or be more becoming—especially with a bit of bang, which is held securely under the knot of the kerchief's corners.

THE KITCHEN MAIDS

The kitchen maids are under the direction of the cook, except the one known colloquially as the "hall girl," who is supervised by the housekeeper. She is evidently a survival of the "between maid" of the English house. Her sobriquet comes from the fact that she has charge of the servants' hall or dining-room, and is in fact the waitress for them. She also takes care of the housekeeper's rooms, and carries all her meals up to her. If there is no housekeeper, the hall girl is under the direction of the cook.

The kitchen maid most often wears a colored cotton dress to match that of the other maids in the house, but she wears a heavier, larger apron and short sleeves. Her dress is given to her. Sometimes she wears white. It is better that she wear color all the time or white all the time, since to dress her in white in the afternoon and color in the morning really means a double supply of clothes.

THE PARLOR MAID

The parlor maid keeps the drawing-room and library in order. The utility man brings up the wood for the fireplaces, but the parlor maid lays the fire. In some houses the parlor maid takes up the breakfast trays; in other houses, the butler does this himself and then hands them to the lady's maid or the housemaid, who takes them into the bedrooms. The windows and the brasses are cleaned by the utility man.

The parlor maid assists the butler in waiting at table and washing dishes, and takes turns with him in answering the door and the telephone.

In huge houses like the Worldlys' and the Gildings', the footmen assist the butler in the dining-room and at the door—and there is always a "pantry maid" who washes dishes and cleans the pantry.

THE HOUSEMAID OR CHAMBERMAID

The housemaid does all the bedrooms, cleans all silver on dressing tables, polishes fixtures in the bathroom—in other words takes care of the bedroom floors. She also takes care of the rooms of the other servants.

In a larger house, the head housemaid has charge of the linen and does the bedrooms of the lady and gentleman of the house and a few of the guest rooms. The second housemaid does the nurseries, extra guest rooms, and the servants' floors. The larger the establishment, the more housemaids, and the more the work is further divided.

In the typical American house in which the bedrooms are taken care of by one person who is possibly waitress too, she is called chambermaid or chambermaid-waitress.

THE CLOTHES OF THE WAITRESS, PARLOR MAID, AND HOUSEMAID

The waitress, parlor maid, and housemaid are dressed alike. Their work dresses are of plain cambric in whatever the house-color may be, meaning the color the lady of the house prefers, with large white aprons with high bibs, plain white rolled-back collars, and just-above-elbow sleeves. Everywhere these short sleeves have replaced the long ones of yesterday which had to be unbuttoned at the cuff and rolled up—only to look very wrinkled when pulled down. These newer above-the-elbow sleeves are edged with a turn-back attached white cuff, and the dresses are finished at the neck with a matching white turned-down collar.

In a formal house, these are exchanged by the waitress and also by anyone who assists her in the dining-room, for long-sleeved, high-necked dresses of taffeta, or silk, either in black or dark colors, with embroidered white Swiss collars, cuffs, and matching aprons. In summer or in hot climates, these dresses are often of light-colored dimity, or dotted muslin, with same accessories as for silk.

Thirty years ago, every service maid in a fashionable private house wore a cap. But little by little when it became the custom to see the most untidy half-grown slavey in every down-at-heel doorway with a mat of whitish Swiss pinned somewhere on her untidy head and as many yards of embroidery ruffling on her apron and shoulders as her person could carry, people of taste began taking caps and rufflings off. In most communities today, caps are rarely seen (and most maids loathe them). The requirement is that a maid's hair must be beautifully smooth and neat. Hair, if bobbed, must be very short. Anything suggesting a faddist hair-cut or curls flying long and loose would be in almost as shockingly bad taste as a butler wearing a mustache!

THE LADY'S MAID

A first-class lady's maid, now most often called "personal maid," is required to be a hairdresser, a good packer, and an expert needlewoman. Her duty is to keep her lady's clothes in perfect order and to help her dress and undress. She draws the bath, lays out underclothes, always brushes her lady's hair and usually dresses it, and gets out the dress to be worn, as well as the stockings, shoes, hat, gloves, handbag, or whatever accessories go with the dress selected.

As soon as her lady is dressed, everything that has been worn is gone over carefully. Everything mussed is pressed, everything suspected of not being immaculate is washed or cleaned with cleaning fluid, and, when in perfect order, is placed where it belongs. Underclothes, as mended, are put in the clothes hamper. Stockings are looked over for threatening runs or holes, and the first stopped, the second darned. Fine stockings, as well as washable gloves, are always washed by the maid.

In many cases, the meticulous maid refuses to let anyone but herself launder items of especial fineness. This is more reasonable than it perhaps appears, since mending these fragile items is her very special task.

Occasionally, maids have to wait up at night, no matter how late, until their ladies return; but the majority are never asked to wait beyond a reasonably early hour. Those who sit up late are permitted to sleep comparatively late in the morning.

In other days the maid for a débutante in the height of the season sat night after night at débutante dances until early morning to see her young lady safely home.

DRESS OF A LADY'S MAID

On duty a lady's maid wears a black skirt, a laundered white waist, and either a small white apron, the band of which buttons in the back, or else a small, round-cornered, black taffeta apron with a narrow self ruffle. This is either tied or buttoned at the back. Her aprons are supplied by her employer; otherwise she always wears her own clothes. These, however, must be very quiet in color and of shirtwaist plainness. She never wears a cap.

A bow of black velvet ribbon is often becoming, as well as correct, if she wears her hair high.

Usually, in the smartest houses, she changes her white waist and black skirt of the morning for an afternoon and evening dress of black taffeta or silk, with a small soft white or cream collar, and a small, black taffeta apron.

Mrs. Gilding, junior, puts her maid, on company occasions when she waits on guests in the dressing-room, in light gray taffeta, gray stockings, black satin pumps, and a very small embroidered mull apron with a narrow, gray velvet waist-ribbon, and collar of mull to match. Customarily, however, and always for ordinary occasions, the lady's maid buys her own clothes. This is a personal matter.

Certain ladies give their maids more than lavish supplies from a scarcely worn wardrobe. Others give them things of small account or nothing. This is especially true of those who have many relatives, or friends, or organizations to whom they feel obliged to give everything.

THE VALET

The valet (pronounced val-et, not vallay) is what Beau Brummell called a gentleman's gentleman. He keeps his employer's clothes in perfect order, brushes, cleans, and presses everything as soon as it has been worn, lays out the clothes to be put on, and puts away everything that is a personal belonging. Some gentlemen, particularly those who are very old, like their valets to help them dress, run the bath, shave them, and hold each article in readiness as it is to be put on. But most merely require that their clothes be laid out for them and in good order to put on.

The valet also unpacks the bags of any gentlemen guests when they come, valets them while there, and packs again when they go. He always packs for his own gentleman, buys tickets, looks after the luggage, and makes himself generally useful as a personal attendant, whether at home or when traveling.

At big dinners he is often required, much against his will, to serve as a footman—in a footman's livery.

The valet wears no livery except on such occasions. At all hours of day or evening, he wears an ordinary business suit, dark and inconspicuous in color, with a black tie.

In this present day a valet is usually a "visiting one" who goes each day to a number of employers to keep the clothes of each in order.

VALET-BUTLER ALONE

In a bachelor's quarters, a valet is often general factotum, not only valeting but performing the service of cook, butler, and even housemaid. When serving meals, he either wears a jacket like that of a steward, or the dress suit of a butler. This last is, as a matter of fact, seldom the choice of a fastidious employer, who usually feels that the jacket of a steward is less pretentious and therefore in best taste for a simple house or apartment.

A serious problem for the valet who cooks is how to prevent spattering grease from getting on his sleeves and cuffs. For this, a thin, washable, seersucker gown, put on with opening in the back like a surgeon's apron, is practical when he broils or fries or takes the roast out of the oven. This is because it is easier to put a thin, long-sleeved gown with elastic bands at wrists over what he wears, than to take off coat, undo cufflinks, roll up sleeves, and then have to reverse this process—just to handle one roast or frying pan.

THE CHILDREN'S NURSE

Everybody knows the children's nurse is either the comfort or the torment of the house. Many an excellent cook has left an otherwise satisfactory job because the nurse was upsetting the kitchen routine.

Everyone also knows innumerable young mothers who put up with inexcusable crankiness from a crotchety middle-aged woman because she was "so wonderful" to the baby. And here let it be emphasized that she usually turns out to have been not so wonderful to the baby at all.

Devotion must always be unselfish; the nurse who is really wonderful to the baby is pretty sure to be a person who is kind generally. In ninety-nine cases out of a hundred the sooner a domineering nurse—old or young—is got rid of, the better. It has been the experience of many a mother whose life had been made perfectly miserable through her belief that if she dismissed the tyrant the baby would suffer, that in the end—there is always an end!—the baby was quite as relieved as the rest of the family when the right sort of kindly and humane person took the tyrant's place. It must never be forgotten that a young child is inescapably imprisoned in the atmosphere made by the disposition of the person in charge of it, and that sunlight is not more essential to a plant than an atmosphere of sympathetic lightheartedness to a child.

It is hardly necessary to add that one cannot be too particular in asking for a nurse's reference and in never failing to talk on the telephone personally with the lady she is leaving. Not only is it important to have a sweet-tempered, competent, and clean person, but her moral character is of utmost concern, since she is to be the constant and inseparable companion of the children, whose whole lives are influenced by her example, especially if busy parents give only a small portion of time to their children.

When the mother of the children cares very much about good taste, their nurse is always dressed in white in the house. With the wonderful wash-and-wear fabrics it is possible for every nurse to dress at all times—even when traveling—in spotless white, since it is entirely possible to rinse out each uniform and hang it over a bathtub to dry very quickly, and it needs no ironing. On the street she wears a very simple suit and hat of either blue or gray. To dress any nurse in the cloak and cap of the English nurse is suitable only if she herself is British.

SERVICE IN FORMAL ENTERTAINING

For a wedding or a formal dance there is an awning from curb to front door. A formal dinner is prepared for by stretching a carpet—a red one invariably—down or up the front steps and across the pavement to the curb's edge. At all important functions there is a chauffeur—or a caterer's man—on the sidewalk to open the doors of cars, and another stationed inside the door of the house to open it on one's approach and to direct arriving guests to the dressing rooms.

DRESSING ROOMS

At every large party it is necessary to have two dressing rooms—one for the ladies upstairs, and one for the gentlemen on the ground floor—each with its lavatory. In houses where dressing rooms have not been installed during its building, two bedrooms have their beds removed, and coat-racks rented from a caterer placed where the beds were.

If the party is very large, coat checks are given to the ladies as well as to the gentlemen, exactly as in public coat rooms. These are, of course, more often given to the gentlemen than to the ladies, whose wraps are all different, whereas those of the gentlemen are for the most part alike. On reclaiming one's hat, coat or wrap, no tip is ever given in a private house.

Whether downstairs or in the bedroom of the hostess, the ladies' dressing room should be supplied with combs, hairpins, bobby pins, powder, individual stacks of cotton, or small individual powder puffs, also safety pins. In the lavatory there must be small new cakes of soap and small fresh towels. The maid who is on duty in the dressing room must also see that any towels when used are immediately replaced. Her principal duty, however, is to look each arriving guest over for anything that may be amiss. If a hook is undone, or the trimming of a dress is caught up, it is her duty to say, "Excuse me, madam (or miss), but there is a hook undone," or, "The drapery of your gown is caught— just a moment, please—I'll fix it!" Which she does as quietly and quickly as possible.

In a great house the valet looks after the gentlemen. But in most houses, the guests put their own coats and hats where they find a place, and can get them again perfectly well by themselves.

THE ANNOUNCEMENT OF GUESTS

The butler or caterer's announcer stands just outside the drawing-room, and the hostess stands just within, and as the guests pass through the door, he announces each one's name. When necessary, he asks, "What name, please?" He then says, "Mr. and Mrs. Jones." If Mrs. Jones is considerably in advance of her husband, he says, "Mrs. Jones!" then waits for Mr. Jones to approach before announcing, "Mr. Jones!"

It is now customary in many houses to have waitresses announce people, but this must not be done unless she pronounces names with ease and a dignified but unself-conscious manner.

THE HOUSE WITH LIMITED SERVICE

The fact that you live in a house with two servants, or very well with only one, need not imply that your house lacks charm or even distinction; but, as explained in the chapter on Dinners, if you have limited service you must devise systematic economy of time and labor or you will have disastrous consequences. If you have no household help at all, you will find many tried and tested suggestions for being a charming hostess as well as cook and waitress. Read Chapter 31 which is devoted to the problems of the servantless hostess.

HOUSE RUN BY ONE MAID

The details of just how much, and just what, one maid should do, constitute a subject of importance to tens of thousands, but one which is almost impossible to treat in a general statement, because her work must be adjusted not only to the needs of the particular family by whom she is employed, but also to her own capability.

Out of every twenty-four hours every normal human being should have at least nine hours for sleeping, dressing and undressing, in addition to plenty of time for eating three meals. During the rest of the day, she must find the time for recreation as well as for work. It is impossible to establish a fixed schedule that can apply to time in and time out, because these are in many cases subject to personal requirements and agreements.

The maid's food and lodging, uniforms and aprons, are part of her pay; and when one considers that the greater part of the average businessman's or businesswoman's earnings goes for food and clothes and lodging, it is not unreasonable that her hours for housework would—at least on occasions—run to longer than ordinary business hours.

ARE MAIDS ALLOWED TO RECEIVE MEN FRIENDS?

Certainly they are! Whoever in remote ages thought it was better to forbid their men friends the house and have Marie, or Bridget, or Selma slip out of doors to meet them in the dark had very distorted notions, to say the least. And any lady who knows so little of human nature as to make the same rule for her maids today is acting in ignorant blindness of her own duties to those who are not only in her employ, but also under her protection. And she probably would not be able to keep a maid!

In every well-appointed house of size there is always a sitting-room which is furnished with comfortable chairs and sofa if possible, a radio, perhaps a television set, good lights to read by, and always magazines (sent out as soon as read by the family). In other words, the employees have an inviting room to use as their own exactly as though they were living at home.

In a smaller house where no sitting-room is possible, the kitchen table has an attractive cover put on it, and a droplight and a few restful chairs are provided.

ADVICE TO THE BEGINNER WHO ENGAGES
A GENERAL MAID

If you have never kept house before and do not know what a maid should be able to do, it might be best to go to a reliable employment office where the clerk will be glad to tell you about hours and wages and an average working plan. On the other hand, if you advertise in the paper, then you could perhaps ask a friend whose own house is run most nearly the way you would like your own to be to give you advice on making a fair and practical schedule.

INTERVIEWING AN APPLICANT

When you interview an applicant, it is a fixed rule of propriety that in your own house she should stand; but if you go to an office, it is proper to invite her to be seated while you talk with her. In either case, the first thing she does—always—is to hand you her written references from her last employer. If she has several, she shows you the last two or three. A good reference should say that she is honest, sober, capable, trustworthy, and of good disposition. If one of these items is missing in each of the references shown you, then you should take this shortcoming into consideration.

However, let us say that the references of a certain applicant are good and that the wages you can pay meet her expectations. Let us say, too, that you find her personality pleasing (perhaps this is not always reliable, but it is a point to consider).

The next move is to give her briefly but *accurately* the schedule of both working and time-off hours. Accuracy is emphasized because careless misrepresentation of facts or intentions is unfair. It is unfair, for example, to assure the maid that she is to have no care of the baby, and then gradually ask that she do just about everything that would be expected of a special nurse.

Another important point is that you should try to visualize what you offer her as well as what you exact of her. Don't say that you are always prompt when you are not; don't say that your meals will be very simple and then expect her to be an expert chef. Don't say that the house is easy to take care of when it couldn't be more inconvenient. Don't say that her work will take a certain number of hours a day without having the vaguest notion of how much work can be reasonably done in this length of time. At the other extreme, it isn't necessary to exaggerate whatever inconveniences there may perhaps be, particularly when there will be much compensating pleasantness that could make her quite happy with you—more so, in fact, than in a house whose shortcomings might be fewer.

HOW MUCH WORK?

As to how much work a general maid can be expected to do, the essential point to consider is that in the working hours of each day one pair of hands can do only so much, and you therefore have to adjust your requirements accordingly. If you live in the country where everything stays very clean and the rooms are not cluttered with ornaments and other time-taking objects, and if your meals are reasonably simple, and you are always prompt, one maid alone should be able to do all the work of the house without difficulty. This, however, would not mean that she could do all the cleaning and cooking and the waiting on extra company in addition to her daily routine of housework if she is often called away from whatever she is doing by an over-busy telephone. When this happens, it is important that *you* make allowances, and not expect that she will be able to finish all her work.

MAKE HER ROOM ATTRACTIVE

But meanwhile let us go back to the day of your new maid's arrival. Try to imagine yourself in her place and take pains to make her room as attractive as possible. Surely nothing could be more dispiriting than for any normal young woman, or older one, to arrive in a strange place, which is to be her "home," and to be taken into a drab and comfortless room which all too plainly shows that you have not given so much as a thought to what these surroundings must mean to her happiness.

After all, a comfortable bed, attractively painted furniture, a little becoming chintz are not very difficult to supply, especially in this day when smooth-flowing paints or enamels in beautiful colors can be put on by the merest amateur, in fact by anyone who has the slightest manual dexterity. In other words, dingy brown and buff are really inexcusable. The same attention to attractiveness and convenience should be evident in the kitchen—in which she is not only to work and to take her meals, but in which she is also to spend many of her hours of leisure.

Let her know that she can count on always having her definite afternoon and evening off. Plainly, it is not fair at the last minute to expect her to change her afternoon and evening out because it happens to be inconvenient to you. This lack of consideration is one of the chief causes of servant trouble.

UNIFORMS FURNISHED BY EMPLOYER

A maid's uniform as well as her aprons and collars and cuffs are furnished by her employer. For morning in a perfectly appointed house she wears a cotton dress, either white or colored, and a big apron with a bib. The long sleeves which were once exacted have now been supplanted by those well above elbow length, which are not only more practical, but much prettier than rumpled long ones, pulled down, to wait on table as well as go to the door! In a simple house it is also in good taste—because suitable—that her uniform for afternoon and evening have three-quarter sleeves with cuffs just below the elbow.

Where the family is very small and the maid's schedule permits her finishing all heavy work before serving the midday meal, she changes for this into her afternoon dress. This dress is usually of one of the new, textured synthetics, or in summer dotted Swiss or dimity in a pastel color and with fine organdy or embroidered Swiss apron, with cuffs and collar to match. In the average house where it is not practical that she dress at such an early hour, it is, of course, necessary that she postpone changing into her afternoon dress until after she serves the noon meal.

PROPER COURTESY SHOWN TO DOMESTIC EMPLOYEES

In a dignified house, a servant is never spoken to as Jim, Maisie, or Katie, but always as James, or Margaret, or Katherine, and a butler should be called by his last name. The Worldlys' butler, for instance, is called Hastings, not John. In England, a lady's maid is also called by her last name, and the cook, if married, is addressed as Mrs., and the nurse is called "Nurse" by the family and "Mrs." by the other servants, whether she is married or not. A chef is usually called "Chef" or else by his last name.

Every courteous person says "please" in asking that something be brought her or him. "Mail these letters, please!" or "Some bread, please." One can, of course, "put a smile" into one's tone and say, "A little more bread!" But usually one who is well mannered instinctively adds "please." No lady or gentleman barks, "Mail this letter!" "Give me the bread!"

In refusing a dish at the table, one says, "No, thank you" or "No, thanks." To be courteously polite is a thing every thoroughbred person knows how to be—and a thing that everyone who would acquire the attributes of a thoroughbred must learn to be.

Any who may think they appear superior by being rude to others who happen to have been less fortunately placed, might as well know that they on the contrary are proclaiming to all who hear their rudeness that they themselves have never had any of the early advantages.

ETIQUETTE OF SERVICE

The well-trained, high-class servant is faultlessly neat in appearance, reticent in manner, speaks in a low voice, and moves silently. In answering a bell, she asks, "Did you ring, Madam?" or if especially well-mannered she asks, "Did Madam ring?"

A courteous maid answers, "Yes, Madam," or "Very good, Sir,"—possibly "Yes, Sir,"—never "Yes," "No," "All right," or "Sure." Grown sons and daughters are called "Miss Katherine or "Mr. Oliver"; half-grown children are generally called by their familiar names with the prefix of Miss or Mr. (Miss Kitty, Mr. Ollie), but never by the nurse, who calls them by their first names until they are grown and if she has been with them since their babyhood—always. To demand that the servants call really little children Miss and Master is unpleasing evidence of social insecurity. Queen Elizabeth II said that Prince Charles and Princess Ann should be called "Charles" and "Ann" by the staff of the royal household.

All cards must be, and small packages should be, presented on a small tray.

SUCCESS IN THE MANAGEMENT OF A HOUSE

It is certainly a greater pleasure and incentive to work for those who are appreciative than for those who continually find fault. Everyone who has ever done volunteer work will remember how easy it was to work for, or with, some people, and how impossible to get anything done for others. And just as the heads of workrooms, or wards, or canteens were either stimulating or dispiriting, so must they and their types also be to those who serve in their households.

It might be well for those who have trouble to remember a basic rule which is often overlooked: Justice must be the foundation upon which every tranquil household is constructed. Work must be as evenly

This, perhaps, explains why some people are always having a servant problem, finding servants difficult to get, more difficult to keep, and most difficult to get efficient work from. It is a question whether the servant problem is not more often an employer problem. I'm sure it is! Because, if you notice, those who have woes and complaints are invariably the same ones, just as others who never have any trouble are also the same. It does not depend on the size of the house; the Lovejoys never have any trouble, and yet their one maid-of-all-work has a far from easy place; and a vacancy at Brookmeadows is always sought after, even though the Oldnames spend ten months of the year in the country. Neither is there any friction at the Golden Hall or Great Estates, even though the latter house is run by the butler—often a cause of trouble. Such houses, where the servant problem does not exist, are alike and range from a house with one maid to one with a staff of twenty.

THOSE WHO HAVE PERSISTENT TROUBLE

divided as possible; one servant should not be allowed liberties not accorded to all.

It is not just to be too lenient, any more than it is just to be unreasonably demanding. To allow impertinence or sloppy work is inexcusable, but it is equally inexcusable to show causeless irritability or to be overbearing or rude. And there is no greater example of injustice than to reprimand those about you because you happen to be in a bad humor, and at another time to overlook offenses that are greater because you are in an amiable mood.

There is also no excuse ever for correcting either an employee or a child in front of anyone else.

If we attempt to analyze the spirit pervading happy houses, I think it will be found in the understanding and fairness that is shown by both sides. Proper pride on the part of every high-minded employee exacts that she give fair value for wages received. On the other side, the obligation of the lady of the house and the other members of the family is to show human understanding and be fair in what they exact. If they are just in their point of view, and if, being themselves kind and trustworthy, they naturally believe that those serving them have the same traits, and are very, very unlikely ever to have any house-keeping difficulties.

THE COMPANION

A companion's position is always one of social equality with her employer. The object of her care may be an invalid, a very elderly person, a widow, or a young girl. In the last case the companion is a chaperon. In the majority of cases the companion is a relative or friend who becomes a permanent member of her employing relative's or friend's household on a salaried basis.

Her duties cannot very well be set down, because they vary with individual requirements. One lady likes continually to travel, and merely wants an agreeable companion to go with her or to accompany her for a drive in the car in pleasant weather. Another will want the papers, her favorite magazines, or books read to her.

Another is a semi-invalid who never leaves her room, and the duties of her companion are almost those of a trained nurse—quite possibly she may have been one and was persuaded to make the house of her ex-patient her permanent home. The average requirement is in being personally agreeable, tactful, intelligent, and—companionable!

A companion dresses as any other lady does, according to the occasion, her personal taste, her age, and her means. If she is expected to go out in public places or to be constantly dressed for company at home she should be given a definite dress allowance. This means that if an employer wants her companion to travel with her or go out with her socially, she should make it possible for her to be suitably and becomingly dressed for each of these occasions, by paying extra for this very considerable personal expense.

CONFIDENTIAL SECRETARY IN RESIDENCE

The most important secretarial position and one that comes into immediate contact with an employer's home and social, as well as public, life is that of resident confidential secretary. By this is more particularly meant a man—rather than a woman—whose employer is either a diplomat or a governor or of other importance in public life and is therefore in need of an assistant who is always on hand. This type of secretary is in every way considered a member of the family. He is always present at business meetings and often present at social ones as well. He always has a secretary of his own and perhaps several stenographers. In other words, he is a deputy who serves as extra eyes and hands and supplementary brains for his chief. A position of this sort is rare, hard to find, and still harder to fill.

THE TUTOR

The social position of a tutor is similar to that of the companion. For reasons which are in many ways unfair, the tutor's social acceptance is much more enthusiastic than that of the governess. The reason is, of course, that he is in all probability an attractive and intelligent young man still in or just out of college and therefore welcomed as an extra man. The governess on the other hand is a usually not-so-young additional woman.

A tutor is expected to be present when wanted and absent when not, to be at all times agreeable and at the same time impersonal, and to remember that so far as his character and behavior are concerned, his job carries on through the hours when he is off duty as well as when he is on.

THE GOVERNESS

The position of governess varies greatly according to her own accomplishments, the ages of the children, and the mode of each family's life. If the house is a large one, she has a sitting room of her own. Otherwise her room should be furnished as an attractive and transformable sitting room, with a day-bed, a desk instead of a bureau, easy chairs, and good reading light. This is not an excessive amount of luxury but a very plain necessity, because otherwise she has nowhere to sit except in the discomfort of a bedroom or else with the family—a situation that is at times as trying for them as for her.

A governess usually comes to the family breakfast, lunch table, and to dinner if her pupils do. But when her charges are half-grown, it is often arranged that they shall dine with their parents while the governess is served in her own sitting room or in the dining room at an hour earlier than that of the family. Arrangement is always made whereby the children and the governess are served elsewhere when formal company is expected. When friends of the family come for lunch or dinner and the governess is to be present, she shows herself ready to be agreeable to anyone inclined to talk to her, but she should rarely lead the conversation. After the meal she withdraws to her own quarters, goes out for a walk, or occupies herself as she wishes until late afternoon, unless she is especially asked to stay.

According to best taste, a governess should not wear unsuitably conspicuous clothes, which does not mean that she cannot wear the latest fashion of the day, but that fashion should be whispered rather than shouted out loud.

THE DUTIES OF A PRIVATE SECRETARY

The duties of a private secretary are naturally to attend to all correspondence, file papers and documents, telephone personal messages, arrange appointments, and also serve as extra hands, and eyes, and intelligence for her employer. She also, of course, writes all impersonal notes, takes longer letters in shorthand, and writes others herself after being told their purport. She also audits all bills and draws the checks for them; the checks are filled in and then presented to her employer to be signed, after which they are put in their envelopes, sealed, and sent. When the receipted bills are returned, the secretary files them according to her own method, where they can at any time be found by her if needed for reference. In many cases it is she, though it may equally well be the butler or waitress or personal maid, who telephones invitations and other messages. (In a house that has menservants it is always the butler who answers the telephone and when he is off duty, a footman in his place; otherwise it is done necessarily by one of the maids.) If there are children in the house of boarding-school age, she may have to attend to details of their tuition, arrivals and departures, etc.

The secretary is sometimes a social secretary who may also be a social manager who devises entertainments and arranges all such details as the decorations of the house for a dance or a program of entertainment following a very large dinner. The social secretary very rarely lives in the house of her employer; more often than not she goes also to one or two other houses, since there is seldom work enough in one to require her whole time.

The position of the social secretary is an entirely clerical one. Her duties are to write all invitations, acceptances, and regrets; keep a record of every invitation received and every one sent out; and enter in an engagement book every engagement made for her employer. Sometimes she is also a bookkeeper who draws checks and audits accounts.

Her dress is that of any business woman. Extremes of fashion that border on the eccentric are out of keeping, as they would be out of keeping in an office.

THE REGISTERED NURSE

The social position of a registered hospital nurse is, of course, that of a deputy physician and, if on a long case, the closest of the family's friends. Always she eats her meals with the family or else has them served to her on a tray in a sitting-room. She never eats in the kitchen unless that is where the family also eats.

When on duty in her patient's room or anywhere in a private house, she wears her uniform. But when going into the street or going downstairs in a hotel, or traveling with her patient, she dresses as does any other lady.

No professional calling except that of clergyman or physician is held in such admiration and respect as that of the trained nurse. So much so in fact, that her uniform is full protection against criticism, no matter how unconventional the situation in which she may on occasion find herself placed.

THE BABY-SITTER

With smaller family houses and small-apartment living, the shortage of a "live-in" staff has, especially for young people, created the demand—and baby-sitters have achieved both an amateur and professional standing.

The age of a sitter may range from the early teens, if he or she is a responsible youngster and fond of children, up to elderly ladies.

In the intermediate group, many high school and college boys and girls, and young business women, are glad to supplement their allowances or salaries by baby-sitting a few times a week.

In many large cities girls who live in residential clubs post their names to indicate their availability for baby-sitting, and mothers in the neighborhood may avail themselves of this service. In some communities there are agencies which provide approved sitters at standard rates.

The rate of payment varies in different localities, and no set schedule can be set up. But the customary rate of the community should be observed, and the sitter should be paid promptly. The sitter should be told that after the children are asleep he or she may use the television set or play the radio, read, or do homework. In other words, it should be clearly understood what he is expected to do and what he may not do. It is thoughtful to leave a snack in the refrigerator—the hours can become long and tiresome. Be specific about where you are going: address and telephone number, as well as the name, address, and telephone number of the children's doctor. Always tell the sitter when you expect to be back—and try to be on time.

Adequate transportation must be provided for the sitter's safe return home, and this applies for sitters of any age.

FLAT SILVER AND
TABLE-SETTINGS

·∘] 27 [∘·

THE FOLLOWING IS A REALLY COMPLETE LIST OF FLAT
silver for any house, with the most important pieces indicated by an
asterisk. In other words, a bride can quite well start out with only these
and put off until later years the purchase of any additional pieces she
finds she needs from the longer list.

1 * *Serving spoon.* An extra large, especially wide spoon with which
 one helps oneself to whatever is passed at table.

2 *Tablespoon.* Its present use is confined almost entirely to serving
 as an alternate to the serving spoon. In fact, its use as an eating
 implement is almost obsolete except in great houses such as the
 Gildings' and the Worldlys' where this spoon is used to eat consommé served in plates with rims.

3 * *Dessertspoon.* This spoon in size is midway between the teaspoon
 and the tablespoon; also used for breakfast cereals.

4 * *Teaspoon.* The great American utility spoon—used in many instances when the dessertspoon would be correct.

5 * *Coffee spoon.* For demitasse or after-dinner coffee service.

6 *Iced-tea spoon.* Necessary only when serving iced tea or iced coffee
 in tall glasses.

7 *Orange spoon.* Really practical for eating orange or grapefruit
 served in halves but segments not cut apart; when the fruit is cut,
 teaspoon can be used just as well.

8 * *Salt spoon.* Necessary only if you use saltcellars instead of shakers.

9 *Serving fork.* Extra large fork correctly used with serving spoon.

10 * *Large dinner fork.* For meat course only, but also used as serving
 fork.

11 * *Small fork* (also called *breakfast, salad,* or *dessert fork*). The general utility fork used for every purpose in most households.

12 *Fish fork.* An unnecessary fork, but not incorrect if you like it.

13 *Oyster fork.* If you serve oysters or clams on half-shell.

THE PERSONALITY OF A HOUSE IS INDEFINABLE

No home of a hostess of cultivation and charm, whether palace or cottage, will fail to reflect the quality of inviting comfort.

1   2   3   4   5   6   7   8   9   10   11

1 After-dinner coffee spoon	5 Dinner fork	9 Butter knife
2 Teaspoon	6 Luncheon fork	10 Fruit fork
3 Dessert spoon	7 Dinner knife	11 Fruit knife
4 Tablespoon	8 Luncheon knife	

FLAT SILVER—ABOUT THREE EIGHTHS OF ACTUAL SIZE

14 * *Large knife—dinner knife.* For meat only.
15 * *Small knife—breakfast and lunch knife.* Also used for fish or salad or dessert.
16 *Fish knife.* Same as "12."
17 *Butter knife.* "Spreader" is the trade term for an often ugly little knife of the present day; it is, however, hard to do without if you have no small knife to take its place.
18 *Fruit knife* and *fork.* They usually come in pairs with silver, gilt, or stainless metal blade and tines.
19 *Sugar tongs.*
20 *Ladle.* For gravies or sauces.

IMPORTANT CONSIDERATIONS IN CHOOSING SILVER

To the bride who wants to choose silver that will meet the permanent standards of good taste, the following rules are suggested. Because silver is something intended to last a lifetime, the rule of safety is to study the old designs which, having had the approval of time, are certain to endure for many years to come; whereas the new designs, no matter how attractive, may prove in a short while to have been but a transient fashion. For one who feels certain of her taste or for one who can again buy new, this precaution is unimportant. Ornate silver is certainly harder to keep clean than a simple pattern.

The silver illustrated in this chapter has stood the test of time. It is beautifully simple. Its surface is brilliant; the corners of the forks are smoothly round; the prongs are slim. On less carefully designed silver the fork corners are sharp, the prongs thick, and something is added to or cut away from what is supposed to be a plain design. For those who do not like plain silver, there are many patterns with ornamentation. Some of these, such as the well-known "King" pattern, which have been available for generations, are very fine. The "King" pattern is available in plate as well as sterling—so that to the foundation pieces in sterling, extra matching pieces especially needed for parties can be had in plated ware (of course at lower cost).

Silver—as explained later in the chapter on dinners—must be kept brilliantly polished. Dingy or unpolished silver belongs in the same category as dirty fingernails.

MIXED PATTERNS TOGETHER

When bought new, silver of one pattern is naturally preferred. This does not mean that a single giver provides the whole service. It is, in fact, customary that the bride choose the pattern she prefers and that her family and perhaps even friends join together to fill out the necessary pieces to complete her service. On the other hand, many, many tables in beautifully appointed houses are set with mixed silver. Meaning by this that dessertspoons and forks, fruit knives and forks, or other implements for special courses need not—in fact preferably do not—match the foundation place-setting silver. This is because too many items of the same pattern tend to become monotonous and lack the sparkle of interest.

HOW MUCH SILVER

It is of course impossible to guess what the requirement for each hostess will be. But very certainly, yesterday's lists as given in the earliest editions of this book were much longer than the modern bride is likely to have need for.

Even so, you who are choosing your silver should go over the list carefully with certain definite questions in mind. First of all, remember that although any big parties you may give will require many small forks and teaspoons, these can be much less expensive than your regular silver which they need not even pretend to match.

Since eight at table is about as big a dinner as most of us are giving today, this means that you will probably need:

3 or possibly 4 serving spoons (tablespoons may be used)
2 or 3 serving forks (large dinner forks may be used)
8 tablespoons (only if soup is to be served in soup plates with rims,
    11 or 12 if three or four are to be used as serving spoons)
8 dessertspoons
8 teaspoons
4 salt spoons (if you do not use saltshakers)
8 large forks (10 if two are to be used as serving forks)
8 small forks
8 large knives
8 small knives
8 individual butter knives
1 gravy ladle
1 pie server
8 after-dinner coffee spoons
1 sugar tongs

EACH PIECE OF FLAT SILVER AND ITS USE

Correctly both a spoon and a fork are placed in every serving dish or platter—unless the fork is really not necessary. Special serving spoons and forks are not necessary since these are replaced by tablespoons, and when needed, by dinner forks.

The tablespoon is for consommé served in a soup plate. Dip the soup away from you, fill two-thirds full, and pour soup between your lips silently from the side of the spoon, not the tip. A soup that is semi-solid, such as a *minestrone* or *petite marmite*, or one that is so thick with rice or vegetables that it is more solid than liquid, may be "eaten" from the end for it is impossible to do otherwise. But in this case the bowl must never be more than half filled because more than a third of the tablespoon must never be thrust into no-matter-how-large a mouth!

Young children whose table manners are past the elementary stage feel deeply the humiliation of having small-sized silver. But to give them full-sized forks and spoons entails the undivided attention of some-one to prevent their becoming too adept at stowing heaped spoon and fork loads into the unsuspected capacities of the young human maw.

The dessertspoon is midway in size between the tablespoon and tea-spoon, and is used for almost everything that is eaten with a spoon, such as dessert, cut-up fruit, berries, cereal, soup in bowls or in cups that are very wide. Teaspoons—or the round-bowled bouillon spoons—are used for small cups of bouillon. The dessertspoon should not be used for soup in plates. If you have no tablespoons, you must not serve consommé or other thin soups in plates. To see people try to sip clear soup dip by dip with a little spoon is irritating.

The teaspoon is used for all beverages served in cups and for grape-fruit, boiled egg, fruit cocktail, etc. One old-fashioned but unbreakable rule to remember: *Never leave a teaspoon standing in a cup.* The instant it is out of your hand, it belongs in the saucer.

The after-dinner coffee spoon is half the size of a teaspoon and is for the small cup of black coffee and for nothing else. You stir sugar with it and possibly taste the coffee. But you drink the coffee from the cup, leaving the spoon in the saucer.

The iced-tea spoon is the ordinary ice-cream soda spoon of the soda counter and is available now in almost all patterns of fine table silver and used for beverages served in tall glasses. If there is a plate under the glass, you lay the spoon on it after stirring or tasting. But if there is no plate, you leave it in the glass. If a teaspoon is used for this pur-pose, you also leave it in the glass, as you can't lay it on a plate used for food and certainly not on the table. At a soda fountain you may lay it on the marble counter or table after tasting; you should not stir your drink around, however, and then let soda or orangeade run in a wet smear on either table or counter.

The orange spoon is a somewhat narrow, pointed-tip teaspoon. Some-times the bowl has grooves. It is not essential, because a teaspoon can take its place.

The serving fork is an extra-large dinner fork and is not necessary.

The dinner or large fork is essential for the meat course at dinner, also for meat served at lunch, and it can also be used in place of a serv-ing fork.

The small fork is the most important of the forks. Its use is for every possible course at breakfast, lunch, and dinner except the meat course.

The special fish fork with a flattened first tine and the silver knife with pointed end and saw-tooth edge, used for no other purpose than eating fish, are a needless extravagance in most families, and are therefore seldom included in a bride's silver chest.

The oyster fork is a very small, slim fork, about six inches long, the prong end of which is about half an inch wide. It is used for oysters or clams and other shelled seafood, and unless you serve them, these forks are unnecessary.

The fruit fork is brought on with the fruit knife, either with or after the fingerbowl.

The large or dinner knife has a steel—now almost always stainless— blade and is used only for the meat course at dinner (whether this be served in the evening or in the daytime).

The small knife has a silver or silver-plated blade or a blade of stainless steel and is used for breakfast, lunch, supper, and every course at dinner except the meat course.

A small, sharp, stainless steel or silver-bladed knife with a pointed end is fine for fruit. It is often different in pattern from the rest of the silver. Its blade may be of silver or gilt, with a handle of porcelain, silver, gilt, crystal, mother-of-pearl, ivory, agate, or other semi-precious material. Usually there is a fork that matches it.

The butter knife is always used to spread butter or jam or jelly on bread of every description; it is used for nothing else. If there is no special butter knife, the small knife will answer. Butter that is mixed with food and condiments such as accompany different meats is spread on the meat with a fork.

SERVING IMPLEMENTS

In most houses an ordinary tablespoon and dinner fork are used for almost every dish, but in the very complete silver chest the special serving spoon and fork are exactly like the tablespoon and dinner fork, but of a slightly larger size. In other days Apostle spoons or other ornate spoons and forks were often used, but today it is preferable that the serving pieces match the silver.

A wooden salad fork and spoon and a wooden bowl are admissible, especially at the family table where father or mother is an expert on salad dressing and mixes it personally. But in very formal houses salad is served with the serving spoon and fork that match the silver.

The serving spoon alone is used in a dish of small vegetables, such as peas or mashed potatoes, or a pudding or cereal—anything easily taken with a spoon in the right hand. Otherwise a fork accompanies the spoon, and you are expected to insert the spoon under a piece of meat or fish, or branching vegetable, something on toast, or whatever it may be, holding the food in place with the fork in the left hand, held prongs down.

Sauces are usually ladled. If there is no ladle or spoon, you pour the sauce from the sauceboat.

With tongs you help yourself to asparagus by pushing the lower tong under a few stalks, grasping the tongs and closing them.

A cake or pie lifter is a flat piece of silver with a handle. You lift the griddle cakes or a piece of pie on it and steady them or it with the fork. Should there be no fork, you lift and balance carefully!

No matter what sort of serving device you encounter, you cut, when necessary, with the edge of a spoon or other broad implement, and then, pushing it under the helping, hold the food in place with the fork-shaped piece.

MISCELLANEOUS IMPLEMENTS

Sugar tongs are needed for lump sugar and a spoon for granulated sugar, unless it is powdered and in a shaker. Ladles are used for gravy —even if there is a sauceboat. If there is a ladle, you dip it full, stop the drip against the lip of the bowl or sauceboat, empty it on the food for which it is intended, and, paying attention to its drip, put it carefully back without letting any drops fall.

The proper way to take salt that is not in a shaker is with a salt spoon, not on the blade of one's knife. If there isn't any salt spoon, then at least be sure the knife blade or the spoon you use is clean.

Grape scissors are of silver, usually ornamented with a grape design. You cut about half a dozen hot-house grapes off a large bunch, which needless to say no one is supposed to take whole. If there are no scissors, you break off a small cluster or two with your fingers. But you do not pull off individual grapes from the bunch!

Nutcrackers and nut picks properly belong on the Thanksgiving and Christmas or any home dinner table where nuts in their shells are to be served. But unshelled nuts have no place at a formal lunch or dinner party, and salted ones have no place after the table has been crumbed.

At the seacoast, or wherever broiled lobsters are a specialty, and have not been sufficiently cracked, nutcrackers and nut picks are indispensable for breaking the claws and extracting the meat.

Silver handles with prongs or a blade to be thrust into the ends of ears of corn on the cob are often included in the silver chest.

Silver ashtrays, containers for cigarettes and lighters should be within easy reach of guests if smoking is permitted at the table.

WHICH FORK?

One of the fears expressed time and again in letters from readers is that of making a mistake in selecting the right table implements. As a matter of fact the choice of an implement is usually unimportant—a trifling detail which people of best position care nothing about.

However, in order that you may make no mistake, you need merely remember that you are to take the outside—that is, the farthest from the plate—spoon or fork first. If the pieces have not been laid in this order, the fault is that of the person who set the table and not yours. If you are in doubt, wait until your host or hostess has picked up his or her implement and follow his or her lead.

The statement above, that people of position do not care about which piece of silver to use, has one qualification. They would not use the dinner fork for oysters or a teaspoon for soup, because they instinctively choose an implement suitable for whatever they are about to eat. But if they happen to choose a medium-sized pronged article for fish when it was intended by the manufacturer to be especially helpful for salad or shredded-wheat biscuit, it makes no difference whatever.

DETAILS OF TABLE-SETTING

BREAKFAST

Small-sized fork at left of plate.

Small-sized knife at right of plate.

Cereal spoon at right of knife.

Teaspoon or, if you prefer, a dessertspoon for fruit, but not for coffee, at right of cereal spoon.

Butter knife at left of fork, or across bread and butter plate, which is to the left and above knife. Butter knife is the preferred word, although butter spreader is what the silver stores like to call it to distinguish it from a serving piece of the same name.

Napkins at left of plates if cut-up fruit compote is at places, otherwise on heated place plates if table is set with hot food.

Coffee cups with spoons lying at right of saucers, at the right of each plate if coffee is served from pantry. If served by the lady of the house, cups and saucers are included with tea or coffee service at her place.

Food is equally often passed in courses or all put in covered dishes on the table.

LUNCHEON OR SUPPER

Salad fork at left, next to plate.

Meat fork at left of salad fork.

Then outside at left, fork for egg dish or entrée or fish, if there is to be a first course requiring a fork.

Silver salad knife at right next to plate. In spite of the somewhat prevalent idea that salad should be eaten with a fork alone, the salad knife always has had its place on the well-appointed table whenever leafy salad or cheese is to be served.

Next to the salad knife comes a meat knife, and at the right of this knife is a bouillon or fruit spoon. At supper the tea or coffee service is put in front of the hostess.

DINNER

Salad fork at left of plate, then meat fork, and left of that a fork for fish or the entrée.

At right, next to the plate, if three knives are necessary, the salad knife first, then a dinner knife, then a fish knife. Then the soup spoon, then the oyster fork, or fruit spoon.

In every case, the implements necessary for each course are arranged in order of their use. The one to be used first goes on the outside, where it is reached first; that to be used last is put nearest the plate, where it is encountered in turn when the outer articles have been taken away. Dessertspoon and fork are brought in on the dessert plate after the table is cleared. The dessert services are explained on page 350. On the properly set table there are not more than three forks (two preferably, but, if needed, three) and two knives. This rule applies only to a strictly formal house. In a simple house, especially one without servants, the hostess necessarily adapts this as well as other rules to her own personal situation.

FORMAL DINNERS

·≈][28][≈·

ALTHOUGH TODAY THE FORMAL DINNER—OR DINNER OF
ceremony—has almost ceased to exist, and the trend is toward the informal or friendly dinner, it is necessary that this chapter be left nearly
as it was originally written because its every detail is a definite part of
the complete set of patterns *from which all details* of even the simplest
dinner-giving are chosen.

To give a perfect dinner of ceremony is the supreme accomplishment of a hostess. It means not alone perfection of furnishing, of service,
of culinary skill, but also of personal charm, of tact.

A DINNER IN A GREAT HOUSE

When Mrs. Worldly gives a dinner, it means no effort on her part
beyond deciding upon the date and the principal guests who are to form
the nucleus. Every further detail is left to her subordinates—even the
completion of her list of guests. For instance, she decides that she will
have an "older" dinner, and finding that the tenth of the month is available for herself, she tells her secretary to send out invitations for that
date on the dinner blank described elsewhere. She then looks through
her dinner list and asks her secretary to invite the Oldworlds, the Emi-
nents, the Learneds, the Wellborns, the Highbrows, and the Onceweres.
She also picks out three or four additional names to be substituted for
those who regret. Then turning to the "younger married" list, she
searches for a few amusing or good-looking ones to give life and charm
to her dinner, which might otherwise be heavy. But her favorites do not
seem appropriate. It will not do to ask the Bob Gildings, not because of
the difference in age but because Lucy Gilding smokes like a furnace
straight through dinner and is miserable unless she can play bridge for
high stakes and, just as soon as she can bolt through dinner, sit at a
card table; while Mrs. Highbrow and Mrs. Oncewere quite possibly disapprove of women's smoking at all and class all playing for money with
gambling. So she adds the Kindharts and the Normans, who "go" with

everyone, and approves her secretary's suggestions as to additional names if those first invited should regret.

The list being settled, Mrs. Worldly's own work is done. She sends word to her cook that there will be twenty-four on the tenth; the menu, which she will probably merely glance at and send back, will be submitted to her later. She never sees or thinks about her table, which the butler will arrange properly.

On the morning of the dinner her secretary brings her the place-cards—the name of each person expected is written on a separate card —and she puts them in the order in which they are to be laid on the table, very much as though she were playing solitaire. Starting with her own place at one end and her husband's at the other, she places the lady of honor at his right, the second in importance at his left. Then at either side of herself she places the two most important gentlemen. The others she fits in between, trying to seat side by side those congenial to each other.

When the cards are arranged, the secretary puts the name of the lady who sits at each gentleman's right in the envelope addressed to him. She then picks up the place-cards, still stacked in their proper sequence, and gives them to the butler, who will lay them in the order arranged on the table after it is set.

Five minutes before the dinner hour, Mrs. Worldly is already standing in her drawing-room. She has no personal responsibility other than that of being hostess. The whole machinery of equipment and service runs seemingly by itself. It does not matter whether she knows what the menu is. Her cook is more than capable of attending to it. That the table shall be perfect is merely the everyday duty of the butler. She knows without looking that her chauffeur is on the sidewalk; that footmen are in the hall; that her own maid is in the ladies' dressing room; and the valet in that of the gentlemen; and that her butler is just outside the door near which she is standing.

So with nothing on her mind—except possibly a jeweled diadem— she receives her guests with the tranquillity attained only by those whose household, whether great or small, can be counted on to run like a smoothly coordinated machine.

A NOVICE ATTEMPTS A FORMAL DINNER

This is the contrasting picture to the dinner at the Worldlys', the picture to show you—particularly a bride—how awful a meant-to-be-"formal" dinner can be when undertaken without experience.

Let us suppose that you have a quite charming house, and that your wedding presents included everything necessary to set a well-appointed table. You have not very experienced servants, but they would all be good ones with a little more training.

You have been at home for so few meals you don't quite know how really inexperienced they are. Your cook makes good coffee, eggs, and toast for breakfast, and the few other meals she has cooked seemed to be all right, and she is *such* a nice person!

So when your house is in order and the last pictures and curtains are hung, the impulse suddenly comes to you to give a dinner! Your husband thinks it is a splendid idea. It merely remains to decide whom you will ask. You hesitate between a few of your own intimates or older people, and decide it would be such fun to ask a few of the hostesses who have been most kind to you. You decide to ask Mrs. Toplofty, Mr. Clubwin Doe, the Worldlys, the Gildings, the Kindharts, and the Wellborns. With yourselves that makes twelve, which is really too many, but you decide that it will be safe to ask that number because a few are sure to regret. So you write notes—since it is to be a formal dinner—and—they all accept! You are a little worried about the size of the dining-room, but you are elated by the wonderful evidence of your popularity, and you prepare lightheartedly for your dinner. You must get Sigrid a dress that properly fits her; and Marie, the chambermaid, who was engaged with the understanding that she is to serve in the dining-room when there is company, has not yet been at table, but she is a very willing young person who will surely look well.

Nora, when you tell her who are coming, eagerly suggests the sort of menu that would appear on the table of the Worldlys or the Gildings. You are thrilled at the thought of your own kitchen producing the same. That it may be the same in name only does not occur to you. You order pink roses, pink cakes and pink candles for the table. You pick out your best tablecloth, but you find rather to your amazement that when Sigrid asks you about setting the table, you have never noticed in detail how the places are laid. Knives and spoons go on the right of the plate, of course, and forks on the left, but which goes next to the plate, or whether the wineglasses should stand nearer or beyond the goblet you can only guess. It is quite simple, however, to give directions in serving; you just tell the chambermaid that she is to follow the waitress, and pass the sauces and the vegetables. And you have already explained carefully to the latter that she must not deal plates around the table like a pack of cards, or ever take them off in stacked up piles. *That* much at least you *do* know. You also make it a point above everything that the silver must be very clean. Sigrid seems to understand, and, with the optimism of youth, you approach the dinner hour without misgiving.

Wearing the dress your husband likes, you come out of your bedroom. The table, set with your wedding silver and glass, looks quite nice. You are a little disturbed about the silver—it does look rather leaden, but perhaps it is just a candle shadow. Then you notice there are a great many forks on the table! You ask your husband what is the matter with the forks. He does not see anything wrong. You need them

all for the dinner you ordered. How can there be less? So you straighten
a candlestick that was out of line and put the place-cards on.

Then you go into the living-room, and after everyone has arrived you
wait a few minutes with no sign of dinner. You wait a little longer and
gradually you become nervous—what can have happened? The dining-
room door might be that of a tomb for all the evidence of life behind
it. You become really alarmed. Is dinner never going to be served? Conversation is getting weaker and weaker. Mrs. Toplofty—evidently des-
pairing—sits down. Mrs. Worldly also sits; both say nothing. At last
the door opens with a jerk, and Sigrid, instead of bowing slightly and
murmuring gently, "Dinner is served," stands stiff as a poker, and
shouts: "Dinner's ready!"

You hope no one heard her, but you know very well that nothing
escaped any one of those present. And between the delay and your
Sigrid's manners, you are already thoroughly mortified by the time you
reach the table. But you hope that at least the dinner will be good. For
the first time you are assailed with doubt. And then comes the soup.
You don't have to taste it to see that it is wrong. It looks not at all as
clear soup should! Instead of being glass-clear amber, it is a greasy-
looking brown. You taste it, fearing the worst, and the worst is realized.
It tastes like dishwater—and is barely tepid. You look around the table;
Mr. Kindhart alone is trying to eat it.

In removing the plates, Delia, the assistant, takes them up by piling
one on top of the other, clashing them together as she does so. You can
feel Mrs. Worldly looking with almost hypnotized fascination—as her
attention might be drawn to a street accident against her will. Then
there is a wait. You wait and wait, and looking in front of you, you
notice the bare tablecloth without a plate. You know instantly that the
service is wrong, but you find yourself puzzled to know *how* it should
have been done. Finally Sigrid comes in with a whole dozen plates
stacked in a pile, which she proceeds to deal around the table. Instinct
tells you that to try to interfere would only make matters worse. You
hold your own cold fingers in your lap, knowing that you must sit there
and that you can do nothing.

The fish, which was to have been a *mousse* with *sauce hollandaise,*
is a huge granulated mound, much too big for the platter, with a narrow
gutter of liquid around the edge and the center dabbed over with a
curdled yellow mass. You realize that not only is the food itself awful,
but that the quantity is too great for one dish. You don't know what to
do next. There is no use in apologizing; there is no way of dropping
through the floor, or waking yourself up. You have collected the most
knowing and the most critical people around your table to put them to
discomfort that you feel they will never forget. Never! You have to bite
your lips to keep from crying. Whatever possessed you to ask these
people to your horrible house?

Mr. Kindhart, sitting next to you, says gently, "Cheer up, little girl, it doesn't really matter!" And then you know to the full how terrible the situation is. The meal is endless; each course is equally unappetizing to look at, and abominably served. You notice that none of your guests eat anything.

You leave the table literally sick, but realizing fully that the giving of a dinner is not as easy as you thought. And in the living-room, you start to apologize and burst into tears!

As you are very young, and those present are all really fond of you, they try to be comforting, but you know that it will be long, if ever, before any of them will be willing to risk an evening in your house again. You also know that without malice, but in truth and frankness, they will tell everyone, "Whatever you do, don't dine with the Newweds unless you eat your dinner before you go."

When they have all gone, you drag yourself miserably into your room, feeling that you never want to look into that dining-room again. Your husband, remembering the many bad lunch counters he often eats at, tries to tell you it was not so bad! But you *know*! You lie awake making plans to let the house, and to discharge your awful household the next morning, and then you realize that the fault was yours.

If you yourself had known every detail of cooking and service, of course you would not have attempted to give the dinner in the first place—at least not until, through giving little dinners, the skill of your household had become expert enough to encourage your giving a big one.

On the other hand, suppose that you had had a very experienced cook and waitress. The dinner would, of course, not have been bungled, but it would have lacked something, somewhere, if you added nothing of your own personality to its perfection. It is almost safe to make the statement that no dinner is ever really well done unless the hostess herself knows every smallest detail so thoroughly that, like a proofreader, she is unobserving of perfection, but unfailingly ready to correct a flaw. The perfect housekeeper is not even conscious of paying attention, but nothing escapes her. She can walk through a room without appearing to look either to the right or left; yet if the slightest detail is amiss, her eyes see it at once.

Having generalized by drawing two pictures, it is now time to take up the specific details.

DETAILED DIRECTIONS FOR DINNER-GIVING

The requisites at every dinner of perfection, whether a great one of two hundred people or a little one of four, are as follows:

Guests. People who are congenial to one another. This is of first importance.

Food. A suitable menu perfectly prepared and dished. Food that is good of its *kind*.

Table furnishing. Freshly laundered linen, brilliantly polished silver—no matter how little of it—and all other table accessories in perfect condition and suitable to the occasion and surroundings.

Service. Competent; expert for *your* requirement.

Living-room. Inviting in arrangement and well-aired.

A cordial and hospitable host.

A hostess of charm. Charm says everything—tact, sympathy, poise, and perfect manners—always.

And though for all dinners these requisites are much the same, the necessity for perfection increases in proportion to the formality of the occasion and the importance of the establishment.

For dinner-giving in the less formal American house and the house without servants, see Chapters 29 and 31 respectively.

SELECTION OF PEOPLE

The proper selection of guests is the first essential in all entertaining. Some people have this "sense"—others haven't. The first are the great hosts and hostesses; the others are the mediocre or the failures.

It is usually a mistake to invite great talkers together. Brilliant men and women who love to talk want listeners, not rivals. Very silent people should be sandwiched between good talkers, or at least voluble talkers. Silly people should never be put anywhere near learned ones, nor the dull near the clever, unless the dull one is a young and pretty woman with a talent for listening and the clever is a man with an admiration for beauty and a love of talking.

Most people think two brilliant people should be put together. Often they should, but with discretion. If both are voluble or nervous or "temperamental," you may create a situation like putting two operatic sopranos in the same part and expecting them to sing together.

The endeavor of a hostess, when seating her table, is to put together those who are likely to be interesting to each other. Professor Bugge might bore *you* to tears, but Mrs. Entomoid would probably delight in him, just as Mr. Stocksan Bonds and Mrs. Rich would probably have interests in common. Making a dinner list is a little like making a Christmas list. You put down what *they* will (you hope) like, not what you like. Those who are placed between congenial neighbors remember your dinner as delightful—even though both food and service were mediocre; but ask people out of their own groups and seat them next to their pet aversions: wild horses will not drag them your way again.

ASKING SOMEONE TO FILL A PLACE

Since no one but a fairly intimate friend is ever asked to fill a place, this invitation is always telephoned. A very young man may be asked by the butler if he will dine with Mrs. Gilding that evening, and very likely no explanation is made; but if the person to be invited is a lady or an older gentleman (except on such occasions as noted above), the hostess herself telephones. "Can you do me a great favor and fill a place at dinner tonight?" The one who receives this invitation is rather bound by the rules of good manners to accept if possible.

IMPORTANCE OF DINNER ENGAGEMENTS

Dinner invitations must be answered immediately; engraved or written ones by return mail, or those which were telephoned, by telephone and at once! Also, nothing but serious illness or an utterly unavoidable accident can excuse the breaking of a dinner engagement.

To accept a dinner at Mrs. Nobody's and then break the obligation upon being invited to dine with the Worldlys proclaims anyone capable of such rudeness an unmitigated snob whom Mrs. Worldly would be the first to cut from her visiting list if she were to know of it. The rule is: Don't accept an invitation if you don't care about it. Having declined the Nobody invitation in the first place, you are then free to accept Mrs. Worldly's, or to stay at home.

There are times, however, when engagements between intimate friends or members of the family may perhaps be broken, but only if made with the special stipulation: "Come to dinner with us alone Thursday if nothing special turns up!" And the other answers, "I'd love to— and you let me know, too, if you want to do anything else." Meanwhile, if one of them is invited to something unusually tempting, there is no rudeness in telephoning her friend, "Lucy has asked us to go to the opera on Thursday," and the other says, "Go, by all means. We can dine Tuesday next week if you like, or come Sunday for supper." This privilege of intimacy can, however, be abused. An engagement, even with a member of one's family, ought never to be broken without good reason, or it becomes apparent that the other's presence is more a fill-in of idle time than a longed-for pleasure.

THE MENU

People are putting much less food on their tables than formerly. The very few rich, still living in great houses with an imposing array of servants, sit down to three, or at most four, courses.

Under no circumstances does a modern dinner, no matter how formal, consist of more than

1. Soup or oysters or melon or clams
2. Fish or entrée
3. Roast
4. Salad
5. Dessert
6. After-dinner coffee

One should always try to choose a well-balanced menu; an especially rich dish is balanced by a simple one. Fish timbale with a thick creamed sauce might perhaps be followed by spring lamb, other plain roast meat, or a *filet mignon*. A broiled fish might be followed by boned capon or another elaborate meat dish. It is equally bad to select peculiar food except as a secondary course. Some people love highly flavored Spanish or Indian dishes, but they are not appropriate for a formal dinner. At an informal dinner an Indian curry or Mexican enchilada for one dish is delicious for those who like it; and if there is another substantial dish, such as a plain roast, which practically everyone is able to eat, those who don't like highly spiced dishes can at least stay their hunger.

It is the same way with Italian dishes. One who detests the taste of garlic and onions would be very wretched if garlic were put into each course—and liberally! With curry, a fatally bad selection would be a very peppery soup, fish with green peppers, and then the curry with chutney and other throat-searing ingredients, finishing with an endive salad. Yet more than one hostess has selected exactly these.

Equally bad is a dinner of flavorless white sauces from beginning to end: a cream soup, boiled fish with white sauce, or a *vol-au-vent* of creamed sweetbreads, followed by breast of chicken and mashed potatoes and cauliflower, palm-root salad, vanilla ice-cream, and lady cake. Or, everything sweet: beet soup, fish with apricot sauce, duck basted with currant jelly, a sweet fruit salad with *Bar-le-Duc* jelly, and a sugary dessert. In these examples each dish is good in itself but unappetizing in the monotony of its combination.

Another thing: Although a dinner should not be long, neither should it consist of samples, especially if set before men who are hungry.

The following menu—one course too long at that—might seem at first glance a good dinner, but it is one from which the average man would go home and forage ravenously in the icebox:

Clear soup (no substance)

Smelts (one apiece)

Individual *croustades* of sweetbreads (holding about a dessertspoonful)

Broiled squab, miniature potato croquette, and string beans

Lettuce salad, with one small cheese straw apiece

Ice-cream

The only thing that had any sustaining quality, barring the potato which was not more than a mouthful, was the last, and very few men care to make their dinner of ice-cream. If the squab had been roast instead of broiled it would have been adequate because more of the flesh of a roast squab can be eaten. Or if there had been a thick cream soup, or a fish with more substance—such as salmon, or a baked thick fish of which he could have had a generous helping—this would have been adequate. But too many women order trimmings rather than food.

SETTING THE TABLE

The one unbreakable rule is that everything on the table must be geometrically spaced: the centerpiece in the actual center, the places at equal distances, and all utensils balanced. Beyond this one rule you may set your table as you choose.

If the tablecloth is of white damask, which for a formal dinner is always the best possible style, a felt must be put under it. (To say that it must be smooth and white, in other words perfectly laundered, is as beside the mark as to say that faces and hands should be clean.) Damask is the old-fashioned but essentially conservative tablecloth, especially suitable in a high-ceilinged room that is either English or French or of no special period in decoration. Lace tablecloths are better suited to an Italian room—especially if the table is a refectory one. Handkerchief linen tablecloths embroidered and lace-inserted are also, strangely enough, suited to all quaint, low-ceilinged, old-fashioned, but beautifully appointed rooms, the reason being that the lace cloth partially reveals the bare table. The lace cloth must also go over a refectory table without felt or other lining. (For bare tables, see Index.)

Whenever a damask cloth is used, the middle crease must be put on so that it is an absolutely straight and unwavering line down the exact center from head to foot. If it is an embroidered one, be sure the embroidery is "right side up." Next goes the centerpiece—usually an arrangement of flowers in either a bowl or a vase, and certainly not too high for guests to see over—but it can be any one of an almost unlimited variety of things: flowers or fruit in any arrangement that taste and ingenuity can devise; or an ornament in silver that needs no flowers, such as a covered cup; or an ornament of glass or china, or perhaps an arrangement of distinctive conversation-piece objects which blend with the rest of the table setting.

Next comes the setting of the places. The distance between places at the table must never be so short that guests have no elbow room and that the servants cannot pass the dishes properly; when the dining-room chairs are very high-backed and are placed so close as to be almost touching, it is impossible for them not to risk spilling something over someone. On the other hand, to place people a yard or more apart so that conversation has to be shouted into the din made by the shouting of all the others is equally trying. About two feet from plate center to plate center is ideal. If the chairs have narrow and low backs, people can sit much closer together, especially at a small round table, the curve of which leaves a spreading wedge of space between the chairs at the back even if the seats touch at the front corners. But on the long, straight sides of a rectangular table in a very large—and impressive—dining-room there may be a foot of space between the chairs.

SETTING THE PLACES

The necessary number of plates, with the pattern right side up, are first put around the table at equal distances—spaced with a string, if whoever is setting the table has not an accurate eye. Then on the left of each plate, handle toward the edge of the table and prongs up, is put the salad fork; the meat fork is put next, and then the fish fork. The salad fork, which will usually be the third used, is thus laid nearest the plate. If there is an entrée, the fork for this course is placed between the fish fork and that for the roast, and the salad fork is left out to be brought in later. On the right of the plate, and nearest to it, is put the silver- or steel-bladed salad knife, or if the salad is one for which no knife is necessary, the knife nearest the plate is the meat knife; next the fish knife, the edge of each toward the plate. Then the soupspoon and then the oyster fork or grapefruit spoon. Not more than three forks and three knives belong on the table when it is set. Additional forks and knives (rarely necessary today) may be put on the table during dinner as they are needed.

THE GLASSES

Which wineglasses shall be chosen depends of course upon the menu, but their table-setting arrangement will have to be according to size, in that little ones cannot very well be hidden behind large ones. Therefore, the goblet or tumbler for water is placed directly above the knives at the right of the plate; next to it, at a slight distance to the

CHAMPAGNE   CLARET   SHERRY   LIQUEUR

WATER   LONG DRINKS   OLD-FASHIONED   COCKTAIL

right, the champagne glass; in front and between these two, either the claret glass or the tall-stemmed glass for white wine. Then, either in front of this, or somewhat to the right again, the sherry glass. If there is to be a glass for burgundy, it would be back between the goblet and the glass for champagne.

Such an array as this is scarcely ever seen, except at a semi-public dinner, which is more properly rated as a banquet. At the typical dinner, three glasses in addition to the goblet is the maximum; at an informal dinner, more likely two; one for sherry and one for claret, or possibly one for a light white wine and one for burgundy. Or, instead of grouping the glasses on the table, some prefer to have them placed in a straight row slanting downward from the goblet at upper left to the glass for sherry at lower right.

NAPKIN SHOULD BE ON THE PLATE

A dinner napkin folded square and flat is laid on each place plate; very fancy foldings are not in good taste, but if the napkin is very large, the sides are folded in so as to make a flattened roll a third the width of its height. Napkins are put at the side or across top of plates only when it is necessary to put food on the table before seating the guests. To put the napkin at the side of the empty plate in order to display it is very much like wearing a ring over a glove—as well as being incorrect for formal table-setting. Bread should not be put in the napkin. Butter plates are never used on a formal dinner table. The place-cards should be put on top of and in the center of the napkin.

When the places have been set, two pairs of silver candlesticks are placed at the four corners about half-way between the center and the edge of the table, or two candelabra at either end half-way between the places of the host and hostess and the centerpiece. How many candles depends upon whether the dining room is otherwise lighted or not. If the candles alone light the table, there must be a candle a person, at least (two five-branch candelabra and one pair of candlesticks for a dinner of twelve). But if the candles are merely ornaments, four candles will be adequate for a table of eight. Candles are used with or without shades. Fashion at the moment says without, which means that, in order to bring the flame well above people's eyes, candlesticks or candelabra must be high and the candles as long as the proportion can stand. If the flames shine into the eyes of those at table, the candles must have shades. Shades, by the way, increase the light on the table if they are flaring in shape.

Dishes, either bowl or basket or paten-shaped, are put at the corners, between the candlesticks or candelabra and the centerpiece, or wherever there are equally spaced vacancies on the table. These dishes, or compotiers, hold candy, fruit, fancy cakes, or other edible trimmings, chosen less for flavor than for decorative appearance. Salted nuts do not belong in any dishes which remain on the table after it is crumbed. Properly, **nuts** are often put on the dinner table, either in two big silver dishes or **in** small individual ones at each of the places. In any case they are removed with the salt and pepper pots after the salad course. The colloquial description of eating "from soup to nuts" could never apply **to** a formal dinner. After-dessert "nuts and raisins" belong only on the family dinner table—at the Thanksgiving and Christmas tables especially.

On a very large table four compotiers are filled with candy, and perhaps two larger silver dishes or baskets are filled with fruit and put on midway between two of the candy dishes. Flowers are also often put in two or four smaller vases, in addition to a larger and dominating one in the center.

Pepper pots and saltcellars should be put at every other place. For a dinner of twelve there should be six and surely not less than four saltcellars and pepper pots.

Olives and celery are passed during the soup course. Each fish, or meat, or salad has its own accompanying condiment, sauce, or relish. Pickles have no place on the correct dinner-party menu, because they are never served except as an accompaniment or garnishing for cold meats, which belong to lunch, supper, buffets, and picnics.

SILVER MUST SHINE

Many people who would not dream of using a wrinkled tablecloth or chipped glass or china seem totally blind to silver that is jaundiced in color and black in the crevices.

WINES

Except during the years of our experiment with prohibition, wines have always had their proper place on the menu of a perfect dinner; let us consider each of them in detail.

Sherry. Customarily this (in a small V-shaped glass) is the first wine served at dinner. It is served with the soup and should always be put into a decanter and served at room temperature. It can stand being decantered indefinitely without spoiling. All wines are poured at the right of each person at table and without lifting the glass from the table. Sherry is also served at lunch, or at supper, or as a hospitable refreshment at any time. Years ago it was invariably offered with biscuits or cakes to guests arriving from a journey or about to depart on one. Nowadays sherry is usually included with cocktails as an alternate choice.

White Wine. A certain few epicures have always insisted that chilled chablis be served with oysters. Otherwise any dry white wine is served with fish, possibly with an entrée, or a dry or sweet white wine may be the only wine at a women's lunch or at the family dinner table.

Claret. At a simple dinner party claret is served with meat. Epicures shudder at its appearance before the meat, but at the family dinner table either claret or white wine is drunk from the beginning of the meal to its close.

Burgundy. Stronger than claret, is especially suitable with red meats, duck, and all game. Claret and burgundy should both be at room temperature or a degree or so warmer rather than colder if the vintage be very fine. The decanting of vintage wines is a very delicate as well as important operation. Clarets and white wines, if not decanted, should be lifted as gently as possible, without changing the side on which the bottles are lying, into straw baskets of the sort that they are served from in restaurants.

The white wines are carried carefully to a cool—even cold—place. Red wines are carried with equal care to the dining-room or pantry, which has a temperature approximating 68 degrees; and all these wines are left in their baskets until as short a time as practical before they are to be served, and then, with all the care and gentleness possible, decanted. Some epicures put them through filter papers—others believe that filtering robs them of some of their bouquet. At all events, care is taken not to let any sediment, which has settled at the bottom of the wine, get into the decanter.

Champagne. Since this is, above all other beverages, that of the formal dinner party, it has, like all other formal details, many exigencies. When other wines are included, it is served with the meat course; but, when it is the only wine, it is served as soon as the first course has begun. Its proper temperature depends upon its quality.

Champagne which is not of especially fine vintage is put in the refrigerator for a day and then frappéed by putting it into a cooler with a very little salt as well as ice, and holding the bottle by the neck turned back and forth a few times. In doing this, take care not to leave the bottle in the salt and ice too long or the champagne may become sherbet! Also, when opening, be sure to wrap the bottle in a towel or napkin as a protection in case it explodes.

A fine vintage champagne, on the other hand, is packed in ice without salt.

Champagne glasses ought to be as thin as soap bubbles. Thick glasses do no harm to poor champagne, which should have its poorness disguised; but a thick glass will lower the temperature at which a really fine champagne should be served and spoil its perfection. If thick glasses must be used, the epicurean thing to do is to chill them in the refrigerator and put them on the table at the moment the champagne is served. For further advice on serving champagne, see page 348.

Whisky. At an informal dinner party (informal in this sense, meaning anything less than a dinner of greatest ceremony) whisky is always proffered to the gentlemen as an alternative. In the South, many people prefer Bourbon and soda. Before pouring the champagne, the butler or waitress asks, "Would you prefer Scotch or rye, Sir?" "Highball" is a term that is frowned upon. One says "Scotch and soda" or "whisky and soda." A tall glass—the same as that for iced tea—should have one large piece of ice in it (small pieces melt quickly and fail to keep the drink cold). The whisky is poured by the servant until the guest makes a gesture to stop. And then the glass is filled with soda or other sparkling mineral water, or water as the guest desires.

Port, Brandy, and Liqueurs. English port and especially fine cognac are not likely to be served in the average American house. If they should be, they are brought to the gentlemen alone, who remain seated at table, drinking their coffee and smoking cigars and eating unsalted nuts. Liqueurs, on the other hand, are always proffered the ladies as well as the gentlemen. Three small decanters are proffered on a tray, which also holds a row of very little glasses. The fashionable list includes cognac always, and two others, chartreuse and benedictine, or kümmel, or green crème de menthe, or Cointreau.

If the mint is chosen, a few of the glasses must be filled with fine crushed ice over which the mint is poured. White mint is served the same way. The green is merely prettier.

When vintage wines are served, an occasional bottle may have turned sour, therefore a teaspoonful or so of each bottle opened is first poured in the glass of the host who tastes it. This also provides for the removal of small pieces of cork that may have broken off in opening. If the wine is good, the bottle is then poured for the guests. If not good, another bottle is opened. For this reason extra bottles should be ready to open.

THE BUTLER IN THE DINING-ROOM

When the dinner guests enter the dining-room, it used to be customary for the butler to hold out the chair of the mistress of the house. The theory is that the host himself will hold the chair of the guest of honor—who sits on his right—and all the other gentlemen will hold the chairs of the ladies on their right except the partner of the hostess, whose chair is held by her servant so that the gentleman of honor need not help her. But, whatever the theory, this has always seemed a discourtesy to the guests. And the polite hostess insists on having the butler stand at the chair of the guest of honor instead of her own. This is much more important at a lunch where there are no gentlemen than at a dinner.

If there are footmen enough, the chair of each lady is held for her. Ordinarily, where there are two servants, it is best that they stand at opposite sides of the room and help those who may seem in need of assistance.

In a big house the butler always stands throughout a meal back of the hostess' chair, except when giving one of the men under him a direction or when pouring wine. He is not supposed to leave the dining-room himself or ever to handle a dish. In a smaller house, where he has no assistant, he naturally does everything himself; when he has a second man or parlor maid, he passes the principal dishes and the assistant follows with the accompanying dishes or vegetables.

CORRECT SERVICE OF DINNER

In every formally appointed house, whether there are two at table or two hundred, plates are changed and courses presented in precisely the same manner.

The so-called "Russian" service is that of every *formally* appointed house. The term simply means that no serving dishes are ever put on the table except ornamental dishes of fruit and sweetmeats. The meat is carved in the kitchen or pantry; vegetables are passed and returned to the side table. Only at breakfast are dishes of food put on the table— or, of course, at a buffet meal of any sort.

THE EVER-PRESENT PLATE

From the setting of the table until it is cleared for dessert, a plate must remain at every place. The plate on which oysters or clams are served is put on top of the place plate, as is also a plate holding fruit or cold fish in a stemmed glass. At the end of the course the used plate is removed, leaving the place plate. The soup plate is also put on top of this same plate. But when the soup plate is removed, the underneath plate is removed with it, and the plate for the next course immediately exchanged for the two taken away.

THE EXCHANGE PLATE

If the first course had been a cold dish that was offered in bulk instead of being served on individual plates, it would have been eaten on the place plate, and an exchange plate would then have been neces-sary before the soup could be served. That is, a clean plate would have been exchanged for the used one, and the soup plate then put on top of that. The reason is that *a plate with food on it must never be exchanged for one that has held food;* a clean one must come between.

If an entrée served on individual plates follows the fish, clean plates are first exchanged for the used ones, as the used ones are removed, until the whole table is set with clean plates. Then the entrée is put at each place in exchange for the clean plate.

DISHES PRESENTED AT LEFT; REMOVED FROM RIGHT

Although dishes must be always presented at the left of the person being served, and it is better that plates be removed at the left too, it is permissible, if more convenient, to remove them at the right.

Glasses are poured and additional knives placed at the right, but forks are put on as needed at the left.

TWO PLATES AT A TIME?

The only plates that are regularly brought into the dining-room one in each hand are for soup and dessert. The soup plates are put down on the place plates which have not been removed, and the dessert plates need merely be put down on the tablecloth. But the plates of every other course have to be exchanged and therefore each individual service requires two hands. Soup plates, two at a time, would better not be attempted by any but the expert and sure-handed, as it is while placing one plate and holding the other aloft that the mishap of "soup poured down someone's back" occurs! If only one plate of soup is brought in at a time, this accident at least cannot happen. In the same way, the spoon and fork on the dessert plate can easily fall off unless it is held level. Two plates at a time, therefore, is not a question of etiquette, but of the servant's skill.

PLATE REMOVED WHEN FORK IS LAID DOWN

Many years ago it was considered impolite to remove any plates until the last guest at the table had finished eating! Then came one or two decades of speed, during which good service required the removal of each plate the instant the fork was laid upon it, so that by the time the last fork was put down, the entire table was set with clean plates and was ready for the service of the next course.

But the protests of the slow eaters were heard throughout the land and the hostess, who a few years ago prided herself on having no used plate left at any place more than a few moments, now does not have the plates removed until the slowest eaters have finished.

MORE THAN ONE SERVICE

At every well-ordered dinner there should be a separate service for each six persons; that is, no hot dish should, if avoidable, be presented to more than six, or seven at most. At a dinner of eighteen, for instance, three dishes, each holding six portions, are garnished exactly alike and presented simultaneously: (1) to the lady of honor, (2) to the lady sitting in the sixth seat to the right, (3) to the lady in the sixth seat— around the end of the table. Study the diagrams on the following pages, which explain seating precedence and partner arrangement.

THE ORDER OF TABLE PRECEDENCE

This order of seating is rigid and unbreakable. The lady of highest rank is on the host's right. The lady of next highest rank is on his left. The third lady sits on right of man of highest rank. The fourth lady on

left of man of the second rank, and so on as marked on the diagram.
The lowest in rank is nearest the center. The "lady of honor" or of first
rank must be "taken in" by the host and seated at his right.

At ordinary dinners therefore the hostess goes in to dinner with the
man of the second highest rank. But if the man of honor is of such importance that she must go in with him as well as place him at her right
(see Very Important Guest of Honor, below), it is necessary to send
the lady who sits on the right of the gentleman of honor and the gentleman who sits on the hostess' left in to dinner together and then
to separate them. He sees her to her place, and, discovering his card is
not next to her, goes around the table until he finds his own. This is
plainly shown on Diagram 1.

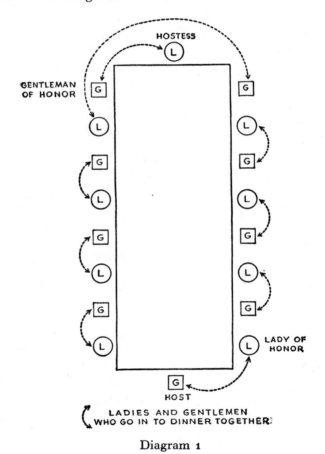

Diagram 1

At dinners of eight, twelve, sixteen, twenty, and twenty-four, where
either two ladies or two men must sit at head and foot of the table, the
hostess usually relinquishes her place and the host keeps his. At a dinner
of twelve it is important that she take the place at her left instead of

at her right, because otherwise she, instead of the lady at the right of the gentleman of honor, will be served first. For an example of this, see Diagram 2.

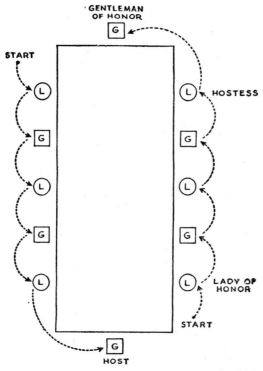

Diagram 2

Hostess relinquishes her place. Dotted lines show normal **service.**

VERY IMPORTANT GUEST OF HONOR

There is one maneuver necessary only on the very exceptional occasion when the guest of honor is a man of such importance (the President of the United States or a foreign ambassador, for instance) that he must not only be seated on the right of the hostess, but also take her in to dinner.

In order to accomplish this, one exception must be made to the rule that each gentleman seats on his right the lady he takes in to dinner. On this occasion it is necessary to separate one lady and gentleman after they walk into the dining room together. The choice obviously falls on the lady who is to sit on the guest of honor's right and the gentleman who will be seated on the hostess' left, who by taking these two odd places restore the balance of the table. This unusual maneuver, puzzling to these about-to-be-separated guests, is easily set straight by the hostess who is standing close beside them. See Diagram 1.

THE COURTEOUS HOSTESS IS NEVER SERVED FIRST

The hostess who has herself served first when another woman is a guest at her table is giving an innocent example of outstanding rudeness still current at the present day. It is only fair, therefore, to give a complete history of the possible origins of this upstart rudeness, some of which are understandable and others not; it will be found at the end of this chapter.

In all first-class restaurants each dish is presented to the host for his approval before it is passed or served to his guests, but he does *not* help himself. Nor should a hostess.

DINNER OF TWELVE IN THE HOUSE OF A WIDOW

Since it is almost impossible to seat twelve in the house of a widow (who will appoint a member of her family or a very intimate friend to sit in the host's place to avoid serving herself from an untouched first dish), it is now considered essential to consider the lady of honor the one who is seated on the right of the gentleman of honor who, of course, sits on the right of the hostess, as in Diagram 3.

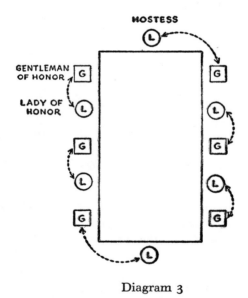

Diagram 3

If the dinner is given for a lady and it is therefore important to have a deputy host so as to seat her opposite the hostess, then the way to avoid serving the hostess first would be to resort to the maneuver shown in Diagram 4.

This reverses service on the right side of the table and awkwardly returns to the omitted gentleman, but there is no help for it without committing the unforgivable offense of serving the hostess to one set of dishes first.

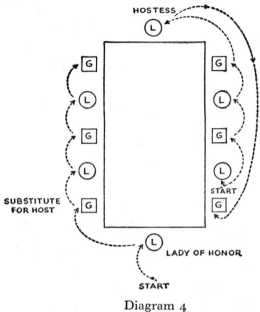

Diagram 4

A DINNER OF EIGHT WHEN THERE IS NO HOST

Gentlemen never take the ladies in to dinner at so small a dinner as eight.

It makes no difference whether or not there is a host, the lady at the foot of the table is generally served first. And the dishes are passed to the right, or passed alternately right and left in order that the same

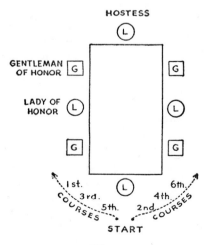

Diagram 5

gentleman shall not always get the last piece on a dish. In many houses the lady at the first gentleman's right is served first, if she is really of more importance than the lady at the end of the table. Service goes around to the right as usual, or reverses for alternate courses, as the hostess chooses, so that there will be two gentlemen who share alternately in being the last served.

While it is thoughtful not to have the same gentleman be the last served all through the dinner, it is not advisable to reverse the direction of service whenever the dinner is large enough to require two services, unless the footmen can be counted on not to become confused by serving first to the right and then to the left, and risk bumping into each other.

FILLING GLASSES

As soon as the guests are seated and the first course is put in front of them, the butler goes from guest to guest on the right-hand side of each, and asks, "Apollinaris or plain water?" and fills the goblet accordingly. In the same way he asks later before pouring wine, "Sherry, Sir?" (or "Madam?"). Champagne is of course the typical dinner-party wine. In fact, it is to many people the evidence of a party, in contrast to the sherry, white wine, and claret of the family table. In France champagne is often not served until dessert, but in the smartest houses elsewhere, sherry is served with the soup (or chablis with oysters), and then champagne is served straight through to the end.

The proper way to serve it is from its own bottle with a napkin around it (put on like a shawl) and wrapped tight. The reason for this is to catch all drops—either of wine or condensed moisture—that might fall, as well as maintaining its proper chill from warming hands. (For other details regarding wines, see page 339.)

WHEN REFUSING, SHOULD A LITTLE WINE BE POURED?

Whether it is best at table—because least conspicuous—to allow a little wine to be poured into your glass before you check the pouring is open for discussion, because, unless your host happened to be looking at your glass when the wine was poured, he will not notice later on that your almost empty glass had never been filled. On the other hand, if he did happen to notice, he could not feel that much wine was wasted. In any case, to turn your wineglass upside down is a needlessly rude way to say "No."

As to this general subject of saying "No" when we want to, one wonders why so many people who feel embarrassed when refusing cocktails have no hesitation whatever in refusing foods—particularly those to which they are allergic! The reason is probably this: The censorious attitude of those who disapprove of alcohol, no matter how temperate its use, has brought about a connotation of disapproval in its refusal. One may refuse to eat bread, or fish, or strawberries, and this may cause

regret on the part of the hostess who knows that her biscuits are super-
latively good, or the fish caught but a few hours before the meal, or the
strawberries picked at just the right hour of the day in her garden, but
no disapproval can possibly be implied on the part of the guest who
says, "No, thank you."

Not so many years ago, when diet fads had not yet come into fashion,
and the scientific study of balanced rations, vitamins, and allergies and
so on, was unknown outside the laboratories, it was considered very discourteous to refuse whatever one's host or hostess proffered. A well-
behaved guest took at least a little of everything passed and ate or drank
that little. Today, the increasing use of the word "allergic" has been
more helpful to the acceptance of the phrase "No, thank you" than anything that ever happened. And after all, if a guest knows that lobster
gives him hives, he would be stupid to eat it even though it has just
been flown in from Maine.

BREAD

As soon as soup is served, dinner (finger) rolls are passed in a flat
dish or a basket. An old-fashioned silver cake basket makes a perfect
modern bread basket. Some of the raffia ones from Italy are very attractive. Or, most popular of all, a shallow wicker basket that has a
fringed napkin laid in it and several sorts of breads displayed. (Finger
rolls, crescent rolls, melba toast, and rye or whole wheat crackers are
typical.) A guest helps himself with his fingers and lays the roll or
bread on the tablecloth, always. No bread plates are ever on a table
where there is no butter, and no butter is ever served at a formal dinner.
Whenever there is no bread left at anyone's place at table, more should
be passed. The glasses should also be kept filled.

PRESENTING DISHES

Dishes are presented held flat on the palm of the servant's left
hand; every hot one must have a napkin placed as a pad under it. An
especially heavy meat platter can be steadied if necessary by holding
the edge of the platter with the right hand, the fingers protected from
being burned by a second folded napkin.

Each dish is supplied with whatever silver is needed for serving it.
In a formally appointed house both a serving spoon, somewhat larger
than an ordinary tablespoon, and a fork of large size are put on all
dishes. In a simpler house the spoon alone is used except on the dishes
that are hard to help oneself to. String beans, braised celery, spinach
en branche, etc., need both fork and spoon. Asparagus has various special lifters and tongs, but most people use the ordinary spoon and fork,
putting the spoon underneath and the fork prongs down, to hold the
stalks on the spoon while being removed to the plate. Corn on the cob
is taken with the fingers, but this dish, delectable though it be, is *never*

served at a *formal* dinner party. For this occasion it should be cut off, buttered, seasoned, and served in a vegetable dish. A galantine or mousse should have both fork and spoon, but peas, mashed potatoes, rice, etc., are offered with a spoon only—except at a formal table.

THE SERVING TABLE

The serving table is usually an ordinary table placed in the corner of the dining room near the door to the pantry, and behind a screen, so that it may not be seen by the guests at table. In a small dining-room, where space is limited, a set of shelves like a single bookcase is useful; best of all are shelves, made by a carpenter, and fitted to the folds of the screen.

The serving table is a half-way station between the dinner table and the pantry. It holds stacks of cold plates, extra forks and knives, and the fingerbowls, and dessert plates. The latter are sometimes put out on the sideboard, if the serving table is small or too crowded.

At small informal dinners all dishes of food after being passed are left on the serving table in case they are called upon for a second helping. But at formal dinners, dishes are never passed twice, and are therefore taken directly to the pantry after being passed.

CLEARING TABLE FOR DESSERT

At dinner always, whether at a formal one or whether a member of the family is alone, the salad plates, or the plates of whatever course precedes dessert, are removed, leaving the table plateless. The saltcellars, pepper pots, unused flat silver, and nut dishes are taken off on the serving tray (without being put on a napkin or doily as used to be the custom), and the crumbs are brushed off each place at table with a tightly folded napkin onto a tray held under the table edge.

DESSERT SERVICE

There are two methods of serving dessert. The first, which used to be known as the "hotel method" and has within the last few years become the accepted one everywhere, is to put the fork and spoon on a china plate. Some people further put a glass plate for ice-cream on top of this, but most use the china plate. After the dessert the fingerbowl is brought in on a plate by itself. In the other service, which used to be that of all private houses, the entire dessert paraphernalia is put on at once.

This single service may sound as though it were more complicated than the two-course service, but actually it is simpler except when fruit is served. People dip their fingers in the fingerbowls (which they have put above their own places) and leave the table. Otherwise each plate has to be exchanged for a fingerbowl on its separate plate.

When fruit is to be served, it is passed immediately after the dessert or ice-cream; and last are passed decorative sweets. Usually these include chocolates, caramels, peppermints, candied orange, or whatever one chooses for decoration as well as taste.

Before leaving the subject of dessert, it may be well to add that the fingerbowl is less than half filled with cold water; and at dinner parties a few violets, sweet peas, or occasionally a gardenia may (or may not) be floated in it. A slice of lemon is never seen in a well-appointed house in an after-dessert fingerbowl. After broiled lobster, at an informal or family dinner, lemon in *hot* water (or soapy hot water) is excellent.

Black coffee is never served at a formal dinner table, but is brought afterward with cigarettes and liqueurs into the drawing-room for the ladies, and with cigars, cigarettes, and liqueurs into the library for the gentlemen.

If there is no library or similar man's room, coffee and cigars are brought to the table for the gentlemen after the ladies have gone into the drawing-room. (For full descriptions of the several varieties of coffee-serving, see Index.)

MENU CARDS

Small, standing porcelain slates, on which the menu is written, are seen on occasional dinner tables. Most often there is only one which is placed in front of the host; but sometimes there is one between every two guests.

Menus on fashionable tables never include obvious accessories, such as celery, olives, rolls, peppermints, radishes, currant jelly, chocolates, fruit, any more than they include salt and pepper or iced water.

PLACE-CARDS

The place-cards are usually plain, about an inch and a half high by two inches long, sometimes slightly larger. Fancy cards, while suitable on special occasions, such as Christmas or a birthday, have gone out of fashion on a formal table. The courtesy title and surname are used except when there is more than one guest with the same surname, in which case Mr. Russell Albright and Mr. Don Albright, for example, should be used to make the distinction.

SEATING THE TABLE

As has already been observed, the most practical way to seat the table is to write the names on individual cards first, and then "place" them as though playing solitaire; the guest of honor on the host's right, the second lady in rank on his left; the most distinguished or oldest gentleman on the right of the hostess, and the other guests filled in between.

WHO IS THE GUEST OF HONOR?

The guest of honor is the oldest lady present, or a stranger whom you wish for some reason to honor. A bride at her first dinner in your house, after her return from her honeymoon, may be given, if you choose, precedence over older people. The guest of honor is *always* she who is taken in to dinner by the host and placed on his right, whether she is one for whom the dinner is given or merely one who was selected at random. This place at table makes her the guest of honor. The lady of next greatest importance sits on the host's left and is taken in to dinner by the gentleman on whose right she sits. The hostess is always the last to go into the dining room at a formal dinner unless the President of the United States or the governor at a dinner in his own state be present. In these exceptional cases the hostess would go in to dinner with the guest of honor, who leads the way, and the wife of the President or governor would follow immediately with the host.

In Washington, for instance, even though the dinner be given for a guest of medium rank, the ladies of highest rank have the honor-places on either side of the host. The lady for whom the dinner is actually given is merely "among those present," unless those of higher rank agree to waive precedence. When Mrs. Frances Perkins was Secretary of Labor, she waived her rank and said always to seat her where no one else wanted to sit.

THE ENVELOPES FOR THE GENTLEMEN

In an envelope addressed to each gentleman is put a card on which is written the name of the lady he is to take in to dinner. This card just fits in the envelope, which is an inch or slightly less high and about two inches long. When the envelopes are addressed and filled, they are arranged in two or three neat rows on a silver tray and put in the front hall. The tray is presented to each gentleman just before he goes into the drawing-room, or in the entrance hall on his arrival.

THE TABLE DIAGRAM

An exceedingly practical method of telling each gentleman where he is to sit at a very large table is to choose a small fold-over card instead of the usual one in an envelope. His name is on its front fold and his partner's name inside, and below her name in the lower half of the fold is a small engraved diagram showing the table and the door of entrance and the location he is to find marked with pen strokes.

Or if it is so big a dinner that there are many separate tables, the tables are numbered with standing placards (as at a public dinner) and the table number written on each lady's name-card. (Do not call it an escort-card.)

A PERFECTLY SET FORMAL DINNER TABLE

Dinner is served. Bread and butter plate is not used.

Rimmed soup plate is placed on service plate. When china, plates are of same color.

Fish plate has been exchanged for soup and service plates, with sherry glass to be removed.

The meat plate has now been exchanged for the fish plate.

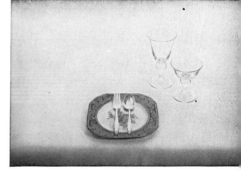

Correctly, a salad fork and knife are provided for the salad course.

Table is cleared before dessert plate, fork and spoon are put on the table.

CORRECT PLACE-SETTING FOR EACH COURSE AT A FORMAL DINNER

A DETAIL OF A FORMAL DINNER TABLE

The after-dinner coffee tray.

The formal service of after-dinner coffee.

AFTER-DINNER COFFEE SERVICE

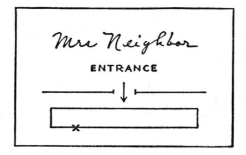

THE HOSTESS AT THE SIDE

When the number of guests is a multiple of four, the host and the hostess never sit opposite each other. It would bring two ladies and two gentlemen together if they did. At a table which seats two together at each end, the fact that the host is opposite a gentleman and the hostess opposite a lady is not noticeable; nor is it ever noticeable at a round table. But at a narrow table which has room for only one at the end, the hostess invariably sits in the seat next to that which is properly her own, putting in her place a gentleman at the end. The host usually keeps his seat rather than the hostess because the seat of honor is on his right; and in the etiquette governing dinners, the host and not the hostess is the more important personage!

When there are only four, they keep their own places, otherwise the host and hostess would sit next to each other. At a dinner of eight, twelve, sixteen, twenty, etc., the host keeps his place, but at supper for eight or twelve, the hostess keeps *her* place and the host moves a place to the right or left because the hostess at supper pours coffee or chocolate. And although the host keeps his seat at a formal dinner in honor of the lady he takes in, at a little dinner of eight, where there is no guest of honor, the host does not necessarily keep his seat at the expense of his wife unless he carves, in which case he must have the end place, just as at supper she has the end place in order to pour.

SIDEWALK, HALL, AND DRESSING ROOMS

In other days, on the occasion of a formal dinner, the entrance to a house often had an awning, especially if much entertaining was done there; but dinners of this formality have become so unusual that an awning now suggests a wedding. Even today, of course, the man on the pavement must, if it is raining, shelter each arriving guest under his doorman's umbrella from car to door. If it does not rain, he merely opens the doors of vehicles. Checks are never given at dinners, unless the guests number fifty or more. "Mr. Worldly's car" is called to the chauffeur on duty at the front steps, and he notifies Mr. Worldly's chauffeur.

In all modern houses of people who do much entertaining, there are two rooms on the entrance floor, built sometimes as dressing rooms and nothing else, but more often they are small reception rooms, each with a lavatory off of it. In the one given to the ladies, there is always a dressing table with toilet appointments on it, and the lady's maid should be on duty to give whatever service may be required. When there is no dressing room on the ground floor, the back of the hall is arranged with coat hangers and an improvised dressing table for the ladies, since people today customarily no longer go upstairs to a bedroom. In fact, nine ladies out of ten drop their evening cloaks at the front door, handing them to the servant on duty, and go at once without more ado to the drawing-room. Gentlemen also leave their hats and coats in the front part of the hall.

ANNOUNCING GUESTS

A gentleman always falls behind his wife in entering the drawing-room. If the butler knows the guests, he merely announces the wife's name first and then the husband's. If he does not know them by sight, he asks whichever is nearest to him, "What name, please?" And whichever one is asked answers, "Mr. and Mrs. Lake."

The butler then precedes the guests a few steps into the room where the hostess is stationed, and, standing aside, says in a low tone but very distinctly, "Mrs. Lake," a pause and then, "Mr. Lake." Married people are usually announced separately as above, but occasionally people have their guests announced, "Mr. and Mrs. Gray."

ANNOUNCING PERSONS OF RANK

All men of high public executive rank are not only announced first, but take precedence over their wives in entering the room. The President of the United States is announced simply, "The President." His title needs no qualifying appendage, since he, and he solely, is *the* President. He enters first, and alone, of course; and then "Mrs. Washington," being announced, follows. The governor of a State is in courtesy announced as "His Excellency" but the correct announcement would be "the Governor of (name the State)" and then "Mrs. Goodland." He enters the room and Mrs. Goodland follows. "His Honor the Mayor and Mrs. Lake" observes the same etiquette; or in a city other than his own he would be announced "The Mayor of Chicago and Mrs. Lake."

Other announcements are "The Honorable the Chief Justice and Mrs. Law," "The Secretary of State and Mrs. Eminent," "Senator and Mrs. Jefferson"; but the senator allows his wife to enter the room first, because his office is not executive. An ambassador must be announced "His Excellency the British Ambassador," and then "Lady Howard"; he enters the room first. A minister plenipotentiary is announced "His Excellency the Swedish Minister." He enters and a moment later "Mrs.

Ogren" follows. But a first secretary and his wife are announced without other title than their own, "Count and Countess European," or "Mr. and Mrs. American."

"Excellency," though strictly a title belonging to none but an ambassador, is always granted by courtesy to a minister plenipotentiary. In many of our embassies and legations, we Americans make ourselves absurd in the eyes of Europeans by exacting that counselors, first secretaries—almost every one in the service—be addressed by subordinates and strangers as "Excellency," which is *not* correct. The only exception is made in favor of a chargé d'affaires. This courtesy is, however, temporary and ceases upon the return to his chief.

The President, the vice president, the governor of a State, the mayor of a city, the ambassador of a foreign power—in other words, all executives—take precedence over their wives and enter rooms and vehicles first. But senators, representatives, secretaries of legations, and all other officials who are not executives, allow their wives to precede them, just as they would if they were private individuals.

Foreigners who have hereditary titles are announced by them. "His Grace the Duke" or "Her Grace the Duchess of Overthere," "The Marquis and Marchioness of Landsend," or "Sir Edward and Lady Blank," etc. Titles are invariably translated into English. "Count and Countess Lorraine," not "M. le Comte et Mme. la Comtesse Lorraine." Archbishops have heretofore been announced "His Grace," but they are now announced as "His Excellency" instead.

HOW A HOSTESS RECEIVES AT A FORMAL DINNER

On all occasions of formality, at a dinner as well as at a ball, the hostess stands near the door of her drawing-room, and as guests are announced, she greets them with a smile and a handshake and says something pleasant to each. What she says is nothing very important; charm of expression and of manner can often wordlessly express a far more gracious welcome than the most elaborate phrases, which as a matter of fact should be studiously avoided. Unless a woman's loveliness springs from generosity of heart and sympathy, her manners, no matter how perfectly practiced, are nothing but cosmetics applied to hide a want of inner beauty, precisely as rouge and powder are applied in the hope of hiding the lack of a beautiful skin. One device is much like the other, very pleasing unless brought into comparison with the perfection of the real.

Mrs. Oldname, for instance, usually welcomes you with some such sentence as "I am very glad to see you," or "I am so glad you could come!" Or if it is raining, she very likely tells you that you were very unselfish to come out in the storm. But no matter what she says or whether anything at all, she takes your hand with a firm pressure and her smile is really a *smile* of welcome, not a mechanical exercise of the

facial muscles. She gives you always—even if only for the moment—
her complete attention; and you go into her drawing-room with a
distinct feeling that you are under the roof, not of a mere acquaintance,
but of a friend. Mr. Oldname, who stands never very far from his wife,
always comes forward and, grasping your hand, accentuates his wife's
more subtle but no less vivid welcome. And either you join a friend
standing near, or he presents you, if you are a man, to a lady; or if
you are a lady, he presents a man to you.

Some hostesses, especially those of the Lion-Hunting and the New-
to-Best-Society variety, are much given to explanations, and love to
say, "Mrs. Jones, I want you to meet Mrs. Smith. Mrs. Smith is the
author of *Dragged from the Depths,* a most enlightening work of
psychic insight." Or to a good-looking woman, "I am putting you next
to Mavro Bey—I want him to carry back a flattering impression of
American women!"

But people of good breeding do not exploit their distinguished guests
with embarrassing hyperbole, or make personal remarks. Both are in
worst possible taste. Do not understand by this that helpful explanations
cannot be made; it is only that they must not be embarrassingly made,
nor overdone. Nor must a "specialist's" subject be forced upon him, like
a pair of manacles, by any power-displaying hostess who has captured
him. In illustration of what I mean by a helpful explanation, Mrs. Oldname might perhaps, in order to assist conversation for an interesting
but reticent person, tell a lady just before going in to dinner, "Mr.
Traveler, who is sitting next to you at the table, has just come back
from two years alone with the cannibals." This is not to exploit her
"traveled lion," but to give his neighbor a starting point for conversation at table. And although personal remarks are never good form, it
would be permissible for an older lady in welcoming a very young one,
especially a débutante or a bride, to say, "How lovely you look, Adelaide
dear, and what an adorable dress you have on!" But it would be
objectionable to say to an older lady, "That is a very handsome string
of pearls you are wearing." And never anywhere nor at any time may
one ask anyone, "How much did it cost?"

THE HOST'S DUTY

The host stands fairly near his wife, so that if any guest seems
to be unknown, he can present him to someone and not let him stand
alone. At formal dinners introductions are never general, and people
do not as a rule speak to strangers, except those next to them at table
or in the drawing-room after dinner. The host therefore makes a few
introductions if necessary. Before dinner, since the hostess is standing
(and no gentleman may therefore sit down), and as it is awkward for
a lady who is sitting to talk with a gentleman who is standing, the
ladies usually also stand until dinner is announced.

WHEN DINNER IS ANNOUNCED

It is the duty of the butler to "count heads" so that he may know when the company has arrived. As soon as he has announced the last person, he notifies the cook. The cook being ready, the butler, having glanced into the dining-room to see that windows have been closed and the candles on the table lighted, enters the drawing room, approaches the hostess, bows, and says quietly, "Dinner is served." Or if she happens to be looking at him, he merely bows.

The host offers his right arm to the lady of honor and leads the way to the dining-room. All the other gentlemen offer their arms to the ladies appointed to them and follow the host, in an orderly procession, two and two; the only order of precedence is that the host and his partner lead, while the hostess and her partner come last. If by any chance a gentleman does not know the lady whose name is on the card in his envelope, he must find out who she is and be presented to her before he takes her in to dinner. At all formal dinners, place-cards being on the table, the hostess does not direct people where to sit. If there was no table diagram in the hall, the butler usually stands just within the dining-room door and tells each gentleman as he approaches, "Right" or "Left." He has plenty of time to reach the chair of the hostess before her, as she always enters the dining-room last.

WHEN THERE IS NO HOST

A hostess who is either a widow or unmarried asks the man she knows best—a relative if there is one present—to act as host. He gives his arm to the guest of honor and leads the way to the dining table, where he sits opposite the hostess. After dinner he leads the men to the smoking room and later to the drawing-room to "join the ladies."

THE MANNERS OF A HOSTESS

First of all, a hostess must show each of her guests equal and impartial attention. Also, although engrossed in the person she is talking to, she must be able to notice anything amiss that may occur. The more competent her servants, the less she need be aware of details herself, but the hostess giving a formal dinner with uncertain dining-room efficiency has a far from smooth path before her. No matter what happens, if all the china in the pantry falls with a crash, she must not appear to have heard it. No matter what goes wrong, she must cover it as best she can, and at the same time cover the fact that she is covering it. To give hectic directions merely accentuates the awkwardness. If a dish appears that is unpresentable, she as quietly as possible orders the next one to be brought in. If a guest knocks over a glass and breaks it, even though the glass be utterly irreplaceable, her only concern must seemingly be that her guest has been made uncomfortable. She says, "I am sorry!

But the glass is *nothing!*" And she has a fresh glass brought (even though it doesn't match) and dismisses all thought of the matter.

Both the host and hostess must keep the conversation going, if it lags, but this is not as definitely their duty at a formal as at an informal dinner. It is at the small dinner that the skilful hostess has need of what Thackeray calls the "showman" quality. She brings each guest forward in turn to the center of the stage. In a lull in the conversation she says beguilingly to a clever but shy man, "Harold, what was that story you told me—" and then she repeats briefly an introduction to a topic in which Harold particularly shines. Or later on, she begins a narrative and breaks off suddenly, turning to someone else, "*You* tell them!"

These examples are rather bald and overemphasize the method in order to make it clear. Practice and the knowledge of human nature, or of the particular temperament with which she is trying to deal, can alone tell her when she may lead or provoke this or that one to being at his best, to his own satisfaction as well as that of the others. Her own character and sympathy are the only real "showman" assets, since no one "shows" to advantage except in a congenial environment.

THE LATE GUEST

Fifteen minutes is the established length of time that a hostess may wait for a belated guest. To wait more than twenty minutes, at the outside, would be showing lack of consideration to many for the sake of one. When the late guest finally enters the dining room it is she who must go up to the hostess and apologize for being late. The hostess remains seated and the guest merely shakes hands quickly in order that all the men at table need not rise. The hostess must never take the guest to task, but should say something polite and conciliatory such as, "I was sure you did not want us to wait dinner!" In other days the newcomer was always served with dinner from the beginning unless she was considerate enough to direct the servant who held her chair, "Let me begin with this course." But today so many of the younger people are carelessly—on occasion even wilfully—late that it has become proper to bring no dish back after it has left the dining-room.

ETIQUETTE OF GLOVES AND NAPKIN

Ladies always wear gloves to formal dinners and take them off at table. Entirely off. It is hideous to leave them on the arm, merely turning back the hands. Both gloves and bag are supposed to be laid across the lap, and one is supposed to lay the napkin, folded once in half across the lap too, on top of the gloves and wrist bag, and all three are supposed to stay in place on a slippery satin skirt on a lap that more often than not slants downward.

It is all very well for etiquette to say, "They stay there," but every woman knows they don't! If you obey etiquette and lay the napkin on top of the bag and gloves loosely across your satin-covered knees, it will depend merely upon chance whether the avalanche starts right, left, or forward onto the floor. There is just *one* way to keep these three articles (including the lap as one) from disintegrating, which is to cover the gloves and wrist bag with the napkin put cornerwise across your knees, and tuck the two side corners under like a lap robe, with the gloves and bag tied in place, as it were.

This ought not to be put into a book of etiquette, which should say you must do nothing of the kind, but it is either do that or have the gentleman next to you groping under the table at the end of the meal; and it is impossible to imagine that etiquette should wish to conserve the picture of gentlemen-on-all-fours as a concluding ceremony at dinner.

A compact can be put on the table or added to the lap collection, as you choose, but a bag of even small size has no place on a dinner table.

THE TURNING OF THE TABLE

The "turning of the table" is accomplished by the hostess, who merely turns from the gentleman on her left probably with whom she has been talking through the soup and the fish courses to the one on her right. As she turns, the lady to whom the "right" gentleman has been talking turns to the gentleman farther on, and in a moment everyone at table is talking to a new neighbor. Sometimes a single couple who have become very much engrossed refuse to change partners, and the whole table is blocked, leaving one lady and one gentleman on either side of the block staring alone at their plates. At this point the hostess has to come to the rescue by attracting the blocking lady's attention and saying, "Sally, you cannot talk to Professor Bugge any longer! Mr. Warren has been trying his best to attract your attention."

Sally, being in this way brought awake, is obliged to pay attention to Mr. Warren, and Professor Bugge, little as he may feel inclined, must turn his attention to the other side. To persist in carrying on their own conversation at the expense of others would be inexcusably rude, not only to their hostess but to everyone present.

At a dinner not long ago, Mr. Kindhart, sitting next to Mrs. Wellborn and left to himself because of the assiduity of the lady's farther partner, slid his own name-card across and in front of her, to bring her attention to the fact that it was his turn. Other hostesses have been known to send a note by a servant saying, "Please talk to Mr. McKaye on your right."

ENEMIES MUST BURY HATCHETS

One unbreakable rule of etiquette is that you must talk to your next-door neighbor at a dinner table. You *must;* that is all there is about it!

Even if you are placed next to someone with whom you have had a bitter quarrel, consideration for your hostess, who would be distressed if she knew you had been put in a disagreeable place, and further consideration for the rest of the table which is otherwise blocked, exacts that you give no outward sign of your repugnance and that you make a pretense, at least for a little while, of talking together.

At dinner once, Mrs. Toplofty, finding herself next to a man she quite openly despised, said to him with apparent placidity, "I shall not talk to you—because I don't care to. But for the sake of my hostess I shall say my multiplication tables. Twice one are two, twice two are four—" and she continued on through the tables, making him alternate them with her. As soon as she politely could, she turned again to her other companion.

ON REFUSING A DISH

It used to be an offense, and it still is considered impolite, to refuse dishes at the table, because your refusal implies that you do not like what is offered you. If this is true, you should be doubly careful to take at least a little on your plate and make a pretense of eating some of it, since to refuse dish after dish cannot fail to distress your hostess. If you are on a diet and accepted the invitation with that stipulation, your not eating is excusable; but even then to sit with an empty plate in front of you throughout a meal makes you a seemingly reproachful table companion for those of good appetite sitting next to you.

STARTING A COMPLICATED DISH

When a dinner has been prepared by a chef who prides himself on being a decorative artist, the guest of honor and whoever else may be the first to be served have quite a problem to know which part of an intricate structure is to be eaten and what part is scenic effect.

The main portion is generally clear enough; the uncertainty is in whether the flowers are edible vegetables and whether the things that look like ducks are potatoes or trimming. If there are six or more, the chances are they are edible, and that very few of a kind are decorations only. Rings around food are nearly always to be eaten; platforms under food seldom, if ever, are. Anything that looks like pastry is to be eaten; and anything divided into separate units should be taken on your plate complete. You should not try to cut a section from anything that has already been divided into portions in the kitchen. Aspics and desserts are, it must be said, occasionally Chinese puzzles; but if, in taking what looks like something eatable, you do help yourself to part of the decoration, no great harm is done.

Dishes are never passed from hand to hand at a formal dinner or even at an informal one in a formally appointed house. Often people pass salted nuts to each other, or an extra sweet from a dish nearby, but not circling the table.

LEAVING THE TABLE

At the end of the dinner, when the last dish of sweets has been passed and the hostess sees that no one is any longer eating, she looks across the table and, catching the eye of one of the ladies, slowly stands up. The one who happens to be observing also stands up, and in a moment everyone is standing. The gentlemen offer their arms to their partners and conduct them back to the drawing-room or the library or wherever they are to sit during the rest of the evening.

Each gentleman then bows slightly, takes leave of his partner, and, with the other gentlemen, follows the host to the room where after-dinner coffee, liqueurs, and cigars and cigarettes are being passed. It is perfectly correct for a gentleman to talk to any other who happens to be sitting near him, whether he knows him or not.

At the end of twenty minutes or so, the host must take the opportunity of the first lull in the conversation to suggest that they "join the ladies" in the drawing-room.

In a house where there is no extra room to smoke in, the gentlemen do not conduct the ladies to the drawing-room, but stay where they are (the ladies leaving alone) and have their coffee, cigars, liqueurs, and conversation sitting around the table.

In the drawing-room, meanwhile, the ladies are having coffee, cigarettes, and liqueurs passed to them.

Coffee is served three ways: 1. The footman proffers a tray of cups, saucers, and sugar; the butler follows with coffee pot alone and pours into the cup held in the guest's hand. 2. A tray is proffered by the butler or the waitress to guests who help themselves. 3. The tray of cups and sugar is held on servant's left hand. The guest puts sugar into one of the cups and the servant pours coffee with the right hand.

Liqueurs are offered exactly as coffee in No. 2 and No. 3. The guests pour their own, or saying "Chartreuse" or "Mint, please" their choice is poured for them.

Cigarettes are arranged on a tray with matches, or a lighter which is burning. There is no modern New York hostess, scarcely even an old-fashioned one, who does not have cigarettes passed after dinner.

At a dinner of ten or twelve, the five or six ladies most often sit in one group, or possibly two sit by themselves, and three or four together; but at a very large dinner they inevitably fall into groups of four or five or so each. In any case, the hostess must see that no one is left to sit alone. If one of her guests is a stranger to the others, the hostess draws a chair near one of the groups and, offering it to her single guest, sits beside her. After a while, when this particular guest has at least joined the outskirts of the conversation of the group, the hostess leaves her and joins another group where perhaps she sits beside someone else who has been somewhat left out.

When there is no one who needs any especial attention, the hostess nevertheless sits for a time with each of the different groups in order to spend at least a part of the evening with all of her guests.

THE GENTLEMEN RETURN

When the gentlemen return to the drawing-room, if there is a particular lady whom one of them wants to talk to, he naturally goes directly to where she is and sits down beside her.

Usually, the ladies on the ends, being accessible, are more likely to be joined by the first gentlemen entering than is the one in the center, whom it is impossible to reach. This is, however, quite simply done. When John Jones particularly wants to talk with Miss Smith, he goes up to her, bows, and asks, "Will you come and talk to me?" Whereupon she leaves her sandwiched position, and goes to another part of the room and sits down wherever there are two vacant seats.

Needless to say, gentlemen should not continue to talk together after returning to the drawing-room, as it is not courteous to those of the ladies who are thus necessarily left without partners.

At informal dinners, and even at many formal ones, bridge tables are set up in an adjoining room, if not in the drawing-room. Those few who do not play bridge spend half an hour or less in conversation and then go home, unless there is some special diversion.

TAKING LEAVE

That the guest of honor must be the first to take leave was in former times so fixed a rule that everyone used to sit on and on, no matter how late it became, waiting for her whose duty it was to go. More often than not, the guest of honor was an absent-minded old lady, or celebrity, who very likely was vaguely saying to herself, "Oh, my! are these people *never* going home?" until by and by it dawned upon her, or someone reminded her, that the obligation was her own!

But today, although it is still the obligation of the guest who sat on the host's right to make the move to go, it is not considered ill-mannered, if the hour is growing late, for another lady to rise first. In fact, unless the guest of honor is one *really*, meaning a stranger or an elderly lady of distinction, there is no actual precedence about her being the first to go.

The guest merely says, "Good night. Thank you so much." The hostess answers, "I am so glad you could come!" She has already pressed a bell for the servants to be in the dressing rooms and halls. When one guest leaves, they all leave, except those at the bridge tables. They all say "Good night" to whomever they were talking with and shake hands, and then going up to their hostess, they shake hands and say, "Thank you for asking us," or else "Thank you for a very pleasant evening."

"Good night!" and "Thank you so much!" are the usual expressions. And the hostess answers, "It was so nice to see you again," or "I'm glad you could come."

In the dressing room, or in the hall, the maid is waiting to help the ladies with their wraps, and the butler is at the door. When Mr. and Mrs. Sewell are ready to leave, he goes out on the front steps and says, "Mr. Sewell's car!" The host's chauffeur signals to Mr. Sewell's chauffeur and then reports to the butler, who in turn says to Mr. Sewell, "Your car is at the door, Sir," and they go out.

The bridge people leave as they finish their games; sometimes a table at a time or most likely two together. (Husbands and wives are never, if it can be avoided, put at the same table.) Young people in saying good night say, "Good night. It was just wonderful!" or "Good night, and thank you *so* much." And the hostess smiles and says, "So glad you could come!" or "Good night!"

THE CURIOUS FAULT OF LATENESS

The point to make is that the habit of lateness is not the result of the inability of the habitually tardy to measure time (as their friends try to believe), but the result of a coldly calculated intention of a selfish woman (rarely a man) to make an entrance wherever she goes exactly as a star of the theatre makes her entrance on the stage. There is, however, an important difference. The entrance of the star is planned by the playwright and the producer; that of the latter by herself alone.

Hostesses have tried to solve the problem of late-arriving guests by advancing the dinner hour from the 7 P.M. of long ago to 8 P.M., but now an 8:30 dinner often stands waiting until 9. In other words, setting the dinner hour later has not been the answer. The one that shows best promise is that of wording the invitation:

Dinner at 8:15
Taking Places at Table at 8:30

In this case, host, hostess, and the majority of their guests take their places at table promptly and follow the Gilding pattern to the extent that a course that is no longer being eaten is not brought back. It is, however, proffered if the majority of the guests are still eating it.

To those who oppose this rudeness of the hosts to their guests, the reply is that it is hardly fair to the many who were courteously prompt to be required to wait overlong for food, which was quite possibly being despoiled of its perfection by this waiting.

THE STAG OR BACHELOR DINNER

A man's dinner is sometimes called a stag or a bachelor dinner and, as its name implies, is a dinner given by a man and for men only. A man's dinner is usually given to celebrate an occasion of welcome or farewell. The best-known bachelor dinner is the one given by the groom just before his wedding. Other dinners are more likely to be given by one man (or a group of men) in honor of a noted citizen who has returned from a long absence, or who is about to embark on an expedition or a foreign mission. Or a young man perhaps gives a dinner for a friend's twenty-first birthday; or an older man gives one merely because he has a quantity of game which he has shot and wants to share with his special friends.

Nearly always a man's dinner is given at the host's club or in a private room in a hotel. But if a man chooses to give a stag dinner in his own house, his wife (or his mother) should *not* appear. For a wife to come downstairs and receive the guests for him cannot be too strongly condemned as out of place. Such a maneuver on her part, instead of impressing his guests with her gracious hospitality, is far more likely to make them think what a "Mr. Milquetoast" her husband must be to allow himself to be henpecked. And for a mother to appear at a son's dinner is, if anything, worse. An essential piece of advice to every woman is: No matter how much you may want to say "How do you do" to your husband's or your son's friends—*don't!*

CHAIRMAN (OR TOASTMASTER) AT A PUBLIC DINNER

The chairman, or toastmaster or master of ceremonies, sits at the center of the most prominent table, usually on a dais.

After the dessert is served, the chairman rises and makes a few remarks, or perhaps a very short address on the association or object of the dinner, and ends with a reference to the first speaker, telling what he or she has accomplished, or is trying to accomplish, and then adds, "I have great pleasure in introducing Mr. Smith," or "It gives me great pleasure to introduce Mr. Smith" (or Miss Jones). The chairman sits down and the speaker stands up.

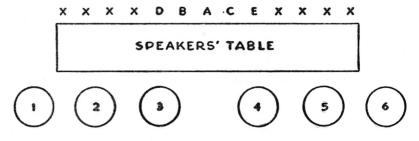

Key: A—Toastmaster; B—Guest of honor or most prominent person present; C, D, E—Other guests, ranking guests; XXXX—Those who will be called on to speak and other honored guests. 1, 2, 3, 4, 5, 6— General guest tables.

When the first speaker sits down, the chairman again stands, thanks the first speaker, and says something pleasant about his talk—that it was interesting, or delightful, or instructive, or whatever most aptly describes it—and then introduces the next speaker—probably with a brief reference to his especial qualifications. Or possibly he says, "Our next speaker is one who is known to, and loved by, us all: Professor Bugge." And so on throughout the list. The principal speaker is usually last on the program.

TOASTS

It is impossible to suggest definite toasts because they ought to be personal and spontaneous. Usually they are scarcely longer than the toast at the bridegroom's dinner: "To the bride!" "To the Professor! May he live to be a hundred and his teaching endure a thousand years." "To the team! Whether it win or lose, may it always be glorious."

At a dinner given by a group of young women in honor of their mothers, the chairman might give this toast: "To those to whom we owe all that we are, and for whom we would like to be all that they believe we are—Our Mothers!" Or, on the other hand, a group of mothers at a dinner given for their daughters might say: "To those of the newer generation who, in blazing new trails, carry our faith, our hopes, and our hearts' encouragement—a toast to our daughters!"

But as noted above, each toast ought to express the sentiment of the person proposing it. And the shorter it is, the better.

THE GREAT AMERICAN RUDENESS

The subject purposely saved for the conclusion of this chapter is one the importance of which cannot be overemphasized. In fact, it has, within the last ten years, become known almost throughout the civilized world as an astonishing American rudeness—or, at best, a sign of ignorance!

The outstanding rudeness is that of the hostess who helps herself first when a woman guest is seated at her table. In fact, if such a custom is to be allowed to continue spreading, what possible meaning remains in the word "courtesy"? Since consideration of those who are her guests is the very first rule of courteous behavior, the hostess who helps herself to the fresh and untouched dishes and then lets her only—or her most important—woman guest take her leavings is either unthinking (which is quite likely), or she is intentionally rude (which cannot be likely).

The custom threatens less than it did a few years ago, but the hostess who permits herself to be served before any woman guest at her table is still encountered in sufficiently numerous localities to make it of importance to try to trace the behavior to its separate origins.

Example No. 1—This goes back to the days of the Borgias, when hosts invited enemies to their tables with the intention of poisoning

them. It therefore became the duty of every innocent host or hostess
to partake of each dish or flagon first, to assure his guests that neither
food nor drink was poisoned. It was and still is customary, when fine
vintage wines are served, to pour about a teaspoonful into the host's
glass to see whether the wine is good. If not good, he orders another
bottle. But his glass is never filled until the last at table.

Example No. 2—In the crude days when frontier towns were rough,
many of the guests invited to a gentlewoman's table were quite unversed
in table manners. Their hostess, therefore, put them at ease not only
by helping herself to each dish first, but by eating first as well, so that
they who might know little about the use of table implements could
follow her example. But this behavior, which was proper then, is not—
and never has been—proper when the guests are quite as skilled as their
hostess in the use of a serving fork and a spoon. This "showing the
guests how" is the reason most often given by those who defend the
hostess-first practice. It would be hard to imagine a reason less polite.

Even if the dish is an architectural masterpiece like those of the
nineties, nothing is simpler for one who is served first than to say to
whoever is waiting at table, "Do I take this?" prodding lightly with
the fork, or "Do I cut here?" This is done every day. In fact, many New
Yorkers can well remember an old-time butler whose dishes were about
three parts ornament to one part food, and who frequently advised one
who had taken a dab of pink hominy foundation and a raw-turnip rose,
"The brown piece at the right, Madam, is very tasty." Or if a hostess
had reason to suppose her guest of honor may be embarrassed—an old
lady perhaps who does not see very well—then the dish might be cut
into and the serving spoon inserted beneath the first helping and the
fork in the hand above it, in the way a dish is prepared for a child who
does not otherwise know what or how much to take.

Example No. 3—There is a line of American tradition which traces
back to the patriarchal system where three or even four generations
lived at the old homestead when great-grandmother sat in her high-
backed, cushioned armchair at the head of her table, and first dishes
and first courtesy were shown to her because she was the matriarch.
When visitors came to meals, they were not likely to be as old as she, for
roads were too rough to entice old ladies from their firesides or gardens.
But this deferential practice of first serving a hostess who was very old
became an example of impropriety when copied by her newly married
granddaughter, who, without taking the trouble to think, jumped to
the conclusion that what grandmother did was right. Quite true! But
what was right for a great-grandmother surrounded by members of her
own family, is far from right for a hostess of twenty—or even of fifty,
at whose table sit neighbors or strangers. There is no difference whatever between the rudeness of a hostess who chooses the piece she prefers
and gives second choice to a guest, and the rudeness of a child who helps

herself to her own choice pieces of candy, and then hands the discarded pieces to the child who has come to play with her.

Example No. 4—Royalty, when seated with the nobility or commoners, is served first (for that matter, is served from set-apart dishes). This has nothing to do with us unless it points out the presumption of one who considers herself royalty and her friends of a lower class!

Example No. 5—The occasional discourtesy in the house of the well-born but absent-minded hostess who is carelessly unaware of what her badly trained butler or waitress is doing. This does not affect those who, knowing better, neither care nor notice, but it does affect Mrs. Littletown, whose worldly experience has not been very wide, and who goes home and unquestioningly copies what she has seen young Mrs. Smartan Careless let her butler do. A number of her friends in turn copy her. And so it goes!

Example No. 6—This is not really so much an example as a contributing cause. Exactly as it is the natural instinct of an office employee to devote his energies to his employer rather than to anyone else, this same impulse is characteristic of the domestic employee. Today wages are paid usually by the lady of the house; therefore those in her employ will be inclined to serve her first unless otherwise directed—and on occasion persistently directed.

Example No. 7—And perhaps the principal offender against good taste is self-styled schools for domestic employees which teach (so it is said) this misbehavior. When a pupil from this school serves the first meal in the house of Mrs. Fastidious, this first rudeness is the last. But a new employer, who is perhaps for the first time engaging a butler, hesitates to criticize his manner of serving, no matter what it may be; and this adds still another link to the chain of rudeness, as she does not dare to insist that he serve another lady first. When only gentlemen are present, the hostess is of course served first, because she is the only lady.

MODERN DINNER-GIVING

IN THE PRECEDING CHAPTER EVERY INFLEXIBLE REQUIRE-
ment of a correctly formal dinner was given in detail. This was not
meant to discourage dinner-giving by those whose houses are not
equipped to comply with its exactions, but was intended merely as the
complete pattern from which each hostess may select or adapt as many
details as are practical for her personal use.

Perhaps in time the term formal dinner may come to mean nothing more exacting than company at dinner, but correctly the term formal
dinner or dinner of ceremony, which means the same thing, can be
applied only to the most exacting and most ceremonious social function
that exists.

THREE CLASSIFICATIONS OF TABLE SERVICE

There are three classifications of table service: the first is formal
service—described in the preceding chapter and permitting no deviation
from ceremonious forms; second, a semi-formal service which may be
as elaborate as the first with a butler assisted by footmen, a butler and
a parlor maid, or the service may be by a waitress with or without
assistance of another maid. This second classification is infinitely flexible and is used for nearly all dinner parties given today; third, hostess-
alone service, which, as the term implies, is the most difficult as well as
most important of the three, since it is practiced in an ever-increasing
number of American homes.

THE SEMI-FORMAL SERVICE

Semi-formal service can be quite as elaborate—in so far as having
many servants and following an exacting ritual is concerned—as that
in the most formally run house. Or it can, on the other hand, be adapted
to whatever is most practical for each family's particular needs.

This semi-formal service is perhaps best illustrated by considering
that in the house of the Squires. Mr. Squire, for instance, carves at table,

and Mrs. Squire pours after-dinner coffee in the living-room. Otherwise every detail of table-setting and dinner service is fromal.

Mr. Squire's practice of carving the meat at the table is more complicated as well as slower than completely formal service. This is because in the latter case the carving is all done by the cook in the kitchen, while the soup or fish is being eaten. But in the almost-formal house of Mr. Squire there is an obstructingly long ritual—preceding the meat course—of exchanging used fish plates for clean plates all around the table; and then putting one hot plate in front of Mr. Squire, waiting for it to be filled, taking it up with the right hand, putting a fresh hot plate in front of Mr. Squire with the left hand, picking up the plate of the one to be served and putting down the filled plate; going to the side table, leaving the exchanged plate, getting a fresh hot plate, returning to Mr. Squire, and repeating the same procedure. Each time a plate is filled, the butler or waitress takes the plate with the serving on it where he or she is told—"For Mrs. Jones," "For Miss Mary," "For Mr. Jones," and so on.

A much simpler method of service for the host who wishes to carve is to put a stack of hot plates in front of him, and let the maid lift each plate as it is served, and take it to the one for whom it is intended. When all have been served with this course, she passes the vegetables in serving dishes.

At the Neighbors' at the opposite end of the scale, the family of eight is waited on by one maid, who sets a stack of soup plates in front of Mr. Neighbor and then the soup tureen. Mr. Neighbor ladles the soup and the maid carries it to each in turn, and then goes back to the kitchen.

Water is in all the glasses and bread and butter on each bread and butter plate when the family sit down. When she is rung for, the maid takes away the plates two at a time, stacks them quietly on the serving table behind the screen, and then carries out the tureen. Then she brings in the stack of hot dinner plates and sets them in front of Mr. Neighbor, who puts a piece of meat—also gravy, stuffing, or condiment—on the plate at the top of the pile, and then, when it is filled, hands it either right or left to be passed from hand to hand to the person for whom it is intended (in front of whom no formal place plate stands); meanwhile the maid brings in the vegetables (a double or triple dish is most practical) and proffers this to each person who has been served the meat. She also proffers bread and pours water as necessary. As she returns to the kitchen, she carries out the used soup plates. Dessert or salad is served by Mrs. Neighbor and passed by the maid, who then carries the coffee tray into the living-room.

For details of dinner-giving in a house that has no servants, see Chapter 31, and also read the sections on buffet parties and big dinners at little tables in Chapter 32.

INFORMAL TABLE-SETTING

The table must be larger than the table set for formal service, because room must be left for the tea service or the soup tureen at one end, and for the meat or fish platter at the other, and quite probably for the vegetable dishes in between. Otherwise the setting is much the same. Table cover of what you please—damask or runners or doilies, or bare table with place mats—centerpiece, candlesticks, or candelabra for evening light.

The first change from the formal arrangement is that, instead of limiting forks to three, all flat silver to be used is put at each place. As always, the silver to be used last is put nearest the plate, the one to be used first on the outside. The service plate, which is an inseparable item of formal service, is put on the informal table only when it is to be used. Otherwise each place at the table is left plateless.

In many houses, the salad ingredients are attractively arranged in a set of bowls and bottles that, with the salad bowl, are put in front of the hostess, who mixes the dressing herself. In one of the loveliest old houses in the South, salad-mixing is a veritable ritual—and goodness only knows what goes into the mixture. A few drops of this, or shakes of that, or spoonfuls of the other, all stirred with a wooden fork and spoon. It is quite wonderful! And surely its deliciousness is accented by the display of its making.

The same idea exactly has made certain restaurants in Paris famous —all because the head waiter, or the proprietor himself, cooks and mixes something before your eyes. The ducks of the "Tour d'Argent," the Crêpes Suzette of Joseph, seem to acquire an added allure by the visible process. In short, preparing a dish at the table (which many servantless hostesses think of as a handicap) may easily become an especially appreciated feature of hospitality.

Many hostesses make a practice of always setting the table for four when there are to be four or any lesser number for a meal. At the extra or "dummy" places, water, bread and butter are not served.

INFORMAL SERVICE OF COFFEE

The most popular informal way of serving coffee is to place a good-sized tray on a coffee-table or stand. On the tray is a percolator or other coffee-making machine—most pleasingly one of glass, which is enticing to watch, whereas an opaque one merely emphasizes the time you have to wait for the coffee to be made. You, when you are hostess, sit near this tray, turn on the switch or light the lamp, make the coffee, pour it, asking each guest "How many lumps of sugar?" and "Cream?"— cream is now offered even with after-dinner coffee—and hand it exactly as at afternoon tea.

CAFÉ BRÛLOT

In many houses of the South of yesterday, making *café brûlot* was an established ritual. On a huge silver tray was arranged a collection of little dishes and boxes holding slivers of lemon rind, cloves, allspice, aloes, granulated sugar, cinnamon, a decanter of brandy, a pot of very black, freshly made coffee, and a deep silver bowl and ladle. Into the bowl went a variety of spices, and over these brandy was poured, lemon rind was squeezed, and the brandied spices pressed and stirred. The brandy was then lighted, and while it blazed high the coffee was poured in little by little and all the time the ladle, stirring and dipping and pouring back, kept the alcohol burning. Often the lamps were momentarily carried out of the room so that the beauty of the blazing coffee was accentuated. When the alcohol had burned out, the lights were brought back (today more prosaically the electric lights could be turned off and on again), and the coffee was ladled into cups. Like salad-making, it was a charming custom. It is almost unknown today, and is described here in the hope of encouraging its return to fashion. See one modern recipe for this old-time favorite on page 412.

DISHES WITH ACCOMPANYING CONDIMENTS

But let us return to further details concerned with the subject of informal dinners in a house with limited equipment. In other words, let us consider the choice of dishes which do not require accessories.

Nothing so delays the service of a dinner as dishes that must immediately be followed by gravy, condiment, or other dishes. If there is only one person to do the serving, it is wise to include no dish on the menu—unless you are only two or three at table—that is not complete in itself.

For instance, fish nearly always has an accompanying dish. Broiled fish, or fish *meunière*, has ice-cold cucumbers sliced thin as a wafer, with a very highly seasoned French dressing, or a mixture of cucumbers and tomatoes. Boiled fish always has mousseline, Hollandaise, mushroom, or egg sauce, and even if covered with sauce when served, is customarily followed by additional sauce and small, round, boiled potatoes sprinkled with parsley.

Many meats have condiments. Roast beef is never served at a dinner party—it is a family dish and generally has Yorkshire pudding or roast potatoes on the platter with the roast itself, and is often followed by pickled or spiced fruit.

Turkey likewise, with chestnut stuffing and accompanying cranberry jelly and giblet sauce. is not a company dish, though excellent for an informal dinner. Lamb has mint sauce or mint jelly.

Partridge or guinea hen must be followed by a tray with two sauceboats—one with browned bread crumbs, and the other with hot bread sauce. Applesauce goes with barnyard duck.

The epicure does not enjoy a wild duck cooked more than sixteen minutes in a very hot oven, but he does like it accompanied by celery salad.

SPECIAL MENUS OF UNACCOMPANIED DISHES

One person can wait faultlessly on many people if dishes which need no supplements are chosen. And yet many housekeepers thoughtlessly order dishes such as those listed above, and then wonder why the dinner is so hopelessly slow when their waitress is really so good.

The following suggestions are merely offered in illustration; each housekeeper can easily devise further for herself. It is not necessary to pass anything whatever with melon, or grapefruit, or a *macédoine* of fruit, or a canapé. Oysters, on the other hand, should be followed by tabasco and buttered brown bread or layered brown and white bread. Soup needs nothing with it (if you do not choose split pea, which needs croutons, or *petite marmite*, which needs grated cheese). Fish dishes, if made with sauce in the dish, such as *sole au vin blanc*, lobster Newburg, crab *ravigote*, fish mousse, especially if in a ring filled with plenty of sauce, do not need anything more. Tartar sauce for fried fish can be put in baskets made of hollowed-out lemon rind—a basket for each person—and used as a garnishing around the dish, though it is preferable, when possible, to garnish the dish with pieces of lemon and pass the sauce separately.

Filet mignon or fillet of beef, duly surrounded by little clumps of vegetables, shares with chicken casserole the distinction of being the dinner-party life-saver of the hostess who has no one to help her one servant in the dining-room. Another dish, but more appropriate to lunch than to dinner, is of French chops banked against mashed potatoes or purée of chestnuts, and surrounded by string beans or peas; or a crown roast of lamb with peas in the center, mint jelly in small pastry cups, and potato croquettes as a garnish. None of these dishes require any following dish whatever, not even a vegetable.

Fried chicken with corn fritters on the platter is almost as good as the two beef dishes, since the one green vegetable which should go with it can be served leisurely, because fried chicken is not quickly eaten. And a ring of aspic with salad in the center does not require accompanying crackers as immediately as plain lettuce.

Steak and broiled chicken are fairly practical since neither needs gravy, condiment, nor sauce.

THE POSSIBILITIES OF THE PLAIN COOK

In giving informal or little dinners, you need never worry because you cannot set the dishes prescribed for a formal dinner before your guests, friends or even strangers, so long as the food that you are offering is good of its kind.

It is by no means necessary that your cook should be able to make the clear soup required for a formal dinner, which is so difficult to make and so expensive; nor is it necessary that she be able to construct comestible mosaics and sculptures. The essential thing is to prevent her from attempting anything she can't do well and let her stick to the dishes she knows how to make. And remember, the more pretentious a dish is, the more it challenges criticism.

If your cook can make neither clear nor cream soup, but can make a delicious clam chowder, better far to have a clam chowder! And the same way throughout dinner. Whichever dishes your own Nora or Selma can do best are the ones you must have for your dinners. And most important of all, let her experiment with new dishes when you are alone with your family and not when you have company.

Another thing: It is not important to have variety. If you gave the Normans chicken casserole the last time they dined with you, that is no reason why you should not give it to them again—if it is the "specialty of your house," as the French say.

A late, and greatly loved, hostess whose Sunday luncheons at a huge country house just outside Washington were for years one of the outstanding features of Washington's smartest society, had clam broth, fried chicken, and pancakes, week after week, year after year. Those who went to her house knew just as well what the dishes would be as they did where the dining-room was situated. At her few enormous and formal dinners in town, her chef was allowed to be magnificently architectural; but if you dined with her alone, the chances were ten to one that Sunday chicken and pancakes would be served.

This illustrates a point that most hostesses fail to take advantage of. Most people like really good "specialty" dishes and look forward to them when dining again in the same house.

DO NOT EXPERIMENT FOR STRANGERS

Typical dinner-party dishes are invariably the temptation no less than the downfall of ambitious ignorance. Never let an inexperienced cook attempt a new dish for company, no matter how attractive her description of it may sound. Try it when you are having family or most intimate friends who will understand, if it turns out all wrong, that it is a "trial" dish. In fact, it is a very good idea to share the testing of it with someone who can help you with suggestions if they are needed for its improvement.

Or suppose you have a cook who is rather poor on all dinner dishes, but makes delicious bread, and cake, and waffles, and oyster stew, scrambled eggs, or even hash! You can make a specialty of asking people to supper. Suppers are necessarily informal, but after all, formal parties play a very small rôle compared to informal ones.

PROPER DISHING

The dishing is almost as important as the cooking; a smear or thumb-mark on the edge of a dish is like a spot on the front of a dress.

Water must not be allowed to collect at the bottom of a dish. That is why a folded napkin is always put under boiled fish and asparagus. And dishes must be hot; they cannot be too hot. Meat juice that has started to crust is nauseating.

Sending in tepid food is about the worst fault (next to not knowing how to cook) that a cook can have.

On the other hand, food that is supposed to be thoroughly chilled must be just that.

BLUNDERS IN SERVICE

If an inexperienced servant blunders, you should pretend, if you can, not to have noticed it. Never attract anyone's attention to anything by apologizing or explaining, unless the accident happens to a guest. Taking the servant to task makes the situation worse, for the original trouble was probably due to nervousness. Speak, if it is necessary to direct her, gently as well as kindly; your object is to restore confidence, not to increase the disorder. Beckon her to you and say quietly, "Mrs. Smith has no fork." Never let her feel that you think her stupid, but encourage her as much as possible; and when she does anything especially well, remember after the guests have gone to tell her so.

THE ENCOURAGEMENT OF PRAISE

Nearly all people are quick to censure but rather slow to praise. Admonish, of course, where you must, but censure only with justice; and don't forget that whether of high estate or humble, we all like deserved praise. When a guest tells you your dinner is the best he has ever eaten, remember that the cook cooked it, and tell her what he said. Or if the dining-room service was silent, and quick, and perfect, then tell whoever served it how well it was done. If you are entertaining all the time, you need not commend your household after every dinner you give, but if any especial willingness, attentiveness, or tact is shown, don't forget that a little praise is not only merest justice, but is a very inexpensive repayment for good work.

GIVING A SUCCESSFUL DINNER

What do we mean by a successful dinner? Does it mean the snob's satisfaction in the importance of those who accepted his invitation? Or does it mean the perfectionist's satisfaction in the knowledge that every detail was smoothly flawless? Or does it mean that every minute of the evening sped by gaily, and that everyone lingered late and at that was loath to go?

DO WHATEVER YOU CAN DO WELL

The last-named success is the real success. The first requirement for successful dinner-giving is skill in selection of a few or many friends who find each other amusing, or entertaining, or at least agreeable, and who have a pleasant evening at your home. And this costs not a cent. A second requirement is provision of food and service, which, since the dinner is not a formal one, can be whatever you choose or whatever you can best provide.

BUT DON'T CALL IT FORMAL!

Of course a hostess may offer her guests steak smothered in onions, Brussels sprouts, and whatever else she chooses for a company dinner. But she must not call this meal "formal" because this word in its proper sense means a dinner of ceremony, for which the menu must be limited to definitely prescribed dishes, which include steak only when cut into small rounds of tenderloin. But if she is actually having a friendly dinner to which she is inviting intimate friends, there is only one objection to her steak, onions, and Brussels sprouts—and that is the penetrating odor of frying or any cooking of the cabbage or onion families. The one thing every hostess tries to avoid is the risk of the smell of cooking. But if her kitchen is so shut off from the rest of her house and so well ventilated that she can avoid this handicap, then that is all right. In fact, as has been said many times in this book, the best menus to provide are those which her own kitchen does best!

DINNER OR SUPPER?

Whether a meal is correctly called dinner or supper depends upon what is served. At dinner, soup is always served in plates (with rims) and eaten with a tablespoon. Coffee is always black and served in half-sized cups after dinner. At supper, soup is served in cups or bowls. Coffee is served with cream in breakfast cups during the meal. There is also a difference in the menu, such as a roast with dinner, and minced or hashed or other made-over meat, or else cold meat for supper.

BREAKFASTS, LUNCHEONS,
AND SUPPERS

·⊰[30]⊱·

ALTHOUGH THE ENGRAVED CARD IS OCCASIONALLY USED
for an elaborate luncheon, especially for one given in honor of a noted
person, formal invitations to lunch are nearly always written in the
first person, and rarely sent out more than a week in advance. For
instance:

> Dear Mrs. Kindhart (or Martha):
>   Will you lunch with me on Monday the tenth at half
> after one o'clock?
>   Hoping so much for the pleasure of seeing you,
>   Sincerely (or Affectionately)
>   Jane Toplofty

The word "lunch" is used in best society much more than luncheon.
"Luncheon" is rarely if ever spoken, but it is written in third-person
invitations, and in books like this one.

If the above luncheon were given in honor of somebody—Mrs. Eminent, for instance—the phrase "to meet Mrs. Eminent" would have been
added immediately after the word "o'clock." If it is a very large luncheon for which the engraved card might be used, "To meet Mrs. Eminent" is written across the top of the card or invitation. It is by no means
necessary to give either a dinner or lunch for anyone. In fact it is probable that not more than one out of a thousand luncheon invitations are
"to meet" a guest of honor.

THE FORMAL LUNCHEON OF TODAY

Luncheon, being a daylight function, is never so formidable as a
dinner, even though it may differ from the latter in minor details only.
Luncheons are generally given by and for women, but it is not unusual,
especially in summer places or in town on Saturday or Sunday, to include an equal number of men.

But no matter how large or formal a lunch may be, the hostess, instead of receiving at the door, sits usually in the center of the room in some place that has an unobstructed approach from the door. Each guest coming into the room is preceded by the butler to within a short speaking distance of the hostess, where he announces the new arrival's name and then stands aside. A waitress does the same only if she can announce names distinctly and with ease and dignity. Otherwise the guests greet the hostess unannounced. The hostess rises, or if standing, takes a step forward, shakes hands, says, "I'm so glad to see you" or "I am delighted to see you." She then waits for a second or two to see whether the guest who has just come in speaks to anyone; if not, she makes the necessary introduction.

When the butler or waitress has "counted heads" and knows the guests have arrived, he or she notifies the kitchen and then enters the room and merely approaches the hostess and bows slightly. But if it is necessary to attract the hostess's attention, he or she says, "Luncheon is served."

If there is a guest of honor, the hostess leads the way to the dining-room, walking beside her. Otherwise, the guests go in in twos or threes, or even singly, just as they happen to come, except that the very young make way for their elders, and gentlemen stroll in with those they happen to be talking to, or, if alone, fill in the rear. The gentlemen never offer their arms to ladies in going in to a luncheon—unless there should be an elderly guest of honor, who might be taken in by the host, as at a dinner. And even then the others follow informally.

THE TABLE

Candles have no place on a lunch or breakfast table, and are used only if there should happen, on a very dark day and in an ordinarily dark room, not to be enough daylight to see to eat comfortably. Also a plain tablecloth, which must always be put on top of a thick table felt, is correct for dinner but not for luncheon. In other words, we dine and breakfast on damask, but we lunch on lace. We also lunch on damask if it be colored. Traditionally the lunch table is "bare"—which may perhaps mean bare between the place mats which may be made in literally unrestricted varieties of linen, needlework, or lace.

If the table is a refectory one, instead of place mats and a bare center, the table is set with a runner not reaching to the edge at the side, but falling over both ends. Or there may be an embroidered table-cloth made to fit the top of the table to within an inch or two of its edge.

The decorations of the table are practically the same as for dinner: flowers or an ornament in the center, and two or four dishes of fruit or candy where they look best. If the table is very large and rather too bare without candles, four slim vases with small sprigs of flowers to match those in the centerpiece—or any other glass or silver ornaments —are often added.

The places are set as for dinner, with a place plate, three forks, two knives, and a small spoon. The lunch napkin, which should match the table linen, is much smaller than the dinner napkin, and is not folded quite the same: it is folded like a handkerchief, in only four folds (four thicknesses). The square is laid on the plate diagonally, with the mono-grammed (or embroidered) corner pointing down toward the edge of the table. The upper corner is then turned sharply under in a flat crease for about a quarter of its diagonal length; then the two sides are rolled loosely under, making a sort of pillow effect laid sideways; with a straight top edge and a pointed lower edge, and the monogram displayed in the center. Or it can be folded in any simple way one prefers. If, as in the house of a hostess who has no waitress (see Chapter 31), it is not practical to put the napkin on the service plate, the best way to fold it when it is to be laid on the table is to fold its square of four thicknesses once again, perpendicularly, like a narrow book, and place it to the left of the plate on which the first course has been put.

Another feature of lunch service, which is always omitted at a formal dinner, is the bread and butter plate.

THE BREAD AND BUTTER PLATE

The bread and butter plate is part of the luncheon service always —as well as of breakfast and supper. It is put at the left side of each plate just above the forks. Butter is sometimes put on the plate before the meal, but usually it is passed. It should be served as butter balls, or curls rather than in squares. Hot breads are an important feature of every luncheon; hot crescents, soda biscuits, bread biscuits, dinner rolls, or corn bread, the latter baked in small shallow pans like pie plates three to four inches in diameter. At all events several breads are passed as often as necessary. Butter is also passed throughout the meal until the table is cleared for dessert. Bread and butter plates are always re-moved immediately before dessert, with the saltcellars and pepperpots.

THE SERVICE OF LUNCH

The formal service is identical with that of dinner. Carving is done in the kitchen and no food set on the table, except ornamental dishes of fruit, candy, and nuts. The plate service is also the same as at dinner. The places are never left plateless, except after salad, when the table is cleared and crumbed for dessert. The dessert plates and fingerbowls are arranged as for dinner.

THE LUNCH MENU

Five courses at most (not counting the passing of ornamental sweets or after-dinner coffee as a course), or more usually four actual courses, are sufficient for the longest and the most elaborate luncheon possible. For example:

1. Fruit, or soup in cups
2. Eggs or shellfish
3. Fowl and vegetables
4. Salad
5. Dessert

In New York the menu for lunch eaten in a private house is seldom more than four courses and would eliminate either No. 1, 2, or 5.

The most popular fruit course is either melon, grapefruit, or a mixture of fresh orange and grapefruit, or a little pineapple; any sort of fruit cut into very small pieces, with sugar and maraschino, or rum, or ordinary preserved apricots for flavor, served in special bowl-shaped glasses that fit into long-stemmed and much larger ones, with a space for crushed ice between; or it can just as well be put in champagne glasses, after being kept as cold as possible in the refrigerator until sent to the table.

Soup at luncheon, or at a wedding breakfast or a ball supper, is never served in soup plates, but in two-handled cups, and is eaten with a teaspoon or a bouillon spoon, or after it has cooled sufficiently it is drunk from the cup which is lifted to the mouth with both hands. It is limited to a few varieties: either chicken or clam broth, with a spoonful of whipped cream on top; or bouillon, or green turtle, or strained chicken, or tomato broth; or in summer, cold chicken, vichyssoise, beef, or tomato bouillon.

Lunch-party egg dishes must number a hundred varieties. (See any cook book.) Eggs that are substantial and rich, such as eggs Benedict, or stuffed with *pâté de foie gras* and a mushroom sauce, should then be balanced by a simple meat, such as broiled chicken and salad, combining meat and salad courses in one. On the other hand, should you have a light egg course, like "eggs surprise," you could have meat and vegetables, and plain salad; or an elaborate salad and no dessert. Or with fruit and soup, omit eggs, especially if there is to be an aspic with salad.

The menu of an informal luncheon, if it does not leave out a course, at least chooses simpler dishes: a bouillon or broth, shirred eggs or an omelette; or scrambled eggs on toast which has first been spread with a *pâté* or meat purée; then chicken or a chop with vegetables, a salad of plain lettuce with crackers and cheese, and a pudding, or pie, or any other family dessert. Or broiled chicken, chicken croquettes, or an aspic is served with the salad in very hot weather. While cold food is both appropriate and palatable, no meal should ever be chosen without at least one course of hot food. Many people dislike cold food, and it disagrees with others; but if you offer your guests hot soup (or at supper, tea or chocolate), it would then do to have the rest of the meal cold.

All of the menus suggested above are for lunch parties. If one invites women one knows are trying to diet, the menu would of course be shorter and simpler. In other words, when lunching with intimate friends one has the kind of food one knows they like.

LUNCHEON BEVERAGES

At women's lunch parties in very conservative houses, cocktails are seldom proffered, and if they are, there are always non-alcoholic as well as stronger ones; but a light Rhine wine, sauterne, or claret, or a fruit cup is served at table. If men are present, cocktails are passed in most communities; but always—at no matter what sort of party—there must be tomato or fruit juice for those who do not like alcohol. Nothing is in worse taste than forcing any guest either to take alcohol or else to sit conspicuously empty-handed.

At the family lunch table it is a widespread American custom for the lady of a house to have the tea set put before her at the table, not only when alone, but when having friends lunching with her, and to pour tea, coffee, or chocolate. Such hot beverages are served only in old-fashioned communities and at the family table, but iced tea, coffee, and chocolate are admitted to summer lunch tables everywhere.

Iced tea at lunch is prepared like a "cup" with lemon and sugar, and sometimes with cut-up fresh fruit or a little squeezed fruit juice, and it is poured into glasses often decorated with sprigs of fresh mint at each place. But coffee should be passed around in a glass pitcher on a tray that also holds a bowl of powdered sugar and a pitcher of cold milk, and another of cream as thick as possible. The guests pour their coffee to suit themselves into tall glasses half full of broken ice, and are furnished with very long-handled spoons.

A BRIDGE LUNCH AT THREE TABLES

If you are one of those who have a very small dining-room or perhaps no dining-room at all, but have a large living-room or perhaps a wide veranda, or if you live in a rainless climate that permits tables to be set either in a patio or out on the lawn, a luncheon of twelve, followed perhaps by bridge, is not only one of the nicest parties imaginable, but not beyond the possibilities of a simple house.

Preparations are much the same as those for a big dinner at little tables (see Index). Each card table should be set with a damask cloth, either white or pastel color, a yard and a half square, which is much the best covering for lunch as well as dinner on small tables. Any other style of small tablecloth will of course do, but they should, if possible, be exactly alike. Better to have simple matched ones than assorted elaborate ones. You set your places as at every table, the amount of silver depending upon your menu.

If you were giving a formal lunch and had two servants to wait at table, there would be no food at the places. But under the usual circumstances of having only one maid to wait on more than eight, it would be much easier for her to put the cold soup in a cup (or hot soup in little individual pots with covers) at each place before people were seated. While they are eating their soup, she passes the rolls and then pours iced tea from a big pitcher into the glasses which are already on the table, with cracked ice in them. A great saving in service would be to have your service plates hot, so that when the maid carries away the last soup cup on its saucer, the service plates are all ready to be used for the main course, which she then passes.

At card tables the main course plates are removed one in each hand, before a salad course previously arranged on each plate, or before dessert if there is to be no salad. After lunch, you and your guests go elsewhere for coffee, which you make and pour.

While you are drinking your coffee, the maid has time to clear the tables and reset them with two packs of unopened new cards, three sharpened pencils (one extra one in case a point breaks), and two score pads. Other bridge parties are listed in the Index.

AFTER-THE-MEAL ICE WATER

On a hot summer day when people have been playing cards for an hour or a little over, the maid should bring in a tray with a large pitcher of ice water and perhaps another pitcher of iced tea and put it down on a convenient table. The one thing that hostesses tend to forget is that five people out of six long for a drink of water in the afternoon more than anything else. In occasional very hospitable houses sandwiches and cookies are brought in in addition to the iced tea, but these are not necessary when bridge is following a luncheon. If you were inviting people to come at three and play for the afternoon, light refreshments would be considered necessary between half past four and five o'clock.

BREAKFAST

The menu of a hunt breakfast can be that of either a breakfast or a luncheon. There may be coffee with cream, cereal and wheat cakes, or typical luncheon dishes. The breakfast may be a buffet with a side board covered with such dishes as grilled kidneys, ham and eggs, scrambled eggs, corned beef hash with poached eggs and, perhaps, broiled sausages.

Regular weekly stand-up breakfasts are given by hospitable people who have big places in the country and encourage their neighbors to drive over on the day when they are "at home"—usually Saturday or Sunday.

SUPPERS

Supper is the most intimate meal there is, and since none but family or nearest friends are generally included, invitations are by word of mouth.

The atmosphere of a luncheon is often formal, but informal lunches and suppers differ in nothing except day and evening lights, and clothes. We occasionally have strangers at our informal luncheons, but we keep our suppers for our families and intimate friends.

THE SUPPER TABLE

The table is set, as to places and napery, exactly like the lunch table, with the addition of candlesticks or candelabra or both, as at dinner. The supper table differs from the usual lunch table, however, in this: in front of the hostess is a big silver tea tray with full silver service for tea, chocolate, or breakfast coffee, most often chocolate or cocoa, and either tea or coffee. At the host's end of the table there may be a chafing-dish—if the host likes to cook.

Many hospitable people, whose houses are run with plenty of servants, love to give informal Sunday-night suppers on their servants' Sundays out, and forage for themselves. And in the thousands of houses which have no servants at all, this same Sunday-night custom is equally possible. The table is left set; a cold dish of something and salad are left in the refrigerator; the ingredients for one or two hot dishes that can be quickly cooked either on the stove or in chafing-dishes on the supper table itself. (For the serious aspects of cooking parties given by chef-hosts, see Chapter 34.)

COOK, WAITRESS, AND
CHARMING HOSTESS!

·◦[31]◦·

THE ESPECIAL INTENTION OF THIS CHAPTER IS TO ANSWER
the problems of the hostess who has not only to cook the dinner but to
serve it without ever leaving the table. This is because at the first
gesture she makes to rise, every man instantly springs to his feet. No
matter how earnestly she asks them to stay where they are, up they
get and after her they go.

The following directions are therefore especially written for you,
my favorite reader, who in addition to being a charming hostess, have
not only cooked the dinner but are prepared to serve it to six—or possibly eight—of your guests, and to do this without once leaving the table.

First of all, you set your table according to the formal pattern.
Centerpiece of flowers or fruit flanked by candlesticks or candelabra.
You set the places with whatever flat silver and glasses will be needed
for your menu.

Service plates (even hot ones which are very useful when the first
course is to be passed by a waitress) must be omitted. It is proper—
because practical—to put the first course on the table just before your
guests go in to dinner.

Two items of equipment that you cannot do without are a pair of
sturdy serving tables: one to stand at the side of your husband's chair
and the other next your own. These are to be used for supplies and discards. The easiest to find are the plain, early American oblong sofa end
tables from 10″ to 12″ deep by 22″ to 25″ wide. They have two shelves
below the top, and they come in every sort of wood, and are for sale in
every furniture department. The bottom shelves are to put the used
dishes on, and the middle shelves for supplies and later-used dishes. On
the top of your own table you probably put the dessert, while the
salad goes on the top of the table next to your husband (half of the
salad plates on top of half of the dessert plates on your second shelf,
the duplicate half of both on your husband's shelf). Also on top of

your table are finger rolls and melba toast in a bread basket (for these no butter is necessary). If you are serving claret or other red wine, it is of course decantered and put on the table in one or more, probably two, decanters. White wine is left in its napkin-wrapped cold bottle in a silver coaster on the table. Thermos pitchers of water on either side of the table are most practical because they don't drip.

FLOOR-STANDING LAZY SUSANS

If you live in an early American or Georgian house and have a fairly large dining-room, a pair of floor-standing Lazy Susans are a double delight. The eighteenth century cabinet-makers called them dumbwaiters. A big round tray at the bottom with two or three others diminishing in size above revolve on a pole that has wide-spread claw feet and a little finial at the top—it looks like a Christmas tree.

Old ones are rare, even in museums, but any competent cabinet maker could make a pair without difficulty and in the height and circumference best suited to your needs.

The pattern of the tray for either type of Susan is that of any Chippendale or Sheraton pedestal table.

Possibly modern reproductions may be found in the better furniture stores.

PLAN YOUR MENU CAREFULLY

If you are fortunate enough to own a silver roast-beef platter with a huge silver cover, you can perfectly well include both soup and roast in your menu, because the silver cover which is also ornamental—when kept polished—will hide the roast and keep it hot during the eating of a soup course. Otherwise you will probably find it best either to omit the soup, or choose a meat course other than a roast.

For example, if you begin with soup, the meat course is perhaps a veal and ham pie, or chicken casserole, or sliced turkey with mushrooms, or chicken à la king—kept HOT in a chafing-dish in front of your husband's place—perhaps a second dish of baked macaroni, or scalloped potatoes, and a green vegetable in a covered dish on your husband's or your second shelf.

IF YOU BEGIN WITH SOUP

If your first course is to be soup, the most practical soup dishes are the individual pots on matching plates with heat-holding lids, put on at each place just before you announce dinner. After the soup has been eaten, you remove the soup plates from the guests on either side of you. If you are eight at table, you also remove the plate from the one beyond the guest at your left. At his end, your husband does the same.

BY, MICHAEL GREER, A.I.D., OF NANCY MC CLELLAND, INC.

PHOTOGRAPH, ALBERT GOLDMAN

A SUPPER TABLE OF UNUSUAL ATTRACTIVENESS

Luncheon is served. The bread and butter plate is used.

The bouillon service has been exchanged for the service plate since it was of a different color.

Plate for entrée follows bouillon. Two courses served before the meat is now unusual.

Meat plate replaces the entrée plate.

The salad plate follows the meat course.

Table cleared of everything except glasses before dessert service is placed.

CORRECT PLACE-SETTING OF EACH COURSE AT LUNCHEON

The fingerbowl service is the same as for dinner; see page 350.

AN INVITING, CORRECTLY SET LUNCH-PARTY TABLE

ALMOST EVERYONE ENJOYS THE BUFFET SUPPER

IF YOUR MEAT COURSE IS TO BE A ROAST

If you have no roast-beef cover, it will be best to begin your dinner with this, and provide the equivalent of a first course in the living-room by serving plenty of substantially satisfying canapés with your cocktails, which should include a choice of vegetable or fruit juices for any guest who does not care for an alcoholic one.

You receive your guests and stay with them until all have arrived; then you leave them with your husband and go into the kitchen, take the roast out of the oven, put it at your husband's place and the vegetable dishes beside it, and then invite everyone to "Come in to dinner."

Your husband carves the roast. Perhaps he also serves the vegetables. But preferably the vegetable dishes are handed around.

At the end of the meat course, your husband puts the meat platter on the lowest shelf of his table and the vegetable dishes beside it. He then removes the plates of the two guests sitting on either side of him, and if you are eight, of the second beyond, on his left. You do the same at your end of the table, putting the used plates on the lowest shelf of your table. You both place fresh plates for salad in front of those next to you; you put the silver at the places when you set the table.

If you were only six at table then you would have no trouble, but the one snag at a dinner of eight is that unless you have an uneven number of men and women, you have to sit at the left of your own place at table. If you take the seat at the right of your place, you will have to reach three persons on your left to keep plates from crossing the guest of honor on your husband's right—which you avoid if you can. When you do sit in this place you must remember to serve only one person on your left and two on your right, because the second on your left is the guest of honor and is served by your husband.

The same plate-changing procedure follows each course.

THE SALAD COURSE

Salad dressing mixed at table is a ritual in many houses; but unless it is a specialty, it is best to have it already mixed and to pass the bowl so that people may help themselves. Each one, in turn, holds the bowl for the next.

Dessert is probably served by you and handed down the table exactly as your husband carved and handed the meat course.

COFFEE IN THE LIVING-ROOM

At the end of dinner after your guests are seated in the living-room, you go to the kitchen, take the cream out of the refrigerator, put it on the coffee tray—which has otherwise been prepared—and carry it into the living-room; you put it down on your coffee table, sit beside it, and make the coffee.

When it is ready, you pour it. When everyone has finished, you collect the cups and saucers and carry the tray back into the kitchen, where you can then take a few moments to put spoilable foods in the refrigerator.

OTHER DINNER-GIVING DETAILS

All other details are the same as at every dinner. The less pretense made, the less risk of criticism.

In selecting your menu, remember that a good dinner is much more dependent upon its preparation than upon selection. It doesn't really matter whether you give people dinner-party saddle of lamb or corned beef hash—what does matter is that it shall be good of its kind. It is much better to serve something simple than to try a dish too difficult to prepare alone. You will not be flustered and when the hostess has a good time, the guests usually do too.

YOUR UNANSWERABLE FRONT DOOR

One of the real problems of having no maid is that of answering your front door. When you do not want to see visitors you can simply not go to the door when the bell rings and then pretend you are not at home; but, unless your really intimate friends have a special pre-arranged ring, you then risk turning them away before your unopened door. And further, there is the possibility that the ring you don't answer may be a telegram, or something else that is important.

Of course, if you are giving a party, either you leave your front door open—except in very cold weather—or else you have to ask one of the guests who was the first to arrive to open the door for you.

For a really big party, it is usually possible to hire a special cook, waitress, or waiter who can cook and serve for every sort of entertainment. But in a small house or apartment that everybody knows is normally run by you alone, suddenly to acquire a staff is likely to give an impression of over-great effort.

RULES OF ESCAPE FOR HELPLESS HOSTESSES

There is a very real need for new rules which can politely effect the escape of a hostess from an interrupting visitor who refuses to listen to her when she plainly explains she is in the middle of her work. Often it is true the visitor says, "Don't let me interrupt you!" and then just sits—leaving the hostess helpless!

And yet nearly all the things we do and say seem polite or rude, proper or questionable, according to the way they are done or said. For example, Mary Warmhart can greet a visitor, "Oh, I'm so sorry! I have to go to Cora's for bridge in five minutes, but I *do* want to see you even for these few moments." Or at another time she can say to someone who stays on and on, "I hate to interrupt our talk, but I have to meet the

2:15." Or "Oh, I can't believe it's ten minutes past eleven! And we have
a Board meeting at eleven."

There are many situations from which every well-bred visitor in.
stinctively tries to protect her or his otherwise helpless hostess. When a
hostess happens to appear in full view, so that she can't possibly be
"not at home," but when it is perfectly obvious that she is very busy,
the considerate visitor says at once, "I'll come again soon!" The quite
proper thing for the hostess to answer is, "Oh *will* you? *Please* do! Because I can't ask you to wait until (whatever it is that is demanding
her time) is finished." But if the hostess replies, "I'm not at all busy,
do come in!" then it is her own fault if the visitor interrupts her.

BUFFET SUPPERS OR COCKTAIL PARTIES

Rather than try to give sit-down dinners, many hostesses find it
easier to confine their entertaining to buffet suppers or cocktail parties.

An advantage of the buffet is that many more guests can be invited
than at a sit-down dinner, but it is important not to have so many that
there will not be places for all to sit. And at a cocktail party to invite
all to whom one is indebted and to "get it over with" is a temptation
that should be resisted. Two or three small parties will not cost much
more for food and drinks than one large, uncomfortably overcrowded
one, and the smaller ones will be infinitely more enjoyable. One thing
to note at today's cocktail parties is that so many people prefer a Scotch
and soda to the classic martini.

A LITTLE JACK HORNER SHELF OF WELCOME

This term is intended merely as a suggestion. It may so happen
that you and your husband love people and that your friends are inclined to swarm into your house late in the afternoon, on holidays especially, when the markets are closed, and to remain until supper time.
John, your husband, shows symptoms which you know very well mean,
"I'm hungry"—and still your friends stay. In your own mind you go
over the contents of the refrigerator. Your perfectly good supper for
two might do for three, but at the moment you are seven or nine.

The answer to those who are often in this predicament is to have a
supply of ever-ready preparations which you call your Little Jack
Horner Shelf of Welcome or some name of your own devising.

This is an emergency shelf of provisions sealed in by having paper
pasted across it like a Jack Horner pie so that its contents shall never
be depleted. Fill this shelf with foods put up in cartons or tins, ready
to eat as they are or as soon as heated. Also, on this shelf, keep stacks
of paper cups and plates and napkins—and perhaps even paper spoons
and forks. Then, when the party is over, all you need to do is to take off
the little remaining food, a few platters, dishes, and pitchers, and dump
everything else into the fire or garbage can.

In stocking your Shelf of Welcome, be sure to remember that a man's idea of a meal is something substantial and hot.

This description has nothing to do with etiquette other than to make it possible to say at any time to any number, "Do stay! We can have a picnic supper ready in a few minutes." After an impromptu lunch or supper, be sure to replenish your shelf so that you will be ready for the next deluge.

HOSPITALITY NOT DEPENDENT UPON WEALTH

The fact that one is able to spend very little is no bar at all to hospitality. A young couple living in a single room that has a folding sofa-bed so that the room can be made into the semblance of a sitting-room, may ask friends they care for—and others are of no importance—to come to their "home in a room."

Where people do things with modest hospitality, and fail, it is not because of their stinted means, but because of their own attitude. They mentally if not actually apologize, which is fatal. They entirely over-look the fundamental fact that hospitality is far more dependent upon personality than upon lavishness of provision.

The real secret of successful party-giving is simply the gift of never outgrowing a child's imagination. In other words, the spirit of "let's pretend," which enters into the play of all children, is the very spirit that animates the subconscious mind of every ideal hostess.

Unless you really love the game of hospitality, unless you delight to have the friends you like share your festival, your party, even though it be given in a palace with rows of lackeys and a ton of choicest viands, will be but a heavy procession of over-richly laden minutes. Whereas if the enthusiasm of your welcome springs from innate friend-liness—from joy in furthering the delight of good-fellowship beneath your own roof—you need have little doubt that those who have ac-cepted your hospitality once will eagerly look forward to doing so again and again.

Solutions to other problems of the lady without a maid will be found in many chapters of this book, particularly those on "Simple Party-Giving" and "Modern Dinner-Giving."

SIMPLE PARTY-GIVING

TO ALL WHO LIVE IN SIMPLE UNPRETENTIOUS HOUSES, successful party-giving amounts to little more than the friendly enthusiasm of the host or hostess. Practically all of us fall naturally into one of two categories. In the first belong those to whom the thought of giving any sort of party is as full of delight (and as empty of qualm) as the prospect of a visit to the circus is to a child. In the second are all those who are literally panicked at the thought of inviting anybody in. They are sure people won't want to come; they are sure they will be bored if they do; they are sure, in fact, that company is a synonym for failure—with the result that these fears all too often come true.

On the other hand, those who love to give parties usually give them with ease, which means an unworried attitude of mind. Even if a dozen things go wrong, they know that few of their friends will notice, and fewer still will care, and after all why should things go wrong?

The point is that sometimes the hostess seems to imagine she is asking enemies to her house, a condition brought about perhaps by those two formidable words, hostess and guest. Perhaps if she would forget that she was to be hostess and that guests were coming and would think instead, "John and I are going to be at home, and Mary, Jane, Jim, and Bob are coming in," the entire situation would clear.

If the hostess and host are relaxed, and seem to be enjoying their party, there is no doubt that the guests will have a good time, too.

GIVING A BRIDGE PARTY

In giving a bridge party, whether of two tables or of ten, the first thing to do is to make a list of those to be invited. And then divide those who accept into groups of four; and try to seat at each table only those who like to play together. The tables may all be different—one with good players, another with beginners, one where the stakes are high, another where they play for nothing—but you must do your best to put those who play about the same game at the same table. Apart from ability as players, it is important to remember characteristics of temperament. Don't put people who take their game seriously (and "play for blood") with others who unceasingly chatter and keep asking, "What's trumps?" Don't put one who plays rapidly at a table with hesitators and dawdlers who take a whole minute to decide upon which card they'll play—and who even then take half a minute more in daring to lay an intended finesse face up on the table!

We all know hostesses who apparently seat players by drawing names out of a hat without the slightest regard to who plays well and who plays badly, or for what stakes they like to play. At an evening party the unthinking hostess will put two men who are the best players in town at a table with one woman who, imagining herself a wit, thinks of nothing but the next bright remark she can make, and another woman who is beautiful to look at but who knows scarcely more than a child of eight about contract. A man will be delighted to find a pretty woman next to him at the dinner table, but at the bridge table he hopes for an expert partner. If she is pretty or charming, or both, so much the better, of course, but these attributes are secondary. The real point is that one poor player spoils the whole evening—or afternoon—for the three who play well, and what she or he does to an unfortunate partner who perhaps cuts her or him all through the afternoon can be left to your imagination.

And now your preparations. It seems scarcely necessary to say that the two packs of cards on each table must be fresh, and that the pencils laid beside the score pads must be sharpened and the leads not broken under the edge of the wood—and it is well to have three pencils, one for each scorer and for a spare in case a lead breaks. On each table you leave a slip of paper on which you have written distinctly the names of the four players who are to play there together. They, of course, cut for their seats and partners. It is also of importance to see that each table is comfortably lighted, because poorly placed light that is reflected from the shiny surface of the cards is just as bad as darkness so deep that red cards are indistinguishable from black ones. If you have any doubt about light, sit in each place, hold cards in your hands, lay a few on the table, and see.

If it is customary in your community to play for prizes, then you, of course, select a first prize for the highest score to be made by a woman and a first prize for the highest score to be made by a man; but at a party to which no men are invited, a second prize is usually given. In any case, all prizes are attractively wrapped before being presented. Those who receive the prizes must, of course, open the packages at once and show some evidence of appreciation when thanking the hostess. Needless to say, a well-behaved person does not show disappointment upon receiving a prize that happens not to please her, nor does she "forget" to take it home. If the hostess chooses to give a present to her guest of honor, this should neither be called nor treated as a bridge prize. (See Chapter 33.)

REFRESHMENTS AT A BRIDGE PARTY

At a bridge party given, let us say, at three or half past three in the afternoon, hot tea, or chocolate, or coffee, or else cold beverages— and with any of these sandwiches and cake—should be served at about five o'clock. At a very large party the table is set in the dining-room exactly as at a formal tea, but under typical circumstances with not more than two tables the everyday afternoon tea-table is set in a corner of the living-room. Sometimes a member of the hostess' family pours tea, or perhaps at the finish of a rubber the hostess herself pours tea. This is always the case when the party is to be concluded at tea time and when prizes are given. Very often enthusiastic bridge players playing for stakes and not for prizes play straight through until six o'clock or later. They need not stop playing. One by one, as each becomes dummy, she goes to the tea-table, drinks a cup of tea or a glass of iced tea or coffee, eats a sandwich or two, and returns to the rubber.

In some communities refreshments are served at the tables when the tables have finished the last game.

If a few neighbors come in to play bridge in the evening, have a tray brought in with one or two cold beverages and a few thin sandwiches. On the other hand, if you are giving a party and the weather is cold, set a light buffet—in the dining-room—of Welsh rabbit or scrambled eggs and sausage, coffee and buttered finger rolls.

BUFFET SUPPERS

There are three delightful things about buffet suppers that appeal to nearly all of us. First, there is no handicap in lack of service. Second, no distress is caused by the hostess who keeps a dozen courteously prompt guests waiting for those who are always late. On the other hand, and third, for those of us who like never keeping others waiting, an invitation to a stand-up (buffet) supper allows us to dress without constantly looking at the clock, and to arrive more or less at our leisure without running the risk of being either rude or breathless.

Those who arrive promptly and like to eat promptly, do so. Those who come late fare almost as well, and no one is made to do anything he or she doesn't want to—and that seems to be the ultimate in present-day hospitality.

YOUR GUESTS

Since every informal party is at its best when people know each other well, it is essential either that you confine your invitations to people in one group or that you ask a reasonable number from each different group so that none will find themselves without friends to sit with.

The invitation is usually written across the top of the face of your Mr. and Mrs. visiting-card.

If request for a reply is added in the lower corner, the invitation should be answered, for otherwise the hostess will have no idea how many to provide for. The answer can be telephoned or sent on a return card merely saying "Sat. Oct. 2 with pleasure."

Very often the invitation is telephoned. "Will you come to a buffet supper next Tuesday at half-past seven?"

"Please answer" may be substituted for R.S.V.P. or even "Please telephone answer" might be used on an informal invitation to a buffet.

SETTING THE TABLE

In preparation, the chairs are taken away from the dining table, which is left in its usual place so that the guests can go all around it. It may be placed against a wall if by doing this there will be enough space left in the dining-room for two or three card tables each with places for four guests to sit.

The difference in the principle of buffet and ordinary table setting is that objects of utility are of first importance, and unless there be ample space for both, objects that are solely for ornament are omitted. Flowers in the center of the table are lovely, of course, but if it is a question of choosing between flowers and fruit, a centerpiece of fruit is preferable.

In the same way, if the table be crowded and candles are not needed to see by, they would better be left off. If candles are needed, candelabra are better than candlesticks because first, they give better light; and second, they are less likely to be knocked over by a guest removing a plate of food.

In setting a buffet table the important dishes of food are often placed in the center at each end, because it is easier to help oneself from platters of hot food near each end of the table than when they are placed about its center. Other items of food such as salad, bread and rolls, butter and cheese, stacks of plates, forks, spoons and knives, if these last are necessary, are placed where they can be reached from both sides of the table.

Generally red and white wine, possibly a punch bowl or other cold drinks, ice water, and beer left in its cans or bottles, together with glasses, are all on the sideboard.

Color plays an enormous part in the beauty of a buffet table. If you have copper bowls, or dishes, or a samovar, or a copper-bound beer keg, red-cheeked peaches, apples, pears, purple grapes, bananas and oranges, even a few tomatoes to add to the coppery red, are effective—especially if you live far from the sea and cannot include the ubiquitous platter of lobster decorated with its claws.

With copper, keep all the autumn tints in mind: green, red, russet, and yellow on a bare table. Or if you prefer, a red, or green, or yellow tablecloth will make a warm and inviting combination. Coarse white damask tablecloth and napkins dyed a fairly strong color make an ideal foundation for a table that you prefer not to have bare. Especially suitable for the buffet table are strong colors like eggplant, russet brown, lobster red, leaf green, and dark blue; or if you are setting your table with chromium, additional colors of tablecloths to choose from include turquoise blue, emerald green, and magenta.

In a modernistic house you perhaps go to the smartest of colorless extremes and have every item black or white or silver, black or white glass, or else everything in brilliant chromium. Or during the holidays, if you are setting your table with pottery and pewter, nothing is nicer than an old-fashioned red damask tablecloth with holly or poinsettia and plenty of colorful fruit. There is no rule about how you place things other than choosing the way that seems to you most inviting.

THE MENU

It does not matter which dishes you happen to choose, so long as they are good of their kind and easy to eat with fork alone—or possibly with a spoon. Otherwise, merely use a reasonable amount of common sense in selecting dishes that will be satisfying to the people invited. In other words, don't feed hungry men bouillon, dabs of *hors d'oeuvre*, samples of fruit salad, and meringues. For women alone, food might be trifling; but for normal men with normally good appetites you should provide three or four dishes that are substantial, and at least two of these should be hot.

Substantial dishes, for example, include all thick soups, eggs, meat, potatoes, puddings, and pie. Nearly everything made in a baking dish or casserole is ideal for a buffet meal, not only because it is substantial, but because it is easily kept hot. Olives, radishes, and celery are nothing but trimmings. Olives and other relishes are typically served with cocktails before dinner in the living-room. This statement is added because hundreds of hostesses seemingly believe that an olive is the first essential—the symbol, as it were—of a party. Have them, of course, if you like, but count them out as items of food.

Buffet menus include such acceptable combinations as these:

1. Fish baked in pudding dish (hot); a variety of cold meats (cut into narrow strips to eat without a knife; even roast beef can be managed if strips are not only narrow, but thin); vegetable salad; hot pudding. (If expense is important, plenty of stuffed hard-boiled eggs can take the place of cold meats.)

2. A thick Italian soup; curry of lamb cut in small bite-sized pieces with noodles or wild rice; vegetable salad; two varieties of pie.

3. Spaghetti Milanaise; beef and kidney or veal and ham pie; scalloped potatoes and mixed green salad; *macédoine* of fruit with some plain cake.

It is true that men are supposed to turn up their noses at any menu that lacks a hot roast, but a good Irish stew, or goulash, or meat pie will make them forget about the missing roast.

Of course, buttered rolls, party sandwiches, a fruit cup and coffee, and perhaps hot chocolate, should be included with each menu.

Each dish should have a stack of plates beside it and the proper silver to eat with in a row beside the plates; cups and saucers or glasses should surround the container of each beverage. But other than using ordinary practical common sense in considering convenient arrangement, there are no table-setting rules.

It is very important that hostesses who give buffet parties collect a supply of small tables so that each guest can put down extra plates, glasses, cups and saucers, and an ashtray. But, of course, if it is not practical to store so many tables, though they come in compact nests of four, guests will just have to hold their plates in their hands and put their cups and saucers and glasses down wherever space can be found —probably on the floor.

THE BUFFET PARTY ITSELF

So let us say that the table is set with all the cold foods and the dining-room lights are lighted and the hot foods are ready to be brought in from the kitchen, or else that they are already in their hot-water-heated chafing-dishes or other containers, and let us go with the host and hostess into the living-room and wait for the guests to arrive.

As people enter the room, the host and hostess go forward to greet them and perhaps introduce any who may for the moment find themselves alone. It must, of course, always be remembered that at every small and particular party (as distinguished from a huge and general one) the roof of a friend's house serves as an introduction, and one talks with those whom one finds nearby, whether we know them or not.

When the majority of those expected have arrived, the doors into the dining-room are opened and people in more or less of a queue file around the dining table and the women as well as the men help themselves, because they like to see what there is to eat and to take just what they want. Otherwise, a man will ask a woman what she would like, fills a plate and takes it to her.

A man seeing a woman sitting and not eating naturally asks her (whether he knows her or not), "Can't I get you something to eat?" If she says, "Yes, please," he brings her whatever it is she would like. But most likely she says, "Thank you, but I'm going into the dining-room in a moment." If people continue to sit and wait to be served, the hostess has to direct them as she would direct children at a party, saying, "Please go into the dining-room and help yourself to what you like." Then, if they stand blockading the table, carrying on a long conversation, she has to say, "Won't you please take your plate and go into the other room again and sit down?"

If there are no little individual stands or tables and guests must put their glasses on the floor (there being no other place), it is rather better to have the iced drink in goblets which are raised on high but substantial stems, because they are easier to reach than low tumblers which sit flat on the floor and make less of a wet ring on the carpet than cold tumblers do. The cup, saucer, and spoon necessary for the coffee, tea, or chocolate must be managed as best one can under the circumstances.

Important item: plenty of ashtrays. For a buffet supper recently a New York hostess went to a ten-cent store and bought a hundred ashtrays. She put two of them on each step of her staircase—one next to the wall and one on the outer edge and the others in every space that could possibly serve as a cigarette parking place.

The only serving detail of importance in a buffet meal is the clearing away of used dishes and the unceasing emptying of ashtrays. In a house with servants every plate is removed as soon as put down and filled ashtrays constantly replaced. Also, if there are servants, the glasses of those seated are refilled from time to time, and the main dishes often proffered. But the only thing the servantless hostess can do is to ask one or two members of her family—or her most intimate friends— to help her put used dishes in several spaces provided, from which she can stack them and take them away as easily and unobtrusively as possible.

The fact that guests must do their own serving is no handicap, since people do exactly the same thing in a great house. In fact, it is thought that sitting for a while here, then going again into the dining-room and foraging for themselves, then coming back to the same place or finding

a place with others is one of the very things that make buffet parties
the informal and popular gatherings that they are. If people are not
sitting beside those they find particularly congenial, women as well as
men are free to move elsewhere. An attractive woman can even escape
the most persistent bore by going to the table and then joining whomever she chooses. So if you have never given a buffet lunch, dinner, or
especially supper, you can't begin too soon to discover the charm and
ease of this delectable form of entertaining.

BIG DINNERS AT LITTLE TABLES

A big dinner or supper at little tables is the buffet party's only
serious rival in modern popularity, because it is equally suitable for
indoors in winter or outdoors in summer, as well as for those who have
many servants and for those who have one or none. Since those who
have many servants merely follow the directions fully given in other
chapters, let us consider the best method of serving a supper of twenty
or possibly thirty with no one to serve it but the hostess and anyone she
can requisition as an aide: husband, perhaps, but more likely sister or
friend.

IF YOU ARE A HOSTESS ALONE

To begin with, the number of guests you can have depends upon
the number of tables that can be fitted into your dining-room, terrace,
and wherever else you choose. But don't crowd too many tables in a
small space. If your dining table is a big one, take it away if you can.
But if you can't, push it flat against the wall. Don't forget, if you are
setting tables in your living-room, to leave plenty of space in which
to receive your guests—even though they may not be able to sit down
until they take their places at the tables. The smallest and cheapest
card tables are excellent unless their legs wobble! And they are easy to
store.

Cover each table with a small damask or other tablecloth, or use
place mats if the table surface is attractive. At each place put a napkin
and the amount of flat silver necessary for your menu, and a glass
for water or for fruit cup. And if your dinner is really a supper, put
a breakfast cup and saucer at each place too. Also put on a saltcellar
and a pepperpot. Put a hot-plate mat in the center of each table and
leave it clear. Set the tables with place-cards, because many people,
without place-cards to guide them, are rather at a loss.

The menu must be short and simple, but substantial. For example,
don't waste energy, dishes, and silver on a cold nothing-to-eat first course
of fruit or canapé that leaves everyone even hungrier than when he sat
down. Begin at once with a substantial hot dish such as chicken à la king
with rice around it, or macaroni with meat balls and a rich tomato sauce,
or a real goulash. Second course, put a mound of vegetable salad on a big

platter and surround it with plenty of stuffed eggs. Third course, pie or any other equally practical dessert.

And now the problem of serving three tables, each seating four—six tables if you have room, and your sister, for example, to help. Using three tables as our one-person unit: a dish of buttered rolls and four hot plates would be put on each of your own three tables before guests sit down, and your sister would supply her three tables in the same way. Therefore, for the sake of clearness, let's think only of your own three-table unit (of which your sister's is a duplicate). As soon as your people are seated, you put the hot course on the place mat in the cleared center of the first table. Then you put a pitcher of fruit punch, or as this type of dinner may equally well be called supper, a pitcher of cocoa or a pot of coffee on a tray with sugar and cream, in the center of the second table. By this time those at the first table have served themselves to the hot dish, which you now carry to the third table. Then those at the second table having served themselves to coffee or whatever the beverage may be, you place the coffee tray or fruit-punch pitcher on the first table. The second table in turn is given the hot course from the third table, at which you now take your own place. Each course is served the same way.

The one difficulty is in finding platters deep enough to supply twelve persons, and at the same time small enough to be put in the center of a card table, because otherwise the platters must be refilled. In taking off the used dishes and plates, this is one occasion when a service wagon is practical and therefore proper.

Details for a bridge lunch at small tables are given on page 380.

A SIMPLE DANCE

A successful dance at least expense rather implies that it will be given at home, though it might perhaps be given at a golf club, an inn, or a tea-room. But let us say that when all the furniture is out of your own living-room, the space will be large enough to dance in. Decorations and supper can be as simple as you like, but one item that is important and must be considered, before deciding definitely to send out invitations, is good music.

INVITATIONS

Invitations, by the way, are written across the top of the visiting-card of the young girl's mother, or whoever is hostess—"Jan. 6. 9 p.m. Small dance"—or possibly, if only her own friends are invited, across the young girl's own card. If a holiday dance is given by a young boy, his name is written on his mother's card. But a man giving a dance writes on his own card. Or, of course, all these invitations may be telephoned.

MUSIC AND PARTNERS

But to return to the question of good music, which means music that is gay and with perfect rhythm, and not necessarily a band with many pieces. Heavy or feeble music will guarantee a complete failure, no matter what all other preparations may be. A perfect dance from a young girl's point of view is *wonderful* music and—lots and lots of partners! In fact, one really ought to put partners before the music, since the best orchestra is wasted if there are not plenty of young men. Ideally there should be about three men or boys to every two girls. But a hand-picked collection of young men who dance with enthusiasm is infinitely more helpful to the success of the party than twice the number, who are indifferent dancers, and most of whom spend the entire evening propped against the walls.

DANCE USHERS

The best plan for a successful party—meaning that every girl shall have plenty of partners—is for the hostess to appoint a sufficient number of young men as floor committee or ushers, as they are sometimes called. Ushers wear white boutonnières or other badges so that they may be easily recognized. An usher needs no introduction to ask a girl to dance. His principal duty is to see that every girl has a partner—and no partner for too long. If he notices that one boy and girl are dancing time and again, he looks questioningly first at one and then at the other and says with his lips, "Want to change?" If both signal "No," he pays no further attention; but if one signals "Yes, *please!*" he cuts in and dances with the girl until he signals to a stag. No stag may refuse the signal from the usher. He has no fear of being stuck with the girl the usher was dancing with because the usher *must* rescue him.

Another of the uses which a boy can make of the floor committee is to tell one of its members beforehand when he is going to undertake an obligation dance. This means dancing with someone whom he knows very slightly or the unattractive daughter of his mother's best friend. Within a reasonable time that member of the floor committee will see that he is relieved. There should be one usher for every ten girls at every big dance.

One might ask why a young man is willing to be an usher. First, because there is a certain social honor in being chosen for that function, much as in being usher at a wedding. And there are also advantages in being an usher! He can dance with anyone he chooses, and the moment he no longer chooses, he signals to a stag to cut in on him.

DANCE HOSTESSES

When a sorority or other girls' club gives a dance—and also at the best-known junior dances given during the holidays in the great cities—

a certain number of girls are sometimes appointed as dance hostesses. Their duties are similar to those of the boys who serve as floor committee or ushers at other dances. When a hostess sees a girl stranded, she takes her own partner to the girl and he dances with her. The hostess then goes to the stag line alone, commandeers a stag, and dances over to the girl. She then asks the stag to cut in and dances with her own partner again.

SUPPER AT A SIMPLE DANCE

As previously said, supper can be very simple. A punch bowl kept filled with some sort of thirst-quenching ice-cold fruit juice, with perhaps a block of sherbet in the bowl, to drink between dances is, of course, important; but sandwiches and coffee passed around on trays are really quite enough for refreshments. Or if you would add more, then have bouillon as well as the coffee with the sandwiches and add ice-cream and cake. Beyond this you can add as much as you may choose. At all events, for a really simple party, something hot to drink, something cold, sandwiches (not sweet), and cakes (sweet) are all that are necessary.

When the orchestra plays "Home Sweet Home" or "Good Night, Ladies," it is time to say good night to the hostess and go home.

PICNICS

From earliest spring until latest autumn the very proposal, "Let's give a party," is almost certain to suggest a picnic to those who enjoy them. In its essential outline, going on a picnic means the packing of a lunch basket—possibly several baskets—with things to eat and drink, and then either walking or sailing, paddling or driving to some pleasant outdoor spot, and eating this lunch or supper.

But although picnics can be utterly delightful when well managed, they can be altogether awful when bungled! Therefore here are a few general directions for the benefit of those who want to give a picnic that will be delightful.

First decide whether you are going to give what is merely an outdoor lunch or supper, meaning you take only things that are ready to serve, such as the basket of sandwiches and thermos variety of liquids, or whether you are going to build a fire and cook.

If the latter, what are you going to cook and who is going to do the cooking? And what about each and every other preparation that must be made? In short, it is important to make as careful preparations as you would were you inviting people to dine or to lunch with you at home.

You wouldn't ask people to lunch at one o'clock and then think it quite all right to serve at three; nor would you be blissfully content to give them fish, or steak, or chicken, one side of which is raw and one side charred to a cinder. Nor would you tranquilly proffer greasy and black-edged scrambled eggs, or ice-cream in cups because it had turned to soup.

In planning your picnic, it is a good idea to make up a list of all items that will be needed, and check it before leaving. This may prevent the salt or the bottle opener from being omitted!

BUILDING YOUR PICNIC FIRE

But for your definite picnic example let us assume that you will cook your food on a grill.

Your first preparation includes acquiring some sort of picnic broiler. There are available portable broilers with folding legs, which are ideal for the picnic enthusiast. A recent innovation is the small disposable broiler that comes complete with charcoal briquets, ready to be ignited. These are so inexpensive that several may be purchased for a large picnic party; they are to be found in most large hardware or chain grocery stores.

Another suggestion is to create your own broiler from two lengths of iron tubing. If the picnic is to be on a beach, remember to take along your own firewood or charcoal. Don't depend on gathering driftwood; probably someone will have been there before you, or the driftwood will be wet. And be sure to bring some excelsior or prepared fire-lighting fluid to quickly get a good cooking fire started.

To make your own broiler dig a basin-shaped hole slightly less than a foot deep, and wide enough to allow for sloping sides that won't cave in. Put your lighting material on the bottom and then your charcoal; stoke it until it is red-hot, and wait patiently until there are no longer any flames or smoke, then spread out the embers evenly. Put your two iron rods across the sand—at the surface, or sunk down a little way. Set your broiler, frying pan or other pot across them, and cook.

PACKING FOR THE PICNIC

The perfect picnic manager, like the perfect traveler, has made simplification an exact science. She knows very well that the one thing to do is to take the fewest things possible and to consider the utility of those few.

Fitted hampers, tents and umbrellas, folding chairs and tables are all very well in a shop—and all right if you have a trailer or a station wagon to take the things in—but the usual flaw of picnics is that there are too many things to carry and to look after, and to clean and pack up and take home again.

Plainly, therefore, the wisest thing to do is to take one big pot of something easily heatable—for example, Irish stew, creamed chicken, or corned-beef hash—rather than raw meat, and potatoes, and vegetables to cook. But this, of course, depends entirely upon who is going to cook. For cold foods, stuffed eggs, each wrapped in wax paper or kitchen foil, are better than plain cold boiled ones. Whole tomatoes and potato salad might be included. Sandwiches of about three varieties, in addition to some of plain bread and butter, seem necessary unless you know the tastes of those who are going. And by all means label each variety. Don't attempt to take bread and fillings separately and let people make their own. The messiest picnic that can be imagined is one at which knives and plates, and bread and butter, and a half-dozen jars of jams and meat pastes are all blown around together and flavored with sand. Also take everything you possibly can in containers that can be burned, and use nothing but paper plates and forks and spoons and cups that can all be burned too.

The best recommendation for a picnic is everything neatly wrapped and labeled, and then everything that has been used burned. And don't leave anything behind you. Be sure that the fire is out and the ashes buried.

DON'T EXPERIMENT WITH AN UNKNOWN PLACE

Advice scarcely necessary to offer is that for your picnic you select a site that you know something about—because you have picnicked there before and know that the ground is not swampy, or that it is not more mosquito-infested than anywhere else, or that it is not covered with poison-ivy. If it is to be on a beach, it is well to remember to make some preparation to shield both your guests and the food they are to eat from sand. For this nothing is better than a few ordinary five-foot garden stakes and a few yards of ticking with a hem at each end of each length, through which stakes are inserted and then thrust into the sand to form a windbreak.

By the way, if you are giving a large picnic and including a number of people of average variety—by this is meant not picnic addicts—it is important to select a site that is easy to get to or away from. This suggestion is made because of a picnic once given on a far-away beach. When the tired company from the city wanted to leave, they found that their hosts had chosen a place reached by a sandbar which could be crossed only at low tide. And the tide would not be low again for several hours.

Nothing is so dampening to the enjoyment of a picnic as the presence of one or more fault-finders who never lift a finger, sit and complain of the heat, of the sun, or the chill of the wind, or a possible shower, or the danger of sitting on the ground, or of their personal sufferings caused by mosquitoes or black flies, as though their tender skins were alone sensitive to these trials. On the other hand, if you select your company from among those who have a genuine passion for picnics (these are really the only ones to invite for an enjoyable time), not only will they make everyone forget blowing sand and inquisitive ants or hungry mosquitoes, but most likely they will work like beavers.

CLAMBAKE

The preparations for a clambake are more specialized; but if you know how a seaweed oven is made (practically, as well as theoretically), or if someone on your beach has had long experience in making it and timing the baking of corn on the cob and potatoes and the clams and lobsters, nothing is more in keeping with a holiday at the seaside than a clambake. In recent years it is necessary to suggest that you make sure there is enough seaweed on your beach before you think of a clambake—and I repeat, do not attempt one at all if you are not an expert.

HOSPITALITY IN A BACK YARD IN TOWN

To the many who overlook the possibilities of the smallest of gardens as a setting for charming hospitality, the following description is offered. In a certain great city there is a certain little house less than eighteen feet wide. Its back yard is naturally the same width and only twenty feet deep. Against the fence surrounding it the vines are tacked flat, and at the far end a painted vista gives an illusion of distance. There is a flagged space next to the open double glass doors of the ground-floor rear room, and an awning drops down, hiding the surrounding buildings and showing only the walls of vines at either side with the painted vista at the end. While the early spring flowers are blooming in the beds in front of the vines, the owners of this garden are at home in it, every afternoon late, to friends who drop in for a glass of iced tea or other beverage, and who find the setting the most attractive in town.

DANCING PLATFORM IN THE GARDEN

A garden in which there is a permanent dance platform affords perhaps the greatest pleasure that can be devised for summer evenings. Such a platform, moreover, can easily be built in any garden where there is an available patch of level ground. For example, in their garden, which is not one of unusual size nor of especial beauty, the Littlehouses have built a permanent dancing floor, painted with four coats of deep blue paint and polished with wax. Around the edge of the floor is a protecting rail hidden by a clipped hedge unbroken except for an entrance on either side. The dance floor can be seen only from the upstairs windows of the house—from which it looks like a pool.

Impromptu dances at the Littlehouses' are as much the center of the summer social life of their neighborhood as are the outdoor swimming pools elsewhere. And since floodlighting, which is necessary to bring out the particular beauties of the garden and to light the dance floor, is part of the permanent fixtures, all the actual preparation necessary when their friends want to dance is to turn on the light switch—or perhaps not, if there is bright moonlight—and find a dance program on the radio or choose dance records for the phonograph.

Of course, rain calls everything off—until the floor has time to dry thoroughly and can be rewaxed.

IF YOU WANT TO GO TO BED, DON'T BEGIN GAMES

It is true that most people beyond their teens are likely to put on an expression suggestive of eating lemons when anyone proposes playing games; but if you can make them begin playing truth or consequences (or with any talent in the party, charades), you'll probably find that nothing short of the appearance of breakfast can stop them.

Of course, if in your own heart you don't want to play games, you won't be able to make anyone else want to—and that is in fact the secret of successful entertaining.

In proof of this, an occasion may be cited when the Normans gave what Mrs. Norman called a "haphazard party" in her cottage at the seashore. Without any regard to who liked or disliked whom, she asked merely those whom she happened to meet in the village post office while the mail was being sorted. The result was one of those nightmare evenings where the quarreling neighbors and the one divorced couple found themselves seated together, and the inflexible conservatives were next to the violent radicals, the highbrows next to morons, the snobs next to those who most despised them.

Fifteen minutes after their arrival everyone was occupied with the problem of how to leave without being rude, when suddenly an irrepressible young man—we'll call him Jonesy—exclaimed, "Let's all play Going to Jerusalem!" Everybody, looking glum, muttered, "Oh, no!" But whether they said it out loud or to themselves mattered nothing to Jonesy, who ordered, "Stand up, please," and took all the chairs of those who stood and put them down the middle of the room. Then he commanded a usually unapproachable pianist to "strum a march," and to Jerusalem half of those present went. The next turn included everyone, and in less than fifteen minutes, a stiff, dull, and utterly unmixable party had become almost a children's romp. Going to Jerusalem was followed by charades, and all those who had been contemplating going home at nine were still, at two in the morning, guessing or illustrating syllables.

Behind the trifling story of this evening lies something of real importance—something akin to a rule for happiness, which might be supposed to read: Let's not pretend that we are old while we are still young. And above all, let us not get actually old, ever, by being lazy or overcritical and always ready to protest, "Oh, no!" It's a thousand times better for us all regardless of our age to encourage the frame of mind that exclaims, "Oh, yes, let's!"

··◦] *33* [◦··

ASIDE FROM THE FIXED RULES FOR SPEECH AND MANNER
and deportment, which are the same for all well-bred persons, people
living in a particular neighborhood follow the customs of that neighborhood. In other words, to *do as your neighbors do* is the only sensible
rule.

SHOWERS

Showers are friendly neighborhood gatherings held usually in
honor of a bride-to-be, or in welcome of a new clergyman or of new
house-owners, or in expectation of the arrival of the stork. In fact, one
may give a shower of almost any variety that imagination can invent.
Presents given at a stork shower include everything for a new baby. A
larder shower includes everything eatable, often given for a new clergyman. The shower for a bride is sometimes specified as a linen shower,
or a kitchen shower, or a stocking shower, or a general shower, to which
each person brings what appropriate item she chooses.

The setting for a shower can be almost anything—a luncheon, a
dinner, an afternoon tea, an evening party, or even a morning coffee.

Invitations to showers are either telephoned—"I'm having a silver
shower for the Newholms on Tuesday at three o'clock"—or written on
a visiting-card—"Larder shower for Dr. Smythe" or "Stork shower for
Helen." Then the day and hour. Or, any shower cards at the stationers'
that appeal to you would be equally proper.

It is not appropriate for the invitations to be sent out by the immediate family of the bride, because each person who accepts must
shower Mary with a present. It is true that gifts are usually sent by
those who accept an invitation to a wedding reception or breakfast, but
even so they are not obligatory. Moreover, a wedding is an outstanding
social event and the present-giving is only a secondary consideration,
whereas the sole object of a shower is the showering of presents.

If the invitation specifies linen, or kitchen utensils, or stockings, the gifts should be those indicated. Sometimes the showered presents are given in place of wedding gifts. Usually however they are an extra expression of generosity and of much less importance than the wedding gifts. Sometimes they are the donation of the bride's bridge club or a small sewing circle of her most intimate friends who have been busy throughout a number of weeks hemming or embroidering a set of friendship table linen or kitchen towels, each piece of which is embellished and signed by the sewer. For those who in this busy age have time for such expressions of affection, such gifts have a charming and personal sentiment that a bride is certain to appreciate.

Although wedding presents are sent from the shop where they are bought, gifts for a shower are brought by hand and given personally—usually upon each donor's arrival; but sometimes the packages are taken at the door and put unopened with the others on a table in another room.

In some localities all the presents are sent to the hostess several days beforehand. She leaves the packages wrapped as they are, but puts each in a uniform gift wrapping so that the whole stack of packages shall be attractively alike. For this purpose the assortments, to be found at all stationery counters, are enchanting. When all are wrapped, the presents are piled on a table, perhaps in another room or behind a screen, or perhaps in full view against one wall of the living-room. Sometimes a pretty little girl wheels the gaily wrapped packages in a child's decorated wagon and places it in front of the bride-elect.

A suggestion to make a few presents go far is to treat each present as a treasure in a treasure hunt and tell Mary to look for them. When she finds one, she will find instructions—but not too obvious—for finding the next present.

When everyone—or almost everyone—expected has arrived, Mary opens the packages one by one and thanks each giver. "Thank you, Susie—how lovely!" "Oh, Margaret, this is just what I need!" "Jane, dear, I never saw anything prettier!" It is better that the cards of donors be enclosed, because if not, each giver must wait and as her present is unwrapped more or less self-consciously say, "That's from me."

After that, if the party is at tea time, the guests are offered light refreshments of tea or coffee and cakes; if in the evening, coffee or punch and sandwiches, or cider and doughnuts.

A shower for a bride may be given at any hour of the day or evening. Evening is chosen when the shower presents take the place of wedding presents, and men as well as girls are invited. Originally shower presents were the kind of things, most often to wear, that girls can give to girls but which would be embarrassing to display if any men were present, and therefore showers were for girls only.

Whether or not a wedding present is sent in addition to a shower gift depends upon the custom of one's own community; it also depends upon how well one knows and how much one cares for Mary. And most of all it depends upon the depth of one's purse.

The shower for a clergyman is usually given in the early evening. A stork shower is always given in the early afternoon and only intimate girl or women friends of the mother invited—that is, when the shower is an anticipation shower. Sometimes a stork shower and surprise party combined is given at the house of the mother when the baby is five or six weeks old. Although a surprise party, this is one occasion when it would be excusable for someone to give her a hint at least half an hour in advance, so that both she and the baby will be found ready for company. Also, usually the guests bring light refreshments with them as at all typical surprise parties. And as they surely would in the case of a surprise shower for a clergyman.

THE SURPRISE PARTY

Popular now as it ever was is a surprise party, given usually to new householders but equally suitable for any neighbors or friends. The general plan of a surprise party is, as everyone knows, the arriving by surprise at a friend's house in the eager hope that it really will be a surprise!

The ways to make preparation are two. One is to find out an evening when John and Mary Neighbor are giving a dinner at home. In this case the company who are to surprise them meet in a house nearby and then troop in a procession, with quite possibly a band leading the way, to storm the house. The second way is to choose an evening when John and Mary are dining with the Greens. In this case the Greens are, of course, in the know; and while dinner at the Greens' is progressing, those who are giving the surprise take possession of John and Mary's house. When they return, a dance is in full swing. In any case, provisions for the late supper are always brought by the Neighbors' unexpected guests.

Such parties, needless to say, always consist of a group of intimate friends and usually take place on John's or Mary's birthday or some other suitable anniversary, particularly the wedding anniversaries that are celebrated in paper, wood, tin, or crystal.

A WARNING AGAINST THE
GOLDEN ANNIVERSARY SURPRISE

A word of warning for those who might be inclined to celebrate a golden wedding anniversary with a surprise party. If the bride and groom are young for their ages, it is possible that they would enjoy this type of party. But if they were not married in their earliest youth, the disturbance of too great a surprise might very well have the opposite of happy results.

SINGING AND SEWING CIRCLES

Singing circles meet usually in the evenings and include men as well as women who enjoy singing together. They sing for a while and then have a buffet supper or light refreshments such as coffee and sandwiches, or Welsh rabbit and beer, or perhaps merely doughnuts and cider. Very often they give a concert at the end of the year. Otherwise there are no rules for singing circles—except to ostracize those who can't keep in tune.

The hostess at whose house a sewing circle meets should have an extra supply of different-sized thimbles, and of needles and several pairs of scissors and spools of thread. What they sew depends upon the purpose of the class, which may be to make garments for a nursery, or hospital, or other organization; or, having no object other than meeting socially, the members sew for themselves—which perhaps means making needlepoint, or darning socks, or, most likely of all, knitting. Very often a sewing circle is also a lunch club which meets weekly or fortnightly at the houses of the various members. They sew from eleven until about one and then have a sit-down or buffet luncheon.

In many of the oldest communities, membership in the sewing circle rates as the hallmark of highest social position.

DESSERT BRIDGE PARTY

As an innovation intended to eliminate tea-drinking and cake-eating late in the afternoon, dessert bridge parties are becoming popular in many neighborhoods. This is a back-to-husband movement especially intended for the woman who should go home and get a husband's dinner, but who instead stays on and on, and eats and eats, until she could not possibly eat any dinner herself, and sets a very poor one before a tired and hungry man. Each guest goes to the dessert bridge party without having eaten midday dessert at home. At the house of the hostess the dining table is set for the dessert course only: a china dessert plate and a lunch napkin on the plate, a fork at the left and a spoon at the right. The table should, furthermore, be set with a coffee tray in front of the hostess; while her friends are finishing their dessert, she pours the coffee, and it is handed around the table. After coffee, they begin playing on tables already set out in the living-room. The game ends at four, or half-past, or five at the latest. The players then go home hungry and provide substantial dinners for themselves and their husbands.

RICH AFTERNOON TEA AT A CARD PARTY

Although a heavy afternoon meal used to be served at a card party in certain American localities, this practice has all but disappeared today when almost everybody is unwilling to risk her lovely slimness of out-

line by eating more than a sliver of a sandwich with a cup of cream-
less tea.

A few however who either have no tendency to fat or who don't care
about their figures still are likely to provide—and enjoy—a heavy tea at
which various dishes with mayonnaise, sandwiches, pastries, whipped
cream, and chocolate are not unusual.

THE GUEST PRIZE

The why and the wherefore of its origin, how it *ever* became a custom, and why it is continued by an appreciable number of otherwise
courteous hostesses are a complete mystery to the writer of this book.

But from the evidence given in countless letters (most of them in
protest) the bestowal of this guest prize is not as it should be—a gift
to the guest of honor provided by the hostess—but a strangely counte-
nanced robbery of the prize actually won by the player with the
highest score who, instead of being permitted to keep what should right-
fully be hers, is obliged to hand it over to the guest of honor (unless of
course she herself happens to be this person).

In any case, it is absolutely essential to fairness that the guest prize
(if one is to be given) be a completely separate gift, presented by the
hostess to her guest of honor. If this same guest should also have high
scores, she should receive both guest and high-score prizes. But the
robbing from the winner of her winnings is from the standpoint of fair
play most incorrect.

HOURS FOR PARTY-GIVING

The hour chosen for a meal, or a party, or a game, or a visit should
always be that of neighborhood custom. To invite friends to dine two
hours later than their habitual meal is far more likely to distress than
impress them with what may be intended as a fashionable innovation.
People dine in London at nine, and in Spain or Mexico at ten or even
later, but this is no reason for upsetting the digestions of those of us
who prefer to dine at seven. If weddings in the evening are customary
in your neighborhood, then have your wedding in the evening too. If,
on the other hand, a nine o'clock dinner hour and a noon wedding are
customary, then even though you forage in the refrigerator an hour
or more before the dinner hour, at nine you dine and at noon you marry.

If neighbors pay visits in the evening—or if morning is the hour
preferred—you take your protesting husband with you in the evening,
or go by yourself in the morning, no matter how inconvenient either
hour may be to you.

THE PATTERN FOR EVERY PARTY IS THE SAME

Every sort of party, whether it be a tea, a wedding, a christening,
a silver wedding, a supper, a dance, a meeting of a sewing or book club,

an engagement party, a shower, housewarming, tea for some one person or for the hostess alone, is governed by the same rules.

The hostess—usually alone, but on occasions with a daughter or a guest of honor who may be receiving with her—always stands in the principal room of the house, or within easy view of the entrance, and shakes hands with each arriving guest. The guests and she then exchange greetings. After this they may devote the time to dancing, or playing games, or looking at television, or listening to music, or to a speaker. Or if it is another kind of party they congratulate the bride and groom, or are shown over the house, or watch the unwrapping of the showered presents. But eventually they go into the dining-room and help themselves—or are helped—to light or substantial refreshments set out upon the dining table. Sometimes, as at a small afternoon tea, the tea or other refreshments are brought into the living-room and served there.

For a between-meal hour the refreshments consist of sandwiches, cake, and tea in the afternoon; or chocolate and cake, or ice-cream and cake, or bouillon and sandwiches at night.

At some parties the guests go home after the refreshments are concluded, at others the refreshments are only an interlude and the dancing, card games, or whatever it was the guests were doing, continues.

HOSPITABLE HOSTS

·⊰[34]⊱·

TO THE OLD SAYING THAT MAN BUILT THE HOUSE BUT woman made it a "home" might be added the modern supplement that women cook as a duty whereas men cook only because they like to. Whether it is true that to men go the laurel wreaths for raising cookery to the heights of a fine art is debatable; the men, of course, always point out that the world's great chefs are men. While this does not make all men good cooks, more and more of them are trying it. And with today's trend toward casual living and informal entertaining, they are even taking an active role in party-giving. These "chef-hosts" like to don elaborate barbecue aprons and tall chef caps and display their culinary achievements. And there are some who will even wash up the pots and pans afterward!

And when the host pursues his culinary interests out of doors, there are no pots and pans to scrub, no kitchen to get messed up—and no objections from the hostess, who can relax and enjoy her party as much as any guest.

SOCIETY MOVES TO THE KITCHEN

It is true that the cooking of an especial concoction in a chafing-dish at table, or the preparation of terrapin or canvasback ducks in the kitchen by the host himself was the practice of many a host of past generations. But the occasional chef-hosts of yesterday, who prepared a specialty for a few appreciative friends, are now being replaced by the scores of men who have organized supper clubs in winter, clambake clubs in summer, barbecues in the fall, and who at the present moment would seem to be leading Society into the kitchen!

For many men, the art of cooking has become a new kind of competitive sport. This description of one "Grill and Saucepan" club (as we shall call it here) may perhaps be interesting not only to those who are organizing similar supper clubs, but also to anyone who would like to hold an unusual party in the attractive kitchen of his home.

410

THE "GRILL AND SAUCEPAN" CLUB HOUSE

The thirty members of this smart club consider themselves con-noisseurs as well as expert chefs. Their club house is an old barn donated by one of the members; together they bought a small piece of land on a roadside in the country and had the barn hauled to its new site.

They took out the partitions, leaving one big, open, raftered room. A board subfloor was laid, and over it bright blue linoleum. They built a big, field-stone chimney at one end of the barn, and at the opposite end a completely equipped kitchen was separated from the room proper by a stainless steel work counter, finished in blue. The walls of the main part of the room, which were the soft, mousy, brownish color of old chestnut wood, were left unpainted. The center of the room was left bare of furniture. Benches upholstered in red plastic fabric, like those in French restaurants, were built along both side walls and around the corners, stopping at either side of the fireplace. In front of the chimney were set wooden tables, covered with bright blue oilcloth. Wooden chairs, painted red to match the benches, were ranged on the opposite side of the tables. Two chandeliers in the shape of wagon wheels, ornamented with sheet aluminum, and six matching wall brackets, were designed to provide electric as well as candlelight.

The feature of the club is, of course, the kitchen end of the room. This is divided into three spaces. On one side a door leads into the men's coat room, and on the other side into the ladies' powder room. In the center space between these two rooms is a large alcove which forms the kitchen and is divided from the main room by the steel-topped counter. The kitchen, in contrast to the weathered-wood color of the main room, is all white, bright red, and chromium. The range, the refrigerator, and cupboards are all white; the grill alone is black. The saucepans are bright red lined with white, and all other receptacles used are of red and white china or of glass or of chromium.

CHEF-HOSTS COOK; THE LADIES LOOK ON

Suppers are given throughout the winter on the first and third Saturdays of every month, and three members are always hosts together. Each chef prepares one course, and each has his own apportioned section of the counter. Behind the counter are three sinks with receptacles underneath them into which all pots or dishes can at once be put out of sight until they are washed later. Or electric dishwashing machines might be installed which would of course speed up the K.P. duties. At one end of the counter is a lifting section that makes passage in and out of the kitchen possible.

The guests are invited to arrive half an hour before supper, and they either stand or draw up chairs on their side of the counter to watch the chefs display their talents. Cocktails are offered them, but not in over-liberal quantity nor accompanied by appetizers, since nothing must take away from the full appreciation which hunger lends to the dishes in preparation.

When supper is ready, the cook of the first course beats a gong. All women guests hurry to their places at the tables and the men line up in front of the counter and carry this first course to their partners. Later, when the gong strikes for the second course, each man carries his partner's and his own dishes to one end of the counter, and then again stands in line for the second course. This is all repeated for the third course. By the time this has been eaten, the fire has purposely been allowed to burn down to embers, so that no bright flame will detract from the ceremonial of the *café brûlot* with which each supper party comes to a climax.

CAFÉ BRÛLOT

For this ceremony the chef-hosts file into the supper room. The first places a small high table in the center of the room. On this another places a big bowl; the third fills the bottom of it with spices. Then the first pours in the brandy. All the lights in the room are turned off and the brandy and spices lighted. Then carefully, little by little, so as not to quench the flame, the coffee is poured into the mixture, which is continuously lifted with a silver ladle whose every motion intensifies the flame until finally it burns out. The lights of the room are then turned up again, logs thrown on the fire, and the coffee ladled into cups. While the lights are out, one of the hosts draws the curtains (of coarse red cotton damask) that run on a rod in front of the kitchen alcove. Women hired for the occasion then do the dishwashing and putting in order behind the scenes.

For those who would like to try this dramatic finale to any meal, here is a recipe for *café brûlot* that will serve twelve. Make four cups of very dark coffee (Continental-style instant coffee may be used) and keep it hot. Measure three-fourths of a cup of brandy. In a large bowl place twenty-four cubes of sugar, three sticks of cinnamon one inch long, three whole cloves, and the grated rind of one lemon and one orange. Pour the brandy over the spices and sugar and ignite it. Then carefully pour in the hot, dark coffee as described above. When the flame has burned completely out, ladle the coffee into half-sized (three-ounce) cups.

LET'S ENTERTAIN IN THE KITCHEN

The popularity of such clubs will suggest to the fortunate owners of houses that have large and attractive kitchens that they make a feature of some part of the actual preparation, not of a whole dinner, but of one or two dishes. Even those whose kitchens are small, as so many are today, can make the preparation of one dish a dinner-table feature. Such small cooking appliances as electric skillets and chafing-dishes make possibe the at-table cooking of a large variety of dishes, from Japanese *sukiyaki* to Welsh rabbit.

THE OBLIGATION OF COURTESY TO THE SERVANTS

When there is a maid, the kitchen should be considered available to the family only when she is out. And in the house with many servants, the kitchen, of course, belongs to them as entirely as the front of the house belongs to the family. Such a family, desiring to prepare its own Sunday supper, may, of course, let its entire household, no matter how many, go out on the same Sunday instead of, as is usual, letting half go one Sunday and half the next.

In any case, there is one exaction which every family should practice without fail: The kitchen should be returned to its rightful tenant, the cook, in just as good order as it was turned over to the family when she went out. The same is true of the pantry and even the dining-room. Leaving a few pots and pans filled with water and some soap or a detergent in an otherwise clean sink in an otherwise tidy kitchen is reasonable. But it would not be fair to the cook, any more than it would be to the maid alone, to leave her a kitchen that requires hours of scrubbing and polishing to get back in order.

COMFORTABLE OUT-OF-DOORS DINING

There are two schools of thought on this subject, and friction is quite likely to occur if both schools are represented in the same family. Such a family is, let us say, divided into one group of outdoor-worshippers who find no heat too great, no rain too wet, and no wind too strong, and an equal number of discomfort-haters who wilt in the sun, grow cross in the wind, and who have, moreover, an antipathy to insects. The enjoyment of the first group is all too often spoiled by the obvious suffering of the second. In this extreme case, the only solution may be to let the hardy outdoor members go picnicking by themselves while the indoor-lovers remain tranquilly at home.

But in the more usual and less extreme cases, this problem can be satisfactorily solved. An aerosol insecticide spray will temporarily remove the insects from the lawn or picnic site. Screened-in and roofed patios or terraces are attractive additions to any house, and certainly will add to the comfortable enjoyment of casual outdoor living. There is a large variety of lovely garden furniture available, ranging from delicate wrought iron and glass to practical plastic and rugged redwood. But the family that is really dedicated to outdoor dining will probably not settle for anything less than a dining table of painted boards, either permanently nailed or removably hooked to "horses" to allow garage storage during the winter months.

If you invite a crowd for an outdoor supper or lunch, make your table as long as you need to but no more than thirty inches wide. The resulting friendliness among the whole company will be magical. At a very wide table a person talks only to his immediate neighbors at right and left, but at a very narrow table one talks not only to one's neighbors on either side, but also to those across the table.

SETTING THE TABLE OUT-OF-DOORS

There is always something friendly and completely informal in the mere fact of dining *al fresco*, but there are certain factors to consider which are unique to the out-of-doors dining room. Glaring sun is one of these. Do not put a white cloth on your table, and do not use white china except in the shade. A table painted green or a soft green table-cloth are obvious possibilities; but since there is green in every direction, a deep blue may be more appealing. Place mats of natural straw are always attractive for casual meals, and are appropriate to the usual picnic or barbecue menus, too.

Wind is the greatest problem in setting an outdoor table. Even an ordinary summer breeze will blow away everything from paper plates to floral decorations. If you use a tablecloth, weight it by sewing pockets in each corner and dropping lead or other weights into each pocket. If the table top is of ordinary wood planks, thumb tacks will secure place mats. If you wrap each setting of heavy flatware in a napkin, airplane-style, and place it on each paper plate, the plates will not be blown away. To keep small, lightweight napkins on china plates where they belong is practically impossible; therefore put the napkin half under the plate instead. For the smokers, deep ashtrays that are weighted with sand or water and have trap tops are essential. Otherwise, ashes blow on everything, even when the breeze is scarcely perceptible.

It is absolutely necessary on a lawn (even more so on a beach) to have cross-stretchers at the bottoms of both chairs and tables, even when these are of wood, since chairs sink down in the earth or sand to wherever their rungs are placed.

Every dish should, of course, have a cover. Candy and salted nuts should be put in glass-covered urns. Flowers must be tied or wired into a bouquet and then put into a very heavy vase with a broad base that will not blow over.

THE COUNTRY HOUSE
AND ITS HOSPITALITY

·=◦[35]◦=·

THE DIFFERENCE BETWEEN THE GREAT HOUSE OF A FEW years ago with its twenty to fifty guest rooms, all numbered like the rooms in a hotel, and the farmhouse or small cottage which has but one guest room is much the same as the difference between the elaborate and simple wedding—one merely of degree, and not of kind. In other words, all people of good taste follow the same standard pattern of living, no matter whether it is followed intact or must be greatly adjusted to fit personal needs. Ill-mannered servants, incorrect liveries or service, sloppily served food, carelessness in any of the details that to fastidious people constitute the well-run house are no more tolerated in the smallest cottage than in the palace. But, because the largest houses are those which furnish us with a complete pattern, let us begin our detailed description with them.

HOUSE PARTY OF MANY GUESTS

A week-end usually means from Friday afternoon or from Saturday lunch to Monday morning. Everyone arrives about five o'clock on Friday or on Saturday at lunch time. Many come in their own cars; others are met at the station.

No hostess should fail to send a car to the station or boat-landing for everyone expected. If she has no conveyance of her own, she must order public ones and have the fares charged to herself.

If she is staying home to welcome those coming by car, she tells her chauffeur whom he is to meet, or she describes them to the driver of whatever car or taxi she has hired, so that each one is greeted by name. "Mrs. Town?—Mr. Doe?—Mrs. Neighbor sent me to meet you."

GREETING BY THE HOST

The host always goes into the front hall to greet everyone who arrives. He asks the guests if they want to be shown to their rooms, and, if not, sees that the men who come give their keys to the butler or valet, so that their bags can be unpacked, and that the ladies, unless they have brought maids of their own, give theirs to the maid who is on duty for the purpose.

GREETING BY THE HOSTESS

As soon as her guests appear in the doorway, the hostess at once rises, goes forward, shakes hands, and tells them that she is glad to see them. This is one of the times when everyone is introduced. If it is at tea time, the newly arrived are supplied with tea and whatever else may be offered.

After tea, people either sit around and talk, or perhaps play bridge, or take a turn around the garden. About an hour before dinner the hostess asks how long each one needs to dress, and tells them when she expects them down for dinner. If any need a shorter time than she must allow for herself, she makes sure that they know the location of their rooms, and leaves them and goes to dress herself.

A ROOM FOR EVERY GUEST

It goes without saying that, in the largest of well-appointed houses, no guest, except under unusual circumstances, is put in a room with anyone else. Some exceptions are:

1. A man and wife, if the hostess is sure beyond a doubt that they sleep in the same room when at home.

2. Two young girls who are friends and have volunteered, because the house is crowded, to occupy together a room with two beds.

3. On an occasion such as a wedding, a dance, or an intercollegiate athletic event, young people don't mind for one night—that is spent for the greater part "up"—how many are doubled; and house room is limited merely to cot space, sofas, and—not unheard of—the billiard table.

In a house of any size, she would be a very clumsy hostess who, for a week-end, filled her house like a sardine box to the discomfort and resentment of everyone.

In the well-appointed house, every guest room has a bath adjoining for itself alone, or shared with a connecting room—and used only by a man and wife, by two women, or by two men. A bathroom in the large house we are talking about should never be shared by a woman and a man. The most usual accommodation for a man and wife is a double room with bath and a single room next.

THE GUEST ROOM

The perfect guest room is not necessarily the last word of a decorator. In fact, a room "to be looked at" is what it is NOT. Its perfection

THE TRAY FOR A GUEST WHO BREAKFASTS IN BED

The tray should be attractively set and well appointed. Often a small nosegay is added—and the morning newspaper.

COURTESY, JAMES AMSTER, A.I.D.

A PLEASANT CITY YARD FOR AFTERNOON TEA AND OTHER ENTERTAINMENT

is the result of nothing more difficult than painstaking attention to every detail for the guest's comfort.

It is by no means idle talk to suggest that every hostess be obliged to try each of her guest rooms by spending at least one night in each of them herself. If she does not do this, she should at least make occasional tests. She should periodically go into the guest bathroom and draw the water in every fixture, to see that there is no stoppage and that the hot water faucets are not seemingly jokes of the plumber. If a man is to utilize the bathroom, she must see that there is an outlet for an electric razor and a hook for a razor strop, in case he uses one, and, furthermore, that there is a mirror by which he can see to shave both at night and by daylight. Even though she can see to powder her nose, it would be safer to ask her husband to bathe and shave both in the morning and in the evening in each bathroom and then listen to what he says about it.

She may have a perfect housemaid, yet it is not unwise occasionally to make sure herself that every detail has been attended to; that in every bathroom there are plenty of bath towels, face towels, a washcloth, bath mat, a new cake of unscented bath soap in the bathtub soap rack, and a new cake of scented soap on the washstand.

It is not expected, but it is often very nice to find eau de cologne, bath salts or bath bubbles, mouth wash, bath powder, almond or other hand or sunburn lotion in decorated bottles on the washstand shelf. But to cover the dressing table in the bedroom with brushes and an array of toilet articles is more of a nuisance than a comfort. A good clothesbrush and whiskbroom are usually acceptable, because guests almost invariably forget these.

A comforting adjunct to a spare room that is given to a woman is an electric heating pad with an outlet for it beside the bed, or a hot-water bottle with a woolen cover, hanging on the back of the bathroom door. If the water does not run sufficiently hot, a card (in the perfect house) also on the back of the door might read, "Please ring bell three times for hot water to fill this."

HOSTESS SHOULD SLEEP IN HER OWN SPARE ROOM

In the spare room the hostess should make sure—by sleeping in it at least once—that the bed is comfortable, that the sheets are long enough to tuck in. If they are not, it is easy to sew a half-yard-wide strip of strong muslin sheeting to the bottom of each sheet. She must see, too, that there are two pillows—one medium hard and one especially soft, so that one may make one's choice. There must also be plenty of covers. Besides the blankets there should be a wool-filled or an eiderdown quilt, of a color to go with the room, laid across the foot of the bed.

She should be sure to ring the bell to see not only that it is in working order, but also that the maid or whoever is rung for understands from the annunciator downstairs which room has rung.

There must, of course, be a night light at the head of the bed. Not just a decorative glowworm effect, but a 30-70-100-watt, three-switch light with an adjustable shade that is really good to lie in bed and read by. Moreover, if there are twin beds, there must be a light for each bed that is shaded from the other bed so that the occupant of one bed can read while the other sleeps. And always there should be books—chosen more to divert than to strain the reader's attention. The sort of selection appropriate for a guest room might best comprise two or three non-fiction books of the moment, a light novel or a mystery novel, a book of essays or poetry, another of modern short stories or "Saki," and a few of the latest magazines. It is very important that this selection be revised for each guest, for even though one may not guess accurately the taste of another, one can at least avoid making the guest room either a waste basket or a catch-all for books selected because their bindings look pretty.

There should be a candle and a box of matches, for even though there is electric light, it has been known to go out. There should also be cigarettes, matches, and ashtrays on the desk, and a scrap basket beside it. In hot weather, every guest should have an electric fan, if the house does not have some type of air-conditioning; and in August, even though there are screens, a fly "swatter"!

DRESSING-TABLE AND DESK

A bedroom sofa is very important—if the room is a large one—in case the lady who is to occupy the room should wish to rest during the day, with a sofa pillow or two and a lightweight quilt across the end of it.

The hostess should do her own hair in each room to learn whether the dressing-table is placed where there is a good light over it, both by electric light and by daylight. A very simple expedient in a room where massive furniture and low windows make the daytime dressing-table difficult to use is the Continental custom of putting an ordinary small table directly in the window and standing a good-sized mirror on it; or, if you have no standing mirror, any small mirror hung on the window frame will answer the purpose of comfort even better.

And the pincushion! It is more than necessary to see that the pins are usable and not rusted. There should be black ones and white ones, long and short; also safety pins in several sizes. Three or four threaded needles of white thread, black, gray, and beige silk are an addition that has proved many times welcome. And supply a thimble of usable size—or better, two or three sizes—instead of the habitual No. 12 into which any woman whose fingers are tapered can put two together. One must also examine the writing desk to be sure that the ink is not a cracked patch of black dust at the bottom of the well, and the pens solid rust, and the writing paper textures and sizes at odds with the envelopes. There should be a fresh blotter and a few stamps. Again, thoughtful hostesses put in some convenient place a card giving the post office schedule and saying where the mail bag can be found. And a calendar, and a clock that goes and shows the right time. Is there anything more typical of the average spare room than the clock that is at a standstill or, worse, a half-hour slow?

PLENTY OF HANGERS

In the closets there must be plenty of clothes-hangers made of wood or plastic and not the thin wire ones from the cleaners that may even be rusty. For women a few hat stands, and for men trouser-hangers or the coat-hangers that have a bar for the trousers.

It should be unnecessary to add that every bureau drawer and closet should be looked into to see that nothing belonging to the family is filling the space which should belong to the guest, and that the white paper lining the bottom of the bureau drawers is fresh.

In a hunting country, there should be a bootjack and boot-hooks in the closet.

People who like strong perfumes often mistakenly think they are giving pleasure in filling all the bedroom drawers with pads heavily scented. Instead of feeling pleasure, some people are made almost sick. But all people—hay fever patients excepted—love flowers, and vases of them beautify rooms as nothing else can. Even a shabby little room, embellished with a few wild flowers or a potted plant, loses all effect of shabbiness and is inviting instead.

When bells are being installed in new houses, they should be on cords and hung at the side of the bed. Light switches should be placed at the side of the door going into the room and bathroom, but the bed light should be on its separate plug, that can be turned on or off from the bed.

BUT NO SHUTTERS THAT BANG!

Guest rooms should have shutters and dark shades for those who like to keep the morning sun out. The rooms should also, if possible, be away from the kitchen end of the house and the nursery.

A shortcoming in many houses is the lack of a newspaper, and the thoughtful hostess who has the morning paper sent up with each breakfast tray, or has one put at each place on the breakfast table, deserves a halo.

At night a glass and a thermos jug of water should be placed by the bed.

It is also well to see that the rain water draining down from the roof does not make a noise like a pneumatic hammer at the bottom of the leader just outside the window.

THE GUEST CARD

Needless to say, guest cards are used only in huge houses that are now extremely rare. But the questions on it are and always have been asked by every competent hostess. At bedtime she asks, "Would you like to come down to breakfast, or will you have it in your room?" If the guest says she would like to have it in her room, she is asked what she would like to eat. She is also asked whether she cares for milk, or fruit, or other light refreshment at bedtime, and whether there is a special book she would like to take up to her room.

The guest card at the Gildings' is as follows:

PLEASE FILL THIS OUT BEFORE GOING DOWN TO DINNER

What time do you want to be awakened? ....
Or will you ring? ....
Will you breakfast upstairs? ....
Or down? ....

UNDERSCORE YOUR ORDERS

Coffee, tea, chocolate, milk,
Oatmeal, hominy, shredded wheat,
Eggs, how cooked?
Rolls, muffins, toast,
Orange, pear, grapes, melon, or orange
  or vegetable juice.

AT BEDTIME WILL YOU TAKE

Milk, orangeade, grape juice?
Cookies, crackers?
Apple, pear, grapes?

Besides this list, there is a catalog of the library with a card clipped to the cover, saying, "Following books for room No. X." Then a few blank lines and a place for the guest's signature.

AT DINNER

Everyone goes down to dinner at a country house party as promptly as possible, and the procedure is exactly that of all dinners.

BEDTIME

At the end of the evening, it is customary for the hostess, rather than the guests, to suggest going upstairs; but etiquette is not strictly followed in this matter. If, at a reasonable time after dinner, anyone is especially tired, he or she quite frankly says, "I wonder whether you would mind very much if I went to bed?" The hostess always answers, "Why, no, certainly not! If you do not find everything you want in your room, please ring for it."

It is not customary for the hostess to go upstairs with one guest if others are still sitting in her living-room. She does, of course, go with an only woman guest, or an elderly one, to make sure that everything has been thought of for her comfort.

THE LITTLE HOUSE OF PERFECTION

As a complement rather than a contrast to the house party in a great house like that of the Gildings (most of which are one by one being razed because very few today have the means to afford the staff of servants such a house requires), the attributes of the completely perfect house cannot be better represented than by Brook Meadows Farm, the all-the-year home of the Oldnames. Nor can anything better illustrate its perfection than an incident that actually took place there.

A great friend of the Oldnames had married a widow from a distant state. Because her husband was a man of gregarious habits and indiscriminating tastes, the new wife had no way of guessing what the Oldnames might be like nor what kind of clothes to pack. So she asked her husband to tell her something about their hosts and their house.

"Oh," said he, "they're wonderful! Their house? It's just a little farmhouse. Oldname wears a dinner coat of course; his wife wears . . . I don't know what . . . but I've never seen her dressed up a bit!"

"Evidently plain people," thought his wife. And aloud, "I wonder what daytime dress I have that I could wear in the evening. The gray voile might do. Perhaps I had better put in my cerise satin . . ."

"The cerise?" asked her husband. "Is that the red you had on the other night? It is much too handsome, much! I tell you, Mrs. Oldname never wears a dress that you could notice. She always looks like a lady, but she isn't a dressy person at all." So the bride packed her plainest clothes, but at the last minute she put in the cerise.

When she and her husband arrived at the railroad station, she found *that* at least primitive enough; and Mr. Oldname in much-worn tweeds might have come from a castle or a cabin. Country clothes are no evidence. But her practiced eye noticed the perfect cut of the chauffeur's coat, and that the car was beautiful.

"At least they have good taste in cars and accessories," thought she, and was glad she had brought her best evening dress.

They drove up to a low white-shingled house, at the end of an old-fashioned brick wall bordered with flowers that were a harmony in color and all in perfect bloom. She knew no inexperienced gardener produced that apparently simple approach to a door that has been chosen as frontispiece in more than one book on Colonial architecture

The door was opened by a maid in a silver-gray taffeta dress, with organdy collar, cuffs, and apron, white stockings, and silver buckles on black slippers. The guest saw a quaint hall and vista of rooms that at first sight might easily be thought simple by an inexpert appraiser. But Mrs. Oldname, who came forward to greet her guests, was the antithesis of everything the bride's husband had led her to believe.

To describe Mrs. Oldname as simple in her environment is about as apt as to call a pearl simple because it doesn't dazzle. Nor was there an article in the apparently simple living-room that would be refused were it offered to a museum.

The tea-table was Chinese Chippendale and set with old Spode on a lacquered tray over a mosaic-embroidered linen tea-cloth. The soda biscuits and cakes were light as froth; the tea a special blend sent from China. There were three other guests besides the bride and groom: a United States senator, and a diplomat and his wife who had lately been liberated from long internment in enemy country. Instead of bridge there was conversation.

When the bride went to her room—which adjoined that of her husband—she found her bath drawn, her clothes laid out, and the dressing-table lights lighted.

That night the bride wore her cerise dress to one of the most perfect dinners she had ever gone to.

When at last they went upstairs and she saw her husband alone, she took him to task. "Why in the name of goodness didn't you tell me the truth about these people?"

"I did tell you it was a little house. It was you who insisted on bringing that red dress. I told you it was too handsome!"

"Handsome!" she cried, almost in tears. "I don't own anything to compare with the least article in this house. And that 'simple' little woman, as you call her, would make almost anyone seem provincial. As for her clothes, they are priceless—just as everything is in this little gem of a house!"

These two houses are extremes, but each an extreme of luxury— from which, however, is derived the perfect pattern that all of us should try to follow as far as we can, but of course no further.

GUEST ROOM SERVICE

Unless a visitor brings her own maid, the personal maid of the hostess (if she has one; otherwise, the housemaid) unpacks the luggage, lays toilet articles on the dressing-table and in the bathroom, puts folded things in the drawers, and hangs dresses on hangers in the closet. If, as she unpacks, the maid sees that something of importance has been forgotten, she tells the hostess; or, in case she has been long in this house and knows where to find a substitute for a missing article, she supplies the guest, without asking, with such articles as comb and brush or clothesbrush or toothbrush. (This last article afterward is packed in the guest's luggage.)

Whoever looks after the host's clothes performs the same service for the men. In small establishments, where there is no lady's maid or valet, the housemaid is always taught to unpack guests' belongings and to press and hook up ladies' dresses, and to send gentlemen's clothes to be pressed, and there are some jewels of maids who can even do this last themselves.

In big houses, breakfast trays for the ladies are usually carried to the bedroom floor by the butler or a footman, and are handed to the lady's maid or to the housemaid, who takes the tray into the room. In small houses they are carried up by the waitress.

Trays for men visitors are less common, but when ordered are carried up and into the room by the butler, or, if there are no men-servants, by the waitress.

BREAKFAST TRAY ADVANTAGES

Unless breakfast is at a set time and everyone comes down promptly, the advantage of having one's guests choose breakfast up-stairs is that no delayed breakfast prevents the dining-room's being put in order or the lunch table set. Trays, on the other hand, can stand all morning "all set" in the pantry and interfere much less with the dining-room work. Many hostesses therefore much prefer guests to have trays.

Every china store carries breakfast sets, of course, but only in open stock patterns can one buy extra dishes or replace broken ones—a fact it is well to remember. A set always comprises a coffee- or tea-pot, a hot milk pitcher, a cream pitcher and sugar bowl, a cup and saucer, two plates, an egg cup, and a covered dish. A cereal is usually put in the covered dish, toast in a napkin on a plate, or eggs and bacon in place of cereal. This with fruit is the most elaborate tray breakfast ever provided.

TRAY SERVICE

When a guest rings for breakfast, the housemaid goes into the room, opens the blinds, and in cold weather closes the windows, lights the fire, if there is an open grate in the room, and turns on the radiator. Asking whether a hot, cool or cold bath is preferred, she goes into the bathroom, spreads a bath mat on the floor, a big bath towel over a chair, and draws the bath. As few people care for more than one bath a day and many people prefer their bath before dinner instead of before break-fast, this office is often performed at dinner time.

TIPS

In the United States, when you dine in a friend's house, you do not tip anyone—ever. But when you go to stay overnight or longer as a house guest, you do give a gratuity. A fixed schedule of the amount to tip is really impossible to prepare, in as much as each occasion will vary.

To an average servant in an average house, two dollars is about right for a week-end. Mrs. Lavender, staying with the Littlehouses and not making more work than the least possible, might quite acceptably give no more than a dollar for a week. Intimate friends in a medium-sized house send tips to all the servants—perhaps only a dollar apiece, but no one is forgotten. In a very big house, this is never done; you tip only those who have served you. If you have your maid with you, you always give her about two dollars to give the cook—often the second one —who prepared her meals and one dollar for the kitchen maid who set her table.

A gentleman (very unfairly) scarcely ever remembers any of the women (except a waitress) and tips only the butler and the valet, and sometimes the chauffeur. The least he can offer any of the menservants is two dollars and the most usually is five. If a gentleman brings his own valet, he gives him money for his tips exactly as a lady gives tipping money to her maid.

In a few houses the tipping system is abolished, and in every guest room, in a conspicuous place either on the dressing-table or over the bathtub where you are sure to read it, is a sign saying:

PLEASE DO NOT OFFER TIPS TO MY EMPLOYEES. THEIR CONTRACT IS WITH THIS SPECIAL UNDERSTANDING, AND PROPER ARRANGEMENTS HAVE BEEN MADE TO MEET IT. YOU WILL NOT ONLY CREATE A SITUATION, BUT CAUSE THE IMMEDIATE DISMISSAL OF ANYONE WHO MAY BE PERSUADED BY YOU TO BREAK THIS RULE OF THE HOUSE.

The notice is signed by the host. The arrangement referred to is one whereby every guest means a bonus of so much per day added to the wages of all employees. This system is much to be preferred for two reasons. First, self-respecting servants dislike the demeaning effect of tips—an occasional few won't take them. Secondly, they can count that so many visitors will bring them precisely such an amount.

HOW TIPS ARE GIVEN

Just before the time for saying good-by to your hostess, when the maid has finished packing your bag and the chambermaid is probably doing up your room, you give each her tip. And you give the butler his or the waitress hers in the front hall. You may always give the butler a tip for any other menservants.

In a small house, if the waitress is not in the hall, you go to the pantry and put the money into her hand. If you are an habitual visitor and know her name, you say, "Good-by, Anna, and thank you." Then you go into the kitchen and do and say the same thing or you may, after giving Anna her own tip, hand her a second sum of money saying, "Please give this to the cook for me." If Anna has pressed your dress, let us say, or sewn something that had ripped or done any special service, you give her fifty cents or a dollar or two extra; and when you say good-by, you add "Thank you" for whatever the service was.

HOUSES WE LIKE TO STAY IN

In houses where visitors like to go again and again there is always a happy combination of some attention on the part of the host and hostess, and the perfect freedom of the guests to occupy their time as they choose. In other words, while we of the modern day like to have some attention paid to us at least now and then, the majority of us would rather go to stay with one who lets us quite alone than ever again go to stay with an energetic one who schedules our every moment and never lets us rest for one minute.

THE ENERGETIC HOSTESS

The energetic hostess is she who fusses and plans continually, who thinks her guests are not having a good time unless she rushes them, Cook's-tourist fashion, from this engagement to that, and crowds with activity and diversion—never mind *what* so long as it is something to see or do—every moment of their stay.

She walks them through the garden to show them all the nooks and vistas. She dilates upon the flowers that bloomed here last month and are going to bloom next. She insists upon their climbing over rocks to a summerhouse to see the view; she insists on taking them in another direction to see an old mill; and, again, everyone is trouped to the cupola of the house to see another view.

She insists on everyone's playing croquet before lunch, to which she gathers in a curiously mixed collection of neighbors. Immediately after lunch everyone is driven to a country club to see some duffer golf—for some reason there is never time in all the prepared pleasures for any of her guests to play golf themselves.

After twenty minutes at the golf club, they are taken to a church fair. Another entertainment that her guests must not miss is a flower pageant of the darlingest children fourteen miles away. Everyone is dashed to that. The pageant is sweetly pretty, but the sun is hot and the guests have been on the go for a great many hours. At last, finally, their hostess leaves. "Home at last!" think they. Not at all. They are going somewhere for tea and French recitations. But why go on? There is still all the evening and tomorrow to be lived through.

THE ANXIOUS HOSTESS

The anxious hostess does not insist on your ceaseless activity, but she is no less persistent in filling your time She is always asking you what you would like to do next. If you say you are quite content as you are, she nevertheless continues to shower suggestions. Shall she turn on the television or shall she play the phonograph for you? Would you like her to telephone to a friend who sings too wonderfully? Would you like to look at a portfolio of pictures? If you are for a moment silent, she is sure you are bored, and insists on talking to you when your only wish is to get back to finish a thrilling story you have started in a magazine.

DON'TS FOR THE HOSTESSES

When a guest asks to be called half an hour before breakfast, don't have him called an hour and a half before because it takes you that long to dress, nor on the other hand allow him a scant ten minutes if the shorter time is all you require. Too often the summons on the door wakes him out of sound sleep; he tumbles exhausted out of bed, into clothes, and downstairs, to wait perhaps an hour for breakfast.

If a guest prefers to sit on the veranda and read, don't interrupt him every half page to ask if he really does not want to do something else. If, on the other hand, a guest wants to exercise, don't do everything in your power to obstruct his starting off by saying that it will surely rain, or that it is too hot, or that you think it is senseless for him to exhaust himself on a golf course or tennis court on the very days that should be for his rest.

Don't, when you know that a young man cares little for feminine society, fine-tooth-comb the neighborhood for young women for his entertainment.

Don't, on the other hand, when you have an especially attractive young woman staying with you, ask a stolid middle-aged couple and an octogenarian professor for dinner who will bore her to death instead of an attractive man that she would like to meet.

Don't, because you personally happen to like a certain young girl who is utterly old-fashioned in outlook, and different from ultra-modern others who are staying with you, try to bring them together. Never try to make any two people like each other. If they do, they do; if they don't, they don't, and that is all there is to it.

THE PERFECT HOSTESS

The ideal hostess must have so many perfections of sense and character that were she described in full, no one seemingly but a combination of seer and angel could ever hope to qualify.

She must first of all consider the inclinations of her guests; she must not only make them as comfortable as the arrangements and limits of her establishment permit, but she must subordinate her own inclinations utterly. At the same time, she must not fuss and flutter and get agitated and seemingly make efforts in their behalf. Nothing makes a guest more uncomfortable than to feel that he is the cause of his host's or hostess's being put to a great deal of bother and effort.

A perfect hostess like a perfect housekeeper gives the impression that she has nothing whatever to do with household arrangements, which apparently run themselves.

Certain rules are easy to observe once they are brought to attention. A hostess should never speak of annoyances of any kind—no matter what happens. Unless she is actually unable to stand up, she should not mention physical ills any more than mental ones. She has invited people to her house, and as long as they are under her roof, hospitality demands that their sojourn shall be made as pleasant as lies in her power.

If anything goes wrong with her household she must work a miracle and keep it from her guests. If, for instance, the cook leaves, then a picnic must be made of the situation as though a picnic were the most delightful thing that could happen. Should a guest be taken ill, she must assure him that he is not giving the slightest trouble; at the same time nothing that can be done for his comfort must be overlooked.

GUEST OR HOSTESS

·•·⟧ 36 ⟦·•··

IN OTHER DAYS WHEN MODES OF TRAVEL WERE SLOW, THE long distances were distressingly fatiguing, and once a guest arrived there was almost no limit to his or her visit. In fact, one young woman who went to spend a fortnight with friends in Virginia stayed thirty years—until she died. But in the present day and age, a hostess should always say quite definitely, "Will you come on Friday for over Sunday?" or "Will you come on the sixth for a week?"

The guest who accepts may shorten her visit, but she must not stay beyond the time she was asked for, unless very especially urged to do so. Even then she would be wiser to go early and be missed rather than to run the risk of outstaying her welcome.

THE ART OF BEING A HOUSE GUEST

Having accepted the invitation and assuming that you want to be an ideal guest, there are four details which demand your attention: selection of clothes to be taken, selection of luggage to put them in, selection of trifling gifts, and selection of the ideal guest's frame of mind.

It is not necessary, but it is always courteous to take your hostess a gift, or better, if she has children, to take presents to them. The conventional list of flowers, fruit, candy, or a book is really not a best choice, unless you know of a book she wants, or that she eats candy, has no flowers in her garden or fruit on her trees. As to the children, if they are young, a collection of small, amusing articles from the ten-cent store often gives them more pleasure than a single present of value.

Your first concern when going on a visit is to condense your luggage in both quantity and size—particularly size. If you are going in your own car this is not so important; but if you are being taken in someone else's car or go by train to a place where there are seldom any porters to carry heavy bags, too much luggage can be a near tragedy.

It is sometimes impossible to go for a week-end without a good deal of luggage. An athletic man, who is likely to ride and play golf and tennis, might easily be taken for a vaudeville star carrying his properties with him. Otherwise a dinner coat, and one, or at most two, country suits with the necessary shirts, shoes, ties, etc. will suffice. Even in Newport a week-end guest is no longer expected to wear white tie and tails—not even if he is going to the most formal dinner or dance.

A guest in someone's home should never suggest taking his hosts to a meal in a restaurant. While you are their guest, you eat the food they provide. You show your gratitude by inviting them to a restaurant sometime when they are in town or by sending a suitable present.

If you have friends in the neighborhood and they invite you and your hosts over for a swim or to play tennis, you should never accept the invitation and then relay it to your hostess. It is better to leave the "door ajar," and make a non-committal reply such as, "May I call you back, as I'm not sure about Joan's plans?"

If you are not needed to make up a foursome at bridge, and you are tired and want to go to bed before your hosts and the other guests do, it is perfectly all right to say to your hostess that you've had a "rugged" week at the office and would like to go to bed.

When you are visiting do not use the staff as your own servants, and unless you have been told to ring for breakfast do not do so. The thoughtful hostess will suggest to an aged guest that if he or she would like any help in dressing, John, the houseman, or Marie, the maid, will be glad to do whatever he or she can.

If the household is a simple one, in which the hostess does her own housework, you may certainly, and indeed you should, offer to help in clearing the table and cleaning up in the kitchen.

TAKE YOUR OWN SPORTS CLOTHES

If you are going where you are to swim or ride or play games, be sure you take your own bathing suit (it is safer to take two in case of damp weather and slow drying; better still, of course, are the quick-drying synthetics to solve this problem), riding habit, racket or golf clubs, and with them your own warm coat. Not only will your hostess be glad not to have her own good things used and perhaps ruined, but you will avoid possibly having yourself to use a wet and mildewed bathing suit, a rotted rubber cap stuck tight as a plaster, a tennis racket that has been left out on the grass overnight, broken golf clubs, and a polo coat spotted with machine oil.

THE GUEST NO ONE INVITES AGAIN

It too often follows that the borrower is likewise an abuser of the lender's property. The guest no one invites a second time is the one who runs a car to destruction and a horse to a lather, who dog-ears books, who burns cigarette trenches on table edges, who uses towels for boot rags, who stands wet glasses on polished wood, who tracks into the house in muddy shoes, and leaves his room looking as though it had been visited by a cyclone. Nor are men the only offenders. Women have been known to commit every one of these offenses and more besides. Think of what they can do to fine linen with the indelible lipstick!

Perhaps the greatest damage that most of us are ever asked to bear is that caused by a lap dog which is taken everywhere and allowed to run free because of its owner's bland unawareness that, although it may be house-trained in its own home, all strange places are "outdoor places" to a dog.

Besides these actually destruction-producing shortcomings, there are evidences of the bad upbringing of modern youth, whose lack of consideration is scarcely less annoying. There are those who are late for every meal; the cheeky ones who invite friends of their own to meals without the manners or the decency to ask their hostess' permission; the casuals who help themselves to a car and go off and don't come back for meals at all; and then those who write no letters afterward, nor even take the trouble to go up and speak to a former hostess when they see her again. This abuse of hospitality is of course more often met with by hostesses of great estates who have general week-end parties than by the hostess of a little house who seldom has anyone staying with her except a really intimate friend.

Needless to say, a young person who is considerate is a delight indeed. A young girl who tells where she is going, first asking whether it is all right, and finds her hostess as soon as she is in the house at night to report that she is back, is the one who very surely will be asked again and often. A young man, of course, is much freer, but a similar deference to the plans of his hostess and to the hours and customs of the house will result in repeated invitations for him also.

The lack of these things, showing want of common civility and decency, reflects not only on the girls and boys themselves, but on their parents, who have failed to set proper examples of good manners to them at home.

THE IDEAL HOUSE GUEST

The laws governing the behavior of the ideal guest are by no means easy to follow; not for some people, or so it seems. Whether it is easy or not, you as a guest must conform to the habits of the family with which you are staying. You take your meals at their hour, you eat what is put before you, and you get up and go out and come in and go to bed according to the schedule arranged by your hostess. *And no matter how much the hours, or food, or arrangements may upset you, you must appear blissfully content.*

When the visit is over, you need never enter that house again; but while you are there, you must like it. You must like the people you meet and the things they do. This is the first and the inviolable law for the guest. If you neither understand nor care for dogs or children, and both insist on climbing all over you, you must seemingly like it, just as you must be amiable and polite to your fellow guests, even though they be of all the people on earth the most detestable to you. You must do your best to appear to find the food delicious, even though it is to you almost uneatable. You must disguise your hatred of red ants and sand, if everyone else is bent on a picnic. You must pretend that six is a perfect dinner hour though you never dine before eight, or, on the contrary, you must wait until eight-thirty or nine with stoical fortitude, though your supper hour is six and by seven your chest seems securely pinioned to your spine.

YOU CAN SEND YOURSELF A TELEGRAM

If you go to stay in a small house in the country, and they give you a bed full of lumps in a room full of mosquitoes and flies, on a floor over that of a crying baby, under the eaves with the temperature over a hundred, you *can* the next morning walk to the village and send yourself a telegram and leave. But though you feel starved, wilted, exhausted, and are mosquito-bitten until you resemble a well-developed case of chickenpox or measles, by not so much as a facial muscle must you let the family know that your comfort lacked anything that your happiest imagination could picture—nor must you confide in anyone afterward (having broken bread in the house) how desperately wretched you were. All you can do is to politely decline the next time you are asked.

TO BE ALWAYS IN DEMAND

If you know anyone who is always in demand, not only for dinners, but for trips on yachts, and long visits in country houses, you may be very sure of one thing—the popular person is first of all unselfish or else extremely gifted, very often both.

The ideal guest not only tries to wear becoming clothes, but tries to get into an equally becoming frame of mind. No one is ever asked out very much if she is in the habit of telling people all the misfortunes and ailments she has experienced or witnessed, though the perfect guest listens with apparent sympathy. Another attribute of the perfect guest is never to keep people waiting. One is always ready for anything—or nothing. If a plan is made to picnic, one likes picnics above everything and proves that liking by enthusiastically making the sandwiches or the salad dressing or whatever she thinks she makes best. If, on the other hand, no one seems to want to do anything, the perfect guest has always a book to be absorbed in, or a piece of sewing or knitting she is engrossed with, or else beyond everything she would love to sit in an easy chair and do nothing.

This ideal guest is an equally ideal hostess; the principle of both is the same: a ready smile, a quick sympathy, a happy outlook, consideration for others, tenderness toward everything that is young or helpless, and forgetfulness of self, which is not far from the ideal of womankind. There is no rule that a man shall be other than a perfect guest in kind.

AN EXPERT VISITOR LOOKS AFTER HIS OWN COMFORT

The most trying thing to people of very set habits is an unusual breakfast hour. When you have the unfortunate habit of waking with the dawn, and the household you are visiting has the custom of sleeping on a Sunday morning, the long wait for your coffee can quite actually upset your whole day. On the other hand, to be aroused at seven on the only day when you do not have to hurry to your own affairs of state, in order to yawn through an early breakfast and then sit around and kill time, is quite as trying. The guest with the early habit can in a measure prevent discomfort. He can carry in a small case (locked, if need be) his own small electric water-heating outfit and a small package of tea or instant coffee, sugar, powdered milk, and a few crackers. He can then start his day all by himself in the barnyard hours without disturbing anyone and in comfort to himself. Few people care enough to fuss, but if they do, this equipment of a habitual visitor with incurably early waking hours is given as a suggestion.

Perhaps the entire guest situation may be put in one sentence. If you are an inflexible person, very set in your ways, don't visit! At least don't visit without carefully looking the situation over from every angle to be sure that the habits of the house you are going to are in accord with your own, or that you have confidence in your adaptability.

WHEN YOU STAY IN A LITTLE HOUSE

When you are visiting a house run with one or even no maid, it is inconsiderate to make your visit a burden through the extra picking up that your careless disorder entails. Even should you be staying in a house where there are many servants, it should be remembered that each has a share of work to do. If the housemaid offers to press a dress that has become mussed in packing, you of course accept her offer and later give her a gratuity—but you should not ask this service unless the pressing is really necessary.

LEAVING A PERFORMANCE EARLY

At a musicale or other performance, when you cannot stay until the conclusion of the program, you should sit as near the door as you can and try to leave as inconspicuously as possible. It is discourteous to the performers (and to other guests) to leave before the conclusion of their offering.

TELEVISION AND RADIO MANNERS

When guests arrive or callers come visiting and you find yourself enjoying a television show or a favorite radio program, good manners require that you (however regretfully) turn the set off. If you are fortunate enough to have another room available—the library or the study—you may entertain your friends there out of earshot, and leave the younger members of the family to enjoy their favorite programs. If your callers had wanted to hear the program, they no doubt would have stayed at home and listened.

But it is discourteous, as a host, to continue a program and so not be able to give your undivided attention to your guests. A family visitor also may do his share in solving this sometimes difficult conflict of interests by saying, "Oh, do leave it on, we can talk after the program is over," or "I do know you want to listen to it. Let me come another time." But this really does not solve the problem, once the program has been shut off and if the visitor has not quickly responded to the situation.

If you are invited to watch a television show and you are not interested in seeing "Billy Bruiser" try to knock out "Tommy Tough," or the horse show, or the dog show, or listen to an opera, it is not discourteous to say, "Thank you, no. May I come some other time?"

THE GUEST ON A YACHT

The sole difference between being a guest at a country house and a guest on a yacht is that you put to a very severe test your adaptability as a traveler. You live in very close quarters with your host and hostess and fellow guests, and must therefore be particularly on your guard against being selfish or out of humor. If you are on shore and don't feel well, you can stay at home; but off on a cruise, if you are ill you have to make the best of it, and a seasick person's "best" is very bad indeed! Therefore, let it be hoped you are a good sailor. If not, do not accept that yachting invitation!

"POT LUCK" HOSPITALITY

A rather typical husband's idea of hospitality is to bring home an unannounced friend with him. And his typical complaint is that his wife's idea of hospitality is to invite people to dine on the eighteenth and have so much of everything brought in for the occasion that he hardly recognizes his own table and certainly doesn't know the hired waiters walking around it. And most of us will sympathize with the man.

Of course, if the day happens to be one of those when there is just enough dinner for two and really not enough for three, and there is nothing in the house to make an extra portion with—and the husband then brings in a friend with a full-sized appetite—his wife would have cause for distress.

The only thing she can do is to say good-naturedly to the unexpected guest that if he doesn't mind short rations this once, he shall have extra long ones next time. Thereupon she at least tries to make the friendliness of her welcome disguise the dinner's shortcomings. If a course consists of two "individual" dinners, there is nothing to do but to pretend she is "on a diet" of whatever she may have found in the larder.

On no account may she let the guest feel that his presence is an inconvenience to her. If necessary to make any comment, it must be done gaily and light-heartedly. And, unless the menu is so meager that he actually gets up from the table as hungry as when he sat down, the chances are that he will never notice the dinner's shortcomings.

WHEN REFRESHMENTS ARE SERVED

If your guests are invited to an entertainment at any time between meal hours, the refreshments are served afterward. But if the invitation is for an hour between twelve-thirty and one, or six and eight, breakfast, lunch, dinner, or supper is served first and the entertainment takes place afterward. At a wedding, of course, the whole reception comes after the ceremony.

FIRST AID TO A SUCCESSFUL HOSTESS

To be able to remember the certain dishes that your friends like, or more especially the ones they avoid, is a wonderful asset that can be acquired by anyone willing to take a little trouble. If you haven't a talent for remembering—and few of us have—then keep a "like and dislike" notebook in which you index: "John Allen—cannot eat shellfish, red meat, or strawberries. Seems to like best chicken Maryland and roast turkey. Took two helpings chocolate ice-cream. Likes coffee very strong." Opposite John Allen's food page you might note that he dislikes Susie Long, dislikes bridge with Major Case. And so on indefinitely for each person you are likely to ask to your house.

One woman particularly disliked black bean soup; her unobserving cousin, otherwise a charming woman, served it every time she was a week-end visitor.

Nothing is a greater help to your success than the use of just such information. The unobserving, uncaring hostess will time and time again invite John Allen and give him crabs, red meat, strawberries, and tastelessly weak coffee, seat him at table next to Susie Long, and at the bridge table with Major Case. John Allen is evidently a dyspeptic, but he illustrates the idea!

When inviting a stranger to your house, you offer him the best you can provide, and if your choice be unfortunate for him, it can't be helped. But there is no excuse for not remembering that a friend persistently refuses certain dishes—that is, if you would be a perfect hostess.

THE GIVE AND TAKE OF HOSPITALITY

It is true that a return invitation should, when possible, be made for every first invitation. We actually, however, return hospitality when and as we can. And if we can't return it—at least, in kind—no great harm is done.

For instance, let us say that the Greathouses invite their friends the Onerooms first to dinner, then to lunch, then to dinner again throughout every month in the year. It is entirely possible that the Onerooms proffer no return invitations whatsoever, and yet the Greathouses may very well feel themselves repaid many times over. Mary Oneroom perhaps puts herself out to do a dozen kindnesses of one sort or another, or quite possibly she and her husband repay the hospitality only with themselves, with their good looks, their amiability, their tact, their wit, or their sympathy. This "payment-of-oneself," as the French say, is an important phase of hostess-and-guest obligation which many people overlook.

Mrs. Greathouse, who likes nothing better than giving parties, cannot possibly give them without guests, can she? The unthinking may imagine that mere money will do. But let us draw the picture of a beautiful background, a splendid house, a perfect butler, a row of smart footmen, floral decorations, an orchestra, beautiful table appointments, a perfectly prepared menu, Mr. and Mrs. Greathouse in flawless evening clothes waiting in a flawless drawing-room—for whom? That's it, exactly! For their guests. And the quality of their party depends first and last upon the people who are coming. It is the guests who make the party a brilliant success or a distressing failure. Every prominent hostess knows that she must more or less depend upon a few especially adaptable and tactful and personable aides, such as the Gaylings who are always smart and amusing, and the Lovejoys who are attractive in appearance, tactful, and charming—as only those are who are keenly interested in people and things in general, and not especially interested in themselves.

Obviously the hostess who says, "We have had the Gaylings four times this year and the Lovejoys time and again, and I'm not going to ask them until they invite us back," is without any sense of values. No wonder her parties are failures. Naturally a hostess does not continue to send invitations to those who repeatedly decline, or to those who show no appreciation or who make no return in whatever way they can. But a hostess of talent would never put the Gaylings, or the Lovejoys, or the Onerooms on the debtor side of her ledger any more than she would put flowers, or music, or professional entertainers there.

This does not mean that those who can make "material" return are not under any obligation to do so. To keep the scales balanced, it is necessary that we contribute something. But that "something" can be anything that opportunity suggests—a cup of tea with someone especially interesting, a trifling present now and then, or the payment made with the cooperative effort of our own talents—whatever they may be.

COURTESY TOWARD ARTISTS AND ENTERTAINERS

Apart from the courtesies that every really well-bred hostess instinctively shows alike to friends, acquaintances, or strangers who are admitted to her house, particular rules that should apply in reference to professional artists do not go very far because so much depends upon circumstances. Generally speaking, all entertainers should be admitted at the front door, of course.

Musicians who play at a dance or at a wedding reception necessarily arrive long before the guests, and are shown at once to a dressing room and then to the place where they are to play. They should be greeted briefly by whoever is in charge of arrangements. Refreshments should be taken to them at the times that fit in best with their program.

Soloists or actors, who are to make their entrance from behind scenery as on a stage, should be shown to dressing rooms and then to the best "green room" the house can provide. They should be greeted as soon after their arrival as possible by the host or hostess or both, who naturally ask whether there is anything that would add to their comfort. Whether after their performance they meet many of the guests or none depends upon their own standing no less than upon their personality and their wishes. When musicians or actresses or actors are especially charming or talented, or both, guests will almost surely ask to meet them.

COURTESY TO A CELEBRITY

A real celebrity, whether a star in the musical world or a notable person who is to lecture, is usually the guest of honor and treated as such in every particular—except that he or she does not take a place in the receiving line and meet the guests as they arrive. Since the hostess cannot leave her place at the door, the host or another member of the family is delegated to greet the celebrity upon his arrival and to conduct him to whichever is the most suitable room in which to wait until it is time to make his entrance. The host or delegate-host remains with the artist or speaker until the hostess herself appears. She greets the celebrity and conducts him to the music room or to the platform and introduces him to the audience. At the end of the program the hostess stands beside the celebrity and introduces those of her guests who come up to be introduced.

But no matter in which category an artist belongs, there is a certain purely business matter-of-factness to the situation of a professional fulfilling an engagement. He goes prepared to do to the best of his ability what he has agreed to do, and at the close of his performance he receives the sum that has been agreed upon. Whether in addition to this he has a delightful evening or a trying one is, so far as his business contract goes, beside the mark.

INEXCUSABLE BEHAVIOR TO FRIENDS WHO ARE PROFESSIONALS

For obvious reasons a most indefensible example is that of the hostess who considers the talents of professional friends—and even bare acquaintances—as assets to which she has proprietary rights. Don't we know Mrs. Hi Wayman, who invites Mr. Barrytone Tops or Mr. Hit-on-Broadway to dine on Sunday evening! After dinner she coyly announces that she just knows that Mr. Tops will be delighted to sing, or that Mr. Hit-on-Broadway will *of course* do that delicious scene which is the only reason why the theatre is packed to bursting every night in the week except this—his one evening of rest!

It is often true that at a party of considerable size a star-ranking professional can, or possibly must, decline on the plea that contracts prohibit his performance. But at an informal dinner at which one or two others of lesser talent have contributed their part, it is often embarrassing to refuse because it seems ungenerous to all those present who so eagerly look toward him. But actually it is distinctly unfair to expect someone to return the courtesy of a little food and a place at table between no matter how pleasant companions with an entertainment commercially valued at something approaching, or possibly surpassing, four figures! And even if he is not at or near the top of his profession, remember your guest is not a trained poodle to be put through a bag of tricks for the entertainment of your other guests.

FAVORS TOO MUCH TAKEN FOR GRANTED

Much might be said about the unthinking casualness with which numberless people ask favors of their professional friends. Put bluntly, one would not go to a bank and ask for money, nor to the shop of a milliner and ask to be given a hat, and yet the friends of a professional artist will think nothing of asking for a sketch or a recital. And the work of every professional is his bank account. If he gives to one person, how can he refuse to give to another—and who will want to buy what is given so freely?

Of much less importance, but merely illustrating the point: The barest acquaintances of an author think nothing of asking him for his books. Apparently most people imagine that books grow like daisies in the field and that an author need merely pick them at random. Doctors and lawyers are constantly asked for professional advice by people they meet casually in the houses of their friends. As for people of the theatre, no others in all the professions in the world are so persistently asked to give their time, their vitality, and their talent. And in nearly all cases they are delighted to give generously to someone they care for or to a cause in which they are interested; but when they are asked to give, a conventional "I'm so sorry" should be respected without forcing them into a position that seems to make them seem ungracious.

If musicians are amateurs, however, their friends can perfectly well ask them to play at a musicale. But they should not be asked to provide a background accompaniment to chatter. No one with any sensibility would invite first-class artists to play or sing and then make no effort to preserve a courteous silence during their performance. On the other hand, professional dance orchestras and other party musicians who play at dances and at weddings do not expect, or even want, to face a room full of completely silent people.

RECEIVING GUESTS AT A CLUB OR HOTEL

When giving a lunch or any party in a club or hotel, the hostess waits for her guests in the lobby or entrance hall. As her guests arrive, they join her and stand or sit near her.

If the room is filled with others, she herds her own group, as it were, a little apart. When all have arrived, they go to the dining-room and to the table, which must always have been prepared in advance for them, and if they are more than four, the food should have been ordered and the meal ready to serve as soon as they sit down.

GUESTS AT A BANQUET

It is only at a semi-public lunch or dinner, at which there is a separate speakers' table, that the guests at the other small tables take their places without waiting for the arrival of the principal guest.

HOSTESS ENTERS LAST

When entering a room or her house with a guest, a hostess goes first only when it is necessary to show the way. And then she usually says, "Excuse me for going first." In a restaurant the head waiter leads the way to the table and the hostess follows her guests.

DON'T!—WHEN YOU ARE HOSTESS

Don't pretend to be other than you are. In other words, don't dress the chore man as butler, or the grocery boy as a footman in the hope of impressing your neighbors. To make too much effort is always a mistake.

On the other hand, don't lazily and incompetently think that no provision at all is plenty good enough.

DO!—WHEN YOU ARE A GUEST

It is not necessary to be told, when going out on the street, to put on a hat and perhaps a coat and gloves, or when going to swim to wear a bathing suit, or when going to a dinner party to wear a dinner or evening dress.

But there are lots of people who, taking great pains to put on becoming clothes, never for an instant think of putting on a becoming frame of mind. When going to a party, it is far more important to put a headache or a worry out of view than to wear a new dress.

TAKING A HOUSE GUEST TO A PARTY

When an unexpected house guest arrives for a week-end it is quite all right for a hostess to telephone to ask if she may bring him to a lunch or dinner at a large house, or to an afternoon party or buffet supper at a small house. But it is much better when the party is a sit-down one at a house of limited size to say, "I find that I will have John Smith as an extra house guest Saturday. If that is too many of us, would it be better for Henry and me not to come either?" The hostess then is perfectly free to say either, "Oh, no, I have plenty of room. Do bring him." Or "Oh, I am *sorry* there is not space to squeeze in even a mouse; it would be better for you and Henry to come another day."

— AND PLEASE KEEP YOUR GERMS TO YOURSELF

How often do we hear Mrs. Cravin Praze explain at length, "I got out of bed to come (a-choo! sniffle, snuffle). I thought I'd never be able to get into my clothes I had such a chill (snuffle, sniffle, cough, cough). My temperature is over 103. I really ought to have a medal for bravery! But I did not think it fair to give up." Helpless Hostess says, "Oh, my dear, I'm so sorry! You ought to go straight back to bed." Unhappily, politeness does not let her say what she thinks, which is, "How *could* you be so thoughtless of others as to come here and breathe flu germs on everybody!"

Therefore, although there is a fixed rule which makes it very discourteous to break a dinner engagement, this rule is canceled when there is any danger of scattering infectious air-borne germs.

Even at home one member of the family who has tonsillitis or a bad cold will go and sit close enough to another to breathe in his face—and then protest violently later, "I *know* Jimmy did not get the grippe from *me!*" Far more considerate to stay quarantined in one's room unless nose and mouth are both covered with a protecting mask of gauze. Feeling utterly miserable themselves, they should try to keep others from feeling likewise—you'd think!

The business angle of this subject is unhappily not so easily solved. A clerk or stenographer or saleswoman or even a school teacher cannot stay at home because of slight ailment. But she *can* do her best—by gargling and inhaling antiseptic medication and by trying not to breathe in close contact with any one except through a piece of fresh gauze or a fresh handkerchief—to keep her germs to herself.

OVERNIGHT GUEST IN A CITY APARTMENT

Today an increasing number of people live in apartments and a guest room is rare. Sometimes a couch in the living-room may be converted into a comfortable bed at night for an occasional overnight guest, or if a child is away at boarding school, his room may be available. No matter how hospitable your host or hostess may be, a guest should remember that an extra person in small quarters is, inevitably, something of an imposition—no matter how charming the guest may be. Household regulations should be meticulously observed, and a guest should not stay any longer than necessary. He should take up as little room with his possessions as possible, and keep his belongings neat. Above all, he should be prepared to fit in with the household schedule and not inconvenience his host or hostess.

COURTESY ON THE TELEPHONE

⋅⋅৹[37]৹⋅⋅

THE MOST DISCOURTEOUS HABIT ON THE TELEPHONE IS that of the businessman who tells his secretary to call Mr. Jones and is then not waiting to take the call.

The secretary, for example, dials the number; a voice announces, "A. B. Jones Company"; the secretary says, "Mr. Brown is calling Mr. Jones." Promptly Mr. Jones says, "Hello, Brown!" but instead of Brown's voice, that of his secretary explains, "Mr. Brown is busy on another wire, he'll be with you in a moment." Mr. Jones listens good-temperedly—a few seconds, and more seconds. Mr. Brown is evidently unaware that seconds seem minutes to a busy person listening to a dead receiver.

It is quite all right, of course, to have someone call a number for you, but you must then be ready to take the receiver the moment the person called speaks. Obviously this annoyance applies only to one who has several telephones on his desk, one of which rings just as he is about to reply. In this case the secretary—while continuing to listen to the Jones wire—should reply, "Mr. Brown is on another telephone. Will you wait or may I call you?" If the new voice says, "I'll wait," they all wait for Mr. Jones. The moment he replies, she hands the first telephone to Mr. Brown and keeps the other wire waiting. As soon as the Jones conversation ends, she tells the waiting caller, "Mr. Brown is here now," and hands him the telephone.

The point is that the person who *has been called* has the "right of way"—even though he has not yet come to the telephone. It is picking up the second telephone after putting in a call on the first that results in rudeness to the one who, having been called to the telephone, is then asked to wait! Usually this absentee telephone-calling comes from a busy office, but I am sorry to say it is not at all unheard of at home.

THE BUSINESS OFFICE "GOOD MORNING"

The familiar business-office salutation, "Smith, Brown Company— "Good morning!," while it is quite pleasant, may not be very efficient.

This salutation is still that of most business firms as well as hotels, and there is great hesitation about criticizing it because it is polite and pleases many. And yet, when we are pressed for time, it is not as pleasing as it ought to be, to be held up even by a voice with a smile—in fact, the lovelier the smile, the more likely is it to impel us to reply, "Good *morning*—er, eh—I'd like to speak to Mr. Smith, please. This is Mr. Jones." All of which is more time-taking than "A. K. Jones calling Mr. Smith." Moreover, it can happen that Aunt Jane from Bright Meadows, hearing the operator's friendly, "Blank Company. Good morning!" replies, "Why, good *morning*. Who is this I'm speaking to?" The operator explains briefly and Aunt Jane explains at length, "I'd like to talk to Mr. Jones—he's my nephew, you know—he's my sister Sarah's oldest boy. She told me to be sure to let him know—" Aunt Jane purrs on, hampering—if not disrupting—the reception desk.

All of this leads to the advice of putting "Good morning" at the beginning of the salutation, which works quite well. A brisk "Good morning, Smith Jones Company" is without discourtesy answered, "Mr. Jones, please."

"HELLO" CORRECT AT HOME

The correct way to answer a house telephone is still "Hello." This is because it is like looking out through shutters, as it were, to see who is there. "Yes" is abrupt and a bit rude. To answer, "This is Mrs. Jones's house," leaves the door standing open wide, and to answer, "Mrs. Jones speaking," leaves her without chance of retreat.

This is not nonsense. It is a really important angle of modern telephone etiquette. In all great cities, telephones are rung so persistently by every type of stranger who wants to sell something to Mrs. Householder, or ask a favor of Mrs. Prominent, or to get in touch with Mr. Official (having failed to reach him at his office), or to ask if you are listening to a certain radio program, that many persons of prominence are obliged to keep their personal telephones unlisted. The last thing that they want to do, therefore, is to announce to strangers, "Miss Star speaking." It is far more practical to say "Hello" and let the one calling ask, "Is this Miss Star's house? Mr. Director would like to speak to her." Or if she herself answers, a friend recognizing her voice says, "Hello, Mary. This is Kate."

In a doctor's office it is proper, of course, to announce, "Dr. Squill's office."

"WHO IS CALLING, PLEASE?"

Everywhere it is correct that the person answering the telephone ask, "Who is calling, please?" If the person says, "I want to speak to Mrs. Brown personally—never mind my name!" whoever answers the telephone replies, "I'm sorry but I can't interrupt Mrs. Brown. May I give her a message later?" If he then refuses to leave a message or give his name, he can hardly expect Mrs. Brown to speak to him, nor is there any reason why she should.

GIVING ONE'S NAME

Whether to give one's name with or without title, is a question often raised.

In business, and also when talking with strangers, titles are always used.

The following rules hold good: An older person announcing herself or even himself to one who is much younger says, "This is Mrs. Elder" or "Miss Spinster" or "Mr. Elder."

Mrs. Worldly, who is middle-aged, says, "This is Mrs. Worldly" to everyone except those who actually call her Edith.

A younger lady, whether married or single, says, "This is Marie Manners." In fact, she makes this same announcement to everyone whom she knows socially, whether that person calls her Marie or Mrs. Manners. (The phrase "this is" is more impersonal—and also less pompous—than "I am. . . .")

If you are a young man calling a friend and the answering voice is that of the friend or a member of the friend's family, you say, "This is Jim Brown" or probably "This is Jim." If the voice is that of a maid or a butler, you say, "Mr. James Brown would like to speak to Mrs. Gray or Miss Mary."

Calling a daughter of the family "Miss Mary" is a point of social etiquette not characteristic of the South alone, but of best society everywhere. To ask for "Miss Gray" or even "Miss Mary Gray" would imply either that she is living away from her home or, if she is living at home, that you are a stranger probably calling on business. But in any case, it definitely would proclaim you a stranger to her family.

In business, it would be in very worst taste for a salesman to announce himself to a customer—a lady—as Sam Sales. Correctly he says, "This is Mr. Sales of the Blank Company." But to a gentleman he leaves off the "Mr."

A young woman in business also says, "This is Miss Caesar of the Wheel Tyre Co." or "Transcontinental Railroad—Mr. Train's secretary speaking."

In business, names must be given as briefly but as explicitly and as clearly as is humanly possible.

INVITATIONS BY TELEPHONE

If Mrs. Smith and Mrs. Jones are themselves telephoning, there is no long conversation, but merely:

Mrs. Jones: "Is that you, Mrs. Smith (or Sarah)? This is Mrs. Jones" (if she is elderly), or "Alice Jones" (if she is fairly young), or

"Alice" (if an intimate friend). "Will you and your husband (or John) dine with us tomorrow at eight o'clock?"

Mrs. Smith: "I'm so sorry we can't. We are dining with Mabel." Or "We'd love to," or "Yes—with pleasure." And probably repeats "Tomorrow at eight" to be sure there is no misunderstanding of date or time.

Invitations for a week-end visit are as often as not telephoned:

"Hello, Ethel! This is Alice. Will you and Arthur come on the sixteenth for over Sunday?"

"The sixteenth? That's Friday. We'd love to!"

If either Mrs. Smith or Mrs. Jones is not telephoning and the message is given by or received by a butler or a maid, see The Formal Invitation by Telephone on page 127.

DON'T ASK "WHAT ARE YOU DOING SATURDAY?"

A bad habit which should be avoided is the prefacing of an invitation with, "Hello, John. What are you doing Saturday night?" Or "Are you going to be busy Monday afternoon?" This maneuver puts John in the position of finding it embarrassing to refuse after having answered, "Nothing," and then being told that he is expected to dine with the Borings or to play bridge with the Revokes. On the other hand, if he answers, "I have an engagement," and is then told that he would have been invited to something he likes very much, it is disappointing not to be able to go—without seeming rude to the person whose invitation he has at first refused. If this situation is bad for a man, however, it is even worse for a woman. A man can perhaps be excused for changing his mind when he hears Louise Lovely is going to be at the dinner or playing at the same table with him. But a young woman who says she has an engagement and is then told, "Too bad you can't come, because John Brilliant was looking forward to meeting you," can't very well change her mind and say, "Oh, then I'll get out of my dinner somehow and come."

TWO IMPORTANT DON'TS

When the number you get is evidently wrong, don't ask, "What number is this?" Ask instead, "Is this Main 2-3456?"

Don't answer and then say, "Wait a minute," and keep whoever called you waiting while you vanish on an errand of your own. If the doorbell is ringing and you can't listen at that moment, say "I'll call you back in a few minutes!" *And do so.*

DON'T LET YOUR SMALL CHILD ANSWER THE TELEPHONE

A custom that is satisfactory to few of us is that of letting a too young child answer the telephone. A lot of time is wasted trying to make the child understand a message and bring an answer that leaves you in no doubt as to its mother's meaning. If there is a long silence, there is no way of knowing whether the child is hunting for Mother, or playing with a friend or his dog, quite forgetful of the telephone which, being off the hook, can no longer ring.

LONG-DISTANCE CALLS

Of first importance, *don't shout!* When you telephone long distance don't raise your voice. You will only distort it. Amplifiers on the long-line circuit step up your voice all the way. Speak slowly and distinctly into the transmitter with the mouthpiece about an inch from your lips. Avoid mumbling or hastily running your words together.

When calling long distance, keep on the tip of your tongue what you have to say, and say it promptly. Receiving the reply, say "Good-by" and hang up. If you have several things to say, write them down and read them off.

If you often call really long distance a telephone timer is a must. It is a small second-counting gadget that rings a bell before each three minutes. If you are making a personal call and the person on the other end of the line likes to talk on and on, ask the operator, when you put in your call, to interrupt when the three minutes are up.

You should, of course, always keep a pad and a reliable pen or pencil beside the telephone. To exclaim, "Wait a minute until I find something to write on!" doesn't give a picture of a well-ordered house.

CONSIDERATION OF EQUIPMENT

A few words about the consideration which we should show to the telephone company by taking care of the instrument itself:

Don't stand it where it may be easily knocked off, or too near a radiator, or in the very hot sun, or where it can be rained on.

Don't let the cord get snarled tight. Material so treated is sooner or later weakened and impaired. Spiral protectors are available in many colors and in white and will keep the cord from tangling.

Don't jiggle the telephone plunger—the futile senseless habit of the impatient. It is as stupid as the impatient driver who presses his horn ceaselessly in a traffic jam where it is perfectly obvious that the car in front of him can't move. If you thrust the plunger up and down slowly you operate a relay which turns on a light on the surface of the operator's board; when you jiggle it, the relay will not work: no light goes on and the operator merely hears a clicking which she cannot identify as to number.

THE OVERWORKING OF INFORMATION

It is quite true that the telephone operator who answers when we dial Information is prepared to answer our perplexities, but it is not at all true that she can be expected to overcome our lazy carelessness.

Strangely enough it is not our oldest generation which finds it difficult to read the small print in the overheavy telephone book (a small magnifying glass near the telephone will help the far-sighted, or a great effort will get you out of the big easy chair to lift the heavy book) that gives Information an overamount of work. On the contrary, investigation by the telephone company has found that the overcrowding calls that are at times literally crippling to the service, especially in our greatest cities, are made by the lazy young who have seemingly neither the strength of muscle nor the sense of fairness to lift themselves off their spines long enough to look up a number, rather than ask Information to do it for them. If for some reason you have to ask for a number, and if it is one you think you will call again, write it down.

RULES OF COURTESY ON A PARTY LINE

When it is realized that the usual number of families sharing a party line is four, the maximum ten, and that for so long as one person is talking, no outside call can reach any other on that line, the consideration required of each sharer is obvious. For this reason the telephone company has taken pains to make and expects the subscribers to keep the following rules:

Ordinarily when you find the line in use, you hang up for three minutes before signaling again. In an emergency it is permissible to break in on a conversation and call out clearly: "EMERGENCY!" and then "Our barn is on fire," or "Johnny's had an accident," or whatever it is. But unless all on the line hang up, your telephone is cut off.

A personal memory: During the last war, a soldier tried to say a few last words to his wife before sailing. For fifty minutes the long-distance operator repeatedly received a "busy wire" signal. He had to go without a word to her.

What he could have done and we can all do is to remember that while the operator is not permitted to cut in on a busy wire, her supervisor can. In this case the husband could have asked for the supervisor of the station called and briefly explained. At her discretion, she could then have cut in and announced a long-distance call for Mrs. Soldier, and would those talking kindly hang up and permit her to take it?

PAYING FOR CALLS ON A NEIGHBOR'S TELEPHONE

A situation of extreme embarrassment and unfair cost to telephone subscribers is caused by neighbors who, having no telephone of their own, add not merely the annoyance of interruption but unpaid-for amounts to the subscriber's bill.

To those who live in a town where local calls are not charged for or the allotted number of calls is seldom used up and no long-distance ones are made, frequent use of your telephone may very well be annoying but it does not add to your bill. In a city where every local call is charged for, and whenever a long-distance call is made, it is just as correct to present an itemized bill for the charges on your telephone bill as it would be to present a bill for eggs or chickens, a thing you would never hesitate to do.

For an occasional short-distance call, you might let it go, but for those who make many long-distance calls, it is simplest as well as most accurate to show your telephone users the toll list and let each check his calls and pay the totals.

It is not too finicky to ask (if they are likely to make many calls) that those, who live where local calls are not charged for, remember, when they are visiting in a city where every call in excess of the daily allowance is added to the subscriber's bill, to leave ten cents (or whatever the charge may be) for each city call, beside the telephone.

Try to avoid making calls from a busy doctor's office, but if you have to, pay the nurse for the call.

TELEPHONE PAYMENT BY VISITORS

Many mistakenly hesitate to proffer payment for their calls. The definite rule is this: Should one be obliged to make a single local call, one would not ordinarily offer payment for it, but it is absolutely required that one pay for every long-distance call. Moreover, it is the only way a house guest can feel free to telephone as often as he or she may want to. One should always call the operator as soon as one has finished speaking and ask for "the toll charge on XY-23 Great Town" and then leave this amount with a slip, giving date and number called. Or if one has made many during a long stay, the complete list of telephone calls and telegrams sent, with the amounts of each and their total, should be handed to the hostess and paid for when one says good-by.

This is not humiliating, and no matter how rich the host may be it is the *correct* way to pay this debt.

TELEPHONE COURTESY TEST

If it interests you to know how good or otherwise your telephone manners may be, the number of times you can answer "Yes" to the following seventeen questions will give you your rating. If every one is "Yes," you deserve not merely a crown, but a halo!

1. Do you make sure of the correct number so as not to risk disturbing strangers by "calling from memory"?

2. Do you make conversations with busy people as brief as possible?

3. When calling intimate friends who do not recognize your voice, do you resist playing a game of "Guess who?" and announce yourself promptly?

4. Do you try to time your calls so as not to interfere with the occupations of those you call most often?

5. Do you make business calls well before the close of office hours, especially if calling a person you know is a commuter?

6. If you call a young mother often, do you take note of her children's meal and bath time so as to avoid these hours?

7. If you want to have a conversation of any length, do you ask whether the other person is free to listen or whether to call back at another time?

8. Do you treat wrong-number calls as a mutual inconvenience and answer, "Sorry, wrong number," in a tone of polite sympathy instead of showing ill-tempered annoyance?

9. On a dial telephone, do you always wait for dial tone?

10. If you are either a fond parent or doting grandparent, do you realize that the charming prattle of your little ones who rush so happily to answer the telephone can be irritating at times rather than delighting to a caller—especially one calling from a great distance?

11. When you call a long-distance number from the house of a friend, do you always ask the toll operator for the charge and leave the correct amount?

12. When you hear an unexpected voice, do you at once ask, "Is this Broad 1234?" instead of asking, "What number is this?"

13. When unable to stop what you are doing, do you explain and offer to call back in so many minutes, rather than say, "I'll be back in a second," and then keep your caller holding the wire much longer than you realize?

14. In reverse of this, do you explain to one calling you that you have a visitor and will call back at a later time and not let the visitor sit listening to your half of what to her must be an unintelligible and boring conversation that runs on and on?

15. When the number you are calling is not answered quickly, do you wait long enough for someone to lay aside what she may be doing so that when she reaches the telephone she will not have been disturbed just to answer the telephone you have already hung up?

16. Do you, when making a number of calls on a party line, space them so that others on the line may have a chance to use their telephones?

17. In a general office, do you explain to personal friends inclined to talk at length that you will call them after hours?

ETIQUETTE FOR THE SMOKER

·:·] 38 [·:·

THE EVER-INCREASING CUSTOM OF SMOKING IN NEARLY all places at nearly all hours and by all sorts of people makes it seem advisable to gather in this special chapter rules that will permit the enjoyment of smoking by those who smoke with the least unhappiness to those who don't.

The first point that must be made is that in all large cities the odds are against those of us who do not like to smoke. If ten people hated it to every one who liked it, that would be one thing; but in nearly all great cities where the smokers outnumber the non-smokers by surely 100 to 1, or so it seems, about the only thing we who also live in these cities can do is to profit by the song sung at the sneezing pig-baby in that pepper-filled kitchen in *Alice's Adventures in Wonderland:*

> I speak severely to my boy,
> I beat him when he sneezes;
> For he can thoroughly enjoy
> The pepper when he pleases!

In other words, at this present time we are all going to have to enjoy "the pepper" or stay in our own homes, and even there admit none but non-smokers.

THE NON-SMOKER SITUATION IS THIS

The situation of those non-smokers who are made actually sick by the smell of tobacco or the discomfort of smoke in their eyes is each year being made harder. Smoking is even now permitted in the best (mezzanine) seats in the movies—and of course in all eating places. It is true that the theatres devoted to plays are still smoke-free. Happily the orchestra seats in the movies are still free from smoke—otherwise there would be only churches and museums where non-smokers can go with complete comfort.

Until very lately parlor cars were smokeless. Now, however, the newest (and finest?) parlor cars upholstered in pale blue and gleaming chrome are built with smoking sections sometimes divided only by a small waist-high partition between the chairs on either side. On occasion it becomes merely interior decoration that in no way separates the smoking end from the non-smoking.

Unless able to secure a drawing-room or roomette for herself or himself alone, the day coach is the non-smoker's best choice—and even there, conductors do not always enforce the no-smoking rule.

Since smoking is not allowed on local buses, riding on one is, up to the present, as comfortable in this respect as ever.

WHEN GUESTS SMOKE

While it may be just to agree that the few have no right to interfere with the pleasure of the many, there are certain requirements of propriety and of consideration for others that those who smoke should observe. It is entirely proper that a hostess or even a host ask that they do so.

The answer to the hostesses who ask how they can protect their possessions from careless guests is that hospitality need never be helpless. It is true that after a guest has burned a hole in the upholstery or a groove on a table edge, nothing can be done about it. But when a hostess sees a smoker pick up an ornament of value to use in place of an ashtray, she can certainly take it away and put an ashtray in its place. Perhaps she says nothing or perhaps she smiles and says, "Let me give you this," as though she were thinking of the smoker's convenience.

The wise hostess will see to it that there is an ashtray within easy reach of every seat in her house that may be occupied by a smoking guest. A thoughtful hostess, even one who does not smoke herself, will see that there are cigarette boxes, with fresh cigarettes in them, and a lighter that is filled and that works for the comfort of her smoking guests. Cigars need be passed only after dinner and when the ladies have left the dining-room.

SMOKING DON'TS

First of all, it is unforgivable to lay a cigarette (or cigar) on the edge of a table or other piece of furniture—ever! Forgetting it and letting it burn a charred groove on a table edge or a brown scar on a marble mantel is merely the result of putting it down on the wrong place to begin with. Find an ashtray to lay it on—or *ask* for one.

Striking a match directly toward someone—most often outdoors and "with the wind"—belongs in the category with a pointed gun, should the head of the match fly off and land on a woman's inflammable dress!

Never press a cigarette out without being sure that the object pressed on is intended for that purpose. Cigarettes put out against lamp bases, ornaments, and almost any surface that presents itself to an unthinking smoker, may mar or destroy objects of value. Most of us do not, but some of us do!

Lighted cigarettes should not be thrown into fireplaces. A roaring fire started on a hot July day may be the reward of such carelessness, though such a result is preferable to having a cigarette tossed out the the window upon an awning or the top of someone's new convertible parked outside.

CIGARETTES AT TABLE

Until the last few years, smoking at a really formal dinner was unthinkable, but today cigarettes are passed at the end of the salad course even in the houses of those conservatives who have heretofore held out against any smoking before or during dinner. It is true that there are numberless women who light their own cigarettes the moment they have entered the room and greeted their hostess, and again as soon as they are seated at table—some of them even greet their hostess cigarette in hand. It is also true that others, following their example, are as likely as not to give the impression that smoking is approved by the most conservative.

When young Mrs. Inconsiderate lights her cigarette even before laying her napkin across her knees and greets the man on her right from beneath an ascending veil of smoke, all others at table, including the men next to her, feel free to follow her example. And to stop this practice there is really nothing that the conservative hostess can do.

NEVER LIGHT YOUR OWN CIGARETTE AT A TABLE WITHOUT ACCESSORIES

Whether it is proper to smoke at table depends upon the setting of the places. If each place is set with cigarettes, a lighter and an ashtray, naturally people may smoke as soon as they choose. But in the houses of those who do not put them on the table or who have them passed only at dessert, it is still bad manners to light one's own cigarette and smoke throughout the meal.

It is also extremely bad manners and thoughtless to pay no attention to whether smoke is blowing into the face of someone who may not be smoking. Be careful too that the smoke from the cigarette you are holding, or have laid down, is not finding its way into someone's face.

INEXCUSABLE UNTIDINESS

Other don'ts include all the untidiness of average smokers, such as spilling ashes on the floor and into any and all the parlor ornaments. Surely you can look around for something that is obviously an ashtray, or, failing to find it, ask your hostess. If she seems reluctant to provide you with an ashtray, or tells you she has none, stop smoking and get rid of your cigarette outdoors, if possible, or wherever you can best destroy its odor. (Remember: Just putting it out does not help at all. Nicotine nausea, which affects some non-smokers, is greatest when caused by cigars or cigarettes *that have been put out*. Dead butts are the sick-making ones.)

TIMES WHEN NO ONE MAY SMOKE

One may not smoke in a church, or during any religious service, or ceremonial proceedings. One may not smoke in a sickroom. One should not smoke in the room of a convalescent unless the convalescent himself is smoking. Good taste forbids smoking by a woman on a city street. It should be unnecessary to say that no one should think of smoking or carrying a lighted cigarette when dancing. To these obvious exceptions should be added those in business (regulated by the rules of each firm) and those of consideration for the customs of the community which you may be visiting, or for the prejudices of the people with whom you personally come in contact.

THE CLOTHES OF A LADY

·≫] 39 [≪·

CLOTHES DO MORE THAN ADD TO OUR APPEARANCE; THEY are our appearance. The first impression that we make upon others depends almost entirely upon what we wear and how we wear it. Manners and speech are noted afterward, and character is discerned last of all.

In the community where we live, character is the fundamental essential; but for the transient impression that we make everywhere in public, two superficial attributes are alone indispensable—good manners and a pleasing appearance. And such an appearance is impossible without an average degree of smartness.

In Europe, where a high title serves in lieu of gold brocade, or in the intellectual circles where talent alone counts, or in small communities where people are known for what they really are, appearance is of esthetic rather than essential importance.

But in the world of smart society, clothes represent not only our ticket of admission but our contribution to the effect of a party.

Not even the most beautiful background could in itself suggest a brilliant gathering if the majority of those present were frumps or vulgarians. Rather be frumpy than vulgar! Much. Frumps are often celebrities in disguise, but a person of vulgar appearance is pretty sure to be vulgar all through.

DO YOU KNOW HOW TO WEAR CLOTHES?

The woman who knows how to wear clothes is like a stage director who skilfully presents—herself. This skill in presentation is something for which it is difficult to give directions, because it is a talent rather than a formula. Naturally one who is young and whose skin is clear, whose figure is size ten or twelve, can quite literally wear any hat or dress she fancies and have both become her to perfection. And yet another girl, lacking the knack of personal adjustment, will find the buying of a becoming hat an endless search through such trials of unbecomingness that she finally buys, not one she likes, but the one she dislikes least.

The sense of what is becoming and the knack of putting clothes on well are the two greatest assets of smartness. And both are attainable by anyone willing to look at herself as she really is.

FOLLOWING FASHION HAS LITTLE IN COMMON WITH BEAUTY

Fashion has the power to appear temporarily in the guise of beauty, though it is the antithesis of beauty as often as not. If you doubt it, look at old fashion plates. Even the woman of beautiful taste succumbs occasionally to the epidemics of fashion, but she is more immune than most. All women who have any clothes-sense whatever know more or less the type of things that are *their* style—unless they have such a temporary attack of "fashionitis" that they are irresponsibly delirious.

There is one unchanging principle which must be followed by everyone who would be well dressed—SUITABILITY.

VULGAR CLOTHES

To define differences between clothes that are notable because of their smartness and clothes that are merely conspicuous is to define something that is very elusive.

Vulgar clothes are those which, no matter what the fashion of the moment may be, are always too elaborate for the occasion, that are too exaggerated in style, or that have accessories out of harmony with the dress and the wearer.

Beau Brummell's remark that, when one attracted too much notice, he could be sure of being not well dressed but overdressed, has for over a hundred years been the comfort of the dowdy. It is, of course, very often true, but not invariably so. A person may be stared at for any one of many reasons. A woman may be stared at because she is ill-behaved, or because she looks like a freak of the circus, or because she is enchanting to behold.

If you are much stared at, what *sort* of stare do you create? Are you sure it is admiring? Or might it be curious? Or could it be disapproving?

THE SHEEP

Frumps are not very typical of America; those who overdress are somewhat more numerous; but most numerous of all are the quietly dressed, unnoticeable men and women who make up the representative background of every city, who buy as good clothes as they can, but not more than they need, and whose ambition is not to be strikingly noticeable but to fit in suitably with their background, whatever that may be.

Less numerous, but far more conspicuous, are the dressed-to-the-minute women who, like sheep exactly, follow every turn of latest fashion blindly and without the slightest sense of whether it is a good one or absurd, or even if it is in the least becoming to her. As each new season's fashion is defined, all the sheep run and dress themselves each in a replica of the other; their own types and personalities have nothing to do with the case. Fashion says, "Wear a three-cornered handkerchief instead of a bodice," and daughter, mother, grandmother, and all the neighbors wear the same. If emerald green is fashionable, all the yellowest skins will be framed in it.

Wherever shorts are tolerated, every cornered and cushioned and nubbined kneecap is hinged in plain view. While evening dresses are cut to the last limit of daring, the ample billows of the fat will continue to vie blandly with the marvels of anatomy exhibited by the thin. Utility, becomingness, suitability, and beauty are of no importance. Fashion is followed to the letter—therefore they fancy, poor sheep, they are the last word in smartness. Those whom the fashion suits *are* "smart" but they are seldom, if ever, distinguished because—they are all precisely alike.

THE WOMAN WHO IS CHIC

The woman who is chic is always a little different. Not different in being behind fashion, but always slightly apart from it. Chic (pronounced sheek) is a borrowed adjective, but unfortunately no word in our language expresses its meaning. Our adjective elegant—which, before it was vulgarized, most nearly approached it—rather suggested the mother of the young woman who was chic. Its nearest description today is the combination of sophistication (in its intentionally deceptive meaning) combined with fastidious taste. By way of comment, the word chi-chi (pronounced she-she) is not a synonym for chic, but a flashy imitation of it.

The woman who is chic adapts fashion to her own personality. This is in contrast to the average woman who will merely buy the latest hat or dress and adapt herself to it, whether the fashion is suited to her or not. When it is conspicuously NOT, it is likely to be chi-chi.

HOW TO WEAR A CORSAGE

There is no rule in existence that is concerned with how a woman may choose to wear a corsage. She pins it wherever and however *she* thinks most becoming to her dress, and to herself, and also to the flowers themselves. In short, she stands in front of her mirror, holds the flowers against her dress in different places until she finds where they are most pleasing, and that is where she pins them.

HOW MANY JEWELS

It has always been the rule of the well-bred not to wear too many jewels in public places, because public display is considered poor taste in the first place and, in the second, a temptation to a thief. But in the present vogue for costume jewelry, the smart world of New York and elsewhere has developed a veritable mania for covering itself in public, as well as at home, with pearls, rubies, and emeralds—of glass! Since jewelry is, after all, ornamentation, glass makes quite as effective trimming as gems—and, like all other trimming, can be overdone and tasteless.

DON'T EXCHANGE A FACE FOR A MASK

To the modern generation it must seem fantastic that not so very long ago all make-up was considered wicked. Today the only restraint in the use of every item in the cosmetic catalog lies in the answer to the question: Are you sure you are not exchanging a face for a mask?

Don't daub on rouge until you look as though you had inflammation of the cheek bones. Don't plaster your face with powder until it no longer has any semblance of skin. Lipstick or lip rouge calls for a skilful hand and keen vision.

Remember that a mask can never take the place of a face. The face of a clown is grotesque, for it is meant to be. If cosmetics are to add to beauty, they must be the allies, not the enemies, of nature. For those whose eyebrows are too heavy or straggling, plucking is to be commended, because neat edges tidy the face just as clipped borders tidy garden paths.

HAIRDRESSING

Hair tumbling loose to the shoulders is all very well on the young, but on an older woman it is as grotesque as though she wore a baby's cap and bib. Moreover, a flowing mane that makes the head disproportionately huge, while becoming to a lion, is scarcely conducive to the distinction of a woman. The best style is the one that enhances the beauty of the face whether it is the latest mode or has the quaintness of an earlier day.

WHEN ONE'S INCOME IS LIMITED

No one can dress well on nothing a year; that must be granted at the outset. But a woman who has talent, taste, and ingenuity can be suitably and charmingly dressed on little a year. First of all, for a woman to mind wearing a dress many times because it indicates a small bank account is to exhibit a false notion of the values in life.

True, it is tiresome everlastingly to wear black on every formal occasion, but nothing looks so well and nothing is so unrecognizable. A very striking dress cannot be worn many times without making others as well as its owner feel bored at the sight of it. "Here comes the zebra" or "the cockatoo" is inevitable if a dress of stripes or flamboyant color is worn often. She who must wear one dress whenever she goes out would better choose black or very dark blue or possibly gray, with effective accessories of one variety or another that go together so that they can be made to do double service.

One who would be well dressed on a moderate budget should be chary of buying dresses fashioned in the whim of the moment, if these must be worn after its "high style" of the moment has passed.

To buy things at sales is very much like buying things at auction. If you really know what you want and something about values, you can often do marvelously well; but if you are easily bewildered and know little of values, you are likely to find your bargain a disappointment, and the money you spent on it unhappily wasted.

WHAT TO WEAR IN A RESTAURANT

Day clothes, tailored suit or dress, with hat and gloves are the proper dress for lunch in the smartest restaurants. Hatless heads and toeless shoes are still seen, but seldom on the well dressed. In New York evening clothes are still sometimes worn to the best restaurants, and occasionally during the first week of a notable play (especially opening night) when one is sitting in front orchestra seats. Cosmopolitan communities follow a similar pattern everywhere.

CLOTHES FOR THE AFTERNOON

The hours between one and six are occasions when important day dresses are appropriate. If you have few clothes, you may perfectly well wear the simplest sort of day dress in which you look well. You need never worry because you are not dressed *as much* as the others! The time to worry is when you are *over*dressed!

At a formal lunch party in town, people usually wear worsteds or dull silks made with tailored simplicity. The same is true for an afternoon tea or concert. For a cocktail party day dresses are correct. A dinner dress is permissible only in the late afternoon when you stop in to visit an intimate friend on your way to a dinner party.

DON'T GET TOO MANY CLOTHES

Choose the clothes which you *must* have carefully, and if you must cut down, cut down on elaborate ones. There is scarcely anywhere that you cannot fittingly go in plain clothes. Very few, if any, women *need* fancy things; everyone needs plain ones.

A very chic Chicago woman who is always perfectly dressed for every occasion has worked out the cost of her own clothes this way: On a sheet of paper, thumbtacked onto the inside of her dress-closet door, she puts a complete typewritten list of her dresses and hats and the cost of each. Every time she puts on a dress, she makes a pencil mark after its notation. By and by, when a dress is discarded, she divides the cost of it by the number of times it has been worn. In this way she finds out accurately which are her least costly and which her most expensive clothes. When getting new ones, she has the advantage of very valuable information, for she avoids the kind of dress that is seldom put on—which is of course the sort of purchase one on a medium-sized allowance can least afford.

WHEN IN DOUBT

There is one rule that is fairly safe: When in doubt, wear the plainer dress. If you don't know whether to put on a ball dress or a dinner dress, wear the dinner dress, or whether to wear velvet or wool to a lunch party, wear the wool.

SHALL I WEAR A HAT?

Notwithstanding the continued practice of certain younger women to go hatless on all occasions, best taste exacts that in a city a hat be worn with street clothes in the daytime. A woman wearing a hat is more chic than if she were hatless. With an evening dress a hat is incorrect.

GLOVES

Always wear gloves as well as hat in church, and also on the street in a city. Always wear gloves to a restaurant, to the theatre, when you go to lunch, or to a formal dinner, or to a dance. Always take them off when you eat. The question of length and color is one of transient fashion and personal taste.

A LADY KEEPS HER GLOVES ON

A lady never takes off her gloves to shake hands, no matter when or where, and *never* apologizes for wearing gloves when shaking hands. On *formal* occasions she should put gloves *on* to shake hands with her guests when she is hostess—and keep them on when she in turn is a guest. Always wear gloves when standing in a receiving line.

The one time she does not shake hands when wearing gloves is when they are riding gloves or earth-stained gardening gloves, which might smudge the fresh gloves of a friend. In such a case she would pull off her glove. Or if it is one that is difficult to take off, she makes a gesture of showing her hands and says, "Sorry! I can't shake hands."

CLOTHES FOR THE COUNTRY

In the country, as everywhere else, very young women wear, on the country-club veranda or at a lunch, every variety of simple one-piece dress or sports clothes *with skirts*. Hats and gloves are optional except at church and at other special occasions.

Slacks or long shorts are proper on a boat, or on the beach, or at picnics. Short shorts (for those who are young and slim) are correct only on tennis courts.

The most appropriate beach costume is, of course, a bathing suit. Choose a style that is becoming to your figure, and that will be comfortable when you swim. The original reason for undress was unhampered freedom in swimming, but this fashion can be carried too far. The extremely abbreviated bathing suits seen on beaches in Mediterranean countries are not in the best taste in this country. After all, even the most beautiful figure is more alluring when something is left to the imagination.

That older or fat women should choose bathing suits that are ample enough to be becoming cannot be too strongly advised.

Evening clothes are the same in the country as in town; in the summer, however, the simpler they are, the prettier.

For a garden party, a country dress is entirely suitable; but, if you have a very elaborate summer day dress, such as a bridesmaid's dress, this is one of the few times you are likely to be able to wear it.

Clothes for church are much the same as in the city. One must wear a hat and should wear gloves.

THE WELL-DRESSED GIRL AT COLLEGE

The girl who would like to know what clothes to take to college and how to be well dressed on a reasonable sum of money should first of all pay particular attention to practicality.

As a tentative list from which you may subtract if you must, or to which you may add as you please, it is safe to suggest one or two suits of tweed or other useful wool material, and several sweater-blouses of varying weights. Knit skirts with matching blouses are very good; but skirts of tweed or dark flannel will give better service, because knit skirts require a fairly long rest, lying flat on a shelf, to straighten the bagging knees or sitting-down bulge to which they are inclined, even though they be turned front-side back every other time they are worn. The closely knit cotton jersey skirts and sweaters hold their shape much better than the more expensive hand-knitted woolen or bouclé ones. In addition to casual clothes, which you wear day after day in class or on campus, you should have a dress or two to wear under a coat to church on Sundays, to town for lunch on Saturdays, and for dinner in the dining-room—and a few smart outfits for dates. See also Chapter 15.

For evening clothes there is little to suggest except the practical idea of buying evening dresses that have accompanying jackets or capes. With its jacket such an evening dress can serve many purposes.

Remember that both fussy dresses with trimmings which must be continually cleaned and pressed and materials which wrinkle like tissue paper or are spotted by a drop of rain are obviously impractical. The type of dress for a moderate budget is one that is plain in cut and that does not have to be sent to the cleaner if anything touches it. Test whatever you are in doubt about by squeezing it into a ball in your hand and then seeing whether the wrinkles stay in or disappear when smoothed out between your fingers.

In addition to dresses, you will also need a heavy country coat—of fur, perhaps—a wool or polo coat, and a raincoat. Hats or caps, though unusual on the campus, depend upon your clothes—and you. You will need gloves for warmth in a cold climate and other gloves for church and for town. But most important of all, do have sensible shoes for day-time use. Wear fancy slippers or sandals with stilt heels in the evening, if you like, but don't walk about the campus in silly shoes.

You will need a house coat and slippers, of course; and pajamas and underthings simply tailored are in best taste. A lot of nightgowns and other things deeply trimmed with lace are all very well in the trousseau of a bride, but neither practical nor suitable in a college dormitory.

CLOTHES FOR THE BUSINESS WOMAN

The first requirement is neatness. The unfailing directions for clothes worn in an office are that they be tailor-made, smart to the last degree and in perfect taste, but in nothing conspicuous. Above all, avoid wearing clothes that need constant arranging. If you have to keep fuss-ing at your belt or your neckline or your wrists, if anything dangling drips into things or catches on knobs or typewriter keys, discard the distracting detail quickly. It is not necessary to sacrifice prettiness to exaggerated sleekness as one must to look well on horseback, but do avoid everything that interferes or catches, or keeps getting out of place.

Also wear clothes that properly cover you. Scant attire may be very alluring in a musical revue, but men do not look for nor want to find that allure in their offices. Conspicuous clothes are entirely out of place for business. In hot weather, very short sleeves are permissible. Deep-mourning clothes are not suitable in an office, but you may wear black and white or gray. Also, it is not unusual for women to wear mourning bands on tailored coats, although not on dresses.

Neat and carefully done hair by all means, but do avoid little-girl effect of hair hanging loose.

One important accessory for beautiful business clothes is a pair of plain sensible shoes of best quality. High-heeled, fancy sandals and heelless slippers not only are inappropriate and extravagant but ruinous to any foot that must be much stood upon. A well-shod foot is much to be prized—and noticed. The hospital regulation for properly supporting shoes was not made to keep nurses from looking pretty, but to preserve toes and arches from damage and collapse.

One can't say to everyone, "Wear flat-heeled, laced boots." To one who has a fallen arch, a flat heel is agony, and a laced high boot is torture. But high-heeled slippers for long hours of walking or standing will not only in time be painful but make the bare foot of the one who insists on wearing them look disfigured and horrible.

ON MOTOR OR TRAIN TRIP

On a motor or train trip, the very best basic color is brown with its dilutions of tan, fawn, beige, and cream. Nothing is so dust-proof, or goes so long without valeting, as a dust-colored tweed tailor-made skirt and jacket with a gay print blouse, a buttonhole flower of its dominating color, and a swagger coat to match the tone of the suit, with well-polished brown leather shoes and a serviceably big hand or shoulder-strap bag of the same leather as the shoes (and both bag and shoes polished again and again, so that they gleam as though varnished, and are well protected against dust and scratches). Nothing could be smarter and more comfortable than a small brown hat with just enough brim to shade your eyes. With this brown-to-tan-to-cream color scheme you can have any number of blouses or sweaters. You can have hats of the soft, uncrushable variety that can easily be packed without being damaged in odd corners of your bag or trunk. If brown is just not your color, as for a few it isn't, then the subtler shades of green or heather might do.

ON AN AIRPLANE TRIP

Clothes for an airplane trip do not differ from those worn on a train except that on a flight from the tropics to the cold of a northern winter, it is most important to have a really warm coat for the trip into the city from the airport.

ON A SHIP

But for shipboard, blue would probably be a better foundation theme than brown: a navy-blue tailored suit, or a blue-mixture tweed, either of these worn with a white blouse. A warm country coat of blue or bluish mixture (to be used also as an evening wrap), a blue hat, bag, and shoes, and white wash-fabric gloves would be your foundation. Then white knit or cotton dresses, with white—or white and blue— sports shoes, would be all you could need for day wear. In addition to this, two very simple semi-evening dresses, or an evening dress with one or two jackets.

Unless you are dancing or there is a Ritz restaurant in which you are dining, it is not necessary to dress in the evening on any ship unless you feel like it.

CLOTHES FOR A CRUISE

But now let us consider an approximate list of things to take on a definite cruise. Whether it is to be a short one of five days or a longer one of eighteen or more, you must first of all have something in which to travel from wherever you live to where you board the ship. Then you must, of course, take with you steamer clothes for cold days and other things for hot days, and something to wear in the evening. To these add a raincoat and a bathing suit, and that is about all.

For going on board, or for going ashore in a city, any plain tailor-made coat and skirt of lightweight wool in a becoming color is the smartest thing you can wear. Or if you are very young, a bright-colored suit with several blouses or sweaters would be the very best choice you can make for wearing on the ship as well as on shore. A skirt and coat are more useful for traveling than a dress and coat because the skirt worn with different blouses or thin sweaters, and perhaps hats, will serve the purpose of several costumes. A second, lighter-weight, lighter-colored skirt is also useful to wear with the same blouses or sweaters. For hot weather the simplest tailored dresses, either of cotton or silk, or the newer mixtures of natural and synthetic fibres, are best.

Wear on a steamer in summer the same sort of clothes that are worn in the country anywhere, as they are most practical and suitable.

On shore as well as on shipboard one-piece knit dresses are ideal daytime clothes. If you have these in different weights, you will need nothing else whatsoever for daytime—or for evening, either, if you do not choose to dress. But remember that knit clothes are not for the fat. One who is more than inclined toward plumpness should never wear a knit dress without a sweater coat—a coat, moreover, which hangs loose enough not to cling around the line of the equator across the back. Or, as a change from knit dresses, nothing is more practical either for ship or shore in very hot weather than simplest short-sleeved dresses of cotton, such as seersucker or a thinner wrinkle-free cotton print. At home white linen or silk tub dresses couldn't be nicer but not out on the sea, where you are away from an ironing board. Many of the new fabrics are practical since they can be tubbed, put on a hanger, and dry very quickly.

For the somewhat older woman, thin foulard—the kind that slithers through your fingers, and that no amount of squeezing can crease—is perfect. Dark neutral-colored ones for town and light or gay ones for coast resorts or on the boat.

Gay colors may sound unconservative for the not-so-young, but it is quite possible to wear a dress and hat of vivid color against the vivid background of a tropical scene and not seemingly imitate either a clown or a cockatoo. But even so, one who is tempted by anything that could be called flamboyant should remember that in any public place to be the most conspicuously dressed is all too likely to be the most vulgar. And a ship (unless it is a yacht) is a public place.

WOMEN WHO REPRESENT US ABROAD

I read with sadness in a newspaper a few years ago that the colonel in command of one of our detachments in Germany found that there have been enough women in the families of United States Army personnel who dress improperly to make it advisable to issue a directive on the subject.

It seems to me that the impression our American women make on people of other countries is so important that I am quoting his directive as something that should certainly be followed by the women who, whether they wish it or not, are the examples by whom all American women are judged by those who see them.

"The attire being worn in public by some American women is not in good taste . . . women dressed improperly will not be permitted to enter United States installations to which the public has access. Included in this restriction are post exchanges, all parental activities, commissaries, theatres and service clubs . . .

"No bare-back, halter-type sunsuits may be worn without a jacket or wrap.

"No bare midriff costumes.

"No strapless, low-cut dresses except in clubs or at appropriate social functions.

"No shorts on teen-agers or women.

"No levis (blue jeans) on mature women.

"No pin curlers, or any curlers on hair unless neatly covered by suitable scarf or headgear. . . ."

RIDING CLOTHES

A riding habit, no matter what the fashion happens to be, is the counterpart of an officer's uniform; it is not worn to make the wearer look pretty! To look well in a habit a woman must be smart or she is a sight! And nothing contributes so much to the sights we see at present as the *attempt to look pretty instead of correct*. The criticism is not intended for the woman who lives far off in the open country and jumps on a horse in whatever she happens to have on, but for those who dress for looks and ride in the parks of our cities, or walk on the stage and before the camera in scenes meant to represent smart society.

A habit is good or it is bad. Whatever the present fashion may be, have your habit utterly conventional. Don't wear checks or have slant pockets, or eccentric cuffs or lapels. Choose a plain dark or dust color. A night-blue that has a few white hairs in the mixture does not show dust as much as a solid color, and a medium-weight closely woven material holds its shape better than a light loose weave.

You may wear a single white carnation or other simple flower in your buttonhole—but no other trimming. Get boots like those of a man, low-heeled and with a straight line from heel to back of top. Don't have the tops wider than absolutely necessary to be able to get the boots on and off, and don't have them curved or fancy in shape. Be sure that there is no elbow sticking out like a horse's hock at the back of the boot. Don't have a corner on the inside edge of the sole. And don't try to wear too small a size! And above everything, have them properly polished, even if you have to do this yourself.

Gloves must be of heavy leather and two sizes larger than those ordinarily worn.

A hat must fit the head and its shape must be conventional. Never wear a hat that would be incorrect on a man, and don't wear it on the back of your head or over your nose.

Wear your stock as tight as you comfortably can, though not too tight. Tie it smartly so as to make it flat and neat, and anchor whatever you wear so securely that nothing can possibly come loose.

If you want to see examples of perfection in riding clothes, look at the pictures of any of the smart meets in illustrated monthly magazines devoted to sports and society, and study the clothes worn by the members of the Hartford or Myopia meets. There are many others that are also admirable, but these are often photographed and never fall below standard.

Remember too that riding clothes like Army clothes are strictly according to regulation. If right they are perfect. But they cannot be even a little wrong without being ALL wrong.

PRINCIPLES OF TASTE APART FROM FASHION

Suppose, since clothes suitable to the occasion are the first requisite of good taste, we take up a few details that are apart from fashion. A formal dinner dress is the handsomest type of evening dress that there is. A ball dress may be exquisite in detail, but it is often merely effective; the perfect ball dress is one purposely designed with a skirt that is becoming when dancing. A long, figure-wrapping type of dress that would make Diana herself look like a toy monkey-on-a-stick might be dignified and beautiful at a dinner. A dinner dress differs from a ball dress only in that it is not necessarily designed for freedom of movement.

THE MEANING OF SEMI-FORMAL

Merely to clear away much confusion: Semi-formal does not mean women in formal evening dresses and men in business suits. In communities where the tail coat is worn, semi-formal means dinner jackets (tuxedos) and simple evening dresses. In others where the dinner jacket is formal, semi-formal would mean men in dark sack suits and women in so-called cocktail dresses. Whenever men wear business suits, women should wear afternoon—not evening—dresses.

FASHION AND FAT

Two things the heavy woman should avoid are big patterns and tight-fitting styles. Fat women look better in feminine but never frilly clothes, that follow but never lead the vanguard of moderate fashion.

They should never wear eccentric clothes or clothes in light colors. Clothes that are what the French call "vague" are always better for any bad figure than those which reveal it precisely, and emphatically.

The tendency of fat is to detract from one's refinement; therefore, anyone inclined to be fat must be ultraconservative—in order to counteract its effect. Very tight clothes make fat people look fatter and thin people thinner. Satin is a bad material, since its shimmering highlights accentuate form. Dull-surfaced, soft materials, dark colors, and small or subdued prints are best. Elaborate details, such as loose-hanging panels and irregular hemlines, should be avoided. A moderate hem length, at about mid-calf, is most flattering to the overweight figure.

DRESSES TO WEAR AT HOME

It is doubtful that the younger generation knows that the tea gown of the put-on-for-company variety was a cross between a ball dress and a coronation robe and nothing at all like a wrapper. Of late years, the phrase tea gown has been given to a wrapper-like house gown worn to rest in rather than to see company in.

Today's alternate to a tea gown is either the tailored house coat, Sunday-night dress, or the hostess gown. All these, including the house coat (if of beautiful material), are suitable for wear at any very informal gathering at home.

CHILDREN SHOULD BE DRESSED LIKE THEIR FRIENDS

Clothes of children need no comment because children should be allowed to dress like their friends. Nothing makes a child, especially a boy, more self-conscious than to look different than the children he plays with. In other words the mother who dresses a boy—or even a girl—in noticeably different clothes may make the child not merely temporarily unhappy but can very easily set him so far apart as to warp his whole future life.

This may even mean permitting your children to wear "blue jeans" instead of the beautiful clothes you would like to see them in.

TEEN-AGE FADS

As noted in the foregoing paragraph, it is the impulse of all young persons to try to be as exactly like each other as biscuits in a pan. The girl who is a leader, for example, starts a fashion and all copy! Sometimes the leader's example is admirable; sometimes less so.

During the war, groups of teen-age girls across the entire country took to the sloppiest of oversized boys' clothes worn in the sloppiest way.

How long it will be before a new craze—perhaps for extreme loveliness—takes its place, no one can say. It can only be hoped that the behavior that tends to go with pants and shirt-tail out will not by that time have become such a habit that it will prove to be incorrigible.

THE CLOTHES OF A GENTLEMAN

⋯⋗[40]⋖⋯

LET US SAY AT THE START THAT, ALTHOUGH THE CLOTHES a man wears (especially his evening ones) are as certain to reveal his background as his speech, fashion is not important. How old a suit may be doesn't matter a bit. The right kind of clothes, the clothes that follow the accepted conventions on the other hand, are very important. The wrong kind, whether new or old, are like illiteracies in speech. By which is meant that the clothes, like the speech, of an elderly gentleman might suggest yesterday rather than today and still be most distinguished. But even the smallest offense to taste in details seems to classify a man as definitely as if he were to say "I seen it," or "drapes," or "pardon *me*."

If you would dress like a gentleman, pay close attention to the clothes of men of about your own age whom you know to be reliably conservative, and try to emulate them, until your own judgment is sufficiently trained to pick out good suits from the eccentric in style.

EVENING CLOTHES

Your tail coat is the last thing to economize on. It must be perfect in fit, cut, and material, and this means a first-rate tailor. Certainly this has always been the rule. In the present day this advice must be qualified, because in the better American stores ready-to-wear clothes have reached such a high degree of excellence that a man with a good average figure can be fitted admirably—even to a tail coat. At all events it must be made of a dull-faced worsted, either black or more likely a midnight blue, which has the characteristic of looking blacker than black. Apart from the silk facing of the lapels, wide braid on the trousers, and the buttons on the sleeves and on the front and back of the coat, it must have no trimming whatever.

Your linen must always be faultlessly clean and your tie of plain white lawn, or piqué, tied so it will not only stay in place but look as though nothing short of a swim in the surf could disarrange it.

Your handkerchief must be white, of very fine linen by choice;

gloves if any, white; flower in buttonhole, if any, white, although in recent years red carnations are being worn by many men whose taste cannot be questioned. White kid gloves used to be obligatory both at the opera and at balls, but it must be confessed that today even very few New Yorkers ever wear them.

When you go out on the street, wear either a silk hat or an opera hat. The opera hat is now more generally worn, probably because of its obvious convenience not only at the opera or theatre or in coat rooms but also in doing away with the need for a hatbox when packing or storing. Wear your hat level on your head, not on the back of your neck, or cocked over one ear. Evening dress coats should be black, but if you choose an overcoat of plain midnight blue, it can be worn both afternoon and evening—that is, if it looks black at night and blue by day.

If you carry a stick, it should be of plain Malacca or other wood, with either a crooked or straight handle. The only ornamentation allowable is a plain silver or gold band or top; but a perfectly plain crooked or a straight stick with the very minimum-sized gold cap for its top is best form. The reason why a band on a crooked Malacca is allowed is that the cost of a single length of wood is prohibitive. The less expensive sticks are made with a joining which is hidden under the band. Avoid carrying a stick with a ball top and above all, unless you are a dancer on the stage, avoid an ebony cane with an ivory top as you would avoid wearing a pink shirt with evening clothes.

Lastly, wear patent leather pumps or ties, and plain or ribbed black silk or nylon socks.

THE DINNER COAT OR TUXEDO

The tuxedo is simply the English dinner coat, which was first introduced in this country at the Tuxedo Club in the early nineties to provide something less formal than the swallowtail, and the nickname has clung ever since. To a man who cannot afford to get two suits for evening wear, the tuxedo is of greater importance. It is proper nearly everywhere, whereas the tail coat is necessary only at balls, formal dinners, and until recently in a box at the opera. The tuxedo suit is made of the same material and differs from a full-dress one in only three particulars: the cut of the coat, the braid on the trousers, and the use of a black tie instead of a white. The dinner coat has no tails and is cut like the coat of a business suit except that it is held closed in front by one button at the waistline. The lapels are silk- or satin-faced, and the collar is made of the suiting; or if it is shawl-shaped, the whole collar is of satin. The shawl collar is supposed to be a shade less formal than lapels.

The dinner coat may be either single- or double-breasted, although a generation ago a double-breasted dinner coat was worn only on informal occasions during the summer, for the express purpose of going without a waistcoat. Worsted, of black or midnight blue, will be suitable all year 'round, although white linen is appropriate for summer or in the tropics.

The trousers are identical with full-dress trousers except that the braid should be narrower.

Evening ties of fancy silks are bad form. A "butterfly" bow shape is correct in plain black silk or satin, and avoid like the plague any colored tie or a black one with a white edge.

With a double-breasted dinner coat it is not necessary to wear a waistcoat. Instead of a waistcoat, a black or midnight-blue silk cummerbund may be worn with either a single- or double-breasted coat. With a single-breasted dinner coat, no fashionable New Yorker wears any but a white waistcoat. Black ones are seen, however, on the past-middle-aged who do not care to advertise an expanded waistline. Never, except in vaudeville, wear a gray one or a yellow one.

As noted in a foregoing paragraph, the most practical hat for town wear in winter, both for full-dress and dinner coat, is an opera hat which collapses, instead of the regular high silk one. In summer a straw is usual, but today a black Homburg is proper in both summer and winter, and indeed has almost replaced the opera hat because it is less conspicuous.

Since even Newport—which was the last summer resort in America that was formal enough to make the wearing of full evening dress the rule—has during the last few years practically given it up, there is now no occasion when a fashionable New Yorker can possibly wear full dress between the months of May and November, because neither opera, nor formal dinners, nor balls are given then, and in New York society an evening wedding is unknown. In San Francisco or Atlanta or other cities where evening weddings *are* fashionable, or elsewhere if balls are given, the full dress is, of course, correct regardless of the season.

THE HOUSE SUIT

The house suit is hardly heard of today, and even years ago was a pure extravagance, avoided by many who wore an old tuxedo suit instead. For many generations a gentleman was expected to change his clothes for dinner, whether he might be going out or dining at home; and for this latter occasion some inspired person created the house or lounge suit, which is simply a dinner coat and trousers cut somewhat looser than ordinary evening ones, made of silk, or preferably for greatest comfort, of vicuña or some other very soft wool—lined with either satin or silk. Nothing more comfortable or luxurious could be devised for sitting in a deep easy chair after dinner, in a reclining position that would be ruinous to formal, finely fitted evening clothes.

A house suit is distinctly what the name implies. The accessories are a silk or cheviot unstarched soft shirt, with turn-down soft collar and a black bowtie. The coat is either double-breasted or made with two buttons instead of one, so that no waistcoat need be worn with it.

The house suit which is worn almost solely by men of fashion must not be confused with the velvet jacket that has no trousers to match, and is typical of studios and Bohemian quarters. Nor must the house suit be confused with the dressing gown that seems to be a certain type of moving-picture director's or stage manager's idea of what a gentleman invariably wears at home!

FORMAL DAYTIME DRESS

Formal afternoon dress consists of a black cutaway or morning coat with black cloth waistcoat to match the coat, and gray-and-black striped, or black with white line, cashmere trousers. A white piqué waistcoat is fashionable at a spring wedding, especially for the bridegroom, best man, and ushers. The coat can be bound with braid but, in somewhat better taste, it is plain. A silk-faced lapel is wrong, although it is the correct facing for the more formal and elderly frock coat.

Very fashionable is a black sack coat instead of cutaway but with other details the same. The cutaway is still correct, however, for members of the bridal party. The black sack coat is equally smart, though not as formal, since it may be worn with a derby hat, which is impossible with a cutaway. A silk hat is correct with either a cutaway or a frock coat.

A black and white, or gray, bowtie or four-in-hand is worn with all three kinds of afternoon coat. A gray silk ascot worn with a frock coat is still supposed to be the correct wedding garment of the bride's father.

Black calfskin oxford ties are correct in best fashion. Spats are not popular with very smart men except at weddings, and very rarely seen even then. Also they must never be in any color except sand or white, or of any material except linen. White spats are for the wedding party. Cloth spats, like the black evening waistcoat, mean merely a man without knowledge of, or probably indifferent to, smartness—like a woman's ankle-length skirt in a knee-length period.

At a spring wedding or other formal occasion a sand-colored double-breasted linen waistcoat with sand linen spats look very well on a man who is slim-waisted and youthful.

THE BUSINESS SUIT

The business or three-piece sack suit is supposed to be an everyday inconspicuous garment and should be. Today's suit usually consists of trousers and a single- or double-breasted coat without waistcoat. A few rules to follow are:

Don't choose striking patterns or materials; suitable woolen stuffs come in endless variety, and any which look inconspicuous at a short distance are safe.

Don't get too light a blue, too bright a green, or anything suggesting a horse blanket. Trousers may be and generally are made with a cuff; sleeves are not. Lapels are moderately small. Padded shoulders are an abomination. Skirt-wide trousers are equally bad. If you must be eccentric, save your efforts for the next fancy-dress ball, where you may wear what you please, but in your business clothing be reasonable.

It is better taste not to wear silk socks in winter, except in the evening; but above everything, don't wear white ones—except wool or cotton with white tennis shoes. Don't cover yourself with chains, fobs, scarf pins, lodge emblems, etc.; and don't wear horsey shirts and neckties. You will only make a bad impression on everyone you meet. The clothes of a gentleman are always conservative; and it is safe to avoid everything that can possibly come under the heading of novelty. If a salesman offers you anything that has "never been seen before," the rule of good taste is shun it unless your judgment is very experienced.

THE BUSINESS SUIT IN SUMMER

Summer clothes are lighter in color as well as weight, and their accessories can be much less conservative. Colored socks are entirely proper not only in browns and grays, but in light bluish colors as well. Ties of printed foulard or handkerchief silks can be gaily colored but the pattern should be small. Handkerchiefs may be of matching color or may be embellished with patterns or whole scenes in brightest colors.

A gray or blue suit in the new lightweight, crease-resistant summer fabrics has the advantage of being correct for the city and not looking out of place in the country.

JEWELRY

In your jewelry let diamonds be conspicuous by their absence. Nothing is more vulgar than a display of them on a man's shirt front or on his fingers.

There is a good deal of jewelry that a gentleman is allowed to wear, but it must be chosen with discrimination. Large pearl shirt studs, real ones, are correct for full dress only. One alone can be worn with a dinner coat; but two, only if quite small. Otherwise you may wear white mother-of-pearl, or black onyx surrounded with a very inconspicuous circle in diamond chips, but so tiny that they cannot be told from a threadlike design in platinum—or others equally modest.

Waistcoat buttons, studs, and cufflinks, worn in sets, constitute a modern custom that is unnecessary but permissible. Both waistcoat buttons and cufflinks may be jeweled and valuable, but they must not have big precious stones nor be conspicuous.

A watch chain if worn at all should be very thin—in the evening preferably of platinum or white gold because less conspicuous against a white waistcoat. A man's ring is usually a seal ring. If a man wears a jewel at all, it should be sunk into a plain gypsy hoop setting that has no ornamentation, and worn on his little, not his third, finger.

A MAN'S WEDDING RING

When a man wears a wedding ring, one who is conservatively fashionable still prefers that it be worn on his little finger. This is true of New York rather especially. Although even here, today, an increasing number of young men, who wear wedding rings, prefer to wear this ring on the third finger as are the rings of the graduates of Annapolis and West Point. Especially is this true since this last war when so many of our service men were impressed by the almost universal wearing of wedding rings on their European comrades' third fingers.

OCCASION FOR GOLD STUD

When a bowtie is worn with a cutaway which necessitates a stiff shirt without wash buttons, the one stud that shows above the waistcoat must be of plain gold.

CIGARETTE CASE SET WITH DIAMONDS

On the cigarette case of a gentleman any monogram or other embellishment in diamonds must be composed of chips that are almost powder-small. Brilliants are beautiful for women, but not for men of good taste.

An amusing European fashion is to have innumerable small devices, each given by a friend, *appliquéd* on a plain gold or silver case. Such devices are minute monograms, or crests of donors, or designs illustrating a nickname, or personal event, executed in enamels or platinum. In the days of our great prosperity they were sometimes in minuscule diamonds.

IN THE COUNTRY

Gay-colored socks and ties are quite appropriate with flannels or golf tweeds. Only, in your riding clothes must you again be conservative. Boot tops must be high on the leg, and snug fitting. And remember that all leather must be polished until its surface rivals a mirror. There is nothing a really smart man abominates more than any leather that *looks* new.

Have your breeches fit you. The coat is less important; in fact, any odd coat will do. Your legs are the cynosure of attention in riding.

In the country men usually wear comfortable slacks, with a contrasting coat or sport jacket, preferably single-breasted. A sweater or waistcoat in a bright color is suitable, as are colored shirts. Rough tweeds and worsteds are popular country fabrics. Crepe-soled shoes, or shoes of nappy or colored leathers, are appropriate only in the country.

On the golf course, slacks or Bermuda-length shorts are now universal, though there are golfers who insist that nothing is so practical as knickerbockers. Not even on the beach are the bright cabana sets so popular in parts of Florida and California in best taste.

Country clothes should always look casual, and never studied. The important thing is always to dress appropriately. If you are going to play golf, wear golf clothes; if tennis, wear flannels. Do not wear a yachting cap ashore unless you are living on board a yacht, or riding clothes unless you are really going to ride.

If some semi-formal occasion comes up, such as a country tea, the time-worn conservative blue coat with white or gray flannel trousers is perennially good.

A serious breach of etiquette is frequently made by those who are ignorant of the fact that nearly all two- or three-color hat bands are not patterns chosen at random, but emblems to be worn by special privilege. If you choose a fancy ribbon instead of a plain black one, you must be very sure that it has no significance; to announce by your hat band that you played on a certain Varsity team, or that you are a member of such a club or association, when you didn't and are nothing of the sort, is precisely the same as wearing the emblem of a fraternity to which you do not belong.

THE ESSENTIAL VALUE OF VALETING

The well-dressed man is always a paradox. He must look as though he gave his clothes no thought and as though literally they grew on him like a rabbit's fur, and yet he must be perfectly groomed. He must be clean-shaven and have his hair cut and his nails in good order (not polished). His linen must always be immaculate, his clothes in press, his shoes perfectly done. His brown shoes must shine like old mahogany, and his white buckskin shoes must be whitened like a prize bull terrier at a bench show.

One reason—a very great one—why the English gentleman is so often better dressed, usually on less money, than his American counterpart, is that the former is perfectly valeted, even though he perform this office himself, while the latter more often than not is indifferent to what proper valeting means. First of all, how typical is it of the American man to put trees in his shoes the instant he takes them off? And does he carefully pull his trousers flat and fold them straight and hang them smoothly over the trouser bar of a hanger or the back of a chair, and hang up his coat carefully, too; or does he fling his clothes any old way upon a chair, and even let his trousers fall into their natural folds?

Even let us say he hangs his suit up neatly. Does he perhaps wear the same things day after day until the shoes turn up at the toes, and his suit grows balloon-shaped at the knees and sags despondently at the pockets? And then, after wearing his clothes completely out of shape, even if he sends them to be pressed, does he send them to a chosen tailor who will skilfully restore them or to one of another variety who would seem to operate a scorching steam roller rather than an accurately heated pressing iron?

The well-dressed man never wears the same suit or the same pair of shoes two days running. He may have only two suits, but he wears them alternately; if he has four suits, he should wear each every fourth day. The longer time they have to recover their shape, the better.

THE CLOTHES OF A VERY YOUNG MAN

As already said in this chapter, no man of inexperience should buy anything the salesman assures him is the newest thing out. This means that—if it looks unlike anything he has ever beheld—he should leave it severely alone. This is, of course, a rule of safety. The man who knows a lot about clothes buys what he chooses, but the young man who does not know anything except that violet as a color appeals to him will quite possibly dress himself like a chorus man in the perfume ballet, in utter unconsciousness of his crashing through every tenet of good taste.

One might make a rule that not only symphonies in violet, but all color combinations, such as socks and handkerchief and tie of precisely the same shade and pattern, are a little too studied.

There is a certain effect of casual negligence that, especially in the country or at college, is the best sort of dressing. It is a suggestion of ease of movement or lack of vanity. The best description of a college man's clothes would be that they suit him. This impression is merely the result of rather loosely fitted clothes that have a comfortably worn look, a collar not too high nor too tight, tie neither too thick nor too stiff, comfortable woolen socks, and thick-soled shoes.

Country wear allows all sorts of colors; the loudest of golf stockings and sweaters, the most cubistic handkerchiefs and ties, all are perfectly permissible to the boy or man *whose type can absorb them.* This question of absorption is an entirely individual one. Fair-haired, loose-jointed, or thin men can absorb strident violences that on thick-set or dark-haired men with "blue" chins look vulgar.

In the city and in the world of work, it must be remembered that the untidy man has a down-and-out appearance, and it may be cruel, but it is true, that good, conservatively chosen clothes get better consideration for their owners than do shoddy ones. Remember, however, a man's clothes need never be new to look well, and happily there are no changes—that matter—in fashion.

A YOUNG MAN BUDGETS HIS CLOTHES

A man who has plenty of money buys what he chooses and when he chooses; if certain items prove not very useful, they can stay on their hangers or on the shelves and no great harm is done. But the young man of the smart world whose pay envelope is as small as his popularity is great must give serious thought to make his limited means provide him with clothes that will look reasonably well in the environment to which he belongs.

Let him consider, then, what he must spend much money on, what he may save on, and what he can do without.

OF FIRST IMPORTANCE—GOOD SHOES

At the top of the list go good shoes. Therefore, spend money on the quality of leather and of workmanship in shoes; then *take care of them*. Putting trees into them the minute they are taken off is more important than polishing. Polishing can be done at any time, but trees should restore shape while the leather is still warm from the foot. *Never* (if you own two pairs) wear the same shoes two days in succession. Loafers are comfortable and fine for a country week-end, but they are sloppy and too casual for an office.

DAYTIME CLOTHES

In these informal days, a very young man, even in New York society—unless the exactions of formality return to the opera and he is likely to be often in a box—can easily do without a tail coat, for the dinner coat with a white waistcoat takes the place of full evening dress almost everywhere.

For daytime clothes, the dark blue business suit is always put at the head of the list because it looks well on perhaps more occasions than any other type of suit; but for hardest wear, it is not as good as a brownish, or grayish, or greenish tweed which is much less inclined to grow dusty, to show spots, or to acquire a highly polished shine.

Let us say a young man has two sack suits, one gray-brown and the other olive-brown, to be worn alternately. With both he wears brown calf shoes, polished as many times as possible to darken as well as to shine; plain brown socks and a darkish tie, either plain or with an inconspicuous pattern; a brown felt hat, and an overcoat that is brownish. If his overcoat is dark blue or gray, he would do better to choose navy blue or grayish suits and wear black calfskin shoes.

As already said, it is always better that his clothes look utterly unthought of rather than to risk their looking thought of too much. The moment a man's clothes even faintly cry out, "Look at us! Are we not perfection? See how our colors blend; see how well we're pressed!" it is obvious that their wearer's studied effort to be well dressed has failed.

To say that clothes make a gentleman is a flippant sophistry, but clothes of the sort that a gentleman ought to wear do make a gentleman look the way he ought to look!

WHAT TO WEAR

If ever in doubt what to wear, the best rule is to err on the side of informality. Thus, if you are not sure whether to put on your dress suit or your tuxedo, wear the latter.

On the other hand, when an occasion is important, and a man for any reason wants to make sure that his clothes will be correct, it is entirely proper that he call his host or his hostess on the telephone and ask, "Do I wear a black tie tonight, or a white one?" Or, if neither host nor hostess answers the telephone, he sends a message by whoever does, "Mr. Jones would like to know whether dinner tonight is to be white tie or black tie."

Or the question may be: "Day clothes or tuxedos?"

CLOTHES FOR VARIOUS OCCASIONS

FULL DRESS (TAIL COAT)

1. At a ball
2. At a very formal evening wedding
3. At a dinner or evening party to which the invitations are worded in the third person, and given in winter season

SINGLE-BREASTED TUXEDO (DINNER COAT)

This is the most essential item in the evening wardrobe of a gentleman.
1. At every evening party except those which are ceremoniously formal
2. On opening nights at the theatre
3. Dining in a *de luxe* restaurant
But the tuxedo is never worn before six o'clock—except when leaving one's home earlier to go to an evening party.

DOUBLE-BREASTED TUXEDO

The double-breasted tuxedo coat is always worn buttoned and is the most informal evening dress for a man since a waistcoat is not worn with it.

A CUTAWAY (MORNING COAT) WITH STRIPED TROUSERS

1. At a noon or afternoon wedding correct for all men of the bridal party; also proper for though seldom worn today by the guests
2. On Sunday for church (in the city) especially on Christmas and Easter
3. On all daytime occasions of ceremony, such as taking part in a dedication, unveiling, review of a parade, or when accompanying an ecclesiastical or civic personage, or when in any way appearing as an official in public

4. As pallbearer; or black sack coat with striped trousers, dull black silk tie, and black kid gloves

Frock Coat

1. For clergymen
2. For older men who prefer it to a cutaway

Black Sack Coat with Striped Trousers

Very popular in diplomatic circles and excellent anywhere as a less formal substitute for cutaway.

Business (Sack) Suits

1. For every ordinary occasion in town
2. For traveling
3. In summer the coat of a blue flannel suit, worn with white or gray flannel trousers for a lunch or to church, in the country
4. In summer at a small or country wedding, a navy-blue sack suit may replace a cutaway for all men—including those of the bridal party

Country Clothes

1. Only in the country
   To wear golf clothes or tennis flannels—and quite obviously, shorts—in town is entirely inappropriate.

ACCESSORIES AT A GLANCE

Full Evening Dress (Tail Coat)

Shirt. Stiff-bosomed, made for one or two studs as preferred; some men have shirt, tie, and waistcoat all of the same piqué

Collar. Wing

Tie. White lawn or piqué

Waistcoat. White piqué with or without revers, single- or double-breasted

Handkerchief. Fine white linen or batiste with white monogram

Socks. Black silk or nylon with or without black or open-work clocks

Shoes. Patent leather pumps or patent leather oxford ties

Jewelry. Pearl studs, otherwise studs as inconspicuous as possible; cuff links of platinum or white gold, or some simple combination such as white mother-of-pearl with thin platinum rims

Boutonnière. White carnation conservative—red one permissible

Hat. Silk or opera

Stick (if carried). Plain Malacca smartest; where necessary to hide joining, plain gold band permitted; ebony with white ivory end

is not permissible; ivory ball, unthinkable outside of a minstrel or
variety show

Gloves. White buckskin with overcoat; white kid evening gloves only
for a ball or when usher at an evening wedding

Overcoat. Either black or night-blue; the latter most useful because
it can serve for both afternoon and evening wear

Muffler. Plain white

DINNER COAT (TUXEDO)

Shirt. Stiff white or pleated

Collar. Wing or turn-down; in very hot weather soft shirt and collar
permitted

Waistcoat. Of same material as coat and trousers or white piqué whenever dinner coat substitutes for full dress; no waistcoat is needed
with a double-breasted dinner coat; black or midnight-blue cummerbund may be substituted for waistcoat with a single-breasted coat

Tie. Black satin or silk

Handkerchief, socks, shoes, also *boutonnière* and *stick* (if any). Same
as for full dress

Gloves. None

Jewelry. Variety less restricted than for full dress; studs, cuff links,
waistcoat buttons, and all to match or in different sets of mother-
of-pearl, with platinum, or onyx, or any jewelry or other variety
in conservative taste

Hat. Black Homburg or opera hat; stiff straw or Panama in hot weather

Overcoat. Same as for full dress, or any tailored coat; in country, any
coat—polo, etc.—and any hat

WHITE DINNER COAT

Intended only for hot weather, it should be double-breasted so as to
avoid waistcoat, or wear a cummerbund; trousers, shirt, tie, socks,
and shoes: same as with dinner coat. All white articles of clothing
must be immaculate and perfectly ironed.

Hat. Straw or Panama or none.

BUSINESS, LOUNGE, OR SACK SUIT

Shirt and *Collar.* Anything you like that is reasonably conservative

Shoes. Any of brown or black leather except patent leather

Socks. Wool, silk and wool, nylon, or lisle, plain or patterned, but avoid
striking mixtures of color

Tie. Plain or figured; avoid flowered designs and stiff satin textures

Handkerchief. Linen or silk or cotton, white or colored

Jewelry. Very little and for utility, not ornament

COUNTRY CLOTHES

Sport clothes suitable to each particular sport or game.

General details. Avoid all clothes that suggest town; country clothes look better when not too new and not too newly pressed

Sport Clothes. Worn only in the country, and special sport clothes suitable to a particular sport worn only by those who are participating in that sport

Shirts. All soft shirts, white or colored, with collars attached; polo type of shirt worn without coat or tie outdoors everywhere in the real country; but coat and tie should be put on before going into dining-room for lunch or dinner

Shorts. Very bad on the old or fat; but all right in the country on the young and reasonably thin

A YOUNG MAN'S FORMAL CLOTHES

Today no young man wears in daytime anything more formal than a dark blue business suit except at a wedding. Moreover many—of those whose fathers once wore cutaways on Sundays and whose grandfathers perhaps still do—go out to the country every week-end.

In the past years of ever-increasing costs, and decreasing use for formal clothes, it has become not only thinkable, but customary, for a large minority (even possibly a majority) of very young ushers at New York weddings and guests at the débutante balls to have not only their cutaways but their tails supplied by certain fashionable tailors who are making a specialty of renting formal clothes completely altered to fit junior customers.

Young men who do not as yet possess a tail coat—let alone a cutaway—no longer have to endure the "hired suit" look, or to be obliged to refuse to serve as usher for a best friend, or to insist that their own weddings be solemnized on a summer morning in the country.

As one college senior who served last spring and again this winter at two of New York's most prominent weddings explained: "A cutaway is certainly of no earthly use to me except when I am an usher at a wedding, and I have by no means reached my full growth. If I had bought one last year I couldn't get into it now. Without the refitted rental cutaway and tails most of us would never be able to usher or accept invitations to balls at which a 'tux' wouldn't do.

"Of course, if we can know ahead that there will be so-or-so many balls, the tailor will put aside a tail coat fitted to each of us and have it kept for us alone."

Happily, therefore, if the wedding is to be a formal one and he does not already possess a well-fitting morning coat—usually called a cutaway—he merely goes to one of the tailors who have an especial lending service for young men—the sons of their customers usually—who at a very reasonable sum will outfit the bridegroom and all his ushers.

In many cases these renting juniors will in time become buying customers. But there is no obligation, either real or implied.

A Boy's Clothes

The following list of clothes is considered complete for a boy going to a representative preparatory (boarding) school:

Suits. Three daytime suits (long trousers): two of tweed for every day, one navy blue for Sunday and dress occasions

Shoes. Two brown or black pairs for every day and one pair of black to wear with navy-blue suit

Socks. Thin wool smartest, or else cotton; plain black for blue suit; otherwise subdued colors

Shirts. Solid colors, light blue or tan, etc.; if the climate is very cold, flannel with fine striped lines; for Sunday and dress, a few white shirts; polo shirts for hikes, etc.

Ties. Plain dark blue for blue suit; others of mixed colors not too gaudy

Casual wear. One or two pairs odd trousers, and sweaters of different weights. Windbreaker leather coat, polo coat and raincoat.

Sport clothes. Slacks, shorts, bathing suit, etc.

Travel. For train and in city: overcoat and felt hat; at school: a knit cap or nothing

In New York and other large cities every boy home from boarding school for the holidays wears a tuxedo to all big holiday parties and dances; following community customs for evening dress is a safe rule.

College Clothes

The same as in the list just given with the addition of evening clothes will meet all requirements of the undergraduate.

THE CLOTHES OF THE PROTESTANT CLERGY

For services in which ecclesiastical vestments are not worn, old-fashioned ministers still wear a frock coat at all hours of day or evening —in church or elsewhere—either double- or single-breasted, with a lay coat collar and waistcoat, or the clerical coat with a low, standing collar. For formal services, certain clergymen wear long single-breasted coats buttoned all the way up to the collar, showing no waistcoat; but the majority of younger clergymen choose a frock coat made to be open in the front, for the full length, over a cassock waistcoat or clerical waist-coat. A cassock waistcoat is without buttons in the front and made either with or without a low band collar of its own material about half the height of the straight white collar and fastened at the back and worn underneath the waistcoat. A clerical waistcoat is buttoned down the front and has a short standing collar which is open in front to the full depth of the plain white collar beneath. The clerical waistcoat is always made of cloth to match the coat. The cassock waistcoat is of cloth in the daytime but of ribbed black silk for evening wear. Most modern clergymen choose the cutaway coat in preference to the frock coat, a clerical waistcoat of cloth and black trousers. But by many others, gray trousers that are almost black are considered permissible.

For everyday wear, the younger clergymen have ordinary sack suits —of black—with a clerical waistcoat; but many high-church Episcopalians prefer a clerical standing collar, forming a notch where the collar fails to meet the top edges of the coat fronts. All these clothes are worn by Episcopal clergymen at home and in public, and during services by clergymen of denominations which do not prescribe vestments.

In the evening many clergymen wear exactly the same clothes that they wear in the daytime. Others merely exchange the cloth waistcoat for a cassock waistcoat of silk. Others, whose parishes happen to be very fashionable, wear evening dress.

At a large evening wedding, for example, at which all men present wear full evening dress, a clergyman, to be suitably in the picture, wears —for the ceremony if he has no vestments, or at the reception after he has removed his vestments—an evening tail coat and trousers and a cassock waistcoat of black ribbed silk. Or at a small evening wedding he wears a tuxedo coat with the same black silk waistcoat.

Not long ago, clergymen wore black clothes always—in the country as well as in town. But the modern love of outdoor sports has brought clergymen as well as laymen out upon the golf links and the tennis courts, and during his recreation hours in the country or at the seaside a clergyman wears clothes exactly like those that are worn by every other man of conservative taste.

SITTING-ROOM CONVERTIBLE INTO A BEDROOM

The modern convertible couch or sofa makes this sitting-room easily a guest-room of distinction.

Tablespoon is used for consommé in a plate. The spoon should be dipped away and the soup sipped silently from side.

The service dish is always presented with its own spoon and fork.

Insert the spoon under the toast and hold it firmly with fork.

To sop bread in sauces or gravies, place it in the center and—

Pushing it down under the sauce with the fork lift the sauce over it with the knife.

This shows that bacon need not be eaten with the fingers.

CORRECT CHOICE AND USE OF TABLE IMPLEMENTS I

Eating with the fork alone.

It is permissible to use the knife as a pusher, with the fork pushed against the steadily held knife.

Bread should be held against rim of plate while being buttered.

Typical use of knife and fork, holding with the fork and cutting with the knife.

On first cutting into a mousse or aspic or patty or similar dishes, turn spoon and cut left side of the portion this way.

Then make cut on the right side and lift out the portion; and next help yourself to the food in the center.

CORRECT CHOICE AND USE OF TABLE IMPLEMENTS II

The expert way is to lift a mouthful on the fork in the left hand without changing to the right.

It is correct to cut salad with a knife having a silver or stainless steel blade.

When plate is passed for a second helping, implements should be placed at one side.

Correct use of dessert fork and spoon. Hold with fork; cut and eat with spoon.

Using the fingerbowl.

When napkin is not to be used again, it is laid loosely folded beside the plate.

CORRECT CHOICE AND USE OF TABLE IMPLEMENTS III

TABLE MANNERS

·◦⟨ 41 ⟩◦·

E DISTANCE FROM THE TABLE AT WHICH IT IS BEST TO
a matter of personal comfort. A child should not be placed so close
.t his elbows are bent like a cricket's, nor so far back that food is
likely to be dropped in transit from plate to mouth.

WHEN CHILDREN COME TO THE TABLE

No child under five can be expected to use a napkin instead of a
bib. No matter how nicely behaved he may be, there is always the
present danger of his spilling something, sometime. Soft-boiled egg is
hideously difficult to eat without ever getting a drop of it down the
front, and it is much easier to supply him with a clean bib for the next
meal than to change his clothes for the next moment. By quietly experi-
menting with the individual child, it can easily be ascertained just when
he is ready for the next step in the training program. But until he is
ready to accept the new way, do not force the issue unduly.

Very little children usually have hot-water plates—made as a double
plate with hot water space in between—on which the food is cut up and
the vegetables "fixed" in the pantry, and brought to the children before
other people at the table are served, not only because it is hard for them
to be made to wait, when their attention is too easily attracted by food
not for them, but because they naturally eat slowly and deliberately.
As soon as they are old enough to eat everything on the table, they are
served, not last, but in the regular rotation in which they come at table.
(Parents interested in teaching table manners to very young children
will find complete directions in *Children Are People*, Emily Post's book
of junior etiquette.)

When children are learning to help themselves, they must especially
try to handle the serving spoon evenly and to guard against "flinging"
it quickly and so spattering the table. In fact, this principal cause for
a spotted tablecloth is something to which occasionally even grown people should pay attention.

THE LEFT-HANDED CHILD

To the many who ask whether it is best to set the place at table in reverse of usual order for a left-handed child who has to "cross over" for every implement, the answer is definitely "No!"

Nothing could turn out to be a greater handicap than letting him become accustomed to reversed place-setting. It is only by being obliged to make this maneuver at every meal at home that he becomes adept in doing this. If his place is set especially for him at home, he will be conspicuously as well as helplessly awkward at every meal he ever eats away from home where his place will not be so set.

TABLE TRICKS THAT MUST BE CORRECTED

To pile mashed potato and other vegetables on the convex side of the fork on top of meat for two inches or more of its length is an ungainly habit dear to the hearts of schoolboys and sometimes of their fathers—a habit that is more easily prevented in the beginning than corrected later. In fact, taking a big mouthful (next to smearing the face and chewing with mouth open) is perhaps the worst offense at table. To prevent this was perhaps the object of zigzag eating. At least it could be a not unreasonable explanation of how this strange custom ever came into being.

The procedure called zigzag eating is this: With knife in right hand and fork in left, the diner cuts a piece of meat. Then instead of lifting the piece to the mouth with fork in left hand—or at least cutting several pieces—the knife is at once laid down, the fork transferred to right hand, turned over, prongs up, and the piece of meat speared and conveyed to the mouth. Then the fork is zigzagged back into the left hand and turned over, prongs down, while the knife is picked up again and another piece of food cut. Again the knife is laid down, fork turned over and zigzagged to right hand—don't let us even picture it. The only serious objection to making the right hand do all the work is that no form of limping, whether it be of foot or hand, expresses effortless ease. And why an able-bodied person should like to pretend that the left hand is paralyzed and cannot be lifted more than three or four inches above the table is beyond understanding.

Although not seen at the tables of fashionable people, zigzag eating is a custom seen often enough in this country to be known to Europeans as "the American way of eating."

To sit up straight and keep their hands in their laps when not occupied with eating is very hard indeed for children, but it should be insisted upon in order to forestall a careless habit that all too readily degenerates into flopping this way and that, and into fingering whatever is in reach. The child must not be allowed to warm his hands on his plate, or drum on the table, or screw his napkin into a rope, or make marks on the tablecloth. If he shows talent as an artist, give him pencils or modeling wax in his playroom, but do not let him bite his slice of bread into the silhouette of an animal, or model figures in soft bread at the table. And do not allow him to construct a tent out of two forks, or an automobile chassis out of tumblers and knives, or tie the corners of his napkin into bunny-rabbit ears. Food and table implements are not playthings, nor is the dining-room table a playground.

Children should be taught from the time they are little not to talk at table about what they like and don't like. A child who is not allowed to say anything but "No, thank you," when offered something he doesn't want at home, will not mortify his mother in public by screaming, "I *hate* spinach. I *won't* eat potato. I want ice-cream and cookies!"

Older children should not be allowed to jerk out their chairs, to flop down sideways, to flick their napkins by one corner, to reach out for something, or begin by eating candy, fruit, or other table decorations, A child as well as a grown person should sit down in the center of his chair and draw it up to the table (if there is no one to push it in for him) by holding the seat in either hand while momentarily lifting himself on his feet. It makes no difference whether he approaches the chair from the left or right. The only rule is to take his place quietly, and not jump or rock his chair into place at the table. In getting up from the table, again he must push his chair back quietly, using his hands on either side of the chair seat, and *not* by holding onto the table edge and giving himself, chair and all, a sudden shove!

EMBARRASSING DIFFICULTIES

If food is too hot, quickly take a swallow of water. Never, NEVER spit it out! If food has been taken into your mouth, no matter how you hate it, you must swallow it. It is offensive to take anything out of your mouth that has been put in it, except dry fish bones and equally dry fruit pits or seeds. If you choke on a fish bone, cover your mouth with your napkin and leave the table quickly. To spit anything whatever into the corner of your napkin is too nauseating to comment on. It is horrid to see anyone spit wet skins or pits on a fork or onto the plate, and is excusable only if you get a bad clam or something similar into your mouth. Even then the best—because least noticeable—method is to take it from your mouth in your fingers—thumb underneath and four other fingers forming a screen over whatever it is from lips to plate. And then gently wipe off any moisture on your fingertips on your napkin.

Peaches or other very juicy fruits are peeled and then eaten with knife and fork, but dry fruits, such as apples, may be cut and then eaten with the fingers. *Never* wipe hands that have fruit juice on them on a napkin without first using a fingerbowl, because fruit juices leave injurious stains.

WHEN HELPING YOURSELF, REMEMBER

When helping yourself, the first rule is to pay attention to what you are doing and not handle a serving fork or spoon in such a way as to scatter food particles over either floor, table, or yourself.

Anything served on a piece of toast is usually lifted off on the toast, unless you don't want the toast, in which case you may take the quail or help yourself to asparagus and leave the toast in the dish. For sweetbreads, mushrooms on toast—foods that seem to be an arrangement— take the toast and all on the spoon and hold it in place with the fork. If there is only a serving spoon and no fork in the dish, you balance the food as carefully as you can.

WHEN YOU HELP YOURSELF TO
CONDIMENTS, GRAVIES, PICKLES, JELLIES

Gravy should be put *on* the meat, and the condiment, pickles, and jelly *at the side* of whatever they accompany. Olives, radishes, or celery are put on the bread and butter plate if there is one; otherwise on the edge of the plate from which one is eating. Salted nuts are put on the tablecloth.

When helping yourself, you say nothing; but when declining a dish offered by a waiter, you say, "No, thank you." Your voice is barely audible and in fact a negative shake of the head and "Thanks" more nearly describes the usual refusal.

WHEN PASSING PLATE FOR SECOND HELPING

Always leave knife and fork on the plate when passing it and be sure the handles are far enough on not to topple off.

THE GRADUATING TESTS IN TABLE MANNERS

A young person is supposed to have been graduated from the school of table etiquette when he or she is able to sit at a formal lunch or dinner table and find no difficulty in eating properly any of the comestibles which are supposed to be hurdles to the inexpert. But the real test of perfect table manners is never to offend the sensibilities of others. Never chew with the lips open; never eat or drink audibly; and never make a mess of either food or implements.

In addition to the directions already given for young children, it may perhaps be useful to list a few details that are sometimes perplexing.

FINGERS OR FORKS

All juicy or soft fruit or cake is best eaten with a fork; in most cases it is a matter of dexterity rather than rule. If you are able to eat a peach or ripe pear in your fingers and not smear your face, let juice run down, or make a sucking noise, you are the one in a thousand who *may*, and with utmost propriety, continue the feat. If you can eat a napoleon or a cream puff and not let the cream ooze out on the far side, you need not use a fork; but if you cannot eat something—no matter what it is—without getting it all over your fingers, you must use a fork, and when necessary, a spoon or a knife also.

GOOD TABLE MANNERS AVOID UGLINESS

All the rules of table manners are made to avoid ugliness. To let anyone see what you have in your mouth is offensive; to make a noise is to suggest an animal; to make a mess is disgusting. On the other hand, there are a number of trifling decrees of etiquette that are merely finicky, sometimes unreasonable and silly. Why one should not cut one's salad in small pieces—if one wants to—makes little sense unless, that is, one cuts up a whole plateful and makes the plate messy! Until a stainless steel was invented, a steel knife blade was not usable for salad or fruit, because it turned black; but silver-bladed knives have always been used for salads as well as for fruits in best-appointed houses, and today stainless has joined its older brother silver.

To condemn the American fashion of eating a soft-boiled egg in a glass or eggcup because it happens to be the English fashion to scoop it through the ragged edge of the shell is about as reasonable as though we were to proclaim English manners bad because they bring on a dish called a "savory" of fish roe, or something that seems to us equally inappropriate, after the dessert at dinner.

Many other arbitrary rules for eating food with a fork, spoon, or the fingers are also really stumbling-blocks rather than aids to ease and smoothness. As said above, one eats with a fork or spoon "finger foods" that are messy or sticky; one eats with the fingers those which are dry; and one eats dessert with fork or spoon as one prefers. It is true that one should not eat French fried potatoes or even—strictly speaking— Saratoga chips with the fingers, for they "belong" to the meat course. Although separate vegetable saucers are never put on a formally set table, if a man in his own house likes a saucer for his tomatoes, he is certainly within his rights in having it. But if children are taking daddy as their pattern, let us hope that should he insist on eating a chicken wing or a squab leg in his fingers he asks for a fingerbowl. The real objection to eating with the fingers is that they become greasy or sticky, and to suck them or to smear one's napkin is equally bad manners.

LEAVING FOOD ON ONE'S PLATE NOT GOOD MANNERS

The suggested saving to be made by eating everything on one's plate and leaving no food for manners' sake is evidently a confusion of the word plate with platter. To leave a portion on the platter (or in the serving dish) because a guest might like another helping was good manners; on the other hand, to deliberately leave a portion of the food on one's own plate has never been accepted etiquette. In fact, food left on your plate is wasted, for it then must be thrown out, whereas food left in the dish can be stored in the refrigerator and used later.

The one food-saving rule of importance is to serve small portions and then pass every dish a second time. Instead of cutting a broiled chicken in four pieces or, if small, in only two as was formerly done at lunch parties, it is now cut in eight pieces, or four, and the platter passed again.

ON THE SUBJECT OF ELBOWS ON THE TABLE

Although elbows on the table are seen constantly in highest fashionable circles, a whole table's length of elbows, planted like clothespoles, and hands waving glasses or forks about in between is certainly not an attractive dinner-table picture. And yet there are some situations when elbows are not only permitted but are actually necessary—especially on tables in restaurants when people are lunching or dining at a small table of two or four, and it is impossible to make oneself heard above music, and at the same time not be heard at other tables nearby, without leaning far forward. And in leaning forward, a woman's figure makes a more graceful outline supported on her elbows than doubled forward over her hands in her lap as though she were in pain! *At home,* when there is no reason for leaning across the table, there is no reason for elbows. And *at a dinner of ceremony*, elbows on the table are rarely if ever seen, except perhaps at the ends of the table, where again one has to lean forward in order to talk to a companion at a distance across the table corner.

Elbows are *never* put on the table while one is eating. To sit with the left elbow propped on the table while eating with the right hand or to prop the right one on the table while lifting fork or glass to the mouth must be avoided.

RUDE TO WIPE OFF TABLEWARE

Sometimes in restaurants one sees people wiping knives, forks, and spoons on their napkins. This is an act insulting to any reputable proprietor and usually inexcusable. If it should happen, however, that you are obliged to eat in a really dirty restaurant and must wipe the tableware, do so as inconspicuously as you can under the table's edge so that the attention of others is, at least, not attracted to your action.

OTHER TABLE DONT'S

Don't encircle a plate with the left arm while eating with the right hand.

Don't push back your plate when finished. It remains exactly where it is until whoever is waiting on you removes it. If you wait on your-self, get up and carry it to the kitchen.

Don't lean back and announce, "I'm through." The fact that you have put your fork or spoon down shows that you have finished.

Don't *ever* put liquid into your mouth if it is already filled with food—this really means filled. You might have a little bread in your mouth when you drink your coffee, if it be so little as to be undetectable to others. But a good habit is *never*.

Don't dunk, although it is an approved practice in lunch wagons according to the movies. Dunking a whole doughnut into coffee can be rated very little above eating with a knife. If you MUST soften your doughnut or slice of toast, at least break it in half and dip an end, or cut the toast into one-inch strips and dip them lightly, or better, break a small piece at a time into your coffee, milk, or soup, and eat it with a spoon.

Don't apologize and thus *call unnecessary attention* to anything so unpleasant as having to blow your nose at table. The only thing to do is to end it as quickly as possible.

Don't wait until all the plates are served; after a few guests have been served, it is perfectly all right to start eating.

THE USE OF A PUSHER

There is no better pusher than a piece of dry crust. Lacking this, the knife is also correct—*if* properly used. Held in the left hand in the same position as it is when held in the right hand, with the tip of the blade helping to guide and hold each mouthful for the fork to lift, it is a natural motion in no way incorrect.

A more conspicuous way of using the knife as a barricade is often dexterously and unobjectionably done by well-mannered men (though rarely practiced by women) by holding the whole length of the knife blade, sharp edge down, as a barrier and then eating subsequent mouth-fuls by pushing the fork against it.

CERTAINLY YOU MAY SOP BREAD INTO GRAVY

But it must be done properly—by putting a small piece down on the gravy and then eating it with knife and fork as though it were any other helping on your plate. A very good sauce may also be finished in this way—in fact to do so is a compliment to the cook.

NO EXCUSE FOR EATING CHOPS AS FINGER FOOD

The wartime excuse for holding chops, as well as chicken legs, in the fingers as a food-saving measure has no justification—not even that of food-saving. It is, on the contrary, wasteful. At home, the conscien-tious carver cuts all the meat on these bones as closely as he can—and serves bones to no one. All bones are set aside on a clean plate. After the meal they are broken apart and put into the soup pot. This is a one hundred percent saving. Letting the children gnaw at them (quite apart from the harm done to their manners) wastes much of their nutritive value.

BONES, PITS, AND SEEDS

Fish bones or other incidental bones are taken between finger and thumb and removed between compressed lips. Pits and seeds must be eaten quite bare and clean in the mouth and dropped into the cupped fist and then into the plate. The pits of stewed prunes or cherries that are eaten with a spoon are made as clean and dry as possible in the mouth with the tongue and teeth, and then dropped into the spoon with which you are eating, and conveyed to the edge of the plate. Even so, people with best manners usually drop the pits even of stewed prunes or cherries into the cupped hand, held close to the lips.

REMOVING BONES FROM FISH

Lift the end of the bone with a fork, and then lift it all the way out pinched between the knife and fork together, or with the fingers. Do not let the fingers touch the fish.

YESTERDAY A SALAD KNIFE WAS NOT ACCEPTABLE BECAUSE—

Comparatively few families of former days possessed silver-bladed salad knives. Those that *did* used them always. But the many whose only knives were steel-bladed, which upon the slightest touch of vinegar turned black as ink, had to get on as best they could with the fork alone. And anything more difficult than managing leafy salad with a fork alone—especially the fresh, crisp, springing variety—is difficult to imagine. At all events, beware of rolling the fork and wrapping springy leaves around the tines in a spiral. Remember what a spring that lets go can do!

At present, and happily ever since stainless steel was introduced, there has been no possible reason why anyone should be denied the efficiency of a salad knife. In fact no hostess of today, whose house might not be equipped with salad knives, would think of serving an endive or lettuce salad to her knifeless guests, but would choose a chopped celery or apple or grapefruit fork-salad instead.

SALT

If there is no spoon in the saltcellar, use the tip of a clean knife. If the saltcellar be for you alone, use your knife or take a pinch of salt with your fingers.

SALT ON THE TABLECLOTH

Putting salt on the tablecloth and then pinching it between the fingers to put on food is a very old custom and therefore not incorrect if it so happens that a saltcellar is not on one side or the other of one's plate. But dipping celery or radishes into this salt on the tablecloth is never permitted. Salt that is to be dipped into should be put on the bread and butter plate or on the rim of whatever plate is before you.

LUNCHEON OR LUNCH BUT *NOT* BRUNCH!

Pretentious people always say luncheon. Most of us prefer to say lunch. The meaning is the same. But do not give encouragement to that single-headed, double-bodied deformity of language, "brunch." The word is an ungracious one which furthermore has a hurried lunch-wagon suggestiveness. Breakfast on the other hand has a homelike, break-of-day friendliness that brings to mind every degree of hospitality from country breakfasts to hunt-meets and weddings. Brunch—breakfast at lunchtime—calls to mind standees at a lunch counter but *not* the beauty of hospitable living.

NAPKIN UNFOLDING DOES NOT MATTER

The only thing that matters is that a napkin shall stay on your lap. In addition to the suggestion on page 358 for keeping a large dinner napkin in place, one who has a shelving lap will perhaps find it practical to carry a pair of small spring clips with which to clip a too little or too heavily starched napkin to her dress or the edge of his waistcoat. After all, it isn't of much use on the floor!

GRACE BEFORE MEALS

The old-fashioned custom of giving a family blessing or thanks before meals is a very gracious one though unfortunately it is not observed as widely as it used to be. Some families are seated with bowed heads and touch nothing until the grace has been said; others remain standing—both forms are correct.

Usually the mother or the father offers the prayer, but it is sweet to allow the youngest member of the family or if there are several to let them take turns in asking grace.

There are a number of shorter and longer variations, but the following three are typical examples.

> Bless us, O Lord, and these Thy gifts, which we are about to receive from Thy bounty. Through Christ our Lord. Amen.

> Lift up your hands toward the Sanctuary and bless the Lord. Blessed art Thou, O Lord our God, King of the universe, who bringest forth bread from the earth. Amen.

Bless, O Lord, this food to our use, and us to Thy service, and make us ever mindful of the needs of others, in Jesus' Name. Amen.

THE FOODS THAT ARE SOMETIMES DIFFICULT

ARTICHOKES

Artichokes are always eaten with the fingers; a leaf at a time is pulled off and the edible portion dipped in the sauce, and then bitten off. When the center is reached, the thistlelike part is scraped away with a knife, and the heart eaten with a knife and fork.

ASPARAGUS

By reputation this is a finger food, but the ungraceful sight of seeing a bent stalk of asparagus falling limply into someone's mouth, and the fact that moisture is also likely to drip from the end, have been the reasons why most fastidious people invariably eat it—at least in part—with the fork. That is, cut the stalks with the fork to where they become harder, and then pick up the ends in the fingers if you choose. But don't squeeze the stalks, or hold your hand beneath the end and let juice run down your arm.

Hothouse asparagus, or any other that has no hard end, is eaten entirely with a fork. All hard ends should be cut off asparagus before serving it at a dinner party, since picking up stalks in the fingers is scarcely compatible with formal table manners.

BAKED POTATO

Baked potato, whether white or sweet and not otherwise prepared before serving, is usually eaten by breaking it in half with the fingers, scooping all the inside of the potato onto the plate with a fork and then mixing butter, salt, and pepper in it with a fork.

Another way to eat baked potato is to break it in half with the fingers and lay both halves, skin down, on the plate. Mix a little butter in a small part of one half with a fork and eat that. Then mix a little more, and so on, eating it out of the skin without turning it out on the plate.

A third way—for those who like and eat the skin as well as the inside—is to cut the baked potato into two halves with the knife and fork. Then cut them again into pieces, a few at a time, of eatable size. Butter the pieces with the fork alone, and eat, of course, with the fork held in right hand, tines up.

BACON—FRENCH FRIED POTATOES—SARATOGA CHIPS

Breakfast bacon should, when possible, be eaten with a fork. But when it is so very dry and crisp that it scatters into fragments when broken by the fork, fingers are permitted, as they are also for dry Saratoga chips. But French fried potatoes are eaten with a fork.

BIRDS

Birds are not eaten with the fingers. You cut off as much meat as you can and leave the rest on your plate. If you know how to manage very small bones, such as joint or wing, or the second joint of a squab, you put the piece of bone with meat on it in your mouth, eat it clean with teeth and tongue, and remove the bare bones between forefinger and thumb, from between compressed lips.

BOUILLON

Drink any thin soup that is served in a cup or sip it from a spoon as you prefer (sipping must, of course, be silent). Usually you sip a few spoonfuls and then, when it is cool enough, drink from the cup, holding both handles or one as you choose. Remember not to hold your fingers curled in exaggerated cockscombs. Imagine the double-curl effect!

BREAD AND BUTTER

Bread should always be broken into moderate-sized pieces—but not necessarily single mouthful bits—with the fingers before being eaten. If it is to be buttered, a piece is held on the edge of the bread and butter plate, or the place plate, and enough butter spread on it for a mouthful or two at a time, with a butter knife. If there isn't a butter knife, use any other knife you find available.

This buttering of bread is not an important rule. There are always common-sense exceptions. For instance, little hot biscuits can of course be buttered immediately, since they please most palates only when the butter is quickly and thoroughly melted. Bread must never, however, be held flat on the palm and buttered with the hand held in the air. If a table knife is used, care must be taken not to smear food particles from the knife onto the butter. Jellies and jams as well as butter are spread on bread with a knife, never with a fork, though you do put butter on vegetables and jelly on meat with a fork.

BUTTER

Every sort of bread, biscuit, toast, and also hot griddle cakes and corn on the cob are buttered with a knife. But corn that has been cut off the cob, or rice, or potato—or anything else on your plate—has seasoning or butter mixed in it with a fork.

CANAPÉS

Canapés served before a meal are eaten with the fingers with cock-tails in the living-room. At table they are eaten, as are other *hors d'oeuvre,* with a fork.

CHEESE

Cheese is one thing that may be spread with either a knife or a fork. If eaten with a salad, with which one is using no knife, one may break off a piece of cheese and put it on lettuce or a cracker with one's fork. Runny or soft cheeses, such as Brie, Camembert, or Liederkranz, should always be spread with a salad knife. A hostess should remember that ever since the coming of stainless steel, salad knives are a modern must of table-setting.

CLAM CHOWDER—THICK SOUPS

Clam chowder is one of the soups that should be served in a soup plate or bowl, but not in a cup. You should be able to drink cup soups easily. Thick soups are eaten by taking about one third of the spoon into the mouth and doing what really amounts to pouring the soup into the mouth from the end of the spoon.

CONDIMENTS

The thought of smearing condiments with a knife on food already impaled on a fork is quite unpleasant if more than a small amount is taken. The proper way to manage a quantity of cranberry sauce, dressing, jelly, pickle, etc., is to lift it onto the fork and either eat it as a separate mouthful or impale with it a very small piece of meat on the tips of the tines.

CORN ON THE COB

To attack corn on the cob with as little ferocity as possible is perhaps the only direction to be given, since from the point of view of grace a series of ferociously snatching, teeth-bared bites that can be heard as well as seen, to say nothing of butter and corn fragments sprinkled on chin and cheek, while delectable to the palate, is horrible to the sight. The only maxim to bear in mind when eating this pleasant-to-taste but not-very-easy-to-manage vegetable is to eat it as neatly as possible. It doesn't matter whether you break the ear in half, or whether you hold it by its own ends or by silver handles. The real thing to avoid is too much buttering all at once and eating it greedily. If you like much butter, then spread it across only half the length about two rows at a time. If you take a moderate amount of butter, you can spread it across the whole length of two rows, add salt and pepper, hold the ends in both hands, and eat those two rows, and repeat the buttering and eating until all is finished.

Cutting corn off the cob is chiefly a question of the sharpness of the knife. Considerate housekeepers should supply small sharp vegetable knives to those who like to cut the corn off. When corn is served for a dinner party, it should be cut off the cobs in the kitchen and creamed or buttered.

CRACKERS OR CROUSTARDS WITH SOUP

Croustards, which are very small forcemeat pastries, are scattered on the soup after it has been ladled into the plate to be served. Croutons (tiny French-fried cubes of bread) are either put on the soup or else passed separately in a dish with a small serving spoon and each person puts a spoonful in his soup. Oyster crackers, as well as any others, are put on the bread and butter plate, or on the tablecloth—and two or three pieces at a time dropped into the soup.

LOBSTER, BROILED

This is called a finger food because otherwise the meat in the claws cannot be eaten, unless the claws have been not only cracked but literally broken in half. Properly, a big paper napkin and a fingerbowl with hot, slightly soaped water should be put at the side of each place at table as soon as people are served, and carried away, of course, as soon as the plates are removed.

OLIVES

Eat with your fingers. Bite off, but don't nibble around the stone! Bite a stuffed one in half. Put only a very small stuffed olive in your mouth whole.

SPAGHETTI

The method of eating spaghetti by winding it on a fork held against a spoon is correct neither here nor in Italy, where indeed only peasants use a spoon. A few pieces are held against the plate with the end of the fork, which is then twisted to wrap the spaghetti around the fork and then conveyed to the mouth. If necessary this can be done against the curve of the plate which will substitute for the spoon in keeping the slippery pieces on the fork while they are being wound around it. An extra amount of grated Parmesan cheese will help a novice succeed with this because it makes the strands less slippery.

OLIVES, ONIONS, AND CHERRIES IN COCKTAILS

Drink the liquid and, when the glass is drained, it is easy enough to tip the glass and drop the cherry, onion, or small olive into your mouth. Since a large olive is too much of a mouthful, lift it out with the fingers and eat it in two or three bites.

SANDWICHES

All ordinary sandwiches not only at picnics but everywhere are eaten from the fingers. Club sandwiches and other inch-thick and whole-meal sandwiches are best cut in smaller portions before being picked up and held tightly in the fingers of both hands, or if literally dripping with mayonnaise they should be served on a plate with a knife and fork. If you are not sitting at table and you have no knife, you bite into an overlarge and hugely thick piece as nicely as you can or, quoting previous advice in the matter of eating corn on the cob, attack it with as little ferocity as possible.

EATING FRUIT AT TABLE

The equipment for eating fruit at table is a sharp-bladed fruit knife and fork, a fingerbowl, and a napkin that fruit juice will not permanently stain. If in a restaurant and no knife is given you, it is proper to ask for one.

PEACHES

A freestone peach or nectarine is broken in half and eaten. A clingstone you can't break apart; therefore only if you don't mind the fuzz, as most of us do, you eat it whole. If you do this you take very small bites to prevent the juice from running down your wrist. Usually you peel the peach whole and then eat it with knife and fork.

CANTALOUPES AND MELONS

The cantaloupes and muskmelons are served in halves and eaten with a spoon.

A honeydew melon is cut into new-moon-shaped quarters or eighths, depending on size, and eaten with either spoon or fork—whichever you prefer. Similarly with Persian or Casaba melons.

Watermelon is cut into large-size pieces or slices and usually eaten with a knife and fork. Or, if with fork alone, remove seeds with tines and then cut piece with side of fork.

BERRIES

Strawberries as well as all other berries are hulled or stemmed ahead of time, served with cream and sugar, and eaten with a spoon. When especially fine and so freshly picked that they are still warm from the garden's sun, they are often served with their hulls on and sugar placed at one side of each person's plate. The hull of each berry is held in the fingers and the fruit is dipped in the sugar and so eaten.

ORANGES

A favorite table orange is the rather rough-skinned firm fruit, the seedless California one. An enjoyable way to eat it is to slice the two ends of the rind off first, then standing it on one end and holding it on the plate with fingers of left hand, cut the peel off in vertical strips with the knife. You then cut the peeled orange in half at its equator. After this, each half is easily cut and eaten mouthful by mouthful with knife and fork together. They can also be halved, the sections loosened with a curved grapefruit knife, and then eaten with an orange spoon or teaspoon.

A thin-skinned orange, filled with seeds, is extremely difficult to eat. About the only way is to cut it into eighths, take out the seeds from the center with the tip of the knife, and eat the new-moon-shaped pieces as daintily as you can in the fingers.

Tangerines seemingly present no problem because the skin is removed easily and the segments separate readily. But the pulp, seeds, and fibers must be taken neatly from between the lips with the thumb and first two fingers (fingers above and thumb underneath).

APPLES AND PEARS

Apples and pears are quartered usually with a knife. The core then is cut away from each quarter and the fruit is eaten in the fingers. Those who do not like the skin pare each quarter separately.

BANANAS

Although it is not bad manners to peel the skin half-way down and eat the fruit bite by bite at table, it is better to peel the skin all the way off, lay the fruit on your plate, cut it in slices, and eat with a fork.

HOTHOUSE GRAPES

Hothouse grapes are eaten two ways: One, lay a grape on its side, hold it with fingers of left hand, cut into center with point of knife and remove the seeds. Then put grape in mouth with left hand. The other way, put a whole grape in your mouth, chew it, swallow the pulp and juice, and drop the bare seeds into your almost closed fist. In this way, the seeds are conveyed unseen from lips to plate.

GARDEN GRAPES

Press the stem end of a grape between your lips and against your almost closed teeth and the juice and pulp will be drawn into your mouth and the seeds be left in the skin. Little seedless grapes are no problem since they are eaten whole.

CHERRIES AND PLUMS

Cherries and plums are eaten in the fingers of course. The pit of the cherry should be made as dry as possible in your mouth and dropped into your almost-closed cupped hand and thence to your plate. The plum is held in your fingers and eaten as close to the pit as possible. On occasion when you do remove a pit in your fingers, be sure that you do it with your thumb underneath and your first two fingers across your mouth, and not with your fingertips pointing into your mouth.

FORMAL CORRESPONDENCE

·⊶[42]⊷·

THE LETTER YOU WRITE, WHETHER YOU REALIZE IT OR not, is always a mirror which reflects your appearance, taste, and character. Today letter writing is something of a lost art for most of us. But a sloppy letter with the writing all pouring into one corner of the page, badly worded, badly spelled, and with unmatched paper and envelope—even possibly a blot—proclaims the sort of person who might have unkempt hair, unclean linen, and run-down heels, or a run in her stockings; just as a neat, precise, evenly written note portrays a person of those characteristics. Therefore, while it cannot be said that one may read the future of a person by a study of his handwriting, it is true that if a young man wishes to avoid choosing a wife in whose daily life he is sure always to find the unfinished task, the untidy mind, and the syncopated housekeeping, he may be quite safe in selecting her from one whose letters are well written, even and neat.

HOW TO IMPROVE A LETTER'S APPEARANCE

Some people are fortunate in being able to make graceful letters easily, to space their words evenly, and to put them on a page so that the picture is pleasing; others are discouraged at the outset because their fingers are clumsy and their efforts childlike; but no matter how badly formed each individual letter may be, if the writing is consistent throughout, the page as a whole will look fairly well. Avoid exaggerated styles of writing, such as dotting "i" with a circle.

You can *make* yourself write neatly and legibly. You can—with the help of a dictionary if need be—spell correctly; you can be sure that you understand the meaning of every word you use. If it is hard for you to write in a straight line, use the lined guide that comes with nearly all stationery; if impossible to keep an even margin, draw a perpendicular line at the left of the guide so that you can start each new line of writing on it. A guide line one-half inch from the right edge of your paper to tell you where to stop each line will also help. You can also make a guide to slip under the envelope. Far better to use a guide than to send envelopes and pages of writing that slide uphill and down, in uncontrolled disorder, so that the recipient has to all but stand on his head to read it.

CHOICE OF WRITING PAPER

Suitability should be considered in choosing note paper, just as in choosing a piece of furniture for a house. For a handwriting which is habitually large, a larger-sized paper should be chosen than for writing which is small. The shape of paper should also depend somewhat upon the spacing of the lines which is typical of the writer, and whether a wide or narrow margin is used. Low, spread-out writing looks better on a square sheet of paper; tall, pointed writing looks better on paper that is high and narrow. Whether the paper is rough or smooth is entirely a matter of personal choice—but let the quality be good, and the shape and color conservative.

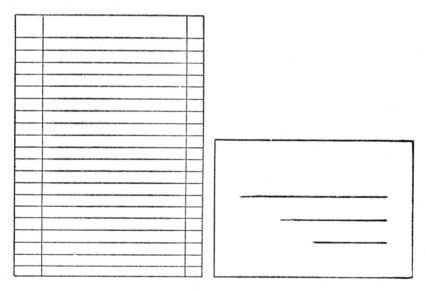

Paper should never be ruled, or highly scented, or odd in shape, or have elaborate or striking ornamentation. Many people use smaller paper for notes, or correspondence cards cut to the size of the envelopes. Others use the same size for all correspondence and leave a wider margin on top and bottom as well as on left and right in writing notes.

The flap of the envelope should be plain and the point neither skimpy nor unduly long. If the flap is square instead of pointed, it may be allowed greater length without being eccentric. When the paper is thin, envelopes with colored linings are used so that the writing cannot be read through the envelope. And the monogram or address may be stamped on the paper in a color to match the lining. Young girls may be allowed quite gay envelope linings, and the device on the paper may be gay to correspond, but must not be so large or loud as to be in bad taste. Oblong envelopes are excellent for business, but those more nearly square are smartest for personal use.

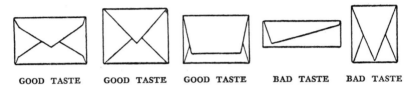

GOOD TASTE   GOOD TASTE   GOOD TASTE   BAD TASTE   BAD TASTE

Linings for Christmas-card envelopes may be as gay as the ornaments that decorate a Christmas tree. This is the time one may go "overboard." But unrestrained masses of red and gold, swirls of purple and green or other striking colors, are abominations at any other time.

Metal-edged paper is not good form. Deckle-edge paper is always suggestive of a studio and for that reason appropriate for artists, but not as good as clean-cut edges for most of us.

PAPER FOR A MAN

Writing paper for a man should always be conservative. Plain white or cream, or gray or granite, or a deep blue (not turquoise) paper of medium or larger size, and stamped with his address or his initials or, for social correspondence, with his crest, if he has one, is in good taste. The color of the engraving (or printing) should be black or gray or navy blue. Writing ink should be black or navy blue, but not green.

A very practical paper for a man's non-social correspondence is a single sheet 7 or 7¼ inches by 10 or 10½ inches marked in plain block letters in navy blue at the top. His name without title, his address and his telephone number—all three appear. This paper can be used for typewriting or handwriting, and is folded in threes to fit into a 7¼ or 7½ by 4-inch envelope. Good stationers supply correctly sized paper and envelopes that match.

PAPER FOR A WOMAN

White, cream, all blues, grays, and mauves are in best taste. Pink is on the fringe of admittance; green is still not admitted. Paper should be of small or medium size, single or double sheets, plain or with any colored border—even green or red if it be extremely narrow—and stamped with either a monogram, initials, address, or both, in color to match the border. Writing ink may be violet as well as any blue, but not green.

FIRST NAME ALONE FOR YOUNG GIRL

A girl's name—either Elizabeth in full or Betty—embossed in color is popular for all personal correspondence of a young girl. But it should not be used by an older woman except when writing to her really intimate friends or relatives, and even then it is not in best taste.

PAPER SUITABLE FOR EVERYONE IN FAMILY

A paper suitable for the use of all the members of a family has the address stamped—or perhaps printed—in plain letters at the top of the first page. Frequently the telephone number is put in small letters under the address, or in the upper left-hand corner under a small telephone device, with the address in the center—a necessary convenience in the present day of telephoning. For example:

350 PARK AVENUE

TELEPHONE PLAZA 4-7572

or

39 EAST 79TH STREET

DEVICES FOR STAMPING

As heraldry with its origins in the Middle Ages is not an institution in America, the use of a coat of arms is as much a foreign custom as the speaking of an alien tongue; but in certain communities where old families have used their family arms continuously since the days when they brought their device—and their right to it as certified by the colleges of heraldry—from Europe, the use of it is proper, but even so, rather conspicuous at the present time.

A WOMAN ALONE MAY NEVER USE A CREST

Notwithstanding the ornamental beauty of a crest and the utter ugliness of a lozenge, a widow has no right to use her husband's crest on her letter paper. Properly she may use the device on the shield of his coat of arms, transferred to a diamond-shaped device called a lozenge. She may also, if she chooses, divide the lozenge perpendicularly into two parts and crowd the device from her husband's shield into the left half and the device from her father's shield into the right half, making a combination such as that in the example at the head of the invitation on page 103.

A spinster uses her paternal arms on a lozenge without crest or motto. A crest is used only by the male member of the family, and therefore its appearance on the paper of a widow or a spinster is as absurd as it would be to put esquire at the end of her name. Surprisingly few Americans, however, seem to be aware of this heraldic rule.

POST OFFICE REQUIRES RETURN ADDRESS ON ENVELOPE

It has always been customary to place a return address at the top left-hand corner on the face of a business envelope; and when necessary to use one on a personal letter, to put it on the flap. Whatever the real reason for making this distinction, it did separate the two types of letters in our mail. Today (in response to requests made by the United States Post Office) it is considered permissible and even advisable to put *all* return addresses on the face of the envelope. If handwritten, it should be very small. Remember also that zone numbers are a part of the address.

PRINTING AS WELL AS DIE-STAMPING

There are certain definite and fairly inflexible rules about marking. Not many years ago, the paper used by a lady was either die-stamped (engraved) or left plain. This was in the same era when the mystery of operating a typewriter was still the special province of the professional stenographer. Today the writing equipment of a busy man or woman is almost as certain to include a typewriter as it is to employ modern pens in place of quills. The convenience of paper upon which one's full name and address are printed has become indispensable to everyone who must write many letters. In short, a few quires of die-stamped paper—at unavoidably higher cost—for formal letters are augmented by dozens of quires of printed papers for informal social correspondence and for business letters.

COUNTRY HOUSE STATIONERY FOR A BIG HOUSE

In selecting paper for a country house we go back to the subject of suitability. A big house, in important grounds, should have very plain, very dignified letter paper. It may be white, or tinted blue or gray. The name of the place should be engraved, in the center usually, at the top of the first page; further information is often given by a single device slanting across the upper corner, or as many as may be necessary are put in a column at the upper left side. Many persons use a whole row of small outlines—the engine of a train and beside it Stirlington, meaning that Stirlington is the railroad station; a telegraph pole, an envelope, a telephone,

 STIRLINGTON, NEW YORK

 RINGWOOD, NEW JERSEY

 SLOATSBURG, NEW YORK, 732

and beside each an address. Instead of, or in addition to, the engine, there may be a boat, or an airplane, or perhaps even a bus. These devices are suitable for all places, whether they are great or tiny, that have different addresses for the railroad, post office, telephone, or telegraph.

If the house is located on winding roads off the main highway, a simple line-drawn map is very helpful to visitors who may be coming by car.

FOR THE LITTLE COUNTRY HOUSE

On the other hand, farmhouses and little places in the country may have very bright-colored stamping, as well as gay-lined envelopes. Places with easily illustrated names quite often have them pictured. The BIRDCAGE, for instance, may have a bright blue paper with a red bird-cage suggestive of lacquer; the BANDBOX, a fantastically decorated milliner's box on oyster-gray paper, the envelope lining of black and gray pin-stripes; and the DOLL'S HOUSE might use the outline of a doll's house in grass green on green-bordered white paper, and white envelopes lined with grass green. Each of these devices loses

its charm unless it is as small as the outline of a cherry pit and the paper is of the smallest size that comes with envelopes 3½ x 5 inches, or paper 4 x 6 inches and envelopes a size to hold the paper without folding.

OFFICIAL WRITING PAPER

An ambassador or minister has the coat of arms of his country—in gold usually—stamped at the top of writing paper and on cards of invitation for official or formal use. For his personal use and for the use of all who live at the embassy or the legation, note paper is engraved merely

AMERICAN EMBASSY
LONDON

The letter paper of a governor is stamped

EXECUTIVE MANSION
COLUMBUS
OHIO

and is usually surmounted by the coat of arms of the state. The letter paper used for social correspondence by a governor's family as well as himself is engraved EXECUTIVE MANSION. But EXECUTIVE OFFICE is often chosen as the heading for official letters.

This same paper, but without the coat of arms, may be used by his family if the address is also that of their home. Otherwise their paper is stamped with their personal address.

It is unnecessary to add that the wife of a senator has no right to use stationery headed THE SENATE, nor may the wife of a congressman write on paper engraved HOUSE OF REPRESENTATIVES.

MOURNING PAPER

The wide borders of former days have been discarded for those which customs of yesterday would have called second mourning. An over-heavy border (from $3/8$ to $1/2$ inch) is unknown in the United States today.

One fourth of an inch is considered deepest mourning, and $3/16$ used as deep mourning by all who are young; $1/16$ and $1/32$ of an inch are suitable width for second mourning.

DATING A LETTER

Usually the date is put at the upper right-hand side of the first page of a letter, or at the end and to the far left of the signature of a note. It is far less confusing for one's correspondent to read May 9, 1955, than 5-9-55. The latter is often confusing because it is not known whether the sequence is month-day-year or day-month-year, a growing usage of Continental origin.

At the end of a note "Thursday" is sufficient unless the note is an invitation for more than a week ahead, in which case write as in a letter, "January 9." The year is not essential for it can hardly be expected that a year will be required for a letter's delivery.

SEQUENCE OF PAGES

If a note is longer than one page but shorter than three, the third page is customarily used next, as this leaves the fourth page blank and prevents the writing from showing through the envelope. With heavy or lined envelopes, the fourth is used more often than the third. In letters one may write first, second, third, fourth, in regular order; or first and fourth, then, opening the sheet and turning it sideways, write across the two inside pages as one. Many prefer to write on first, third, then sideways across the second and fourth. The sequence is not important. Certain people have the habit of repeating the last word on a page at the top of the next. It is undoubtedly a good idea derived from old manuscripts when it was customary, but it does make a stuttering impression upon a reader not accustomed to it.

FOLDING A LETTER

To fold a letter in such a way that the recipient shall be able to read the contents without having to turn the paper is giving too much importance to nothing. It is sufficient that the paper be folded *neatly*— once, of course, for the envelope that is as deep as half the length of the paper, and twice for the envelope that is a third as deep. The paper that folds twice, by the way, should be used only for business purposes. Social letter paper should fold only once and be fitted into a square envelope. Note paper which is smartest at the moment is the same size as the envelope and goes into it flat without folding.

SEALING WAX

Although sealing wax—like the title esquire—is almost never used in America, both look very nice when properly placed. In short, if you use sealing wax, let us hope you are an adept at making an even and smoothly finished seal, and that you choose a plain-colored wax which can be persuaded to pour smoothly and colorfully and not to look like a blackened, streaked blob of colored dough.

SALUTATIONS

The most formal beginning of a social letter is "My dear Mrs. Smith." The fact that in England "Dear Mrs. Smith" is the more formal opening does not greatly concern us in America. "Dear Mrs. Smith," "Dear Sarah," "Dear Sally," "Sally dear," "Dearest Sally," "Darling Sally" are increasingly intimate.

Business letters begin

> Smith, Johnson & Co.
> 20 Broadway
> New York 4, N. Y.
>
> Dear Sirs:

In this modern day of informal business letters one written to an individual begins

> Messrs. Smith, Johnson & Co.
> 20 Broadway
> New York 4, N. Y.
>
> Dear Mr. Johnson:

THE COMPLIMENTARY CLOSE

It is too bad that, for personal letters and notes, the English language does not permit the charming and graceful closing of all letters in the French manner, with those little flowers of compliment that leave such a pleasant fragrance after reading. But ever since the eighteenth

century English-speaking people have been busy pruning away all ornament of expression; even the last remaining graces, "kindest regards,"
"with kindest remembrances," are fast disappearing, leaving us nothing but an abrupt "Sincerely yours."

The close of a business letter should be "Yours truly" or "Yours very
truly." "Respectfully" is used only by a tradesman to a customer, by an
employee to an employer, or by an inferior; *never* by a person of equal
position. No lady should ever sign a letter "Respectfully," except as part
of the long, formal "have the honor to remain" close of a letter to the
President of the United States or, of course, to a bishop or a mother
superior.

The best ending to a formal social note is "Sincerely," "Sincerely
yours," "Very sincerely," "Very sincerely yours," "Yours always sincerely," or "Always sincerely yours."

"I remain, dear madam," is no longer in use, but "Believe me" is
still correct when a degree of formality is to be expressed in the close
of a note.

Believe me
Very sincerely yours,

or

Believe me, my dear Mrs. Worldly,
Most sincerely yours,

This last is an English form, and although it seems somewhat affected today, it is used by quite a number of Americans.

APPROPRIATE FOR A MAN

"Faithfully" or "Faithfully yours" is a very good closing for a man
when writing to a woman or for any uncommercial correspondence,
such as a letter to the President of the United States, a member of the
Cabinet, an ambassador, a clergyman, etc.

THE INTIMATE CLOSING

"Affectionately yours," "Always affectionately," "Affectionately,"
"Devotedly," "Lovingly," "Your loving" are in increasing scale of
intimacy.

"Lovingly" is much more intimate than "Affectionately" and so is
"Devotedly."

"Sincerely" in formal notes and "Affectionately" in intimate notes
are the two adverbs most used in the present day. Between these two
there is a blank; in English we have no expression to fit sentiment more
friendly than the first and yet less intimate than the second.

NOT GOOD FORM

"Cordially" was coined no doubt to fill this need, but its condescension puts it in the category with "residence" and "retire," and all the other offenses of pretentiousness.

"Yours in haste" or "Hastily yours" while not bad form is rather carelessly rude.

"In a tearing hurry" is a termination dear to the boarding-school girl; but its truth does not make it any more attractive than the vision of that same young girl rushing into a room with her hat and coat half on, to swoop upon her mother with a peck of a kiss and, with a "—by, Mom!", whirl out again!

OTHER ENDINGS

"Gratefully" is used only when a benefit has been received, as to a lawyer who has skilfully handled a case, to a surgeon who has saved a life dear to you, a friend who has been put to unusual trouble to do you a favor.

In an ordinary letter of thanks, the signature is "Sincerely," "Affectionately," "Devotedly"—whatever your usual close may be.

The phrases that a man might devise to close a letter to his betrothed or his wife are limited only by the extent of his imagination, and they are too personal to be set down in this, or any, book.

THE SIGNATURE

Abroad, the higher the rank, the shorter the name. A duke, for instance, signs himself Wellington, nothing else, and a queen her first name, Elizabeth.

But in America, it is not customary for a man to discard any of his names. So John Hunter Titherington Smith, finding that name too much of a penful for the one who unendingly signs letters and documents, chooses J. H. T. Smith instead, or perhaps, at the end of personal letters, John H. T. Smith. And in addressing him others naturally follow his lead. (That he is likely to become "J.H." to his business associates is another story.)

A married woman should always sign a letter to a stranger, a bank, business firm, etc., with her legal name, and add, in parentheses, her married name. Thus:

> Very truly yours,
> Mary Jones Mathews
> (Mrs. John Mathews)

Of course if for all general purposes her writing paper is marked with her full name and address, her signature, Mary Jones Mathews, needs no further explanation.

NEVER SIGN A LETTER WITH "MRS."

Although this rule is fully explained on page 527, it is actually one of the most important rules in this book and cannot be too strongly emphasized.

Thousands upon thousands of well-bred, courteously intentioned women, writing to those whom they admire and respect, unthinkingly sign themselves

Sincerely,

Mrs. John Mathews

or

Mrs. Mary Mathews

This second signature is just as rude as the first and is also lacking in good taste.

A lady writing to another lady, or to a gentleman, should sign her name this way to every friend and acquaintance who perfectly well knows her married name

Sincerely,

Mary Mathews

To acquaintances who may not know which Mrs. or possibly Miss Mathews she may happen to be, she signs her name

Sincerely,

Mary Mathews

(Mrs. John Mathews)

An unmarried lady signs her name

Sincerely,

(Miss) Mary Mathews

Those who fear to sign their names "Mary" because they think someone might then feel privileged to call them "Mary" can write clearly beneath their signature, "Kindly reply to Mrs. John Smith." And they may moreover sign their name "M. J. Smith" instead of "Mary Jones Smith."

Never under any circumstances sign a letter with "Mr.," "Mrs.," or "Miss" as an unseparated part of one's signature unless one is willing to be considered ignorant or unpardonably rude.

WHEN THE TITLE "MR." IS CORRECT

As unconventional as it may sound, it is at times permissible and often desirable that a man use "Mr." in parentheses before his signature to indicate that such a name as Leslie, Sidney, Shirley, or Marion is not that of a woman.

CORRECT USE OF ESQUIRE

The postscription Esq. has gone almost out of general use in the United States—except among the conservative members of the older generation and by lawyers and justices of the peace. Its correct use is, furthermore, confusing. For example, formally engraved invitations are always addressed to Mr. Stanley Smith. Written invitations, as well as all other personal letters, may be addressed to Stanley Smith, Esq. The title of Esquire is of British origin and formerly used to denote the eldest son of a knight or members of a younger branch of a noble house. Later all graduates of universities, professional and literary men, and important landholders were given the right to this title, which even today denotes a man of education—a gentleman. John Smith, Esquire, is John Smith, gentleman. Mr. John Smith may be a gentleman or may not be one. And yet, as noted above, all engraved invitations are addressed "Mr." There is no "required" usage for the term Esquire, either as a courtesy or otherwise.

CORRECTLY A WIDOW KEEPS HER HUSBAND'S NAME

According to best taste no note or social letter should ever be addressed to a married woman—even if she is a widow—as Mrs. Mary Town. Correctly and properly a widow keeps her husband's name for *always*. If her son's wife should have the same name, she becomes Mrs. James Town, senior, or simply Mrs. Town, if there is no other in her community with the same name.

Of course if, in a certain community, it is customary for widows to use Mrs. with their Christian names and they themselves have no objection, their names are certainly their own to use as they choose. But to those of you who want to keep your husband's name, best taste and truth agree that the man gave his name when he gave the wedding ring —both were for life, or until the woman marries again.

NAME OF DIVORCÉE

A divorced woman takes her own surname in place of her ex-husband's Christian name. Supposing her to have been Mary Simpson before her marriage, she calls herself Mrs. Simpson Johnson.

DAUGHTERS, SONS, AND CHILDREN

The eldest daughter is Miss Taylor; her younger sister, Miss Jane Taylor. Today this right to Miss Taylor is considered rather suggestive of a spinster of uncertain age, and the moderns prefer Miss Alice and Miss Jane Taylor.

Envelopes to children are addressed: Miss Katherine Taylor, and Robert Taylor, the latter with no title.

Do not write The Messrs. Brown in addressing a father and son. The Messrs. Brown is correct only for unmarried brothers.

WRITE ADDRESS PLAINLY

Write the name and address on the envelope as precisely and as legibly as you can. If your writing is poor, PRINT. Remember that the post office has enough to do in deciphering the letters of the unlettered without being asked to do unnecessary work for you!

When you are writing to someone who lives in an American city that uses postal zones, try to learn the zone your correspondent lives in, and write it on the envelope as it is an essential part of the address. Zone numbers are used in many foreign cities too and are an integral part of the address.

LETTERS ON BUSINESS MATTERS

If you are writing to someone at his home address, you will properly assume that no one else will open the letter, and it is rude to write "Personal" on it. But if you are writing a social note to a friend's business address, it is entirely correct. "Please Forward" is correct if you know only a former address but not the current one.

Preferably a business letter is typewritten; anything bordering on the unconventional is out of place. The correct beginning for an impersonal business letter is:

> Mrs. Richard Worldly
> 257 Park Avenue
> New York 17, N.Y.
> Dear Madam:

A personal business letter, meaning a letter from a business or professional man to a customer or client he knows personally, begins

> Mrs. Richard Worldly
> 257 Park Avenue
> New York 17, N.Y.
> My dear Mrs. Worldly:

Business letters written by a customer or client differ very little from those sent out from a business house. A business letter should alway be as brief and explicit as possible. For example:

TUXEDO PARK
NEW YORK

May 17, 1955

H. J. Paint & Co.
  22 Branch St.
    New York 7, N.Y.
Dear Sirs:
  Your estimate for painting my dining-room, library, south bedroom, and dressing-room is satisfactory, and you may proceed with the work as soon as possible.

                    Very truly yours,
                      C. R. Town
                    (Mrs. James Town)

An order letter to a store should contain precisely this information:

1. Name or description of article, *including*
2. Quantity, size, color and *necessarily*
3. Price.
4. How paid for (C.O.D., check enclosed, or charge account).
5. How sent, when necessary.
6. Address and date.

Example:

Brown, Green and Company
Dear Sirs: (the "Dear Sirs" is often omitted)
  Please forward by American Railway Express C.O.D. to
                    Mrs. J. B. Greatlake
                    20 Lakeshore Drive
                    Chicago, Illinois
3 jars Black's Clensen Cream—50¢ size
1 chair (No. 4433 in your catalogue), price $59.50
1 quilt (No. 1746) in rose color, price $22.00
                      Yours truly,
                      A. K. Greatlake

LETTER OF INQUIRY TO A HOTEL

101 PARK AVENUE
NEW YORK

May 22, 1956

Proprietor of Ocean House
  Beach Haven, Maine
Dear Sir:
  I would like to know what accommodation you can offer me for the month of August. I require one double room with bath for my husband

*and myself, a single room for my daughter, and a single room for my
son.*

Your hotel was recommended to me by Mrs. Arthur Norman.

*If you will send me floor plan and prices, I will let you know my
decision promptly.*

Very truly yours,
Mary Newhouse
(Mrs. John Newhouse)

COURTEOUS LETTER FROM THE POINT OF VIEW OF A COLUMNIST

When writing to an "answer column" it is obvious, if you think
about it, that briefly and clearly put questions, which are easily and
quickly read and can be briefly answered, are chosen of necessity because of the obviously limited time which can be given to the reading
of each one of scores of letters. In other words, several pages of illegible
handwriting requiring a half-hour to decipher and answer cannot be
chosen instead of twenty short, clearly typed letters. It is not a question
of *don't want to*, but of *can't*.

THE SOCIAL NOTE

The form of a social note differs from a business one in that the
full name and address of the person written to is written only on the
envelope; the sender's address, if given, is die-stamped. Better-quality
stationery is used, and the salutation is "My dear ——" or "Dear ——"
instead of "Dear Sir." Example:

350 PARK AVENUE

Dear Mrs. Robinson,

I am enclosing the list I promised you.

*I do hope the addresses will be of some use to you, and that you will
have a delightful trip.*

Very sincerely,
Martha Kindhart

Thursday.

SIRS OR MADAMS

The salutation "Dear Sir" or "Sirs" is a much better form than
"Gentlemen." When writing to a firm or organization composed of
women, the salutation is "Dear Madams." Never write "Mesdames."
any more than you would write "Messieurs" instead of "Sirs."

THE NOTE OF APOLOGY

Examples:

I

BROADLAWNS

Dear Mrs. Town,

I do deeply apologize for my seeming rudeness in having to send the message about Monday night.

When I accepted your invitation, I stupidly forgot entirely that Monday was a holiday and that all of my own guests, naturally, were not leaving until Tuesday morning; Arthur and I could not therefore go out by ourselves and leave them!

We were disappointed and hope that you know how sorry we were not to be with you.

> *Very sincerely,*
> *Ethel Norman*

Tuesday morning.

A note of apology should really offer some excuse for breaking an engagement. Although you may have telephoned or sent a telegram, a note should follow.

II

Dear Mrs. Neighbor,

My gardener has just told me that our chickens got into your flower beds and did a great deal of damage.

The chicken netting is being built higher at this moment and they will not be able to damage anything again. I shall, of course, send Patrick to put in shrubs to replace those broken, although I know that ones newly planted cannot compensate for those you have lost. I can only ask you to accept my contrite apologies.

> *Always sincerely yours,*
> *Katherine Sedwick Pennybacker*

LETTERS OF THANKS

In the following examples of letters that are intimate and from young persons, such profuse expressions as "divine," "awfully," "petrified," "too sweet," "too wonderful" are purposely inserted, because to change all of those enthusiasms into "pleased with," "very," "feared," "most kind" would be to change the validity of the "real" letters into smug, stilted, and self-conscious utterances at variance with anything ever written by young men and women of today. Even the letters of older persons, although they are more restrained than those of youth, avoid anything suggesting prolixity, pedantry, or affectation.

Do not suppose from this that well-bred people write poorly! On the contrary, perfect simplicity and freedom from self-consciousness are possible only to those who have acquired at least some degree of cultivation. Pretentiousness in a letter of thanks or sympathy is an infallible sign of insincerity and lack of taste. For simplicity of expression, such as is unattainable to the rest of us, but which we can at least strive to emulate, read the Bible first, then at random such writers as Robert Louis Stevenson, John Galsworthy, Max Beerbohm, Somerset Maugham or A. A. Milne! E. V. Lucas has written two novels in letter form—which illustrate the best type of letter writing. Today's generation will doubtless provide new writers of distinguished letters that in turn will serve for time to come.

LETTERS OF THANKS FOR WEDDING PRESENTS

All wedding presents are sent to the bride, but she generally words her letters of thanks as though they belonged equally to the groom, especially so if they have been sent by friends of his.

TO INTIMATE FRIENDS OF THE BRIDEGROOM

Dear Mrs. Beck,
    To think of your sending us all this wonderful glass! It is simply divine! Jim and I both thank you a thousand times!
    The presents are, of course, to be shown on the day of the wedding, but do come in on Tuesday at tea time for an earlier view.
    Thanking you again, and with love from us both,
                                                    Affectionately,
                                                        Joan

FORMAL

I

Dear Mrs. King,
    It was more than thoughtful of you and Mr. King to send us such a lovely clock. Thank you very, very much.
    Looking forward to seeing you on the tenth,
                                            Very sincerely,
                                                Joan McCord

Sometimes, as in the example above, thanks to the husband is definitely expressed in writing to the wife. Usually, however, "you" is understood to mean "you both."

II

Dear Mrs. Potter,

All my life I have wanted a piece of jade, but in my wanting I have never imagined one quite so beautiful as the one you have sent me. It was wonderfully sweet of you and I thank you more than I can tell you.

Affectionately,
Joan McCord

III

Dear Mrs. Hardwick,

Thank you for these wonderful prints. They go too beautifully with some old English ones that Jim's uncle sent us, and our dining-room will be quite perfect—as to walls!

Hoping that you are surely coming to the wedding,

Very sincerely,
Joan McCord

INTIMATE

Dearest Cora,

That you should have taken days and days to make this marvelous needlepoint for ME—really, darling, I can't tell you how much I love it, and appreciate it, and thank *you!*

Sally

FOR A PRESENT RECEIVED AFTER THE WEDDING

Dear Mrs. Chatterton,

The mirror you sent us is going over our drawing-room mantel just as soon as we can hang it up! It is exactly what we most needed and we both thank you ever so much.

Please come in soon to see how becoming it will be to the room.

Yours affectionately,
Mary Smith Smartlington

THANKS FOR CHRISTMAS AND OTHER PRESENTS

It was too adorable of you, dear Lucy, to have a chair like yours made for me. Jack says I'll never get a chance to sit in it if he gets there first. In fact we both thank you ever and ever so much.

Affectionately,
Sally

Dear Uncle William,

I know I oughtn't to have opened it until Christmas, but I couldn't resist the look of the package, and then putting it on at once! So I am all dressed up in your beautiful clip. It is one of the loveliest things I have ever seen and I certainly am lucky to have it given to me! Thank you a thousand—and then more—times for it.

Love,
Rosalie

Dear Kate,

I am fascinated with my utility box—it is too beguiling for words! You are the cleverest one anyway for finding what no one else can— and everyone wants. I don't know how you do it! And you certainly were sweet to think of me. Thank you, dear.

Ethel

THANKS FOR A BABY PRESENT

Dear Mrs. Kindhart,

Of course it would be! Because no one else can knit like you! The sweater you made the baby is the prettiest thing I have ever seen, and is perfectly adorable on her! Thank you, as usual, dear Mrs. Kindhart, for your goodness to

Your affectionate
Sally

Dear Mrs. Cooper,

Thank you ever so much for the lovely afghan you sent the baby. It is by far the prettiest one he has; it is so soft and close—he doesn't get his fingers tangled in it.

Do come in and see him, won't you? We are both allowed visitors, special ones, every day between 4 and 5:30!

Affectionately always,
Lucy

BREAD-AND-BUTTER LETTERS

When you have been staying over Sunday, or for longer, at someone's house, it is absolutely necessary that you write a letter of thanks to your hostess within a few days after the visit.

Bread-and-butter letters, as they are called, are the stumbling blocks of visitors. Why they are so difficult for nearly everyone is hard to determine, unless it is that they are often written to persons with whom you are on formal terms, and the letter should be somewhat informal in tone. Very likely you have been visiting a friend and must write to her mother, whom you scarcely know; perhaps you have been included in a large and rather formal house party and the hostess is an acquaintance rather than a friend; or perhaps you are a bride and have been on a first visit to relatives or old friends of your husband, but strangers, until now, to you.

As an example of the first, where you have been visiting a girl friend and must write a letter to her mother, you begin "Dear Mrs. Town" at the top of a page, and nothing in the forbidding memory of Mrs. Town encourages you to go further. It would be easy enough to write to Pauline, the daughter. Very well, write to Pauline then—on an odd piece of paper, in pencil—what a good time you had, how nice it was to be with her. Then copy the note you composed to Pauline on the page beginning "Dear Mrs. Town." You have only to add "Love to Pauline, and thank you again for asking me," sign it "Very sincerely" or better "Affectionately"—and there you are!

Don't be afraid that your note is too informal; older people are always pleased with any friendly and spontaneous expressions from the young. Never think, because you cannot write a letter easily, that it is better not to write at all. The most awkward note that can be imagined is better than none—for to write none is the depth of rudeness, whereas the awkward note merely fails to delight.

TO A FORMAL HOSTESS AFTER AN ESPECIALLY AMUSING WEEK-END

Dear Mrs. Oldname,

Every moment of the week-end was a perfect delight! I am afraid my work at the office this morning was down to zero in efficiency; so perhaps it is just as well, if I am to keep my job, that the average week-end in the country is different—very. Thank you for the wonderful time you gave us all, and believe me

Faithfully yours,
Frederick Bachelor

Dear Mrs. Oldname,

Again I realize that there is no house to which I always go with so much pleasure, and leave on Monday morning with so much regret, as yours.

Your party over this last week-end was simply wonderful! And thank you ever so much for having included me.

Affectionately,
Constance

Dear Mrs. Oldname,

Thank you more than I can tell you for my very happy week-end.

I enjoyed every minute of it, and think you were very kind to include me in such a delightful house party.

Very sincerely,
John Huntington Smith

FROM AN OLD BACHELOR TO HIS YOUNG RELATIVES

Dear Janice and Tom,

Why do I so much like to stay with you? I thought of this as the train carried me away this morning.

I like to stay with you—because I love you both. But that is not quite enough. I love other members of the family but I abhor staying with them. Either they fuss too much—or they rigidly exact that I force my lifelong habits into a pattern strictly theirs. But you have the art of effortless adjustments that are exceedingly soothing to the crotchets of

Your affectionate
Uncle Tom

FROM A BRIDE TO HER NEW RELATIVES-IN-LAW

A letter that was written by a bride after paying a first visit to her husband's aunt and uncle won for her at a stroke the love of the whole family. This is the letter.

Dear Aunt Abigail,

Now that it is all over, I have a confession to make! Do you know that when Dick drove me up to your front door and I saw you and Uncle Bob standing on the top step—I was simply paralyzed *with fright!*

"Suppose they don't like me," was all that I could think. Of course, I knew you loved Dick, but that only made it worse. How awful, if you couldn't like me! *The reason I stumbled coming up the steps was because my knees were actually knocking together! You remember, Uncle Bob said that it was good I was already married, or I wouldn't be this year? And then, you were both so perfectly adorable to me and made me feel as though I had always been your niece—and not just the wife of your nephew.*

I loved every minute of our being with you, dear Aunt Abigail, just as much as Dick did, and we hope you are going to let us come again soon.

With best love from us both,

Your affectionate niece,
Eloise

This type of letter would not have served perhaps if Dick's aunt had been a forbidding and austere woman; but even such a one would be far more likely to take a new niece to her heart if the new niece herself gave evidence of having one.

AFTER VISITING A FRIEND

Dear Ellen,
It was hideously dull and stuffy in town this morning after the fresh coolness of Strandholm. A back yard is not an alluring outlook after the beauty of your garden.
It was good being with you and I enjoyed every moment.
                                        Devotedly,
                                            Caroline

FROM A MAN WHO HAS BEEN CONVALESCING
AT A FRIEND'S HOUSE

Dear Martha,
I certainly hated taking that train this morning and realizing that the end had come to my peaceful days. You and Warren and the children, and your place, which is the essence of all that a home ought to be, have put me on my feet again. I thank you so much—much more than I can say—for the wonderful goodness of all of you.
                                        Fred

FROM AN OLD FRIEND TO HER HOSTESS

Dearest Ginny,
You were simply wonderful to me! I can see you look up from your petit point and smile and shake your head and say, "But, my dear, I did nothing!"
All right, then, let us leave it at that—that "nothing" is to listen without ever a sag of interest, with never less than complete under-standing.
So thank you, Ginny, for the nothing which is everything to your
                                        Devoted
                                            Clara

Dearest Sally,
Words can't tell you how comfortable you made me and how happy I was the whole time I was there. It was all so nice! And such a lovely, lovely holiday! for which I thank you much.
                            Affectionately and appreciatively,
                                            Peggy

Lucy, darling,
You know I loved staying with you—I always do!
I hated to go—as always, too!
Thank you and best love to you both.
                                        Devotedly,
                                            Catherine

Darling Betty,
We both had a wonderful time!
You were very good to ask us so soon again, and we thank you very,
very much.

Yours,
Mary

TO AN ACQUAINTANCE

After a visit to a formal acquaintance or when someone has shown you especial hospitality in a city where you are a stranger:

My dear Mrs. Duluth,
It was more than good of you to give my husband and me so much pleasure. We enjoyed, and appreciated, all your kindness to us more than we can say.
We hope that you and Mr. Duluth may be coming East before long and that we may then have the pleasure of seeing you at Strandholm.
In the meanwhile, thanking you for your generous hospitality and time, and with kindest regards to you both, in which my husband joins, believe me,

Very sincerely yours,
Katherine Hill Starkweather

AN ENGRAVED CARD OF THANKS

An engraved card of thanks is proper *only* when sent by a public official to acknowledge the overwhelming number of congratulatory messages he must inevitably receive from strangers when he has carried an election or otherwise been honored with the confidence of his State or country. Executive Mansion is the established name of the house in which a governor lives; but if he prefers, all professional letters may be sent from the Executive Office. A recent and excellent example follows:

EXECUTIVE MANSION

My dear . . . .
I warmly appreciate your kind message of congratulation which has given me a great deal of pleasure, and sincerely wish that it were possible for me to acknowledge it in a less formal manner.

Faithfully,
(signed by hand)

THE LETTER OF INTRODUCTION

A letter of business introduction can be much more freely given than a letter of social introduction. For the former it is necessary merely that the persons introduced have business interests in common—which are much more easily determined than social compatibility, the necessary requisite for the latter. It is, of course, proper to give your personal representative a letter of introduction to anyone to whom you send him.

On the subject of letters of social introduction there is one chief rule:

Never *ask* for such letters of introduction, and be very sparing in your offers to write or accept them.

Seemingly few persons realize that a letter of social introduction is actually a draft for payment on demand. The form might as well be, "The bearer of this has (because of it) the right to *demand* your interest, your time, your hospitality—liberally and at once, no matter what your inclination may be."

Therefore, it is far better to refuse in the beginning than to hedge and end by committing the greater error of unwarrantedly inconveniencing a valued friend or acquaintance.

When you have a friend who is going to a city where you have other friends and you believe that it will be a mutual pleasure for them to meet, a letter of introduction is proper and very easy to write; but sent to a casual acquaintance—no matter how attractive or distinguished the person to be introduced—it is a gross presumption.

THE MORE FORMAL NOTE OF INTRODUCTION

Dear Mrs. Miller:

Julian Gibbs is going to Buffalo on January tenth to deliver a lecture on his Polar expedition, and I am giving him this note of introduction to you. He is a very great friend of ours, and I think that perhaps you and Mr. Miller will enjoy meeting him as much as I know he would enjoy knowing you.

With kindest regards, in which Arthur joins,

Very sincerely,
Ethel Norman

If Mr. Norman were introducing one man to another, he would give his card to the former, inscribed as follows:

Introducing Julian Gibbs
Mr. Arthur Lees Norman

Also, Mr. Norman would send a private letter by mail, telling his friend that Mr. Gibbs is coming.

Dear Miller,

I am giving Julian Gibbs a card of introduction to you when he goes to Buffalo on the tenth to lecture. He is delightfully entertaining and a great friend of ours. I feel sure that Mrs. Miller would enjoy meeting him. If you can conveniently ask him to your house, I know he would appreciate it; if not, perhaps you will put him up for a day or two at a club.

Faithfully,
Arthur Norman

INFORMAL LETTER OF INTRODUCTION

My dear Ruth,

I am giving this letter to George Perrin, a great friend of ours, who is going to be in Chicago the week of January seventh.

I want very much to have him meet you, and hope that this will find you in town.

Affectionately,
Louise Hill

At the same time a second and private letter of information is written and sent by mail.

My dear Ruth,

I have sent you a letter introducing George Perrin. He is young, about thirty-five or so, good-looking, very good company, and an altogether likable person.

He has only one flaw. He does not play a very good game of contract, which is not important; but, knowing the game you play, it is only fair to him, as well as to you, to ask you to invite him to something other than cards.

I know you will like him; you would like him even at the card table, for that matter, but less than elsewhere.

Affectionately,
Louise Hill

INTRODUCTION BY LETTER

An introduction by letter is far more binding than a casual spoken introduction, which commits you to nothing. Obviously, therefore, you should never ask anyone not a really intimate friend of yours to put a friend of his under the obligation which such a letter imposes.

A letter of introduction is always handed you unsealed. It is correct for you to seal it at once in the presence of its author. You thank your friend for having written it and go on your trip.

If you are a man and your introduction is to a lady, you go to her house as soon as you arrive in her city, and leave the letter with your card at her door, without asking to see her. She should—unless prevented by illness—at once invite you to tea. or to lunch or dinner, or at least name an hour when she will be at home.

If your letter is to a man, you mail it to his house, unless the letter is a business one. In the latter case you go to his office, and send in your card and the letter. Meanwhile you wait in the reception room until he has read the letter and calls you into his private office.

If you are a woman, you mail your letter of social introduction and do nothing further until you receive an acknowledgment. If the recipient of your letter leaves her card on you, you in return leave yours on her. But the obligation of a written introduction is such that only illness can excuse her not asking you to her house—either formally or informally.

When a man receives a letter introducing another man, he calls the person introduced on the telephone and asks how he may be of service to him. If he does not invite the newcomer to his house, he may put him up at his club, or ask him to lunch or dinner at a restaurant, as the circumstances seem to warrant. But it is absolutely necessary that he show this stranger what courtesy he can.

THE INDIRECT LETTER OF INTRODUCTION

When the Newcomers go to live in Strangetown, an indirect letter of introduction is better than a direct one. By indirect is meant a letter written by Mrs. Neighbor at home to a friend of hers in Strangetown. As already explained, a letter of introduction presented by Mrs. Newcomer to Mrs. Oldhouse puts Mrs. Oldhouse in a position where she *must* do something for the Newcomers, no matter how inconvenient or distasteful it may be. Her neglect of them can be construed as nothing less than a repudiation of friendship for the writer of the letter and an unforgivable rudeness to the Newcomers.

If, on the other hand, Mrs. Neighbor merely writes to Mrs. Oldhouse, "My friends, the Newcomers, are going to live in your neighborhood," the former is free to make advances only in so far as she feels inclined.

Mrs. Newcomer, knowing nothing about this letter and expecting nothing in the way of hospitality, is far more likely to be pleased when Mrs. Oldhouse calls on her, and to feel that it is because she is liked for herself, than when she is invited to whatever it may be because Mrs. Neighbor made the invitation obligatory. A letter of introduction is usually an inconvenience and on occasions a very real burden. If you are ill or in mourning—the only excuses possible—you *must* send a note explaining your lack of hospitality, and even then, if possible, send a deputy. Your husband, or your sister, or even your nearest friend goes to explain—and in so far as possible to take your place.

A transient visitor is soon gone again and your obligation quickly ended; but when someone comes to live in the neighborhood permanently, it is obvious that a letter of introduction involves you in a sponsorship that can conceivably become irksome and even embarrassing.

With the indirect letter, you and the Newcomers have the same opportunity to know each other well, if you like each other, but you are bound only by inclination.

THE LETTER OF RECOMMENDATION

A letter of recommendation for membership in a club is addressed to the secretary and should be somewhat in this form:

To the Secretary of the Town Club.
My dear Mrs. Brown,
   Mrs. Titherington Smith, whose name is posted for membership, is a very old friend of mine.
   She is a person of much charm and distinction and when you meet her I am sure you will agree with me in thinking that she will be a valuable addition to the club.
                                        Very sincerely,
                                          Ina Jackson

LETTER OF RESIGNATION FROM A CLUB

Mrs. James Town
Secretary Colonial Club, New York
My dear Mrs. Town,
   It is with great regret that I find it necessary to resign from the club, and to ask you therefore to present my resignation at the next meeting of the governors.
                                        Very sincerely,
                                       Mary Smartlington

REFERENCES FOR EMPLOYEES

Although the written recommendation that is given to an employee carries very little weight compared to the slip from the employment agencies, where either "yes" or "no" has to be answered to a list of specific and important questions, one is nevertheless put in a trying position when reporting on an unsatisfactory servant.

Either a poor reference must be given—possibly preventing the employee from earning his or her living—or one has to write what is not true. Consequently it has become the custom to say what one truthfully can of good, and leave out the qualifications that are lacking, except in the case of a careless nurse, where evasion would border on the criminal. It is not necessary to say of a cook that her soufflé never rises more than an inch and that her angel food cake is tough.

That solves the poor recommendation problem pretty well; but unless one is very careful, this consideration for the "poor" one is paid for by the "good." In writing for a very worthy employee, therefore, it is of the utmost importance in fairness to him or her to put in every mark of merit that you can think of, remembering that omission implies demerit in each trait of character not mentioned. All good references should include honesty, sobriety, capability, and a reason, other than their unsatisfactoriness, for their leaving. The recommendation for a nurse cannot be too conscientiously written.

A lady does not begin a recommendation: "To whom it may concern" nor "This is to certify," although housekeepers and head servants writing recommendations are very partial to both these forms.

A lady in giving a good reference should write:

TWO HUNDRED PARK SQUARE

Selma Johnson has been in my employ as cook for two years and a half.

I have found her honest, sober, industrious, neat in her person as well as her work, of amiable disposition, and a very good cook.

She is leaving—to my great regret—because I am closing my house.

I shall be very glad to answer personally any inquiries about her.

Josephine Smith

(Mrs. Titherington Smith)

February 17, 1955

The form of all recommendations is the same.

.... has been in my

employ .... months/years as ....

I have found him/her .... He/She is

leaving because ....

(Add any special remark of recommendation or one showing especial interest.)

....

(Mrs. ....)

Date ....

LETTERS OF CONGRATULATION ON AN ENGAGEMENT

Dear Stella,
While we are not altogether surprised, we are both delighted to hear the good news. Ted's family and ours are very close, as you know, and we have always been especially devoted to him. He is one of the finest—and now luckiest—of young men, and we send you both every good wish for all possible happiness.

Affectionately,
Nancy Jackson

Just a line, dear Ted, to tell you how glad we all are to hear of your happiness. Stella is everything that is lovely, and, of course, from our point of view, we don't think her exactly unfortunate either! Every good wish that imagination can think of goes to you from your old friends,

Nancy and Arthur Jackson

All the good wishes in the world to you, dearest Stella. Give Ted my love and tell him how lucky I think you both are, and how much I hope all good fortune will come to you.

Your loving
Aunt Kate

LETTER FROM MOTHER TO SON'S FIANCÉE

When it is impossible for a mother to pay the conventional visit upon her son's new fiancée, a letter should be written to her. The general outline is:

Dear Mary,
John has just told us of his great happiness which, of course, brings joy to us. Our one distress is that we are so far away (or whatever else) *that we cannot immediately welcome you in person.*
We do, however, send you our love and the hope that we shall meet very soon.

Sincerely and affectionately,
Martha Jones

FROM A CLASSMATE TO A GROOM-TO-BE

Dear Bob,
So you've got her! Wonderful news! I know how crazy you have always been about her—and she's something to be crazy about.
In short, I think it's great, and send congratulations to you both.

George

Dear Phyllis and Tim,

So that's *why you had no interest in the Junior Assemblies! You were preferring a little assembly of two in front of the fire, or driving up hill and down dale, or skating off by yourselves down at the ice-house end of the lake! I did notice this last, and wonder now that I was not awake to all the other evidence!*

Anyway—having taken a breath after the surprise of your letter— I am enchanted. That the nicest girl I know is going to marry pretty much the nicest man, is very, very good news. And if you are half as happy as I wish you, life will be all silver, not only as a lining, but on every cloud—all around.

Much love to you both, in which Janet and Jonathan join.

Always affectionately,

Tuesday, Jan. 8.   *Caroline*

OTHER LETTERS OF CONGRATULATION

Dear Mrs. Steele,

We are so glad to hear the good news of David's success; it was a very splendid accomplishment and we are all so proud of him and happy for you. Please give him our love and congratulations, and with full measure of both to you.

Affectionately,

Mildred Bowen

Another example:

Dear Michael,

We all rejoice with you in the confirmation of your appointment. The state needs just such men as you—if we had more of your sort, the ordinary citizen would have less to worry about. Our best congratulations!

James Bowen

THE LETTER OF CONDOLENCE

Intimate letters of condolence are like love letters in that they are too sacred and too personal to follow a set form. One rule, and one only, should guide you in writing such letters. Say what you truly feel. Say that and nothing else. Sit down at your desk; let your thoughts dwell on the person you are writing to.

Don't dwell on the details of illness or the manner of death; don't quote endlessly from the poets and Scripture. Remember that eyes filmed with tears and an aching heart cannot follow rhetorical lengths of writing. The more nearly a note can express a handclasp, a thought of sympathy, above all a genuine love or appreciation of the one who has gone, the greater comfort it brings.

Write as simply as possible and let your heart speak as truly but as briefly as you can. Forget, if you can, that you are using written words. Think merely how you feel—then put your feelings on paper—that is all.

Suppose it is a young mother who has died. You think how young and sweet she was—and of her little children, and, literally, your heart aches for them, and her husband, and her own family. Into your thoughts must come some expression of what she was, and what their loss must be!

Or maybe it is the death of a man who has left a place in the whole community that will be difficult, if not impossible, to fill, and you think of all he stood for that was fine and helpful to others, and how much and sorely he will be missed. All you can think of is "Dear Steve— what a prince he was! I don't think anything will ever be the same again without him." Say just that! Ask if there is anything you can do at any time to be of service to his people. There is nothing more to be said. A line into which you have unconsciously put a little of the genuine feeling that you had for Steve is worth pages of eloquence.

A letter of condolence may be abrupt, badly constructed, ungrammatical—never mind. Grace of expression counts for nothing; sincerity alone is of value. Do not say to one whose life has been made forever desolate by the loss of one of outstanding character or genius, "I remember the big brimmed hat she wore" or "seeing him reading his paper on the train"! Nothing more unappreciative can be imagined. The only things of the least comfort at such a time are letters which show appreciation of the character, talent, charm, or any quality whatsoever that was actual and outstanding in the personality of the one mourned.

The letters from friends and associates, expressing genuine affection for a man's personality or admiration for his character and unreplaceable ability, are the only ones that *share* a widow's or a mother's grief.

An occasional letter from one who has suffered an undeniably equal loss, who in sincerity writes words of encouragement and assurance that in time the pain will grow less instead of greater, is of genuine help. But such a letter must never be written by anyone whose own suffering has not been equally devastating. Glibly listed qualities that did not exist are as meaningless as attributes of true greatness entirely overlooked.

EXAMPLES OF NOTES AND TELEGRAMS

As has just been said, a letter of condolence must, above everything, express a genuine sentiment. A few examples are included here merely as suggestive guides for those at a loss to construct a short but appropriate message.

My dear Mrs. Neighbor,

We are so very shocked to hear of the sorrow that has come to you.

If there is anything that either my husband or I can do, I earnestly hope that you will ask someone to call upon us.

Alice Rivington Blake

or

My dear Mrs. Neighbor,

I know how little words written on a page can possibly mean to you at such a time. But I must at least tell you that you are in our thoughts and in our hearts, and if there is anything *that we can do for you, please send us a message—whatever it may be.*

With deepest sympathy,

Mary Newling

Or this to a near relative or friend

DARLING! WORDS ARE SO EMPTY! IF ONLY I KNEW HOW TO FILL THEM WITH LOVE AND SEND THEM TO YOU. ALL MY THOUGHTS. MARY

LETTER WHERE DEATH WAS RELEASE

The letter to one whose loss is for the best is difficult in that you want to express sympathy but cannot feel sad that one who has long suffered has found release. The expression of sympathy in this case should not be for the present death, but for the illness, or whatever it was that befell long ago. The grief for a paralyzed mother is for the stroke which cut her down many years before, and your sympathy, though you may not have realized it, is for that. You might write: "Your sorrow during all these years—and now—is in my heart; and all my thoughts and sympathy are with you."

REPEATED DETAILS OF GREAT IMPORTANCE

NEVER under any circumstances sign a personal letter "Mr.," "Mrs.," or "Miss." The proper signature for a married woman is "Mary Smith," and then underneath or to the left in parentheses "(Mrs. John Smith)." The name in parentheses is for information only, and is not a signature (see also page 506 on this point). The proper signature for an unmarried woman is "Helen Jones," and when necessary put "Miss" in parentheses to the left. The proper signature for a man is "John Smith." If he has an official title it can be added underneath, "Mayor of the City of New York" or, "Captain, U. S. N."

The only times when a lady of quality signs her name "Mrs." are these: in a hotel register, to a business telegram, or to an order letter to a tradesman. And then it must be "Mrs. *John* Smith." To a servant in her own employ it is "Mrs. Smith."

LONGER LETTERS

·∘][43][∘·

THE PRACTICE OF GENERAL LETTER WRITING TODAY IS shrinking to such an extent that the letter threatens to become a telegram, a telephone message, or just a postcard. Since the events of the day are communicated by newspapers, radio and that newcomer television with far greater accuracy, detail, and dispatch than ever they could be by the single efforts of a Voltaire himself, the circulation of general news—which formed the chief reason for letters of the stagecoach and sailing-vessel days—has no part in the hurried correspondence of today.

Of course, love letters are probably as numerous as need be, though the long-distance telephone and telegrams must have lessened their number, too. Young girls write to each other as much and as imprudently as they have always done, and letters between young girls and young men flourish like unpulled weeds in a garden where weeds were formerly never allowed to grow.

It is the letter from the friend in this city to the friend in that, or from the traveling relative to the relative at home, that is gradually dwindling. As for the letter which younger relatives dutifully used to write—it has gone already with much of the old-fashioned grace of speech and deportment.

Still, people *do* write letters in this day and there are some who possess the divinely flexible gift for a fresh turn of phrase with which to express a delightful keenness of observation. It may be, too, that in other days the average writing was no better than the average of today, as naturally it was the letters of those who had possessed unusual gifts which have been preserved for us all these years.

Nevertheless, you who find letter writing an utterly impossible chore, and you who are quite content to believe that you are lacking in all power of thought or humor, of observation or facility of expression, you may be quite right in joining the ever-growing group of people who confess frankly, "I can't write letters to save my life!" and in confining your literary efforts to picture postcards with the engaging caption "X is my room," or "Beautiful weather. Wish you were here."

USING THE TYPEWRITER FOR
PERSONAL CORRESPONDENCE

The personal use of portable or standard typewriters has created a certain amount of confusion concerning the occasions when it may or may not be used in writing letters.

First of all, the typewritten letter is not only proper but also *preferred* for all personal letters of any length. Yesterday's objection to the typewritten personal letter was the result of the practice of dictating such letters to a secretary or stenographer. But now, when almost everyone can use a typewriter himself, the objection no longer holds, and the ease with which a typed page can be read is, for most of us, more than compensation for the loss of a handwritten letter that is difficult to decipher.

Whether the letter is written by hand or on the machine, the manner of composition is the same.

THE DIFFICULTY IN BEGINNING

For most people—when they are faced with a wordless sheet of paper and they wonder how in the world they will ever fill it—the difficult parts of a letter are the beginning and the closing. The instruction of a professor of English to "Begin at the beginning of what you have to say, go on until you have finished, and then stop" is just about as much help as was the instruction of the celebrated artist who proclaimed: "You simply take a little of the right color of paint and put it on the right spot." Let us see if I can give a few more helpful suggestions.

HOW NOT TO BEGIN

Even one who loves the very sight of your handwriting could not be expected to find pleasure in a letter beginning, "I know I ought to have written sooner, but I haven't had anything to write about." Or one's saying, "I suppose you have been thinking me very neglectful, but you know how I hate to write letters."

Such sentences are written time and again by persons who are utterly unconscious that they are really expressing an unfriendly and unloving thought. If one of your friends were to walk into the room and you were to receive him stretched out and yawning in an easy chair, no one would have to point out the rudeness of your behavior; yet countless kindly intentioned people begin their letters mentally reclining and yawning in just such a way.

HOW TO BEGIN A LETTER

Suppose you merely change the wording of the above sentences, so that, instead of slamming the door in your friend's face, you hold it open.

"Do you think I have forgotten you entirely? You don't know, Ann, how many letters I have planned to write you." Or "Time and time again I have wanted to write you but each moment that I saved for myself was always interrupted by—*something*."

One of the difficulties frequently encountered in beginning a letter is that the answer has been so long delayed that it must be begun with an apology, which at best is an unhappy beginning. These examples, however, show how even an opening apology may be attractive rather than repellent.

If you take the trouble to write a letter, you have remembered some-one in a friendly way, otherwise you would not be writing at all.

It is easy enough to begin a letter if it is to be an answer to one that has just been received. The news contained in it is fresh and the impulse to reply needs no prodding.

Nothing can be simpler than to say, "We were all overjoyed to hear from you this morning," or "Your letter was the most welcome thing the postman has brought for ages," or "It was more than good to have news of you this morning," or "Your letter from Capri brought all the allure of Italy back to me," or "You can't imagine, Ann, how glad I was to see an envelope with your writing this morning." And then you take up the various subjects in Ann's letter, which should certainly launch you without difficulty upon topics of your own.

Remember to answer any of her specific questions. It is certainly not only unflattering to be given the impression that you read them hurriedly, but often very upsetting to have long-awaited information one has asked for completely overlooked.

ON ENDING A LETTER

Just as the beginning of a letter should give the reader an impression of greeting, so should its ending express friendly or affectionate leave-taking. Nothing can be worse than to seem to scratch helplessly around in the air for an idea that will effect your escape.

"Well, I guess you've read enough of this" or "You're probably bored by now so I'd better close" are stupid.

HOW TO END A LETTER

When you leave the house of a member of your family, you don't have to think up an especial sentence in order to say good-by. Leave-taking in a letter is the same.

Goodby, dearest, for today.
　　　　　　Catherine

or

Will write again in a day or two.
　　　　　　Martin

or

Lunch was announced half a page ago!
So good-by, darling, for today.

　　　　　　Nancy

LETTERS THAT SHOULD NOT BE WRITTEN

Even in so personal a matter as the letter to an absent member of one's immediate family, remember not to write *needlessly* of misfortune or unhappiness. To hear how ill or unhappy those we love are is to have our own distress intensified by the number of miles which separates us from them.

LETTERS OF GLOOMY APPREHENSION

The chronic calamity writers seem to wait until the skies are darkest, and then, rushing to their desks, luxuriate in pouring out all their troubles and most especially their fears of trouble-to-come on paper to their friends.

"My little Betty ["my little" makes it so much more pathetic than saying merely "Betty"] has been feeling miserable for several days. I am worried to death about her, as there are so many sudden cases of polio. The doctor says the symptoms are not alarming, but doctors see so much of illness that they don't seem to appreciate what anxiety means to a mother," etc.

Another writes: "The times seem to be getting worse and worse. I always said we would have to go through a long night before any chance of daylight. You can mark my words, the night is hardly more than begun."

THE BLANK LETTER

The writer of the blank letter begins fluently with the date and "Dear Sara," and then sits and chews his penholder or makes little dots and squares and circles on the blotter—utterly unable to attack the cold, forbidding blankness of that first page. Mentally, he seems to say, "Well, here I am—and now what?" He has not an idea! He can never find anything of sufficient importance to write about. A murder next door, a house burned to the ground, a burglary, or an elopement could alone furnish material; and that, too, would be finished off in a brief sentence stating the bare fact.

A person whose life is a revolving wheel of routine may have really very little to say, but a letter need not be long to be welcome.

Dear Lucy,

Life here is as dull as ever—duller if anything! Not even a fire-engine out or a new face in town. But this is to tell you that I am thinking of you and longing to hear from you.

THE DANGEROUS LETTER

A pitfall that those of sharp wit have to guard against is the thoughtless tendency toward exercising that wit by writing clever but cruel things. Ridicule is a much easier and more amusing medium for the display of wit than praise, which is always rather bromidic. The amusing person latches onto human foibles and exploits them, and it is all too easy to forget that wit sparkles irresistibly at the expense of other people's feelings, and the brilliant tongue is all too often pointed to rapier sharpness. Admiration for the quickness of a spoken quip somewhat mitigates its cruelty. The exuberance of the retailer of oral gossip eliminates much of the implication of scandal, but both quip and gossip become deadly venom when transferred permanently to paper. For all choleric emotions, the written word is a bad medium. The light jesting tone that saves a quip from offense cannot be expressed; and remarks, spoken remarks that would amuse, can pique and even insult their subject when written. Without the interpretation of the voice, gaiety becomes levity, raillery becomes accusation. Moreover, words that should be of a passing moment are made to stand forever.

Anger in a letter carries with it the effect of solidified fury. The words spoken in reproof melt with the breath of the speaker once the cause is forgiven; the written words on the page fix them everlastingly.

Love in a letter endures forever in our memories.

Admonitions from parents to their children may very properly be put on paper—they are meant to endure and be remembered—but momentary annoyance should never be more than briefly expressed. There is no better way of insuring his letters against being read than for a parent to get into the habit of writing in an irritable or fault-finding tone to his children.

One point cannot be overstressed: Letters written under strong emotion should be held for twenty-four hours and reread before being sent—and then probably torn into small pieces and not sent at all.

THE LETTERS OF TWO WIVES

Do you ever see a man look through a stack of mail and notice that suddenly his face lights up as he seizes a letter from home? He tears it open eagerly, his mouth up-curving at the corners, as he lingers over every word. You know without being told that the wife he has had to leave behind puts all the best things she can devise and keep for him into his life as well as on paper!

Do you ever see a man go through his mail and see him suddenly droop—as though a fog had fallen upon his spirits? Do you see him reluctantly pick out a letter, start to open it, hesitate, and then push it aside? His expression says plainly, "I can't face that just now." Then by and by, when his lips have been set in a hard line, he will doggedly open his letter to see what the trouble is now.

If for once there is no trouble, he sighs with relief, relaxes, and starts the next thing he has to do. Usually, though, he frowns, looks worried, annoyed, harassed, and you know that every small unpleasantness is punctiliously served up to him by one who probably would be shocked beyond words if she could know the effect her unrelieved letters of complaint and calamity have upon the man she thinks she loves and cherishes.

THE LETTER EVERYONE LOVES TO RECEIVE

The letter we all love to receive is one that carries so much of the writer's personality that she seems to be sitting beside us, looking at us directly and talking just as she really would, could she have come on a magic carpet, instead of sending her proxy in ink-made characters on mere paper.

Let us suppose we have received one of those perfect letters from Lelia, one of those letters that seem almost to have written themselves, so easily do the words flow, so bubbling, so effortless is their spontaneity. There is a great deal in the letter about Lelia, not only about what she has been doing, but what she has been thinking, or perhaps feeling. And there is a lot about us in the letter—nice things that make us feel rather pleased about something that we have done or are likely to do, or that someone has said about us. We know that all things of concern to us are of equal concern to Lelia, and though there may be nothing of it in actual words, we are made to feel that we are just as secure in our corner of Lelia's heart as ever we were. And we finish the letter with a very vivid remembrance of Lelia's sympathy, a sense of loss in her absence, and a longing for the time when Lelia herself may again be sitting on the sofa beside us and telling us all the details her letter must needs have left out.

THE LETTER NO WOMAN SHOULD EVER WRITE

The mails carry letters every day that are truly H-bombs should their contents be exploded by falling into wrong hands. Letters that should never have been written are put in evidence in courtrooms every day. Many cannot, in any way, be excused; but often silly girls and foolish women write things that, when for instance they are read to a jury, sound quite different from what was innocently, but stupidly, intended.

Of course the best advice to young girls who feel impelled to pour out their emotions in letters to men can be put in one word, *don't!*

However, if you are a young girl—or even a not-so-young woman—and are determined to write a letter to a man, who is neither your husband nor your betrothed, that contains any possibility of emotion, then at least put it away overnight in order to reread it and make sure that you have said nothing that may sound different from what you intended to say.

Remember this above all: Never write a letter to anyone—no matter whom—that would embarrass you were you to see it in a newspaper above your signature. Not that this means *you*, but thousands upon thousands of women, inspired by every known emotion, have poured words on paper, but few of the many made public have had charm or beauty. There were, as many may remember, a certain few letters read in a Pacific Coast divorce court not long ago, which revealed a woman's character of unforgettable loveliness; but such characters—as well as such letters—are rare indeed.

The point to remember, then, is that written words have permanency, and that thoughts carelessly put on paper when not destroyed by accident in the course of time can exist for hundreds of years.

PROPER LETTERS OF LOVE OR AFFECTION

If you are engaged, of course you should write love letters—the most beautiful that you can—but don't write baby-talk and other sillinesses that would make you feel idiotic were the letter to fall into cynical unromantic hands.

There is no objection to the natural, friendly. and even affectionate letter from a girl to a man she knows well. Instead of "Dear Jim" it perhaps begins "Dearest Jim," but not "Dearest!" Then follows all the news she can think of that might possibly interest him—about the home team's new players, Betty and Tom's engagement, the political disagreement between two otherwise friendly neighbors, who won the horseshoe-pitching tournament, how many trout Bill Henderson got at Duck Brook . . .

Probably she also tells him, "We all missed you at the picnic on Wednesday—Ollie made the flapjacks and they were too awful!" Or

. . . We all hope you'll be home in time for Carol's birthday. She has at last inveigled Mother into letting her have an all-black dress which we suspect was bought with the purpose of impressing you with her advanced age! Mother came in just as I wrote this and says to tell you she has a new recipe for chocolate cake that is even better than her old one. Laura will write you very soon, she says, and we all send love.

Affectionately (or *Ever devotedly*),

Ruth

THE LETTER NO GENTLEMAN WRITES

One of the fundamental rules for the behavior of any man who has the faintest pretension to being a gentleman is that he never writes a letter that can be construed, even by a lawyer, as damaging to any woman's good name.

DETAILS OF GENERAL IMPORTANCE

Although long letters to friends may, and all business letters should, be typewritten:

Never typewrite an invitation, acceptance, or regret.

Never typewrite a formal social note.

Be sparing with underscoring, exclamation marks, and postscripts.

Do not ever, if you wish your words to be read, carry paper economy to such lengths that you write over the same sheet twice—once horizontally, and then vertically, and do not write on both sides of semi-transparent paper.

Do not use unmatched paper and envelopes or write with a pencil if you can possibly help it.

Never send a letter with a blot on it.

Never sprinkle French, Italian, or any other foreign words through a letter written in English unless the foreign word has no English equivalent, or has become anglicized. If you are hesitating between two words, always select the simpler, more familiar word.

There has been no great writer in English who has not acknowledged his unreserved debt to the great beauty of the English Bible as the foundation of his art.

HOW TO ADDRESS
IMPORTANT PERSONAGES

·∘] 44 [∘·

AT ONE TIME OR ANOTHER NEARLY EVERY ONE OF US
either meets, or has to write a letter to someone of importance, such as
a senator or judge, a clergyman or president of a university, and we
certainly do not want to be thought ignorant by addressing him or her
improperly. Neither can we remember all the proper forms of address
for all the personages we might ever need to speak or to write to.

For this reason the chart in this chapter has been prepared. It tells
what to call the personage when you speak to him, how to begin and
close both a formal and an informal letter to him, how to address the
envelope and how to introduce him.

TITLES—ROYAL AND LESSER

The very first requirement of proper behavior is to learn enough
about rank to know the difference between royalty, nobility, and titles
that are personal honors, but not inheritable. The most conspicuous
mistake made by us in the United States is that of believing a baron
and a count, and their American wives, royalty.

A study of the last page of the chart and its footnotes should make
the divisions clear enough to know that royalty is set quite above and
apart from all others. It is plain, therefore, why etiquette requires that
special deference be shown them.

Upon being presented to royalty—meaning by this a king, queen,
emperor, empress, or any of their children—a gentleman bows. If the
royal hand is offered to him, he takes it and bows as he does so. Whether
or not a lady curtsies depends upon whether she has lived much abroad
and makes this motion naturally. In this country, however, it is not
expected that a lady do more than bow, much as a courteous hostess
does when greeting her guests.

It is a strict requirement that we wait for royalty to speak first and
to choose the topic of conversation.

Were we their subjects, we would address them in the third person. But since this form of speech is not used by us, we are not considered discourteous when we say "you."

A royal prince is always addressed "Sir" and a princess as "Ma'am" (not Madam), and these titles are repeated from time to time during a conversation.

When a royal prince or royal princess marries one who is not of royal birth, neither the wife nor the husband is accorded thereby the title of Royal Highness. For example, countless Americans have been introduced to the Duke and Duchess of Windsor. He of course is addressed formally "Your Royal Highness" and addressed by those who meet him socially as "Sir." The Duchess is addressed "Your Grace" by those who serve her, and by her friends as "Duchess," but never "Royal Highness" or "Ma'am." Together they are listed as His Royal Highness the Duke and Her Grace the Duchess of Windsor.

When they are dining in the house of others, the hostess gives her place at the head of the table to the Duke and seats herself on his right. The Duchess is seated on the host's right—as is every guest of honor— and he keeps his own place at the end of the table.

It should be added that persons of royal birth usually have themselves the simplest, most unself-conscious manners imaginable. They accept the perfection of the accomplished or the awkwardness of the untutored with equal grace. Even so, it is more pleasant to be the former than the latter.

Our manners to all members of nobility are precisely the same as those we show to our own citizens.

PERSONAGE	ENVELOPE ADDRESS (including wife or husband) □ shows where wife's name is to be inserted	FORMAL BEGINNING OF LETTER	INFORMAL BEGINNING OF LETTER
The President	(*If the letter is sent from abroad*) The President of the United States of America (*If sent from within United States*) The President □, Washington, D. C. (and Mrs. Executive)[1] (*3-line address*)	Sir:	My dear Mr. President:
The Vice President	The Vice President □, Washington, D. C. (and Mrs. Hisname)	Sir:	My dear Mr. Vice President:
The Chief Justice of the Supreme Court	The Honorable, The Chief Justice,* □, Washington, D. C. (and Mrs. Hisname)	Sir:	Dear Mr. Chief Justice:
Associate Justice of the Supreme Court	The Hon.* C. K. Fairplay, Justice of the Supreme Court, □, Washington, D. C.† (and Mrs. Fairplay)	Sir:	Dear Mr. Justice Fairplay:
Member of the President's Cabinet	The Secretary of State □, Washington, D. C. (and Mrs. Eminent) *or* The Hon. David C. Eminent, Secretary of State** □, Washington, D. C. (and Mrs. Eminent) *or* *Same as above* □ The Hon. Mary Onerown (Mr. John and)	Sir: *or* Dear Sir: *or Madam:*	My dear Mr. Secretary: Madam Secretary:
United States or State Senator	*Socially:* Senator □ Chester H. Widelands (*His house address*) (and Mrs.) *On official business:* The Hon. and Mrs. Chester H. Widelands, Senator from Texas, Washington, D. C. *or* The Hon. Mary Widelands	Sir: *or* Dear Sir: *or Madam:*	Dear Senator Widelands:
Member of Congress *or* of State Legislature	The Hon. □ H. C. Wellcome, House of Representatives, Washington, D. C. (and Mrs.) *or* The Hon. □ H. C. Wellcome, State Assembly, Albany, New York (and Mrs.)	Sir: *or* Dear Sir: *or Madam:*	Dear Mr. Wellcome: Dear Mrs. Jones: *or* Dear Miss Smith: *Do not write* *Dear Congressman* *or* *Dear Representative‡*
Governor	His Excellency the Governor □, Lansing, Michigan (and Mrs. Goodland) *or* The Honorable □ L. G. Goodland, Governor of Michigan (and Mrs.) *or* Her Excellency the Governor □ (and Mr. Hisname)	Your Excellency: *or* Sir: Your Excellency: *or Madam:*	Dear Governor Goodland:

* Alternate acceptable form: The Chief Justice, The Honorable John Page and Mrs. Page. This form may be used for any Honorable and his wife.
** Persons of fastidious taste prefer the abbreviation "Hon'ble" instead of "Hon."; the latter, though suggestive of Great Britain rather than the United States, is also acceptable here; best usage is the unabbreviated form.

FORMAL CLOSE OF LETTER	INFORMAL CLOSE OF LETTER	IF YOU ARE SPEAKING TO HIM YOU SAY	CORRECT TITLES OF INTRODUCTION
I have the honor to remain, Most respectfully yours, *or* I have the honor to remain, Sir, Yours faithfully,	I have the honor to remain, Yours faithfully, *or* I am, dear Mr. President, Yours faithfully,	Mr. President, *and occasionally throughout a conversation,* Sir	*Only the name of the person being introduced is spoken.*
Same as for the President	Believe me, Yours faithfully,	Mr. Vice President, *and then,* Sir	The Vice President
I have the honor to remain, Yours respectfully,	Believe me, Yours faithfully,	Mr. Chief Justice, *and then,* Sir	The Honorable, The Chief Justice
Believe me, Yours very truly, *or* I have the honor to remain, Yours very truly,	Believe me, Yours faithfully,	Mr. Justice	Mr. Justice Fairplay
Same as above	*Same as above*	Mr. Secretary *(If necessary to differentiate)* Mr. Secretary of State	The Secretary of State
Same as above	*Same as above*	Madam Secretary *(whether Mrs. or Miss)*	*Same as above*
Same as above	*Same as above*	Senator Widelands *A servant or subordinate says:* Mr. Senator *Same; and* Madam Senator	Senator Widelands *(On very formal and official occasions,* Senator Widelands of Texas)
Believe me, Yours very truly,	Yours faithfully, *or* Sincerely yours,	Mr. Wellcome *(Mr. Congressman is not correct)* *or* Mrs. *or* Miss	Mr. Wellcome *(If the introduction is official you add* Congressman from Ohio) *or* Mrs. *or* Miss
I have the honor to remain, Yours faithfully,	Believe me, Yours faithfully,	Governor Goodland *(The Governor is rarely called* Excellency *when spoken to and when he is announced except in States where this title is official. But in all States letters are addressed and begun with this title of courtesy.)*	The Governor *(in his own State) or* The Governor of Michigan *(out of it)*

† Alternate acceptable form: Associate Justice of the Supreme Court, The Honorable C. K. Fairplay and Mrs. Fairplay.
‡ "Congresswoman" is colloquial and not in current formal usage.

Numbered footnotes are on last pages of this chart.

PERSONAGE	ENVELOPE ADDRESS (including wife or husband) □ shows where wife's name is to be inserted	FORMAL BEGINNING OF LETTER	INFORMAL BEGINNING OF LETTER
Mayor (Mayoress is English, not American)	His Honor the Mayor □, City Hall, Chicago (and Mrs. Johnson) *or* Her Honor	Dear Sir: *or* Sir: *or* Madam:	Dear **Mayor Lake:**
Officers of the Navy with grade of Commander or higher, and officers of the Army, Air Force, and Marines with grade of Captain or higher	Admiral □ George Highseas Captain □ David Greenwave (and Mrs.)	Dear **Sir:** *or* Sir:	Dear Admiral Highseas: Dear Captain Greenwave:
Junior officers in Navy, Army, Air Force, and Marines	Ensign □ Arthur Ripple 2nd Lieutenant □ John Gun (and Mrs.)	Dear **Sir:**	Dear Mr. Ripple: Dear Mr. Gun:
Bishop (*Protestant*)	To the **Right Reverend Thomas A.** Churchleigh *or* The Bishop of Rhode **Island,** Providence, **R. I.**	Right Reverend and dear Sir:	My dear **Bishop** Churchleigh:
Clergyman (*Protestant*)	The Rev. George Saintly (*If you do not know his first name, it is better to assume that he is a D.D. than to commit the bad taste of writing The Rev. Saintly without his Christian name*)	Sir: *or* My dear **Sir:**	Dear Dr. Saintly: (*or* Dear Mr. Saintly *if he is not a D.D.*)
Rabbi	Dr. J. A. Temple *or* Rabbi J. A. Temple *or* Rev. J. A. Temple	Dear Sir:	Dear Dr. Temple: *or* Dear Rabbi Temple:
Cardinal (*Roman Catholic*)	His Eminence Michael Cardinal Angelus, Archbishop of Baltimore, Baltimore, Md.	Your Eminence:	Your Eminence:
Archbishop (*Roman Catholic*) (*There is no Protestant Archbishop in the United States*)	The Most Reverend John Kindhart, Archbishop of San Francisco, San Francisco, California *But letter to British Archbishop,* His Grace the Right Honourable The Archbishop of Canterbury	Your Excellency: *or* Most Reverend Sir:	Most Reverend and dear Sir:
Bishop (*Roman Catholic*)	The Most Reverend Henry Jones	Most Reverend Sir:	My dear Bishop Jones:
Monsignor	The Right Reverend Monsignor [4] Ryan	Right Rev. and dear Monsignor Ryan:	Rev. (*or* Very Rev.)[4] and dear Monsignor Ryan:

Numbered footnotes are on last pages of this chart.

FORMAL CLOSE OF LETTER	INFORMAL CLOSE OF LETTER	IF YOU ARE SPEAKING TO HIM YOU SAY	CORRECT TITLES OF INTRODUCTION
Believe me, Very truly yours,	Yours faithfully,	Mr. Mayor *or* Madam Mayor	Mayor Lake
Same as above	*Same as above*	Admiral Highseas Captain Greenwave *(When introducing a Captain of the Navy, it is important to add "of the Navy" because his rank equals that of a Colonel in the Army.)*	Admiral Highseas Captain Greenwave of the Navy
(In Great Britain junior officers are always introduced as Mr. except when wearing civilian dress. But in the United States best custom tolerates the use of their titles in introductions and on place-cards at table.)		Mr. Ripple Mr. Gun*	Ensign Ripple Lieutenant Gun
I have the honor to remain, Your obedient servant, *or* to remain, Respectfully yours, *(To the Bishop of the Church of England)* I have the honor to remain, Your Lordship's obedient servant,	Faithfully yours,	Bishop Churchleigh	Bishop Churchleigh
I have the honor to remain, Yours faithfully, *or sincerely,*	Faithfully yours, *or* Sincerely yours,	Mr. Saintly *(If he is D.D. or LL.D., you call him Dr. Saintly; or Pastor Nordic if he is a Lutheran)*	Dr. *or* Mr. Saintly *(If a Lutheran, Pastor Nordic)*
Same as above	Yours sincerely,	Rabbi Temple *(If he holds a doctorate, he is called Dr. Temple.)*	Dr. Temple *or* Rabbi Temple
I have the honor to remain, Your Eminence's humble servant,	Your Eminence's humble servant,	Your Eminence	*One is presented to* His Eminence, Cardinal Angelus
I have the honor to remain with high respect, Your Excellency's humble servant,	*Same as formal close*	Your Excellency *(In England, Your Grace)*	*One is presented to* The Most Reverend, The Archbishop of San Francisco
I have the honor to remain, Your obedient servant,	Faithfully yours,	Your Excellency	Bishop Jones
Respectfully yours,	Respectfully yours,	Monsignor Ryan	Monsignor Ryan

* This is formally correct. Since the last war, however, lieutenants are more generally addressed "Lieutenant."

PERSONAGE	ENVELOPE ADDRESS (including wife or husband) □ shows where wife's name is to be inserted	FORMAL BEGINNING OF LETTER	INFORMAL BEGINNING OF LETTER
Priest	The Rev. John Matthews [8]	Reverend and dear Sir:	Dear Father Matthews:
Mother Superior	Reverend Mother Superior *or* Reverend Mother Mary (*and the initials of her order*)	Reverend Mother:	Dear Reverend Mother Mary:
Member of Religious Order	Sister Angelica O.S.D. (*initials of order*) Brother James, O.B.M.	My dear Sister: My dear Brother:	Dear Sister Angelica: Dear Brother James:
University Professor	Professor, *or* Associate Professor *or* Assistant Professor . . . *or* Dr. *if holding a doctorate*	Dear **Sir:**	Dear Professor Learned: *or* Dear Doctor Learned:
Instructor	Mr. *or* Dr. Book	Dear Sir:	Dear Mr. Book: (*or* Dr. *if he holds a doctorate*)
Ambassador [1] *Same for woman* (Ambassador preferable to Ambassadress)	His Excellency, The American Ambassador □, American Embassy [5] *or* Embassy of the United States of America,[6] London (and **Mrs. Plum**)	Your Excellency:	Dear Mr. Ambassador: Dear Madam Ambassador:
Minister [1] Plenipotentiary	His Excellency, The American Minister, □, Copenhagen, Denmark (and **Mrs. Lovejoy**) The Hon. □ J. D. Lovejoy,[7] Legation of the United States of America (and Mrs.) *or* Her Excellency	Sir: *is correct but* Your Excellency: *is customary by courtesy.*	Dear Mr. Minister: *or* Dear Mr. Lovejoy: Dear Madam Minister: *or* Dear Mrs. *or* Miss Lovejoy:
Consul	John Smith, Esq., American Consul, Rue Quelque Chose, Paris, France	Sir: *or* My dear Sir:	Dear Mr. Smith: *or* Mrs. Smith *or* Miss Smith
High Federal [7] official	The Honorable * James J. Jones, *official or home address*	Sir: *or* My dear Sir:	Dear Mr. Jones: *or* Mrs. Jones *or* Miss Jones

* He himself should never use this title either on his stationery or visiting-cards.

FORMAL CLOSE OF LETTER	INFORMAL CLOSE OF LETTER	IF YOU ARE SPEAKING TO HIM YOU SAY	CORRECT TITLES OF INTRODUCTION
I beg to remain, Yours faithfully, *or* I remain, Reverend Father, with high respect, Yours faithfully,	Faithfully yours,	Father *or* Father Matthews *or* Your Reverence	The Reverend Father Matthews
Yours respectfully,	Yours faithfully,	Reverend Mother	Reverend Mother, may I present Mrs. Jones
Same	*Same*	Sister Angelica Brother James	Sister Angelica, *same.* Brother James, *same.*
Believe me, Sincerely,	Yours sincerely,	Professor *within the University or College.* Mr. *elsewhere—or* Dr. *if he holds a doctorate*	Professor, *or* Dr. Learned
Sincerely,	*Same*	Mr. Book—or, *if he holds a doctorate,* Dr. Book	Mr. *or* Dr.
I have the honor to remain, Yours faithfully, *or* Yours very truly, *or very formally:* I have the honor to remain, sir, (*or* madam) Respectfully yours,	Yours faithfully,	Your Excellency *or* Mr. Ambassador Madam Ambassador (*meaning she herself was appointed*)	The American Ambassador *when he is in the country to which he is accredited. Elsewhere* Our (*or* The American) Ambassador to ——:
Same as above	Yours faithfully,	*In English he is usually called* "Mr. Lovejoy" *though it is not incorrect to call him* "Mr. Minister" *or, if you know him well,* "Minister." *The title* "Excellency" *is also used by courtesy, though it does not belong to him. In French he is always called:* Monsieur le Ministre	Mr. Lovejoy, the American Minister, *or merely* The American Minister (*Everyone is supposed to know his name or find it out.*) *or* Mrs. *or* Miss Lovejoy
I beg to remain, Yours very truly, *or* Yours very sincerely,	Faithfully,	Mr. Smith *or* Mrs. Smith *or* Miss Smith	Mr. Smith *or* Mrs. Smith *or* Miss Smith
Faithfully yours, *or* Yours sincerely.	Faithfully,	Mr. Jones *or* Mrs. Jones *or* Miss Jones	*Officially* The Honorable James J. Jones; *otherwise* Mr. Jones

Other footnotes are on last pages of this chart.

PERSONAGE	ENVELOPE ADDRESS (including wife or husband) ☐ shows where wife's name is to be inserted	FORMAL BEGINNING OF LETTER	INFORMAL BEGINNING OF LETTER
A reigning Sovereign	His Most Gracious Majesty, The King Her Most Gracious Majesty, The Queen	May it please Your Majesty	*There can be none.*
Member of a Royal Family	To His Royal Highness the Duke of Realm (*or* Crown Prince Olan of Nordia, *or* Grand Duke Paul, *or* Prince Berwin, *etc.*) Each name prefixed by H.R.H. *or* H.I.H. *or* H.S.H. *as required.*	Your Royal Highness:	Sir: (*or* Ma'am) "Dear Sir" *only by a friend to whom this special permission has been given personally.*
Duke ⁹ and Duchess ¹	To His Grace the Duke of Overthere (*or* Her Grace the Duchess of Overthere)	*Officially,* My Lord Duke: *or* Sir: *Socially,* Dear Duke of Overthere:	Dear Duke: Dear Duchess:
Marquis ⁹ and Marchioness	*Officially:* To the Most Honourable The Marquis of Greystone *Socially:* The Marquis of Greystone (*or* The Marchioness of Graystone)	My Lord: *or* Sir: *or* Madam:	Dear Lord Greystone: Dear Lady¹⁰ Greystone:
Earl ⁹ and Countess Viscount ⁹ and Viscountess	The Earl of Alwin *Officially,* The Right Honourable The Earl . . . The Countess of Alwin Viscount and Viscountess Blunt	Sir: *or* Madam:	*Same as above*
Baron ⁹ Lowest rank in the Peerage always called Lord	Lord Heath Lady Heath	Dear Sir: *or* Dear Madam:	*Same as above*
Baronet ⁹	Sir Cecil Brown, Bt. and Lady Brown ²	Dear Sir *or* Dear Sir Cecil	
Knight ⁹	Sir Samuel Shillings and Lady Shillings²	*Same as above.*	

TITLES OF CHILDREN OF PEERS

Eldest son of a Duke is in courtesy called by his father's second title—whether Marquis or Earl.

All younger sons of a Duke or Marquis have Lord prefixed to the given name (not surname). Envelope is addressed to The Lord John Jones, ordinarily called Lord John. His wife is called Lady John (not Lady Alice).

All daughters of either a Duke or Marquis are The Lady Mary.

All sons of an Earl are called The Honourable John, daughters The Honorable Mary.

¹ A wife never shares her husband's official titles. The wife of every American is Mrs.—"The President and Mrs. Executive." "His Excellency the American Ambassador and Mrs. Highrank." Also the wife of a Duke or a Lord, who may be "His Excellency," is addressed and announced as "The Duchess of this" or "Lady that." She is "Excellency" or "Ambassadress" only occasionally and by courtesy unless she herself received the appointment.

² The wife of a Peer, a Baronet, or a Knight is NEVER Lady Mary unless she is also the daughter of a Duke, a Marquis, or an Earl. A serious mistake often made is giving an American woman the title of Lady followed by her own Christian name, which is proper only when she herself is the daughter of a Duke, a Marquis, or an Earl. For example: Lady Mary Broadlands could not possibly have been Mary Green, daughter of an American.

When the daughter of a Duke, Marquis, or Earl marries a commoner they are called Mr. George and Lady Mary Doe.

Mary followed by Lady is under many circumstances correct. A widow is called Mary, Lady Broadlands. Or Mary, Duchess of Overthere.

It is important that "The" be put before "Lady" as the title of a wife of a Peer (exercising his own Peerage) to distinguish her from the wife of a Baronet or the wife of a Knight.

⁹ When a priest is a member of a religious order the envelope is addressed: Rev. John Matthews, S. J. *or* O. P., according to the initials of the order of which he is a member.

FORMAL CLOSE OF LETTER	INFORMAL CLOSE OF LETTER	IF YOU ARE SPEAKING TO HIM YOU SAY	CORRECT TITLES OF INTRODUCTION
I remain, Sir, with the greatest respect, Your Majesty's most obedient servant,[8] (*or* Ma'am)	*There can be none*	Your Majesty Throughout a conversation, Sir (*or* Ma'am—*not* Madam)	*Only the name of the person introduced is spoken*
I remain, Sir, with the greatest respect, Your Royal Highness's most obedient servant,[8] (*or* Ma'am)	I remain, Sir, (*or* Ma'am) Respectfully yours,	Your Royal Highness (*In long conversation*) Sir *or* Ma'am	Your Royal Highness, may I present Mrs. Worldly
I have the honour to remain,	*Same as to any friend*	Duke (*or* Duchess) (*Your Grace is for servants and retainers*)	Mrs. Worldly, may I present the Duke of Overthere Duchess, may I present Mrs. Worldly
I remain yours very sincerely, Sincerely yours, (*Beginning, close, same for remainder of peerage.*)	*Same as to any friend*	Lord Greystone *or* Lady [10] Greystone	Mrs. Worldly, Lord Greystone Lady [10] Greystone, Mrs. Worldly
In the world of society all persons of title below Duke and Duchess are spoken to and of as Lord and Lady.[10] To speak of the Marquis or Marchioness, the Earl or Countess announces the speaker as ignorant of social usage. This mistake is made by many writers. *Honourable is used only on envelopes and place-cards[7] never on visiting-cards or spoken.*		Lord Alwin Lady Alwin [8] Lord Blunt Lady Blunt Lord Heath *Same as above* [8]	*Introduction same for remainder of peerage, baronet, and knight.*
	Same as to any friend	Sir Cecil	
	Same as to any friend	Sir Samuel	

[4] There are two classes of Monsignori in the Roman Catholic Church: Right Rev. Monsignor Ryan and Very Rev. Monsignor Ryan. Right Rev. takes precedence.

[5] In South America alone, where out of courtesy to those who also consider themselves and are "Americans," our Embassies and Legations are known as those of The United States of America. But in all other countries of the world we are known simply as "Americans"—*e.g.*, the only name we have. We are not United Staters or United Statians—there is not even a word to apply to us! To speak of the American Minister to this country or that, or of the American Embassy in Paris is correct.

[6] Although our Ambassadors and Ministers represent the United States of America, it is customary both in Europe and Asia to omit the words United States and write to and speak of the American Embassy and the American Legation. In addressing a letter to one of our government representatives in countries of the Western Hemisphere, "The United States of America" is always specified.

[7] Federal usage bestows the title "Honorable," first officially and then by courtesy for life, on the following: The President, Vice President, U. S. Senators, U. S. Congressmen, Members of the Cabinet, all Federal Judges, Ministers Plenipotentiary, Ambassadors, and Governors of all States. But this title is not used by the person himself on his visiting-card and letterhead, or in his signature. The people in the State address State Senators as "The Honorable Lawrence Hamilton, State Senator" as a courtesy title, but officially he is "Lawrence Hamilton, Esq., State Senator."

[8] This form of closing address to a Sovereign or a Royal Prince is varied according to the social and personal status of the writer. An American citizen would close: "I remain, Sir (*or* Ma'am), Respectfully yours,".

[9] An official or military title is given precedence over a title of rank, as General Viscount.

[10] IN OTHER COUNTRIES, NOT BRITISH, the wife of a Marquis or a Count or a Baron is called Marquise, Countess, or Baroness. Lord and Lady are British titles.

MANNERS AND ETIQUETTE
IN BUSINESS

·➳[45]ɕ··

EVERY EXECUTIVE KNOWS HOW IMPORTANT ETIQUETTE
is, both in managing his office and in dealing with other businessmen.
No man can ever tell when a knowledge of it may turn to his advantage,
or the lack of such knowledge may turn the scale against him. The
man who remains "planted" in his chair when a lady speaks to him,
who receives customers in his shirt sleeves, who does not take off his
hat when talking with a lady nor take his cigar out of his mouth when
addressing her, impresses others, not so much by his lack of good manners
as by the business incompetence that his attitude suggests.

THE WELL-RUN OFFICE

In the well-run business office, the more important the executive,
the greater courtesy does he seem to show to those who come to see him.
A certain president of a great industry, for example, employs several
assistants chosen purposely because of their tact and good manners. If
an unknown person asks to see Mr. President, one of these deputies goes
out to find out what the visitor's business is; and instead of telling him
bluntly that the boss can't see him and to write a letter, the deputy not
only says, "Mr. President is in conference just now," but adds, "I know
he would not like you to be kept waiting. Can I be of service to you? I
am his junior assistant." If the visitor's business is really with the president, he is admitted to the chief executive's office, since it is the latter's
policy to see everyone that he possibly can.

The president has a courteous manner that makes everyone feel
there is nothing in the day's work half so important as what his visitor
has come to see him about! Nor is this manner insincere; for he has
made it a lifelong practice to give anyone he talks with his undivided
attention. Should his time be short and the moment approach when he
is due at an appointment, his secretary enters a few minutes ahead of
the time necessary for the close of the present interview, and apolo-

getically reminds him, "I'm sorry, Mr. President, but your appointment with the traffic committee is due." Mr. President, with seeming unconcern, uses up most of these few minutes in a completely unhurried close of the previous conversation, giving his visitor the impression that he may, perhaps, be late at his appointment and wholly so because of his interest in the subject that his visitor brought before him.

This is neither sincerity nor insincerity, but merely bringing social knowledge into business dealing. To make a pleasant and friendly impression is not alone good manners, but equally good business. That this is understood by modern business is shown by the importance they give to public relations. The less experienced man would quite likely show his eagerness to be rid of his visitor, and after offending the latter's self-pride by the discourtesy of inattention, possibly even be late for his own appointment! The man of skill saw his visitor for fewer actual minutes, but gave the impression that circumstances over which he had no control forced him unwillingly to close the interview. He not only gained the good will of his visitor, but had plenty of time for his own appointment.

GOOD MANNERS AND GOOD MIXERS

When one thinks of a man who is known in politics and business as a good mixer, one might imagine him as a rough diamond rather than a polished one. But a good mixer is not a "back-slapper." A good mixer among uncouth men may quite accurately be one who is also uncouth; but the best mixer of all is one who adjusts himself equally well to finer as well as to plainer society. Education that does not confer flexibility of mind is an obviously limited education; the man of broadest education tunes himself in unison with those in whose company he finds himself, whoever they are and whatever their intellectual level may be.

THE SELF-MADE MAN AND WORLD-WIDE MANNERS

It is not in order to shine in society that grace of manner is an asset; comparatively few people in a community care a rap about society anyway! A man of affairs whose life is spent in doing a man's work in a man's way is not likely to be thrilled at the thought of getting dressed up and going out with his wife to a tea or a ball.

But what many men do not realize is that a fundamental knowledge of etiquette is no less an asset in business or public life, or in any every-day contact with people, than it is in society.

Just as any expert, whether at a machine bench, an accountant's desk, or at golf, gives an impression of such ease as to make his accomplishment seemingly require no skill, a bungler makes himself and everyone watching him uneasy. And as inexpertness is quite as irritating in personal as in mechanical bungling, so there is scarcely anyone who sooner or later does not feel the need of social expertness.

Some day he will envy the accomplished manners of men he thought of as being "soft" when he felt himself strong and manly and perhaps American in his crudeness!

THE "X" MARKERS

But let success come to an untutored man. Let him be appointed to high office. Let him then shuffle from foot to foot, never knowing what to do or say; let him meet open derision or ill-concealed contempt from every educated person brought in contact with him; let opprobrium fall upon his State because its governor is a boor; and let him as such be written of in the editorials of the press and in the archives of history! Will he be so pleased with himself then? Does anyone think of Theodore Roosevelt as soft or effeminate because he was a great master of etiquette? Washington was completely a gentleman—and so was Abraham Lincoln. Though Lincoln's etiquette was self-taught, it was no less mastered for that! Whether he happened to know a lot of trifling details of pseudo-etiquette matters not in the least. Awkward he may have been; but the essence of him was courtesy. No "rough, uneducated" man has command of perfect English, and Lincoln's English remains supreme.

One thing that some Men of Might forget is that lack of polish in its wider aspects is merely lack of education. They themselves look down upon a man who has to make an "X" mark in place of signing his name—but they overlook entirely that to those of cultivation they are themselves in degree quite as ignorant.

BUT THE SON OF A SELF-MADE MAN—!

And yet many a self-made man changes his attitude completely when his own son is growing up. Almost invariably he takes special pains to make sure the boy will not be handicapped by the disadvantages which the father has never acknowledged but knows very well are his.

In fact, no one can miss the pride of Mr. Self-made, sitting in his office with a visitor—one whom he considers important—when his son comes into the room with an entire lack of self-consciousness. As his father introduces him as "My son!" he puts out his hand in a frank and easy way and yet with deferential friendliness. Then, having quickly and easily said whatever he came to say, as quickly and easily he makes his way out again. Is Mr. Self-made sorry that the big man thinks, "Fine boy, that!"? Does he regret having sent his son to college?

BUSINESS WOMEN

The president of a great manufacturing concern supported his objection to women employees by the following criticism: "A man comes into the office at nine sharp, hangs his hat on a peg, and sits down at his desk ten seconds after coming in the front door. A woman comes in just as conscientiously at a minute to nine, goes into the dressing-room, and it is anywhere from ten to twenty minutes before she has finished brushing her dress, and fixing her hair, and powdering her nose—and heaven alone knows what!"

Nevertheless, women have come to stay in not only every branch of business but every profession as well. Women are the successful heads of their own offices in many businesses and in almost all the professions. There are today very few offices that do not have women secretaries, bookkeepers, receptionists, switchboard operators, clerks, and typists.

Women who work have learned not to waste their employers' time. And employers have learned that the effect on morale of a ten-minute hair-combing or coffee break more than makes up in increased efficiency for the actual loss in time. No employer, however, will stand for a coffee-break atmosphere throughout the working day. Women should avoid wasting time in idle conversation during working hours, since this only interrupts the office routine and is a very unbusinesslike habit.

SEX BANNED IN BUSINESS

A woman who goes into an office because she thinks herself pretty and hopes to meet romance in the form of her employer, or at least to rise quickly because of her physical charm, has clerkship and chorus work mixed up. Sex is one thing that has no place in business. Much as a man may admire a pretty, or magnetic, or an amusing woman in his leisure hours, in his hours of work he wants someone to help him with that work. The more help she can give him, the more he values her and the more salary he is willing to pay.

Naturally he likes one whose personality is attractive, rather than one who is strikingly the reverse—but business personality and leisure personality are two different things. They are sometimes combined in one person, and sometimes romance is an outcome of business, but that is the exception that proves the rule. And every time the prospect of romance intrudes into a business situation, think not just twice but a dozen times before allowing an office relationship to become a personal one. The woman who happens to work in an office with her husband should remember to be as impersonal and efficient during working hours as any other woman would be.

Every businessman likes a woman who is neat, impersonal, and efficient, just as he likes an automobile that is ready to go any distance without any danger of breaking down. A successful business personality has as its first attribute *efficiency*, not sex appeal.

THE PERFECT SECRETARY

The function of the perfect secretary is to complement her employer's endeavor, and not make any intrusions which would be more likely to impede than help.

She should respond to his requirements exactly as a machine responds to the touch of lever or accelerator. If he says "Good morning," she answers "Good morning" with a smile and cheerfully. She does not volunteer a remark, unless she has messages of importance to give him. If he says nothing, she says nothing, and she does not even mentally notice that he has said nothing. In fact, when she notices his preoccupation, she waits, if possible, holding back irrelevant messages until he has finished the letters he wants to dictate or whatever business it was that made him ring for her. She should never interrupt but wait until her employer has finished; then, if there is something she doesn't understand, is the time to ask questions. An employer would prefer a secretary to ask rather than guess.

Needless to say, a secretary must not betray the secrets of her employer. His business dealings must be regarded as professional secrets that it would be dishonorable to divulge—no matter how inconsequential they may seem to her.

THE CORRESPONDENCE OF HER EMPLOYER

Business training surely teaches every secretary to know everything she can that will be of service to her employer, but to know as little as possible about the things that are not her concern. When sorting his mail, she leaves unopened the obviously private letters—envelopes written by hand on stationery not suggestive of business—and having opened his other letters and clipped them in whatever order he likes to have them, she should then clip a sheet of blank paper on the top of each pile, or put the mail in a manila folder, so that visitors—or others who have access to his office and who may accidentally stand behind his desk—will not have the contents of letters displayed before them.

TAKING DICTATION

When a stenographer enters a man's office in response to his summons or because it is the hour set for her appearance, she should take a chair and place it near enough to hear him easily. Where she sits depends very much on the office—where the light comes from, and where she can best hear his voice. It is not expected that he get up and offer her a chair or show her the sort of personal attention that a man in social life shows to a woman.

QUALITIES OF THE IDEAL BUSINESS WOMAN

The ideal business woman is accurate, orderly, quick, and impersonal, whether she is a typist or top executive of a great concern. By "impersonal" is meant exactly that! Her point of view must be focused on the work in hand, not on her own reactions to it, or to anyone's reactions to her. If she is an executive, she avoids being dictatorial and still maintains her dignity.

At the very top of the list of women's business shortcomings is the inability of many of them to achieve impersonality. Mood, temper, jealousy, especially when induced by a "crush on" her employer or a fellow worker—these are the chief flaws of the woman in business and a constant source of annoyance in every office where she exists. The greatest handicap to woman's advancement in business is her inability to leave her personal feelings and affairs at home! An anonymous expert on business gave as the recipe for success: "The ability to work efficiently and pleasantly with other people." The recipe is perfect—there is nothing to add except to acknowledge that it takes no small amount of will and self-control to get on with any constant companion under the daily friction of an enforced relationship that is unrelieved day after day, week after week. It is wonderful that human nature stands the strain as well as it does, especially in situations where one's own work is dependent upon the cooperation of others for its complete efficiency. One would need a disposition made in heaven not to become surly when another's lagging makes one's own energy futile. One horse in a team always pulls better than the other. It is pretty hard on the better one, especially when the slow one seemingly prevents the better from getting ahead. But just as the driver of a team knows the better horse, the foreman or the manager or the president will almost surely know the better work—in time.

It is also very important for a woman who has anyone under her authority, especially if it be a man, not to give unnecessary orders—just to show her authority!

THE REASONS FOR LOST POSITIONS

One basic reason for many lost positions is inability to work pleasantly and cooperatively with associates and superiors. The woman who is dissatisfied and announces her unhappiness to her co-workers is quite likely to lose her job. The junior executive who persistently goes over his superior's head, or who constantly tells his associates that he knows better than his superior, is just asking for his "walking papers." On the other hand, the man who respects his immediate superior, and realizes that he too has a position to protect, will never be considered unpleasantly "pushy."

It is needless to add that the surest way to lose a position is lack of personal cleanliness. Appearance, neatness, and fastidiousness are of first importance to everyone. A man or woman who dresses carelessly and is unclean will surely have difficulty in remaining employed, and will certainly be hindered in advancing in his or her chosen field.

When being interviewed for a new position, it is most important to be at ease. Wear comfortable and appropriate clothes. Be polite (but never humble); answer all questions completely and frankly. When the interviewer indicates that the conversation is over, leave promptly.

OFFICE DISCIPLINE

A business organization is, in one sense, like a military one. You should take as much pride in helping to keep up the tone of the office you work in as you take pride in your own efficiency.

An employee ought to have that same feeling for the spirit of the organization or the office he works in that is characteristic of the "school spirit" of young people. He and his associates, his superiors, his inferiors, are fellow members who can all add to or detract from the firm's importance.

The possession of tact whereby you know how to please people and make them pleased in turn with your firm is one of the surest ways of getting an increase of salary. Putting on airs and thinking of yourself as too good for your job is pretty close to asking for a job not half as good as the one you hold.

Do not bring your personal problems to the office. You may rest assured no one is interested. Leave them at home, or, if you must, discuss them with a friend during lunch.

No matter how well an employer may know her out of business hours, he must in the office call his stenographer "Miss Jones" and not "Katie." It is still more necessary that she address him as "Mr. Smith," and that, when she enters his office and is asked a single question, she either say "Yes, Sir," or "No, Sir," or if she objects to "Sir," "Yes, Mr. Smith," or else follow her monosyllable with a short sentence.

When a young woman who holds a subordinate position meets an officer of the company, she does not speak unless spoken to. When a woman clerk meets her department manager in the hallway, she would naturally say "Good morning," but not invite any longer conversation.

There are, however, varying degrees of formality in business organizations. Offices today tend to be more casual than formerly. Some employers feel that in a more relaxed atmosphere employees will be more efficient, more reliable, and more loyal. These employers try to hire personnel who will be congenial, and who will work well together to the benefit of the company. The employer or ranking executive determines the degree of formality in his office. He may, for instance, prefer to be on a first-name basis with his staff; the informality does not itself imply a too-familiar relationship.

LUNCHING WITH ONE'S EMPLOYER

A young woman in a subordinate position does not go out to lunch with her superior or employer. But if she holds a responsible position and has matters of business to discuss, there is no reason—unless her own—why she should not on occasion lunch with him. It would however be courting criticism should their going out together become a habit.

A CHEERFUL DINING ALCOVE FOR MAIDS IN AN APARTMENT

It also could serve as a pleasant breakfast nook for a small family.

HOUSEMAID IN A ONE- OR TWO-MAID HOUSEHOLD

A morning dress. The afternoon or evening dress is shown facing page 353.

THE TELEPHONE IN AN OFFICE

Personal messages over the telephone are at times unavoidable, but long chatty conversations are not only out of place, but wasting time which does not belong to the employee. Social "chatter" annoys other people in the office who can't help but overhear your discussion of the movie you saw last night. Personal calls that interfere with the routine of office procedure, either incoming or outgoing, are inexcusable except in genuine emergencies.

Discourage visits from your family and friends at the office. Your baby brother may be a most enchanting child, but his place is not in the office in which you work.

BUSINESS GIFTS

Gifts from a firm are usually in the form of a bonus or a proportion of one's salary. At Christmas a man may give his personal secretary a present. Candy is conventional; although, when she has been with him for some time, he might choose something he thinks she would rather have. It is hardly necessary to add that wearing apparel is NOT suitable. A private secretary known well to a man's wife is sometimes, but not usually, remembered by the wife at Christmas. Occasionally employees give presents to their employers, but it is not usual. There are exceptions: If there is a wedding in the employer's family, or if a baby is born, then the employees may all contribute and send a gift. They also as a group may send flowers to a funeral. A committee could collect contributions and select an appropriate gift.

Gift-giving to one's fellow-workers who are also personal friends should always be arranged for out of office hours.

CHARACTER AND TACT WITH CUSTOMERS

A tactful person at the reception desk in an office is of great importance. Neither a condescending nor gushing attitude is suitable—anywhere! A pleasant, quiet, but cordial attitude can do much to further the good will of the firm for which you work.

When a recumbent, gum-chewing office boy flings at you from behind a locked gate "Who d'ja wanna see?" and then shuffles off and returns with: "Mr. Brown's busy. Can't see ya t'day! Y' c'n try t'morrer if ya like!"—the customer will *not*, unless he really must see Mr. Brown and cannot take his business to anyone else. Many offices—especially those which have many personal contacts—are putting middle-aged women and men at the reception desk because it has been found that people do not resent being refused admittance by a tactful older person as they resent being barred by one who is young and callous! Good public relations has become an important part of good business management.

A woman, on going to a man's office, sends in her visiting-card, or

her business card. This is one of the few occasions when a woman leaves
her card upon a man.

A man does not rise when a stenographer or other woman employee
comes into his office. But he must stand to receive a woman visitor, and
stand until she is seated. He stands again when she prepares to leave
and usually goes with her to the door, opens it for her, and "bows
her out."

SHOULD A STENOGRAPHER RISE?

A question often raised is whether a stenographer should rise when
visitors to the office approach her desk. Many a young woman thinks
it very rude not to meet the friendliness of such persons as she would
do were she at home.

The answer to this is that unless the visitors are persons of importance to her employer—so that the time she takes from her work is
spent in her employer's interest—it would not be expected of her, or
even proper, to greet them in such a way as to encourage their talking
to her at length. On the other hand, if she were the private secretary of
an executive and it were part of her job to make a pleasant impression
on behalf of her employer, or perhaps to act as his deputy, she would
naturally leave her desk to greet a stranger or a very occasional customer; but not (if she is otherwise busy) to greet one who comes into
the office constantly. A secretary's duties do not include helping a
visitor off and on with his coat, unless he actually needs help. This
same approach to these problems applies to all similar office personnel.

ANNOUNCING NAMES ON TELEPHONE

A man calling a woman on business says, "This is Mr. Smartling
of Dash & Sons." If he were calling a man, he should say, "This is
Smartling of Dash & Sons."

A young woman (no matter how young) calling a lady (no matter
how old) would say, "This is Miss Jones of Blank & Company." And
of course she would say the same were she calling a man.

SPORTSMANSHIP IN GIVING AND TAKING

A situation often met in business is the following: In Oldclerk's
department Newhire is given a piece of work to do and he tells the
former frankly that he is unable to cope with it. Oldclerk generously
takes the sorry mess and works it out. Newhire then writes it into final
form and presents it to his employer for approval. When he is con-
gratulated, he remains silent about Oldclerk's part in the matter. The
question is: Should Oldclerk be sport enough to help him again? Should
he be inclined to make an issue of the incident, or should he consider it
better to say nothing and let the final tally speak for itself?

The answer to this is that John Newhire could probably not be expected to announce his own incompetence—perhaps even lose his job—nor, let it be hoped, did Oldclerk help him in order to have him laud his own ability and generosity. Generosity is not thus expressed! A kind and outgiving person would help him, and of course say nothing. If Newhire continues to abuse the generosity of Oldclerk, the latter would certainly be justified in letting him meet his own handicaps.

If Newhire had had faith in his abilities he might in all honesty have admitted that he had asked for help but that he believes he understands how to do that job now.

THE PROBLEM OF PROTECTING
AN EMPLOYER'S INTEREST

Frankness which springs from tact and loyalty to one's employer must not be confused with the ordinary and despicable habit of talebearing. For example, let us say Miss Bright is secretary to Mr. Brilliant, a man of rare ability and character. She learns that a glib-tongued colleague, whom her employer trusts implicitly and with whom he frankly discusses his ideas, is taking these ideas as fast as he can to the partners of the firm as his own, in the hope of getting Mr. Brilliant's place. Mr. Brilliant is beginning to notice that things are not going well for himself, but he does not suspect that his supposed friend is to blame. Should Miss Bright tell Mr. Brilliant about his friend's treachery or go to his employers? In this specific case, the wisest course would be to do neither until she has collected evidence exactly as she would were she a prosecuting attorney preparing a case for trial in court. What she merely suspects, or believes, or has been told, is not evidence. But if she knows that on such a day Mr. Cheater showed the Smith representative an outline of Mr. Brilliant's plan, and that on another day he casually suggested to the head of the firm that they handle the Jones account in the way Mr. Brilliant was at that moment trying to perfect before submitting it himself, loyalty to her own employer demands that she lay these facts before him in order that he shall be able to act in his own defense. In other words, collecting definite facts in her employer's interest must, of course, not be confused with ordinary talebearing.

A somewhat similar situation, but one far more difficult to handle, is one involving an employer's wife. Should she find out that his young and beautiful wife is having, or at least is on the road toward having, a serious affair with another man, the answer to "What can the secretary do?" is *nothing!* She has no right to tell her employer anything about his wife, and certainly she can't go to the wife. Nor, for that matter, may she meddle in his private life at all.

BUSINESS WOMEN IN UNCONVENTIONAL SITUATIONS

Situations which women of other days were never called upon to meet have made it evident that something in the way of a modern code of propriety for young women following business or professional careers is essential. Certain jobs—particularly those of responsibility leading to the heights of success—carry with them the paradoxical responsibility of upholding a moral code of unassailable integrity while smashing to bits many of the long-established rules of propriety.

The young woman who is a confidential secretary to an executive may very well on occasion be required to stay late into the evening working with him alone; or if the nature of his business or profession requires that he go on long tours of investigation or conference with firms in distant cities, it may quite possibly be necessary that she accompany him on this purely business trip. Theoretically and according to the normal conventions of etiquette, nothing could be more improper than that a young woman—an attractive and personable one, no doubt —should go traveling about the country with a man alone. But practically, and according to the exactions of the modern business world, it is necessary that every professional or business woman shall write her own code of propriety. She must! In the case of Miss Secretary, no one in the world can advise her as well as she can advise herself. She knows exactly how necessary she is or is not to the work her employer must do; she knows his attitude toward her, and certainly she knows her own attitude toward him. Therefore, she knows beyond the shadow of a doubt whether she must or whether she need not go with him.

The point to be made is this: Between breaking conventions in pursuit of a good time and breaking them only in so far as her profession exacts, lies the whole width of the moral code.

The most conspicuous illustration is that of the trained nurse who is necessarily called upon to break many rules of the social proprieties, and yet gossips would stoop low indeed to criticize the unconventional exigencies of her profession. If her own attitude is above reproach, no scandal can touch her, no matter how unconventional the circumstances.

It is true that a nurse is set apart, more so than the business woman; but even so, both are free from criticism—unless they themselves give cause for it. It isn't the bald fact of taking trains and staying in hotels and being off in a farthermost state alone with Mr. Employer that will hurt Miss Secretary's good name. Nothing will hurt her good name except her own or Mr. Employer's unprofessional and therefore improper attitude of mind. If his attitude of mind is IMPERSONAL, as it should be, everyone will know it; if it isn't, then that is another story, since by some inexplicable waves of mental telepathy everyone will know that too.

A SECRETARY MAKES PREPARATIONS FOR JOURNEY

And now having said that Miss Secretary may defy convention, it is necessary to add a fairly formidable array of qualifying exactions that the critical world expects her to follow.

In preparation for the journey, she orders whatever accommodations he always expects. On trains, she engages a drawing-room or a section for him, and a section or a lower berth for herself in the same car; but in hotels she engages a suite for him, and a room and bath for herself on another floor. To put herself in another car or in another hotel would be a mistake, because she will make her employer conscious of the fact that she is conscious of him.

IF SECRETARY IS SHOWN INTO ROOM IN EMPLOYER'S SUITE

If she should by a most unusual chance find herself shown into a room adjoining that of her employer, the question of what to do depends somewhat upon the type of man he is. Perhaps she says as a matter of fact, "This is not what I ordered. I'm sorry!" Or maybe she says, "This is stupid; I'll go and change it." She then goes down to the desk and tells the clerk that her room is not the one that was ordered, and tries to get another.

To those who may think it stupid as well as prudish to do anything about this at all, since everyone must know as well as she does that the relationship between Mr. Employer and herself is one of professional necessity, the worldly answer is that much more is at stake than a question of social gossip. The greater his prominence, the more seriously could carelessness of propriety endanger his career, and this not at the moment but years later when exaggeration of the fact of their adjoining rooms can without limit distort the truth.

HER BEHAVIOR OUTSIDE BUSINESS HOURS

Questions concerned with whether Miss Secretary may lunch, or dine, or dance, or go to the theatre or a movie with her employer are over the line where professional propriety crosses into dangerous territory. It is almost certain that she will lunch with him or have dinner with him—especially on trains, or boats, or in hotels in smaller towns. On rushed days she may have to eat in his rooms where they are working; in other words, she takes eating alone or eating with him as incidental to convenience. The danger mark is when the pleasure of dining becomes social.

This sounds overstrict perhaps, but these are the rules that even a business woman must consider when she writes her code. It is up to the woman to keep the relationship on the level she wishes.

IMPORTANCE OF APPEARANCE WHEN TRAVELING ALONE WITH EMPLOYER

As noted in the chapter on The Clothes of a Lady, the best directions for clothes are—tailor-made. Smart to the last degree and in perfect taste, but in nothing conspicuous. Neat, carefully done hair, but no ultrasophisticated or conspicuous little-girl effect of hair hanging loose down to the shoulders. Little girls do not go on business trips! No bare-backed evening dress, no dangling bracelets, no obvious make-up, no strong perfume, no earrings the size of a silver dollar, and no champagne. In short, she must be obviously what she is: an attractive, competent, intelligent, and impersonal secretary.

STORE ETIQUETTE

The technical aspects of salesmanship are much too specialized to be discussed by anyone who has not learned the subject at first hand and practiced it with success—success, moreover, that is measured by the tangible proof of satisfactory sales slips, and best of all, an increasing number of customers who ask for Mrs. Keen or Miss Personable when they come again to buy. A saleswoman can be very helpful, and she can also be a nuisance.

But the aspects of salesmanship that depend for their success upon tactful and pleasing manners belong very decidedly in a book such as this. Also very decidedly belong good manners that are to be expected of all customers who make any pretense to being well-bred.

SALESWOMEN *VERSUS* CUSTOMERS

The behavior of the customer is a far more responsible matter than that of the saleswoman. The distress inconsiderate customers can inflict, or the pleasure considerate ones can give, is plainly of greater concern to one who waits on them than any annoyance or satisfaction that the saleswoman can cause the customer.

To the customer nothing is at stake further than the satisfaction or irritation—or most often the completely negative impression—that is made upon them by the woman who waits on them during a few moments of time, the length of which the customers themselves control. But a saleswoman is, so to speak, at the mercy of any customer who is ill-bred or unreasonable for so long as that customer chooses to keep her in attendance.

Moreover, every displeased customer is a mark against a saleswoman's value, and, whether deserved or not, many such marks mean loss of a job.

FROM THE CUSTOMER'S POINT OF VIEW

First, however, let us consider the point of view of a customer, since this is something that we all know from personal experience. We surely do not all agree as to the type of saleswoman we like or dislike. A clever saleswoman must have different methods with different customers. After all, if customers were identical, perfect salesmanship would not be the difficult accomplishment it is. It is quite possible that methods which are unendurable to some of us are acceptable to others.

But I do not think any of us like high-pressure salesmanship or that it ever pays in the long run. One wonders how many customers who have been high-pressured into buying what they did not really want or into spending more than they could afford have thereafter avoided not only that particular salesperson, but that particular store as well.

THE SUCCESSFUL SALESWOMAN

Really great saleswomen have cultivated not only an expert knowledge of the commodities they sell, but an equally expert ability to appraise each of the customers to whom they sell.

It is essential to know, therefore, whether a customer likes to be "dearied" or "madamed," or chatted to about every topic under the sun; and whether she is one who likes to have her mind made up for her, or whether she is one who, knowing exactly what she wants, prefers to have her own questions answered intelligently without any unasked-for advice.

But the saleswoman an intelligent customer is certain to like best— the one in fact to whom she always returns—is one who listens to what she says and tries to give her what she wants, instead of trying to sell her what the store seems eager to be rid of.

For example, when you ask for something she can't supply, the ideal saleswoman would listen attentively to what you say and answer, "I am very sorry we have nothing at all like that in the color you want; but I could give you something in a small pattern of yellow," and then with certain eagerness she would ask, "Have you time to let me show it to you?"

You are pleased, because the saleswoman showed eagerness to help you find what you want, and you as a customer would be very lacking in courtesy not at least to let her show you what she so much hopes may please you. When she brings it, you are inclined to be pleased because, though you know it is not just what you want, you are sure it is not going to be thrust upon you. And the possibilities are that if you can make it do, you will take it. And even if you do not, you will certainly come back to that saleswoman another time when you are looking for something else.

A POOR SALESWOMAN

Of all the varieties of poor saleswomen, the worst is she who simply brushes aside what you say you want and blandly spreads before you something that is exactly what you have explained to her you do NOT want, at the same time trying to force you to like it by extolling its beauties or its bargain values, and capping the climax by telling you that Mrs. Uppity thinks this is exquisite! That kind of saleswoman would have difficulty in selling a steak to a starving man.

We can all understand seeking to guide a customer who doesn't know what she wants. But what can result except irritability against a clerk—and, because of the clerk, against the store—when a customer of intelligence is treated as a moron?

TACT ESSENTIAL TO CUSTOMERS AND CLERKS ALIKE

In social life tact is an asset, but in business, almost as much as in diplomacy, tact is essential. Why tact and good temper and courteous consideration of others is exacted of one who sells is understood by everybody. But there exist some pretenders to gentility who think that because they are customers the precepts of courtesy need not apply to their own behavior. The test of a lady is nowhere greater than in situations where the advantage is her own. It isn't possible to advertise lack of quality more blatantly than does the overbearing, inconsiderate shopper who rudely criticizes everything a saleswoman shows her, who treats her as though she were of a completely inferior class, who keeps her for an entire afternoon pulling material about, and then buys nothing.

THE INCONSIDERATE CUSTOMER

As a guess, one might say that an inconsiderate customer can be at her worst and cause the greatest strain upon a saleswoman's sportsmanship and good temper in the ready-to-wear clothing department. And what a careless customer often does to model dresses is scarcely believable. Perhaps she smears the fronts of the dresses with lipstick as she pulls them on or off. Or, if the day is very hot and she wears scant underclothes, she dampens them with perspiration. Perhaps she tears them in haste or sheer carelessness; perhaps she scorches one with her cigarette although smoking is not permitted in stores. Rarely does she think *she* did the damage. And in the end she orders none or perhaps she buys and then returns everything looking still more shopworn the next day.

It is true that we all at some time buy something which for one reason or another we are obliged to send back. But this is not the chronic practice of any considerate person; and neither is being inconsiderate of salespeople nor of the merchandise belonging to the store.

Another lack of consideration is shown by those who go shopping ten minutes before closing time. The salespeople have had a long day and have routine chores to do before they can leave.

Another fault—but probably only belonging to women of leisure who have had no business experience—is to think it fair or honest to expect favors from their friends who are no longer women of leisure and who are not in a position to give below-cost prices, or to put all other customers aside and spend their time in gossiping with a former friend.

Is the customer always right? It would not seem likely. Unfailing patience and good temper are qualities exacted of every saleswoman, whereas there is nothing to restrain the ill-humor or unreasonableness of a customer—except her own good breeding.

And finally it is hard to believe but there are women who, with no thought of buying anything, will go into a dressmaker's salesroom solely to pass an hour or so before a lunch date, and waste the time of a saleswoman who is paid at least in part by commissions on the dresses she sells—and not on the ones she shows.

CLUBS AND CLUB ETIQUETTE

·◦[46]◦·

A SOCIETY IS AN ORGANIZATION COMPOSED OF PERSONS who band together for a common purpose and are not infrequently obligated to one another by bonds of brotherhood. A club is an organization composed of persons who have joined it for their individual convenience or pleasure.

A club's membership, whether composed of men or women, or both, may be limited to a dozen or may include several thousands, and the procedure in joining may be easy or difficult, according to the type of club and the standing of the would-be member.

Membership in many athletic associations may be had by walking in and paying dues; also many country golf clubs are as free to the public as country inns. But joining a purely social club of rank and exclusiveness is a very different matter. To be eligible for membership in such a club a man must have among the members friends who like him enough to be willing to propose him and second him and write letters for him; furthermore he must be disliked by no one—at least not sufficiently so for any member to raise any serious objection to his company.

There are two ways of joining a club: by invitation and by having application made for you. To join by invitation means that you are invited when the club is started to be one of the founders or charter members, or if you are a distinguished citizen, you may at the invitation of the governors become an honorary member; or in a small or informal club you may become an ordinary member by invitation or at the suggestion of the governors that you would be welcome. A charter member pays dues, but not always an initiation fee. An honorary member pays neither dues nor initiation fee; he is really a permanent guest of the club. A life member is one who pays his dues for twenty years or so in a lump sum, and is thereafter exempted from dues even though the annual dues should be greatly increased in later years or he should live to be a hundred. Few clubs have honorary members and none have more than half a dozen; so this exceptional type of membership may as well be disregarded.

The ordinary members of a club are either resident—meaning that they live or have their office within fifty miles of the club—or non-resident—living beyond that distance and paying smaller dues but having the same privileges.

In certain of the London clubs, one or two New York ones, and a leading club in several other cities, it is not unusual for a boy's name to be put up for membership as soon as he is born. If his name comes up while he is a minor, it is laid aside until after his twenty-first birthday and then put at the head of the list of applicants and voted upon at the next meeting of the governors. In the same way an ex-member who puts his name up for reelection always precedes new applicants.

HOW A NAME IS "PUT UP"

Since no well-bred man is likely to want to join a club in which the members are not his friends, he says to a member of his family or an intimate friend, "Do you mind putting me up for the Nearby Club? I will ask Dick to second me." The friend answers, "Delighted to do it!" and Dick says the same.

More likely the suggestion to join comes from a friend, who remarks one day, "Why don't you join the Nearby Club? It would be very convenient for you." The other says, "I should like to," and the friend replies, "Let me put you up, and I'll ask Dick to second you." And he arranges with Dick to do so.

It must be remembered that a gentleman has no right to ask anyone who is not really one of his best friends to propose or second him. It is an awkward thing to refuse in the first place; in the second it involves considerable effort, and on occasion a great deal of annoyance, to say nothing of responsibility.

For example, let us suppose that Jim Smartlington asks Donald Cameron to propose him and Clubwin Doe to second him. Jim's name is written in the book kept for the purpose and signed by both proposer and seconder:

> Smartlington, James
> Proposer: Donald Cameron
> Seconder: Clubwin Doe

Nothing more is done until the name is posted—meaning that it appears among a list of names put up on the bulletin board in the clubhouse. It is then the duty of Cameron and Doe each to write a letter of endorsement to the governors of the club, to be read by that body when they hold the meeting at which Smartlington's name comes up for election.

Example:

Board of Governors,
The Nearby Club
Dear Sirs:

It affords me much pleasure to propose for membership in the Nearby Club Mr. James Smartlington. I have known Mr. Smartlington for many years and consider him qualified in every way for membership.

He is a graduate of Yalvard, class of 1941, and rowed on the Varsity crew. He is now in his father's firm, Jones, Smartlington & Co.

Yours very truly,
Donald Cameron

CANDIDATES MUST MEET GOVERNORS

Cameron must also at once select with Smartlington six or more of his friends who are members of the club (but not governors) and ask them to write letters endorsing him. Furthermore, the candidate cannot come up for election unless he knows several of the governors personally so that they can vouch for him at the meeting. Therefore, Cameron and Doe must take Smartlington to several governors (at their offices generally) and personally present him, or very likely they invite two or three of the governors and Smartlington to lunch.

Even under the best of circumstances it is a nuisance for a busy man to have to make appointments at the offices of other busy men. And since it is uncertain which of the governors will be present at any particular meeting, it is necessary to introduce the candidate to a sufficient number so that at least two among those at the meeting will be able to speak for him.

In the example we have chosen, Clubwin Doe, having himself been a governor and knowing most of the present ones very well, has less difficulty in presenting his candidate than might many other members who, though they have for years belonged to the club, have used it so seldom that they know few of the governors even by sight.

At a leading women's club of New York, the governors appoint an hour on several afternoons before elections when they are in the visitors' rooms at the clubhouse in order to meet the candidates whom their proposers must present. This would certainly seem a more practicable method, to say nothing of its being easier for everyone concerned, than the masculine etiquette which requires that the governors be stalked one by one, to his extreme inconvenience and loss of time.

As already said, Jim Smartlington, having unusually popular and well-known sponsors and being also very well liked himself, is elected with no difficulty.

IMPORTANCE OF GOOD LETTERS OF ENDORSEMENT

But take the case of young Breezy. He was put up by two not too well-known members who wrote half-hearted endorsements themselves and did nothing about getting letters from others. They knew none of the governors, and trusted in the fact that two members who knew Breezy slightly would do. His casual proposers forgot that enemies write letters as well as friends—and that, moreover, enmity is sometimes active where friendship is often passive. Two men who disliked his "manner" wrote that they considered him "unsuitable." As he had no friends strong enough to stand up for him, he was turned down. A man is rarely blackballed, as such an action could not fail to injure him in the eyes of the world. (The expression "blackball" comes from the custom of voting for a member by putting a white ball in a ballot box, or against him by putting in a black one.) If a candidate is likely to receive a blackball—two disqualify him; in some clubs, one—the governors do not vote on him at all, but inform the proposer that the name of his candidate had better be withdrawn, which is almost invariably done, rather than run any risk of the stigma of a blackball. Later on, if the objection to him is disproved or overcome, his name may again be put up.

QUALIFICATIONS FOR ELECTION

The more popular the candidate, the less work there is for his proposer and seconder. A stranger, if he is not a member of the representative club in his own city, would need strong friends to elect him to an exclusive club in another community, and an unpopular man has no chance at all.

However, in all but very rare instances, events run smoothly; the candidate is voted on at a meeting of the board of governors and is elected.

A notice is mailed to him next morning, telling him that he has been elected and that his initiation fee and his dues make a total of so much. The candidate at once draws his check for the amount and mails it. As soon as the club secretary has had ample time to receive the check, the new member is free to use the club as much or as little as his predilection suggests.

THE NEW MEMBER

The new member usually, though not necessarily, goes to a club for the first time with his proposer or his seconder, or at least an old member. Let us say he goes for lunch or dinner, at which he is host, and his friend briefs him on such unwritten information as, "That chair in the window is where old Gotrox always sits. Don't occupy it when you see him coming in or he will be disagreeable to everybody for a week." Or "They always play double stakes at this table, so don't sit at it, unless you *mean* to." Or "That's Double coming in now. Avoid him at bridge as you would the plague." "The roasts are always good and that waiter is the best in the room," and so on.

A new member is given or should ask for a copy of the Club Book, which contains, besides the list of the members, the constitution and the bylaws or "house rules," which he must study carefully and be sure to obey.

COUNTRY CLUBS

Country clubs vary greatly in both characteristics and expense. A few, like the Myopia Hunt, the Tuxedo, the Saddle and Cycle, the Burlingame, and several others in this class, are more expensive to belong to than any clubs in London or even in New York, and are precisely the same in matters of membership and management. It is also quite as difficult to be elected to them as to any of the exclusive clubs in the cities—more so if anything—inasmuch as they are open to the family and friends of every member, whereas in a man's club in a city his membership gives the privilege of the club to no one but himself personally. The test question always put by the governors at elections is, "Are the house guests the candidate may have as well as his family likely to be agreeable to the present members of the Club?" If not, he is not admitted.

Nearly all country clubs have, however, one open door—unknown to city clubs. People taking houses in the neighborhood are often granted "season privileges"; that is, on being proposed by a member and upon paying a season's subscription, new householders are accepted as transient guests. In some clubs this subscription may be indefinitely renewed; in others a man must come up for regular election at the end of three or six months' or a year's time.

Apart from what may be called the few representative and exclusive country clubs, there are hundreds—more likely thousands—which have very simple requirements for membership. Merely having one or two members vouch for a candidate's integrity and good behavior is sufficient.

Golf clubs, hunting clubs, political, or sports clubs, as well as business and professional clubs, have special purposes and membership qualifications. All good golf players are, as a rule, welcomed at all golf clubs, all huntsmen at hunting clubs, and yet the Myopia, for instance, would not think of admitting the best rider ever known if he were not socially eligible. As a rule, however, the great player is welcomed in any club devoted to the sport in which he excels.

WOMEN'S CLUBS

Except that the luxurious women's club has an atmosphere that a man rarely knows how to give to the interior of a house, no matter how architecturally perfect it may be, there is no difference between women's and men's clubs.

In every State of the Union, there are women's clubs of every kind and grade: social, political, sports, professional. Some are housed in enormous and perfect buildings designed especially for them and others in only a room or two, usually in some hotel.

When the pioneer women's club of New York was started—a club that aspired to be in the same class as the most important men's club— various governors of the latter were unflatteringly outspoken. Women could not possibly run a club as it should be run—it was unthinkable that they should be foolish enough to attempt it! And the husbands and fathers of the founders expected to have to dig down into their pockets to make up the deficit, forgetting entirely that the running of a club is merely the running of a house on a large scale, and that women, not men, are the perfect housekeepers. Today, clubs nowhere are more nearly perfect in appointment or more smoothly run than the best women's clubs.

CLUB MANNERS

Good manners in clubs are the same as good manners elsewhere— only a little more so. A club is for the pleasure and convenience of many; it is never intended as a stage setting for a star or clown or monologist. There is no place where a person has greater need of restraint and consideration for the reserves of others than in a club. In every well-appointed one there is a reading room or library where conversation is not allowed. There are books, and easy chairs, and good light for reading both by day and night, and it is one of the unbreakable rules not to speak to anybody who is reading or writing.

When two people are sitting by themselves and talking, another should on no account join them unless he is an intimate friend of both. To be a mere acquaintance, or, still less, to have been introduced to one of them, gives no privilege whatever.

The fact of being a club member does not (except in a certain few especially informal clubs) grant anyone the right to speak to strangers. If a new member happens to find at the club no one whom he knows, he goes about his own affairs. He either reads, writes, or looks out the window, or plays solitaire, or occupies himself as he would if he were alone in a hotel.

It is courteous of a governor or habitual member, on noticing a new member or a visitor—especially one who seems to be rather at a loss—to go up and speak to him; but the latter should not be the one to speak first. In the dining-rooms of many clubs there is a large table, sometimes known as the social table, where members who are lunching alone may sit, and where the conversation is general, and all are expected to talk whether they are friends or total strangers. Certain New York and Boston clubs, as well as those of London, have earned a reputation for snobbishness because the members never speak to those they do not know. Through no intent to be disagreeable, but just because it is not customary, New York people do not speak to those they do not know. It does not occur to them that strangers feel slighted, until they themselves are given the same medicine in London, or, going elsewhere in America, appreciate the courtesy and kindness of the rest of the country.

The fundamental rule for behavior in a club is the same as in the drawing-room of a private house. In other words, heels have no place on furniture; ashes belong in ashtrays; books should not be abused; and all evidence of exercising should be confined to the courts or gymnasium, and the locker or dressing room. There is often a small room reserved for members who wish to change their clothes or dress for dinner, and in which no exercising clothes are allowed. Many people who wouldn't think of lolling around the house in unfit attire come trooping into far too many carelessly managed country clubs with their steaming faces, clammy shirts, and rumpled hair, giving extremely unpleasant evidence of recent exertion and present readiness for the bath. The leading country clubs are of course as perfectly run as those in cities.

THE PERFECT CLUBMAN

The perfect clubman never allows himself to show irritability to anyone. He makes it a point to be courteous to a new member or an old member's guest. He scrupulously observes the rules of the club. He discharges his card debts at the table. He pays his share always, with an instinctive horror of sponging. And lastly, he treats everyone with the same consideration he expects and demands from them.

THE INFORMAL CLUB

The informal club is often more suggestive of a fraternity than a club, in that every member always speaks to every other. In one of the best known of this type, the members are artists, authors, scientists, sportsmen, and other thinkers and doers. Every day a long table at which the members gather and talk, everyone to everyone else, is set for lunch. There is another dining-room where solitary members may sit by themselves, or bring in outsiders if they care to. None but **members** sit at the round table—which isn't round in the least!

The informal clubs are always comparatively small and the methods of electing members vary. In some there is no list of applicants and membership is gained only by invitation as the result of the spontaneous vote of the whole club; in others members are elected by the governors first and then asked to join.

THE VISITORS IN A CLUB

The best known and most distinguished club of New England has an annex having dining-rooms to which ladies as well as gentlemen who are not members are admitted; and this annex plan has since been followed by other clubs elsewhere.

When a club moves into a new clubhouse, it is quite usual for the members to give an opening reception to which ladies are invited to see the house. After this, women are barred.

All men's clubs have private dining-rooms where members can give dinners to which men who are not members may be invited even though they live in the city in which the club is situated.

In every club in the United States a member is allowed to introduce a stranger—living at least fifty miles away—for a varying length of time determined by the bylaws of the club. In some clubs guests may be put up for a day only; in others the privilege extends for two weeks or more.

Many clubs allow each member a certain number of visitors a year; in others visitors are unlimited. In many city clubs the same guest cannot be introduced twice within the year. In country clubs members may usually have an unlimited number of visitors.

As a rule, when a member introduces a stranger, he takes him to the club personally, writes his name in the visitors' book, and introduces him to those who may be in the room at the time—very possibly asking another member whom he knows particularly well to look out for his guest. If for some reason it is not possible for the stranger's host to take him to the club, he writes to the secretary of the club for a card of introduction.

Secretary
The Town Club
Dear Sir: (*Or* "Dear Mr. Jones," *but not* "Dear Jim." *This is because it is not a personal letter, but a formal request to be put on file.*)

Kindly send Mr. A. M. Strangleigh, of London, a card extending the privileges of the Club for one week.

Mr. Strangleigh is staying at the Carlton House.

Yours very truly,
Clubwin Doe

The secretary then sends a card to Mr. Strangleigh.

The Town Club
Extends its privileges to
Mr. Strangleigh
(*Name handwritten*)
from Jan. 7   to   Jan. 14
(*Dates handwritten*)
Through the courtesy of
Mr. Clubwin Doe
(*Name handwritten*)

Mr. Strangleigh goes to the club by himself. A visitor who has been given a card to a club has, during the time of his visit, all the privileges of a member except that he is not allowed to introduce others to the club and he cannot give a dinner in the private dining-room. The guest must arrange at the club's office to have his charges rendered to himself —he must be punctilious about asking for his bill upon leaving, and pay it immediately and *without question*. Otherwise his bill must be paid by the member who put him up, and putting a man up at a club never means that the member is his host.

The visitor's status throughout his stay is founded on the courtesy of the member who introduced him, and he should try to show an equal courtesy to everyone about him. He should remember not to obtrude on the privacy of the members he does not know. He has no right to criticize the management, the rules, or the organization of the club. In short, he behaves exactly as a guest would behave in the private home of his host.

UNBREAKABLE RULES

Failure to pay one's debts, or behavior unbefitting a gentleman, is cause for expulsion from every club, a disgrace that is looked upon in much the same light as a dishonorable discharge from the Armed Forces. In certain cases expulsion for debt may seem unfair, because one may find himself in unexpectedly straitened circumstances, and the greatest fault or crime could scarcely bring down upon a man a more severe penalty than being expelled from his club.

If a man cannot afford to belong to a club, he must resign while he is still in good standing. If later on he is able to rejoin, his name is put at the head of the waiting list; if he was considered a desirable member, he is reelected at the next meeting of the governors. But a man who has been expelled—unless he can show that his expulsion was unjust— can never again belong to that, nor probably can he be elected to any other club, because the fact he has been expelled from one club will almost certainly come up should another club ever consider him for election. And this would cancel his chances for membership.

Membership in a club must never be used as a business asset or introduction. A man's club, like his wife, is not talked about to strangers. A member may, of course, receive his business associates there. But the club must not be brought into publicity, nor must business letters be written on club stationery.

RESIGNING FROM A CLUB

When one wishes to resign from a club, it is necessary to write a letter of resignation to the secretary well before the date the next yearly dues will be due. For an example of such a letter, see page 522.

MEETINGS OF WOMEN'S ORGANIZATIONS

There is hardly a woman in the country today who is not a member of a local club affiliated with a national organization. Although some men may scoff, we all know that these organizations accomplish a great deal of good. But most members of these clubs have discovered that procedural problems can hinder if not halt their work.

If you have been elected president of your club, be sure that you know how to conduct a meeting. Read a good handbook of parliamentary procedure, and take it with you to every meeting. And always remember that the presiding officer should not offer her own opinions in discussion unless she temporarily relinquishes the chair to the vice president, who will then recognize her.

THE CONVENTION DELEGATE

If you have for the first time been chosen to go as a delegate to a national convention, your biggest problem is likely to be about clothes. Don't be overly impressed by the frightening list of sessions and entertainments. To imagine that you must wear a different dress three times a day is nonsense. You can perfectly well wear the same day clothes to every session, and a dressy afternoon dress will probably do for most evenings. However, in almost every hotel pressing is done expertly; therefore don't leave your prettiest dress home because it doesn't pack well.

Be sure to take appropriate clothes for the season and place of the convention. And remember that if your fellow members had any fear of your shortcomings they would not have chosen you to represent them.

ARRANGEMENTS FOR GUEST SPEAKERS

The committee on arrangements should detail a definite usher to each speaker, entertainer, or other guest of honor at each session or entertainment. These ushers should wait at the door of entrance. Each greets her own particular charge and stays beside her or him throughout the meeting—or at least until she or he is seated on the platform or at table.

FLOWERS FOR GUESTS

Corsage bouquets are always presented to the woman guest of
honor at formal luncheons and at banquets. If there are to be any other
women speakers, smaller corsage bouquets should be put at their places
because it is rather slighting to see one person—no matter how prominent—covered with flowers, and others with none. Before choosing the
bouquet for the guest of honor, someone on the committee should ask
her what colors she is going to wear and choose flowers accordingly.
Purple orchids look well with very few colors. Even white gardenias
do not look well with everything; moreover, although to most of us it is
delicious, some people find their perfume oversweet.

PLACE-CARDS

There are place-cards, of course, at the speakers' table, and when
possible it is better that the committee take pains to have place-cards
for all people expected, because a general scramble to sit where one
can find room is apt to be confusing.

LABELS SERVE AS INTRODUCTIONS

At all large conventions it is of great importance that the committee on arrangements supply each member or guest with a badge
plainly displaying her name, home town, and State, so that members
may talk to each other with intelligence. Otherwise, we perhaps make a
remark to Miss or Mrs. Total Blank from Nowhere; instead, we might
be thrilled to find ourselves next to someone with whom we have long
corresponded, or someone whose work we admire, or someone from our
old home, about which we'd like so much to hear. Or, even if we sit
among strangers, labels take the strangeness away and increase fellow-
ship.

IF CALLED UPON TO MAKE A SPEECH

The trite direction for making a speech—as we all know—is to
say what we have to say as clearly and briefly as possible and then
stop!

When you begin to speak, it is in the very worst taste to contradict,
out of flustered embarrassment, the speech of the chairman who graciously introduces you. To say, "I'm afraid the chairman has greatly
exaggerated my abilities," is a very natural impulse of modesty, but
actually is not only discourteous to the chairman but all too seldom
rings true.

After all, if you really thought yourself incapable of saying anything of interest, or winning approval or friendly regard—you certainly
ought not to have agreed to speak! Of course if it really happens that
you are called upon unexpectedly and completely unprepared, you can

in all sincerity say, "I'm sorry, but I'm not a speaker!" and sit down.

If you *are* prepared—or naturally able—to speak, you should bow and smile and THINK (whether or not you say the words): "How *kind* of you to say that."

The delightful speaker is never one who is trying to make an impression or, as a matter of fact, thinking about herself at all, but the one who *is* interested in her subject and eager to interest *you* in it too.

For more details about speech-making, see Chapter 5.

GAMES AND SPORTS

·∘[47]∘·

THE POPULARITY OF "BRIDGE WHIST" BEGAN ALMOST three-quarters of a century ago and has increased slowly but steadily until it is scarcely an exaggeration to say that those who do not play the current form of bridge or contract are, in many communities, seldom asked out in many circles. And the epidemic is just as widespread among girls and boys as among older people.

CARD PLAYERS, PLEASANT AND UNPLEASANT

That no one likes a poor partner—or even a poor opponent—goes without saying.

The ideal partner is one who never criticizes or seems even to be aware of your mistakes, even though you trump his ace; on the contrary, he recognizes a good maneuver on your part, is pleased over a clever finesse, and gives you credit for it whether you win the hand or lose. The inferior player is likely to judge you merely by what you win, and blame your "make" if you "go down," though your play may have been exceptionally good, and the loss occasioned by wrong information which he himself gave you. To be continually found fault with makes you play your worst, whereas appreciation of your good judgment acts like a tonic, and you play seemingly better than you know how to.

Nothing more quickly reveals the veneered gentleman than the card table, and his veneer melts equally with success or failure. Being carried away by the game, he forgets to keep on his company polish. If he wins, he becomes grasping or overbearing because of his skill; if he loses, he complains constantly about the cards he has been holding and sneers at the luck of others.

A trick that is annoying to moderately skilled players is to have an overconfident opponent (who usually is a better player than they are) throw down his hand, saying, "The rest of the tricks are mine!" Often it is quite possible that they might not have been his if the hand had been played out. Knowing themselves to be poorer players, the others are not likely to challenge the move, even though they feel that their rights have been taken away.

A rather trying partner is the nervous player who has no confidence in his own judgment and will invariably pass a good hand in favor of his partner's bid. If, for instance, he has six perfectly good diamonds, he doesn't mention them because, his partner having declared a heart, he thinks to himself, "Her hearts must be better than my diamonds, and if I have to play the hand I'll probably butcher it." But a much more serious failing—and one that is far more common—is the habit of over-bidding.

OVERBIDDING

In poker you play alone and can therefore play as carefully or as recklessly as you please; but in contract bridge your partner has to suffer with you, and you therefore are in honor bound to play a sound game—the best you know how—and the best you know how will surely keep you from overbidding more than very occasionally indeed.

Remember that your partner, if he is a good player, counts on you for certain definite cards that you announce by your bid to be in your hand, and raises you accordingly. If you do not have these cards, you not only lose that particular hand, but destroy your partner's confidence in you, and the next time, when he has a legitimate raise for you, he will fail to give it. He disregards you entirely because he is afraid of you! *You must study the rules for makes and never under any circumstances give your partner misinformation.* This is the most vital rule there is, and anyone who disregards it is detested at the bridge table, or for that matter at any game. No matter how great the temptation to make a gambler's or what is sometimes called a psychic bid, don't do it!

The next essential, if you would be thought charming, is never to take your partner to task, no matter how stupidly he may have "thrown the hand."

DON'TS FOR THOSE WHO WOULD BE SOUGHT AFTER

Don't hold a post-mortem on anybody's delinquencies, unless you are actually teaching.

If luck is against you, it will avail you nothing to sulk or complain about the awful cards you have been holding. Your partner is suffering just as much in finding you a "poison vine" as you are, in being one— and you can scarcely expect your opponents to be sympathetic. You must learn to look perfectly tranquil and cheerful even though you hold nothing but poor cards for days on end, and you must on no account try to defend your own bad play. When you have made a play of poor judgment, the best thing you can say is, "I'm very sorry, partner," and let it go at that.

Always pay close attention to the game. When you are dummy, you have certain duties to your partner, and so do not wander around the room or look into your opponents' hands. If you don't know what your duties are, read the rules until you know them by heart and then— begin all over again! It is impossible to play any game without a thorough knowledge of the rules that govern it.

Don't be offended if your partner takes you out of a bid, and don't take him out for the glory of playing the hand. He is quite as anxious to win the rubber as you are. It is unbelievable how many people really seem to regard their partners as third opponents.

ANNOYING MANNERISMS

Mannerisms must be avoided like the plague. If there is one thing worse than the horrible post-mortem, it is the incessant repetition of some jarring habit by one particular player. The most usual and most offensive is that of snapping down a card as played, or bending a trick one has taken into a letter "U," or picking it up and trotting it up and down on the table.

Other pet offenses are drumming on the table with one's fingers, making various clicking, whistling, or humming sounds, massaging one's face, scratching one's chin with the cards, or holding the card one is going to play aloft in the air in Smart Alec fashion as though shouting, "I know what you are going to lead! And my card is ready!" All mannerisms that attract attention are unpleasant—and in the long run even unendurable—to one's companions.

Many people whose game is otherwise admirable are rarely asked to play because they have some such silly and annoying habit.

THE GOOD LOSER AT CARDS

The good loser makes it an invariable rule never to play for stakes that it will be inconvenient to lose. The neglect of this rule has been responsible for more bad losers than anything else, and needless to say a bad loser is about as welcome at a game table as rain at a championship tennis match.

Of course there *are* people who can take losses beyond their means with perfect cheerfulness and composure. Some few are so imbued with the gambler's instinct that a heavy turn of luck, in either direction, is the salt of life. But the average person is equally embarrassed in winning or losing a stake that matters and the only answer is always to play only for what one can easily afford.

A THOUGHTFUL HOSTESS PROTECTS HER GUESTS

There is one point of consideration which every hostess owes her guests: protection from being forced into playing for stakes which can embarrass them. Giving a guest a chance to decline her invitation beforehand is really much more important in the case of a man than in the case of a woman. A woman usually feels free to say, "I'm sorry, but I never play for more than so much." But a man sometimes feels that his refusal is an embarrassing confession of financial failure—a position into which no hostess of good breeding would ever put him. If people coming to her house, for instance, are known to play together, nothing need be said; but if strangers are invited to play with others who play for certain stakes, the hostess should say when she invites them, "The Smiths and Browns and Robinsons are coming. They all play for a cent. Is that all right?" The one invited can either say, "I'm sorry. I don't play for money," or "My limit is a tenth of a cent," or "They must be way out of my class! Do ask me again when you are having people who play for less."

There is one hardship sometimes met in certain communities of the very well-to-do: The more expert players set stakes that bar one who plays a first-class game but has a small income from meeting first-class opponents. This, however, applies only to those who want to play with those who rank as top class. Further down the scale, stakes grow smaller and parties with prizes instead of stakes more numerous. Often three who play for high stakes will carry a fourth who plays for less because they like to play with him or her. The three then share that part of the winnings or losses of the fourth which are in excess of what they would have been had the game been played at the fourth's usual low stake.

THE POOR PLAYER WHO INSISTS ON PLAYING

The poor player who thrusts himself into a game made up of good players is the one worst annoyance that the good player—especially in a game such as bridge—must endure. The inexpert bridge player will unperceivingly spoil evening after evening for three other players, blandly believing that his habitual losses are due merely to his bad luck. Of course, the best player can have a long run of poor cards, but the player who persistently loses about twice as much as he wins would be wise—and more popular—if he took accurate stock of his game instead of fixing his attention on the fickleness of luck. For further details about bridge stakes, bridge prizes, and bridge parties, see the Index.

GOLF

Golf is a particularly severe strain upon the amiability of the average person, and in no other game, except probably bridge, is serenity of disposition so essential. No one who is easily ruffled can keep a clear eye on the ball, and exasperation at lost balls seemingly bewitches successive ones into disappearing like puffs of smoke. In a race or other test of endurance a flare of anger might even help, but in golf it is safe to say that he who loses his temper is pretty sure to muff his shot and to lose the game.

Golf players, of course, know the rules and observe them; but it quite often happens that idlers, having nothing better to do, walk out over a course and watch the players. If they know the players well, that is one thing; but they have no right to follow strangers. A player who is diffident is easily put off his game, especially if those watching him are so ill-bred as to make audible remarks. Those playing matches of course expect an audience; and erratic and nervous players ought not to go into tournaments—and certainly not into two-ball foursomes where they will handicap a partner.

In following a match, onlookers must be careful to stand well back of the play and neither talk nor laugh nor even move when a player is addressing his or her ball.

The rule that you should not appoint yourself mentor holds good in golf as well as in bridge and every other game. Unless your advice is asked for, you should not tell another player what he did wrong on a certain shot, nor give him advice on what club to use, or how to play the next shot.

A young woman must on no account expect the man she happens to be playing with to provide her with golf balls or to caddy for her, nor must she allow him to pay for her caddy. If she can't afford to hire her own, she must carry her clubs herself.

OTHER GAMES AND SPORTS

There are fixed rules for the playing of every game—and for proper conduct in every sport. The details of these rules must be studied in the books of the game, learned from instructors, or acquired by experience. A small boy perhaps learns to fish or swim by himself, but he is probably taught by his father or a guide how and how not to hold a gun, cast a fly, or ride a horse. But apart from the technique of each sport, or the rules of each game, the basic principles of good sportsmanship are always the same.

In no sport or game can any evasion of rules be allowed. Sport is based upon an impersonal and indiscriminating enforcement of all rules on everyone alike.

SPORTSMANSHIP

The training schools for sportsmanship are three: first, easiest and best, the nursery; secondly, school and college; thirdly, the adult school of competitive tournaments. Heart-break School the latter might be called, because a young man or woman is often irrevocably broken and labeled "yellow" when lack of knowledge, not weakness of character, is the sole cause.

The quality which perhaps more than any other distinguishes true sportsmanship is absence of any show of temper. It should not be temper brought along and held in check, but temper securely locked and left at home. The usually accepted pattern of a sportsman is the stoic who never by expression or gesture betrays either satisfaction or chagrin. Although this type of player is by all means the one which every beginner should emulate, he is admirable but not supreme, nor will he ever be a hero to the spectators who follow his games. Stoicism is often a means, not an end. The imperfect sportsman, whether he has traits of character that he cannot otherwise control, or whether he is a child or novice at the sport and still uncertain of his own reactions, learns that stoicism is the rule of safety.

The perfect sportsman meets every situation with easy grace. In fact, only when a player's long-tested impulses can be trusted to take care of themselves does he attain to such inbred serenity that he can seemingly break all fundamental rules. He shows chagrin; he shows elation, but only for the briefest moment and always with a smile. The onlookers always choose him their favorite because he is "human." Every now and then his expression lights with a quick smile, a distinctly happy grin, or creases into a grimace at a bit of bad luck or a bungled play. There is no reason whatever why a player may not on occasions smile, unless the smile broadens into triumphant affront or verges on the smugness of conceit. When he wins, he takes his satisfaction lightly or perhaps the better term is transiently. If he loses, he takes it good-naturedly—and still more transiently. Furthermore, when the game is over, the subject is finished. And why he won or lost, or how he felt or played, is not to be talked about.

It is entirely proper, even advisable, for the tournament player to win popularity if he can. One often notices that a player does almost better than he knows how to when the public is cheeringly friendly—no champagne is equal to it. On the other hand, silence for himself and cheering for his adversary are quite as real a handicap as extra pounds strapped upon his back—a weight that every player must at least sometimes steel himself to bear.

For the benefit of those who seem to believe that a man is rated a good sport because he spends money freely, it should be stated clearly that they have confused the term "sportsman"—one who competes fairly in any contest—with "sporting man," a man of far from admirable habits. A player's reputation as a good sportsman is the one thing that money can *not* buy. Neither by giving away boxes of tennis and golf balls, nor by offering colossal silver cups, nor even by a million-dollar endowment, can the richest man that ever was increase by the thickness of a leaf of beaten gold his rating in sportsmanship.

This bribery impulse of the untutored is met with at every club, except the most exclusive few where his kind are not admitted to membership. Being more or less snubbed by those he wants to impress, he is made gradually aware of the somewhat iced atmosphere that surrounds him. Instead of trying to find out what he has done—and is undoubtedly continuing to do—to induce this chilling atmosphere, he attempts to buy the approval of players, or directors, or critics with the impulse of a savage who believes that a string of beads can make friends.

As a matter of fact, an admirable sportsman is merely one who can be counted on to play and to behave like a gentleman.

FRANKNESS OF TODAY

A young man playing tennis with a young girl, just learning the game, a generation ago would have been forced patiently to toss her gentle balls and keep his boredom to himself; or he would have held her chin in his hand, while he himself stood shivering for hours in three feet of water, and tried his best to disguise his opinion as to the hopelessness of her ever learning to swim.

Today he would frankly tell her she had better play tennis for a year or two with a marker or take swimming lessons from the instructors at the beach, lake, or pool. And any sensible girl takes that advice!

RULES OF SPORTSMANSHIP

After all, if you can't take sports with grace and good temper, don't go in for them. Cursing out your faults or your luck, excusing, complaining, protesting against unfairness, won't get you anywhere—except in wrong. You win or you lose; that is all there is to it! To throw down your clubs or racket in temper is to throw down your chances of ever holding them again without penalty. Never to display ill-humor is the first rule of sportsmanship.

The second rule is always to give your opponent the benefit of the doubt! Nothing is more important to your standing as a sportsman, though the loss of the particular point in question may seem very important at that moment. Never argue with the umpire. If he rules a line ball on the tennis court is out, it is out, and do not turn toward the spectators with an expression that says, "See how unfairly I am being treated!"

Among the lesser shortcomings of an unsportsmanlike player is his practice of understating his ability before a match. It is not necessary to point out the lack of fair play of this procedure before the handicaps are given out; but it is a commonplace occurrence to hear from a man who is perfectly satisfied with his skill, "I am not much of a player," or "I know I'll make a poor showing; I've got a 'bad' arm!" The motive is not necessarily dishonest—though on many occasions it is difficult to see it as anything else—but is often a show-off impulse to create admiring surprise should he play brilliantly on the one hand and on the other to save face should his game be off. The only time a player may declare himself unskilled is when he really is and would otherwise be a source of annoyance in a game beyond his class.

For instance: A poor player, upon being invited by experts to make the fourth, whether at tennis, or golf, or bridge, refuses, saying, "Thank you, but I don't play well enough." If the experts persist, because no other fourth is available, the poor player says nothing further, either then or later. He does his bungling best, and that is all there is to that—except that he must never himself volunteer to play with them again. If they invite him, he can, if he cares to, accept, and because they know how he plays, he says nothing.

One last and earnestly urged "Don't" is the loser's practice of complaining of illness after having lost a match. This is one real flaw in many a woman's sportsmanship. "I had such a pain in my side (or knee, or back) that I don't know how I ever got through the match!" is heard so frequently that one consciously resists the temptation to taunt every woman loser, "I'm *sure*, poor dear, you were in such pain you could not see the ball!"

Sportsmanship can be very well acquired by following a few simple rules. Keep your mind on the game, but not on your feelings. If you win, don't at once begin to fancy yourself a star in the firmament. A gloating winner is detested even more than a bad loser. But when you lose, don't sulk, or protest, or long-windedly explain. If you are hurt, whether in mind or body, don't nurse your bruises. Get up and light-heartedly, courageously, good-temperedly get ready for the next encounter. This is playing the game—and the only successful way to take life!

MANNERS AND MOTORISTS

·◦[48]◦·

JOHN CITIZEN IS COURTEOUS IN ALL HIS DAILY CONTACTS
with people, but becomes suddenly transformed into a bad-mannered
autocrat when he is driving his car, particularly his *new* car!

SOCIAL RATING—BY CAR VALUE

Is it because, by virtue of the highly reputable make of his car and
its horsepower, he feels that he has become automatically the equal of
every owner of a similar car, and the superior of the owners of all cars
of less importance? One wonders. Is this importance—according to the
car—perhaps the reason why so often the man in moderate circumstances will stint himself in every way to buy a car actually beyond his
means, thus to gratify his desire to go one better than his neighbor?

GOOD AND BAD DRIVERS

There is another effect that ownership of a high-priced car produces upon John Citizen: It makes him believe that his rating as a great
driver is above question. Really fine drivers do exist, and very good ones
are not uncommon; and, moreover, both of these are fully aware of their
own expertness. But this chapter is certainly not for either of these, but
for the tens of thousands who in ever-increasing numbers swarm out
upon the highways to have their lives saved time and again (though
they don't know it) by the experts who step in between the Grim
Reaper and the bad driver. And if we think seriously of the power in all
of these machines running freely upon our streets and roads and realize
that no examination in driving courtesy is required of one applying for
a license, the wonder is not that there are accidents, but that there are
not more.

BAD ROAD MANNERS CAUSE ACCIDENTS

Of course the type of driver who ought to be given a nice long time
to think it over in jail is the one who, when the road is crowded, pulls

out of a solid line of cars to steal his way forward. Finding himself in sudden danger of a head-on collision, he makes a frantic effort to push his way back into the line he has left—possibly forcing someone off the side of the road, or at the least marring fenders. Or perhaps the newspapers carry one more story of a fatal motor crash—caused by the bad manners of a driver who shoves to get ahead, tries to beat the lights, crowds another off the road, never considering anybody's rights but his own.

THE DRIVER'S SEAT CAN BREED BAD MANNERS

It is hard to understand, but nevertheless quite true, that these same drivers are under other circumstances perfectly behaved people. The man who tried to force his way ahead of the line of cars would not think of trying to force his way ahead of others in a box-office queue; nor would he shove a fellow pedestrian off the sidewalk. Or should he by unhappy accident do such a thing, he would be abject in his apology, mortified by his own rudeness. But in his car, with a firm palm pressed on the horn, he is quite likely to swear roundly at his victim for getting in his way.

DRINK AND DRIVING

It is unnecessary to emphasize the menace of the drunken driver; certainly there is nothing to be said in his defense, nor can anyone want him to escape the full penalty of the law. And furthermore, not half enough emphasis is laid on the exhilarated driver who has had one or two cocktails and certainly cannot be called drunk by any standard but who with overjoyful recklessness takes chances that he would not think of taking when he has had nothing to drink. Alcohol and gasoline do not mix!

THE SNAIL

In contrast to the dangerous driver might be noted the annoying snail—long known by other unflattering sobriquets because of his insistence upon crawling along in the mid-center of the road, or on the left, or in the passing lane of a four-lane highway. Behind him horns can blow but he does not budge an inch. Or if he does, beware of his pet trick of starting for his proper side and then not going there but right back, so that the passing car is forced to brake so suddenly that he risks being rammed by a third car whose driver is not expecting him to jerk to a stop. And yet this same snail, when he is walking on the street, does not refuse to let another pass him by. Needless to say, courtesy demands of one who likes to crawl that he stay far over on the right side to let faster cars go by; and if he won't, there ought to be a special truck of largest size detailed to push him—and keep him pushed.

MR. MILQUETOAST CAN BE A MENACE

Timid Caspar Milquetoast, seeking safety, drives at ten miles below the speed limit on a narrow, twisting road through hilly country and accumulates a long line of impatient drivers behind him. These in their exasperation end by taking desperate chances in passing him when too close to a curve or the top of a hill, and the net result is that Caspar is much more likely to be involved in a serious crash than if he were to drive a little faster and not exasperate a line of car drivers behind him.

HEADLIGHT MENACE

At night a not only annoying but also dangerous driver to meet is one who will not dim his headlights, although knowing perfectly well that other drivers facing him are helplessly blinded by the glare of his lights in their eyes.

ADVICE TO A NOVICE DRIVER

A certain driver whose rating is at the very top told a novice, whom he was teaching, to keep the idea firmly fixed in mind that every car he had to pass or meet was being driven by a fool. At the time, the pupil thought this remark exaggerated. But since then he has realized that it is the very best possible advice on driving, because trusting to the other man's quickness and skill to get out of the way, or to understand an erratic signal, or worst of all a sudden change of mind, is a most prolific cause of accidents. This driver did not mean that all others were really fools, but that one must think so in order to realize that the responsibility was entirely one's own, and that one could not depend on another to save him from the consequences of his own foolish driving.

And this means not only paying attention to what you are doing but remembering to tell others what you intend to do. In short, don't take it for granted that the driver of the car behind you is psychic and able to guess what you are going to do, unless you signal to him with sufficient distinctness and deliberation. To jab your hand out as though it were a hen pecking and draw it quickly in again is scarcely enlightening. And whatever you do, don't let the man behind you think you are going to do one thing and then change your mind. Of course, there is always the contingency of the countless drivers who disregard signals and heedlessly dash forward.

SIGNALS

Practically all cars now have an automatic stop light to warn a following car when the brake pedal is depressed. Cars built in recent years have, also, electric directional signals which permit a driver to indicate the direction in which he is going to turn. It is up to all drivers to get the habit of invariably using these signals.

A point to emphasize is that hand signals unfortunately still differ in different localities. This in spite of the approval by the President's Highway Safety Conference in 1947 of the system of signals specified in a proposed "Uniform Act Regulating Traffic on the Highways." This requires that signals be made with the left hand and arm. Before making a left turn the hand and arm are extended horizontally; before a right turn they are extended upward; and before a stop or even a decrease of speed they are extended downward.

Gradually more and more people are learning and using these signals. Therefore use them! It is however just as important to get over into the right-hand lane before making a right turn or into the left or center lane before turning to the left.

AVOID FALSE SIGNALS

This means, don't put your arm down outside the car and shake ashes off your cigarette. Don't put your hand out when you throw away your cigar. Don't put your hand out and point at the scenery, and don't let anyone else in your car wave his hand out of a window. All these actions only confound drivers of cars that follow.

STOP LIGHT

Although you have a stop light, remember that it does not go on until your brakes are applied; therefore, put your hand out the moment you know you intend to apply the brakes.

DISCOURTEOUS HORN BLOWERS

Trumpet horns—those raucous, penetrating signals designed for use on the open road—are as out of place in city driving as hobnailed shoes in a ballroom. Another impoliteness is the unnecessary blowing of any horn in a traffic line when it can do no good and is merely annoying to others.

The sounding of a horn at pedestrians caught midstreet by a changing light is not only unkind, but may even cause the pedestrian to jump into the path of another car.

If more people realized that the horn, as the voice of the car, is in reality the voice of the driver, there would be less raucous thoughtlessness in its use. People who would never dream of bawling a vocal protest at a moment's delay blast away on their motor horns at every hesitancy of the car ahead. No young man of good taste would announce his arrival to a lovely lady by standing at the curb outside her door and yoo-hooing. Yet this is the identical offense which so many commit who, arriving by car, sit at the wheel and blast away at the horn. A well-mannered visitor will of course alight and ring the bell.

CITY DRIVING MANNERS

When driving in a city, remember that discourtesy to pedestrians can turn out to be manslaughter. Don't rush traffic lights; that is, don't start suddenly in the no-light interval before your light has changed to green and possibly frighten pedestrians or find yourself in a collision with a crossing car whose driver has been slow in stopping. A gentleman will no more cheat the lights than cheat at cards. Don't fail, at a crossing where the lights have turned against you, to stop far enough back to be sure that you are not blocking the proper path of pedestrians crossing the street. Don't, if you can possibly help it, run through puddles and splash pedestrians or other cars, and if you cannot avoid a puddle, at least slow down as much as possible. Don't almost run over someone who is trying to signal a bus or a trolley car when a little consideration requires only a few seconds. Courteous drivers should, before starting on the green light, give pedestrians who are caught in the middle of the roadway a chance to get across. Be sure to avoid starting with a jerk to pass an elderly woman. Instead of hastening her, fright is likely to root her to the spot. Be sure to slow down to a crawl when you see a sign, "School Crossing." You simply cannot tell when a moppet might appear out of the blue.

DRIVERS WE LIKE—AND DISLIKE

The best test of a perfect driver is that with him you never find yourself driving the car. When you see a passenger involuntarily tensing his muscles and pressing his own feet on an imaginary control, this evidence subtracts by just so much from the driver's rating. Certainly the outstanding characteristic of an abominable driver is that of showing no courtesy to his passengers at all, almost jerking their heads off every time he stops, scaring them half to death, and frequently getting into a position that makes the next move he should have been preparing for impossible.

We are all made nervous by the driver who keeps looking out all the time, expatiating on the view and paying no apparent attention to what is happening on the road. Or the one who turns around to talk to those on the back seat (who can't hear what he says because they are so busy praying that the car will stay on the road). Or the one who carelessly lets go of the wheel while he lights a cigarette or tries to get a new station on the radio, meanwhile letting his car meander toward the ditch or else cut over toward the wrong side of the road.

Another bad-mannered driver is the one in a hurry. Among the thousands of car accidents listed on the police blotters, at least half are said to be made by people who have not learned to discipline themselves to be on time. The driver, suddenly becoming conscious that he should have left home earlier, flings his good driving manners to the wind, starts weaving in and out of lines, clipping red lights, pushing his way, and taking chances which he would never take if he were not in a hurry!

CERTAIN BAD MANNERS OF WOMEN DRIVERS

There are, of course, thousands of women drivers who are on every count first-class, but there are certain others who deserve all the criticism that can be given them. Among the worst of these should be put the window-shopper, who crawls along a crowded thoroughfare with her gaze fastened upon the store windows.

A not unfamiliar sight, in smaller towns, are the stop-to-talkers who park side by side and hold long conversations while other cars wait or maneuver their way past the blockade as best they can. There is no reason why Cissy Chatter may not talk with Penny Prattle as long as she chooses, but one of them must draw over close to the curb and wait. The other must park her car in a proper place and then come back to the first car, and either stand on the sidewalk or get into the car.

DRIVING SPORTSMANSHIP

The good sportsmanship of all well-bred drivers is indicated in the following exactions:

It is just as unfair and unsporting to lag when the traffic light turns green (holding up the cars behind you) as to beat the light by starting while it is still red.

The fair-minded driver, if driving slowly, keeps well over to the right so that another, who may be anxious to get somewhere, may overtake him safely. When making turns, it is not much to ask of a driver to turn the steering wheel enough to enable him to stay on the right when he turns right and on the left when he turns left. The boorish driver who swings to the left before a right turn, and vice versa, shows plainly a person so selfish or lazy that he would rather risk his own and the following driver's life, than turn the steering wheel the little extra required to make the sharper turn from the proper lane.

Well-bred people neither monopolize space for two parked cars nor park so close to others that they are prevented from pulling out. In marked parking places, well-bred people stay within the marks.

It shows thoughtfulness to slow up a little and let a car, whose driver has been trying to join the unbroken line of cars you are in, come into the line ahead of you from a side road.

AS TO THE MANNERS OF PEDESTRIANS

When anyone is run over by an automobile, the driver's guilt is *invariably* taken for granted. Often the blame belongs to him, but often again it does not. In other words, motor manners are every bit as important to those who want to escape being injured as to those who want to avoid injuring them. First rules for pedestrians include:

Don't cross before the light turns green. Don't cross streets in the middle of a block. Don't dart forward after hiding behind a parked car and imagine that an oncoming driver, whom you yourself could not see, could know by means of clairvoyance that you were there! Don't, when the lights change while you are in the middle of the street, turn and run back to the side you started from. If you keep on going exactly as you were, drivers will automatically wait and give you time to pass in front of their cars. But not one of those you have already passed can possibly be prepared to have you about-face and suddenly dash back again in front of his wheels.

WHEN YOU WALK ON A ROAD

One of the serious causes of automobile accidents is the practically universal (and a very natural) habit of walking on the right side of a quiet country road.

This habit, obviously acquired from the correctness of this position on a sidewalk, is a not infrequent cause of accidents as well as annoying delays to car drivers. A pedestrian on the right side cannot see a car overtaking him. If another car is coming from the other direction, the pedestrian unfortunately stays on his right-hand half of the road, directly in the path of the unseen or unheard overtaking car. Pedestrians should walk on the left-hand side of the road.

THE CODE OF A GENTLEMAN

⋅⋅◦[49]◦⋅⋅

IN A BOOK SUCH AS THIS, IT IS IMPOSSIBLE WITHOUT USING
the often abused words lady and gentleman to make any directions clear.
For instance, to say that a man never beats a woman is to invite many
to say that the statement is untrue, but no one will question the truth
of saying that a gentleman never beats a woman. The qualifications of
a gentleman are definite; those of a man mean no more than that he is
a male of the human species. A man may be fine, he may be vile; but
when you call him a gentleman, it means he has the qualifications of
one.

Far more important than any mere dictum of etiquette is the fundamental code of honor, without strict observance of which no man, no
matter how polished, can be considered a gentleman. The honor of a
gentleman demands the inviolability of his word, and the incorrupti-
bility of his principles.

DECENCIES OF BEHAVIOR

A gentleman does not, and a man who aspires to be one must not,
borrow money from a friend other than in exceptional circumstances,
and money so borrowed must be returned promptly. All money borrowed without security is a debt of honor which must be paid without
fail and as promptly as possible. The debts incurred by a deceased parent, brother, sister, or even a child are assumed by honorable men and
women as debts of honor.

One who is not well off does not sponge, but pays his own way to
the utmost of his *ability*.

One who is rich does not make a display of his money or his possessions. Only a vulgarian talks ceaselessly about how much this or that
cost him.

A well-bred man intensely dislikes the mention of money and never
speaks of it (out of business hours) if he can avoid it.

A gentleman never discusses his family affairs either in public or

589

with acquaintances, nor does he speak more than casually about his wife.

Nor does a gentleman ever show awareness of the bad behavior of his wife, even though it be scandalous. What he says to her in the privacy of their own apartment is no one's affair but his own, but he must never treat her with disrespect before their children, or a servant, or anyone else.

It has for generations been an exaction of best society that no gentleman goes to a lady's house if he has had too much to drink.

A gentleman calls upon his self-control under difficult or dangerous circumstances. Exhibitions of anger, fear, hatred, embarrassment, ardor, or hilarity are all bad form in public.

A gentleman does not show a letter written by a lady.

A man whose social position is newly self-made is likely to be detected by his continual cataloging of prominent names—name-dropping it is nowadays called. Mr. Parvenu invariably interlards his conversation with, "When I was dining at the Bob Gildings' " or even "at Lucy Gilding's," and quite often glories, in his ignorance, in those of rather second-rate though conspicuous position. "I was spending last week-end with the Richan Vulgars" or "My great friends, the Gotta Crusts." When a so-called gentleman insists on imparting information that is of interest only to the Social Register, *shun him!*

A gentleman never boasts about his friends or connections.

A gentleman's manners are an integral part of him and are the same whether in his dressing room or in a ballroom, whether in talking to Mrs. Worldly, or to the laundress bringing in his clothes. He whose manners are put on only in company is merely a veneered gentleman.

A man of breeding does not slap strangers on the back nor even so much as lay his fingertips on a lady. Nor does he punctuate his conversation by pushing, or nudging, or patting people, nor take his conversation out of the drawing-room!

All thoroughbred people are considerate of the feelings of others no matter what the station of the others may be. Thackeray's climber, who "licks the boots of those above him and kicks the faces of those below him on the social ladder," is a very good illustration of what a gentleman is *not*.

A gentleman never takes advantage of another's helplessness or ignorance and assumes that no gentleman will take advantage of him. And lastly, a gentleman not only respects the reserves of others, but demands that others respect those which are his.

SIMPLICITY AND UNCONSCIOUSNESS OF SELF

These words have been liberally sprinkled through the pages of this book, yet it is doubtful that they convey a clear idea of the attributes meant.

Unconsciousness of self is not so much unselfishness as it is the mental ability to extinguish all thought of oneself—exactly as one turns out the light.

Simplicity is like it, in that it also has a quality of self-effacement, but it really means a love of the essential and of directness. Simple people put no trimmings on their phrases nor on their manners. But remember—simplicity is not crudeness nor anything like it. On the contrary, simplicity of speech and manners means language in its purest, most limpid form, and manners of such perfection that they do not suggest "manner" at all.

THE INSTINCTS OF A LADY

The code of a lady of honor is much the same as that of a gentleman. She is equally punctilious about her debts, equally averse to pressing her advantage, especially if her adversary is helpless or poor.

As an unhappy wife, her dignity demands that she never show her disapproval of her husband, no matter how publicly he slights or outrages her. If she has been so unfortunate as to marry a man not a gentleman, to draw attention to his behavior would put herself on his level. If it comes actually to the point where she divorces him, she discusses her situation, naturally, with her parents, or her brother, or whoever are her nearest and wisest relatives, and of course her lawyer. But she shuns publicity, and avoids discussing her affairs with anyone outside her immediate family. One cannot too strongly censure the unspeakable vulgarity of the woman who confides to reporters the details of her private life.

ONE SURE SIGN OF A CLIMBER

Nothing more blatantly proclaims a climber—man as well as woman—than the repetition of prominent names, the owners of which she must have struggled to know. Otherwise, why so eagerly boast of the achievement? Nobody cares whom she knows—nobody, that is, but a climber like herself. Perhaps they live to swap names back and forth to see which can outbrag the other. To those who were born and who live, no matter how quietly, in the security of a perfectly good ledge above and away from the social ladder's rungs, the evidence of one frantically climbing and vaunting an exalted position is merely ludicrous.

All thoroughbred men and women are considerate of others less fortunately placed. One of the tests by which to distinguish between the woman of breeding and the woman merely of wealth is the way she speaks to dependents. Queen Victoria's duchesses, those great ladies of grand manner, were the very ones who, on entering the house of an intimate friend, said, "How do you do, Hawkins?" to a butler, and to a sister duchess' maid, "Good morning, Jenkins." A Maryland lady, still living on the estate granted to her family three generations before the Revolution, is quite as polite to her friends' servants as to her friends themselves. When you see a woman in mink and diamonds speak to a little errand girl or any other untrained helper as though they were the dirt under her feet, you may be sure of one thing: she hasn't come a very long way from the ground herself.

THE EXPERIENCED TRAVELER

⋅⋅⊰[50]⊱⋅⋅

TO DO NOTHING THAT CAN EITHER ANNOY OR OFFEND THE sensibilities of others is the principal rule of conduct, abroad as well as at home. In order to neither annoy nor offend, it is necessary for us to consider the point of view of those with whom we come in contact; when traveling we should know something of the customs which determine the foreign point of view, if we would be thought cultivated and charming instead of boorish and objectionable. The best way to learn about the customs of other lands is also the best way to plan a trip· read books about the people and places you intend to visit.

BASIC ADVICE TO ALL TRAVELERS

No matter how you are traveling or for how long, your luggage should be neat and compact. There is no excuse for bags that look as if they'd been with you on a ten-year safari, since durable and light-weight luggage is available at moderate cost. Nothing looks worse or makes a traveler so uncomfortable as broken-down bags and numerous bundles.

TRAIN TRAVEL

In a dining-car on a day's journey—especially on the Atlantic seaboard—you do not usually speak to your companion at table, beyond a possible "May I have the salt, please?" But in a country hotel or on a transcontinental journey, if you happen to sit next to the same person for a number of meals, it is extremely snobbish and bad-mannered to sit in wooden silence.

During the day in a Pullman section, the seat which faces forward belongs to the occupant of the lower berth; the occupant of the upper berth rides backward. It would be an act of courtesy for the lady who has the right to the seat facing forward to ask her companion whether she minds riding backward—and if she does, to make a place at her side. The window seat would naturally belong to her—unless she prefers the other.

GOING TO BED IN A PULLMAN

Whether you have a drawing-room, compartment, or bedroom, a roomette, section, or berth, you ring for the porter to make up your berth when you are ready to go to bed. If you have a roomette, drawing-room, compartment, or bedroom, you shut your door and go to bed. In every variety of room, all dressing facilities are included so that you do not go to the public dressing room at all. If, however, your berth is in the open car, you finish for the night in the dressing room while the porter makes up your bed. This is especially necessary if you have an upper berth, so that when you have gone up the stepladder the porter brings for you, you will not have to come down again. In the morning when you want to get down, you ring the bell inside your berth and ask for the stepladder. You dress as much as you can in your berth, because there is no privacy—and less space—in the dressing room. Try to limit the number of items you take to the dressing room.

IF YOU MUST TAKE THE CHILDREN

If you can possibly avoid it, do not travel with very small children. If it is necessary, try to maintain their regular schedule of meals, naps, and bedtime.

Any number of people not only let small children on trains eat continuously so that the car is filled with food odors, but some mothers have been known to let a child with smeary fingers clutch a nearby passenger by the dress or coat and seemingly think it cunning! Those few who are sufficiently well-to-do usually take a drawing-room or a compartment and keep the children in it. Those who are to travel in coaches should take especial pains to plan diversions for the children ahead of time; it is unreasonable to expect little children to sit quietly for hours on end and just "be good." But don't let them race up and down the aisles.

Two little girls on the train to Washington the other day were crocheting dolls' sweaters with balls of worsted in which "prizes" were wound. The amount of wool covering each might take perhaps half an hour to use up. They were allowed the prize only when the last strand of wool around it was used. They were then occupied for a while with a new object—a little book, then a puzzle, then a game. When they grew tired of its novelty, they crocheted again until they came to the next prize. In the end they also had new garments for their dolls.

TRAVEL BY AIRPLANE

Airplanes leave their airports—weather permitting—with the regularity of trains and ships. General rules of courtesy are, of course, the same in a plane as in a Pullman or bus.

It is wise to make your reservations well in advance, for space on a plane is limited. If you are obliged to cancel the trip, sufficient notice should be given to allow someone else to obtain the cancelled seat. Popular flights often have a list of stand-bys.

Some airlines which operate tourist travel have a cancellation charge of twenty percent of the fare if space is cancelled less than three hours before departure.

Tourist ships are less expensive than first-class passage. The equipment is the same, but the service is limited. There are fewer stewardesses aboard and no complimentary meals are served aloft with the possible exception of sandwiches and a cup of coffee.

On a plane you are rarely given a seat number as in a Pullman. The space sold you assures you that a chair or a berth will be reserved for you. Passengers assemble in the airport and are escorted to the plane, after having their luggage weighed, their tickets validated, and other formalities attended to, unless this has already been done at an air terminal before taking a bus to the airport. On boarding the plane if you are the first comer you have the first choice of a seat. You must not, however, claim one which has a card marked "occupied" on it, for this indicates that it belongs to an earlier-arriving passenger who has temporarily left the plane. To hold your place at future stops, ask the stewardess for a similar card. Usually there is one in the pocket in front of your seat for your convenience.

The especial consideration for the feelings of others which shows itself in a general spirit of friendliness among the passengers is so characteristic of air travel that it has, in fact, brought about certain newly accepted rules of traveling etiquette. The on-the-ground custom of paying no attention to fellow travelers is not observed in the air. Those who are willing to talk—and in a plane nearly all are—are entirely free to do so. On the other hand, one who wishes to be left alone can avoid conversation with the explanation, "I'd rather not talk, I'm very tired," which is never resented.

A FEW AIR TRAVEL DETAILS

There are a few ways in which travel by plane is different from travel by train.

When the sign flashes on to "Fasten Seat Belts," do so promptly. The stewardess has to check on each passenger. Also be prompt in obeying the "No Smoking" sign when it is flashed on. Only cigarette smoking is permitted in planes.

No animals are allowed in the cabin of a plane except a Seeing Eye dog. If you wish to take your pet, he must be in a carrier. His weight is counted as part of the amount of luggage you are permitted, and he rides in the luggage compartment.

On most commercial transports service crews consist of stewards and stewardesses. The member of the crew whom you will see most is the stewardess, who is prepared to do everything possible for the passengers' comfort, even to helping mothers with the care of babies or young children. She is not given a tip—ever. In fact tipping is strictly forbidden by airline regulations.

Meals on planes (except tourist) are included in the price of the ticket, and are served by the stewardess or steward. An outstanding Continental airline, for example, true to the tradition of fine French cooking, serves hot course-by-course meals with apéritifs, champagne, and vintage wines included in the bill of fare.

Some airlines provide sleeper service for overnight flights. There is an extra charge for this berth service which varies in amount with the different lines. Berths are assigned at departure time and preference for lower berths is given to women. Breakfast is served in bed for those who wish it.

On an overnight flight, a woman prepares for bed in the "powder-room"—up-in-the-air name for a dressing room. But whatever its name, good manners in it are the same as in the dressing room on a train. When there are many passengers, you must wait patiently for your turn, and when it comes, try to take as short a time as possible—unless you are the last. Even so, you should leave the washstand and the dressing table in perfect order. When you have finished washing, wipe out the basin thoroughly with your used towel, which you then throw into the towel basket. Before combing your hair, lay a fresh towel over the shelf of the dressing mirror. Leave it there until you have finished your hair-do and put on your make-up. Then gather up that towel and throw it into the towel basket. Complete neatness is a first essential of good manners. Never leave any unpleasant trace of untidiness *anywhere!*

Friends should not send any bon voyage presents to one leaving by plane, because unlike a steamer-passenger, the weight of what he takes with him is strictly limited.

THE YOUNG GIRL TRAVELING ALONE

In America, a young girl can go thousands of miles by rail, bus, boat, or airplane without the slightest criticism if she conducts herself with sufficient reserve.

She should be careful about entering into a conversation with any strange man who seats himself beside her. She should not play cards with men or women for money, but a friendly game of cards can help to while away the tiresome hours on a long journey. It is unnecessary to mention that she should not go into a man's drawing-room or accept an alcoholic drink. Above all, she *must not* be persuaded by the kindness of a stranger, whether man or woman, to get into a car to be driven to her destination. If a stranger on the train offers to open a window for her, or to get her a chair on the observation platform, he has **earned** the right to no more than a civil "thank you."

TO ASSURE ACCOMMODATIONS IN HOTELS

It is well to write or telegraph to a hotel in advance for accommodations. A typical telegram reads:

PLEASE RESERVE OUTSIDE SINGLE ROOM WITH BATH AFTERNOON DECEMBER THIRD TO FIFTH. MRS. JOHN HAWKINS.

(Another of the few occasions when "Mrs." belongs with a woman's signature.)

A letter is a little more explicit:

Manager of the _____ Hotel,
  Chicago, Illinois
Dear Sir:
Please reserve two single rooms with baths or with a bath between for my daughter and me. We are due to arrive in Chicago at five o'clock on the afternoon of December sixth, and shall stay a week.
I prefer average-priced outside rooms not higher than the fourth floor.

Very truly yours,
Mrs. George K. Smith

Kindly confirm reservation to
Brightmeadows, Ill.

Both letter and telegram should state clearly the hour of your arrival, number of persons, the accommodations you wish, and the approximate length of your stay.

THE ARRIVAL AT A HOTEL

Your arrival at a hotel is always precisely the same unless you walk in without baggage. Otherwise, a doorman opens the door of your car or taxi and deposits your luggage on the sidewalk. If the hotel is crowded, this individual will ask, "Have you engaged rooms?" If you say, "Yes," all is well; but if you say, "No," the reply is, "Very sorry, but there is not a room left." This means that you have to go to another or maybe to several other hotels. So you should not only wire or write, but ask for a confirmation.

Usually a day or two is sufficient notice, but at the time of a political convention or a big football game, or any other occasion of crowded hotels, you must sometimes write months in advance, and not think of going to the hotel unless you receive word that you will be accommodated.

However, let us suppose it is an ordinary occasion and that you have your room. A bellboy dashes or saunters out, takes your bags from the sidewalk, and carries them into the lobby and deposits them not far from the desk. In a typical hotel there is a counter with one man or two behind it. In the gigantic city hotels there are divisions of desks, labeled "Rooms," "Accounts," "Inquiry," etc.

In either case you go to the desk, or to the division marked "Room Clerk," and say, "I am Mrs. Smithers Greene. I telegraphed you Friday." If you have had no answering telegram, there is always the chance that the clerk may say, "Very sorry, but we have not had a vacancy. The Bankers' Convention is meeting here. We would have telegraphed you but you gave us no address." Which means that you will probably have to go hunting for a place to sleep.

However, let us suppose your room is waiting for you. The clerk turns the register around—or more probably in a modern hotel he presents a form—for you to fill in and sign.

REGISTERING IN A HOTEL

A gentleman writes in the hotel register:

John Smith, New York.

Never under any circumstances "The Hon." (meaning the American title) and not "Mr." if he is alone. But if his wife is with him, the title to their joint names is correct:

Mr. and Mrs. John Smith, New York.

He should not add his street and house number. If instead of a book he has been given a registration card or form, he fills in the blanks, which usually include the house address. But his signature is exactly the same whether written in a book or on a card. Neither "John Smith and Wife" nor "John Smith and Family" is good form. If he does not like the "Mr." before his name, he can sign his own without the title on one line and then write "Mrs. Smith" on the one below. The whole family should be registered.

John T. Smith,	New York
Mrs. Smith	
and maid (*if she has brought one*)	"
Miss Margaret Smith,	"
John T. Smith, Jr.,	
Baby and nurse.	"

Or, if the children are very young, he writes:

Mr. & Mrs. John T. Smith, New York, 3 children and nurse.

"Miss" precedes the names of girls over five, but small boys are registered John or Henry.

One exceptional occasion when a lady signs her name "Miss" or "Mrs." is in a hotel register. "Miss Abigail Titherington" is correct, or "Mrs. John Smith"; never "Sarah Smith."

If Mrs. Smith arrives first, she fills in the blank for both of them. Then when he arrives, he says to the room clerk, "Mrs. Smith has already arrived and registered. What is the number of our room, please?"

As soon as you have registered, the clerk hands the key, not to you but to the bellboy, who gathers up your bags and starts in the direction of the elevators. You follow. If you have many bags, there will be two boys. In some hotels they send a maid as well as a bellboy upstairs with each woman guest. (Whether the guest is to be protected from entering a room alone with a bellboy, or the bellboy protected from being left alone with the guest, has never been explained.) In any case, the bellboy puts down your bags, turns on the lights, and tests the air-conditioning unit. He receives a quarter or a half dollar, depending on the amount of luggage. The maid brings in fresh towels and checks the linen and soap supply; she receives a quarter or, since she is most likely the regular chambermaid, you tip her at the end of your stay.

Any service that you really require you telephone for. You tell the operator if you wish to be called at a certain time, or ask for the Desk if you want to inquire about mail or give the name of a visitor you are expecting. You call the Porter's Desk if you have any inquiries about luggage or trains—a hotel will always send for luggage, also dispatch it. You call the Starter if you want a taxi at a certain hour, the Newsstand for magazines, newspapers, or theatre tickets, Room Service when you want food sent up to you, and Valet Service if you need a dress or a suit cleaned or pressed.

BREAKFAST IN YOUR ROOM

In the morning, for instance, if you want to breakfast in your room, you say, "Room Service, please." Then, when this answers, you say, "Please send a waiter to Room 1117"; or, if you know exactly what you want, you say, "Please send coffee and buttered toast and orange juice for one." Presently the waiter brings in a tray with your order. In a first-class hotel he carries in a long, narrow table that fits between twin beds or stands beside a single one. It is completely set: damask cloth, china, glass, silverware, and thermos pitchers, and possibly chafing-dishes to keep the food hot.

It is entirely proper to receive the waiter when you are sitting up in bed or clad in a tailored housecoat. Waiters are used to carrying breakfast trays into the presence of all varieties of pajamas and negligées, and it is not necessary for even the most old-fashioned lady to be completely dressed to receive him.

In a small hotel he puts the breakfast tray on the bed, and then immediately leaves the room. He returns later for the table and check, which can be paid in cash or signed and put on your bill. The room waiter receives from twenty-five to fifty cents, according to the amount of the breakfast check and whether it is for one or two. In addition to this the hotel makes an extra charge for meals served in your room; room service charges are usually indicated on the menu.

ADDITIONAL SERVICE

To have your clothes washed, telephone that you want your laundry sent for. Pressing is usually done by the regular valet or lady's maid. In a small hotel, a woman's dress as well as a man's suit is sent out to a tailor. It is against the rules in most hotels to use your own iron; therefore, when you don't know where to have any pressing done, you ask a chambermaid tactfully, "Where can I have my dress pressed?" She answers, "I will do it for you," or tells you who will.

HOTEL'S WRITING PAPER

Nowadays all well-run American hotels, the smallest as well as the largest, give their guests as much writing paper as they need. It is not only bad manners but actually dishonorable to take it away in bulk or even to waste it.

HOTEL RULES OF PROPRIETY

It is strictly against the rules of every reputable hotel for a guest to receive a visitor of the opposite sex in a bedroom without speaking to the desk clerk on his particular floor and leaving the door ajar. If you have a private sitting-room, you can have everyone you please take a meal in it with you, or you can receive whomsoever you please, so long as you break none of the ordinary conventions of behavior. Noisy parties, men visitors at unconventionally late hours, or anything that suggests questionable behavior is not permitted in any high-class hotel.

The woman, however, staying alone in a hotel and having no sitting-room of her own receives her men visitors in any one of the public sitting-rooms that all hotels provide. She is also free to ask whom she will to the restaurant or dining-room. There is not the slightest reason why a woman—even though she be very young and very pretty—may not stay in a hotel by herself and have men come to see her and be invited by her to lunch or to dine. It is not so much a question of suitable age as of suitable behavior. A girl who is dignified, whose friends are the sort that pass that sharpest of character readers, the house detective, will never even approach an uncomfortable moment. The woman, on the other hand, who thinks a hotel is a brier-patch where she can hide away all the things she oughtn't to do, will find that she might as well have chosen to hide in a show window.

TIPS

The usual tip for a waiter in a first-class restaurant is between fifteen and twenty percent of the bill, but never less than twenty-five cents in a restaurant with tablecloth on table. If you are staying in an American-plan hotel, you give the waiter or waitress at the end of each week about ten percent of the week's board if for one person, but less if the family is large. When going to stay in a hotel, you give from two to ten dollars to the headwaiter, if you would like a table in a particular location. And you tip him, when you leave, in proportion to the service rendered. You give him one or two dollars a week, if he has done little, and five dollars a week for a family that he has been especially attentive to.

The room waiter receives ten to fifteen percent of the bill, but his fees are slightly larger than those of the dining-room waiters, because a small amount is usually added to the prices on the room-service menu.

In an American-plan hotel, a set sum of twenty-five or fifty cents is charged for each meal taken to a room.

The chambermaid in a first-class hotel is given about one dollar a week a room, fifty cents a week in a small inexpensive hotel, or a dollar a month in a boarding house. If you stay one night only, fifty cents for each room in a large hotel, or twenty-five cents in a small one, is left on the bureau—in the hope that the chambermaid and not an inquisitive bellboy will get it!

Other tips: (Nothing to the doorman for putting bag on sidewalk.)

Twenty-five cents if the bellboy carries baggage to room; fifty cents if the bags are many or very heavy.

Twenty-five cents for paging.

Twenty-five cents to a porter for bringing a trunk to the room, or fifty cents if there is much baggage.

Twenty-five cents for ice water, newspapers, packages, telegrams, etc.

Twenty-five cents for checking a man's coat and hat.

Twenty-five cents for checking a woman's wrap in the dressing room of a high-class hotel or restaurant, or twenty-five cents for the coat rack at the entrance to the dining-room.

Fifty cents or one dollar to the elevator starter when you leave, or fifty cents a week to an individual elevator man. If staying long in a hotel that has many elevators, a dollar a month for each operator.

Taxi drivers are tipped about ten cents for a fifty-cent drive, fifteen cents for a dollar drive, and fifteen percent for a long wait or distance.

The official rate for a porter to take luggage from the entrance of a railroad station to a train is twenty-five cents for each piece, and an additional tip is optional but expected.

Tipping at some steamship piers is not required, and large signs are displayed to that effect. Otherwise, on arrival at a pier, there is a porter to put your luggage on the escalator to the upper level, for which a tip of twenty-five to fifty cents is given depending on the amount of luggage. Having seen your luggage all put on the escalator, you then take the elevator or walk up the stairs to the receiving end of the escalator, where there is another crew of porters who put the luggage on trucks for delivery to the escalator where the luggage goes on board the ship. Tips are given to these porters. The luxury liners, for instance, the *Queen Elizabeth* and the *United States* have ship's stewards at the first-class "Passenger Entrance" who will take small pieces of luggage that you do not want to put on the escalator or lose from sight, and, after waiting for you to show your ticket and passport at the pier booths, will accompany you to your cabin on board ship.

The porter in a Pullman car is given twenty-five to fifty cents a day, and fifty cents a berth a night. If you occupy a roomette, compartment or bedroom space, the tip is in proportion.

Bootblacks are tipped ten cents, and barbers, manicurists, and beauty-parlor specialists on the basis of ten percent of the bill, but not less than twenty-five cents.

Smart-looking people, who frequent expensive hotels and take drawing-rooms on trains, are expected to give larger tips than people traveling economically. The latter may easily be richer, but tips are expected according to appearance.

One piece of advice: You will not get good service unless you tip generously but not lavishly. If you do not care to order elaborate meals, that is nothing to your discredit; but you should not go to an expensive hotel, hold a table that would otherwise be occupied by others who might order a long dinner, and expect your waiter to be contented with a tip of ten cents for your dollar supper! He will be enchanted to serve you a ten-cent supper if you will give him the dollar tip!

Tipping is undoubtedly an undesirable and undignified system, but it happens to be in force; and that being the case, travelers who like the way made smooth and comfortable have to pay their share of it.

DINING ALONE

A hotel guest—whether a woman or a man—going down to the dining-room alone, usually takes a book or newspaper, because nothing is duller than to sit eating bread and butter and looking at the table-cloth, which is scarcely diverting, or staring at other people, which is impolite, while waiting for one's order.

It is always proper for a woman to wear a hat in a restaurant, but she may go into the dining-room without one if she is staying at the hotel. In the evening if she is dressed in evening clothes she does not wear a hat.

GOING TO SEE FRIENDS IN A HOTEL

When going to see people stopping at a hotel, you ask for them at the desk and the clerk telephones to their rooms. If they are receiving you upstairs, you are told the number of the room you are to go to, and you go up in the elevator alone and find it yourself. Or you may be asked to use the house telephone and announce yourself. You can ask the elevator boy which floor Room 616 is on; in practically every modern hotel this would be the sixth floor.

If the friends you are waiting to see answer that they are coming down, you sit in the lobby or the lounge, in view of the bank of elevators, until they join you.

WHEN YOU LEAVE THE HOTEL

The courteous guest tells the management when he arrives that he intends to stay overnight only, or several days, or a week or two, as the case may be. When he is ready to leave, he goes to the cashier—or telephones—asking that his bill be made out. When he has finished packing, he telephones for a bellboy to carry down his luggage. Then he goes to the desk, pays his bill, and leaves his key and a forwarding address if he wishes any mail sent after him, and departs.

ADVANTAGES OF A TRAVEL BUREAU

The easiest way to travel is to go to a travel bureau. If there isn't one in your own town, write to one that has been recommended to you by a well-traveled acquaintance or friend.* Tell them just where you want to go and when and how—in fact, give all the details you can, and let them work out the best possible plan for you. This is their business, and they can do it not only better but much more economically than you can and at no extra cost to you. Except for railroad tickets and Pullman reservations for which there is a regulated charge, most travel agencies do not exact a charge for their services since they get a commission from the transportation company, the resort hotel or dude ranch.

There is one important point that should be explained to the inexperienced traveler: A competent travel bureau will engage best rooms in de luxe hotels and secure automobiles by the week or month, either with or without chauffeurs, or provide any other service, but he is quite likely unaware that they will, with equal interest, provide the same quality service for those traveling on a limited budget.

They will also arrange for telegrams or telephone calls where the train pauses. Another service, if you are going to a resort such as

* Grateful acknowledgment is again made to Miss Dorothy Shepard, my personal friend and travel adviser.

Bermuda or Nassau: they will rent a cottage, hire servants, and your favorite cocktail will be ready when you arrive. These agencies have visited most of the places they recommend.

The value of the service of a reliable and competent travel bureau cannot be too strongly emphasized. It is almost indispensable in these days of increasingly complex conditions of travel.

PREPARATIONS FOR TRAVEL BY SHIP

Let us say your plans are made to sail on such a day. If you are going to foreign countries, items included in your preparations before sailing are various and change at times, which adds to the importance of their being attended to well in advance of time of departure. If you go to a travel bureau, they will advise you of all the requirements depending on where and how you are going, and will attend to the details, and tell you about those you will have to take care of yourself. There are a very few matters that have to be attended to in person, such as applying for a passport and getting a doctor's certificate, etc. Everything else can be done for you; and for anyone obliged to go on a suddenly planned trip, a great deal of valuable time can be saved by having someone else who knows the ropes make your reservations anywhere in the world and deliver your tickets to you.

It is advisable to get some foreign money in small bills and change to have in your hand when you land, and there are restrictions as to the amount you are permitted to take in or out of some countries to be observed. It is also very important to take your money in American Express or other traveler's checks, which are accepted everywhere as readily as cash. Even though you have a letter of credit, which is advisable if you want to have something to depend on for extra and unexpected expenses, there are many occasions when it is inconvenient or even impossible to go to a bank.

Whether you are going to a foreign country or traveling at home, make your list of clothes, not only with utility and becomingness in mind, but with serious attention to the utmost elimination of bulk and weight.

You must of course see that your luggage is suitable and either new or in perfect repair.

ON THE DAY YOU SAIL

On the day you sail be sure to arrive at the steamer in plenty of time to be certain your luggage is on board. Any trunks sent to the pier by express or being checked by rail will be covered by numbered checks, the stubs of which will be given to you. These stubs should be turned in to the baggage-master, or whoever is in charge of his desk, on the pier. The luggage taken on airplanes is limited as to the free amount you can take. This varies for domestic and foreign travel, and special allowances are made for combined domestic and foreign flights. Recently new rates for excess baggage have gone into effect; this is another way your travel bureau can give helpful advice.

RESERVING DINING-ROOM TABLE AND DECK CHAIR

Immediately after being shown to your cabin, it is well to hurry to the dining-room and reserve the table you wish for the voyage. Next, go to the main deck and see the head deck steward about a steamer chair. If you have a preference about the location, this is your chance to get it.

WHAT YOU WEAR WHEN TRAVELING

The first thing to remember on the day you select your clothes is not to let that day's weather upset your judgment. Unless you remember about this, should the day you pack be freezing and stormy, you are as likely as not to start to the tropics with rubbers and galoshes, a slicker and a raincoat as well as an ulster, and very little for days which are warm and sunny. On the other hand, should the day on which you go out to get clothes for a trip to the North be torrid, you will be a very unusual person if you remember that a wardrobe selected solely for the tropics may result in your having to go around wrapped in a steamer blanket on more than a few occasions.

Another mistake made by all novice travelers is taking too many things. It is true that knowing how to select the most practical minimum possible is an achievement that is the result of long experience and rather special skill. But ask your friends who have made the trip you are planning—they should be of great help.

AMOUNT OF BAGGAGE

For ordinary travel, having only a few pieces of luggage is an important consideration. But when going on a ship where you will occupy the same cabin the entire time, particularly if you are to have it alone, the number of pieces you take does not matter. On the other hand, if you are sharing a cabin, you must limit your luggage to one small trunk and possibly a bag or box. In other words, you have no right to expect your cabin-mate to live in a baggage room. Luggage not needed en route is of course checked.

TIPPING ON SHIPBOARD

There are definite minimum amounts that passengers are expected to give. If you are traveling first-class give your cabin steward and stewardess each five dollars. The dining-room steward receives five dollars and his assistant three dollars. One dollar to the bus boy, if there is one, would make him very happy. The smoking-room stewards are tipped at the time of the services they render. The chief deck steward receives five dollars, and his assistant who takes care of you, three dollars.

Ten percent of the amount of the wine bill is given to the dining-table wine steward.

To the bath steward you give a dollar.

All of the above suggestions for tipping are per person, on a transatlantic trip. On a cruise, the usual custom is to tip weekly.

To anyone on the ship who has taken pains to please you, you show by your manner in thanking him that you appreciate his efforts, as well as by giving him a somewhat more generous tip when you leave the ship. Obviously passengers occupying suites are expected to tip more generously than those in modest accommodations.

It should be unnecessary to add that you must on no account attempt to tip a ship's officer! Thank the purser as you would any other acquaintance for courtesy. If you go to see the doctor, or if he is brought to see you, he will probably send you a bill for his services. If he does not and you have had a real illness, it is proper to send him, in an envelope when you leave the ship, the amount that probably would have been charged by your own doctor. If you are ill enough to be hospitalized, an extra charge will be added to your fare.

Tipping in the cabin and tourist classes is less in proportion to the difference in the passage fare. A good general rule for shipboard travelers is to allow approximately ten percent of their fare for tips. Divide about half of this allowance between the cabin and dining-room stewards, and distribute the rest to others who have served you.

KNOWLEDGE OF A COUNTRY'S LANGUAGE
HELPS UNDERSTANDING

As a result of travel by airplane and now even jet, people of the farthest reaches of the earth have become our neighbors. Every traveler will increase his enjoyment of his trip if he attempts to achieve neighborly understanding and friendship. We should try to acquire an understanding of the customs of each country we visit, and never presume to set our behavior up as a pattern to be followed.

It is obvious that the etiquette of each country differs as does its language. We Americans have for years been greatly criticized for our ignorance of both. Not even our diplomats have been required to learn to speak the languages of the countries to which they are accredited. It is really amazing! And then we naively believe that wherever we go we will be loved on sight "because we are Americans!"

We don't love all the foreigners who come to our shores. We do love those individuals who are appreciative of our country and courteous to us. It is quite plain, then, that similarly complimentary requirements are exacted of us in the countries where we are foreigners.

It is, of course, true that good manners are good manners everywhere, except that in Latin and Asiatic countries we must, as it seems to us, exaggerate politeness. We must, in France and Italy, bow smilingly; we must, in Spain, South America, and the East, bow gravely; but, in any event, it is necessary to *bow*—though your bow is often little more than a slight inclination of the head, and a smile—and to show some ceremony in addressing people.

EVEN IF EVERYONE SPOKE ENGLISH

At first thought, it would seem that there could be no difficulties of understanding between us and those whose language is the same as ours—especially the Australians and New Zealanders, who are said to be so much like ourselves. But slight frictions which developed during World War II suggest that thoughtful observance of other people's reactions to the things we do and say would be helpful.

It was said of our soldiers, for example, that not only did they have more money than those of other nations, but that the American troops looked upon foreign currency as being make-believe money—of no value at all.

To our credit it can be said—we are straightforward; we honor our obligations; we keep our word. But sometimes we make overoptimistic promises, and tact is not one of our virtues. Sensitive perception of the feelings of others is something that few of us possess instinctively. It is necessary, therefore, that we train ourselves to perceive the point of view of the people of each country we visit, remembering that it is always the stranger who must adapt himself, just as the visitor does to the ways of the house in which he is a guest.

The English, the Scots, the Welsh, and the Irish are like us in so many ways we can easily be thrown out of balance by a few differences. The best type of Britisher, for example, has just as keen an appreciation of his own ability as we have, but the code of a British gentleman exacts understatement and personal reserve. Therefore, if you would be liked by the well-bred Britisher, *don't* be a show-off or a braggart or a back-slapper. He detests all three. Also, you might remember not to make the mistake of thinking that he hasn't any sense of humor. (Read *Punch*—at least until you have changed your mind on this.)

COURTESY EXACTED IN NORTH AFRICA
AND THE FAR EAST

North Africa has quite definite customs; to smoke or let a pet dog run loose near a mosque, to enter a house either in shoes or barefoot, to let bread fall to the ground, or to cut it with a knife, or to hold it in the left hand—above all to stare at or attempt to talk to a veiled woman— are all not merely discourteous, but grave offenses against the religion of a deeply devout people.

In the Far East, the principal advice is this: *Never* lose your self-control. Only by showing unfailing dignity, tranquillity, and poise combined with good nature can you hope to take the first steps toward earning liking and respect.

AN AUDIENCE WITH THE POPE

It is possible for American tourists visiting Rome to be granted an audience with the Pope for, although there are often hundreds of people in a day who wish an audience, no one is denied. Obviously only relatively few can be granted one of the three types of audience that are considered to be personal; group or collective audiences are arranged for the great majority.

In the latter case the Pope appears, sometimes seated on a portable throne called the *Sedia Gestatoria*, and is carried at shoulder level by eight men, or he may be seated on one of several other fixed thrones, or again he may appear on a balcony overlooking the multitude. He usually delivers a short address and gives his benediction to all those who have assembled.

Requests for these group audiences as well as for the personal ones must all be made at the Office of the Master of the Chamber known as *Ufficio Del Maestro Di Camera Di Sua Santita*, which is in the Vatican. Here all must fill out a form requesting the kind of audience wished and show their credentials which for a Roman Catholic may be simply a letter of introduction from his parish priest. The length of their stay in Rome, their addresses and telephone numbers are also included on the form so that they can be notified of the day and hour of their audience. Non-Catholics as well as Catholics are granted audiences.

The "private" audience is reserved for cardinals, heads of state, ambassadors, or others of first importance. The second type of audience is the "special," which is almost as important as the "private," and is also granted only to people of high rank, or those who have an important subject to present to the Pope. The third type of audience is the "baciomano" which is also considered as a personal one, as each comes into the personal presence of the Pope, kisses his ring, and exchanges a few words with him.

In this third type of audience, visitors stand in a single file around the room and when the Pope enters they bend one knee or kneel and do not stand again until the Pope leaves the audience chamber or makes a sign for them to rise. He passes from one visitor to another extending his hand to each so that all may kiss his ring. He also asks a question and exchanges a few words with each. It is customary for visitors to take with them one or more rosaries or other small religious objects which, after the visitor has received the Papal blessing, are also considered to have been blessed.

The rules of dress for visitors to the Pope are not so strict as they once were. But even now for a private or special audience, men wear evening dress with tails, and women long-sleeved black dresses and veils over their hair. For lesser audiences it is only required that everybody be dressed in a sober and suitable manner. Women must have their hair covered, must not wear dresses with low necks, short skirts nor have bare arms or legs.

CRUISE MANNERS

Customs on shipboard depend upon the difference between a "crossing" and a "cruise." A short transatlantic crossing may lead to very little friendliness. A cruise, on the other hand, always has a sociable atmosphere, a holiday spirit, like that of a large house party where the guests speak to each other as a matter of course.

On every cruise there is a "director" who acts as hostess (but the modern name is director) and tries to see that the passengers have a pleasant time. Any young girl or man on board who is without friends is expected to go to the director and ask him or her to be introduced to congenial people. This means, if they play deck games, or bridge, or like to dance, he or she arranges for games and introduces them to partners. On the smaller ships, the purser or possibly the chief steward assumes the office of director.

If you are seated next to those who respond with friendliness to your greeting, then you may continue to talk. But if they make little response, you then leave them alone until they show friendliness to you. Occasionally, strong and lasting friendships are made on a cruise, but don't be too disappointed if once the cruise is over, the friendly relationship vanishes into thin air.

Good manners are everywhere the same in principle. Courtesy demands that you avoid using a strong scent or, still worse, giving evidence of a strong accumulation of nicotine. Everyone realizes the offensiveness of a man's dirty pipe or stale, over-chewed cigar. But many women's cigarettes, smoked down to the last inch, are equally distressing to those who do not smoke.

CLOTHES FOR A WOMAN ON A CRUISE

One or two simple lightweight suits in your favorite color or colors. (Remember, bright colors look fairly subdued in sunny climates.) They should have accessories such as an odd belt or two, scarfs, or extra blouses. Two or three cotton or silk, nylon or Dacron "spectator" sports dresses. Slacks (only if you are young or at least slim!) and a jacket to wear with them. And speaking of slacks, it is an excellent rule to follow never to wear them ashore unless the ladies who live in the place you are visiting appear in them. At present costume jewelry adds smartness and brightness, especially in the evening when a so-called "cocktail dress" has taken the place of a low-cut evening one which is only worn for "gala dinners." Remember that overdressing on shipboard shows ignorance of good taste.

When going ashore, be sure that you have comfortable foot-supporting shoes, not wobbling stilt heels or clumping high platforms. (If you must wear these, then wear them when sitting in your deck chair.)

Remember that nights on the water are always cool and that a loose, long, warm coat such as a polo coat is essential. A bathing suit will be necessary, if you like either swimming or "sunning." If your cruise is to the South, remember the sun is very strong and burns fast even on a hazy day. Use sunglasses and toast your bare skin only a few minutes each day in the direct sunshine, until you find how much sun you can take without blistering painfully. A few drops of suntan oil will deepen your tan and prevent your skin from drying out.

By the time you arrive at your first port, it is probable that you will have made a number of friends. Perhaps you especially like someone who was introduced to you by the director, or who sits next to you on deck or at table, and you can go ashore with her or him. If this is not the case, then you just go along in the general group.

Nothing is more mysterious than the way a group of people develops as in a photograph. At first you see a crowd of faces and none of them stands out. Little by little they take on identity, and more often than not some inconspicuous person whom at first you hardly noticed is the one who becomes your most delightful friend.

At the end of the cruise comes the bewildering moment of giving the right tips to those who have served you. The fixed rates of yesterday are no longer in force. But a dollar a day to your room steward and also to your table steward is approximately the amount for a short cruise— somewhat less if the cruise is longer. An encouraging fact, however, is that a novice can always ask the advice of a seasoned fellow traveler, who will almost certainly be glad to share his expert knowledge as to the proper tips to give.

IF WE WOULD BE WELCOMED BY OUR NEIGHBORS

Because of the happily increasing friendships between ourselves of the United States and our neighbors of the Latin-American countries to the south of us, it is of vital importance that we make a serious effort to acquire at least an understanding of the meaning of good manners as they are practiced by all people of Latin origin.

To give anything like a complete list of the courtesies that perfect visitors to Latin countries should observe is of course impossible in these paragraphs. But among the few everyday manners that are expected of a guest the following are of first importance:

In every Latin country abruptness is looked upon as a first step toward rudeness. Their peoples are more leisurely inclined than most of us. What most of us of northern climes fail to comprehend is that

courtesy is not an accomplishment of the few but a fundamental requirement of existence like seeing, and hearing, and breathing. Manners
in all Latin countries, whether Spanish, Portuguese, Italian, or French,
are more clearly defined—also slower paced—than ours. A gentleman's
bow is gracefully made. His hat is lifted off the head and not merely
lifted the fraction of an inch and clamped down again.

Rising is always important. When a person enters a room all of those
who are younger instantly stand, even when the older person is a gentleman and the younger ones present are ladies. It is considered very
rude if any persons not enfeebled remain seated.

A situation difficult for a visitor, who might himself be considered
"important," to understand is that it is not his or her place to rush forward and take the initiative. He is expected to wait for others to greet
him or her first.

The Latins have a great love of giving presents; not only at Christmas time or at someone's birthday, but unendingly. Such gifts are usually foods or flowers, especially those baked in their ovens or grown in
their gardens. Or they may be any trifling but pretty things.

In accepting these, we on our part must learn how to bow and smile,
and show our pleasure in accepting the gift—and as soon as possible
thereafter we should show our friendliness by a simple but courteously
proffered gift to interpret our courteous intentions when grace of speech
is lacking.

If it so happens that you can speak not a word of Spanish, or Portuguese, or it may be French, or Italian, remember that you can *smile* and
give a genuine handshake with confident assurance that your gesture
will be received with a cordial welcome.

FRIEND-MAKING IMPORTANCE OF ANOTHER'S LANGUAGE

It is always "friend-making" to show *your wish* to speak the language of the people you visit, even if you can say no more than "Bon
jour" or "Buenos días." Surely you can learn to say it with a smile and
an indication of a bow whenever you may be a visitor in one of our
sister republics to the south of us.

In attempting to acquire good manners according to Latin standards,
the very first lesson is to learn to remember that if we try to be twice
as polite as seems to us courteous, it is just possible that we can escape
being labeled "rude!" Even the British (who are noted for their unbend-
ing reserve) are more courteous than we are. They do say "Good morning" when they go into a store, and they are always generous with their
"Thank you."

Our greatest fault (so it is said) is that we think the best of everything should be eagerly handed to us—even without our asking. When
we're asked "Why?", we believe (even if we are not so rude as to say it)

that it is because we can *pay* for it! If this were true, *could* anything be more ill-bred?

TO "PAY FOR" IS NOT ENOUGH

That we must learn *how* to pay for it *graciously* is the true answer. The fact is that some of us have still to learn that the payment we should make is something more and quite apart from dollars—that is, if we are going to be given more than just what dollars can buy!

Dollars, pounds, francs, pesos, liras, yes—all these buy objects of ornament or utility, but they don't buy a single gesture of welcome, of admiration, of sympathy.

A little thought, a little preparation, a very great wish to learn and to understand, will alone reap the beautiful reward—their friendship.

NOVICE TRAVELERS

The following items of courtesy are those which inexperienced travelers are most likely to neglect:

Don't forget to write thank-you notes for gifts sent you to the steamer so that they will be postmarked the earliest date possible. It is not necessary to write long letters. An appreciative message on a postcard will answer in most instances better than an overlong delayed letter.

If you have lent a book to a fellow passenger, it is entirely proper on the day before landing to say, "I hope you have finished *Green Leaves* as I'd like to pack it in the luggage that I'm sending through to Paris" (or whatever your destination).

If you should be seated at the captain's table, you are expected to ask the steward at what hour the captain dines and be prompt at this one meal. It is likely that you will be invited to meet in his cabin a few moments before the dinner hour he has named and go in to dinner with him. It must be noted that this direction is merely "likely" and not at all "certain."

At the end of your journey, should some of your fellow passengers give you their cards, you say, "Thank you." If you have any of yours with you, you give them yours in exchange. Failing to have any is not rude. Many friendly people dislike handing out cards. Many others forget to take theirs traveling. In fact, most of us are more likely to write the names and addresses of those whom we hope to meet again in our address books than to exchange cards.

If the captain has shown you any special hospitality, it would be courteous certainly to invite him to your house if you live in New York or whichever city is his ship's port.

PROTOCOL IN WASHINGTON

⋅⊰[51]⊱⋅

ALTHOUGH MOST PEOPLE ARE KIND, AND THOSE WHO have been long in service instinctively try to help the inexperienced, it is imperative that each new arrival in Washington, whether an official or a private citizen who expects to take part in the social life of the Capital, learn first of all the proper title by which each diplomat, government official, and military officer is addressed and the order of his rank. When a man has been promoted to high position, the respect due his office should not be overlooked; and placing a foreign representative below his proper seat at a dinner table is showing less than proper concern for his rank and may actually endanger diplomatic feeling between nations.

PRECEDENCE

Precedence is the bane of the Washington hostess; it is as difficult as a cryptogram and social death if not strictly observed. It is easy enough to know that a general outranks a lieutenant, a duke a count, or a member of the President's cabinet a State assemblyman. The difficulty begins, for instance, in determining whether a general of the army should rank the governor of a State, or whether a rear admiral, or a mayor or a justice of a State court should go in to dinner first, or where to seat the Archbishop of X and the Duke of Y.

The hostess who plans to entertain several government officials, military officers, or foreign diplomats has to arrange her seating without slighting any of her guests. But she should realize that her dinner is a private occasion, and that her charm and hospitality are of more importance than any quite minor and unintentioned errors in precedence. As the Protocol Staff of the Department of State recently explained, "The White House and the Department of State prescribe the protocol to be used only for ceremonies of state. The protocol differs somewhat for each ceremony, and the rules used are not considered as binding at private functions. For this reason it is the policy of The White House not to make the rules public or to give out the order of precedence of Government officials."

In an American house the ranking foreigner should in so far as pos-

sible be given precedence. He could never be a rival of the President of
the United States since he would either be a presidential guest of honor,
or the host at his country's embassy and thus never outrank him.

The order of rank in Washington therefore is:

The President of the United States
The Vice President
The Chief Justice and retired Chief Justices
Ex-Presidents of the United States
Foreign Ambassadors (in order of their length of residence in the
    United States)
Widows of ex-Presidents
The Speaker of the House of Representatives
The Secretary of State
The United States Representative to the United Nations
Foreign Ministers Plenipotentiary
Associate Justices of the Supreme Court and retired Associate
    Justices
The Cabinet (in order of establishment; Secretary of State above)
    The Secretary of the Treasury
    The Secretary of Defense
    The Attorney General
    The Postmaster General
    The Secretary of the Interior
    The Secretary of Agriculture
    The Secretary of Commerce
    The Secretary of Labor
    The Secretary of Health, Education and Welfare
Director of Defense Mobilization (Cabinet rank)
Director of Foreign Operations Administration (Cabinet rank)
Director of the Bureau of the Budget (Cabinet rank)
Special Assistant to the President, Council of Foreign Economics
    Policy (Cabinet rank)
Governors of States (in order of seniority)
Senators
The Assistant to the President
Acting Heads of Executive Departments
Former Vice Presidents
Members of the House of Representatives
Under Secretaries of State
The Secretary of the Army
The Secretary of the Navy
The Secretary of the Air Force
Under Secretaries of the Executive Departments and Deputy Secre-
    taries

Chargés d'Affaires, pro tempore, of Foreign Powers
Chairman, Joint Chiefs of Staff
Chief of Naval Operations
Chief of Staff of the U.S. Army
Chief of Staff of the U.S. Air Force
Generals of the Army, and Fleet Admirals, U.S.N. (5 Star)
Special Counsel and Secretaries to the President
The Secretary General of the United Nations
Foreigners with Ambassador's rank, not accredited to the United
  States
The Secretary General of the Pan American Union
Chairman, Atomic Energy Commission
Economic Stabilization Administrator
Federal Civil Defense Administrator
Defense Production Administrator
Judges, United States Court of Appeals
Chairman, Federal Reserve Board
Deputy Under Secretaries of the Executive Departments
Assistant Secretaries of the Executive Departments
The Chief of Protocol
Under Secretaries of the U.S. Army, Navy, and Air Force
Commandant of the Marine Corps
Generals and Admirals, U.S. Army and Navy (4 Star)
Assistant Secretaries of the U.S. Army, Navy and Air Force
Lieutenant Generals and Vice Admirals (3 Star)
Chairman, Red Cross
Director of the Monetary Fund
President, International Bank for Reconstruction
United States Ambassadors and Ministers
Archbishops and Bishops
United States ex-Ambassadors and ex-Ministers
Director, Central Intelligence Agency
Commissioners of the District of Columbia
President, Export and Import Bank
The Treasurer of the United States
Ministers of Foreign Powers (not accredited)
Deputy Assistant Secretaries of the Executive Departments
Deputy Chief of Protocol
Special Assistants to the President
Directors of Offices of Executive Departments
Administrative Assistants to the President
Counselors of Foreign Powers
Consul Generals of Foreign Powers
Major Generals and Rear Admirals (2 Star)
Vice Presidents, Export and Import Bank and Monetary Fund

Assistant Chiefs of Protocol
The Secretary of the Senate
Brigadier Generals and Commodores (1 Star)
First Secretaries of Foreign Powers
> (Military Attachés of Foreign Powers immediately before their
> American colleagues of same rank)

Usually during the social season there are five or more official dinners—one for the Cabinet, the Supreme Court, one or two diplomatic dinners, the Vice President's, and the Speaker's dinners.

In addition to the official dinners, there are usually five state receptions—diplomatic, judicial, departmental, Armed Forces, and Congressional.

IN A FOREIGN EMBASSY OR LEGATION

In a foreign embassy the ranking American, or any other stranger is given precedence. The President of the United States takes precedence over the representative of the country which is receiving him. In the President's absence, the Vice President, the Chief Justice, or the Secretary of State—whichever represents the United States—outranks all foreign Ambassadors. In the diplomatic service, the dean or highest ranking Ambassador is the one who has been longest in residence—not longest in service of his country—in Washington. Next come the Ministers in the same order, then the Counselors, First Secretaries, then the Second and Third Secretaries.

THE USE OF TITLES

Rank is always official; this means that plain Mr. Smith who has become "His Excellency the Ambassador" ranks above a Prince or a Duke who is officially a Secretary of Embassy.

In addition to the information given in the chart in Chapter 44, the following sentences indicate the way persons in the diplomatic world are introduced, announced, and spoken of and spoken to.

"Mr. Ambassador, may I present Mr. Worldly?" (Mr. Worldly finds out for himself, if he does not already know, *which* ambassador.)

But in the case of Mrs. Worldly the order is reversed.

"Mrs. Worldly, may I present The Speaker?"

"Mrs. Worldly, may I present Mr. Justice Law?"

"Mrs. Worldly, may I present the British Ambassador?"

or more formally "—his Excellency the British Ambassador?"

"Mrs. Worldly, may I present the Governor of Colorado?"

"Mrs. Worldly, may I present the Secretary of the Interior?"

Unless she herself holds a diplomatic position, a woman is never introduced to a man lower in rank than a sovereign or president, a member of a reigning family, or a high prelate. A man of lesser rank is always introduced to one of greater.

The governors of certain states, such as Massachusetts, for example, have the official right to the title of "Excellency." But even in States which do not confer this title upon their governors, it is courteous, in speaking about him, to say, "His Excellency has just remarked—"

Speaking to the governor on a single or formal occasion: "Does your Excellency think—" (The title is not repeated throughout a long conversation.)

"May I ask you, Mr. Speaker?"

"How do you do, Mr. Chief Justice."

"I am so glad to see you, Mr. Secretary."

"I appreciate the honor, Mr. President."

"Thank you, Mr. Vice President."

"Thank you, Mr. Ambassador." Or about him: "As his Excellency has explained—" (In this case "Excellency" is his official right.)

"Have you met Senator Brown?" (The phrase, "The Senator from New Jersey," is used only in the Senate itself.)

When introducing or addressing a letter to one who has both a military and an inherited title, military rank is put first, thus: Colonel, Lord London.

It is utterly improper to call a governor "Mr." no matter how informal and simple his own inclinations may be. Only those who know him well say "Governor." In public, he is addressed "Governor Jones." Informally he is introduced or referred to as "Governor Jones" or "The Governor." On formal occasions, such as a public ceremony, he is introduced "His Excellency, the Governor." This is not used repeatedly but on first presenting, announcing, or referring to him. Thereafter, "The Governor" is correct. Outside his own State, the State is added to the title: "The Governor of New York."

It is very important to remember that no matter how well you may have known a man outside of office, you must treat his office with unfailing respect. To slap a governor on the back in public and call him "Jim" is belittling to his office, to him, and to you.

In illustration of the traditional dignity of office: One of the justices of the United States Supreme Court was President McKinley's lifelong and most intimate friend. But after Mr. McKinley's inauguration, this friend, whose own office was an exalted one, always addressed him, even when they were alone, as "Mr. President." It was only in grief upon hearing of his death that he cried out: "Bill! Oh, Bill!"

Members of the Cabinet are usually "Mr. Secretary," but if several are present, one is designated "Mr. Secretary of State," the other "Mr. Secretary of Commerce." And you say, of course, "Mr. Chief Justice" or "Mr. Justice Law"—even after he has retired. You also say "General Pershing," and "Admiral Sims," and "Senator Lake," and not merely "General," "Admiral," or "Senator." You should also say "Doctor Brown" rather than just "Doctor," and never under any circumstances "Doc."

Officers below the grade of captain in the army and commander in the navy are written to by their titles, but prior to the last war were correctly spoken to as "Mister." At present this custom has changed, and it is now unusual to hear lieutenants called other than by title. And this is now considered socially correct for civilian use. Captains and commanders and those of higher rank are addressed by their title and name: Captain Brown, Commander Gray, Colonel Steel. To call them by title alone is not objectionable, as it would be in the case of a governor.

Military and naval titles are used only by officers in active service or retired "regulars." It is not in good taste for reserve officers or those who held temporary commissions during the war to continue having their cards engraved Captain, Major, or Colonel. Often a man is affectionately called "Colonel" by his friends, but he should not have the title engraved on his visiting-cards, neither should he use it as a part of his signature. A civilian staff officer, such as a colonel on a governor's staff, shows very poor taste in using his title, or rank, when his political chief is out of office.

Announcement or official introduction (or when called upon for an address or speech):

"His Excellency, the French Ambassador."

"The Chief Justice" ("Honorable" is not used).

"The Honorable, the Secretary of Agriculture."

"The Honorable, the Speaker of the House of Representatives."

"Count Torla, the Military Attaché of the Swedish Legation."

"His Honor, the Mayor of New York."

OFFICIAL AND SOCIAL FORMS

An invitation to lunch or dine at The White House is a command and automatically cancels any other engagement.

The acceptance must be written—by hand of course. Furthermore, it must be left at the door and may not be sent by mail. It may be folded once in the ordinary way and not fitted to a full-page-size envelope as is necessary in answering court invitations abroad.

There are very few acceptable excuses for refusing an invitation to The White House, and the reason must be stated in the note of regret—such as extended absence in a foreign country (since obviously it would be impossible to return in time), the recent death of a close relative, or actual illness.

AN EXAMPLE OF BEST TASTE

Mr. and Mrs. Richard Worldly
have the honour to accept
the kind invitation of
the President and Mrs. Washington
for dinner on Thursday, the eighth of May
at eight o'clock

A form to be avoided:

Mr. and Mrs. X
present their compliments to their Excellencies
the Ambassador of France and Mme Thoreau
and are most happy to accept their courteous invitation
for dinner on Thursday, May eighth
at eight o'clock at the French Embassy

The above incorrect form is actually being received in Washington embassies. The proper form is

Mr. and Mrs. Richard Worldly
have the honour to accept
the kind invitation of their Excellencies
the French Ambassador and Madame Thoreau
for dinner on Thursday, the eighth of May
at eight o'clock

The note to a disappointed hostess:

Mr. and Mrs. Richard Worldly
regret extremely
that an invitation to The White House
prevents their keeping
their previous engagement for
Tuesday, the first of December

INFORMAL INVITATIONS

Informal invitations to dinner or luncheon at The White House are now used more frequently than formerly. They may be sent by letters, telegrams, or telephone messages from the President's secretary or his wife's secretary. The replies should be sent in the same form to whoever issued the invitations.

Acceptances or regrets (provided the reasons are valid) should be written on house paper, either engraved or plain.

A typical invitation might be worded something like this:

Dear Mrs. Heathcote,

Mrs. Harrison has asked me to invite you to have lunch with her at The White House on Thursday, the sixteenth of May. Luncheon will be at one o'clock.

Yours truly,
Eleanor Smithers
Secretary to Mrs. Harrison

The reply might read:

Dear Miss Smithers,

Will you please tell Mrs. Harrison that I shall be delighted to lunch with her at The White House on Thursday, the sixteenth of May. Thank you very much.

Sincerely,
Frances Heathcote

DETAILS OF WHITE HOUSE ETIQUETTE

Although customs vary somewhat during different administrations, the following details represent the conventional pattern from which each administration necessarily adapts its own procedure.

When you are invited to The White House, you must arrive several minutes at least before the hour specified. No more unforgivable breach of etiquette can be made than not to be standing in the drawing-room when the President makes his entry.

Exactly as at a European court, the President, followed by his wife, enters at the hour set and makes a tour of the room, shaking hands with each guest in turn. When your turn comes, you bow deeply and address him—if he talks to you—as "Mr. President." In a long conversation it is proper occasionally to vary "Mr. President" with "Sir." You call the wife of the President "Mrs. Washington," and treat her as you would any formal hostess. You do not sit down as long as either the President or his wife remains standing. No guest, of course, ever leaves until after the President has withdrawn from the room.

Requests to see the President should be made through one of the Presidential aides—the one closest to the subject you wish to discuss. Your reason should be a valid one, and you should be sure that no one else can solve your problem. It should be stated in your letter so that if possible it can be solved without a personal interview.

DINNER DETAILS FOR WASHINGTON HOSTESSES

During a busy social season, unofficial hostesses give dinner parties, and each tries to obtain as many important people among the high officials and diplomatic corps as possible.

When seating her table, the Washington hostess addresses the dinner-cards of the following notables by titles alone:

The President
The Vice President
The Archbishop of ——
The —— Ambassador
The —— Minister
The Chief Justice
The Speaker
The Secretary of —— (for members of the Cabinet)

Other notables have their names in addition to their titles:

Mr. Justice Fair
Senator Essex
Governor Lansing
The Bishop of Milford
Rev. Father Stole
Dr. Saintly

All other names on place-cards are titled merely by "Mr." at dinners given by a fashionable host and hostess in their own house. The object of a dinner-card is twofold: first, to show the owner of the name where he is to sit; second, to give his neighbors at table (if they have a chance to read the card) a clue to how to address him.

GIVING HIS NAME TO HIS NEIGHBORS

A certain noted lawyer, who being a man of unusual charm dines much in society, makes it a habit when sitting between strangers to lay his place-card on the table at his right and later at his left. There is no rule for this, but it is an act of consideration for which the neighbors of most officials would often be grateful.

At public dinners place-cards are inscribed "His Excellency, the Archbishop of New York," "His Honor, the Mayor of Chicago," etc. "The Assistant Secretary of the Navy" and similar titles are never used because there is more than one Assistant Secretary in all executive departments. One might possibly use "Assistant Secretary of the Navy Smith," but this, though used from necessity, is not really good form.

At a private dinner, the hostess writes the names of her guests as she would if she were speaking to them. "Governor Sweet, will you sit here? Father Stole, will you sit there?"

Undoubtedly the best advice to a Washington hostess is to avoid ever asking those of conflicting importance together. If she is giving a dinner in honor of some guest of lower rank than another, it is imperative that she ask the latter to waive his right for this one occasion. The one requested cannot very well refuse—and does not as a rule object—but if he is unwilling to cede his right, he can send word that he is prevented for some reason from being present at the dinner. As a matter of fact, giving a party in honor of an average friend is extremely difficult in official circles, for no one may be invited "to meet" another of inferior rank.

After a dinner or lunch in Washington each guest must wait his turn—according to rank—and not take leave until all those ranking above him have departed. A recognized exception is made after a lunch that is not too formal, for the benefit of government officials whose duties demand their return in the early afternoon. A busy man, therefore, can quite properly plead necessary work and go—whether lunching in the house of Americans or of foreigners.

The wives of members of the nobility are always addressed by title —"Lady This," "Countess That," "Princess the Other." But the wives of men holding official titles, no matter how exalted, remain "Mrs." if British or American, and "Madame" if of another nationality. Lord and Lady are British titles. In all other countries the wife of a Baron or a Count is Baroness or Countess—never Lady.

CARD-LEAVING A DECLINING CONVENTION

Since custom necessarily determines the proper etiquette of the day, yesterday's unlimited card-leaving is no longer a requirement. This is because the great number of army officers who have been brought to Washington since the war and kept there has resulted in the army directive to officers not to call on their superior officers, because it had become impossible for the highest ranking generals to receive more than a fraction of their hundreds of visitors.

For the same reason unlimited card-leaving is no longer practicable in Congressional circles. People have too much to do in too little time! Moreover the wives of officials are no longer able to keep open house or have fixed reception days since they simply get out of hand. Any stranger in the street of passably genteel appearance might walk in to see what he could see and to eat and drink aplenty.

It is true of course that there is a certain amount of card-leaving on the appointed days of well-known hostesses. But at the houses of most of these, the visitor is unlikely to find anyone at home. One or two host-esses whose houses are overlarge and who prefer a few unassorted cas-uals among the strangers who were expected, rather than sit alone, do receive as usual.

Cards are left, of course, in almost uncountable numbers at The White House, because everyone coming to, as well as living in, Wash-ington, wants to be invited there.

Anyone who has dined at The White House must leave cards within a few days or a week. They should be left by the guest rather than de-livered by a chauffeur or a messenger.

Obviously it is important that the people from the same State get to know each other and it is also fitting that members of the same committees, who will have to work together, cultivate mutual understanding.

CALLING ON THE EMBASSIES

Calling on the Embassies is most popular since invitations to the Embassies are the thrilling delight of visitors to Washington, and they give the biggest, best, and most frequent parties. And when you count up the more than sixty missions, it is no wonder that they add so much to the Capital's gay life.

At these one is apt to find officials of the Cabinet, Supreme Court, Capitol Hill, State Department, etc., so that one doesn't have to resort to a small, quietish "at home" to see, be seen by, and to meet, top officials and "brass."

WASHINGTON'S SOCIAL HOUR

From six to eight o'clock is Washington's most social hour. This is obviously to attract men, most of whom cannot get to a party at five.

OFFICIAL VISITS AND DAYS AT HOME

In Washington, as in European capitals, it is the newcomer's place to make the initial visit. Every official's first duty is to call at The White House. But neither the President nor the President's wife ever returns visits; and leaving one's card at The White House is simply a form of respect. After leaving cards at The White House, which is still correct, it has been the long established custom for the wife of a new official to call upon the wives of all those who rank above her husband. But since the last war, there have been no fixed visiting days and except for appointments or going to see personal friends, very few are at home to formal visitors and their cards are merely left at the door.

If you have a business appointment with the President, it is most important that you arrive a few minutes ahead of the appointed time. No doubt you will be told how much time you are allowed. Make your call brief, and if possible, take less time than that allowed.

Don't take a present unless you have cleared it with an aide, because a small package taken from a briefcase or a handbag will alarm the Secret Service men who are always present unless you happen to be recognized as a personal friend.

Don't smoke unless you are invited to by the person with whom you have an appointment. If a buzzer should ring and you are in a corridor, an attendant will ask you to step behind a closed door. The buzzer means that the President or members of the family are leaving or entering. This precaution is for their safety and their privacy.

Gentlemen always remove their hats as they reach the portico.

GIFTS TO THE PRESIDENT

Not only should you not take a present to the President unless it has been cleared with an aide (as mentioned above), but you should not *send* anything to The White House without receiving permission from his secretary or one of his aides.

You may have had a successful hunting trip and wish to send the President a brace of pheasants. The gift must be cleared with the proper authority, otherwise he will never see or taste it. The housekeeper is responsible for the safety of any food that is accepted.

Sometimes a President agrees to accept a dog, other pets, and various things. They of course must be vouched for before they are shipped. If they are not, they will not be accepted.

WHEN PAYING VISITS IN WASHINGTON

Except that you may be—unless prepared—at a loss to know how to address each official and foreigner, and except that precedence is a thing that must never be lost sight of, you behave in diplomatic and official circles as you do in best society everywhere. A man calling upon an ambassador or a minister asks at the door whether "His Excellency" is at home; but a lady going to see his wife asks whether "Madame Telque," or "Lady London," or "Countess Thatone" is at home. Upon being told that she is, the visitor lays her cards—one of her own and two of her husband's—upon the tray offered her and follows the servant to the drawing-room. Her hostess greets her and indicates where she is to sit. In New York a visitor would merely take any available seat, but in Washington a visitor should not, with others of higher rank present, sit upon the empty chair on the hostess' right vacated perhaps by an ambassador's wife who has left; she should try to find a place less obviously prominent.

For those who are at the bottom or very near the top, it is comparatively easy to remember the rank of the very few below or the equally few above; but for the wife of a new official of in-between rank the strain upon her memory for faces and names duly classified is heavy. In fact, at first this mastery of the rank list seems nearly impossible. To some it remains so, and they are social failures. To others, practice soon makes for perfection.

An invaluable aid, if your memory is not especially good, is to carry a sheet of thin writing paper folded into a notebook with an attached pencil—the whole so small that it can be cupped in the palm of your left hand, and whenever an unobserved chance comes, write quickly the names just heard; or later perhaps you can ask someone present to tell you the titles you did not hear. It is a good idea to add if possible *something* to fix each one in memory:

"Senator Brown, Montana: very tall, thin, gray beard, black eyes."

"Madame Jamand: wife of Finnish Minister, small, round, ash blond, pretty dimpled hands."

"Mrs. Mumford: wife of Congressman from New York, tall, thin, dark, wears glasses, nice smile."

Then when you go home, you find where each belongs on the official list. After a little while your mind gets into the habit of classifying names with appearances. After that, if you have a "talent for people," you elaborate your mere "identification" to a "personality" list.

"Senator Brown: great love of justice. Convince him a thing is right, and he will stand by it through thick and thin."

"Madame Jamand: talks amusingly about people. But not too accurate in what she says."

This last habit of testing and listing people's traits of character is of great value to anyone in any branch of public life.

AT THE WHITE HOUSE

An engraved invitation to The White House means black tie unless white tie is written on the invitation. For black tie the men wear stiff shirts and collars and a dinner jacket.

Women wear evening clothes, and if it is a white-tie dinner, they wear long gloves. At any luncheon—formal or informal—women wear hats, stockings, and gloves.

All the names of guests expected at The White House are posted with the guards at the gate. You announce your name and wait a few seconds until you are recognized.

After the guests arrive, the President and his wife enter and speak to each guest and shake hands. Guests of course remain standing. The President is called "Mr. President" or, if the conversation is long, "Sir" is substituted by men. The President's wife is called Mrs. Jackson.

At a formal dinner, the President goes into the dining-room first with the highest ranking woman guest. His wife follows with the highest ranking man guest.

After dinner when the President and his wife decide to leave, all guests rise and, when they have left, bid each other good-by and leave.

AT THE UNITED NATIONS

Since its founding, the United Nations has presented an element of fluidity in organization that is characteristic of its international nature. For this reason no order of precedence has been finally or definitely established that will adequately reflect its official or social organization. On those occasions, therefore, when guests of almost equal rank are being entertained, the host and hostess may consult the Chief of Protocol (Protocol and Liaison, Room 8537, United Nations, New York).

It is quite understandable that members of an organization comprised of persons from countries of widely varied systems of diplomatic protocol and social custom will largely follow the customs of their home countries in such matters. On the other hand, since the United Nations Headquarters is located within the United States, it is often, even usually, the case that they follow American custom. However, it should be pointed out that the established protocol of Washington cannot possibly reflect the diverse problems of such an organization and would not therefore serve as a guide in matters of social and official etiquette.

There are three broad principles that in general are followed. First, the order of diplomatic precedence—prime minister or chief of state, cabinet minister, ambassador extraordinary and plenipotentiary, envoy extraordinary and minister plenipotentiary, counselor of embassy, and attaché. Second, no seniority in terms of rank or service is recognized; the various member countries are listed alphabetically as they are spelled in the English language. Third, delegates and personnel are selected to serve in an international capacity by the eighty-two nations solely on personal merit, and regardless of nationality or diplomatic status.

As there is a system of rotation employed in many of its component organizations which reflects the international aspect of the United Nations, the determination of precedence is often qualified by a date, as in the Security Council, for instance, where the presidency is rotated monthly. The Secretariat itself characteristically differs from that of the embassies of one nation to another, for they serve as international civil servants and not as representatives of a single country.

The membership of the United Nations is:

Afghanistan, Albania, Argentina, Australia, Austria, Belgium, Bolivia, Brazil, Bulgaria, Burma, Byelorussian Soviet Socialist Republic, Cambodia, Canada, Ceylon, Chile, China, Colombia, Costa Rica, Cuba, Czechoslovakia, Denmark, Dominican Republic, Ecuador, Egypt, El Salvador, Ethiopia, Finland, France, Ghana, Greece, Guatemala, Guinea, Haiti, Honduras, Hungary, Iceland, India, Indonesia, Iran, Iraq, Ireland, Israel, Italy, Japan, Jordan, Laos, Lebanon, Liberia, Libya, Luxembourg.

Morocco, Mexico, Nepal, Netherlands, New Zealand, Nicaragua, Norway, Pakistan, Panama, Paraguay, Peru, Philippines, Poland, Portugal, Rumania, Saudi Arabia, Spain, Sweden, Sudan, Syria, Thailand, Tunisia, Ukrainian Soviet Socialist Republic, Union of South Africa, Union of Soviet Socialist Republics, United Kingdom of Great Britain and Northern Ireland, United States of America, Uruguay, Venezuela, Yemen, Yugoslavia.

Remembering that those serving at the United Nations are in a sense the guests of our country, and some are very distinguished guests indeed, the thoughtful host or hostess will ascertain from the Chief of Protocol the necessary information about his or her guests-to-be.

OUR CONTRIBUTION TO THE
BEAUTY OF LIVING

·◦ᢀ[52]◦·

HOW MANY TIMES HAS ONE HEARD SOMEONE SAY, "NO ONE is coming in. That old dress will do!" Old clothes! No manners! And what is the result? One wife more wonders why her husband neglects her! Curious how the habit of careless manners and the habit of old clothes go together! And how many women really lovely and good—especially good—commit esthetic suicide by letting themselves slide down to where they feel natural in an old house coat, not only physically but mentally.

THE OLD HOUSE-COAT HABIT

She who dresses for her children and for her husband's home-coming is sure to greet them with greater charm than she who thinks whatever she happens to have on is good enough. Any old thing good enough for those she loves most! In any case she might well remember that someone may drop in.

So many people save up all their troubles to pour on the one they most love, the idea being, seemingly, that no reserves are necessary between lovers. Nor need there be really. But why, when their house looks out upon a garden that has charming vistas, does she never show them to him instead of insisting that he look into the clothes yard and at the ashcan?

She who complains incessantly that this is wrong or that hurts, or that some other thing worries or vexes her, so that his inevitable answer to her greeting is "I'm so sorry, dear," or "That's too bad," is getting very decidedly into an old house coat!

If something is seriously wrong, if she is really ill, that is different. But of the petty things that are only remembered in order to be told to gain sympathy—beware!

There is a big deposit of sympathy in the bank of love, but don't draw out little sums every hour or so—so that by and by, when perhaps you need it badly, it is all drawn out and you yourself don't know how or on what it was spent.

It should be unnecessary to add that a man and his wife who quarrel before their children or the servants deprive the former of good breeding through example, and publish to the latter that they do not belong to the better class through any qualification except the possession of a bank account.

THE PROBLEMS OF DIVORCE

No rule of propriety has been more completely changed than that which formerly required all divorced people to meet as unspeaking strangers. The reason for the strictness of this convention was that a generation ago a divorce was unthinkable unless there was irreparable injury or such antipathy existed that tranquil encounter could never again be possible.

Experience has, however, made it plain that serious readjustment of many rules must be made—particularly in those cases where conventions and humaneness are in conflict. And as no thinking person could rate the former above the latter, it has been the conventions that have had to be changed. In the thousands of cases where children are involved, it is far, far better that the parents make every effort to remain on friendly terms. Nothing in all the world is so devastating in its destruction of character and of soul as living in an atmosphere infused with hatred. Anything is better for children than that!

The most bitterly unhappy situation that can come to a child is to be the victim of a court decree which condemns it to the continual shifting, like a human shuttlecock, between parents who hate each other, or —even worse in its emotional effect—to feel that one parent has inflicted unmerited cruelty on the other. Emotional disturbance such as this should not be the portion of any child.

There are cases, of course, where divorce is the best—sometimes the only—solution for everyone concerned. If two persons are truly mismated they certainly and perhaps their children too are better off if they part. The only consideration of vital importance is that they shall not part because of a love-for-another attack that might prove to be transient.

Even so, the epidemic of divorce which has been raging in this country for the past forty years must be rated as a catastrophe along with floods, dust bowls, and tornadoes.

One wonders what part divorce has played in the point of view of many of a now-grown "younger" generation. Their brittle hardness, their lack of consideration for any opinions but their own, and their indifference toward family obligations! How many of the thousands of children who have lived through this experience have suffered spiritual injury, and to what degree? No one can know for certain. Nor can one know to what degree other children, who have been witnesses to the broken homes of their playmates, live in fear of the same thing happening to them.

At present the breaking up of homes is so widespread it may be that those who grow up never having known the completeness of home will find it inessential! Or will it be the other way around? And the children of today's divided houses will be twice as earnest in their efforts to provide their own children with the priceless security of a father and mother together in one place called HOME!

RESPECTING THE PRIVACY OF OTHERS

We should never walk into the house of another as though it were own own unless such behavior has been and still is encouraged. And even so, we should try to acquire sufficient alertness to notice anything that might make our presence inopportune.

Should we, for instance, find a visitor at Nancy's—especially a visitor who is an intimate friend of hers but not of ours—we should leave promptly. This is easily done by saying, "Nancy, would you lend me . . . ?" (whatever we can think of that will imply that we have not come to stay). Or if we find evidence of family discussion, any situation indicating that the family would like to be alone, we should make an excuse or even say, "I'll be back later!" and leave.

Out in public it seems scarcely necessary to add that if we see two people engrossed in a discussion, we must not interrupt unless they make a definite motion that invites us to join them.

TACT

Certainly we've all been thankful—at times—that other people could not read our thoughts—thoughts such as "How very ill you look!" or "How old you've grown!"—thoughts to be locked away quickly in the silence of our own minds. The tactless person seems compelled to say exactly such things as these out loud, even when there can be absolutely nothing to be gained by such brutal frankness.

Of all the qualities that make us likable, none is greater than tact. If there were no tact, there would be little friendship in the world, and social life would revert to stone-age crudeness. Tact, of course, means quick awareness of the feelings of others, and consideration for them. There is only one flaw in this otherwise most charming of human attributes, the possibility of insincerity. We don't know where we stand with one who diplomatically tells us only what he thinks we'd like to hear, instead of giving us a frank, straightforward answer. The social climber is one who misuses this aspect of tact because he seeks only to please those who can help further his ambitions.

On the other hand the tactless person causes nothing but distress wherever he goes. At this point it may be well to point out that, as in the case of many other attributes, excellence is dependent upon motive. The motive of real tact is kindness. When the motive is self-advantage, as it is in the case of the climber on society's ladder, tact and truth are apt to part company.

It must be agreed that it's often more than hard to be tactful and truthful at the same time. Let us say you go to see a friend who has just refurnished her house. You think she has spoiled it completely. And *what* do you say? You can only distress your friend if you tell her, "Well, I think the room is hideous." It's finished; she has to live in it, and criticism can do no good. Of course, if she had told you about it before redoing it, you would have been lacking in interest not to give her your thoughtful and true opinion.

There may be people who, suffering from some personal bitterness or unhappiness, uncaringly say things that hurt the feelings or the pride of others. But most tactless people are merely those who won't stop and think. There are certain people whose minds seem to be drawn as by a magnet to the very subject they ought to avoid.

"Of course," they say, "everybody but you knows your husband is crazy about Laura Lovely!" Or "Well! Your daughter didn't marry the Gilding boy after all!" It sounds unbelievable, but I have actually heard both of these remarks made.

Tact, which is merely appreciation of other people's sensibilities, is just as important to each of us in every contact of life as it used to be to every member of the diplomatic corps. A few rare persons are born with quick perception and innate kindness; but in greatest measure tact, like most of the social graces, is the result of training. At least half the rules of etiquette are maxims in tact. But don't make the mistake of thinking that tact means veering like a weather vane with each breeze that blows. It means trying to cultivate the habit of paying attention and making the effort to find the pleasant or the encouraging side of truth.

IN-LAW SITUATIONS

One is likely to overlook the fact that when John Jones marries Mary Smith, a number of Smiths and Joneses are suddenly forced into the closeness of family relationships. Even when a bride or bridegroom has no family, he or she becomes son or daughter, sister or brother, to those who often have hitherto been total strangers.

The two difficult situations to meet happily and successfully are those between the husband and his father-in-law and between the wife and her mother-in-law. The other positions are easy and there is little reason for failure.

But, in any case, the very first rule that every father-in-law—and especially every mother-in-law—must learn is DON'T INTERFERE. Never mind what small blunders your daughter or daughter-in-law, or your son or son-in-law may make; remember that it is their right to live and do and think as they please. If you are *asked* what you think, answer truthfully, of course; but don't, upon being given one opening, cram in every item of good advice that you've been storing up for just this chance—or you will risk never being asked again.

YOUNG WIFE WHO LIVES WITH MOTHER-IN-LAW

When a young wife, for any one of many reasons, goes to live with her husband's people, she must in this usually difficult situation adapt herself not only to their mode of living, but also to the dispositions of the various members of the family. In this way alone can she herself be happy. On the other hand, it is essential that the mother-in-law encourage the younger woman's efforts to become adjusted to completely new surroundings instead of showing irritation over the shortcomings of which she will certainly have at least a few.

PARENTS WHO MUST LIVE WITH THEIR GROWN CHILDREN

When a mother or father *must* live with a married child, the situation demands the wisdom of a Solomon, the tact of a Récamier, and the self-control of a stoic. Moreover, she or he must conscientiously practice the art of "invisibility" at frequent and lengthy intervals. This does not mean that the mother, for example, must scuttle out of sight like a frightened mouse, but that she shall have or make occupations of her own which keep her from being idly, plaintively, or forcefully present —particularly when especial friends of her daughter-in-law or even old friends of her son are present. Perhaps she can find some friends and play bridge or canasta one evening every week or two. Her room should be equipped with a small radio and possibly television so that she can enjoy her own favorite programs which the others may not care for.

On the other hand there is no excuse for the ruthless unkindness which certain wives show when they are obliged to have a parent-in-law live in their house. This attitude, did they but know it, is not only distressing to the helpless victim of their cruelty, but is certainly resented by all who see it.

IN-LAW RELATIONSHIP AT ITS BEST

An in-law relationship should be unhampering, uninterfering, uncriticizing.

Whether we be mother or father, bride or groom, the safe rule for our own happiness is to take things as we find them, take pleasure in the assets, not go searching for flaws, and not ever for a single second permit ourselves the happiness-destroying weakness of feeling sorry for ourselves.

If we who are of yesterday or the day before that would have the affection of those of today given to us freely, we must ourselves be impersonally independent. Nothing is harder to build than this impersonality of mind, and one moment's relaxed indulgence in self-pity can bring it all crashing down. The first step in the achievement of impersonality is keeping our thoughts away from every trend that is sentimentally focused upon ourselves by thinking of something else—never mind what.

The one great struggle that each of us who of necessity are alone—by that is meant all those who are widowed or single and whose children or sisters and brothers have married—must make is never to give clinging impulses a chance to develop. We hear much about dieting and taking daily dozens and doing all sorts of other irksome things to preserve physical beauty, and relatively little about the unrelenting exercise of plain common sense in achieving mental beauty by adjusting the capital I to its relative proportion.

THE SMITHS AND JONESES SHARE A HOUSE

When two families—no matter how congenial—decide to go housekeeping together, a point few people prepare for but which is of very great importance is this: They should decide upon at least one evening a month when the house is the Smiths' and another evening a month (probably two weeks later) when the house belongs to the Joneses.

Obviously this means that each may give a party for their *own* friends or stay by themselves alone on each of these evenings. Even when the house-sharers are invited to stay, it should be the unbroken practice of the one whose turn it is to go out, to *go!* When they want to have mutual friends and be at home together, this party should be given on any of the other evenings when they would normally all be in. The feeling that the house will be yours alone, even if it is only once a month, is of great importance in this situation.

FLOWERS FOR YOUR FRIENDS

How many charming, friendly, and sympathetic impulses have been smothered by our American mania for the superlative! Why must the flowers we send be the largest and the finest that many dollars can buy—or else none at all? The poets sing of "a rose," but young John America cannot think of roses as fewer than a dozen!

This does not mean that a big box of the most gorgeous flowers is not an enthralling gift. But why must it be supposed that we haven't the spirit or the sentiment to appreciate *the loveliness of little things*? Entirely apart from any question of cost, would we give more pleasure to a dearest friend who lives in the tiniest of apartments by sending her a constant supply of sweet little roses and other short-stemmed flowers?

Or once in a year or so by crowding her small, low-ceilinged room with a twenty-bloom plant of Easter lilies?

On the other hand, we know that when Lucy Oneroom wants to send flowers to Mrs. Richling, who has shown her repeated kindness, to *have* to choose a little pot of African violets is disheartening. But we know, too, that Mrs. Richling is one person to whom a large box of four-foot stemmed roses is not one bit more welcome than the fewest little buds with four-inch stems. In fact, nothing could distress her so much as evidence that too large a part of Lucy's weekly income had gone into long stems, which would quite possibly be cut off in the pantry in order to go into a vase of reasonable height.

WHEN HE GIVES HER FLOWERS TO WEAR

Why does every man take it for granted that the only flowers possible to send are gardenias? Why doesn't *he* at least find out whether *she* might prefer something else? Why can't *he* at some time ask *her* casually whether it is true that every woman's idea of flowers to wear begins and ends with gardenias? And then why can't *he* listen to *her* answer—and remember it? This is added purposely because the other day a certain young man asked this question, and the young woman told him she loved purple violets best of all flowers, and purple sweet peas next. Two evenings later he was taking her to a dance and sent her gardenias!

For the benefit of the man who believes that less than half a dozen gardenias or two hundred violets would be too few to think of, it might be well to explain that, according to *best taste*, two gardenias worn on an evening dress are perfection. Three are possible only if they are very small. On the street dress, one gardenia is correct. Therefore, three gardenias are the very most a really smart woman can possibly wear— ever. And yet, unless Babs manages to let Bob know that two flowers are a perfect number and not thought skimpy by anyone except a "gold-digger," the chances are that, not realizing this, he will go on wishing to send a dozen—and as he cannot afford the price of a dozen, he probably sends none.

WHEN A WOMAN SENDS FLOWERS TO A MAN

It is always proper that a woman send flowers to any man she knows when he is seriously ill or convalescing. Cut flowers or plants are equally suitable. A cactus garden in a shallow container or a terrarium is particularly good since it requires very little care. But sometimes she sends him flowers that have far more sentiment. Should John Strongheart be convalescing, let us say, Louise Lovely might send him a very few flowers—perhaps only one especial flower—every day at the same hour, and tied to it a note or a message or a daily collection of clippings of whatever might interest or amuse him. The value of

this suggestion, it must be acknowledged, does depend upon his sentiment for her. So in a situation where there is doubt, a young woman
had better confine her efforts to clippings sent occasionally, and only one
offering of flowers or a plant.

WE MUST SEND FLOWERS IF WE CAN

There are certain occasions when sending flowers, if we can possibly afford them, is really obligatory. We must send flowers to the
funeral of a friend, or a member of an intimate friend's family. We also
send flowers to an intimate friend who is or has been seriously ill, to
a new mother, to a débutante on her coming out, to a guest speaker
when we are hostess, and on anniversaries—either joyous or tragic—of
our nearest friends. Certain thoughtful people are constantly sending
flowers; others seldom do. Certainly the majority of us send them much
less often than we might, usually because we think those we can afford
to buy or those growing in our garden are not good enough.

For funerals for which it has been requested that no flowers be sent,
it is suggested page 285 be referred to.

In a certain neighborhood a certain flower lover has an entrancing
habit of sending flowers arranged in containers which are also donated
with the flowers. They are usually inexpensive, but her expert eye is
constantly on the lookout for small containers becoming to flowers. Some
are of glass; some are of pottery; but often they are ten-cent kitchen
utensils of tin—even tin cans and boxes from her own kitchen turned
into tôleware with the simplest amount of painting done by herself.
She also keeps a supply of dried moss and small lead flower holders.
Then in winter she buys—or in summer she picks—a careful selection
of flowers, puts a holder in the bottom of pot, bowl, or box, arranges
the flowers, and covers the holder and the stems with soaking-wet moss.
Later the person who receives it adds as much water as the container
can hold.

A lovely Easter present that can be afforded by almost everyone is
a bowl of pebbles in which lily bulbs have been started. These, bought
dormant, are not too expensive, and plain pottery bowls that are inexpensive may be found everywhere.

Only those who have greenhouses can give the very real pleasure
that a certain thoughtful old gentleman gives to a number of his
younger neighbors every Easter, but it is worth including here—just
in case! He sends one or two flats of small seedlings grown in his green-
house. These are to be kept indoors, of course, until the weather permits
their being transplanted in the garden. Heliotrope, snapdragons, annual
phlox, and lupins are his favorite selection.

At all events, there is scarcely any situation in which flowers are
not a suitable as well as probably the most beautiful messengers of
friendship or sympathy or love that can be chosen.

AT THE HOSPITAL

As we have just been talking of flowers, it brings to mind one subject that certainly is at one time or another in the thoughts of all of us. Fortunately, most of us visit hospitals only when members of our families or our friends are ill. But there are times when we ourselves have to go there as patients.

The whole routine of a hospital is highly organized and kept in smooth running order by the doctors and nurses and staff. Whether we go as a patient or visitor, we must behave so that our presence there, when we are visitors, fits into an orderly pattern and so that, as a patient, the hospital's staff can do its best for us.

Far too often visitors are thoughtless and careless. One should think of the problems that a visitor makes under the busy, crowded hospital conditions of today. Courtesy to nurses and the other hospital personnel, quietness of manner and approach in the hospital buildings, avoidance of asking for special attention from busy people, these we can show— and above all we must not act in any way that will be tiring or harmful to the patient we are visiting. We must make our visits short and friendly, leaving our small gifts without fuss or any expectancy of more than a simple thank-you for them. We must not engage the patient in long discussions, nor ask questions about his or her illness that properly are in the sphere of the doctor and the nurse. We must time our visits so that the patient neither becomes tired nor anxious and, of course, we must always follow the rules as they are given to us by the nurse. A surgeon that I know claims that visitors kill more patients than do operations, certainly an overstatement, but be sure that you are not one of those visitors.

When we ourselves are ill there are times when we are apt to forget that doctors and nurses are people too and that they are doing their very best to help us. Unless one has private nurses, we must realize that the hospital staff serves many people and only so much of their time can be devoted to us. We, therefore, should not ask for services that are not really necessary. Simply remember that the doctors and nurses, from professional pride if for no other reason, do their best for you. But if you are as considerate as possible in your demands on their time and sympathy, they will probably on their own give you an extra amount of both, and the patient who is irritable without cause will surely receive little of either.

Here are a few don'ts which may be helpful for visitor and patient.

Don't bring as your gift elaborate floral arrangements or foods that the patient is not permitted to have.

Don't forget, whenever it is possible, to bring your flowers with their own container and let them be of a size that can easily be handled. It should be clear that heavily scented flowers have no place in the sickroom.

DON'T be fault-finding and constantly critical over small and trivial things, and be sure that those attentions which really will be helpful to you are asked for politely and in a friendly manner.

DON'T think that the hospital routine has been devised to bedevil you as it is only a part of a long-range plan carefully worked out to serve you.

DON'T as a visitor overstay your welcome. Visit briefly, cheerfully, and leave the patient rested and encouraged.

DON'T fail to remember that the average patient is not his normal self and the burden of good behavior is on your side, not his.

DON'T talk about his illness in front of the patient. Ask the necessary questions quietly from those who are competent to answer them for you, out of his hearing and sight.

DON'T worry a patient about anything which you feel might upset or disturb him.

DON'T fail when you are in a semi-private room or in a larger ward to remember that there are others there who are ill and who may be disturbed by your talking.

THE FLAG OF THE UNITED STATES

·≫[53]≪·

THERE ARE CERTAIN RULES AND CUSTOMS THAT ALL OF US who love this symbol of our country should know and always follow because it shows our true respect for our country.

Every day in the year between sunrise and sunset is a proper time to fly the flag, though customarily it is not flown in inclement weather unless there is a particular occasion that requires its display.

On Memorial or Decoration Day, May 30th, the flag is displayed at half-staff until noon and at full staff thereafter till sunset. Flag Day is June 14th—the day when we especially celebrate this emblem. It is a widespread custom also for most of us to display the flag on other holidays which are celebrated throughout the country.

There are certain situations under which the flag should never be used, such, for example, as decoration on a portion of a costume or athletic uniform, as embroidery on cushions, scarves, or handkerchiefs, or on paper napkins or boxes. Of course, it should never be used as a covering for articles on a speaker's table or so placed that objects may be placed on it or over it. When the flag is used in the unveiling of a statue or monument, it should not be used as a covering of the object to be unveiled. Everyone knows that it is unlawful to use the flag in a registered trade mark which comprises "the flag, coat of arms, or other insignia of the United States or any simulation thereof." When festoons, rosettes, or other draperies are desired, bunting of blue (uppermost), white, and red should be used, and of course never the flag itself.

DISPLAYING THE FLAG

1. When displayed over the middle of a street, the flag should be suspended vertically with the union (the blue field) to the north in an east-west street, or to the east in a north-south street.

2. When displayed with another flag from crossed staffs, the flag of the United States should be on the right (the flag's own right) and its staff should be in front of the staff of the other flag.

3. When it is flown at half-mast, the flag should be hoisted to the peak for a moment and then lowered to the half-mast position; but before lowering the flag for the day it should again be raised to the peak.

4. When flags of States or cities or pennants of societies are flown on the same halyard with the flag of the United States, the latter should always be at the peak. When flown from adjacent staffs the National flag should be hoisted first and lowered last.

5. When the flag is suspended over a sidewalk from a rope, extending from house to pole at the edge of the sidewalk, the flag should be hoisted out from the building, toward the pole, union first.

6. When the flag is displayed from a staff projecting horizontally or at an angle from a window sill, balcony, or the front of a building, the union of the flag should go clear to the peak of the staff (except when at half-mast).

7. When the flag is used to cover a casket, it should be so placed that the union is at the head and over the left shoulder. The flag should not be lowered into the grave or allowed to touch the ground.

8. When the flag is displayed in a manner other than flown from a staff, it should be displayed flat, whether indoors or out. When displayed either horizontally or vertically against a wall, the union should be uppermost and to the observer's left. When displayed in a window it should be displayed in the same way, with the union to the left of the observer in the street.

9. When carried in a procession with another flag or flags, the American flag should be either on the marching right or, when there is a line of other flags, it may be in front of the center of that line.

10. When a number of flags of States or cities or pennants of societies are grouped and displayed from staffs with our National flag, the latter should be at the center or at the highest point of the group.

11. When the flags of two or more nations are displayed, they should be flown from separate staffs of the same height and the flags should be of approximately equal size. International usage forbids the display of the flag of one nation above that of another nation in time of peace.

12. When the flag is used in a church, on the chancel or on a platform, it should be placed on a staff on the clergyman's right, other flags on his left. When displayed in the body of the church, the flag should be on the congregation's right as it faces the chancel.

13. When used as an identifying symbol on an automobile, it is flown on a small staff affixed on the end of the front bumper, on the right looking forward and within the line of the fender. When used this way, the staff should be tall enough so that the flag clears the car hood. Alternately, a small flag may be flown from the radiator cap. Care should be taken that if the flag has become soiled or wind-torn that it should be promptly removed and replaced.

CARE OF THE FLAG

The flag of our country should be carefully protected in storage and in use so that it will not be damaged. Every precaution should be taken for preventing it from becoming soiled or torn. Care should always be taken that the flag be not permitted to touch the ground, or water, or a floor, or in handling to brush it against objects.

It goes without saying that the National emblem is **never** displayed **in** connection with advertising of any kind.

FOR AND ABOUT YOUNG PEOPLE

·◦[54]◦·

I HAVE OFTEN BEEN ASKED HOW BEST TO TEACH RULES OF etiquette to young people or, as they are so often called today, teenagers, and whether there are special rules which they should be taught. The most important thing for all of us to realize is that etiquette applies to everyone, old or young, and that the best way to teach etiquette to children is the best way to teach anything—by precept, consistency, and gentle firmness. I have written a book on this subject, *Children Are People*. Indeed they are, and parents and teachers will do well to remember it.

LEARNING THE RULES OF ETIQUETTE

Children can scarcely be too young to be taught the rudiments of etiquette, nor can the teaching be too patiently or too conscientiously carried out. Any child can be taught to be beautifully behaved with no effort greater than quiet patience and perseverance, whereas to break bad habits once they are acquired is a herculean task.

The first requisite in table manners is neatness. The child can be taught, just as soon as he can hold a spoon in his tiny hand, to put the spoon pointed end foremost in his mouth, and to take only small mouthfuls; to hold his small glass carefully and not spill his milk; and to eat without smearing his face with everything on his plate. It is possible for even a two- or three-year-old to master these simple lessons, if his mother takes the time to teach him correctly from the very beginning. A child of this age can also be taught not to begin eating until he has been served, and not to leave the table until he has asked, "Please may I be excused?" and received permission to get up.

As soon as a child has learned these lessons he should be allowed to come to the dining table with adults. He may even eat with company, but it is best to correct a child as little as possible in front of guests, since nagging in the presence of strangers may lessen a child's incentive to behave nicely. If he refuses to be good, the best course is to say nothing but lead him as quietly as possible from the table. The child will learn much more quickly to be well behaved if he understands that good behavior is the price of admission to grown-up society.

More specific information on dining-room etiquette will be found in Chapter 41 on Table Manners.

FAIR PLAY

Even quite young children are able to understand the principles of justice, and they should be taught, even before they go to school, to "play fair," to respect each other's property and rights, to give credit to others and not to take too much credit to themselves. They should learn to share their playthings, and to take good care of toys that belong to other children. Every child can be taught never to call attention to the meagre possessions of another child whose parents are not as well off as his own. A bright, observing child should never be encouraged to pick out other people's failings, or to tell her mother how inferior other children are compared with herself. If she wins a medal at school or is praised, her mother naturally rejoices with her, and it is proper that she should, but a wise mother teaches her child that selfishness and conceit can win no place worth having in the world.

The older child will learn the rules of sportsmanship in adult Games and Sports, Chapter 47.

CHILDREN'S PARTIES

A children's party that has been well planned can be enjoyable to everyone. It is necessary only to think of a child's birthday party to see the picture of little ones arriving in their best party clothes, each clutching a paper-wrapped package, each disposition clearly evident in the shy or reluctant or delightful gesture with which each proffers the gift he has brought and says, "*This* is for you!"

The birthday child, standing beside his or her mother at the door, says, "Oh, thank you!" The child should learn at an early age that as host or hostess he must think of his guests rather than himself, and not want the best toys in the grab-bag. He must try to help his guests have a good time.

When a child goes to a party, he must say, "How do you do?" to his friend's mother, and "Happy birthday!" to his friend. When it is time to go home, the child should say, "Good-by, I had a very good time," or "Good-by, thank you ever so much."

The birthday child says, as his young guests leave, "Good-by, thank you for coming." His mother may say to a guest, "Good-by, give my love to your mother!" The child then answers, "Yes, Mrs. Smith."

If the birthday child is old enough, he may help in deciding on the guest list, sending out invitations, and setting the table. A girl may even help prepare the refreshments—mixing the cake batter or making sandwiches.

Parents should not ask too many children, which can lead only to chaos. Refreshments should be kept simple, to enable the hostess to supervise games, and to prevent any possibility of illness from a combination of excitement and too-rich food. Entertainment and games should be provided, in enough variety to prevent boredom and restlessness.

ETIQUETTE FOR THE OLDER CHILD

As the child grows older, he participates in an increasingly wider variety of social activities, in school and out. Many chapters in this book discuss the etiquette of specific situations young people encounter. The teen-ager will want to consult Chapter 17 on "Dating," Chapter 15, "At College," and Chapter 16, "The Chaperon and her Modern Counterparts." Chapter 37, "Courtesy on the Telephone," will help teach telephone manners to the young.

Today's young people often go traveling with their parents. Chapter 50, "The Experienced Traveler," describes etiquette for the traveler at home and abroad. Those teen-agers who are old enough to get driver's licenses can learn about "Manners and Motorists" in Chapter 48.

Teen-agers may also have occasion to refer to Chapter 42 on "Formal Correspondence," and Chapters 39 and 40, "The Clothes of a Lady" and "The Clothes of a Gentleman," respectively.

Young people today, as a consequence of movies, radio and television, in addition to magazine articles and books written for them as well as about them, have a self-awareness and self-knowledge that was not possible to young people a generation ago. These words, therefore, are addressed as much to our young people themselves as they are to their parents.

"BECAUSE EVERYONE ELSE DOES"

All young people feel a need for conformity with the activities of others of their age. This they express in their speech, their play, their choice of clothing, and their relationships to each other. This conformity is quite normal, and is to be respected as part of the development of individual personality as well as social responsibility. Adults, after all, conform to their world too. Young people in time learn that through conformity with most of the social customs of the adult world they will be able to take their place in that world.

Earlier in this book I have recommended that children should be permitted to follow the customs of their community, so as not to differ too radically from the other children in the neighborhood. However, there are necessary and obvious qualifications to this advice. It is possible for children to be well brought up even though the community where the family lives may seem to have accepted lower standards of behavior than the family's own. The phrase one hears so often from children, "everyone else does thus-and-so," is not sufficient excuse for lowering standards. Surely, to take an extreme example, no one could condone cheating at games or on examinations just "because everyone else does."

Of course, parents sometimes must make a decision at the risk of having their children a little different in some particular from their friends. Certainly there are times when children should be required to set an example for others to follow, rather than be just like all the rest. There is a certain element of risk involved in this position, but there is also an element of discipline which is far more important.

Parents and teachers must never underestimate the problems that a teen-ager has in adapting himself to a world full of contradiction which can only be explained by experience. Precepts and lectures are never a substitute for understanding and sympathetic guidance.

ACKNOWLEDGMENTS

Grateful acknowledgment for friendly cooperation in the preparation of the photographic illustrations is made herewith:

To American Institute of Decorators, Dix-Make Uniforms, Florists' Telegraph Delivery Association, and Franciscan fine China. And also to International Silver and James Robinson, Inc., for sterling silver, except where photographs were taken in private homes.

For Plate *"The Bride's Table."* To Franciscan fine China; Plummer, Ltd., for crystal; International Sterling; Robert Day-Dean, for wedding cake; Florists' Telegraph Delivery Association; and Irish Linen Guild.

For Plate *"A Dinner Service of Simplicity and Pleasing Charm."* To Franciscan fine China; Fostoria, for crystal; International Silver; Florists' Telegraph Delivery Association; and Irish Linen Guild.

For Plate *"A Perfectly Set Formal Dinner Table."* To Franciscan fine China; Plummer, Ltd., for crystal; International Silver for flatware; and James Robinson, Inc., for bowl and candelabra.

For Plate *"A Supper Table of Unusual Attractiveness."* To Baccarat, for crystal.

For Plate *"The Tray for a Guest Who Breakfasts in Bed."* To B. Altman & Co., for breakfast tray and appointments.

For Plate *"Almost Everyone Enjoys the Buffet Supper."* To Franciscan fine China; and James Robinson, Inc., for silver.

To Frances L. Orkin, photographic consultant.

INDEX